D21
S56
Shotwell
The long way to freedom

c. 2

Date Due

JAN 1 9 '68			
MAR 7 '68			

THE LONG WAY TO
FREEDOM

Books by JAMES T. SHOTWELL

THE RELIGIOUS REVOLUTION OF TODAY

INTELLIGENCE AND POLITICS

HISTORY OF HISTORY

THE SEA OF PETER (with Louise Loomis)

WAR AS AN INSTRUMENT OF NATIONAL POLICY AND ITS RENUNCIA-
TION IN THE PACT OF PARIS

THE PACT OF PARIS

THE HERITAGE OF FREEDOM

ON THE RIM OF THE ABYSS

AT THE PARIS PEACE CONFERENCE

TURKEY AT THE STRAITS (with Francis Deak)

WHAT GERMANY FORGOT

THE GREAT DECISION

POLAND AND RUSSIA (with Max Laserson)

A BALKAN MISSION

LESSONS ON SECURITY AND DISARMAMENT FROM THE HISTORY OF
THE LEAGUE OF NATIONS (with Marina Salvin)

POEMS

THE UNITED STATES IN HISTORY

THE LONG WAY TO FREEDOM

BY JAMES T. SHOTWELL

THE **BOBBS-MERRILL** COMPANY, INC.

A SUBSIDIARY OF HOWARD W. SAMS & CO., INC.

Publishers • INDIANAPOLIS • NEW YORK

Copyright © 1960 by James T. Shotwell

Printed in the United States of America
First Edition

Library of Congress Catalog Card Number: 60-7143

To

COLUMBIA UNIVERSITY

which, more than half a century ago, encouraged a young professor to study and teach what seemed to him most important in the history and destiny of mankind.

TABLE OF CONTENTS

THE LONG WAY TO FREEDOM

INTRODUCTION

This book deals with the age-long history of a problem which, when viewed in all its aspects, outranks any other in the world today: that of the way by which the freedom of the individual can be not only maintained but increased, parallel with a continual, and apparently inevitable, increase in the scope of government. How can men be free and yet yield so much of their lives to the judgment of others as set forth in the laws and prescriptions of the State?

Although this problem is as old as organized society, the solution of it has remained an aspiration or a theory. Now it is forced home upon us by the pressure of events, not only by ruthless tyranny and war but also by that inescapable master of human destiny, modern science. The revolution which this has caused in the conditions of life has only just begun, but already it has changed the nature of the problem of freedom. Formerly its solution was chiefly sought by limiting the action of governments, erecting barriers against acts of oppression or arbitrary rule. Thus, a realm of private liberties was carved out of the prerogatives of the rulers, and the citizen was safeguarded in his individual rights, which were those of escape from molestation as he sought to live his life in his own way.

This development, registered in bills of rights, writs of *habeas corpus* and the like, has been a precious gain in the history of freedom; but now we are reaching beyond this conception of freedom as an escape from oppression to that of its integration in a better balance of government and people. Henceforth, government must be an instrument by which the individual can find a more perfect adjustment to the society in which he lives, taking into account its economies and its culture as well as the formal element of law.

Freedom, as defined in this volume, is not escape from responsibility but the acceptance of it. It is a social as well as an individual fact. It must therefore be sought in the equilibrium between the needs and desires of the individual and those of other people. It is in this way that we speak of freedom as a function of justice.

While the goal ahead of us is becoming increasingly clear in the crises of today, the background remains overshadowed by many unsolved problems, because the history of freedom has not been written. It is more than the history of the freedom of thought, for it must include as well all the activities

15

of life, many of which are carried on in the unconscious realm of habit. In the Western world it has now become more closely associated with the history of politics, but that has not always been the case, as the narrative of this volume shows. The controls which have governed conduct have their roots in prehistoric societies. Therefore this survey begins with an analysis of those elements of primitive life which keep recurring throughout history.

It is an almost incredible paradox that the greatest impediments to freedom have been created by the three chief agencies of liberation: religion, politics and economics. Religion, while clearing away the grosser forms of superstition, has often blocked further progress by the very intensity of its sense of the sacredness of its mission. Politics, born of war, cut in upon the sphere of taboo, but the war system, by which the secular state was established, became the chief enemy of its own creation. Freedom maintained by a warrior class was, after all, as incomplete as the freedom maintained by shaman and priest.

Wider in its liberation than either of these was that of the economic advance in commerce and industry. But ultimate freedom is more than the elimination of superstition, war and exploitation. It is positive, not negative; the fullness of life under the rule of law, which guarantees the fundamental human rights of thought and expression.

The present volume therefore begins with a survey of primitive society, pointing out its three main elements, the organization for safety against the supernatural terrors in religion, the organization against physical dangers in the war bands, and the organization for welfare, primarily by slaves to do the necessary work. These elements of primitive life continue in various disguises and with varying strength throughout history.

Asia is then examined, although only hurriedly, as the great reservoir of religion. India is, from this point of view, the most primitive of all the great countries of the world. Japan, combining religion with militarism throughout its history, was ill-prepared to prevent economic exploitation in the industrial era; but military defeat may have broken the mold, at least in part. China offered elements of emancipation in its philosophic teachings which reveal an inherent dislike of militarism, but recurring wars presented obstacles to progress. It is against this background that the revolutionary changes taking place in Asia must be measured.

The history of the West begins with the history of the politics of the city state, a fundamentally secular conception. But, while taboos no longer ruled — although they were still recognized — in affairs of state, militarism was dominant. The constant resort to war and the danger of war prevented the sound development of politics in both Greece and Rome. In Greece, where peace was little more than a truce between the city states, politics continued to the very last to concentrate upon a strategy of that anarchy which ultimately weakened and destroyed the cities that were the earliest pioneers of freedom. In Rome the war system reached its highest development, overcoming the anarchy in a world of city states and erecting a structure which bore the outward marks of enduring strength. But where militarism rules it takes command of policy and the civil government, losing all initiative, and becomes a mere framework of bureaucracy, rigid and nerveless. In economics, the effect of antique militarism was equally disastrous, not only because of reliance upon booty from the wars, but even more because of the disastrous effects of slavery.

As the power of Rome extended over the various peoples of Italy and then of the Western world, it enlarged the scope of law to cover all the nations under its sovereignty, and it is hardly too much to say that in this law of nations (*jus gentium*) the peoples of the ancient world, through the cooperative efforts of the Roman jurists, made the greatest single contribution of ancient history toward the emancipation of law from tribalism and superstition. Its positive principles were based on Greek philosophy and ultimately included the teachings of the Church Fathers. Thus the new freedom of the law of nations registered a turning away from primitive society toward principles of civilized life — principles so soundly wrought that they could be regarded as the Law of Nature. Thus even as the political and economic world of antiquity fell into ruins, the concept of justice remained, and with it a decent respect for the empire of the mind.

Alongside these developments in the secular world came the revolution in religion created by Christianity. Freedom from taboo was the outstanding feature of its attack upon both the scribes and pharisees of the Jews and the religions of the pagan world. Its emphasis upon the brotherhood of man under the fatherhood of God gave the sanction of religion to ethics in the conduct of daily life. But its denunciation of war remained uncertain because war was also an instrument of law and order. The "just war" was permissible, but the definition of what constituted a "just war" was inadequate as long as it was held to be war in support of established rule. In this way the war system was left to be an instrument of tyranny. The problem therefore remained unsolved throughout the Middle Ages. The same kind of compromise with secular reality was made in the Christian acceptance of slavery. Thus, in both war and peace the early Church avoided revolutionary doctrines.

With the Dark Age, Europe returned to primitive conditions, and the same problems which confronted the early city states of antiquity had to be worked out once more. The prevalence of taboo and superstition in antiquity, with which the fathers of the Church had struggled, was repeated in the popular mythologies of the north, and the efforts of theologians to combat them culminated in the great system of theology known as Scholasticism. But this application of logic to theology replaced superstition by dogma, which discouraged freedom of thought. Even when the Protestant revolt challenged the authority of medieval orthodoxy, it was not fighting the battle of freedom of belief, but only freedom from that form of belief which it denied. It was not until the eighteenth century that ideas of religious toleration became dominant and the secular state began to guarantee religious freedom.

It was not theocracy, however, but the anarchy of feudalism which was the chief rival of the medieval kingship. The process by which the local sovereignties were fused into a single monarchy is long and obscure, and varies by centuries in different countries. But everywhere kingship was recognized as something more than the greatest of feudal suzerainties, and when the king became strong enough to police his realm institutions of law-making and justice were developed to safeguard his rights and those of his subjects upon whom he had to rely as the basis of his power. In course of time these developed into two great systems of law. On the Continent the jurists in the universities and in the courts of kings revived the principles of Roman law and applied them to the government of the national state, while churchmen and Scholastic philosophers not only safeguarded the rights of the Church, but invoked once more the Stoic ideas of Natural Law as a bulwark of human rights. In England this process was paralleled by the growth of the common law in the king's courts, systematizing law for the realm and yet preserving much of the homely wisdom of the folkways of town and country in remembered and established precedents.

But neither in England nor elsewhere could royalty by itself ensure respect for its authority without the support of national assemblies. Thus parliaments and law courts developed alongside and under the aegis of royalty. But this development was constantly checked by its own protectors as the military power of kings gained the upper hand in the struggle with feudalism. The power of the purse, which was the political weapon of parliaments, was not strong enough and its owners not yet sufficiently experienced to cope with the monarchs of unified national states. The result was that at the close of the Middle Ages medieval politics, like the politics of Rome, developed despotisms. The culmination of this process, as evidenced in the England of Henry VIII and the France of Louis XI, was summed up in the political philosophy of Machiavelli.

Throughout all the Middle Ages, economic life was simple to the point of being rudimentary. Hand labor and agricultural economics offered little chance for social evolution. But with the opening of trade, first through the eastern Mediterranean and the land routes of Asia and Europe, and then by the newly discovered seaways to America and India, the increase of money economy challenged the existing economic system and finally overthrew it. This was the commercial revolution, culminating in the sixteenth and seventeenth centuries.

A new middle class emerged, jealous of its control of the purse and refusing to accept the claim of the "divine right of kings," a claim which would, at least in theory, have made the national state a modernized theocracy. The movement of protest and revolt against this reactionary trend which imperiled not only the freedom of the individual but the institutions of self-government, attained its full force in England in the seventeenth century.

Then, at last, politics came to grips with the fundamental nature of the problem of freedom. Not only the life, but also the property of the individual, must be safeguarded against the tyranny of government. The influence of English revolutionary thought was carried to the Continent through the French *Philosophes* of the eighteenth century, and both directly and through them affected the thought of the leaders of the American Revolution. The way in which this current of protest became a new concept of government is a matter of fundamental importance for us today.

The commercial revolution had been largely instrumental in creating modern capitalism, through both the increase of commerce and, more especially, that of gold and silver; but the new owners of wealth still thought of it in terms of economic warfare, based on the idea that one's advantage lay in taking advantage of those with whom one dealt. As long as this mercantilism remained dominant in national politics, economics was too closely linked with the war system to serve as a genuine liberating principle in the structure of civilization. Adam Smith's *The Wealth of Nations*, published in 1776, based on the principle that the welfare of a commercial country is increased by the welfare of its customers, was as much a declaration of freedom in the economic sphere as was the American Declaration of Independence of the same year in the sphere of politics.

With the beginning of the nineteenth century and the Napoleonic wars breaking down the structure of Continental society, a great new chapter was opened in the history of freedom, too vast and too complicated for any single narrative. The motive force in this development was nationalism, reaching its triumphant fulfillment in the national state system which had been foreshadowed in the breakdown of the medieval system too centuries earlier. Within each country, except for intervals of reaction, institutions of self-government developed, with a new sense of the right of the citizen; careers were opening to talent, and it was growingly evident that the firmest basis of the state lay in the support of a free citizenship.

But the national state system retained the fundamental fallacy of the ancient city state. The freedom of each country was maintained by a balance of power, and the symbol of its independence was the sovereign right to use war as the instrument of its policy. The glorification of the war system in the Germany of Bismarck's day was but a grosser form of a common fallacy. The World Wars were for the national state system what the Peloponnesian War was for Athens.

Meanwhile a far greater force than any of those we have been dealing with began to show itself in the Industrial Revolution. The factory system, based on capital instead of land, began to create a demand for freedom from the tyranny of a society which had become rigid along pre-industrial lines. This was achieved in the economy of *laissez-faire*, which demanded economic freedom for the capitalists in a national state dominated by them. The demands of the workers for freedom from wage slavery were embodied in two separate movements: social reform by process of law, in which there was slow but steady progress; and socialism, striking at the very basis of capitalism itself, but with only slight effect until the advent of Russian communism after the nineteenth century had passed into history.

The end of the era came when the First World War showed that war itself had been fundamentally changed by the advent of modern science and that it could no longer be used as a controllable and directable instrument of national policy. That being the case, resort to it henceforth becomes an international crime. The Second World War reinforced these conclusions, and the Nuremberg trials brought them within the scope of international law. But the elimination of the war system calls for a new international structure capable of making freedom secure under law and of continuing and strengthening the evolution which began in seventeenth-century England and flowered so auspiciously in the nineteenth century in spite of its political imperfections.

Finally, then, we come back to the fundamental problem of freedom in the regime of peace in the daily lives of common people. Civilization has not yet attained this ultimate goal by the mere elimination of taboo or authoritarian teaching or by the elimination of the out-worn war system of the past. Much more difficult than even these vast steps in the progress toward freedom is the prevention of exploitation of honest, decent people by those in positions of economic advantage and their oppression by the cunning or the strong. These are henceforth supreme issues in human life and destiny. It is but natural that the communists should attempt to solve them by resort to violence or force, for that is the way in which most revolutions have been carried through in the past. But all history shows that there is no permanence in institutions which rest upon such a basis. Economic freedom achieved by the sacrifice of every other freedom results in nothing else than the degradation of the individual and the undoing of that long process of emancipation of the intelligence which we have been tracing from the beginnings to our own time.

The present volume traces these issues in broad outline from the beginning of time, not with the detachment of the historian who is interested only in the past, but with a vivid sense of the way this problem confronts us in the world today. Science, sure of its growing mastery over the forces of nature, is now extending that mastery to force new human relationships which call for emancipation from taboo, war and exploitation. Like all other agents of emancipation, however, it can be an instrument of oppression as well as of freedom through the overwhelming use of power. Nevertheless, it is mobilized intelligence, by which science itself is outlawing war by changing its nature from a controllable instrument of policy to senseless, criminal and universal destruction. It is also intelligence which finds the only sure basis of enduring welfare in social justice for others. In other words, we are being forced to discover the true nature of civilization.

This constitutes a turning point in the long processes of history, the significance of which none of us can fully discern in the murk and confusion that have followed two world wars. The battle with superstition, war, exploitation and injustice is by no means over. But the promise of ultimate victory already shines before us. The taboos are yielding to the ministrations of science, and military leaders themselves are recognizing the futility of war.

There still remains, however, the hardest task of all: that of the elimination of exploitation and the establishment of social and economic justice. Just how this can be done and still preserve the heritage of freedom so long fought for and so dearly prized is the outstanding problem of today. Communism attacks this problem by a revolutionary doctrine that would sweep away the capitalism in which the new industrial system has grown up. The result has been a cold war with the threat of hot war menacing the destruction of civilization. But the lesson of history, as set forth in this volume, is that, given time, such rigid and antagonistic doctrines dissolve under new conditions, — and science, the greatest dynamic force in history — is bound to create ever new conditions which make rigid doctrines no longer applicable. The world of the future will be neither the communistic world of the nineteenth and twentieth centuries nor that of capitalism as it exists today. The doctrines will remain for those interested in them; but just as Catholicism and Protestantism, the two most rigid doctrines in history, three centuries ago, ceased their hot and cold wars under the impact of new interests and a new conception of the world, so the present doctrinal dispute will change its nature in an ever-changing world.

Already there are signs that on both sides of the iron curtain new attitudes are developing toward the problems of both war and peace. It is growingly recognized by intelligent people everywhere that, as between the two great aggregations of power, war is no longer war; but renunciation of it, expressed in the only meaningful language, disarmament, is an operation which can only take place if it increases, instead of lessening, national security. This involves much more than the inspection of armaments. Spying and counter-spying are police actions which of themselves do not tend to breed good will and mutual confidence, the only sound basis for disarmament. This makes all the more important the statement of Secretary of State Herter in a notable address before the Foreign Trade Council on November 17, 1959, in which he expressed the belief that the United States and the Soviet Union would find "a common language" for the ground rules of co-survival. Chairman Khrushchev had said the same thing in other words a short time before. But, while he ruled out resort to war, he claimed for communism the victory of peace, in its extension over the majority of mankind. This is not the "common language" which the West uses, as Ex-Secretary of State Acheson strongly and eloquently protested a few days after Secretary Herter's address. Mr. Acheson was right in insisting that we remain on guard against diplomatic manoeuvering, but wrong in the implication that negotiations should be barred because of past failures. It would be a strange turn of affairs if the free nations denied themselves the freedom to negotiate. Sooner or later the "common language" will become universal. The increase in cultural and scientific as well as economic exchanges will give it a new content, voicing new interests.

There is no one definition of freedom which covers all the varied, and often apparently contradictory, aspects of its history, as it is traced in the following pages. This is so self-evident that it should not be necessary to say so but for the fact that the social sciences have been so largely invaded by those who mistake definition for understanding. History is denatured when it is systematized in terms of any one of its many manifestations in the human spirit.

21

This protest against the misuse of the social sciences in the interpretation of history is borne out by the origin and history of the words, "freedom" and "liberty," themselves. The origins point to quite different backgrounds. "Free" is linked in Gothic and Sanskrit with the word "love" as applied to the tie of kinship in family or clan. The German *Friede* ("peace") is from the same root. On the other hand, the Latin *liber* (Greek *eleutheros)* goes back to the Sanskrit *rodhati*, "to grow." *Libertas* has in it the fulfillment of the rights of citizenship. Without pressing the etymological history too far, it seems as though something of these divergent origins still clings to the words. "Freedom" seems to be more personal, "liberty" to be a more civic condition or privilege. Somehow "freedom" seems to hold more of the Anglo-Saxon directness of speech than its Latin synonym "liberty," although the plural "liberties" regains some of the concreteness of "freedom."

From these traces of primitive ideas in the words, we turn to the long and varied history of freedom itself.

CHAPTER I

BEFORE HISTORY

The Human Animal

IN SPITE OF the splendor of his achievements during the last five thousand years, man is still largely a creature of the unnumbered centuries which lie the other side of the ice age. It is a sobering thought that each of us possesses not only the aptitude for civilized life but also the instincts of animals. All history is full of reminders of this; for history is a reservoir of unreason as well as a register of conscious thought. Reason is but a surface covering for mile-deep emotions in us; emotions slumbering in the quiet routine of daily life, but, when stung by crises, dominant for good or ill.

The domain of human relations with which this study deals is the one which offers the most constant reminder of these far-off beginnings. For it is in the mass rather than in the individual that the animal mind chiefly manifests itself. Only the disciplined mind can overcome these primitive impulses which abound in us, and even for it there are more failures than successes. The structure of civilization has not been built by measured thought like the architecture of a building or the engineering of a machine. It is an organic growth capable of disease and deformation as well as normal development, and to understand it properly one must know something of its embryology and early formations and keep these fundamental facts in mind when dealing with the vast and complex problems of today.

The first textbook of history which lies open before us is that illustrated by the specimens in a museum of natural history. The spark of life which found its way from the ocean ooze to Mesozoic jungles faced from the beginning the two chief problems of all life, survival and welfare — in other words safety for the species, if not for the individual, and food with livable conditions of climate and environment. The animal that triumphed was the one that could adjust itself most swiftly and successfully to a world of danger and uncertainty.

This called for a kind of specialization other than that of mere strength, as in the case of dinosaur and mastodon, or of mere swiftness, as in the case of antelope or bird. What was needed was specialization in versatility, and this was to be found in the development of nerves, quick to respond to danger and to meet surprise by surprise. Success in the long process of evolution was found, therefore, not by a development of bone and sinew which culminated in rigid might, nor in the delicate capacity for flight. While both strength and speed were called for, they were less important than capacity for rapid adjustment.

It is important in any study of history to remember that this fundamental equipment of mankind is a basic equipment of animal life — indeed of all life. It is the reaction to stimuli by tingling apprehensions that finally center into that nervous system we have schooled into an instrument of the intellect.

Unfortunately for our understanding of the early history of mankind, the nerves themselves leave no lasting trace, and we must infer from bones or implements their development from the protoplasmic squirm of unicellular life to the guiding brain of the animal. No one knows, and perhaps no one will ever know, just how this happened, but the gap between the lower animals and man has now almost been bridged by studying the fragmentary remains which have been recovered from Java, the hills of Peiping, South Africa, and in our own western states.

In addition to the rich endowment of the nervous system, man had two organic advantages over other animals. The enlargement of the head made possible more varied sounds from the throat, and so the single call of the animal could develop into complicated languages; and the claw became a hand when the thumb slipped down the side to touch other finger points. It is surely unnecessary to recall the role played by the voice in the formation of society, the stimulant as well as the expression of thought; but the evolution of the hand was almost equally important, making possible not only strength of grasp but adjustability as well. It is only when we watch the animals that have no hands fumbling their awkward and circumscribed way through a world that offers so little to fang and hoof, that we can really appreciate what an incomparable instrument it is.

From the hand's solid hold on sticks and stones to the use of tools was a long, slow but inevitable advance; and then with just a little chipping of the rough stone which nature supplied, the hands of prehistoric men, long before the ice age, fitted themselves around the fist hatchet, and mankind began to leave its record in the preglacial soil and rock. The tool had become an adjunct of mankind, not a substitute for the hand but an extension of it, and an imperishable inheritance to be used from generation to generation through the immemorial past.

Down to our own times when modern science opened a wholly new era for mankind, it was with these rudimentary gifts of nerve and muscle, developed into skilled and delicate organisms, that practically all the achievements of history were made. To be sure, from the earliest beginnings it was the brain, with its vocal instrument — the speaking brain — if we may term it so for short, which took the primacy and made such effective use of the substitute for a claw. But without the hand man would never have been more than an agile and supersensitive animal, if indeed he could have survived; for an equipment of nerves alone, however keenly sensitive and coordinated to translate impressions into rudimentary thought, would not have enabled him to overcome the brute force of his foes in the animal world.

It was the speaking brain and hand together which ensured the empire of man. But the mind was capable of a far greater range of experience than the body, because it could mingle past and present in what we call memory. The all important thing was that the register of impressions lasted; for in this way, from the crude experiences of current happenings, man built up a third dimension of life called thought. It was still limited and will always be limited by his experience. But its great advantage is that it is not limited to what is taking place at the time when the thinking is done, but can make its own the experience of other events, other times and places. Thus the interplay of mind and body furnishes the long and halting prelude for the drama of intelligent life.

Throughout the millenia in which this evolution was taking place, man continued to live very much like other animals, at least like the more intelligent of them. The primitive world was one of tooth and claw, of brutish life. The animal mind remained in man as an inheritance from his origins, just as much as bone and muscle.

Nor have the conditions of the human drama ever wholly changed. Psychology is growingly aware of the persistence of the animal mind in even the most intelligent of the human species. The high creations of thought rest upon foundations moored in a nervous system that responds to the electricity of attraction and repulsion, such as stir the microscopic amoeba. This is only another way of saying that all life is one; but it is sobering to realize what that implies. The emancipation of mankind from the dominance of his own unintelligence remains the unfinished task of the ages. The brute continues to prowl dumbly in the subconscious background of even the civilized mind, ready to assert itself by force and violence, cruelty and crime, and to justify oppression and war by an appeal to innate animal tendencies too strong for man.

It would be wrong, however, to concentrate our attention so intently upon

24

the inner as well as the outer impediments to progress as to fail to appreciate how great that progress has been. For, after all, mankind has made his animal equipment serve other than animal purposes. Somewhere in the dim, unnumbered centuries, our ancestors crossed a great divide and entered upon a new world of experience in which they found escape from dumb fears by ceremonies and an artistry in magic, the far off origin of both art and religion. Human history has no more fundamental theme than this escape which led through mimicry to a sense of beauty and from superstition to critical analysis in the search for truth. For this groping of primitive man became the heritage of the civilized, a way kept open through recurring dark ages by one of the noblest efforts of the race: the effort to establish justice — which with beauty and truth is the third of the great trilogy of human ideals.

This glimpse of the trend of history must not mislead us, however, into premature or short-sighted optimism. It is a long road upon which we are travelling, one which leads from crude savagery to a mind freed from the imprisoning centuries. It is also a road upon which the individual cannot travel alone, for the goal is one in which his personal needs are held in equilibrium with those of the rest of the society in which he lives.

Freedom does not lie in escape from society, but in a perfect balance between what the individual comes to think of as his rights and the rights of other people. It is true that in isolation one may gain new perspectives cleared of the trivial happenings of daily life, but such perspectives are always limited by the narrowing confines of an experience that loses contact with reality. Therefore the movement toward the emancipation of the mind is not just that of a few leaders, because, by themselves alone, they cannot create the conditions of a perfect life. Neither is it enough for a single community or nation to achieve progress by itself, for it is in the relations with other people that the animal mind tends to reassert itself. Even when it no longer dominates human conduct in domestic affairs, as in the crude impulses of savagery, it comes to the fore in the relations of one nation or people with another.

Never has this fact been more evident than in the world today, when the nations that regard themselves as the leaders of civilization have turned upon each other with all the ferocity of beasts. War was a function of the organism that man acquired before he became man. The fact that it remains a technique of highly cultured peoples is the outstanding evidence of the frailty of a culture that fails to embrace the whole scope of human relationships. There is no true freedom for either mind or body in a society that uses intelligence for destruction; because the greater the intelligence the greater the capacity to destroy and the greater the apprehension of danger.

The task with which we are now confronted is, therefore, one of education, but not just of the elite within a nation or of those peoples who are already far advanced. It must ultimately include all mankind. This does not mean that the movement of progress will ever be uniform throughout the world. It is merely a recognition of the fact that the very existence of backward peoples hampers the progress of the more civilized. Such a condition offers a temptation to exploitation which, in turn, breeds rivalries, and thus maladjustments, which are so often the cause of war.

There is nothing fanciful in reminding ourselves that the road which we are travelling is that of all mankind; for it has been so since the beginning of time. The travellers are slow-footed, confused, uncertain, fettered by habit and custom; some are far swifter than others, some even so far ahead as to lose sight of those who follow after. But the road we are describing is that of history itself, and the goal which we have termed freedom is also called justice. Neither of these terms conveys its full meaning, however, which is the realization of that deepest of all the aspirations of mankind, that of the spiritual life.

Although the advance of civilization will always remain varied according to the circumstances and capacities of people, the rate at which it moves is no longer the same as in the past. The conquest of time and space by modern science has accelerated the pace and will forever continue to increase it. We, of this age, are standing at a turning point which has no parallel in history. After millions of years of groping, we are at last coming face to face with intelligence as the dominant force in the world,— dominant for good or evil. This is all so new that we cannot yet have any clear conception of the possibilities which lie ahead either in the speed of attainment or the scope of achievement.

Already, however, in the techniques of life, we are leaving our animal inheritance behind. We are finding substitutes for those aids to the brain which the body supplies, opening the eye and ear to the limitless rays that are neither light nor sound, and offering the strength and the forces of nature as substitutes for the hand itself, or at least for the muscle which made it so valiant a tool. This has come upon us with a suddenness which finds us unprepared for its consequences.

The scientific revolution has begun to make a new place in the universe for man by using nature against itself with the ultimate possibility of so mastering its powers that some day he can stand aside while the energy of the sun, out of which his life came, will make all things contribute to his welfare. From atom to stardust, the human mind is now pioneering on the frontiers of the universe and making it more and more its own.

But across the pathway of this alluring prospect lie the obstacles of our own creation: maladjustments in the relation of man to man. The fundamental theme of history is not this conquest of the material world, which is after all but the theatre for human experience. The real theme is freedom — whether it is applied in the practice of justice by which life finds its equilibrium in society or in the creative capacity of the mind itself as it becomes more and more capable of mirroring that ultimate reality of which the prophets and the poets have given us glimpses in the past, divine reason — or whether it degenerates into anarchy, to be employed as the agent of passion and destruction.

From this short survey, it is evident that the study of society must always rest on the foundation of history, because society is the guardian of those things which mankind has cherished, even when he has failed to understand them. In the world of politics the motive force is that which has lain unsuspected but potent in common experience. A Mussolini or Hitler is never the individualist that he seems to be to his followers, for what he creates has its roots in far-off things as well as in the experience of the age in which he lives. A Lenin or Stalin, viewing freedom as an economic fact, ignores and violates personal and political freedom because the world in which he lived never had known it. The clue to these almost unending paradoxes lies in the study of the age-long forces which have so long balked intelligence, and with which it is at grips today.

The Beginnings of Religion

It is no wonder that the social sciences lag behind those which deal with the material world, for of all the mysteries in the universe the greatest is man himself. The chemist and physicist have no such obdurate and elusive phenomena to deal with as those which find their expression in the history and daily life of this strange creature, which adds to the mysteries of external nature the supreme achievement of the reasoning mind. No drama of the imagination can rival this one of sheer human reality in which the creatures of a passing hour carry out their tragic parts from generation to generation, century to century, millenium to millenium.

The social sciences have so far been able to deal only with the merest externals of this vast episode of life; and yet within the last century the whole content of history has been drastically revised. The perspective now makes even the building of the pyramids an event in modern history, as archeology merges the story of man with that of the geological ages. The unrecorded past has been revealed by the comparative study of primitive tribes, and the meager annals of recorded history have been enriched with social data which left their obscure traces in the trend of events.

But through this bewildering enrichment of our knowledge of mankind one striking fact stands out above all the rest: the almost incredible fact that in fundamentals the chief problems of mankind have never changed. From prowling hordes in the earliest stages of primitive life, through the prehistory of savage tribes, into the history of the nations of today run constant trends and fundamental impulses. The problems of life vary in their external forms, but at bottom they are much the same as they have always been, and our instinctive ways for meeting them remain the same as well. The plot of the human drama has remained substantially the same from the first emergence of mankind to our own day, woven out of the two great themes of survival and welfare.

The key to it all lies in one fact, the need of life to perpetuate itself. This at once shapes itself in two directions: protection against danger and the maintenance of a supply of food and of livable conditions. These were the two chief interests of primitive man, and they remain today the basis of the varied activities of the civilized world. Round about them we have raised the emotional and intellectual life which finds expression in the arts and sciences; but we never have escaped from their dominance as a condition of life itself, and we never can. In the simplicity of early society they were not marked off from each other as they are in the modern world, and yet from the beginning the organization of society itself was either directly or indirectly determined by them.

The instinct for survival is universal and ever present, but it is chiefly active in times of crises, especially in the face of danger. For most of the time men as well as animals are only partially aware of what they are doing or of the conditions under which they are living, for they follow to a large extent the unconscious repetition of the things of habit. The sense of danger breaks into this routine with quick reactions against the things of fear. Safety must be found or death and destruction follow. The sudden awareness which this brings may be mistaken as to what the realities are, but this blundering sense of things at hand is the starting point on the long road to intelligence and ultimate freedom. It is here, therefore, that we must begin, where mankind itself first began.

The dangers with which mankind has been confronted have always been of two kinds: one physical, the other psychic. The physical dangers were mostly from the beasts of prey, of whom man was one. By stratagem and by the use of weapons he not only survived but proved his superiority as a fighter over all the animal world. The hunt was more than a means of subsistence, however; it was a cause of social formation. The hunters were followed by those who lived off them, like the pack of animals which they displaced. Thus migratory hordes were kept together in some loose connection.

But these earliest of rudimentary groupings were held together less by the common needs of the chase, or even by war, than by sharing in defense against the haunting dangers of superstition. For primitive man faced psychic dangers, fully as real, if more elusive, than those of the actual world, in the crises of life itself and in the strange, new or unaccountable things that forced themselves into his keen but bewildered consciousness. While routine could go on much the same as with us, there were times when the nerves were set vibrating in blank confusion. Mysterious potencies were felt, as yet too vague and unformed to be invested with spirit life, but fraught with good or ill for all those coming in contact with them.

Therefore, the magician priest, who claimed to know the secret way of dealing with these supernatural, or unnatural powers, had an even greater chance to control the destinies of savage society than the warrior chieftain, except when both offices were united in one. Safety in this uncanny world could never be wholly assured; for sooner or later, the dread things caught up with one, no matter what protective rites were performed. But primitive man did his best to postpone that evil hour and to clear the pathway of lurking danger by resorting to a technique to which the nerves themselves would respond. It is impossible to reduce this technique to any single formula; but its two outstanding features were magic and sacrifice.

In the world of primitive man, all "sacred" things may either curse or bless. They discharge some power, some radiation in the psychic universe, and the man who comes in contact, whose nerves receive its shock, is the victim or beneficiary. Such motor forces are the basis of "contagious magic." Whatever shocks the primitive nerves will set such forces going.

It now transpires that primitives in many parts of the world have a distinct sense of this mysterious power behind contagion and have gone so far as to give it a name. It is the Algonquin *manitou*, the *atua* of the Maoris, the *mana* of the Melanesians. The Latins, that one people of antiquity whose state religion remained even in the time of its highest culture a clear perpetuation of magic, called it *sacer*, or the sacred — the thing with power to bless or curse, the nameless, formless force which even in historic times took to itself form and shape as god or goddess.

Here, then, is the clue which anthropology supplies to open up the origins of religion and trace it through primitive superstitions to the great conceptions of theology. For *mana* does not die out when animism appears, nor where animism grows into anthropomorphism, nor even when polytheism passes away before monotheism. Its maleficent elements grow less and less apparent, and its beneficence more, until, as divine grace, it nourishes the faith and strengthens the moral purpose of the Christian world. In the realm of faith, it has at last left the material media of its long historic phase.

Religion was no special creation midway along the centuries of human groping; it was but the more intense action of that mysterious power which lay at the heart of magic. The action changes with changing society. At first the recoil from things of terror, the sense of wonder at their awful power, the thrill that came to the confused senses from any imagined cause, this psychic reaction adjusts itself, reaches out to further and undreamed possibilities as the reflex of the widening experience of man, until at last it compasses the whole range of religious emotion. Made a blessing instead of a curse by those first specialists in psychology, the medicine men, and surrounding society with taboos which are the basis of most early jurisprudence, the results of our ancestors' fears and awe-struck wonderings are to be seen on every side in our institutions and civilization today.

In religion itself, the potency of mysterious things becomes the adumbration of the noblest of its concepts; for, in spite of the discoveries of science, the mystery of life and the world remains, and all the universe is still a sacrament.

It is essential that, as we turn to trace the secular story of mankind through its changing patterns, we should not lose sight of the vivid and enduring background which we have just been surveying. For the world of the taboo lay not only on the pathway of religion and of intellectual development, it was one of the determining facts in the structure of society as well. The crises of life are recurring and inescapable, and to prepare for them the daily routine as well as the enterprises of war and the chase have all to be kept free from the contagion of unlucky things.

"Luck" is not mere chance when it can be conjured into sticks and stones, and things have to be "purified" by ritual acts from any possible taint of "uncleanness." Only experts can handle this primitive medicine which is brewed in witches' kettles. The shaman in early societies is the one whose hand does not falter, whose eyes do not water, as he touches things too dreadful for others to approach. He is then "sacred" as long as his "luck" — or potency — works. The sacrificial victim also shares the sacredness of things devoted to the gods, and so his sacrificers humor his desires in the interval before the sacrifice. In this connection, by ways too remote for us to follow, the victim may even take on the functions of priesthood, and from this strange union assume the attributes of a "divine kingship."

While the leadership for dealing with things and times of danger furnished crisis organizations, mostly with clan insignia or "totems," there was another underlying tie which held a primitive society together, that of kinship; and the core of society was then what is still the central core of human association everywhere, the family; not the family of today, however, for this earliest of the stable groupings of mankind was worn thin in the course of ages and lost its primitive meaning. The dreaded power of taboo was especially present in the rules for marriage, especially that of exogamy, prohibiting marriage within the totem group. This made the boundaries of kinship something different from the simple blood relationship of the civilized.

The intimate associations of daily life by cave or forest dwellers could be shared by others who, through intermarriage according to the complicated prescriptions of exogamy or by adoption, were enabled to cross the taboo frontiers. The artificial nature of these limitations resulted in systematizing external relationships, and so families found their places in clans, phratries or kin-brotherhoods, and finally in tribes. The process of expansion or interplay of membership thus reached the largest unit recognizing kinship and its associated taboos.

These kinship groups had close memberships. Each person had his definite place in society. Responsibility for crime or the violation of taboo was shared in by one's "relatives" and redress of grievance was either by the individual feud or by drawing in the whole group against the violator. The individual was by no means that carefree man whom romantic writers once imagined and described. The revolutionary challenge in the opening chapter of Rousseau's *Social Contract*, "Man is born free and is everywhere in chains" was both false in itself and in the philosophy of history built upon it. His "noble savage" was not born into a family where all (father and children alike) "being born free and equal, alienate their liberty only for their own advantage." On the contrary, as we have seen, all relationships within the primitive kinship group were closely circumscribed.

But if this was the case within the "family," clan or tribe, it was all the more so in their relations with others. For the outsider was doubly dangerous, as a possible violator of taboo and as a possible enemy in war. When one tribe conquered another, even if it settled down on the same territory, it was careful to preserve the essentials of its original unity by absorbing only those elements of other blood or rites which could be safely and properly brought within its own taboos. The primal law of life, that of the exclusiveness of

30

magic ceremonies, could never be violated with impunity. The most intimate customs of the kinship group were kept safe from pollution by outsiders. The emphasis so strongly placed upon common ancestry or legendary heroes was something more than human interest in the story of the past. It meant that the ancestral customs were also a common possession which could not be readily shared with outsiders.

The "weight of antique custom" thus lay heavily upon the shoulders of mankind. There was almost no provision for change in early society, but only deep concern to prevent it. And yet three ways of escape developed, wholly different from each other.

First of all, there was war, the most imperious force for change because the least humane. The second was the revolutionary influence of great religious and spiritual leaders, capable of defying both belief and traditional conduct. The third was the leverage of economic forces in the social and political structure, working both within it and without, but more especially in the insidious influence of traders settling by the nearest market place and exchanging custom and law along with the goods of commerce.

Of these three influences, the first two, by a paradox without parallel, are inherent in the very "technique of safety" which maintains warrior and priests to keep things as they were. The data of economic life are also those of immemorial repetition, for the daily needs of men can only be satisfied a little at a time and have to be met in the self-same way, day after day, year after year, generation after generation. Yet it was especially in this field that the greatest influence for change made itself felt. The outstanding proof of its greater potency is that, down to our own day, the chief differences between Asia and Europe lay in the fact that while Asia felt the shock of war and moved to the appeal of prophetic leaders, Europe found the pathway of advance through varied experiment in the economic mastery of human needs. This opens long and distant perspectives; it is also a clue to the relative forces in the world today.

The interplay of hunt and war was natural, and perhaps inevitable, when scarcity of game led to expeditions on the ranges of other hordes or tribes. More dangerous, however, than any animal was man himself. Migration, spurred by hunger, was another incentive to fighting. The needs of war, in turn, brought about a rudimentary organization for the crisis which it involved. It was not enough to be the wiliest fighter with the best weapon. The horde had to work together under the guidance of the bravest or most experienced leader. The training for such a profession began by sorting out the best, from earliest manhood, so that in time a warrior class could work together in the loose discipline of the savage foray. In the interval between wars or the chase, the leaders of this soldiery were sure to have a privileged place among those dependent upon them for safety.

Naturally, also, the whole body of fighting men left to others as much as they could that kind of work which is drudgery to healthy and lazy alike. Most primitive war was for plunder. It must also have been a great boon to the women and children when the warriors, instead of killing the conquered,

31

brought them home as slaves; and yet such a step forward in the prosperity of the tribe could not amount to much until they were settled on the soil and began to cultivate the arts of peace.

War and Economics

If freedom was curtailed in the lives of the uncivilized by the restrictions imposed by superstition, it also suffered from the threat and fact of war. The idea of peace was as foreign to early man as that of freedom, and the techniques for safety in both cases were the first of all disciplines. The warrior, however, needed no such psychic qualifications as the medicine man. It was taken for granted that every physically fit young man would be drafted into the profession of arms, for that was the condition of his full membership in the councils as well as the wars of his tribe.

Formal ceremonies of induction into the warrior class take place in all primitive societies. We need cite only one example. Tacitus tells us that in the Assembly of the early Germans, the father, or a relative, decorated the young man with shield and spear, without which he could not carry on either private or public business. This was his *toga,* the first honor of youth. Before this he was just a part of the family; now he belonged to the state.

The *Germania* of Tacitus is a classic of the literature of history. It will always remain a puzzle to critics how this historian of the Rome of Tiberius who evidently never crossed the Rhine, should have written a description of the tribal life of the early Germans which has stood the test of archeology and comparative anthropology. A factual account, utterly devoid of theorizing, it furnishes us with a detailed description of a people who are in the very midst of a revolutionary change in which the taboo of kinship is being broken down by the impact of war. The tribes still fight in families, with the women and even the children urging on the warriors and ministering to them. But this tribal formation is already cut into by bands of warrior companions who rally to the call of a chieftain to join in expeditions for plunder and glory. This institution of the *comitatus* was destined to furnish a model for feudalism in the early Middle Ages, and as described by both Tacitus and Caesar was evidently a sign of the breaking up of the early tribal formations in which the patriarchal blood tie relationship had dominated. If so, we are witnessing the first major change in German society with war acting as the catalyst in the dissolution of its most primitive form.

The laws of taboo are still strong, with a priesthood to ensure their observance, and the function of the king is more that of priest than warrior. Tacitus says that the kings are chosen according to birth, but the chieftains according to valor. This means, of course, that the king comes from a royal family which in all early life means one invested with the secrets of magic practices. By the time of Tacitus the priesthood had taken over the administration of the laws of taboo: . . . "no one has the right to punish, imprison or even to strike but the priests, and they do it as obeying the orders of the gods." But the chief interest of the tribesmen was war, and Caesar tells us that if a German youth held back from joining the *comitatus* he was "accounted in the number of deserters and traitors to whom confidence in all matters was henceforth refused." A society wholly organized for war exerts the same kind of social pressure as the taboo. In the case of the early Germans, peace — the one condition for freedom — was a disgrace.

We shall have further glimpses of early German society later on in our history, but these are of special interest because they exemplify the general law of history, to be provided in almost every known instance of tribal development. It is a strange fact, one which even seems to challenge reason, that war, in spite of its barbarism, may carry society out of the dark background of superstitious savagery into the secular world in which the fate of family or tribe ultimately rests upon the capacity of the individual. It would be wrong, however, to regard this breaking down of the taboo as more than a very limited step towards freedom, for the demands of war are imperious.

Like the Spartans or the Japanese, the Germans of the war bands had to choose victory or death. "In battle line," says Tacitus, "it is shameful to a chieftain to yield in valor and shameful to the members of his war band [*comites*] not to equal the valor of the chieftain, but it is most infamous for them to leave the field without the leader, for their most sacred vow is to defend him, to cover him with their bodies and to attain to his glory by their own deeds. The chieftains fight for victory; the *comites* for the chieftains."

Their whole lives are devoted to war. "If a tribe [*civitas*] languishes in peace, these young men go off to offer themselves elsewhere. Their warhorse and the bloody, victorious spear [*framea*] is given them by their chieftain. He also keeps them at his table, offering them a livelihood from the spoils of war and pillage in place of pay. If you try to persuade them to work or await a harvest, they would listen much less to you than if you engaged them to challenge enemies and merit wounds. They hold it base to acquire by sweat what can be got by blood."

In the tribal Assembly, which met in full battle dress, the place of distinction and influence was held by the chieftain who had the largest war band. His fame spreads to neighboring tribes who send embassies to him loaded with presents, for by "his renown alone wars are terminated."

It is evident from the detail of this description of the German war bands that Tacitus was deeply interested in an institution which had no parallel in Roman history. In his rigidly objective narrative he does not draw the lesson implicit in it, that the primitive German state [*civitas*] which he describes was on the path to anarchy, when the powerful chieftains waged, not merely warlike raids for plunder, but war itself against the neighboring tribes. Within the tribe itself the effect of this development must have been greater still, especially in curtailing the power or at least lessening the dignity of the king.

We shall treat this problem of the role of war as a catalyst of primitive society in further detail where it was most clearly operative, in the histories of Greece and Rome. We must turn now to the third element in social formation listed above, that of economics. The word is a misnomer as used here, for it implies a highly organized articulation of the processes of production and distribution — which never existed until our time. Even Aristotle used it only with reference to the management of an estate. But, while the word economics hardly applies to the work and property of early societies, the fact played its revolutionary part from the beginning of settled life, and before.

The starting point for history lies, as we have seen, in those crises which from time to time disturb the ancient routine. But over against these extraordinary activities of mankind there has always existed a wholly different set of interests, those which deal with the ordinary events of daily life. These are the things which seldom get into history, or at least have seldom got into the histories of the past, for it is the crises that men remember, not the routine of the day's work.

The old chroniclers noting wars and plagues as the chief content of their story, used to pass by any year that did not register disaster with the significant remark, "nothing happened." The things they celebrated in song and story were the things that do not happen often, tragedies, achievements, sufferings, narrow escapes from danger, or triumphs to be registered in pride. History was born in romance; in the myth in which the gods played their part and in the heroic epic dealing with the prowess and skill of man. There is an enduring charm in themes like these because the listener or reader can by proxy and in perfect safety share in the emotions of the actors. This is surely one of the reasons why crimes furnish most of the content of journalism today. Kindly, mild-mannered people to whom the years have brought only routine recover some of the flavor of their barbaric past as they read stories of atrocity, safe from its actual menace.

Yet, in spite of all the attraction of "old, unhappy, far-off things and battles long ago," the great ages of history are not named after the exploits of war but after the mastery of the materials used in the day's work by that class of society which throughout the past has been ignored in history; the slave, the serf, the artisan, the worker in home or field — those who created comfort and supplied food. The stone age with which prehistory begins dates its milennia by the form of its axes and hammers, the tools of daily work. Then metal shared with stone in the growing capacity for controlling and changing life's environment. The age of bronze merging into the age of iron secured a widened area of economic mastery.

There is, after all, nothing strange in the fact that this decisive force which conditioned the ways of living should have for so long remained in the shadows of history, for it shared nothing of the excitement of the chase or of war or the thrill of mysterious powers and presences in religion. Adventuring in politics or in the realm of thought has a charm not only for the adventurers but for all who know about them. But, from the ice age down, the deadening routine of work, forever repeating itself, has been left to those who could not escape from it, or, at best, escape only partially. For this is the story of the underprivileged and unfree, the women of savage life, the slaves, the serfs and their modern successors wherever social and political justice is denied them. It is the darkest chapter in the annals of mankind; cruel, inhuman.

Where freedom does not exist, its full significance at last appears. It is the victims of oppression who know best what it means; unfortunately their lips are sealed, except for a few, like the Stoic Epictetus, whose mind was never enslaved and whose lot was not typical of slavery. Yet while the record, if inadequate, is a searing comment on the innate inhumanity of man, it also shows how he can rise above himself, with newer and clearer conceptions of justice, which is the basis of true freedom.

The Unfree

The origins of slavery as a basis for economic life were similar the world over: it developed in military societies which settled in the lands they had conquered but which still regarding war as their chief occupation and supreme concern. Under these circumstances, slavery seems to have been inevitable, for it was a universal rule wherever warrior peoples turned from sheer savagery to acquire and accumulate property. Mere robbery or spoliation was not enough; work had to be done to ensure food supplies, increase the store of goods and build defense works against possible enemies. These were not the tasks to which warriors would willingly turn from lives of adventure or privileged ease, as long as forced labor was at hand to bear the burden of never-ending drudgery.

So it was the labor of the unfree that, under the direction of the freemen, supplied most of the material creations of early civilization, built its cities, its pyramids, its temples, and cultivated its fields. It was under the lash that the rowers of its ships brought, indifferently, pirates or merchants to foreign shores. Along the routes of raiding armies, forts grew into walled centers of commerce, but Mesopotamia, the first cradle of civilization, both Babylonians and Assyrians carried slavery to its climax in the enslaving of whole nations.

It is hard to think of the utter cruelty which underlay the regime of slave rule as constituting anything but a heinous crime; yet it must be remembered that behind it lay still more ruthless cruelties. When the Tartars and Mongols and their neighboring nomadic hordes rode in savage conquest through Central Asia, and the Huns penetrated the heart of Europe, having no use for slaves, they killed men, women and children in indiscriminate slaughter. If Tamerlane the Tartar in the course of his ravages through Russia and Western Asia celebrated his massacres at Damascus by building a pyramid of sixty thousand skulls, it was but a monument to the unnumbered dead of countless atrocities through centuries of raiding, where slaves were worthless because only free men fought. The crime was war itself.

Slavery as an institution was not a part of the earliest form of society. It is a product of settled life, and however barbarous it appears in the retrospect of history, it really constituted a step forward from the mere savagery of that earlier stage, cannibal or otherwise, when the human enemies were hunted and killed like beasts. The first to be spared were the women, but only to a limited extent; for, as long as the food supply is dependent upon the chase, there must not be too many nonhunters at the fireside of the hunter-warrior.

In the next stage of advance, that of the pastoral nomad, some slaves were kept, won in fights with other hordes, to help tend the flocks, but their chief value was that they might be sold or traded for horses or cattle, which contributed real and substantial wealth.

Yet, we must not generalize too much. The nomads did not all withdraw from their conquests into their tents beyond the mountain barriers of Central Asia with only such booty as could be carried by horse. Already these "shaggy demons of the wilderness" as Carlyle called them, were being drawn out of their careers as destroyers to share in the culture they attacked. Thus Kublai Khan, grandson of Genghis, in completing the conquest of China, stopped the practice of indiscriminate massacre and treated the conquered with humanity. Such a revolution in the history of Mongol warfare laid the basis of a Chinese dynasty which made the new city of Peking the capital of the greatest empire in the world. Persia and India also yielded to the Mongol invaders, who, in turn, yielded to the allurements of the civilizations over which they ruled, with slavery and forced labor as recognized necessities for the enjoyment of leisure and luxury.

In Asia, individual slavery was less a feature of social life than the subjection of a whole class held apart from society by taboos like those of the untouchables of India — the scavengers and outcasts, who to orthodox Hindus cause defilement by their touch or even their presence, and who throughout history have lived apart in slums on the outskirts of towns or villages, denied even the use of the common village well.

In Japan, below the commoners called *Heimin* — farmers, artisans and traders — were the *Eta,* or defiled ones, and the *Himin* mendicants. The *Eta* were in all probability originally war prisoners or the enslaved families of criminals. They had the defiling tasks of tending tombs, disposing of the bodies of the dead, slaughtering animals and tanning hides. They were forced to live in segregated sections and were forbidden to intermarry with the commoners, or even to eat or drink with persons above their own class. They remained under the ban of ostracism from generation to generation. After the Meiji restoration, in 1871, however, they were admitted to the ranks of the commoners and generally relieved from proscription. At the time of their enfranchisement they numbered 287,111. The outcast *Himin* were given the humiliating task of burying executed criminals.

The taboo prescriptions in the European nations never went as far as those in Asia, seldom beyond such limitations on the rights and privileges of citizenship as the Plebs of Rome suffered — denial of the knowledge of those sacred formulas and usages which were rooted in religion, and which qualified for political office. The history of the Plebeian escape from this inferior status filled much of Roman history for two or three centuries. Similar, though less well defined, movements have taken place in the history of other Western nations. We may summarize them all in one generalization: where society was based on kinship and religion, freedom was limited to a ruling caste or class.

The Beginnings of Economics

The desire of men for comfort and for goods is balanced by their desire to escape doing the things which produce the comfort and the goods. While the chief sources of supply for primitive peoples were the booty of war or the chase, and the labor of slaves, there was also barter, as venturesome foreigners opened their "corded bales" from boats or caravans. Bartering was more than mere exchange of articles, it was a sharpening of wits to get the better of the other person, as in horse-trading in modern times. It was used in commercial transactions all through primitive and early antique society, and was so close to brigandage that the Greeks, without giving offense, could ask sailors landing on their shores if they were merchants or raiders.

But trade was also hampered as long as one object had to be exchanged for another, and so in the early market places of Asia Minor, metal pieces began to be used to represent the value of the goods themselves. Thus money came into trade, a universal register of value which could be used in any bazaar or for any purpose. It made property exchangeable not only from counter to counter, but from country to country. In ancient times, however, and indeed down to the discovery of gold and silver in the New World which helped bring Europe out of the Middle Ages, money was very scarce, and its absence was one of the determining factors in the nature of politics as well as of economics.

As long as there was little money and only hand labor to make things with, this aim to escape the drudgery of work could be gratified only by compelling the services of others, through slavery or serfdom, to make the goods or perform the necessary tasks. Whenever money is lacking, politics must remain on the basis of a personal relationship between the rulers and the ruled; neither obedience nor power can be passed along from one to another like coins in the hand. For without money to pay wages or buy goods, there cannot be taxes to pay for government works or for soldiers to protect the people.

This creative role of money in keeping societies coherent in spite of the increased fluidity of human relationships was not limited to internal, domestic history. It was also true of the interchange of one society with another. Trade had to become more than mere barter if it was to spread from people to people in a web of business enterprises. It had to be three-cornered at least, bringing in other parties who were interested in what each had to sell or might buy. The growth of trade, therefore, offers an index of the general growth of both wealth and security, for it could take place only where some measure of safety was assured for both goods and traders. We shall see that the rise of the merchant class brought with it the rise of laws about property and a revolution in the status of citizenship which, in Europe, produced the great new experiment of politics.

The listing of the elements of social and political evolution, however helpful it may be in the understanding of political development, is by no means

37

adequate as an introduction to history. For history is the record of no one of these things by itself but of their constant interplay. The warrior and the priest used the prerogatives they obtained from their services in time of crisis to have their economic wants supplied. The warrior got the booty of war, that is, tribute or slaves to make goods and perform services. The priest received the offerings of the religious. In either case a high rate of pay was exacted. Theirs was the most serious and most dangerous work. In primitive life only a few were qualified to be entrusted with the handling of crises. The tests for leadership of the war band or of the religious life of the people, to which we have referred above, were severe enough to eliminate the less gifted, ordinary people.

On the other hand, conquest begun by the soldier was often finished by the trader. Gaul was finally and personally conquered not by the legions of Rome but by the merchants who followed them, and who set up their bazaars, with glittering beads from Rome or Alexandria, to tempt the Gallic warriors and their families. It is this exploiting form of barter which has so commonly been used by highly civilized peoples in dealing with those of a lower culture. To help in the transfer of goods, metal counters were used like those in the Mediterranean cities, inscribed with a few Roman words, and the language of the market place was Romanized.

Those communities which developed into historic kingdoms and empires were located where the organization of safety and the chance for economic growth were found together. Egypt was a country isolated from the world except for the river valley, where the separate communities could trade with each other, exploiting the rich resources of the Nile. At time of flood, vessels could very easily go up and down the river, so that these communities eventually united under a theocratic organization and then remained secure against the outside world for centuries.

Babylonia and Assyria lay in the fertile crescent of the Tigris-Euphrates between desert and mountains, and were in addition on the caravan routes from India and Central Asia. They were more open to attack from invading nomads and had to develop artificial substitutes for defense. They safeguarded themselves by taking in those people who might be their enemies, as in the case of the Jews during the Babylonian captivity. But under the protection of highly organized armies and great walled cities, they built their canals and worked the richest soil in all the countries of the ancient world. Large forts, like those of ancient Babylon and Nineveh, planted at strategic points along the caravan routes, became the busy centers of the bazaar trade, which in turn stimulated handicrafts; and protected against dangers, property developed with police and law.

But neither armament nor priesthood could keep these antique civilizations safe from the dangers that came in upon them as new bands of tribesmen gathered in the hills to form new empires, like those of the Medes and the Persians. As human defenses failed, the dependence upon superstition grew to greater proportions as an instrument of self-protection. The closer one's relations with the Power or Powers ruling the universe, the more a people might feel assured of ultimate deliverance.

Thus the techniques of safety and of welfare interworked in the ancient past as in the modern world, although in different proportions. The antique dominance of king and priest remained the characteristic of Asiatic society while Europe came to concentrate more and more upon the purely secular needs of daily life. The Asiatic peoples have for the most part clung to their ancient customs and taboos, regulating life according to religious prescriptions and kinship ties throughout the centuries in which the West was slowly ridding commerce, government and even education of the primitive practices and institutions which have been both the strength and weakness of Asia.

The Beginnings of Government

Still we are only on the threshold of history; or rather within that long dim corridor which leads from the jungle of the savage to the city of the civilized — a corridor which has taken mankind thousands of years to traverse. Although the organization of society, of the blood tie, and of welfare, interact upon each other in primitive life, and, by the interplay of common interests in war, the chase, food and shelter, produce cohesion, nevertheless something else was needed before these elements of blind nature, developed from our animal inheritance, could be welded into agencies of social progress.

For the organization of society for safety met one danger by involving itself in another. Supernatural terror was overcome by spiritual power as in the great religions, and while this opened the way from magic to religion, it also hindered the free progress of thought by the persistence of taboos, even when turned to beneficent purposes. Similarly, the danger of war was met by increased or more efficient war-like establishments. In both cases, the primitive cure for danger was to meet it on its own terms. This was not wholly futile because it could make malevolent forces beneficent, if only in a limited way. The step from the shaman to the priest was one of the greatest gains in all our history, for religion could become the nursery of morals, shaping folkways (mores) from the taboo-guarded routine of immemorial custom towards more rational conduct based on ideals of social betterment.

The savage war band also had in it possibilities of a similar, if more limited, development as the embodiment of an institution of government. There never was a time when authority was not enforced; but it is a long step from the assertion of the personal ascendancy of chieftains in horde or family to the use of a permanent body to which one may apply the name "police force." And yet its origins go back to these prehistoric beginnings.

The history of civilization, however, is much more than that of these two processes of institutional change. As the word civilization itself indicates, it is rather a history of the escape from them; not only a process of secularization, but also, in spite of the doctrine of force so widely preached today, of pacification. While war is not necessarily anti-social, but may be used to protect life, to extend liberty and to safeguard the pursuit of happiness, yet as the history of welfare shows, mankind's problem has been to find out how to achieve safety, peace and justice by other and less dangerous ways.

This has been — and will continue to be — the problem of the ages, to find a guidance which is dominated neither by war nor superstition, nor held down by the rigidly recurring routine of daily life. A control has to be established which, while preserving the lessons of experience, will be capable of adjustment to changing situations. In short, society, like the individual, must place intelligence in command of its faculties.

—This seems an axiom too obvious even for passing mention, and perhaps for that very reason it has played but little part in the thought of those who have given us the philosophies of history or politics. It may also be due to the fact that what history has to record is less the expression of reason than of all the varied instincts and desires which lead mankind to action. The weight of ancient custom is seldom lifted except by the explosive action of impulses that spring from emotion rather than reason. Then the old primitive instincts come to life again to mock achievement and threaten disaster. The rational control and direction of society is still an ideal and a dream. But in the swift schooling of these last years of tragic history we are learning as never before that the organization of safety if left to itself can be more dangerous than the dangers it is created to avert, and that the growth of intelligence in a people may prove their undoing if it is not directed toward securing the enthronement of reason in the domain of government.

By reason is not meant logic. Nothing could be more unreasonable than to attempt to make logic the master of politics; for politics is an expression of life, and life eternally escapes from the control of that stern school of unimaginative logic which demands that effects should follow causes without regard to how people feel about them.

Rational control is a different thing; it does not try to get rid of the irrational by pretending that it is not there, but rather by substituting other things for it. It takes advantage of the fact that all society is a natural growth as well as an artificial creation, and that conscious planning must find its place alongside the unconscious acceptance of immemorial things. We must be on our guard against the fallacies of the doctrinaire who spins his theories out of academic thinking detached from human experience and human failings. The institutions which nations develop for these purposes may differ fundamentally from each other even when the terms in which they are cast seem to be identical. The real test of their nature is the use to which they are put.

If government is thus to be defined as including not only the place and functions of rulers but also the interplay of rulers and ruled, its origins lie even further back than the developments of the techniques of safety and welfare which we have been tracing. They are to be found in the undifferentiated authority of heads of families, chieftains of clan or tribe, who had prerogatives over and above the leadership of the war band or the performance of religious rites. These are the forerunners of kings; although not all of them reached that dignity, they are accorded a respect and obedience which marked them off from everyone else. They were both soldiers and priests, but in addition they were the recognized embodiment during their lifetime of the enduring unity which is found in myth and legend.

This patriarchal leadership was not an incidental product of tribal life; the fact that it is found in the history of every people the whole word over shows that it is an unavoidable and necessary expression of a certain stage of social evolution. This means that it lies behind forms of society which we have got rid of, as well as behind those in which it still persists. In the self-confidence of young democracies, it is almost shocking to us to have to admit how much we owe to kings, under whom tribes became states or nations and politics the act of government.

Now what are the qualifications and attributes of this less narrowly technical leadership than that of the warrior or priest?

There is no answer to this question because they differ not only in the different parts of the world but even among neighboring peoples. Yet, upon the whole, the qualifications for that kind of leadership which produces kingship is superior capacity. Inheritance often plays a directing part, as in the case of patriarchal chieftainship, which normally goes to the oldest of a family which has furnished leaders in the past; but this holds true only when the candidate is recognized as competent in himself. Prowess, cunning, a knowledge of both history and the religious secrets are necessary qualifications for an office upon which even the life of the society may depend.

Few tests of leadership are more exacting than those of primitive societies, and they applied equally to early kingship. But, as the problems of the society became more varied and more exacting, consultation with other men of experience, generally the elders, played a large part because these "wise men" knew not only what was right and proper to be done according to taboo and custom, but also what was expedient in time of crisis. The Council which meets to decide on questions of war is naturally composed of those who have to do the fighting or who know how best it should be done, just as the strategist in the field of magic or religion consults the masters of the technique.

Thus even in primitive society we see the roots of the later developments of government. Those who took part in the direction of affairs, no matter in what field it lay, had to establish by certain well recognized tests their right to speak. The organization of society for normal purposes lacked clear-cut separation of functions; but when a crisis called for action, those fitted to act, whether in the field of war or magic, played their special parts.

Now, we have only to recall the fact mentioned above, that the normal purposes of life are merely to keep things going, to see that it is chiefly by way of crises that government has made progress; for crises tend to bring into action the more technical organs, those suited to the solution of the difficulties or emergencies of the time. As the most constantly recurring crises as well as the most varied ones were those of war, it was the military organization which was the chief agent of change. This was true in Asia as well as in Europe, but in the Orient this specialization for war was not made a first step in the breaking down of the sphere of government into certain major fields of operation, whereas the military leaders of ancient Greece and Rome, who were also statesmen, made it the basis for that unique product of western civilization called politics.

This growth in the specialization of government seems to us to be the application of intelligence to the problems of society, lifting them out of the undifferentiated mass of antique custom, to be solved on their own terms. But even with us, politics has never become a science; the technician finds himself eternally limited by the fact that even the most highly technical society is still a vast reservoir of primitive reactions; often incalculable in advance. The Asiatic felt this so strongly that most of the old structure of society survived, in spite of war and conquest.

While the routine of ordinary things is so strong in the "unchanging" East as to limit the scope of government more than in the West, the ruler who established himself as warlord or emperor takes over to the full that un-differentiated power or control which we call sovereignty and holds it by the sanction of religion. The all-important fact is that the two techniques of safety, that of the priest and the soldier, never underwent in Asia that revolu-tionary process by which each in turn was transformed in the West: the Christian revolution which brought ethics to the forefront of religion by its emphasis upon the brotherhood of men, and the secular revolution, begun in the Greek city states, which brought government within the reach of the common man and thus made possible a new and as yet unfinished chapter in the history of civilization, that of Freedom.

From this short sketch of the origins of government, it follows that we should pause a moment to look at the life and thought of Asia, where the oldest folkways still persist in spite of the newer trends recently copied from Europe and America. A moment's pause over the greatest of all reservoirs of human experience! It is a parochial outlook which keeps only to the charted course of European and American history, and one which may be quite mis-leading in its conclusions; for while the peoples of the West suffered the long eclipse of the Middle Ages after the initial brilliance of antique civilizations, the varied cultures of Asia continued to flourish, with philosophies, litera-tures and arts of their own. As we of today come into ever-closer contact with them, it is well to know something of the basis of their enduring strength and the nature of their appeal to many generations of intelligent men.

CHAPTER II

ASIA

The East and the West

THE GREATER PART of mankind lives "east of Suez." This phrase of Kipling's soldier marked the point on the sea route to India where, to the English traveler, the Orient began. But from this focal point the frontiers which divide Asia from Europe stretch over many hundred miles of sea, mountain and plain westward in Africa to the shores of the Atlantic and northward through eastern Europe to the Danube and the steppes of Russia. No other frontier has been more fought over than this from long before the days of Darius or Alexander to those of Mohammed the Conqueror and Suleiman the Magnificent. And each conquest left its impress — Semitic, Egyptian, Hellenic, Roman and Islamic — so that the great crescent which extends around the eastern Mediterranean and beyond, has a culture of its own.

The western fringe of Asia is also the Middle East. The chief tie linking it to the Orient is its religion, Islam, which has also been the chief barrier to penetration by Europe. But now, in the era of modern science, a different kind of penetration is under way, and the frontiers are breaking down. Already the process had begun in the nineteenth century, in the decline of Turkey and the rival extensions of power by Russia and Great Britain. The Asian society still held out, fragmented, in places like Fez and Cairo, with their great theological schools and in far off Balkan centers like Sarajevo — name of evil omen — where broad streets and buildings, planned by architects from Vienna, look out on domed mosques and crowded bazaars, like those of Persia and India. Along the Danube, from Budapest eastward there are faint hints of Asia, lingering echoes in music in the plaintive minor key of the Orient. One detects the Asiatic touch in the folkways of the Balkan peasants who lived for centuries under the Turkish yoke.

North of the Carpathians, the frontier with Asia lacked the background of ancient history. But the Mongol invaders, Huns and Tatars (or Tartars) swept back and forth across southern Russia or settled there for a thousand years, from the fifth to the fifteenth centuries, and Muscovy was made secure from the Asiatic invaders only by Ivan the Terrible in the sixteenth century. The westernizing of the Slavs themselves which followed, was also part of the history of the Asian borderlands, one of the greatest cultural movements of modern history covering northern Russia from the Baltic to the Urals and then northern Asia itself, finally blocking the Asiatic trek to the West by their own trek to the Orient.

The historic boundaries of Asia are thus different from those of its physical geography. This has been the case as far back as the records go. The word "Asia" was coined by the ancient Greeks from Assyrian or Hebraic roots that signified the rising sun, and was used in somewhat the same vague way that we still use the term "Orient." To the Greeks, it was the inland country which began east of the coastline of Asia Minor along which their trading cities were planned and to them, as to us, the real frontier was cultural and historical, the dividing line between two fundamentally different ways of living.

Though no one knew, until modern times, the vastness of the Asiatic continent, there was always a sense of its power and mystery. It was not by chance that these two aspects of the Orient forced themselves upon the attention of the West, because it was chiefly in war and religion that the two made contact. There was as well the commerce which came by caravan which gave the West the idea that the Orient was the home of luxury and wealth. But the commerce was secondary to war and religion. It was not until the seaways were used for exploration at the beginning of modern history that the West really began to reach Asia. But even then and for over three centuries afterward, the Asiatics remained for Western peoples one great incomprehensible mass of mankind known as "the heathen." In this regard the outlook of the Western world was much the same as that of the ancient Greeks to whom non-Greeks were barbarians. The "heathen" Asiatics were, until recent times, alien to our way of life, a people of strange beliefs, inhabiting a continent vast and mysterious, of incalculable power, but devoid of our most cherished ideals, and especially of freedom.

While this was largely the generalization of ignorance, it has been largely justified by the fuller knowledge of today. For the tyrannies of Asia extended over both the realm of the mind through the continuing strength of superstitions, and over the body by the ruthless use of the sword. While there was escape from both in the great periods of culture in different Asiatic countries, there was no thorough-going movement of emancipation from them. History tended to repeat itself rather than to move away from its ancient moorings. In spite of the contributions of philosophers and religious leaders, the past lived on in Asia, until with breathtaking suddenness the ancient structure of society was broken into by modern science, wielding a greater power than that of any conqueror.

The term "heathen" was applied indiscriminately to all who did not share

44

the Christian faith; but it was especially the grosser superstitions which the missionaries sought to combat, and of these the Orient was full. Worship in the temples, the droning of prayers by shaven priests, the use of bells and light and music, bore striking resemblance to the rituals of the West. But magical incantation and primitive beliefs marked the continued dominance of the taboo, either in crude forms, as in India, or refined and disguised, as in the cultured circles of China. "Devil screens" barred the evil powers from even the courtyard of philosophers. Devices like these might be merely inconveniences in daily life, but they held the mind in bondage with a rigidity which blocked the path of progress.

In such a world the history of freedom could not even make a beginning. For, underlying all these superstitions lay the initial tyranny of the taboo, that oldest and strongest and most universal of the tyrants of the mind. The superstitions of Asia which today seem to us almost fantastic in their absurdity, and which are destined rapidly to yield before the march of intelligence, are but the development by ingenious minds of the simple beliefs of primitive peoples the world over, beliefs in the magical potency of unfamiliar things and the danger which may lie in the contagion of things accursed or sacred. The history of Asia is proof that the way of escape from primeval bondage is not by further refinement of myth, for that brings no release to the critical spirit which is the basis of reason. The emancipation of the mind from superstition to religion comes from influences of a wholly different character which, for the most part, do not even lie within the sphere of either superstition or religion. As we shall see in the course of this survey, the great steps forward in religious emancipation were definitely revolutionary, protests which tended to deny the legitimacy of the oldest and strongest orthodoxies in the world, those which turn to magic for their ritual and to animism for their mythology.

While the countries of Asia have varied in their attitude to the taboo from the enslavement to it in India to the relative rationalism of Chinese intellectuals, the fact remains that superstition of the kind indicated here has been an outstanding characteristic of Asian society.

But these impediments to freedom were not what the Greeks had in mind in their ideas of Asia. The Asiatic forces which they feared were those which brought enslavement by the sword, for that had been the fate of the peoples of western Asia with which they were in contact. West of that great mountain barrier, the roof of the world, which forms the heart of Asia, there was less of the continuity of history than in the countries of the farther East. Although Babylon reached back to one of the earliest civilizations of mankind, its earthen defenses proved in the long run unable to offer any such protection against the tribesmen of the north. These defenses were not comparable to the Great Wall, reaching from the sea to the inner mountains, which was built by China many centuries later. The series of empires which followed, the early Babylonian, the Assyrian, late Babylonian and Persian, were like pulsations of power reaching over vast areas, and establishing the rule of a single monarch over western Asia. In doing so they brought new devices in government, but most of them were based upon oppression and exploitation. It is true that by ruthlessly transplanting peoples from one territory to another they cut in upon many of the old primitive beliefs. The best known example of this is the impact of the Babylon captivity upon the religious history of the Jews; for out of it and the subsequent efforts at enslavement came the new high note of religious ethics in the later prophets. But on the whole, the Greeks were right in regarding even the Persian Empire, which freed the Jews from Babylon, as a denial of human liberty through the conquest of the nations which composed it.

These warrior states lessened the primitive servitude of fear but added to it a combination of priestly rule and military force. The kingship was surrounded with symbols of divinity, and in the hands of the priesthood there could be little distinction between heresy and treason, because, in spite of all its disguises, the taboo continued as a support for the kingship. Under these conditions one would hardly expect to find the efficiency in government which developed in the great empires of the Near East, in Egypt, Babylonia, Nineveh, and especially under the great Persian kings. The reason lies in the strength of military organization which has behind it the greatest of all imperatives, choice between victory on the one hand or death or servitude on the other.

There could be little chance for the development of the institutions of freedom in such an organization of power. There could be little personal initiative except in the hands of the king. Therefore, all great enterprises depended upon the strength or wisdom of the monarch. This was less true in the Persian Empire because of the extent of local privileges which were enjoyed by various nations under its rule and of a political organization which spread its web of something like a federal system over the whole vast empire. Yet even with this lessening of arbitrary despotism, the reaction to it of the people who were really free, was shown in the Greek resistance to the invasions of Darius and Xerxes, a national uprising of city states, often at war with each other, uniting to throw back from the soil of Hellas an alien rule utterly repugnant to its history and spirit.

The attitude of the Greeks mirrored in Herodotus is the familiar judgment of subsequent ages: Greece had saved the West from oriental tyranny. But this sweeping generalization needs qualification. The Persians had a genius for political organization different from that which developed within the narrow confines of a city state. It is a vague speculation, but an interesting one to which we refer later, to imagine what might have happened if the Persians had won. Could the free spirit of Greece have had a greater or lesser chance to stir the world with its unique creations? Could the intellectual gifts, which challenged Western thought but failed to prevent political anarchy at home, have realized a better organization within a reformed Persian Empire than it succeeded in creating in a fragmentary way after Alexander had overrun it? In any case, the fact remains that both Greeks and Persians regarded their conflict as one between the weighted centuries of Asia and a Western society in which service to the state is not servitude, but the very attribute of freedom.

While it would be wholly wrong to think of the East and West only in terms of contrast — for, as we shall see, there is much that is primitive and static in the Western world and much that is dynamic in the East — it was not until the advent of modern science that the peoples of the Orient began to face the problems of life and society in the same terms as our own. This change in attitude is one of the fundamental changes of our time. Within a single lifetime it has almost completely reset the drama of East and West; and now both in Asia and Europe there are those who are wondering if it has not gone too far, or at least too fast. The tendency to deny or to obscure the historic differences between the peoples of the Orient and the Occident leaves much out of account with which we have still to reckon. To outward appearances "the brooding East" has ceased to bow its head to the ancient symbols of an immemorial past as the younger generation of Orientals accepts the secularized West and attempts to substitute its institutions for those in which Oriental society was so deeply rooted. In some ways Japan attempts to be more modern than its Western mentors; China seems to be leaving for all time the shelter of its complacent philosophies; and India, even though with uncertain steps, is adjusting its faiths to social reform.

But the static East cannot wholly and at once move into the tracks of the dynamic West. These vast reservoirs of human experience cannot be emptied of a sudden. We must not be misled by externals. Those who look deeply into the structure of Oriental society warn us of the extent to which it still guards and cherishes the ancient ways of living and the things which made the Orient what it was and has been until our own time. The temple bells are still ringing by the old pagodas and the people still make pilgrimages to holy places. The tomb of Sun Yat-sen, the leader of the forces of secularization in China, becomes a sacred spot for his followers, though less sacred than the tomb of the Meiji Emperor of Japan who presided over the modernization of that country. In places like these the moving tides of history break on rocky shores, however fast they may rush by them to the harborage of commerce and the seats of modern learning.

The Foundations of Oriental Society

The foundations of society are much the same the world over. If we go back far enough into the history and prehistory of civilized peoples, we find everywhere traces of habits and customs similar to those of primitive peoples today. Archaeology, the science of human remains of the distant past, is thus closely linked with anthropology, which chiefly studies the cultures of the uncivilized. How is it, therefore, that out of this common past, so largely shared by all mankind at one time or another, there have developed two great divergent trends in the course of history, the one which we term Asiatic and the other European? The chief reason for it lies, as we have already indicated, in the fact that Asia, although it started its great career so much earlier, never until our own time turned away, as the West did centuries ago, from the all-pervading influence of the primitive taboo. This

47

not only lasted on as a superstitious background of religion but deeply affected the structure of Asiatic society as a whole.

The other technique of safety, that of the organization for war, did not attempt to break these taboo customs down, as was the case in the West. On the contrary, the peoples of the Orient, through war and conquest, maintained their sense of terrors greater than those of the sword and of potencies for good or ill determining human destiny. The institutions of society embodying these reactions to the mysterious world in which we live differed, therefore, in fundamentals from those which Europe developed for practical purposes and purely secular interests. It is true that the peoples of Asia differ much among themselves. In general, one may say that India remains the country of preponderant primitive beliefs, especially for that vast portion of mankind which accepts and practices that strange, undefinable religion called Hinduism. Perhaps next, but by no means so completely dominated by cult and belief, are the Japanese, whose religious experience is still vital and a guide to conduct, although it has lost its grosser forms. The Chinese, deeply rooted in their past, have, until recently, seemed to European observers more profoundly sunk in religious primitivism than any other nation. But it is now evident, as those who knew them best have asserted, that, while superstitions and the practice of magical cults widely persist, their traditional culture is more rationalist and capable of easier and more complete assimilation of Western civilization than that of almost any other non-European people.

In the long confusion of Asiatic history, it is impossible to trace with the simplicity of outline of Western history, the interplay of warrior and priest, and their effect upon society. Conquest, it is true, transplanted tribes, and both victors and vanquished were influenced by the new contacts. But this process did not reach deeply enough to bring about that cooperative relationship or fusion upon which the European states were built. Although warring tribes pushed their way along the plains and river valleys of China and India, as they did in the West, killing and enslaving as they went, and although some of them laid the foundations of mighty and enduring empires, yet their power was seldom able to penetrate within the frontiers of that mysterious realm where kinship and religion held sway. The ruler, who was more than a tribal chieftain, had no thought of interfering with the management of social life, because no one thought of doing things any other way than they had always done. The central fact in the life of an Asiatic, therefore, remained his place in the family and after that his membership in clan and tribe. The father of the family was priest and magistrate, and the elders knew the rules of proper conduct which were rigorously applied. It was only when this routine broke down that the ruler interfered and then only to reassert the established order.

The political structure of Asiatic states was thus reduced to a minimum, being chiefly concerned with the collection of taxes and tribute in goods or money by the ruler to pay his followers and maintain his prestige. The splendor of Oriental countries was as much a part of the technique of ruling as the use of soldiery. The tribute bearers from all over eastern Asia, who came to the court of the Chinese Emperors at Peking and who passed through the mile-long courtyards flanked by towering battlements into the presence of the Son of Heaven, carried back home the sense of imperial power which would assure the continuance of the tribute.

The same was true in a different way of the emperors of India; but neither Manchu nor Mogul sought to regulate the lives of the many millions who accepted their overlordship by attempting the kind of legislation which has been and is the business of European governments. Even when the kings or feudal rulers were overthrown, the revolution did not involve the idea of a change in the social structure because that was something quite outside the sphere of government. For the most part it meant only a change of dynasty, not the replacing of royalty by some other form of government, as has been the case with revolutions in European countries. It is true that republics are not unknown in Asiatic history, especially in that of India, but they did not, any more than royalty, break down the fundamental framework of society and were regarded as successful only as they reinforced that primitive structure.

Viewed from the standpoint of the West, therefore, it was the weakness, or rather the slightness, of political organization in Asiatic countries which resulted in the subordination of the individual to the family and the clan. The fact that in the course of history family ties were seldom disturbed, which was constantly the case in the Western world, gave a sense of permanence and, therefore, of authority to this most intimate relationship. This made for conservatism, a trend accentuated by reverence for ancestors, especially in China under the influence of Confucian teaching, and in Japan through the vital appeal of the Shinto religion. Although both lack the sanction of a great theological system of belief, the religious basis of Japan's life made all the subjects of the divine Mikado mythical kinsmen. No such claim could be made for the more than four hundred million subjects of the Chinese Emperor, yet they were taught to think of themselves, in the familiar phrase of Confucius, as "one great family under Heaven." This external similarity, however, should not be over-stressed; so great are the differences in attitude toward both religion and secular matters that observers have remarked how much less Chinese and Japanese seem to understand each other than that creation of a unified Orient in opposition to the West, which has been the dream of a small but vocal section of Orientals. Still farther apart from this unity lies India, where the patriarchal monarchies never included all the people in each state; where large sections of the population were forever excluded, not only from government, but even from daily contact with the rest. For there, to a greater extent than anywhere else in the world, the caste system divided mankind by its impassable barriers.

Caste, the European term for a hereditary class marked off from all others in society, comes from the Latin *castus,* meaning pure, and thus bears witness to the role of the taboo. But the strength of the caste system in India is due to more than those religious scruples which prescribe conduct. Warriors as well as priests helped to fasten it upon the population. While its origins are lost in that twilight of history preserved in the Rig-Veda, which may be termed the Homeric poems of India, there already existed in the era of the Aryan conquest three grades of conquerors — the sacrificing priests, the nobles of high lineage, and peasants — and one of non-Aryan descent, the Sudras, who were the lowest in the scale.

It was apparently not the conquest, however, which fastened these class distinctions into the rigid, iron-bound system of caste. Succeeding centuries of settlements in a world dominated by Hinduism wrought that chemical change upon Indian society. There is, perhaps, some hint of the influence of the native population upon this development in the fact that the Hindu word for caste is *varna,* meaning color, which seems to point to the racial line of cleavage between the light-complexioned Aryans and the dark aborigines whose lands they overran, as the basic origin of caste distinction. But it would be oversimplifying a long and complex process to offer so slight an explanation for its adoption as the Aryan conquest alone.

Whatever its origins, the caste system of India has been the greatest single obstacle to the adoption of modern forms of government and of social reforms under them. In Hinduism and Brahmanism the rules for conduct were determined, with all the sanctions of the mysterious world of magic and miracle behind them, to obstruct and thwart the movements for such far-off things as liberty and representative government. For liberty does not consist in giving these blind and devastating scruples of superstition full sway in the land, and representative government implies equality of citizens before the law.

As we look over this Asian world as a whole, we see it at a disadvantage, compared with the West, in its lack of adjustability. The immemorial past dominates the present even when the taboos wear off, for habit carries on within the rigid structure of prescribed action. All people have subconscious memories, and where change has been feared for the supernatural dangers it may bring, there remains a natural reluctance to accept it, long after the primitive beliefs have passed away. It was from this dead weight of custom that Greece relieved the ancient city state by setting up a political society, which may be defined as one endowed with institutions for changing things as well as for keeping them going. The advantage to the West of having such instruments for keeping pace with new conditions was not fully evident to the Orient until the era of science, mastering time and space, began to substitute for the eternal round of repetition the eternal urge of variation. The effect of this glacial movement of our time lies beyond our ken.

Government Without Politics

This brings us to the outstanding paradox of Oriental history: that while kinship and religion have continued to play a larger part in the determination of the structure of society than royal or imperial government, nowhere else has monarchy reached such heights of power and splendor. Indeed, it was this aspect of the Orient which down to our own day was chiefly in the minds of the peoples of the West whenever they thought of Asia. The descriptions of the courts of Asiatic monarchs glow like the colors of their tapestries, and fill the eye with the rich trappings of romance. But now a closer knowledge of Asia reveals the tough enduring fiber of Oriental life out of which the fabric was woven.

It is no part of this study to inquire why this basic element in human society which finds expression in the most intimate relations of mankind, those of the family, should have proved so much stronger in Asia than in Europe. When we look at the European side of the picture we shall find many reasons there for the change which shifted most of the controls of society from the family to the state; but practically all of these same reasons can be found at one time or another in the history of Asiatic countries. There, as in the West, invasions mingled populations or blotted them out, and there also science began its disturbing and disruptive processes by invention and discovery that long antedated the pioneering inventions of Europe.

Nevertheless, the deep roots of social custom remained for the most part undisturbed in Asia through its thousands of years of history. Kingdoms rose and fell and feudalism flourished through long periods of turbulence, but still the patriarchal heads of families and the elders of the clan carried on the affairs of the local communities on the basis of their ancestral rights.

Perhaps the chief difficulty in understanding the processes of Asiatic history lies in the fact that it did not develop any single pattern or set of patterns as was the tendency in Western lands. The philosophy of history which began with the Greeks has had its frontiers marked out for it by politics — a frontier line never drawn in the Orient — with successive stages of development and only three or four forms of government. In the Orient, on the other hand, the absence of this systematizing trend which we call politics makes any such logical analysis of government misleading. Aristotle's classification of the great divisions of government into monarchy, aristocracy and commonwealth and their perversions into tyranny, oligarchy and democracy cannot be applied to Asia without injecting a foreign note into that confused aggregation of relationships which found its highest expression, not in the abstract terms of law, but in the teaching of the sages and the practice of morality.

From what has just been said it is clear that the government of Asiatic peoples down to our own day lies outside the scope of a book that deals with politics as we of the European tradition understand that word. In recent years the Asiatic peoples have been passing through a great revolution, the greatest in their history, which has attempted to replace the ancient customary methods of social control by importing institutions of the European model. The process, once begun, is bound to continue with an ever-increasing approximation to the methods of the West. But this "modernization" will not affect all Asia alike, as a glance at the past history and present circumstances in the three greatest countries, India, China and Japan, will show; much less will it make Asia a simple replica of Europe.

India is still a world of its own in which primitive ties of kinship and re-ligion have vastly predominated in spite of the intrusion of foreign rulers, of whom the British were only the latest arrivals. If the voice of native India spoke in Gandhi, its quiet tones were answered by the challenging call of the Muezzin from the Mohammedan minaret and the imposing accent of authority of the native princes. But this revolutionary movement in the history of India brings all the more to light the newness of the idea of a government based upon institutions rather than upon personal relationships. From the beginning of time, those who governed and dispensed justice did so, not according to written codes, but as individual rulers applying the customary law, which the patriarchs of village or clan applied in their turn.

This personal rule is indeed the one characteristic of government that has been common throughout Asia. This does not say much, however, because it offers no clues to the understanding of how the governments of the differ-ent countries are actually run. That clue, as we have indicated, lies rather in social structure and history than in the character or place of the ruler. No two neighboring nations are more unlike than the Chinese and the Japanese. Yet down to the Chinese Revolution of 1911, both accepted, in theory at least, the absolute rule of emperors whose title and authority were based on their divinity or semi-divinity and their patriarchal headship of their people. The sacred functions of the Chinese emperor were symbolized by his sacrifice at the Altar of Heaven where he alone, mounting the last steps of the temple, became the intermediary between man and all the supernatural forces of this mysterious world. The Mikado offered a closer link with divinity as the descendant of the creator of Japan itself — the sun goddess whose mirror, seal and sword are still preserved in the Temple of Ise, the most sacred of all Japanese shrines.

Evidently the difference between Chinese and Japanese history is not to be explained by the character of the monarchy. It lies, rather, in the fact that the patriarchal system of society was capable of two divergent and even opposite lines of development and that China followed the one and Japan the other. These may, for purposes of contrast, be summarized in two great categories, the way of the man of peace and the way of the warrior; the teaching of Confucius and that of Bushido.

Confucius

Had all Asia been alike, it would have turned to the one teacher to whom China paid its greatest reverence, Confucius (Kung Fu-tse), for in his phi-losophy we have the most consistent guide to conduct in a society where the relationships are personal and not generalized into abstractions, as is the case in the West. So high a place has been accorded to him in the culture of China as to make him seem almost divine; but in spite of the fact that temples were erected in his honor and a cult developed from his teaching, he was a purely secular figure, a philosopher and teacher, not even a prophet, and his maxims apply, not to a spiritual world hereafter, but to the conduct of daily life. So profound has been the influence of his teaching that it may be taken as the highest expression of the Oriental mind in the analysis of purely human affairs. More interesting for us, however, is the comparison with the thought of his Western contemporaries, those Ionian Greeks who were at that very time beginning the greatest age of Western philosophy, based on the entirely different principle of fearless, penetrating criticism of the orthodoxies of traditional thought.

The basic principle of the philosophy of Confucius — the product of an era of feudalism and unsettled conditions — was to secure an ordered society by the exercise of the most deeply rooted instincts, those rooted in family relations. Within the family itself this meant subordination of women to men and of sons to fathers; applied to the state as the "one great family of Heaven," it stressed the virtue of loyalty to the sovereign and a due recognition of the authority of the vast hierarchy of officials representing him. The insistence upon the patriarchial family system as the one alternative to anarchy was strengthened by a high regard for ancestors and a reverence for their tombs. Equally effective in securing respect for the established order were the prescriptions of etiquette and ceremonial. According to Chinese thinking, there is no better way to preserve one's place in society than to keep other people at a distance by formal manners, frowning down on undue familiarity. In this way the individual recovers something of what he has lost by submergence in the social group, for by dignified conduct, showing a knowledge of the rules of etiquette, he carries with him in his daily life the outer marks of place or preferment.

By the prescriptions for daily intercourse Confucius thus furnished a bridge between the family and the state which has no parallel in Western history, and for that matter in Oriental history either. Ancestral custom and kinship structure received a political completion without politics, sanctioned by a reverence which had all the weighted sanction of religion. But no one knew better than Confucius that a mere agglomeration of families did not make a nation. For a people to be a coherent whole, there must either be strong control from above or an understanding and willing cooperation among all members of society. Lasting controls could not be merely those of force but of justice, and the ideal society would be that in which the innate goodness of mankind could have a chance to show itself under a ruler seeking the same end as his people.

Confucian teaching was, therefore, a set of morals based upon the one fundamental principle of man's inherent goodness. He left behind him, not laws, but admonitions. It is significant, however, of the practical bent of his mind, that he stated the Golden Rule in negative and limited form, "Do not do to others what you do not like when done to yourself." This precept is worth examining, for it bears the mark of Chinese habits, or perhaps Chinese habits bear its imprint. One waits to see what the other person does. The contrast with the positive teaching of Jesus is stronger than the similarity.

From this high moral plane Confucius looked out on all mankind as one.

It is true that the only world he knew was that of the Chinese, but this sense of a universal human society based upon mankind's innate goodness gave strong support to ideals of peace between rulers, as well as within their states. For the influence of Confucius is one of the miracles in the history of thought. Both in the family and the state Confucianism strengthened the moral sense of emphasizing faith in man, not for progress or future reform but for that maintenance of the established order which he, as a conservative, found so rich and beautiful.

The teachings of Confucius, drawn from comments on a great variety of things, personal, social and political, all tend toward one direction: the insistence on the golden mean in thought and conduct. "While there are no stirrings of pleasure, anger, sorrow or joy, the mind may be said to be in a state of Equilibrium; when these feelings have been stirred, and they act in their proper degree, there ensues what may be called the state of Harmony. This Equilibrium is the great root, and this Harmony is the universal Path. Let the states of Equilibrium and Harmony exist in perfection and a happy order will prevail throughout heaven and earth, and all things will flourish." In other words, true freedom lies in self-control, for both the individual and society. The same thing was said by the Greeks, but it never could be taken over and applied to affairs of state by a people whose restless minds challenged the very idea of equilibrium maintained in a static world. In China it acquired the weight of an alternative to religion.

In place of formal law, which was lacking in China, Confucius' precepts, along with the teachings — some widely variant — of other sages, became the Chinese classics which for centuries furnished almost the entire content of Chinese learning. Thousands of the literati could recite every sentence in a literature which became as canonical as that of the Hebrew scriptures. By way of the system of examinations, the bureaucracy was filled with those upon whom the old masters of Chinese morals had laid the impress of high and noble sentiments. Nowhere else in history is there anything to compare with the extent of this substitution of morals for law.

And it must be admitted that when the balance is struck between the Western system of politics, with its repression of violence by the law, and the stable Chinese social system of mutual responsibility, the evidence of history in the realm of human relations is in China's favor. In business dealings, the old adage of the Romans that the buyer should beware of trickery and deceit seems barbarous compared with the traditional honesty of the Chinese merchant. But, in both politics and the ordinary business of daily life, there were, in China, practices which to Westerners seemed like corruption. It was a recognized and accepted practice that income, whether derived from the state or from individual employers, be supplemented by perquisites to help meet the exigencies of the unemployed members of the family group. This is what, among Westerners was known as "squeeze." Its basis was ethical, a recognition of social solidarity in its most intimate unit, that of the family; but in the larger areas of government it was applied, as in the Western world, to enhance the emoluments of office, in other words, for corruption. The total effect of reliance upon Confucian philosophy, without adequate political machinery to insure its fulfillment, was to perpetuate in politics exploitation of the masses by those in power, so that, while China presents much that is magnificent, the total picture one gets of it is one of wealth mixed with penury. A situation which, under the impress of modern forces, demanded redress and bred revolution.

It needed but the touch of modern science and the schooling of young Chinese in Western methods to reveal this incompleteness of the age-old theme of Chinese philosophy. Yet in the teachings of Confucius the heritage of the oldest, continuous culture of mankind was phrased in terms that seemed final. Undisturbed by the passing dynasties it offered no revolutionary scheme for constitutions, but sought to reform administrative as well as social organizations by placing the responsibility for justice and welfare upon conduct within the group or state, so that the social structure remained not only the most intimate but the most real thing in civilized life. It was but a natural consequence that the administrators of China should not be soldiers but scholars trained in the Chinese classics. They were not there to bring change but to keep the static world running smoothly in its ancient grooves.

Bushido

Although Chinese civilization played a dominant part in the molding of that of Japan, and through China both Buddhism and Confucianism established their hold on religion and ethics, yet it was not the priest nor the scholar, but the warrior, who became the ideal for Japan. The warriors were tribesmen, members of a great system of clans, serving as retainers of noble houses. Richly endowed Buddhist monasteries, like the monasteries of the Christian West, fitted into feudalism, sometimes with their warrior-monks and their own war-bands. Such a society, in which the profession of the warrior was held in highest esteem, was the very opposite of that of China, in which the soldiers ranked lowest.

The warrior class which developed under feudal lords, which in time became a hereditary caste, the *bushi*, with a code of conduct of their own, *Bushido*, "the way of the *bushi*." Nowhere else, not even in ancient Sparta, was there such stern self-discipline as was practiced by the knightly retainers (*samurai*) of the great feudal nobles (*daimyo*), indifferent to pain or death in the performance of loyal service to their lords. Yet Japanese feudalism did not destroy the tribal basis of society, as in the West. Even at the time of the revolution which modernized Japan, the military reforms which in 1872 supplanted feudal levies by conscription following upon the restoration of the sovereign power of the emperor, were carried out by three of the great clans; and in the new era of parliamentary rule, the ties of loyalty to clan lasted on in political party organization.

The persistence of this mixture of tribalism and feudalism was probably due to the conditions of life which confronted these island people. Instead of the broad plains of China, their homes were in the mountain valleys, shut in by volcanic ranges from their neighbors. Whatever the reason, the fact remains that Japan maintained, down to our own time, the strongest and most outstanding example of clan organization and feudal militarism, and that the influence of these institutions continues to give color to Japanese political life today. For both have contributed to the central tie of the Japanese, that of loyalty to the emperor who, although he has formally renounced the divinity which had become the object of a national cult from the Middle Ages, yet remains the living embodiment of the nation.

The strength of the blood tie was made fundamental and enduring by the worship of ancestors. The Japanese are a deeply religious people — in striking contrast to the Chinese, who wear their religion so lightly. It is in Nippon that the temple bells are almost forever ringing. Buddhism, which has almost died out of its native India and is little more than a religious philosophy in China, has its temples and shrines that are thronged with worshippers in Japan.

But the most intimate religion is that which has no system of theology, Shintoism, "The Way of the Gods," involving reverence for the living dead that binds the past with the present and makes family piety the fundamental basis of society. It is a religion of cult, not of abstract ideas; but by its emotional appeal it makes of Japanese patriotism something more vibrant than the West has ever known. To die for Japan is to continue to live in it, in that spirit world in which an unquestioning faith projects the immortality of the individual as a member of family, clan and nation.

If religion buttressed the solidarity of the social structure in Japan, the profession of war, that of the *samurai* class, furnished the code of morals which was honored and respected above all others. Here the accent was on the unquestioning performance of loyal service, not as a casual and incidental ideal, but as a stern rule of conduct to be followed undeviatingly through life and death. "The way of the warrior" *(Bushido)* stressing — as fundamental virtues of the samurai — frugality, loyalty and filial piety, became a code of ethics so strict within its limited sphere as to outrange most codes of law, and it was applied with the full sanction of society. The supreme penalty which it imposed for the violation of its code was *hara-kiri* (suicide by disembowelment), which was carried out unhesitatingly, with oriental stoicism; but it must be remembered that the death thus suffered was not thought of as severing the tie of the individual with his people, but as the pathway of honor to the spirit world, leaving no taint upon himself or his family for his conduct. The way of the warrior was therefore that most honored when kinship and religion reached out not merely over clan or tribe but over an entire nation, making its members doubly conscious of the bond which unites them as citizens of today and the ancestors of those of tomorrow.

While *Bushido* is literally "the way of the warrior," or more narrowly "of the military knight," it is not a mere code of fighting; like the European term "chivalry" it covers the whole life and becomes an ideal for all. This widening of its application was particularly noticeable when feudalism was abolished in the Restoration, and the moral code of *Bushido* gained, rather than lessened, in the nation. So much was this the case that the distinguished interpreter of Japanese culture, Dr. Nitobe, although a devout Quaker, described this product of the purest militarism as the very "soul of Japan." The reason for it is that — as Dr. Nitobe saw it — it was rooted in Buddhism, which furnished a sense of calm trust in fate, a quiet submission to the inevitable, and a stoic composure in face of danger or calamity. The Zen sect of Buddhism, with its accent on meditation, carried these qualities still further; but they were negative, and what they failed to give in inspiration for action Shintoism supplied in its two tenets, patriotism and loyalty, which struck deeply into the emotional life. Devoid of theology, it fell back on Confucianism for its ethics, as that worldly-wise system, with its aristocratic and conservative tone was well fitted for the guidance of a knightly society, and ultimately, as in China, for everyone. The ideals were courage, right conduct or justice, benevolence, politeness, honor, honesty and sincerity, loyalty and self-control, as well as a fatalistic and stoical attitude toward death. None of these were to disturb, but rather to maintain, the order of society. It was a kind of non-Christian parallel to the life and thought of Europe in the Middle Ages.

CHAPTER III

THE GREAT RELIGIONS

In the Ancient World

IF ASIA, in spite of its antiquity, failed to lead in the evolution of politics, it produced in the great religions another conception of man's place in the world and another guide to conduct. So far, we have dealt only with the primitive cults which retained and still retain the impress of the taboo, the expression of nervous reactions to the strange and unaccountable in the world around and in life itself. But from this dark soil of superstition has developed some of the richest flowering of the human spirit, as faith supplants fear and the rude fragments of primitive imaginings make way for the ecstatic vision. Here, in a world of its own, the mind of man, groping through mysteries, finds another freedom than that of the secular life in the material world.

This movement of emancipation from superstition has been shared to greater or lesser extent by all civilized peoples, forming one of the most important chapters in the history of intelligence. And its leaders, although differing greatly in outlook and achievement, have not been speculative thinkers but intuitive reformers who either re-interpret the orthodoxies of their day or repudiate them, in order to establish new beliefs and ideals of conduct. Their message, it is important to note, has this one thing in common, that it has cut through the crass confusion of primitive cults to concentrate upon some fundamental truths, relatively simple but profoundly felt.

But then again, in every case this accent upon eternal verities has proved hard to keep. For the process tends to reverse itself as the teaching of the religious leaders is worked into the pattern of daily life. Once more the freedom gained from discarding outworn cults is obscured by new and elaborate ceremonies, and the theologians — the philosophers of the realm of mystery — develop systems of thought as vast as the temples which house both deities and ministrants.

There have been many such movements, but among the great orthodoxies, three are especially significant, not only because of their importance as religions, but because they embody in varying degrees the escape from the clogging superstitions against which their founders protested. Buddha, Christ and Mohammed were, each in his own way, revolutionary heretics to the beliefs and practices they challenged. In no case was their victory complete, for the dark shadow of superstition still obscures the outlook of multitudes of professed followers. Here, however, we are not concerned with distinctions in theology, but with the effect of the religion as a whole upon the history of civilization. For with all their limitations, these great empires of belief have been more lasting and have exerted a far greater influence than any empire founded by the sword.

While Asia has been the nursery of religions, two of the most important of them, Christianity and Mohammedanism, arose in that western fringe of the continent which, as we have seen, was partly European as well, and the subsequent history of Christianity was so identified with that of Europe as to win for it the title, Christendom, which it proudly wore but never wholly deserved.

Here, however, we come upon it in its original Asiatic setting, to revert to it later when it was moving on its triumphant course around the northern shore of the Mediterranean, over the Alps and beyond. But neither it nor Mohammedanism has ever won mastery in eastern Asia. The type of religion which found its way to widest acceptance there was one which put the accent neither upon charity nor upon the unity of God, but upon an ascetic renunciation of the pleasures of the physical world and the attainment of spiritual purity, Buddhism.

To trace the varying content of these theologies would carry us too far afield from the history of freedom, although much of the world's history was determined by them. They do come fully into our survey in two contradictory, opposing ways, imprisoning the mind by superstitions and freeing it by reformations.

The history of religion begins before thought, in cults that ward off or manipulate taboos. Beliefs come later, when a widening consciousness plays upon the world of the mystic potency of primitive life. Religious beliefs are not like other beliefs, those of the accepted routine, but carry along the sense of sacredness, to the point that disbelief is sacrilege. Its suppression is, therefore, justified in the eyes of the orthodox; and, by a sinister paradox, the reformers, treasuring their new beliefs, tend to be as intolerant as those whose guidance they reject. Thus it has happened that the highest of all religious beliefs, monotheism has persecuted as much if not more than the religions whose pantheon is filled with deities.

This does not mean that the development of religious thought leads away from freedom; such a conclusion is both rationally and historically untenable. Rationally, because the highest concept of the Deity is one of mercy and compassion; historically because the suppression of religious persecution, instead of its infliction, is now recognized as a duty of all civilized states.

Egyptian Monotheism

It is a sobering fact, however, that the first of all monotheisms was founded and maintained by persecution. Although it proved to be only a strange interlude in the long annals of Egyptian magic and superstition, the revolutionary reforms of the Pharaoh Amenophis IV[1] of the middle of the fourteenth century B.C. constitute a unique chapter in the history of religions. For twelve years of his reign he carried out a fanatic warfare against the national god Amon Re and the rest of the oldest of all pantheons, that of the gods of the Nile Valley, blotting out their names from the monuments and finally deserting the capital city Thebes, with its great, mysterious temple of Karnak, to found a new city at El Amarna on the edge of the desert, free from the polytheistic influence of the ancient shrines. Changing his name to Akhenaton (or Ikhnaton) in honor of the sun god Aton, the one and only deity, he proceeded with relentless vigor and all the might of a Pharaoh to overthrow the old religions and establish the new one. But in spite of these sweeping measures, successfully carried out against the most firmly established priesthood of history, after his death the great reform was blotted out, never to be retried, and the priests of Karnak could again worship the more tolerant sun god, Amon Re, who admitted other gods as well to the pantheon of Egypt.

The Religious Cults of Mesopotamia

It is strange, stranger than at first appears, that no such religious revolution as that of Ikhnaton was ever attempted by the kings of Babylonia or Assyria. For Mesopotamia, even more than Egypt, was a mother of religious cults, and her kings were more powerful than the Pharaohs.

The chief reason for this undoubtedly lay in the nature of the land. Unlike

[1] Also called Amenhotep.

59

Egypt, Mesopotamia lay open to shifting populations, and its rich soil was a constant temptation to raiders, against which the local deities could not guarantee safety, unless the warrior chieftains were strong in their defense and the cities as well as the temples provided with protecting walls. With busy workers in town and country, the market places drew merchants from near and far, and there was a mingling of peoples as well as of goods. Therefore, when history dawns in Babylonia, the kingship is not only supreme over the priesthoods, but the government is largely secular in both laws and administration.

The code of Hammurabi, that first of all law codes, is anything but the product of religion; it is in many ways as modern as the Code Napoléon. Although the stele in the Louvre on which the code is inscribed shows the great king receiving the law from Marduk, the patron deity of Babylon, the laws themselves have left behind almost every trace of primitive or even tribal custom. It is state-law, enforced by royal power. And yet, in the light of the subsequent history of Mesopotamia, the modern touch in the laws of Hammurabi must not mislead one into thinking that ancient Babylonia was ever a secular state like those of today.

The temple of Marduk outshone the royal palace in magnificence, and as time went on, the priestly class developed, by way of astrology, a place for itself unrivalled by any other priesthood. For both gods and men had their assigned places in the universe, according to a reading of the heavens which only the priests were able to decipher. Nowhere else was superstition so codified, with libraries of records of portents and omens. And in no other cosmogony was the freedom of the individual more positively denied. For the fate of men and nations was to be calculated, if one were sufficiently learned in the meaning of the stars, with all the inevitability of the laws of mathematics. But fate was also luck. Behind all lay the dark sinister forces of the taboo, making both things and times lucky or unlucky; a fact still mirrored in those divisions of the calendar which we have taken from the priestly lore of Babylon.

Zoroastrianism

Wholly different was the reading of the heavens — and of human fate — in the tribesmen of the mountains and uplands which fringed Mesopotamia in the East. These were of that Aryan stock, which carried out the greatest of all invasions, or rather expansions, reaching out, in successive waves of conquest and at different times, over India on the southeast and over northern Europe to the Atlantic on the west. Their primitive beliefs and ways of living were much like those of any other people in an early stage of culture, but against their background developed two of the great religions, Zoroastrianism and Buddhism.

The life of Zoroaster is shrouded in myth, and even the date of his life is uncertain. But the central thesis of his teaching, the struggle between good and evil, reflects the stern conditions of living in the uplands, where sunlight and darkness are the very symbols of good and evil, of life and death. The supreme being, the "Lord of Wisdom," Ahuramazda, later known as Ormazd, existed before the world, which he created and which he has continued to govern.

Yet the universe is threatened by the evil spirit, Ahriman, who, though banished to hell, sends his devilish agents to corrupt mankind. It is a struggle of law and truth against falsehood. The battle is as long as history. Ormazd wages it like an Oriental king, with spirit agents, or angels, of light against the hosts of darkness. Because the prize of the contest is man himself, he must have some freedom to choose evil instead of the good, otherwise the powers of evil would have no chance whatever. But, having the responsibility for his own fate, man faces reward or retribution after death, because his thoughts and actions are all recorded for a day of judgment.

In this regard, Zoroastrianism is almost identical with the creeds that sprang out of Judaism, Christianity and Mohammedanism. Moreover there is a further resemblance in the Zoroastrian confidence that the good would triumph, and that the end of this imperfect world was near at hand. How closely parallel to early Christianity was the cult of the creeds of all the angels of light!

The sun god Mithra won its way through the Roman Empire as the most important of the Oriental mysteries. Although it concentrated upon the utterly un-Christian myth of the slaying of the bull of Ormazd by which Mithra brought life upon the earth, its ceremonies resembled those of the Christians, for it purified by baptism and celebrated the sacrament of a sacred meal, which were the two outstanding ceremonies of the Christian church. Moreover it was a religion of stern morality and self-denial, and it is a striking fact that it spread most widely in the track of the Roman legions, until it reached throughout the whole empire. Fortunately for Western history, however, the popularity of the Mithra among the soldiery stopped short of official recognition and the suggestion has been made that this may have been partly due to the fact that women were excluded from its rites, so that it never entered deeply into the social life of the Empire as Christianity was able to do.

It was not only by way of Mithraism that Zoroastrianism reached into the Roman West, for centuries later, in the third century A.D., a prophet, Mani, made a synthesis of the teachings of Zoroaster, Buddha and Jesus, and his teaching, Manichaeanism, became the most dangerous of the heresies in the history of the early Church, so powerful indeed that for a time it was doubtful whether the religion of the West would be Christianity or Manichaeanism. Carrying the dualism of Zoroaster to still greater lengths, it built up a theory of world history in three great areas: the first, before creation, in which light and darkness were kept apart; the second, which is the age of man, in which they are in constant conflict; and the third, in which darkness will be overcome, and light — the symbol of goodness and the spirit life — will rule alone in the world. Mankind, therefore, must fight as the ally of light in a continual struggle, by absolute self-denial.

No more rigid system of conduct, suppressing all natural desires, was ever promulgated by any creed, and yet, whatever we may think of it, this seems to have been its chief attraction, an attraction which lasted on down into the heart of the Middle Ages.

Buddhism

We turn now from these religions of the past to the great religions of to-day; on the one hand, Buddhism, the greatest religion of the Orient and the one with the greatest number of adherents in all the world; on the other hand, the group of three religions which were related in their origins, and in their history, Judaism, Mohammedanism and Christianity. This latter group, the parent stock of which was Judaism, arose in the far western fringe of the Asiatic continent, and until recent years has had little to do with the religious history of the Far East.

The founder of Buddhism, Gautama (563-483 B.C.), a contemporary of Confucius, was born of princely stock in that portion of India which lies between the Ganges and the Himalayas, and therefore in the very heart of Brahmanism, the priestly development of primitive Hindu cults. His renunciation of wealth and the pleasures of the senses reminds one of St. Francis; but his struggle ended, not in such joy in God's creation as was voiced in the hymn to the sun; instead it led to Nirvana. This final goal is not, however, the pure and blank negation which the Western mind has conceived it to be. Buddhism is not merely negative.

There are eight "noble paths" for mankind to traverse on its way to "Enlightenment": Right Views; Right Aspirations; Right Speech; Right Conduct; Right Mode of Livelihood; Right Effort; Right Mindfulness; and Right Rapture. Vast literatures have grown up to expound these virtues, but the earliest documents furnish all the clues we need to judge the fundamental contribution of Gautama's gospel. It is that we should follow neither the "low and pagan" ideas of the worldly-minded, nor the "painful and ignoble" way of extreme asceticism. Like the Greeks, he choose a Middle Path "to peace, to insight, to the higher wisdom, to Nirvana." And yet with all this sense of moderation, the purpose of Buddhism is essentially that which has underlain the monastic movement of all religions — the offer of an escape from the responsibilities and burdens of life by concentration through meditation upon the spiritual world.

To summarize this teaching in a single paragraph does violence to one of the subtlest and most difficult of philosophies; but at least one may say that the teaching of Gautama is the supreme embodiment of the Oriental point of view with reference to the individual, because he finds salvation through the acceptance of his own subordination not merely to the social order but to a divinely ordered universe.

But Buddhism is more than this central core of doctrine, just as Christianity is more than the Sermon on the Mount. There is also this further external parallel with Christianity — there is no inner affinity between the two religions, although efforts have been made to prove it — that Buddhism prospered most outside of the land of its origin. Only once was it made the official religion of an Indian empire, when Asoka, in the third century B.C., carried on "conquest by religion" in mass conversions of the populace, establishing monasteries for the study of canonical works of the Buddha and sponsoring the completion of the sacred text. This effort to replace the popular cults of Hinduism with a state religion of relatively simple design, lasted only a short time, however. The native superstitions, wielding the terrible weapon of the taboo, triumphed over the reform, and Buddhism was almost entirely forced out of India. There are some nine million Buddhists among its three hundred millions, the majority of whom accept the disordered pantheon of Brahmanism with its rigid rules for ceremonial and caste.

Beyond the Himalayas, however, in Tibet, China and Japan, Buddhism took deep root, and today its devotees number over five hundred millions, or some 35 per cent of the population of the world. This does not mean that all these multitudes are attempting to follow, even from afar, the Middle Path of Gautama. For in the Buddhist shrines, scattered from Russia to the islands of the Pacific, can be traced the history of over twenty centuries of growth and decay, of variation of creed and worship.

In Tibet the Lamas developed it into a theocracy as stern and isolated from the everyday world as the mountain fastnesses around the sacred city of Lhasa. In China, Buddhism linked up with Taoism, another cult which had degenerated from the teachings of the philosopher, Lao Tse, into a confusion of magical rites and ceremonies. In Japan it developed the Zen Sect, which, rejecting doctrinal subtleties, concentrated on a stern, stoical discipline which commended itself to the warrior class. The Buddhism of the monasteries still held its own and paralleled the ancestor worship of Shinto with an organized theology. In all these lands, the temples still resound with the deep-toned chanting of the priests as they perform the sacred rites and ceremonies in the dark, candle-lit interior. Its monasteries still offer the attraction of a life of meditation and escape from the trammels of a suffering world.

If freedom were merely escape, not only from the evil in the world but also from social responsibility, the largest chapter in its history would be that of these Oriental religions, of which Buddhism is the best example. But escape from reality and from responsibility means escape from most of life itself. Oriental society reflected this imperfect measure of mankind because it did not attempt to get rid of the impediments to a free life in a free world, but only to accommodate itself to them. For this reason, the road to freedom in the Orient, that wide road upon which all people may travel, has still a longer way to go before it reaches its goal, than in the less religious but more socially conscious West.

Judaism

Barriers higher than the Himalayas or the Hindu Kush shut off these religious developments of the Orient from that of the Semitic tribes of Israel, in which the basic tenet of Western religions was developed: monotheism. In the beginning, these nomads of the desert fringe held much the same kind of beliefs as other primitive peoples. There was the same fear and avoidance of uncanny things, a keen sense of the protection or curse of the taboo, magical practices to bring luck and avert evil and sacrifice at sacred places.

Their strongest bond of union, however, was the worship of their tribal god, Yahweh. This became of special importance in the struggle against the Philistines, when bands of prophets voiced the need of loyalty to Yahweh as a defence against war and oppression. These early prophets recall the background of nomadic life by their dervish-like frenzies, but they furnished a medium of expression outside of the priesthood, which was destined to reach the highest levels of moral and intellectual power.

The conquest of Palestine, or most of it, by these semi-nomads, with their consequent change to settled life, threatened for a time to strengthen rather than lessen the local superstitions, for the Philistine worship of Baal, most dangerous rival of Yahweh, was that of fertility cults, which are the normal expression of early settled life. The contest, therefore, bore some resemblance to a struggle between the stern dictates of a religion of war and the varied pantheon of a religion of peace. This is admittedly giving the cruelly inhuman cults of Baal an undeservedly high place, but in the eyes of the people of that time, accustomed to barbarous cults, the religion of Baal had by far the wider appeal among the Semite peoples.

It was, therefore, vital for the history of the Israelites, and for the rest of the world, that the religion of Yahweh should cease to be primarily a cult of defense for a few small tribes, and take on the two fundamental qualities of religious morality: the advocacy of peace and the change from the taboo purity of things accursed or sacred to the purity of the inner life of the human spirit. These two, taken together, constitute the greatest of all revolutions in religious history. Yet this is what was achieved by the later prophets of Israel.

In place of the warrior god of the days of the massacres of their neighbors, the Philistines or the Amalekites, Yahweh, as taught by the later prophets, was a god of justice and mercy; in place of burnt sacrifices and "vain oblations" his favor was to be won by caring for the widow and the fatherless and by kindliness and charity. In this way the prophets of Israel tore away the shackles of superstition from the free life of the spirit, not to rest in the Nirvana of Buddhism, but to make religion a guide for the common man in the trials and difficulties of an everyday world.

The scene of this religious revolution, Palestine, the homeland of the Israelites, was on the track of great empires. Fierce tribal fighting marked the course of its early history. It held a frontier position between the kings of Egypt and those of Mesopotamia, and in the hard school of oppression the

Jews learned, from both of these centers of ancient civilization, precepts and principles of law. Their spiritual leaders translated these in terms of inner experience until in the course of the centuries they developed an ethical concept of religion itself. Thus it was by an evolution which became revolutionary at the close, that the prophets of Yahweh ceased to be exponents of a tribal deity.

It is significant — and inexplicable — that this welding of religion with social ethics made little progress in the Orient while the West gave it general, if often hypocritical, acceptance. Here again, as in the case of ancient Greece, and for that matter as in the whole evolution of civilization from the days of primitive savagery down, there has been an utter disparity between the ethics of domestic relationships and those with outsiders. Even in the revolutionary teachings of the later prophets, who interpreted the religion of Israel in terms of morals instead of ceremonial, there are still continuing strains of the worship of a chosen people.

This is clearly the case in the prophecy of Amos, who dates from about 750 B.C. Each strophe of his poem begins and ends with the same refrain, the denunciation of the enemies of Yahweh, predicting punishment for them one and all. The higher ethical note came only when he turned on his own people, to denounce their sins and corrupt living in the same terms. This gave him the vision of a universal human situation and a universal Deity.

The thought of Amos was, however, still cast in warlike mold, the religion of retribution and the sanction of the moral law. The next step was taken by his contemporary, Hosea, who carries Amos' escape from primitivism to ethics still further. The note of doom is sounded in the beginning of his message also, but from it the poem turns to a yearning for righteousness, as the very essence of the religion of Yahweh, who is a god not only of justice but of mercy.

These pioneers of the ethical, non-sacerdotal religion were soon followed by a greater, Isaiah. It is only when one recalls the circumstances of the time that one realizes the boldness of this assertion of the moral order in the Divine plan. The Assyrians were ravaging the lands of the Hebrews, and, in line with all prophetic teaching, Isaiah held that the sufferings of the people were due to their violation of Yahweh's laws. But, intermingled with warnings of impending doom if the laws are not obeyed, there is a note of triumph because of the deliverance of Jerusalem from the besieging, but plague-stricken army of Sennacherib. Yahweh, the protector of Israel, is so much greater than Assur, the god of the Assyrians, that "the whole world is full of his glory." From the text it is clear that it is more than the boasting of an adherent of Yahweh over against the claims of his rival. Isaiah really means the whole world! His ultimate vision is that of monotheism when the God of Israel becomes the acknowledged God of all nations. From this point of view, therefore, the universal outlook becomes the sublimation of Jewish nationalism.

But Yahweh's world is to be different from any other in all history, it is to be a world at peace. In homely phrase that recalls the things one cherishes most — and therefore a phrase which has never been forgotten in any Jewish or Christian land — he envisages the time when the people of the earth "shall beat their swords into plowshares and their spears into pruning hooks; nation shall not lift up sword against nation nor shall they learn war any more." Utterly unfulfilled, this prophecy has nevertheless rung in men's minds as an inspiration ever since its first utterance in old Judea. But it must be admitted that much of its force has been owing to the fact that it has been quoted out of its context. For Isaiah was no pacifist. The time will come when "the whole earth is at rest and is quiet, and they break forth into singing," but not until the empires and cities of the unbelievers are laid waste. Instead of the fulfillment of this glowing prophecy, however, Jerusalem was destroyed and the Israelites were carried off to Babylon.

From that captivity, some two centuries after Isaiah, a greater prophet than he gave voice to the highest spiritual note in Old Testament prophecy. The author is unknown, but his text is to be found in Isaiah 40-55, and his date is about 540 B.C. Here at last Jewish thought not only crossed the great divide into complete monotheism but achieved as well a new conception of God. The Ruler of the Universe is no longer thought of in political terms as an Oriental monarch triumphing over his enemies. Although there is a constant reminder that his warfare is not over, the vision of power and splendor constantly melts away into one of loving-kindness and of tender concern over the welfare of his followers. There is an intimate personal relationship between God and man. The creator of heaven and earth with power "to form the light and create darkness, make peace and create evil" rules the lives of men more like a father than a king, for he is also the consolation of the oppressed, giving power to the faint and leading his followers like a shepherd.

This great chapter in the history of religion is also of vital interest in the history of freedom; for it is a voice out of slavery. Although the Babylonian captivity of the Jews was already over, as the second Isaiah so proudly notes, when he welcomes Cyrus, the Persian conqueror of Babylon as "the Lord's anointed," nevertheless the prophet's thought had been shaped in the years of the captivity. Only one who had witnessed such suffering could rise to the height of Isaiah 53, in which the intermediary between God and man is one who seemingly is not a fitting representative of either the divine or the human. He is "stricken, smitten of God and afflicted," and "despised and rejected of men." There is exultation mixed with poignancy in this great poem in which "a man of sorrows and acquainted with grief" becomes the living exponent of the Deity, for in this way the greatest link between mankind and God is not through the manifestations of divine power in which mankind cannot share, but through one of the deepest and commonest experiences of mankind.

No such high emotional content had existed before in religious history. Often enough, in even the most barbarous cults there had been an identification of the victim with the god to whom he was sacrificed. But in all such ceremonies in the world, the priestly ritual had demanded that the victim was to be "without spot or blemish" and the god was placaded by offering only the richest and best in the prescribed ceremonials. Here we have the absolute opposite of such conceptions of sacrifice. The requirements of taboo are left far behind. Nevertheless there is the confident assertion that it is acceptable to the Deity and is the guarantee of inward peace to the human spirit.

Isaiah 53, in which this passage occurs, was to prove of the utmost importance to Christian theologians who interpreted it as the prophecy of the coming of Christ, whose life so largely fitted into this description of the spiritual redeemer of Israel. Subsequent Jewish history, however, turned from this development in the leadership of prophets to that of priests. It would be hard to say how much of this was due to the rebuilding of the temple and how much it was to be attributed to the inherent strength of compliance with "the Law," of which the priests were the supreme guardians.

In any case, after repeated conquests by the greater kingdoms of the east, following the Alexandrine empire, and with but short intervals of independence, the priests created the most absolutely theocracy in world history. For, instead of kings, the high priests were to be the rulers, and "the Law" was supreme. This included not only the written law of the Old Testament but the "Tradition" codified in the Talmud which, with its elaborate commentaries, contains the most detailed prescriptions for conduct to be found anywhere in all the literature of religion and law. For the student of anthropology it furnishes the best example of the persistent power of the taboo with its rules of life covering every common occurence, with inescapable penalties for any violation. Rigid, automatic and unyielding, it survived through conquest and persecution and was the dominant characteristic of Jewish life from the Babylonian captivity to the Roman conquest and beyond.

From the standpoint of the history of freedom, in view of the Talmudic society at which we have just been looking, it must be admitted that the Jews, in spite of the fact that they were the supreme proponents of monotheism — or perhaps partly because of that fact — failed to achieve either religious or political freedom. This was not only because they were a conquered people throughout most of their history, but also because they remained in tribal formation, held together by the blood tie instead of developing politically, as was the case of Greece and Rome, by ties of common interest with neighbors. When, after the Babylonian captivity, Nehemiah and Ezra restored Jerusalem, it was a fortress city for the Jews alone. The more than religious toleration which Cyrus and Darius showed in contributing to the rebuilding and refurnishing of the Temple awakened no such generous religious attitude on the part of the Jews. The priests maintained the rituals of the ancient orthodoxy and Jewish nationalism bore the stamp of theocracy instead of secular politics.

This conception of a theocratic state lasted on in orthodox Jewry but wore thin in the Jewish people as a whole, as is evident in the new State of Israel, where the theocratic party represents a relatively minor grouping in a large number of blocs. Their contribution to the history of freedom does not lie in this effort to realize once more Jewish nationalism, for that, as we shall see, is but a recrudescence under other forms of one of the strongest elements of primitive society. It was not the kings or priests but the prophets who made the major Jewish contribution to human freedom. Throughout the long history of persecution the Jews continued to cherish a mystical hope and faith which, in the judgment of the Western world, was realized in the life of Christ.

Christianity

It is a great mistake, yet one frequently found in Christian writings, to regard this priestly rule of the Jews as something imposed upon them by their religious oligarchy. No such theory would explain the fanatic tenacity with which the people as a whole held to their worship of Yahweh in the way prescribed for them or observed to the minutest detail the rules for daily life set forth in the Law. Instead of an external religion, it was the very heart and life of Jewish nationalism which was nurtured as well by their hope drawn from prophetic writings, of a messiah who would be sent by Yahweh for the reconquest of Jewish freedom.

In the five hundred years betwen the Babylonian captivity and the destruction of Jerusalem by the Romans, this priestly Judaism held the loyalty of its devotees through every form of adversity, between the short intervals of independence. The Romans, with that supreme political gift for rule through compromise with local customs, left practically untouched the Jewish priestly cult and the Law. This, however, but enhanced the sensibilities of a devoted and humiliated people, so that it was something worse than treason in their eyes for a Jew to violate the Law or challenge its authority.

Yet this is exactly what was done by Jesus of Nazareth. Worse still, if possible, in the eyes of the orthodox Jews, was the insistence that the Messiah, the deliverer of Juda, was not a warrior prince restoring it by force of arms, but a spiritual leader proclaiming that Yahweh's kingdom is not of this world. The challenge to established authority at Jerusalem was complete. The penalty resembled the one exacted by all societies which are held together by fanaticism, whether religious or any other kind.

The founder of Christianity was, however, only the first of a long line of martyrs. The systematic persecution by the Romans, lasting three centuries, was a vastly greater chapter in the history of the church than the sporadic outbursts of Jewish nationalists who were soon forced into impotence by the legions of Titus. But in both cases the causes were the same; the denial of the ultimate sovereignty of the state, the insistence upon a higher law than that of the civil magistrates and a refusal to sacrifice, even for the safety of the state, according to the established rites. Yet the persecutions, with all the might of Rome behind them, failed, and "the blood of the martyrs became the seed of the church." There is no other chapter in the history of freedom to match this victory for freedom of conscience and worship over the mightiest empire in the world at that time. What, in terms of human experience, is the explanation?

The full answer to this question would take us too far afield; some of the compelling elements of the new religion must be left for later chapters in which we trace its history in the Western world. For, although it sprang from Judaic origins, Christianity became a distinctly European religion. The connection with Judaism was, as has already been implied in the previous section, by way of the later prophets and especially of the second Isaiah. So definite and clear was this connection that it more than anything else served to link together the Old and New Testaments to form the Christian Bible. There were, however, two elements in the Christian faith which marked it off definitely from that of Judaism: a new conception of life after death, and the divinity of Jesus.

The Jewish religion had never envisaged the life to come as anything more than a shadowy existence in the abode of Sheol. But Jesus said that the poor and disinherited of this world would find in the world to come a "house with many mansions," prepared and held in readiness for them by the loving Father of all mankind. This was more than any of the prophets had said, more definite and more humanly appealing than the promise of any other religion. And the appeal was to the little people of the world who had never had a share in kingly splendor except at a distance and except as they maintained it by their own slavery or exploitation. Here was a vision beyond what men had dared hope, and it was no extravagant fancy of poet or dreamer, but something promised by the word of God Himself.

For, combined with the belief in immortality, was that of the divinity of Jesus, a combination which made the new religion invincible. This was not the first time that a cult had developed around a religious leader. It had happened to the Buddha and even to a reformer like Confucius. But that was long after their lives, when mythologies began to form about the great but indistinct figures of the past. With Jesus the case was wholly different, for it was His closest associates who became the witnesses of His divinity and of His resurrection.

The strength of this conviction of the apostles and the earliest converts was such that the unique personality of Jesus as a human being who taught humility and practiced it as a supreme virtue, was for a time obscured by concentration upon the divinity whose short stay on earth was after all of less importance to them than his second coming in power and glory in the not-distant future, when he would sit in judgment on all mankind. Such a faith was enough to give vitality to the new religion; but in addition the converts could share in the gift of prophecy or, as it is called, "the gift of tongues," of the Holy Spirit, for such meetings as the first one at Pentecost were, as Paul testified, so common as to threaten the early church with an emotionalism difficult to control. It was Paul himself who saved it from any such fate by insisting that everything should be done with regard to the rights of other members present, and that the fundamental doctrine should never be lost sight of — the gift of immortal life through the sacrifice of the son of God.

But Christianity was more than a doctrine. It was Paul himself, the apostle of faith, who pointed this out. Of the great trilogy, faith, hope and charity, "the greatest of these is charity." Therefore, the preparation for the life to come is the love of one's neighbor, as well as the love of God. Nowhere else in literature is there a more powerful portrayal of the purely ethical content of a religion. It is only to those who suffer long and are kind that the ecstatic vision is vouchsafed. Jesus had said this in bold terms that remained — and still remain — a supreme challenge to experience: the meek and not the powerful shall inherit the earth, and one should love even one's enemies.

A message like this was revolutionary in the fullest sense of the word. The protest against tyranny and violence by the later prophets had now become a doctrine which welded love of God and man into one single test of salvation. Peace was henceforth to be sought not merely in prayer or meditation but by actual practice, in dealing with one's neighbor. No one else had ever gone so far in the denunciation of force and violence as to proclaim that the governance of God rested upon the denial of their validity. The doctrine of Jesus was therefore the absolute culmination of ethics.

Yet Christianity is not just a system of ethics. It is a religion rooted in faith and concentrated upon the world to come, for which life in the present is only a preparation. Viewed from this standpoint it is a genuinely Asiatic expression of the interest of mankind in the eternal mystery and of the poignant sense of its own powerlessness and shortcomings. The fact that it never made much progress in Asia was perhaps due to its revolutionary challenge to the world of taboo which made it less rather than more of a religious movement in the eyes of the Orientals.

This very fact, however, fitted Christianity for the conquest of the West where Greek philosophy and Roman organization had already prepared the way. While primitive taboos persisted in the West and found expression in law as well as in custom, they have not dominated as in the Orient. Christianity is adjustable to progress not only because it is fundamentally a religion of the individual, but also because its theology is based upon a theory of history in which the governance of God is revealed through successive stages of human development. This theology, while parts of it are at times illiberal and even reactionary, has, upon the whole, not prevented it from keeping pace with experience, both intellectual and material. With increasing if cautious speed it follows and sanctions the discoveries of science in its concern for the social justice of a work-a-day world.

Islam

Some seven centuries after the rise of Christianity, Islam, the last of the great religions, burst into a flame of conquest across that part of Asia which had been left untouched by the reforming gospels of Buddha and Christ. This was that great stretch of desert and grassland which reaches from the Red Sea into the central mountain ranges of Asia, the home of Bedouin nomads still in the early stages of tribal society and of low-grade superstitions.

Although on the border of great civilizations, Arabia remained a world apart, successfully protected from the neighboring empires of Egypt and

Babylon by both its desert barriers and its poverty. Then, suddenly, these age-old silences were filled with a cry which still greets dawn and dark from every minaret, the call to prayer to Allah and the homage of his prophet, Mohammed. Within a single lifetime the new religion had reached from Morocco to India, a movement without parallel in history, and all the more remarkable because, within this vast area, it has remained unshaken by Christian crusade and internal wars, and is still one of the vital religions of the world today.

The last of the great religions is first in the singleness of its faith, because it is the last compromising with any other loyalty than that to Allah. There is no text in the Koran which says that one should "render unto Caesar the things that are Caesar's and to God the things that are God's," which justified in Christendom a division of loyalty, to secular as well as to spiritual rule.

To the Mohammedan, everything is Allah's; there is no Caesar to share his lordship over men. The keynote to life is "Islam," which means complete surrender to the will of God. This is not something sought after by a saintly few, for while Islam has its saints or holy men, everyone recognizes the direct control of Allah in the affairs of life. This finds expression in the common phrase of everyday life, "if God wills it," a constant reminder of dependence upon Allah. Indeed this conviction of God's oversight and governance is so strong as to make for fatalism, accepting whatever may be the lot of the believer because it is Allah's will that it should be so.

Not only in its creed, but also in its forms of ritual, Islam is an intensely personal religion. It has no priesthood to serve as intermediary between man and God, for the imams are rather prayer-leaders than a clergy in the Asiatic or even in the Christian sense. Although some sects still offer sacrifices, as in the days before Mohammed, these instances of the persistence of primitive cults are foreign to the spirit of a religion which concentrates upon prayer as the medium of communication with Allah. No other religion puts such an emphasis upon the universal observance of this rite, for it is not a ceremony delegated to the priesthood, to be used vicariously for the benefit of others.

Mohammedan prayer is shared in by all, in what might be termed a spiritual democracy. Five times a day the Moslem prays: at dawn; just after noon; before and after sunset; and again after night has come. The prayers are preceded by ritual ablutions of face, hands and arms, and feet, and as they pray the worshippers prostrate themselves toward Mecca. It is not easy for the world that calls itself Christian to realize the extent to which these ceremonies frame the daily life of every "believer" within the structure of religion. Their very simplicity adds to their impressiveness, especially when every man participates in the Friday meetings in the mosques.

No other religion, not even Christianity, is so exclusively that of its founder as Islam. There is no Old Testament to which the new dispensation looks back. It is true that there are borrowings from the Jews, and that Mohammed claimed his revelations confirmed the Jewish and Christian scriptures, but his knowledge of Judaism was limited and, except for the

71

dominant theme of the resurrection and the day of Judgment, there is little parallel with Christianity.

Although Allah is "the Compassionate," the keynote of Islam is power, not loving-kindness. There is no slightest echo of the virtue of nonresistance or peace except as won by the sword. For the sword was the readiest and surest instrument of conversion. While it is true that this was the way in which the Saxons were "converted" by Charlemagne and most other northern peoples by their war-lords, and that throughout most of their history the Christians have been as warlike as the Moslems, the teachings of the Koran lack that accent on peace which is the distinctive note of the Gospels.

The real source from which Islam drew its strength was the revolutionary crusade of Mohammed himself against the primitive paganism of Arabia which still preserved the tribal society of the legendary days of Abraham, to which it continually looked back. The religion of the Arabs of Mohammed's time continued to be that of the earliest ages, fetish worship overlaid with a veneer of animism in which good and evil spirits played wilfully with destiny. It was, with the usual local adaptations to environment, the universal orthodoxy of primitive life, that of the taboo.

To break down these beliefs, rooted in antiquity and encrusted in the customs of daily life, to destroy this richly variegated and intimate pantheon of idolatrous worship, there was only one way, and that was by bringing to bear against it a still stronger spiritual force. And the only spiritual force strong enough was that of the omnipotent ruler of the universe, Allah (the name is apparently a local one from Mohammed's Koreish tribe), the one and only God. Mohammed never claimed to be more than his mouthpiece, reciting from a trance-like condition the messages conveyed from the seventh heaven to the first heaven by the angel Gabriel. The author of the Koran is not the prophet, but Allah himself.

Compared with the paganism which it replaced, the creed of Mohammed would have seemed as bare and bleak as the Arabian desert that saw its birth if it had not been for the constant reminder of the rewards awaiting the believer after death, and the exaltation of that act of faith which defied the old beliefs: "There is no God but Allah; and Mohammed is his prophet." Daily the faithful are reminded of the sovereignty of God and the sinfulness of anything but absolute monotheism, in the call to prayer and homage to the prophet which is still heard throughout Islam. It is this emphasis upon faith and the puritanical prescriptions of conduct, which have given to Mohammedanism that unyielding quality of aloofness, so that it stands out, imposing and severe, unshaken by Christian crusade and, unlike Buddhism, unsubmerged in its environment. In spite of sectarian divisions, it has an inner unity which gives it vitality in the world today.

Faith was never so glorified, even by St. Paul; but it was denatured of its humanity by its very fanaticism and by the use of war to force its acceptance. In his early prophecies, Mohammed maintained a highly religious tone, with the accent upon the unity of God, but after his flight to Medina in 622 A.D. — the year I of the Mohammedan era — the prophet took on more and more the character of a warrior, or chieftain of warriors. The turning point, a fateful day for civilization, sems to have been when he decided to attack the caravan of traders headed from the north for Mecca, in order to live off the spoil.

The warlike tribesmen of the desert found in the new faith a force for discipline which secured victory, first over the defenders of Mecca and then over their neighbors. Once launched upon this career, they could look forward to greater spoil than from inter-tribal feuds. Fanaticism did not have to await the rewards of the hereafter; it could take for its plunder the decadent but still splendid centers of ancient culture.

The drama of conquest was breath-taking. Eight years after his flight, Mohammed had taken Mecca and had won over its warriors, so that almost immediately he became the dominant figure in all Arabia. At his death in 632 his armies were passing the frontiers of Arabia and within a quarter of a century, the Arabians who had never played any decisive role in history before, had conquered a greater empire than any since Alexander, almost a thousand years earlier. Damascus was taken in 635, Jerusalem in 636, Egypt in 640, Persia in 643, and by 712, Spain and Northwestern India. Islam had become the new great world power.

But the speed of this conquest was matched by its permanence. For almost a thousand years Islam retained its crusading force and, in spite of continued wars and rebellions, showed its power of organization in the great caliphates of Damascus, Bagdad, Constantinople and Cairo and the emirate of Cordova in Spain. From the seventeenth century onward, however, the countries of Mohammedan rule lost their importance as the sea routes supplemented the old caravans; and, while the prophecies of Mohammed still exert their spell and Islam continues to spread through the tribes of Africa, there is no longer any likelihood of a revival of the splendors of Bagdad or Cordova. For the iron laws of economics are stronger than Damascus steel.

But Islam is more than a religion; it is a theocracy, and theocracy is a form of government. The name Mohammed himself gave to his movement was Islam, which means submission to God, and the prophetic utterances gathered together in the Koran are not to be regarded as Mohammed's, but as coming direct from God through the Angel Gabriel. Alongside this sacred book a less but still fundamental role is played by the "traditions" gathered together from his followers. Together the sacred writings make up an extensive encyclopedia of directions for daily life and business conduct. It is law as well as creed, and those who expound it are jurists as well as theologians. Nowhere else in the world is there anything to compare with this effort to measure the conduct of life directly by the standards of a revealed doctrine.

Fortunately, the apparent incoherence and contradictions in the sacred texts open the door to compromise and adjustment in social and political affairs. In comparison with the social system which prevailed among the backward peoples who were the first converts to Islam, it marked a very definite advance. Polygamy was preserved but under much more favorable circumstances than before. Although the blood feud still persisted, the

Prophet tried to limit it and substitute blood money for vengeance. In these, as in most other matters, he set a trend toward conservative moderation.

But it was in their dealings with the new Moslem civilizations that the Mohammedan rulers showed how far theocracy could go in adjusting itself to a secular world. For the most part, the Arab conquerors took over and applied the administrative systems of the countries they over-ran; and not the least of the influences which such a policy imposed upon their system of government was the study and practice of Roman law in the conquered provinces. The army and the highest offices of state were reserved for the faithful, but the unbeliever could take over all of that complicated machinery of bureaucracy which is the inevitable accompaniment of militarism. Moreover, alongside the jurists and the civilian officials, a place was found at the courts of the Mohammedan rulers for Greek scholars and scientists, the only place open to them while Europe was under the eclipse of the Dark Ages.

Behind the grim outlines of tyranny lie experiments which far outrange the contemporary statesmanship of the Western countries. These bright pages of Moslem rule are, it is true, interspersed with others of cruelty and oppression; and are never wholly free from the uncertainties of arbitrary rule. But the fact remains that it was at the courts of the Moslem rulers that Greek philosophy was revived and scientists began to lay the mathematical basis, not only for engineering, but for the measurement of the world. The intellectual freedom which these studies demanded meant personal freedom for Christian as well as for Moslem scholars and thinkers, and yet the government under which they lived was the strongest theocracy in history.

The explanation — at least one explanation — seems to be in the very fact that Islam was never a political movement in the Western sense of the word. As we have pointed out above, it recognized no Caesar as a secular rival to the representative of the prophet. The result was that the Arab conquerors made sure of but two things in their conquests: security against uprisings, and tribute. While they themselves looked after their security, being warriors first of all, they wisely refrained from destruction of the sources of future income from the vanquished. In most cases this meant keeping most of the administrative systems of the conquered countries. A place was found at the court of the Caliph for jurists and civilians who knew how to make the old fit with the new so as to ensure prosperity and contentment.

Not the least striking of these adoptions of non-Moslem principles of government was the way the Abbassid caliphs, from their newly founded capital at Bagdad, took over the administrative machinery of those greatest of Asiatic organizers, the Persians. In like manner the Roman law was studied and practiced in the conquered provinces, as well as the customary law of the non-Moslem inhabitants. Like the canon law of the Catholic Church, the Koran and the *Sunna* or tradition of the prophet furnishes one vast system, dealing with private and religious affairs, but alongside it is the law of the land, based on secular life. So long as they paid the dues levied on them and made no trouble for their rulers, non-Moslem communities were generally permitted to judge themselves and administer local affairs.

Moslem tolerance must not be rated too highly, however. It was partly due to a contemptuous disregard of the conquered peoples, who could be left to their own devices as long as they paid their full quota of tribute, and partly to the inexperience of the Moslem rulers in the vastly difficult task of governing peoples of older and richer cultures than their own. The Moslems themselves profited least from a freedom they despised, and the caste-like distinction between believers and nonbelievers prevented the full development of the capacities of each. In short, the combination of religious fanaticism and militarism proved an impossible ground for the full development of either intellectual or political freedom.

CHAPTER IV

THE GREEK CITY STATES

The Beginnings of Politics

ALTHOUGH the civilization of the Orient, especially that of China, bear the mark of great antiquity, it seems likely that the earliest origins were not in the Far East but in the lower reaches of the Euphrates Valley, triply favored by the rich soil for farms and gardens, by the caravan routes that crossed it and by the ease with which its defensive earthworks could be thrown up against invaders. This most ancient chapter of history, and that of Egypt which paralleled it, lie outside our survey, however, because the drama of history on a continental scale for both Asia and Europe does not go back beyond the second millenium B.C. It was then that the Chinese were moving down the Yellow River into the Central Plain of China and the Aryans were pushing through the mountain gaps of the northwest frontier into the heart of India.

Almost at the same time similar movements of conquest and migration brought the Greeks and Romans into the drama of Western history. As in Asia, the northern tribesmen found earlier civilizations that reached back beyond history. The Minoan culture of the Aegean Islands and the mainland, and that of the Etruscans in Italy, linked culturally with Babylon. The history of the pre-conquest peoples does not come within our survey, because it was unknown even to the ancients, although now research and archeology have shown how rich were the spoils of war taken over by the northern invaders. The commerce of the Aegean which had centered at Crete never wholly ceased, although the Homeric warriors played no part in it, settling around strongholds that protected the farm lands strung along sheltered valleys. Despite their cultural borrowings from the people they conquered, they held stubbornly to their forms of society and it is from these simple beginnings of government that the political history of the West begins.

The movement of these ancestors of the Greeks was not a single migration but a series of tribal incursions, which, in the course of time, took over the settlements along the broken contour of the northern shores of the eastern Mediterranean, the islands of the Aegean, the coasts of Asia Minor and even trading posts on the Black Sea. As the settlements were mostly shut off from each other by rugged, rocky barriers, progress in the arts of peace was slow, because peace itself was never firmly established. There was always the temptation to go out on forays against neighboring settlements, a temptation to which the Greeks continued to yield to the very end of their history. In addition to raids by land, the character of the Mediterranean favored sea raiding as well. While it can be rough in winter, it is almost tideless, and supplied with innumerable harbors. But the advantages of trade over piracy led, in the course of time, to a mingling with foreign traders, for if they could be induced to come back there would be more and more chance of mutual profit as the primitive bazaars developed into market places by the gates of the settlements.

This Aegean world was a vastly different home for tribal life than the lush plains of India or the great river valleys of China. It was a small world of separate settlements or groups of neighboring settlements in which the kinship groups of family, clan and tribe furnished a natural basis for society, but where the urgent needs of war and the changes due to commerce and the arts of peace prevented stagnation. Greek life as described in the Homeric poems is cast in much the same mold as that depicted in the legends of the Aryans or even that preserved in the persisting structure of society in both China and Japan. There is nothing extraordinary in this for it was substantially that of early society the world over.

But whereas in the Orient the primitive kinship-taboo elements continued and were never wholly displaced by even the most powerful of monarchs, in Greece and Rome the practical problems of war and peace, especially of war, forced upon the city states a new device for government, to which in course of time the older basis of society was subordinated. We still give this new device the name the Greeks gave it, "politics," that is to say, management of affairs of the *polis* or city state. It is this, more than anything else, which is the distinctive mark of Western history in contrast with that of the Orient.

The earliest pictures we have of Greek society, those of the Homeric poems, show that, even in its primitive state, it differed from the oriental. It is true that the taboo was dominant in all critical affairs, both of individuals and of the tribes, but this rule was in the hands of "Kings," whose chief function was the practical direction of affairs of peace and war. It is true that the king was chosen from a royal family, which claimed to trace its descent from the gods. But, unlike the oriental kingship, that of these primitive Westerners was held in check by the fact that the leading warriors, who in council elected him, also claimed divine ancestry, so that the taboo of royalty did not separate the King from his comrades in arms. For the King had to qualify and even to excel as a warrior to face the constant danger of wars with neighboring tribes or lead in incursions on them. He had to be wealthy enough to provide the best of weapons, with retainers to use them, and personally maintain his prestige as the bravest of the brave. He had also to be wise in council and keen in debate, for, not being a despot, he had to persuade in order to command.

The Kingship, however, was not wholly secular. As both the affairs of state and the fortunes of war depended on the will of the gods, the King had to see to it that the taboos were not broken, and that the proper ceremonies were performed, either by himself or by a qualified priest. But he himself was not a god, however closely he might claim relationship to them. No temples were dedicated to him or identified with his divine descent, as was the case in Egypt or Japan, where the symbol of the sun or of heaven, as the supreme ruler of the universe, was applied to Pharoah or the Emperor. It was only after the great age of the history of the Greek states was over that Alexander, consciously yielding to oriental influences, accepted the utterly unhellenic practice of the Pharoahs and claimed divinity for himself. How completely foreign this was to the native thought of the West is proven by the parallel of Roman history, where the same kind of oriental influences ultimately falsified the ideals of that greatest of all schools of politics, the Roman Republic, by the introduction of the worship of the emperors.

Even in its origins, therefore, as well as throughout its entire history, there was a striking difference between Western and Asiatic societies. However much the taboo interfered in the affairs of men or nations, it did not determine the structure of their societies, as in the East. The limitation on the power of the early Kings by need to win the loyal support of his followers was an effective influence for progress toward a rational and secular society. Even in the Homeric age, patriarchal kingship with its sacerdotal functions was making way for the qualifications of good generalship or the possession of weapons that excelled. Agememnon was "more of a king" than the "kings" who formed his council, but in neither case was it the priestly character of office or descent from divine ancestors which determined the choice of leadership. The final decisions were made by the council in open debate. In short, the decline of tribal kingships had already set in and we are witnessing the rise of oligarchy, the typical form of government in the Greek city state at the turn of history.

It was not until the sixth century B.C., however, that this secular movement, long in preparation, was finally brought to a head, at the very time when Buddha and Confucius were recasting — with less success — the old trends in religion and social life. By that time the Greeks were ready for the second great stage in their political development, that which challenged and partly overthrew the oligarchy of chieftains whose rise was already discernible in Homeric times. The next step, which broke down the remaining trammels of taboo in politics was that which created the first democracy in history, Athens, when the old patriarchal leadership was discarded for an organization based upon the idea of government by all the free citizens of the city. This was a fundamental change, not merely an episode, in the history of government. It was not shared equally or at the same time by Greek city states, and there were some, like Sparta, in which it never developed the revolutionary quality which made the history of Athens unique in the antique world.

No such development as this ever took place in the Orient. Just why this should have been so, why the Orient remained so firmly planted on its primitive foundations and the West, largely under the tutelage of Greece, moved away to other interests and other ways for satisfying them, raises a question of fundamental importance for this survey. The difference in outlook and in intellectual achievement was not due to a difference in mental endowment, for the Asiatics have shown a capacity equal to the Westerners. It was due chiefly to the fact that the Greeks had the advantage of living in a small but varied world which called for constant ingenuity as the price of safety. Where nature did not provide the means for ready fusion into great empires, which by their very nature would maintain only superficial control, the ancient Mediterranean dwellers had to work out artificial means for their immediate safety and welfare, and the very difficulties which they faced were their stepping stones to progress. Had the problems in government in Greece or Rome been easy to solve by the strengthening of old taboos, as in India, or the submission to a universally accepted authority, as in China, or the fusion of both, as in Japan, Western civilization might never have discovered its ultimate ideal in human freedom.

Life in small communities like those of the early Greeks and Romans, had one definite advantage in that everyone could meet in public places, and that quite apart from formal assemblies they could exchange comments and gossip, not only about the day's events, but also about the affairs of the city. One could sharpen one's wits in debate or show what capacity one had for leadership by an appeal to public opinion that was all the more prompt to respond where everyone knew everyone else or at least something about them. In the cities of the Orient there was also discussion of local and public affairs, but thy were parts of a much larger whole — a vast impersonal empire — and public opinion had no chance to register its direct effect upon the mass of the population as was the case in the little city states of the Mediterranean. The smaller the public the better the chance for changing, not only the policies of the rulers, but the institutions of government itself. In Greece and Rome the conditions were ideal, and it was not long before the primitive society began to change.

The council of the chieftains was at first composed of what we might call the spiritual aristocracy of primitive peoples, that is to say that those who were leaders in what has been termed the "organization of safety": warriors and patriarchs who could best aid the king in defense against the real and imagined dangers confronting the community. In the earliest days one of the council's chief duties was to make sure that the established routines were not violated. But the routine had to be changed when new situations arose, which meant disaster for those who kept to the old technique. For example, when iron supplanted bronze and new methods of defense were used against the new weapons, the strategy of war had to be revised, and with it the provisions for organizing a defense. Then, if one's own settlement remained untouched by change, new developments in neighboring states had to be weighed and the council of the chieftain strengthened to make it more able to deal with the practical problems of security. But changes could not be thorough-going while the old taboos protected the prerogatives of the chieftain and the qualifications for leadership had henceforth to be, not proficiency in the primitive orthodoxy of sacrifice and ritual, but ingenuity in combat and common sense in council.

In such communities as these the needs of war were direct and compelling for the threat of it was never absent. Even in the intervals of peace there was constant preoccupation with war because one never knew when the peace might be broken. In this regard the Greek city states resembled all other settlements in semi-barbaric, semi-tribal life the world over, and even the organization of life among the nomads like the Arabs. In all such early societies the warriors are priviliged members of society because they may at any time be called upon to protect it from invasion and also because they are the ones who bring home the booty from the invasion of others. The old kinship tie supplies all that is necessary for the organization of the fighting men as long as the fighting is carried on by individual combat, and courage and strength carry the day. But when the army begins to form in solid ranks, as was the case with those innovations which made Sparta a terror to its neighbors, and in which Thebes led for awhile, the old careless reliance upon courage and cunning no longer avails.

This military development in the case of small states is a very different thing from that of the creation of great armies like the semi-feudal, semi-mercenary forces of Asiatic monarchs. Small though they were, the armies of the city states were solid companies of marching men, shield to shield, moving like a bristling fortress, and inspired by a common cause. The contrasts between them and the hosts of Xerxes is not unlike that between the archers of England and the cavalry of France on the field of Agincourt. A major change was taking place in the art and science of warfare which, in turn, affected the structure of the city state. For the council of the chieftains had to call in all those who could come in full armour and place them in the ranks of honor on the battlefield even if their ancestry did not qualify them for full participation in the religious ceremonies. The result was that they had a place in the council meetings when the decisions were made on the problems of war or peace.

In this way the structure of politics was largely the creation of military science. There was nothing extraordinary in this, for throughout all history war has played the dominant role in the formation and policies of governments. Strangely enough, however, the analysis of war — as such — is a sadly neglected field in the social sciences. This is perhaps partly due to the fact that when these sciences were developing, during the nineteenth century, war was apparently being narrowed down to a hoped-for vanishing point to make way for the processes of peace.

Now, however, when war is striking not only at the safety of every land but civilization itself, it is well to study the contributions which it has offered to the ultimate calamities which it invariably has brought. This can best be seen in the histories of Greece and Rome which here, as in so many other fields, are an intimate part of our history. Between the period of tribal organization and that of mercenary soldiers under professional leadership in the days of imperial Rome, there was a stage of social formation which was the chief political contribution of antiquity to politics, and which retains lessons of the first importance for all time. In Greece this was the period of the supremacy of Athens, in Rome it was that which witnessed the rise of republican institutions, between the decline of the kingship and the rise of the empire.

It was not only the small size of the city states, however, nor the discipline of military organizations, which made the politics of Greece so great a contribution to the history of freedom. For the Greeks had also another advantage in the paradox that their very isolation tempted their citizens to venture abroad and those of them who could travel shared their experiences with those who stayed at home, stimulating curiosity and an open mind in spite of the narrow confines of their daily life. The intercourse within Greece itself, if sporadic and more or less unfriendly, was still sufficient to maintain a feeling of Greek solidarity against the barbarian world outside the confines of Hellas, a solidarity which found expression in games and religious festivals. But from long before the day of Homer it was the "wine-dark sea" which led them to explore lands as far off as those of the Crimea on the north and Egypt on the south. Ulysses, the wanderer, was typically Greek, both in his daring and his curiosity, finding in the surprises of discovery a substitute for the excitement of battle.

More important than adventure, however, was the movement of colonization. No other people of antiquity spread their settlements around the Mediterranean to the same extent, their only rivals in this regard being the Carthaginians. This movement, whether due to overcrowding or to that mixture of motives which we now call imperialism, scattered Greek outposts as far west as Marseilles and as far east as the Crimea; each settlement cherishing its Hellenic culture but insisting, generally with success, upon independence from the city and the homeland which had founded it. Thus the way was prepared for that extension of Hellas which ultimately, under the aegis of Alexander and his successors, was to transform or at least to touch with Hellenic influence the cultural life of western Asia.

In their contact with other people the Greeks remained strongly nationalistic, but their pride in their common heritage of culture never prevented them from adjustments to foreign influences so long as they did not violate the sense of the integrity and the dignity of human life. In this way the experience of other peoples enriched their own, especially when it challenged the accepted ways of thought and conduct.

It would be wholly wrong, however, to think of the ancient Greeks as cosmopolitan in the modern sense. Down to the last period of their history, they continued to regard non-Greeks as barbarians and to treat them with intellectual arrogance, an arrogance justified by the fact that they improved upon practically everything they took from the non-Greek world. For the adventurers who thus pioneered on the fringes of the barbarian world, having no powerful monarchs to support them or protect them, had to rely upon themselves, as had been done at home by those whose small groups made up the ancient city states.

Self-reliance, joined with enterprise and curiosity, became the outstanding characteristics of the Greek throughout the antique world. How much of it there had been in the earliest days of Greece before the Greeks were there is a question to which history has no answer except in the fact that the sailors of Crete, centuries before the founding of Athens, were in touch with Asia and Egypt. This would seem to indicate that the Greek temper was not due to race so much as to circumstances. But in the light of subsequent history of Hellenism this easy generalization seems quite inadequate. The Greeks stand forth wherever they are as a specially endowed people, whether it be in the Athens of Pericles, the cities of Alexander's planning, or as slaves at Rome. They are the leaders of culture in their own right.

The cities which led in what was destined to be a new era of human culture were not those of the European mainland — for their great era came a little later. They were the Ionian seaports which nestled between the headlands of Asia Minor, whose explorers and traders ranged through the Near East before the days of Herodotus and established trading posts which grew into city states along the lines of trade. Sooner or later the citizens of these Hellenic centers were bound to compare their small cities and especially their tribal lore with the great civilizations of Egypt and Mesopotamia, to the south and east, with which Europe had lost touch since the Minoan age of Greece. The vast spectacle of the antiquity of Egypt with its thousands of years of settled life and the enduring creations of its art and culture made the traditions of the Asiatic Greek seaports seem trivial and laid their tribal taboos open to question. An intellectual revolution without parallel until the days of modern science began in the six century B.C. when Hecataeus of Miletus, the first of the historians, coming back from his travels to Egypt, challenged traditions and orthodoxy by a declaration as sweeping as that of any of the skeptics: "I write what I deem true, for the beliefs of the Greeks are manifold and ridiculous." This is something very different from the reforms set in motion by the religious leaders and philosophers of Asia. Even the secularly-minded Confucius never cut himself off from the past with such a denial of its validity as was the case with these pioneers of the history of Europe. Instead, he emphasized the reverence for the past because in it and not in a divergent civilization of the present, he found the basis for morality.

A new door was opening upon the world, one forced open by the curiosity of inquiring minds. Curiosity is a universal attribute of life, to be found among animals as well as among men. But its peculiar characteristic is that it is highly individual and not a social function of the group. If carried to an extreme, it is frankly antisocial when it questions the truth of what everyone else believes. In the history of Europe it played this double role of stimulating thought by the development of the critical faculty. The pathway to progress which it opened was therefore a dangerous one, because the denial of rooted beliefs weakens a society unless there are substitutes for them that can be relied upon to maintain the common mind in the routine of life and strengthen it in time of crisis. Therefore, such a daring kind of skepticism did not make for political stability. This apparent contradiction between individual freedom of thought and the needs of state was never wholly solved in antiquity — as the death of Socrates and the persecution of the Christians bear witness. It remains the fundamental problem of freedom today.

If Asia Minor was the original home of critical history, it is hardly too much to say that it was also the original home of philosophy. The *histor* was the inquirer or truth seeker as well as the "truth-teller." In Rome, with its trend toward law, he became *questor* or magistrate. But in Greece he was the critic who investigated the evidence of what happened before he ventured to tell his story. Similarly, critics of life and the world around, those whom Plato later called philosophers, began a pioneering movement of the liberation of the mind by questioning and studying the ways of the people with whom they came in contact. Of these, we can mention only one. Almost at the same time as Hecataeus, Xenophanes or Colophon, launched a still more thorough-going critique of the Homeric orthodoxy which, up until then, had been accepted with easy acquiesence by Greeks everywhere.

There are few romances in the history of thought more alluring than the life of Xenophanes. Exiled from his home in Asia Minor, he traveled from city to city, to settle at last in southern Italy at Elea, reciting his poems after the manner of the ancient bards, not to recall the exploits of the gods, but to deny the stories of those exploits as set forth in the Homeric poems. Thus at the dawn of ancient history in the Mediterranean world, we find a philosopher denouncing the traditional beliefs as superstitions, in which men create the gods in their own image, whether they be the fair-haired, blue-eyed deities of Homer or the black gods of the Ethiopians. "Homer and Hesiod," runs a fragment of his teachings, "attributed to the gods all that is a shame and reproach among men — theft, adultery, deceit and other lawless acts." No one really knows for certain about the gods, for all things are matters of opinion. Nevertheless, this skeptic stated as his own belief that "there is one God, greatest among gods and men, neither in shape nor in thought like unto mortals . . . without an effort he rules all things by thought." It is hard to realize that this ringing challenge to accepted beliefs

82

on the basis of critical reasoning comes to us from a distance as far as those forgotten cities of Magna Graecia, before the Parthenon was built in Athens and while there were still kings in ancient Rome; for it comes to us not as a faint echo of unfamiliar things such as we still hear in the literature of Asia, but as a voice of today challenging that greatest of all servitudes, superstition. We lose the sense of its unique quality because, in the years that followed, it was not unique among the Greeks. In this connection the fact that is next in significance to Xenophanes' teaching is the fact that as far as we know, he was never persecuted for his belief.

The citizens of the Mediterranean city states undoubtedly had no clear idea of the extent of the revolution which they had begun in human affairs, that which was destined in the course of centuries to overthrow the taboo as the directing element in human society and substitute for it politics, that is to say, the secular functioning of organized societies. It would be wholly misleading to interpret ancient history as the conscious embodiment of any such secularizing movement. The emancipation from superstition which marked the trend of intellectual history was by no means taken over by the mass of the citizens. There was never any general movement of popular enlightenment through public education — that is a phenomenon reserved for modern times. However much the cultured Greek or Roman freed himself from superstition, and however much the statesmen based their policies upon practical issues of the day, the society of the city states was in its origin and structure deeply religious.

The religion of the family, which looked to the patriarch as priest, was paralleled in each city state by the worship of the special deities that watched over them and whose home in the temple crowning the highest hill or by the market place, was a prouder symbol of sovereignty than that of the secular ruler. The gods themselves might be chosen from a universal pantheon, like Athena on the rock of the Acropolis in Athens or Jupiter on the Capitoline Hill of Rome, but the deities could be counted upon to favor those whose hospitality they could most surely count on. Thus the religion of the city states tended to remain, as in all primitive societies, a science of serving the gods, nicely calculated so as neither to neglect nor overdo the required ceremonies. There is more magic in this than religion, although the word religion itself, in its Latin form *religio,* meant, as Cicero pointed out, the reconsideration (rather than the practice) of all that pertained to the worship of the gods.

The extent to which the ancient city was a repository of magic and religion was not clearly seen until the rise of critical scholarship at the close of the nineteenth century. The pioneer work of Fustel de Coulanges, *The Ancient City,* presented another picture of the city state than that in the school textbooks of the day. The study of social history, analyzing the daily life of the citizens of the ancient world, has now reached the dimensions of encyclopedias, and it reveals a world in which magic and religion interplay with the daily activities as a part of the common scene of the town and countryside. This persistent, deep-rooted mixture of polytheism and magic was, in the eyes of the Christian fathers, the very essence of pagan society. Nowhere else has that gigantic company of uncanny presences been more clearly portrayed than in the pages of St. Augustine's *City of God*. There they are presented as the army of Satan and therefore still alive and active in the affairs of men.

The antique man lived in the presence of these beings. It was therefore but natural that magic and religion continued to play a major role in the affairs of state, with omens and auspices as in ancient Babylon. This situation was not overcome by the rationalization of the philosophers. Battles continued to be won by miracle or lost by the failure to perform the proper ceremonies to appease the gods. Politics itself yielded to their anger in the time of crisis, but in the contest of city with city, those were likely to win who learned the best way to serve both human and divine purposes at the same time. This led to a reorganization of the citizenry, insofar as this could be done without endangering the safety of the state by an undue lack of respect for the gods. The way to do this was therefore to retain the religions structure for the purposes of religion and to set up alongside it a new organization chiefly designed for purposes of war. The patriarchs and those who knew the ancient ceremonies could continue to meet or to exercise their functions in the sphere of taboo, but practical men had more definite things to do. The process of secularization, by which they took over the business of the state, was therefore purposely disguised so that the gods would not notice what was happening.

Incomplete as the process of secularization was, the important point remains that the inhabitants of these Mediterranean cities, in Italy as well as in Greece, never fell under the tyranny of priests, as was the case in Egypt and the empires of Mesopotamia. Those who served the temple did not form a caste which overawed the civil authorities, nor were the beliefs of religion set forth in a sacred text. The Homeric poems were the nearest to a bible that the Greeks produced, yet they were never thought of as inspired writings. Indeed their chief interest was secular rather than religious, mingling myth and legend, the story of gods and men, in what was a substitute for history rather than theology. The way for freedom of thought and speculation lay, therefore, more open before the ancients of the Western world than was the case in the more ancient civilizations of the Orient, where the authority of the past sanctifying sacerdotalism blocked the path to free inquiry. Viewed from the angle of today, the steps which were taken may seem slight, but they were steps out of that primitive world which had been handicapped by an orthodoxy of superstitious fear for untold centuries.

The drama of ancient history was repeated in different terms in the Middle Ages and Modern Times; for the geographical setting which made Sparta, Athens and Rome at once so like and so utterly unlike each other, was continued in the larger theatre of European history, owing to the dissimilarities of one country from another. As in the antique world, war continued its potent role in the relations of state with state and its needs largely determined the form as well as the content of politics down to modern times. But these are the externals of history; neither the institutions of war nor those of peace which it fathered, have any meaning in themselves. Their meaning lies in the uses to which they are put in the poverty or enrichment of human lives. And this in turn is no abstract statement of institutional history. It is the living assertion of the individual's life and place in society. Thus it turns out that in the long run the most important contribution of Greece was not the creation of politics by the remaking of its armies and its policies, in ways which we are about to examine, but its awakening of human reason by the eternal questioning of the great verities of life and the world, including society itself.

Here, then, we have come upon a great new ideal for mankind, that of freedom as the exercise of reason in the conduct of life. This is something wholly different from the escape to nirvana and, in spite of all the work of the church fathers intent upon relating it to theology, its approach to the problems of life is from a different angle from that of the theologians. But human reason is still a feeble and often frustrated guide. The primitive world lasts on in us all and to an extent that none of us would like to admit. As true freedom lies in the application of reason to human affairs, we have still a long road to follow in its ultimate attainment.

Sparta, the Politics of Power

Unfortunately for the modern student of politics, the scenes of its origins in the Western world were so small that its early history seems trivial in contrast with the vast interests and energies engaged in it today, and its devices for government so varied and confused that they have little interest for any except specialists in Greek history. But in that little laboratory of experience a fundamental advance in the management of human affairs was made, which set the model for all the centuries of Western history down to our day.

The best starting point for understanding how politics developed in ancient Greece is the city state which developed it least, Sparta, because it preserved in simplest form the impress of that major force in its creation: war. The origins can only be surmised, for the Spartans did not trouble over history, but it seems quite clear that their Dorian ancestors who overran the central Peloponnesus some time after the Trojan war, either did not wholly conquer the earlier inhabitants or fought among themselves, as so often happens in barbarian conquests, and that those in the settlement of Sparta saved themselves, not by stone-walled fortresses, but by the strictest military discipline and by a political organization planned for war. Little advance was made in the arts of peace because the militarism on which they depended for security could not be safely relaxed — any more than the walls of a city could be pulled down, so long as the Spartans were apprehensive of war — for one of the chief obstacles to progress, in either politics or the arts, is the sense of insecurity. The fallacy in the Spartan system was that defence was found in a rigid system of discipline. Militarism unqualified proved to be as much of an obstacle as taboo. Indeed it preserved much of the primitive taboo, as when the Spartans failed to join in the battle of Marathon because it was the time of a religious festival during which warfare was forbidden.

The Spartan was first and foremost a soldier, trained in rigid discipline from a childhood from which every softening influence of humane custom was removed. This produced a fighting caste of youths who were messmates in the barracks, debarred by law from trade or manufacture, forbidden to possess either gold or silver, but maintained by the state for the one supreme purpose of war. The old military virtues of warrior heroes were instilled in the minds of the warriors by self-inflicted punishments and the admonition to those leaving for battle to return either with their shields or upon them. In short, Sparta was a training camp of armed men, settled in the midst of a farming world far enough inland from the sea to be safe from invasion, and secure there only because of its great army. Thucydides, coming from the splendor of Athens, described it in these terms: "The city is not built continuously and has no splendid temples or other edifices, it rather resembles a group of villages, like the ancient towns of Hellas, and would therefore make a poor showing" (if its remains were excavated in later centuries). Nevertheless Thucydides did not despise Sparta, for there was in its stability and unity an element of greatness, and although its militarism blunted its appreciation of the common heritage of Hellas, it had, nevertheless, taken the great step in the art and science of government which marked it off from the Asiatic world. Its affairs were run by the citizens themselves.

The Spartans attributed the constitution of their city to a legendary lawgiver, Lycurgus, whose figure was already so dim, or rather confused in classical times that Plutarch said there was not a single statement about him that was not called in question, and that this applied not only to his travels and the date of his death, but "above all" to his law-making. Yet there must have been at least one Lycurgus in Sparta, if not more, for so strict a regime must have been imposed by someone strong enough to beat down the opposition of those whose freedom it curtailed. The story of Herodotus that Lycurgus brought back his ideas from his travels in Crete, certainly offers no explanation why they were accepted by the warring factions. He, or someone, had force behind him. But apparently the reform was partly to be explained by the breakdown of the old society or its inherent weakness to attack.

In any case, some time in the seventh or eighth century B.C. the old Homeric council of the chieftains seems to have made way for the larger influence of the assembly of citizen soldiery, a reform which later historians connect with the redistribution of the land. The primitive kingship of two hereditary kings, who in the beginning combined the functions of chief priests and judges with those of generals, lost their semi-military powers to other magistrates such as the five *ephors* who were the inspectors of the five wards or districts. The military function of the kingship remained, however, so that at the close of Sparta's history it is described by Aristotle as "a kind of unlimited perpetual generalship."

It is not worth our while pursuing this analysis of Spartan institutions farther except for two reasons. The first is that it left its mark on the history of the West not only because of the unique discipline of the Spartan citizen, but also because that very discipline enabled the soldiers to move in line of battle with solid ranks, shield to shield, a wholly new device in warfare and one which saved a place in history for Greece itself. Heavy infantry, composed of well-drilled spearsmen could stand the shock of cavalry and defy the prowess of the individual fighter. No taunting champion like Goliath of the Philistines could tempt the Spartans to break rank. The day of the noble chieftain had given way to solidarity and equality of risk and achievement. The Spartan formation of battle might, therefore, be called the introduction of democracy in military organization. This leaves us with a strange paradox — that the first practice of democracy was in that very field which throughout history had most opposed its development, that of militarism. It would be misleading, however, to make too much of this, because it was not democracy under the regime of freedom, which is the only real democracy. Equality and rigid solidarity under discipline has only a misleading and external resemblance to the voluntary coordination of a citizenry in which the individual preserves his freedom.

The second lesson which Sparta left the world is that where the arts of war were so highly developed those of peace were almost wholly left aside. The soldier must not be distracted by any other interest, and so the Spartans, like other primitive peoples, left the day's work for the other, the non-Spartan inhabitants of town or countryside, the *perioeci* or dwellers around, as they were called, and the slaves or *helots*, the underprivileged and the unprivileged. Never were the defects of militarism more clear. There was no free play of ingenuity, no interest in further change. The present dangers were adequately met, but by the use of familiar weapons in familiar ways. New devices should not be risked, only better and if possible larger battalions, and these should be drawn only from the warrior class.

But war wastes manpower as well as weapons, and the Spartans were few. In the last days of Greek history there were only about a thousand of them left. Whether this decline could have been prevented by paying more attention to Sparta's economic development or to the problems of public health is an open question. Because of its inland location and the backward farming country in which it was set, it could never be a "large city." There was no challenge to the mind of the Spartans as there was to that of the Athenians to meet rapidly changing conditions by social and economic, as well as political, change within the state. The fact that the Spartans themselves left the problems of their economic welfare, the tiresome, persistent problems of daily life, to those who had no share in the determination of policy was one of the chief reasons why the influence of Sparta made no contribution to Greek civilization to rival its influence, often malign, as a military power. The rigidity of mind which could not adjust itself to changing circumstances failed to appreciate that intelligence is after all the chief asset of a people. That discovery was left for the Athenians.

It is in the light of the contrast with Athens that the un-Hellenic quality of Sparta takes on its full meaning. It lacked not only the tone of modernity of the city of Pericles, but it suppressed the development of freedom by the kind of police suppression which militarism always employs, or longs to employ, over the civilian population. Even the Romans, the supreme militarists of antiquity, early learned the value of extending their citizenship, making non-Romans comrades in arms and in council. But the Spartans remained enslaved by their denial of freedom to others.

The bearing of this upon the world today has been brilliantly brought out by Arnold Toynbee in his volume on the international crisis of 1938, when the Nazi march of aggression had begun to threaten the liberties of Europe. Commenting on the difference between liberal England and Nazi Germany, he says:

Much the same impression must have been made on the mind of the Athenian observer who visited Sparta at any time during the four hundred years' duration of a Lycurgean "way of life" *(agôge)* which was at last forcibly eradicated by an act of foreign intervention in 189-188 B.C. The most horrifying feature of the Lycurgean system in non-Spartan Hellenic eyes was not in its militarism, which, like Prussian militarism, differed to a degree that hardly amounted to a difference in kind from the warlike propensities of the rest of a society from which Sparta had differentiated itself in the one case, and Prussia in the other. The most appalling aspect of Spartanism was the iniquitous repression of an odiously penalized subject population; and the most monstrous of all Spartan institutions was a Secret Service *(crypteia)* that was the euphemistic official designation of an official murder-gang in which adolescent Spartan boys, during the last two years before their coming of age, were trained to carry out a stealthy patrol of the countryside for the purpose of making away with any Helots who had shown symptoms of restiveness or perhaps even only vestiges of character and ability. This Nazi-like public iniquity was the characteristic of the Lycurgean régime that fixed the impassable gulf between Lycurgean Sparta and the rest of Hellas. But there was one difference of structure, ethos and aim between a Lycurgean Sparta and a National-Socialist Germany that was of crucial importance from the standpoint of these two inquitous communities' neighbors, Hitler knew that the Third Reich must either conquer the world or perish, while the rulers of Lycurgean Sparta were equally well aware that the conquest of an empire would spell the doom of the Lycurgean régime. This difference explains why the Third Reich's term of life was of twelve years, in contrast to a Lycurgean Sparta's run of four centuries.[1]

The parallel which Toynbee draws between Lycurgean Sparta and Nazi Germany is borne out by the following account which Thucydides gives of a mass murder of the helots, which for cold blooded planning rivals the atrocities of Buchenwald and Dachau.

Fear of their members [of the Helots] and their obstinacy led the Spartans to the action which I shall now relate, their policy at all times having been governed by the necessity of taking precautions against them. The Helots were invited by a proclamation to pick out those of their number who claimed to have most distinguished themselves against the enemy (of Sparta), in order that they might

[1] *Survey of International Affairs for 1938*, Vol. II (London: Royal Institute of International Affairs, Oxford University Press) p. 1.

receive their freedom; the object being to test them, that the first to claim their freedom would be the most high-spirited and most apt to rebel. As many as two thousand were selected accordingly and went round the temples, rejoicing in their new freedom. The Spartans, however, soon afterwards did away with them, and no one knew how each of them perished.

There is no indication here that Thucydides shared in a sense of moral indignation against this atrocity, which he describes as an incident in his history of the war. This might be explained by the impartial temper of the historian; but the treaty which closed the first war, the text of which Thucydides gives without comment, provides that "should the slave population rise, the Athenians shall help the Spartans with all their might, according to their power."

The conclusion is clear. A slave-owning state is doubly insecure when its relations with its neighbors are based on militarism; and insecurity — the sensing of danger — is the greatest obstacle to freedom, as is shown, for one thing by the denial of freedom under military discipline. The prevalence of these two elements, slavery and militarism, in the rest of Greece, including Athens, prevented a clear-eyed criticism of what was wrong.

There is no better witness to the unique spell which the disciplined life of Sparta cast over Greeks of other cities than that of the soldier historian, Xenophon, both in turning from Athens to the service of Sparta after the great retreat from Asia, and in his glorification of Spartan institutions in his *Constitution of the Lacedaemonians.* "I recall the astonishment" he says, "with which I first noted the unique position of Sparta among the states of Hellas, the relatively sparce population and at the same time the extraordinary power and prestige of the community. I was puzzled to account for the fact. It was only when I came to consider the peculiar institutions of the Spartans that my wonderment ceased." Then he describes the education of the Spartan youth, contrasting the softening influences of Athenian instruction in music and literature with the Spartan discipline in which "a body of youths in the prime of young manhood [or young bullies] are provided with whips to inflict punishment when necessary, with this happy result that in Sparta reverence and obedience go hand in hand, nor is there a lack of either."

Xenophon's reactionary militarism might be satisfied with this distortion of Hellenic political ideals, but Aristotle was more critical. While he recognized that "there are many elements of virtue in a soldier's life" the constitution of Sparta was defective in exhausting its population in wars. The ownership of land was in the hands of a few, government by the ephors was corrupt, and some of them even "did their best to ruin the state." Bribery was practiced by the members of the council of elders; "the revenues of the state are ill-managed; there is no money in the treasury, although they are obliged to carry on great wars and they are unwilling to pay taxes."[2]

Such was the judgment of the greatest authority on Greek politics. Yet the fact that the Lycurgcan institutions lasted for centuries, while other states

[2] *Politics* II, 9.

were subject to revolutionary changes, furnished a spurious argument for the iron-bound structure of Spartan society, when in reality its stability was chiefly due to the unchanging nature of an agricultural economy isolated from the impact of commerce or foreign influences. Naturally laws and customs based on taboo and security played a part in this history, but their continuing strength was conditioned on the nature of Spartan economy and environment. Even Plato was not clear on this, and lesser minds than his concentrated their attention upon the merits of the close-knit, communist Dorian mode of life, when compared with the looser, ever changing, ever growing response to intelligence of the Ionians. As the execution of Socrates shows, Athens was equally ready to suppress freedom even of philosophic thought, when it felt menaced by a sense of insecurity. From Lycurgus to today, here lies the greatest danger to freedom.

Athens and the Beginning of Democracy

Had the development of politics in Greece remained on the level of the constitution of Sparta, it would not be worth more than passing notice; for, in spite of the intensely practical purposes of an organization designed for war, it hardly more than opened the door to escape from the primitive taboo. Superstitious scruples such as those which kept the Spartans from the battlefield of Marathon still dominated policies of state. That is bound to be the case where the process of emancipation stops at the first step which leaves the soldiery supreme; where the servitude of fear still mocks the progress toward freedom. It was in Athens that the Greek genius really came to grips with this fundamental problem and where its solution was worked out in what has aptly been termed the most incredible chapter in all human history.

There have been many attempts to explain this unique achievement which gave a new meaning to life by revealing its capacity to explore both nature and the mind itself and which provided as a home for such high enterprise the first experiment of democracy. But no one explanation will suffice. The Ionian Greeks who built up the Athenian city and empire were highly endowed by nature, as they showed wherever they settled. But was their intelligence a birthright, or did it acquire its sharpened edge by fencing with others in the market places of the Aegean and in the contact with strange customs and strange people? Surely the quality of Athenian history cannot be explained away as the product of trade and colonization.

But, granting that the Ionian stock was of the best, the stimulus of contact with the outside world certainly was a dominant factor in bringing out the native capacity. The contrast with Sparta is enlightening. There the contempt for trade resulted in stagnation. Athenian society, on the contrary, was dynamic, because it was open to the constantly changing influences of a varied world. That intellectual mobility is stimulated by trade is a commonplace in history. Modern times began when the world of medieval life was broken by the rise of capitalism and the opening of the world market.

In Athens, as the world of business grew, the institutions of democracy developed to assure not only justice but also freedom for the common man. There was the great exception of slavery, and trade was only partially distinguished from plunder — for the war system dominated economic as well as political life — but compared with other antique societies, the history of Athens was that of a revolution in freedom.

The origins of the revolutionary movement which we are tracing go back in Athens, as in Sparta, to the dawn of history when the "lawgiver," Draco, of the seventh century, codified and published the laws of Athens, thus preventing them from remaining the secret lore in the possession of the priestly patriarchal government. How much of this story is mythical is not a matter of concern here. Suffice it to say that such a writing down of the law registers the emergence into history of that other dominant interest of mankind, which we have noted in the survey of primitive life, the daily welfare in the common pursuits of life. Whenever a society advances beyond the primitive stage, its first interest, the organization of safety against both the visible and the unseen dangers of life, has always to yield ground to the more persistent demands of food, shelter and well-being. These have chiefly to do with social and economic justice at home, setting limits to the oppression by the strong, and offering some guarantee for the enjoyment of worldly goods and their increase through the work of the artisan or farmer and the exchange of goods in trade. While primitive man is just as fond of comfort (as he understands it) and as greedy for property (as he understands it) as the more civilized, his satisfactions are more immediate, in idleness or in delight at the glitter of beads or the flash of color. Such easy satisfaction does not call for any disturbance of taboo or habit. But in the course of settled life, property accumulation and the relationships of the members of the tribe become more complicated and the rules of conduct which were administered by the elders must be made known to all. Only by this means can the society continue to be knit together as it was in the old days of kinship tribalism, for the ownership of property is seen to be a means of power which can rival and, ultimately, displace the prerogatives of primitive chieftainship.

It is in this connection that in the history of almost every country, the figure of a great lawgiver appears, enhanced by the myth-making faculty which tends to attribute to him what may have been a long process or a series of reforms. The laws thus gain in strength by this attribution to a single author because they carry the authority of a great personality which is always an asset in lawmaking. Thus Hammurabi stands out in the annals of early Babylon to establish justice and mete out punishment for wrong doing, and thus the Deuteronomist exalted the figure of Moses in the dim antiquity of the Jews. We have already seen the same process at work in Sparta where Lycurgus was looked back to as the founder of a constitution which probably took a century or two to form. We shall find it again in Rome, in the Ten Tables of the law. There is nothing unique, therefore, in finding the lawgiver Draco at the dawn of Athenian history.

The unique character of Athenian history, however, especially in contrast with that of the Asiatic model, is apparent in the rapidity with which it changed this first code of laws. Later Greek historians are somewhat at odds as to just what happened and how. But it would seem that the writing down of the law had the result of showing up all its faults and the pressing needs of a rapidly changing economic situation in which trade was beginning to disrupt primitive society, forced an almost complete repeal of Draco's laws only a generation or so later. This was the work of his great successor, Solon, who stands out in the narrative of Greek history as one of the most revolutionary statesmen in the history of the world.

The details of Solon's reforms are matters of controversy among historians, because the Greek sources themselves do not agree. But the basic principle was that the most important rights and privileges of citizenship in Athens were no longer to depend upon the old kinship ties of the primitive tribal relationships, but upon the income from landed property. Thus, although the gods were left their place in the religious and social structure of society, the basis of the constitution of the state was shifted from religion to economics. There was to be no more slavery for debt, the mortgages were cancelled on Athenian farms and the amount of land which a citizen might hold was limited. The poorer citizens, thus freed from economic bondage, became members of the Assembly and participants in the law courts. So important indeed had the common people become, that it was they who gave the name by which this form of government by universal participation was to be known in all the subsequent languages of Europe, for the people were the *demos,* and their society democracy.

There was only one factor weighty enough to carry an economic reform over into the field of politics to such an extent as to recast the structure of the state. That was the need of strengthening the army. The demand for social welfare was insistent, but it was a slower force than the demand for safety. For the defence of Athens and for its wars, the rocky citadel that watched over the plain of Attica was not enough, nor the walls which reached around the city itself. The only safety for Athens lay in having an army similar to that of Sparta with its heavy armed foot soldiers, the *hoplites,* wearing cuirass, greaves and helmet, armed with spear and sword and carrying a large shield. Such weapons cost money, and so the main battle line of the new army would have to be composed of those who could afford to buy them. Wealth, rather than birth, determined one's place in the organization of safety. The citizens were therefore divided into four classes, the first of which owned land which produced five hundred measures of corn, oil and wine; the second, those who could provide a war horse; the third, those who tilled their land with oxen; and the fourth, freemen, artisans, fisherman and the like, who could man the fleet.

Viewed from this angle, the reform of Solon was but a more complicated development of the war system of Sparta; but the economic life of Athens, upon which the new structure of the state was based, was not that of a static farming community, protected by a war band. It was a swiftly-changing world, in which, although agriculture remained basic, the artisan and smith, the builder and the trader edged their way into the state alongside the older privileged classes. This process of transformation by economic forces is never a simple one, and in Athens, although the main steps in its progress stand out clearly enough, the details of its history are complex and multiform. The new institutions did not wholly displace the old ones, for the Athenians, like the English, appreciated the fact that it is more important that the machinery of politics should be adjusted to meet practical ends, rather than to comply with the strict requirements of logic.

The Council of Athens (Boule) had originally been the Homeric Council of the King, and throughout all Athenian history it retained reminders of its origin. When, therefore, Solon, if indeed it was he who did it, reorganized it on the basis of wealth, with a hundred from each of the four classes described above, it was rather as a check upon radicalism than a contribution to it. Nevertheless, it was not a sovereign body, for that was left to the general assembly of all the freemen of the state, the ecclesia. Alongside these reforms Solon instituted courts of justice (Heliaea) to which appeal could be made from the old court of the Areopagus, and even from the magistrates. Thus democracy took over the processes of justice itself. The jury was chosen by lot, and all citizens, including the freedmen were eligible, so that the same people acted both as electors of the magistrates and as their judges if they came to trial.

The reform of Solon remained the fundamental law of Athens for almost a century, although in that interval city bosses, whom the Greeks called tyrants, gave the Athenians an object lesson in the way the demagogues can, with the consent of the citizens, undermine the safeguards of liberty. Then, in the year 509 B.C., the final outlines of the Athenian constitution were drawn by Cleisthenes, who recast the tribal organization to meet the changing citizenship of the growing state. Army service and civil administration were opened more widely to the poorer classes. The Council, composed of Five Hundred, fifty from each of the ten tribal divisions of the citizens, was in course of time provided with boards of ten to deal with military as well as civil matters.

All this looks artificial from the distance but the simplicity of these broad divisions probably made their adoption easier. In both Athens and Rome, however, they seemed to have remained more military than civil, a distinction which could hardly be made with any definiteness so long as war, particularly local war, was so frequent as to be almost the normal state of affairs. In any case the sovereign body in Athens was not this Council but the general assembly of the citizens (the *ecclesia*) which seems to have been first definitely organized in Solon's day and which became the central organ of Athenian democracy. Here were discussed not only plans for war but all the interests of the state. It was the school for oratory and intrigue, and a new profession arose, that of the politician, whose arts of persuasion could win not only applause but power. Politics as we know it began in the theatre or the market place or wherever the Athenian Assembly was meeting.

As the city grew, however, the broader basis of democracy was lacking because the poorer classes lacked the leisure to attend the meetings at which policies were decided which affected them. From the relatively small state of the days of Cleisthenes, Athens was becoming a metropolitan center and the interest of the citizens in public affairs naturally ceased to be as direct. It was no longer a glorified neighborhood but a great city with varied activities. This was the kind of situation which opened the path to tyranny, which was the Greek term for the seizure of power by illegal means. But the sense of freedom developed in the practical exercise of politics had become so strong, that the tyrants of Athens did not establish a monarchy. Instead, democracy was reorganized and stimulated to do its duty by payment for services.

The new deal in Athenian politics was carried out by the greatest of all Athenian statesmen, Pericles. For the time being it made democracy complete (except for the slaves), and Athens a phenomenon unique in world history. But there was danger that the grant of full political rights to the poorer classes along with pay for exercising them would merely make democracy a proletarian demagoguery, by outvoting the much smaller number of wealthier citizens, who could temper with conservativism any too radical measures involving the stability of the state. This possibility was met by a measure which shows how Pericles kept his statesmanship within the field of practical politics. The number of those in the "third estate" who were permitted to share in the extension of political privilege was limited to those who could claim Athenian parentage on both sides and it was held down to 14,000 citizens, which was almost the number of those in the upper classes.

It is impossible to describe this great experiment in self-government in further detail, but we cannot leave it without pointing to its inherent weakness: its provision for pay put a premium on idleness, for it was only by idling in the Assembly that the democracy as a whole could participate. It was not until many centuries had passed that the principle of representative government was worked out in place of government by all of the people meeting and discussing problems together.

It would be an ungenerous judgment of history, however, to demand of Pericles an experience in the art of government for which the city state was inherently ill-qualified. Without exception, history has accepted as essentially true Pericles' own proud tribute to his city as recorded for us by Thucydides in the funeral oration for those who died in its defense in the Peloponnesian War:

Our government is called a democracy because its administration is in the hands, not of the few, but of the many; yet while as regards the law all men are on an equality for the settlement of their private disputes, as regards the value set on them, it is as each man is in any way distinguished that he is preferred to public honors, not because he belongs to a particular class, but because of personal merits; nor, again, on the ground of poverty is a man barred from a public career by obscurity of rank if he but has it in him to do the state a service.

And not only in our public life are we liberal, but also as regards our freedom from suspicion of one another in the pursuits of everyday life; for we do not feel resentment at our neighbor if he does as he likes, nor yet do we put on sour looks which, though harmless, are painful to behold. But while we thus avoid giving offense in our private intercourse, in our public life we are restrained from lawlessness chiefly through reverent fear, for we render obedience to those in authority and to the laws, especially to those laws which are ordained for the succour of the oppressed and those which, though unwritten, bring upon the transgressor a disgrace which all men recognize.

This passage, one of the noblest in the world's literature, is a panegyric not merely of democracy but of freedom. For Pericles makes it clear that freedom is not to be found in the institutions of government, essential as they are for its creation and protection, but in the way of life of the people themselves. It is to be found in a sense of tolerance and understanding, of neighborliness and justice. Never was the ideal of freedom better expressed. After over two thousand years of history we can still look back to it not only for inspiration but also for guidance.

It is, therefore, fitting to pause for a moment over the full meaning of these words. In the mind of Pericles — or of Thucydides who is the author of the text before us — freedom is more than the sum of human rights which the state can guarantee. It is to be found in the way in which the citizens use those rights for their own and the common good. It is public spirit, not merely patriotism. This means, however, that the home for freedom is only where the citizen feels that he participates in public affairs and is to that degree the master of his fate.

The history of Periclean Athens stands out as a gleaming episode on the long, dark road to freedom. Alongside the tribute of Thucydides (or of Pericles himself) we add that of the most learned of modern historians, Lord Acton. In his *Essays on Freedom and Power,* he says:

The epoch of doubt and transition during which the Greeks passed from the dim fancies of mythology to the fierce light of science was the age of Pericles, and the endeavour to substitute certain truth for the prescriptions of impaired authorities, which was then beginning to absorb the energies of the Greek intellect, is the grandest movement in the profane annals of mankind, for to it we owe, even after the immeasurable progress accomplished by Christianity, much of our philosophy and far the better part of the political knowledge we possess. Pericles, who was at the head of the Athenian government, was the first statesman who encountered the problem which the rapid weakening of traditions forced on the political world. No authority in morals or in politics remained unshaken by the motion that was in the air. No guide could be confidently trusted; there was no available criterion to appeal to, for the means of controlling or denying convictions that prevailed among the people. The popular sentiment as to what was right might be mistaken, but it was subject to no test. The people were, for practical purposes, the seat of the knowledge of good and evil. The people, therfore, were the seat of power. . . .

The idea that the object of constitution is not to confirm the predominance of any interest, but to prevent it; to preserve with equal care the independence of labour and the security of property; to make the rich safe against envy and the poor against oppression, marks the highest level attained by the statesmanship of Greece. It hardly survived the great patriot who conceived it; and all history has been occupied with the endeavour to upset the balance of power by giving the advantage to money, land, or numbers. A generation followed that has never been equalled in talent — a generation of men whose works, in poetry and eloquence, are still the envy of the world, and in history, philosophy, and politics remain unsurpassed. But it produced no successor to Pericles, and no man was able to wield the sceptre that fell from his hand.

The Tragedy of Greece

The eloquence of Pericles is deeply moving, both because of the greatness of his theme and of its inherent tragedy. In praising the dead Athenian warriors he was also praising a dying city, for the Peloponnesian War was to bring about the end of Athenian greatness and the note of foreboding is already in the panegyric on democracy. Thucydides had felt this when the war began, but like Pericles himself and all the poets and philosophers who witnessed that supreme drama, he accepted the ultimate reason as something beyond the control of politics. It was the use of war as an instrument of politics. Even in Athens, the prevalence of war or the threat of it in the relationship of one Greek city state to another was so constant as to prevent the development of a healthy economic life.

The effect of war on trade and industry can never be stated in a single sweeping generalization, for there are many kinds of war and their effects on the warring peoples vary with time and circumstances. From savage life to civilization the raider and the victor in war have always seemed to have the easiest if the most hazardous of gainful occupations. Taking the goods of others or seizing men as slaves, brings not only power but ease and comfort. The ancient world never — to the very end — fully saw the fallacy of this short cut to wealth, how it ultimately exhausts the sources of supply and makes no provision for either its replacement or that of the diminishing body of warriors themselves. These are facts of war which do not reveal themselves at once but only in the long, slow process of decay. If, therefore, the Greeks did not clearly foresee the ultimate disaster to their common economic life which was inherent in the unique prevalence of war, we who have not fully learned that lesson ourselves cannot blame them for shortsightedness. Nevertheless, as we look back over the economic history of Greece, the ultimate effect of war economy is abundantly clear.

Although the Greeks were always traders, yet in the anarchy of the seas in the Homeric age, and even in the great days of Athens, the hazards of war added to the trader's risk as its booty competed with the goods of peaceful barter. Not the least in the achievements of the Greeks was the way in which they met and overcame these obstacles to commerce, and stretched an economic web over land and sea, which became the chief source of wealth for cities with poor agricultural resources. The advantage in the battle of wits in the markets of Greece, as in the oriental bazaars, was on the side of those who could undersell their neighbors, and the one best way to win that advantage in the antique world was by the exploitation of the slaves which war supplied to do the day's work. Industry, therefore, did not have a chance to develop in freedom, but was given over to slave labor. This was the universal situation in the ancient city states, the inevitable step by which peoples living under the economy of war attempted to use it for the betterment of their peacetime conditions.

In one important way, slavery in Greece was limited by the fact that, although prisoners of war were enslaved, it was the practice to allow Greek captives to be ransomed, so that most slaves in Greece were non-Greeks, regarded as barbarians, whose rights were not recognized in any case. In addition to war, piracy furnished an abundant supply of slaves, the slave trade drawing chiefly on Asia Minor and the shores of the Black Sea. At Athens and other cities there were regular slave markets. Freemen, when reduced to extreme poverty, also sold themselves or members of their family into slavery. The total number of slaves was very great; in Attica and a commercial center like Corinth, they apparently sometimes outnumbered the citizens. By the time of Pericles they did most of the farming and had begun to displace free labor in industry and trade. They were not only artisans and builders, but bookkeepers in business concerns, and entertainers. In short, Athens, and all Greece, depended on slave labor.

The treatment of slaves in Athens was exceptionally mild. They were generally treated almost as part of the family, were not denied access to religious rites, and were permitted to accumulate savings to apply on their emancipation or otherwise. They had redress in law against cruel masters, but the use of the lash was permitted and the slaves were legally held as property, like any other commodity to be bought or sold. Those working in the fields, and especially in the mines, were often in irons, fettered to prevent their escape. Even under the best of conditions, there was always the haunting menace of the use of torture to extract evidence if their owners were involved in criminal, or even civil, proceedings. Torture was a common practice, often over trivial cases.

Yet no Greek philosopher ever thought that the slave system was wrong. The most that Plato provided for his Republic was that no Greeks should be held as slaves by Greeks; slavery was for barbarians only, but that was not a point to quibble over in an ideal state. Aristotle, with customary directness, came straight to the problem with a defense of slavery as a divine institution, due to difference in race — the Greeks being free by the law of nature, the barbarians subject to slavery by the same criterion. Like Plato, he insisted that both master and slave should keep to their places, the master not acting too harshly, the slave rendering loyal service. The lack of any moral denunciation of slavery was shared by the later schools of Greek philosophy. It might have been expected that the Stoics, denying any difference between Greek and barbarian, bond or free, would have applied their cosmopolitanism to a movement for emancipation in the city states. The basic tenets would seem to call for it — that virtue governs the universe, that justice is the natural expression of the law of reason ordained by God, that in the city of God (Zeus) all its members work for one another's good. Yet the Stoics kept their philosophy aloof from the practice of politics in their city states until after Christian influence interworked with it in the vital embodiment of Roman law. Even there, Stoicism, the most highly moral influence in antique life, raised no voice against slavery as an institution.

The extent to which slave labor limited that antique culture which was largely dependent on it cannot be overestimated. It was by slave labor that the materials were furnished for the great monuments, for the art of antiquity, and the comfort of daily life enhanced to resemble externally that of modern times. But when work is done by slaves, there can be no interest in applying to it the ingenuity of invention. Therefore, science in the antique world remained, for the most part, speculative interest of privileged thinkers and, if applied, devoted to art instead of industry. Here we have the missing clue to the fundamental difference between antique and modern society. Where slavery prevails, the problems of the common man are utterly falsified; and it is from the reservoir of the common life that the intellectual as well as the material advance of society is drawn.

Alongside the exploitation of slavery in the economy of war, was the exaction of tribute in kind and in treasure. In this regard the record of Athens itself rivals that of oriental potentates, especially in the way in which it used the treasure of its associates in the Delian League against the Persians. The need for maintaining the fleet furnished the pretext of seizing the funds exacted for common defense, and it was only a step from that to applying the treasure for the use of Athens itself, to pay for its magnificence. But such a misuse of funds prevented a knowledge of the wholesale use of capital. Although, spurred on by the inflation of war economy, Athens learned to circulate gold and silver in coins, but instead of making it work as an economic stimulus, it stored it in the temples, hoarding it in the way the oriental rulers did. Aristotle stated the common view of the Greeks, when he stated that money is "barren." Thus, while the political structure of Athens bore the impress not merely of maturity, but of modernity, its economic life remained antique.

More obvious than the effects of war on the economy of Greece, was that on the interrelation of the city states. The explanation commonly given for the disunity of Greek city state system is that the individuality and independence of the Greek spirit were far too strong for any greater bond than that of immediate loyalties. Even if this were true, it is not an explanation, it is a description. The subsequent history of Europe shows that the sense of citizenship is not lost when local unities fuse into the larger unity of the nation. Never has this been shown more clearly than today, not only in the matured democracies of the United States and the British Commonwealth of Nations, but also in the new unity of the people of China and of Russia. There was a sense of cultural unity in Hellas and the recognition that the Greeks were different from the "barbarians" who made up the rest of the world; but there could be no real development of Greek nationality as long as war was taken for granted as an inherent and inevitable element in their relationships one with the other.

The disunity in Greece itself was accentuated by the planting of colonies. These offshoots from Hellas, which extended from the shore of the Black Sea to the coasts of what are now France and Spain, broke their political ties with the homeland. The colonies took their language, their religion, their customs, their ideas of art, music and literature with them from the home city, but they set up a new *polis* wherever they established themselves. In Greece itself, the movements for greater unity, when they were something more than merely temporary alliances, either developed imperialistic aims, as in the case of Athens' transformation of the Delian League into its own empire, or were the tragic efforts of a well-meant federalism too weak to stand against the might of a strong neighbor like Macedon.

The early form of intercity league was a confederacy grouped around an outstanding military champion. Of these the most notable was the Peloponnesian League that looked to Sparta as its chief member. But in the closing period of Greek history, especially in the third century, a genuine movement of intercity cooperation produced for a period all too short, a new political experiment, that of federalism, which in theory at least, is the culmination of Greek political creations. The Aetolian and the Achaean Leagues were more than military organizations. In them was developed, as nowhere else in Greece, the principle of representation. While the member states were left their internal independence and the League dealt only with foreign politics and war, there was an assembly in which each individual citizen had the right to vote, while a council appointed by the states (at least in the Aetolian League) held the reins of power.

Thus, in the last period of its history, Greece made a contribution to politics which, had it been set to work in the early days or in the period of Athenian greatness, might have done for it what the Roman system did for Italy — developed the city state into a republic extending over the country as a whole. But by the third century it was already too late. The horsemen of Macedon were on the way, and the failure of the experiment in the policy of peace but heightened the tragedy of Greek history.

Looking back over that history, we see that "the glory that was Greece" did not fade because of foreign invasion. It had already begun to decline in the recurring anarchy of intercity strife. The preoccupation with war which prevented the development of a wholesome sense of economic laws, blocked social reforms as well, with the result that the people who prized physical strength and beauty most, died victims of malaria. Because the creators of cities of such marvelous beauty turned over to slaves the fulfillment of their dreams, craftsmanship declined. Finally, the manhood of the country left it to follow the profession of arms as the mercenaries of the Persian kings or in the track of the armies of Alexander. Greece was left impoverished and depopulated. This failure to escape from even the effects of war in peacetime would have ensured the failure of Greek civilization, even had there been no Macedonian or Roman conquerors.

Politics in Theory

In this analysis of the history of Greek politics emphasis has been put on the creative, as well as the destructive, role of war. Strangely enough Greek thinkers paid little attention to it, at least in the setting which it takes today in the perspectives of city state organization. Greek philosophy reached its climax in the period after the Peloponnesian War when the data were at hand for a study of its effect in the upbuilding and destruction of the Athenian empire, but neither the greatest historian of antiquity, Thucydides, nor its greatest philosophers, Plato and Aristotle, attempted in their analysis of society to isolate the phenomenon of war and see the part that it had played and was still playing in the evolution of society. As we have just seen, it called forth, in the revolutionary reforms of Solon and Cleisthenes, the framework of the first democracy in the history of the world.

But this change in the internal structure of the state did not bring with it any change in the relation of one state to another. So far as its military purpose was concerned, it was to make Athens more efficient in the age-old relationships with foreigners, those of war and armed truce. Even by the end of its history, Greece had not made any great contribution to international relations. Its treaties, alliances and federations were tentative arrangements compared with the strength which Rome developed out of the same origins. Although Greek philosophy learned to speak in universal terms, the chief interest of all Greeks was in the fortunes of their own city state and their duty as citizens of it. Even Socrates accepted the political anarchy of Hellas as a condition to be bettered by better living, rather than by any far-reaching political reform. He had been a soldier, with a reputation for courage in the army of Athens, and although he questioned almost everything else in the conduct of men and states, we have no record of his questioning the legitimacy of war itself. How could it be otherwise when the fate of the state and, therefore, the existence of the individual depended so often on success in war? Only a purely individualistic philosophy could deny the legitimacy of the war system as long as the whole social order was so closely conditioned by it.

It is this that furnished us with the clue to the failure of Greek philosophy to come squarely to grips with the greatest question that confronts the world today, that of the place of war in the field of politics. For the Greek thinker put all the accent on man as a social, that is to say, a political being. Greek individualism never robbed him of his sense of citizenship. It was but natural that he should concentrate on politics at home because political argument was always within earshot. The voice of the orator reached the passerby and furnished a rival interest to the theater and athletic games. The theme of these discussions was, therefore, chiefly concerned with ward politics and the immediate issues of the day.

And yet the three incomparable leaders of Greek philosophy — Socrates, Plato and Aristotle — did succeed in drawing from their doctrine of civic duties doctrines of universal application, which in one form or another have challenged the intelligence of all thoughtful men. Socrates lived through the Peloponnesian War and the period of tyranny which followed after Pericles. By the "restoration of the constitution" in 403, democracy was restored to power, and it adds to the tragedy of his death that it was under it, and not under tyranny, that he was put to death on the charge that he was denying the gods and corrupting the young. In reality, he was what we would call today a liberal conservative, opposing the pay for political service, which Pericles had introduced and insisting on rule by the intelligent and limiting the fanchise of the irresponsible mob. His influence was that of an educator with a distinctly moral point of view. He defined good as that which is useful: knowledge of it comes from practicing it or observing the effects of good and evil in the daily life of men in the community in which one lives. His sense of duty and of patriotism was based on the idea of a supreme being, a beneficent and intelligent creator of the universe; therefore his patriotism, while centered in Athens, was capable of being extended beyond even Hellas to a conception of a universal citizenship under divine guidance. The far reach of this idea was never fully developed by him, however. His aim was the practical education of Athenians and not the exploration of political theory.

It was Socrates' great pupil, Plato, who gave the classic answers to the questions raised by Socrates: "What is a state?" "What is a statesman?" "What is justice?" "What is government?" Like his teacher and his own great pupil and associate, Aristotle, Plato dealt with these fundamental problems in terms of ethics. The difference being that while Socrates kept more to the analysis of individual motives, Plato's imagination carried him over to the ideal with which imperfect reality stands out in such strong contrast. Aristotle welded the ideal and the particular together into a vast system of comprehensive political history. Plato's ideas on politics are chiefly to be found in the *Republic* and the *Politicus*. It is impossible here to do more than touch upon the externals of his great structure of political thought.

The *Republic* begins with Socrates' question: "What is justice?" and finds it in the education of the individual as a citizen, especially with reference to the right division of labor between the classes of the state. There are faculties which correspond to these duties, and the culmination of the whole process is to be found in placing rule in the hands of the highly educated men, the "philosopher kings." In these higher realms of intelligence, justice could be practiced to the point where there would be something approaching communism for the guardians of society.

In the *Politicus* Plato leaves this optimistic world of hope and dreams and aspirations for more practical problems in the field of scientific statesmanship, that kind of control which can maintain a strong grasp upon recalcitrant human nature and which, on that account, needs to be checked within recognized limits. The constitutional monarchy is the best of all forms of government, and then follow, in the order of descending merit, constitutional oligarchy, law-abiding democracy, and tyranny. At the end of his long life Pato attempted to make this manual of politics still more definite and to leave a code of law sufficiently practical to be adopted by some of the Greek states if not by all. Exiled from Athens, he had studied the Dorian law of Sparta as well as the Ionian law of Athens. But this wider outlook was gained at the loss of the whole of the Socratic method, for Plato now taught that the existing laws were not to be open for free and general criticism, but to be revised only by commissioners appointed for that purpose, who would travel and study the experiences and devices of other states and bring back their suggestions for those who stayed at home. The disciple of Socrates, that arch critic of the common mind, had traveled a long way.

Finally Greek thought reached its encyclopedic culmination in the work of Aristotle, Plato's pupil and the teacher of Alexander the Great. So weighty and so widespread has been his influence upon succeeding centuries that even more than in the case of Plato it seems hardly fitting to summarize his teaching on politics. Like Socrates and Plato he reached it through ethics, but unlike either of them, he was interested as well in the actual history of the city states and the result was a much more realistic picture of society, that of a historian even more than a philosopher. We know that he made a comparative study of many constitutions but the only one of such studies which has come down to us is that of the constitution of Athens, and the text of it had been lost until fifty years ago. Here we have a modern mind at work in a scientific way on problems and practices of politics. His outlook was still limited to that of Greece, even at the very moment when his pupil Alexander was building a greater Hellas throughout the Orient. But it was a world so rich in variety of political experience, so keenly felt by all who had been touched by its proud sense of superiority to other peoples, that from its confused pattern he was able to present an outline of a political structure clearly cut, logical and attuned to the moral forces of the world to a degree that made it a real and lasting embodiment of Greek history.

In his treatment of Ethics and the unfinished treatises on *Politics*, government is characterized in terms at once suggesting the controversy between responsible and autocratic governments today. The test of good government is that it aims at the general good of those under its rule. It may be monarchy, aristocracy or commonwealth, but in each case, the ruler or ruling class must excel in virtue, that is to say in their attitude toward the common welfare. All of these governments may be denatured, as for instance, when democracy aims only at the good of the majority, oligarchy at the good of the few, and tyranny exists for the benefit of the tyrant. Nevertheless, this denaturing of the categories of government does not justify the denial of the fundamental principle, upon which all legitimate authority is based, that of the moral order of the universe.

In Aristotle's mind the world was very different from that of the wayward mythology of Homeric days; it was a world of natural law with which human laws must be in harmony. It was this concept elaborated, from a different angle by the Stoics, which had such a notable effect on Roman philosophy and ultimately found a lasting lodgment in Roman law.

It is a perilous undertaking to generalize as to the nature of anything so varied and far-reaching as the intellectual life of Greece. But there is one generalization which can safely be made. It is that with all the genius of great leadership at its disposal Greek thought failed to grapple with the two chief problems which confront the world, the place of war in human society and the adjustment of economic and social justice. The Greeks never reached beyond the threshold of these problems. Even the Stoics, those sternest of moralists, never really learned to turn from their painted corridor (The Stoa) beside the market place of Athens, to study the bearing of that busy scene on the society of their time. The one outstanding lack in Aristotle's great treatise on politics is the failure to deal with economics; the only "art of wealth-getting" which he regards as legitimate is agriculture.

There are two sorts of wealth-getting; one is a part of household management, the other is retail trade: the former necessary and honorable, while that which consists in exchange is justly censured; for it is unnatural and a mode by which men gain from one another. The most hated sort, and with the greatest reason, is usury, which makes a gain out of money itself, and not from the natural object of it. For money intended to be used in exchange and not to increase at interest.[3]

The contrast between this summing up of economics in the closing period of Greek history and the early picture of farm life in Hesiod's *Works and Days* is hardly more than the difference between simple living and the life of a gentleman farmer. This is a poor showing compared with the splendor of Greek achievements in philosophy; but even this is better than the almost complete absence of intellectual interest in the problem of militarism. We have already indicated the reason for it, however, in the fact that war as an industry of exploitation falsified the very nature of politics which it was largely instrumental in creating.

It would not do, however, to end this short sketch of the politics of Greece with only a reminder of its shortcomings. In spite of the war system which offered no real security, and an inadequate understanding of economics because of exploitation and slavery, the Greeks succeeded beyond all other peoples of the ancient world in asserting and maintaining the love of freedom. This was the new and high note which Greece threw into that ancient symphony of mixed desire which formed the theme of Asian history. Life no longer moved to a minor key but took on the confidence, hope and self-respect of citizens who were pioneers of freedom. It is only when one recalls the splendor of that vision, in contrast with a past shrouded in shadow and haunted by fear, that one realizes the full extent of the tragedy which lay in the failure of the Greeks to grapple with the fundamental weakness in their social and political structure, that which was rooted in the war system.

Nowhere else in Greek history is this sense of tragedy more poignant than in Plato's account of the death of Socrates. It has been called "the

[3] *Politics*, Book I, Chapter 10. It would be misleading however to conclude that Aristotle ignored economics in his analysis of the state. *Cf.* Book 3, Chapter 8. "Tyranny, as I was saying, is monarchy exercising the rule of a master over the political society; oligarchy is when men of property have the government in their hands; democracy, the opposite, when the indigent, and not the men of porperty, are the rulers. And here arises the first of our difficulties, and it relates to the distinction just drawn. For democracy is said to be the government of the many. But what if the many are men of property and have the power in their hands? In like manner oligarchy is said to be the government of the few; but what if the poor are fewer than the rich, and have the power in their hands because they are stronger? In these cases the distinction which we have drawn between these different forms of government would no longer hold good."

earliest justification of liberty of thought," but Socrates did not address it as a protest to the state which had condemned him but rather as a personal defiance to those who would either suppress or turn him aside from what he believed to be the truth:

In me you have a stimulating critic, persistently urging you with persuasion and reproaches, persistently testing your opinion and trying to show you that you are really ignorant of what you suppose you know. Daily discussion of the matters about which you hear me conversing is the highest good for man. Life that is not tested by such discussion is not worth living.

Thus Socrates met death not in defense of any creed, but of the right to think things through with the full freedom of an unbiased mind. In the history of freedom of thought his life stands out as that of its greatest pioneer, and his death that of one of its greatest martyrs. The accusations brought against him — the denial of the gods recognized by the state, the teaching of heresy, and the corruption of youth — reveal that the same kind of intolerance persisted in Athens as had resided in the primitive taboo, and which lasted on through the Middle Ages to our own days. There is a reminder here, in this most poignant episode of antique history, that freedom of thought may find, any time, anywhere, even in the most enlightened societies, that same fierce, blind reaction against the questioning mind as in the case of Socrates.

If the Persians Had Won

In this account of the contribution of the Greeks to politics and freedom, nothing has been said about that great chapter of their history which, from that time to this, has been regarded as a supreme crisis in the history of freedom — the war with the Persians. If Persia had won in the invasion of Greece, both the Greeks themselves and most historians since them have held that all the West would have been orientalized. Herodotus, with that deft touch which adds so much charm to his narrative, has Xerxes himself say this in his war speech to the Assembly of the Persian Nobles:

Once let us subdue his people [the Athenians] and those neighbors of theirs [the Spartans], we shall extend the Persian territory as far as God's heaven reaches. The sun will then shine on no land beyond our borders; for I will pass through Europe from one end to the other, and with your aid make of all lands which it contains one country. For thus, if what I hear be true, affairs stand. The nations whereof I have spoken, once swept away, there is no city, no country left in all the world which will venture so much as to withstand us in arms. By this course then we shall bring all mankind under our yoke, alike those who are guilty and those who are innocent of doing us wrong.

Whatever Xerxes may or may not have said to his officers, here is the issue of the Persian Wars as stated by their Greek historian. And it must be admitted that as we follow the fortunes of Darius and Xerxes in the pages of Herodotus, the chances for world empire seemed good. The conquest of all western Asia had been quickly accomplished, from India to the Mediterranean and the Nile, overthrowing military empires the like of which did not exist in the West, the Assyrian, the Babylonian, including Palestine and Tyre, the Lydian, including the Greek cities of Asia Minor, the Egyptians on the south and the Scythians on the north, beyond the Black Sea.

Conquest was only the beginning of the Persian achievement, however. Darius spent the first ten years of his reign quelling revolts, then he took the next six years "resting" at his capital, Susa, organizing the empire on a new pattern of government. In boldness of conception and magnificence of design, there is nothing in history to equal it. Instead of treating the conquered kingdoms as vassals to be held down by garrisons, he created twenty-three provinces, "satrapies," with governors in control of civil administration, judges to apply the laws impartially to all, and generals in command of the local troops.

The whole vast structure centered in the person of the king, who had a secretary in each satrapy reporting to him. Although royalty as the keystone of the arch was inevitable in Asia, there were checks to despotism such as that recorded in the Book of Daniel when the king could not do anything against the "laws of the Medes and Persians." If the king reserved to himself the assessment of tributes from the satrapies, the realm profitted in the prevention of corruption and extortion by provincial authorities, which was common in the other vast oriental empire, China. Within the satrapies the subject peoples were allowed a large degree of independence, deciding their law suits among themselves, meeting in their own assemblies and, along the Mediterranean, organizing in city states like those of Greece. Although the king kept close oversight of the administration by his local officials, he used his wars as civilizing missions. "He was no more a conquestador than Augustus."[4] Yet the system was faulty which left the final power in the hands of the king; for however well he might use the machinery of government, it lacked the motive power which lies in the sense of individual responsibility of the citizen for his own welfare and that of the state.

The fault in the Persian system should not be exaggerated, however. We should not confuse freedom with democracy, as the Athenians tended to do. Aristotle's statement that Asiatics are slaves by nature is unworthy so keen an analyst of politics; for, in grouping Persians in with Babylonians and Assyrians, he shows no appreciation of their fundamental differences which had been fully appreciated by the Persians. It is in line with the racial prejudice of the Greeks, that all but they are barbarians. It was incredible that the tutor of Alexander should not have in mind the fact that the Persian Empire was the first to use freedom as an instrument of statecraft, in delivering peoples who had been enslaved, restoring to them their lands and

---

[4] The phrase is that of Eduard Meyer, whose *Geschichte des Altertums* did much to readjust the perspectives of ancient history.

possessions.[5] The account of the liberation of the Jews from their Babylonian captivity in the Books of Ezra and Nehemiah has no parallel in Greek history. The proclamation of Cyrus was in the first year of his reign. It was part of his plan of empire-building, both to weaken Babylonia and to create a loyal Jewish state which would be a source of strength on the southwestern fringe of his empire. The generosity of Cyrus paid well, as was evidenced by the added support given Nehemiah by Darius when the walls of Jerusalem were rebuilt. The neighboring tribes warned the king that the Jews might use their new military power to rebel, but the Persian confidence in the Jews remained unshaken; and also, it must be supposed, their ultimate confidence in their own strength.

The problem which the Persians faced and solved in the unification of their empire — the use of freedom in the interests of law and order for all — was an issue which Greece never faced until the days of Alexander; and he solved it, for the time being at least, in the Persian way, retaining a structure of government which could take on the trappings of oriental splendor while holding largely to what we may now call "the modern way," of a Hellenized version of Persian statecraft.

Greek citizenship, such as Pericles so eloquently defined it, meant devotion to one's own city. Although there were religious and racial ties that gave all Greeks a sense of kinship, they kept up constant feuds with their neighbors. Their disunion showed itself even in the gravest crises of the Persian wars. The Ionians of Asia Minor suffered as much from intercity wars as from the Persians, whose intervention they sought at times against their neighbors. The Spartans were absent from the battle of Marathon, the Athenians from Thermopylae, and Salamis was an Athenian victory. Such a record leaves much to be explained. If, as everyone agrees, the Greeks were the defenders of freedom and drew their strength from this fact, what kind of freedom was it?

The answer is, of course, that it was the kind of freedom which was suitable for small communities where people know one another — individual liberty. This is what we have found in Pericles and Plato. The unit is man; not every man, but the kind of man one knows or can know intimately, and with whom one can live on an equal footing. It was this sense of freedom which made it almost like a religion to the Greeks, a personal possession about which one could be passionately aware, and in that awareness, discover one's own self. Philosophy thus became a secular study, freed from

[5] An interesting illustration of the benevolent aspects of Persian rule is furnished by an inscription of a letter by Darius to an official of the Ionian province of the empire, quoted in *Hellenic Civilization* (Botsford and Sihler, New York: Columbia University Press, 1915.), p. 162: "The king of kings, Darius, the son of Hystaspes, to his slave Gadatas says thus: — I learn that thou dost not obey my commands in all respects. In that thou cultivatest my land by transplanting the fruits (of the country) beyond the Euphrates to the lower parts of Asia, I commend thy purpose, and by reason of this there shall be laid up for thee great favor in the king's house. But, in that thou settest at naught my policy towards the gods, I will give thee, if thou does not change, a proof of my wronged feelings; for thou didst exact a payment from the sacred gardeners of Apollo and didst command them to dig unhallowed ground, not knowing the mind of my forefathers towards the god, who hath told the Persians the whole truth."

the religious background of ancient thought, and a precious heritage of the West, when Hellenism was recovered in the Renaissance.

The difference between this and the kind of freedom which the Persians allowed to the peoples whom they liberated lies, not in the nature of the government, but of the governed. For example, it was the Jews themselves who, when liberated from Babylon, reverted to the tribal theocracy of their ancestors instead of trying to explore their more modern world, as the Greeks would have done. Cyrus, Artaxerxes and Darius, wisely did not try to interfere; on the contrary, they helped in the restoration of the temple. Ahuramazda, the God of all mankind, whom the Persians worshipped, was not forced on the worshippers of Jehovah. Religious tolerance went along with political autonomy. Indeed the use of freedom as an instrument of politics was so successful that in Isaiah 14:1 Cyrus the pagan is the "anointed" one, the Messiah.

All this is utterly un-Greek; but the difference is less between freedom and democracy than between a respect for an established way of life, rooted in religion, and the challenge of it, which makes for science. Would Darius have been as tolerant of the Greek way of thinking about the world and man, as he was of the ancient beliefs? Probably not. He stood for law and order. The troublesome Greeks must have seemed to the Persian overlords of Asia — if they bothered to try to understand them — almost the way revolutionary Marxian communism strikes the capitalist world today. But Rome began its world conquest by a disregard of Greek liberties and ended by incorporating the finest statement of them in the Roman law and applying them in Roman policy when the Roman Empire was at the summit of its power. Perhaps a Persian West would not have been very different.

CHAPTER V

THE ROMAN WORLD

Politics in Early Rome

ALTHOUGH the history of Greece, and particularly that of Athens, furnished the first great chapter in the history of politics, the lessons of Roman history were of far greater importance in the subsequent development of Europe and Western civilization. Down to our own day the daring achievements of Athenian democracy have remained an inspiration for the thoughtful and studious rather than a model for practical application in world affairs. On the other hand, the Roman experience in government was the largest single influence upon the minds of those who, throughout the long centuries of European history, created the state system of today.

However lacking the Romans may have been in the versatility and ingenuity which characterized the Greeks — indeed, perhaps largely on that account — they far excelled them in political capacity. For they recognized the hard fact that institutions can live and grow only if they are based upon existing reality and compromise with it. It was the recognition of this fact which was the distinctive mark of Roman polity. While the result was often confusing in its disregard of theory and logic, it is the starting point for any history of the problem of government in Western Europe.

The chief contribution of Rome to the history of freedom was in the extension of citizenship, from the early tribal beginnings of the settlements in and around the city, to the whole of Italy and then to the whole of the imperial conquests. It is impossible to trace this political transformation in detail, but the way in which it was begun in early Rome furnishes the clue to the later story.

Rome began as a city state, similar to those of Greece. It was a little kingdom centered in the fortress-like enclosure of a group of hills a few miles inland from the mouth of the Tiber. Its government and social life were based on the old clan organization. There were patricians, people who belonged to the clans that composed the ruling class, and plebeians, those who did not. The origin of the latter is obscure. Some of them may have been clans who, as the shifting tides of fortune changed, lost caste with their neighbors; some of them may have been members of the peoples who, whatever their origin, were there before the coming of the tribesmen who conquered and settled in the Tiber valley; some of them were possibly freedmen from these conquests, and some of them the descendants of foreign settlers. The Greeks, it may be remembered, had colonies in Sicily and other surrounding territories before the "founding of Rome," and the Etruscans had moved in, perhaps from an unknown land beyond the seas. The mixture of peoples is parallel to that in early Greece.

At any rate, the difference between the patricians and plebeians was marked by taboo barriers of the most exclusive sort. Plebeians could not marry patricians nor hold public office over them nor vote in the meetings of the recognized tribesmen, while only patricians could qualify as city fathers, *patres,* from whom was formed a sort of advisory council to the king. The religious secrets and the laws of taboo were in the keeping of this kinship class and its head.

The story of the origins of Rome is the story of the Greek city states over again, but this time in a more favored setting. For the situation of Rome combined to some extent the advantages of those of Sparta and Athens, and its early history bore resemblance to both. The concentration upon the army and the constant recurrence of war in the hills developed a martial spirit like that of Sparta and a joint leadership to prevent it from getting out of the hands of the ruling oligarchy. But the economics of war and peace wrought the same kind of change as at Athens, supplementing, and then largely supplanting, magical formula and ancient custom by secular law and replacing tribal organization by politics. It was a long and slow process, lasting throughout the whole history of Rome, but the beginnings were made about the same time as the transformation of Athens.

The starting point is much the same. Under the old kingship the Roman people (*populus Romanus*) were united in clans (*gentes*) having common sacred rites and bearing a common name. Ten of these clans formed a division known as the *curia,* and the meeting of the heads of the families of the clans was called the council of the *curiae (Comitia Curiata)* which had the right of choosing the king, although he was nominated by the council of the elders, the Senate. There is no need for us to analyse this complicated constitution further than to point out that this grouping of the clans was the decisive unit for military service as well as for the vote. The whole organization was surrounded by religious services which sanctioned every important act of life. The *populus* was therefore not a citizenry as in the modern world, but rather a religious association in which the gods counted at least as much as men. For tutelary deities, watching over the welfare of clan, family and individual, watched as well over their own welfare, by punishing any lapse or any mistake in the ceremonies by which their favor could be won and kept. In all of this organization under the mystic law of taboo (the *jus sacrum),* the plebs, not knowing the secrets, had no part.

The decisive step in political history is that attributed to the king Servius Tullius by the reorganization of the army and of the constitution, on a property qualification rather than on the old tribal and clan relationship. How long it took to accomplish this revolutionary change and just how it actually happened is of less importance than the fact that some such change did take place, and that this new military organization, arranged in companies or "centuries" was based on land ownership. Therefore it included some plebs as well as the patricians, although it still excluded the foreign merchants whose booths stretched along the Tiber and in the valley between the seven hills.

In order not to violate the religious sanctity of the city itself by any seeming slight to the gods, such as that of an association organized not on a religious but on a military basis, and also, perhaps, because of its size, this new Assembly of the Hundreds (*Comitia Centuriata*) met outside the ancient city walls in what was appropriately called the Field of Mars. Its essential military preoccupation was shown by the fact that it placed in the front rank those who could bring a horse and provide themselves with suitable armor for the annual foray against their neighbors, the Sabines, while next to them were the ranks of the better-armed footmen, and so on down until the whole assembly included the larger body of poor but free-born citizens.

At first this body had only one political function; it was consulted by the king when he proposed to use it in a war of offense which would involve sending the farmers of the Latin plain off into the hill country. But from it there developed in the Republic the right to elect the consuls and to accept or reject the legislation laid before it. Never was there a clearer case of the transformation of a military to a political body.

The old clan organization, the *Comitia Curiata,* continued to lose importance and a new body, the *Comitia Tributa,* appeared as further means of ensuring justice for the plebs and a greater degree of equality for the poorer citizens. The complicated needs of the growing state thus produced a growingly complex political structure. At the same time its chief activity was war, which calls for singleness of purpose and persistence in action. This in the early days of the Republic was supplied by the Senate, composed for the most part of ex-magistrates, which meant experience in both war and peace. In course of time, however, this body proved unable to deal with the vast new problems of empire and, while it always retained something of its ancient dignity, it had to make concessions to the generals in the field and lost all but the outer semblance of its political power.

The Republic and the Division of Power

Under the old kingdom, all power had resided in the king. It was undifferentiated — that is, the power to legislate or make laws was not distinct from the power to administer them, or from the power to lead the army in war, or from the power to settle disputes between citizens, or from the power to preside as high priest of the state religion. Power was not thought of as being divisible. The king was the head of the state, and the head of the state was the source of all authority. In the Orient he remained the source of all authority. But under the Roman Republic, power came to be separated, and to be lodged according to its functions, in different officials and councils, and a series of checks and balances grew up to keep anyone from having too much authority.

First of all, the power that had resided in the king was given to two magistrates, called consuls, who shared the power equally and held office for a year only. They were elected, as were other magistrates, by the assembly of the people, the *Comitia Centuriata.*

The business of the state soon reached the point, however, where two magistrates were not enough to care for it. The religious powers of the kingship had been transferred to the pontifices, or bishops. Financial supervision was put in the hands of censors and quaestors. Most important, the administration of justice was given to praetors, secular magistrates. Military authority and certain other prerogatives were left with the consuls. Thus did the Roman Republic differentiate the powers of the old kingship, keep them apart and yet relate them all to the supreme authority of the state. But it is unlikely that the Roman people thought of their government as being divided up into military authority, religious authority, judicial authority, administrative and consultative authority, financial authority, and so forth. They probably thought of it as an organization consisting of the magistrates, the Senate and the various assemblies of citizens.

According to custom, the consuls had to ask the advice of the Senate on important matters, as had the king before them, but in both cases it was left to executive judgment whether or not the matter was important and whether or not to follow the advice. However, as the Senate was a permanent body, it gradually gained and held the ascendancy over the executive in the government during the period of the Republic. For one thing, it nominated the magistrates to be elected in general assembly.

The Senate was not a legislative body, as is the Senate of the United States. Laws (leges) were supposed to be voted by the people in the *Comitia Centuriata,* but as the awkwardness of that system was apparent in the growing size of the Roman populace and in its general ignorance of public affairs, matters were largely left to the Senate to decide upon by decree *(Senatus Consultum).* Moreover, it had the authority to approve the laws voted by the people. As a body of about three hundred men, it was generally better fitted for debate and consultation than the *comitia.* The Senate thus became the central and dominant body under the Republic. The standards which the armies bore in the field held the singular device SPQR *(Senatus Populusque Romanus),* "the Senate and the Roman people."

But while this parliament of select and experienced men was well fitted to supervise civil government and determine the larger issues of policy, it was ill adapted to direct the conduct of war. Military command must be vested in commanders whose strategy is not interfered with during the conduct of actual warfare. This was recognized by the Republic in the resort to a dictator in time of extreme danger. But so long as the wars of Rome were not in distant lands, the Senate kept its hand on the consuls in the field and their substitutes. In this it made itself the champion of the Republican constitution.

The Expansion of Rome and the Decline of the Republic

While Rome was developing its internal government, it was also expanding externally, and this external expansion was mirrored in its administration of the home city states. First it was able to dominate the lowlands surrounding it — the territory known as Latium. The city states comprising this territory lost their status as confederates and became Latin colonies in the war of the Latin Allies, 340-338 B.C.

The famous motto, divide and rule, applied to these conquered units. Each colony made a separate agreement with Rome. Though the arrangements varied in detail, as a general thing the colony was allowed home rule and was supreme within its own borders. But it had to supply soldiers to the Roman army and to leave all questions of war and peace, alliance and treaties to Rome. There was no political connection between the separate colonies; the connection was directly and wholly with Rome. As the Romans had differentiated and kept apart the powers of government within the state, so they kept the Latin colonies and yet related them all to the supreme authority of the state. All roads led to Rome.

As Rome spread out over Italy, the picture remained the same. There were Roman colonies filled with Roman citizens, established by the Senate and having all the rights of Rome; Latin colonies with the same rights as the original Latin colonies from which the settlers came and municipalities of other kinds, sometimes with almost complete liberty, sometimes with very limited. But the basic principle of government was the old city state, where it had existed, or the tribal system, where it had not. The Romans did not bring great revolutionary changes as they conquered, which is one of the reasons why they held their colonies so easily. Yet they did not loosen the tight rein of their hegemony. No elements of federation crept into the picture.

Failing to obtain equal rights with Roman citizens, the Italian colonies finally resorted to rebellion in 90 B.C. This attempt, called the Social War, to regain their independence, was mostly a military failure, but a political success, for it led Rome to grant citizenship to all Italy, a revolutionary step of the greatest magnitude and importance. Hitherto citizenship in a city state belonged only to the people of the city, and it had been a long, difficult fight even for all the free-born citizens of Rome to gain equal rights.

But to exercise their new-won rights of citizenship in a political way, the Italians had to come to Rome. Voting could not be done anywhere else; there was no representative government. Politically the power was still concentrated in Rome, and remained concentrated there throughout its history. But Roman civil rights, the right to own and exchange property under the same laws as the Romans, the right to be judged in court as were the Romans, was spreading.

The occasion for conflict with her neighbors increased with widened frontiers. Sicily had always been half in the hands of the Greeks and half under the power of Carthage, who held the islands of Corsica and Sardinia as well. The details of Rome's conflict with either the Greek or Carthaginian worlds are not important to our story, but it is important to note that between 262 and 133 B.C. she waged three fierce wars with Carthage, utterly destroying that power and also the kingdom of Macedonia, and that by the latter date Corsica, Sardinia, Spain, the territory immediately surrounding the city of Carthage in Africa, and the whole Greek and Macedonian world, including those parts of it in Sicily and Asia Minor, were in the hands of Rome.

Now all of this had enormous repercussions on the government and people at home. We have already mentioned the consuls, magistrates who held office for one year and had charge of the army, and the Senate, which as a body of ex-magistrates acted as the general staff in directing the wars of conquest and the disposition and government of the conquered peoples. This system worked well as long as the wars were confined to the Italian peninsula or when fighting was for one season only. The whole citizen body could be called out to bear arms against the enemy, a *levée en masse* we would call it today. They fought for a few weeks or for two or three months and then came home to carry on their peacetime tasks. If the war lasted longer, the soldiers could be sent in relays, so that a farmer might have time to come home and plant his crops.

But with the struggle against Carthage the situation changed. During the second Punic War (218-204 B.C.), Hannibal had used the Carthaginian dominance of the Spanish peninsula as a base from which to precipitate himself and his troops into Italy for a sixteen-year period of fighting and ravaging. Rome, therefore, felt the necessity for subjugating Spain to the point where it could never be so used again. This was not accomplished in a single campaign and demanded an army of a different type from the *levée en masse*. Spain was too far off for periodic reliefs. More thorough training was needed than the citizen-soldier could give the time for. Men were taken into the army and paid for their services, and to their pay was added booty. Fortunately, as it seemed at the time, this was made possible and even easy by the spoils from victories, both over Spanish patriots and Macedon — for at the same time Rome had begun to spread out to the east of the Adriatic. This led to the professional soldier and to the gradual disarmament of the ordinary Roman citizen. It also led to a body of men whose chief allegiance was to their general, not to the magistracy of the Republic in Rome itself.

Other changes took place during this period of change from a local city state to a military organization for conquest. Many of the poorer farmers lost their farms because of the plundering of Hannibal. As the war continued, others lost them through long service in the army when there was no one at home to look after the farms. Still others found it difficult to compete with the large estates of the newly rich who had, as in every war, made fortunes and bought up as much land as possible. The number of poor grew constantly. The existence of slaves in large numbers, brought home from the wars, made free industry not only profitable but also menial in character.

The Senate, which had provided a check on the wartime activities of the consuls, was not in a position to supervise very closely what went on so far from home. Moreover, it could not manage the newly acquired provinces well. Unlike the Italian cities, they were ruled by a governor who was allowed a fairly free hand in administering them. They were subject to taxes or tribute, the collection of which was farmed out to individuals who seldom failed to take advantage of their position to add heavily to their own profits while collecting revenues. The system, in fact, put a premium on extortion, and had back of it the moneyed interests of Romans who grew more wealthy each year and who fought any effort at reform taken by individual governors or consuls.

But, probably, most important of all, was the change the new conquests made in the office of consul. The one-year period of the consul was hardly long enough to permit a leader who was directing a campaign of major proportions to carry it out. And so in specified cases, where the term was temporarily extended or where the circumstances called for action which the consul was unable to take, the practical Romans appointed a pro-consul, technically a substitute for the consul, whose powers were not so closely circumscribed by the constitution, and who could become the military leader for the duration of a war or a campaign.

While in office the consuls were the heads of the army, except as the proconsuls cut in upon them, and as such they had *imperium,* a Roman word which has played a large part in the description of the structure of modern states. At first, it meant simply military authority, the kind of authority the old kings had had, personal and general. It could not be divided into the special departments of government like those we have been tracing in Republican Rome. At the front, the command of the general, *imperator,* applied to all.

With the increasing difficulty met by the Senate and the consuls in taking care of the vast region under their power, the office of pro-consul became more and more important. However, it was in the army that talent and genius for leadership had a chance to rise to the top. The capacity of the general was often put to the test by an equally competent enemy. In the north of Africa a half barbaric leader by the name of Jugurtha defied the Roman power; in Asia Minor King Mithridates challenged the best of the Roman generals and, before his defeat by Pompey, had massacred over 80,000 Romans. There were risings in Spain and among the barbarian tribes on the borders.

This situation offered a career to men like Marius, Sulla, Pompey, and finally Julius Caesar, *imperatores,* who went out from Rome not only to protect the state, but to add new conquests in Africa, in the Near East and in Gaul and finally to achieve the empire of the Western World. As pro-consuls they became sole masters of the *imperium* of the state on the frontiers, and they had only to exercise this power in Rome itself to undo the long process of the separation of the powers of government on which the safety of the Republic had depended.

It was not necessary to destroy the offices themselves. By the open or implied threat of force, a master of the legions like Caesar could practically control the state with an even freer hand than if he had accepted the "kingly crown" which Anthony offered him, and the undifferentiated power of the old kingship. The military revolution was completed by Augustus when he "restored the republic" and paid it the derisive honor of calling himself its "first citizen" or "prince." With pro-consular authority in far reaches of the outer provinces, from which most of the tribute came, and with no rival power at home, it was only necessary to retain some of the vaguer offices of state to control the situation. The farce fooled no one, and the realistic Romans, going to the heart of the matter, used the term for military commander, *imperator,* to describe the sovereign who succeeded to the dominion of Caesar. Under Augustus there were approximately twenty legions, or 225,000 men.

Pax Romana — The Nature of the Roman Empire

Few conquests were added after the time of Julius Caesar — Britain, Trace to the south of the Danube and, for a while, Dacia to the north of it, some territories in Asia Minor and the Holy Land. During the reign of Augustus attention was directed mainly to the establishment of a secure frontier protected by the natural barriers of water or desert. At these frontiers stood the legions of Rome, keeping back the barbarian invader on the north and the Oriental despots on the east, preserving the culture and civilization that had been handed down in turn from Homer to Pericles, to Alexander, to Caesar.

We have to think of the endless wars of the Greeks, of the strife between the generals over the remnants of Alexander's empire, of the perpetual fighting of the tribesmen to the north, of the piracy that was the scourge of the Mediterranean trade, to realize what it meant to the antique world for Augustus to establish and his successors to maintain the Roman peace, the *Pax Romana*. There had never been anything like it in the history of the world. No wonder thoughtful people for the next thousand years were to look back to it as to a paradise lost.

Within the shelter of the outer defenses lay a world more securely at peace than the West had ever known. For centuries men could come and go from the borders of Scotland to the foothills of the Himalayas, from the Gates of Hercules to the Black Sea, without fear of attack because the legions of Rome policed that world and her ships swept the sea free of pirates. This strange interlude of peace between the backgrounds of war did not seem to the people of that time to be something temporary which the world would one day look back to as to something almost unreal. For four hundred years the *Pax Romana* lasted, and while four hundred years may be but a moment in all history, it is a considerable space of time as measured by individual lives. Four hundred years ago today Europe was just emerging from the Middle Ages.

But the Empire, the *Pax Romana,* could never have been attained if there had not developed in Rome an attitude towards citizenship entirely different from that of the original freedom-loving pioneers of the Mediterranean in Greece or in early Italy. Mommsen, in his *History of Rome* written long before fascism, has contrasted the Roman's attitude toward government at the period of the end of the Republic with that of the Greeks.

Whereas in Hellas whenever a tendency towards national union appeared, it was based not upon elements directly political, but on games and art; the contests at Olympia, the poems of Homer, the tragedies of Euripides, were the only bonds that held Hellas together.

Resolutely on the other hand, the Italian surrendered his own personal will for the sake of freedom, and learned to obey his father that he might know how to obey the state. Amidst this subjection individual development might be marred, and the germs of fairest promise in man be arrested in the bud; the Italian gained in their stead a feeling of fatherland and of patriotism such as the Greek never knew, and alone among all the civilized nations of antiquity succeeded in working out national unity in connection with a constitution based on self-government — a national unity which at last placed in his hands the mastery, not only over the divided Hellenic stock, but over the whole known world.

It was this sense of obedience of the Roman, his acceptance of the subordination of the individual to the state, that made it possible for Augustus to organize the government so as to gather to himself the full elements of kingship without its being so designated. As a final touch, in 12 B.C., he became Pontifex Maximus, the chief priest, and paid divine honors to Julius Caesar. The worship of the Caesars, both living and dead, developed first in Asia Minor, where divinity was still an attribute of kingship. It gradually spread through the provinces where the emperor's authority was maintained unchallenged and came at last to Rome. Taking the oath at the altar of the Emperor became a test for Christians.

It was not that the Emperors were intolerant of religions other than that of the Caesar worship. The city contained a temple to nearly every god worshipped in the world at that time. But imperial policy rather than religious scruple refused to tolerate anyone unwilling to bow down before the supreme authority of the Emperor to govern the citizens of the state in all the avenues of life, civil, military and religious. This, indeed, was the essence of the mastery over the whole known world for which the Roman gave up his individual desires. The Roman Empire, with the process of conquest completed, was a war organization turned to the purpose of peace, a hierarchy of control which divided the authority of magistrate from magistrate, and linked all of these different prerogatives in the person of the Emperor. It was fascism in its most splendid form.

The true significance of the government as it existed from Augustus on was not apparent for a long time. The Republican forms were kept until 284 when Diocletian became Emperor and frankly substituted a monarchy of the Persian pattern for the existing system. His reorganization of the civil and military administrations of the Empire, as later elaborated by the Emperor Constantine, clearly revealed the hierarchial principle of government. The civil and military administrations were completely separated. For purposes of civil administration the Empire was divided into four prefectures, which in turn were divided into dioceses and these into provinces. At the head of each of these divisions was an official, responsible to the official immediately preceding him in rank, and at the same time also directly responsible to the Emperor. The whole resembled a pyramid with the Roman people at its base, its sides the carefully graded officials, and its apex the Emperor.

The improvement of the government of the provinces under the Empire was marked, even as early as Augustus. Under the Republic, Rome had been the heart of the system; its welfare had been the chief concern of the government. The provinces existed only to pay the expenses of Rome. Under the Empire, the provincial governors no longer had things to themselves. They were responsible for what they did, generously paid and carefully supervised.

And the roads, the famous roads of Rome, were improved everywhere, not only to make trade easier, but also to render the passage of troops from one part of the Empire to another a simple matter, in case a governor of an outlying province should be tempted to cut off a slice of territory for himself. These outlying provinces proved to be a real check on the Emperor. If he kept too small an army at the frontier, the barbarians could break through, but if he kept too large a one a general somewhere might acquire so much power, so much *imperium,* as to enable him to descend on Rome with his loyal legions and take the throne for himself. This repeatedly happened, especially during the second century. The Praetorian guard, encamped at Rome to protect the person of the Emperor might at any time turn against him if its privileges were curtailed. More than once the fate of the Empire was settled in a conspiracy of the military leaders, and the army, the creator as well as the guardian of the Empire, ceased to be its reliable defender.

Pax Romana, however, was something more than a military truce. Outwardly the empire took on more and more the character of a police state; but it was never fascist in the sense in which that word has been used in recent years. Even at the very time that it was becoming hierarchial and absolute and the old republican institutions of government were being discarded, its jurists were continuing to develop the principles of civil law, and however debased the customs of the populace might be, the outlook on life and the political philosophy of thoughtful men were on a high plane of Stoic philosophy or Christian faith.

The purpose of the state was peace and justice *(pax et justitia),* and the conception of human rights was growing even when the attainment was lessening in the weakening economic structure of the empire. Upon the whole, the human outlook remained a generous one. Intolerance was chiefly against the intolerant as when the fires of revolt broke out in Judea in an attempt to re-establish the narrow nationalism of earlier Jewish history. Revolts like this were suppressed in blood and the vanquished were either dispersed or added to the slaves of victorious Rome.

From the standpoint of Rome, the suppression of revolts like these or the wars along the frontiers were police action for the maintenance of law and order. But from the standpoint of the armies themselves it was war. And the more they were called upon for such services the stronger grew their reliance upon their own strength, and the greater was the temptation to use it. Thus it was by the very exercise of power that Rome developed its fatal weakness, the inherent weakness of an authoritarian state.

The Roman Law

The permanent contribution of Rome to the Western world was not this prodigious structure of empire, however lasting its impression on the minds of statesmen and peoples of succeeding centuries, but the development of a vast and splendid system of law. The history of this great juristic creation runs parallel with that of Rome itself from the days of kingship of the little city state to those of the Emperor Justinian when the barbarians were already ruling in the West and the last citadel of the ancient world was Constantinople. It began with the process of secularization under the kingship, and the first sign of its independent life was the creation of the office of praetor to take over the administration of justice within the limits allowed it in a society that was still primitive.

The process of secularization was a long one and is still going on; we still have magic in our law; the oath (sacramentum) goes back to the primitive idea of bad luck if the pledge to the god is violated. But with the establishment of a court of law the tendency is to concentrate upon rules of evidence and technical methods to be applied to all alike. The advantage of this is that it offers a greater chance for impartiality and prevents arbitrary decisions. Justice for the Roman, therefore, became a formal proceeding following precedent and thus developed a learned profession, that of the jurist.

In course of time the courts multiplied, both because of the number of suitors and also because of the growing diversity of problems confronting the magistrates. Even in the early days it had been necessary to have alongside the praetor for the citizen (*praetor urbanus*), a praetor for the foreigner (*praetor peregrinus*), and as Rome extended her dominion the administration of the law became more and more necessary and influential in the transaction of the business of so many peoples.

This development of the law as a technical scheme of things more or less set apart from the rest of the social and political organization was never paralleled in the Orient, a fact of great importance in dealing with Oriental peoples down to the present time. The administration of justice for the Oriental was personal, depending for the most part on tribal, ancient or local custom or on the moods and whims of a despot. This was also the case, as one might expect, in early Germanic law because it was the perpetuation of the undifferentiated rules of primitive society.

Roman law, however, passed out of this stage when the city state was merged into Italy, after the Social War. Then, with the spread of the Empire, under Roman tutelage, the West acquired institutions administering an impersonal set of rules of conduct on the basis of actual cases tried in the past and formulated with an undeviating logic. The importance of this distinctive invention for regulating private as well as public affairs according to a set pattern cannot be overestimated in dealing with the development of Western civilization.

Our first definite knowledge of the early law of Rome goes back to the famous Twelve Tables drawn up in the fifth century B.C. They became a part of the schoolboy's education which he could recite just as the Greek schoolboy could recite the Iliad, and what a difference in outlook from that of the Greek must have been produced in the Roman by memorizing legal forms instead of heroic romance! The Twelve Tables consisted of the same undifferentiated collection of customs, traditional rules and religious ordinances which characterized most primitive codes, but in addition they did lay emphasis on the necessity for a proper trial, the presentation of evidence and of proof, and the illegality of bribery in judicial proceedings, all of which are such fundamental parts of present day court proceedings that we seldom ask how they originated.

It was a long time before the Roman jurists worked their way to a denial of the original principle that men should not have equal rights. As we know, Rome began with a distinct denial of the equality of mankind, as had all the other early cultures. The great struggle between the plebeians and patricians went on for years. But the ruling classes of Rome perceived what the Greek cities never learned, that a city state cannot resist its foreign enemies if torn by dissension within. They yielded, reluctantly and bitterly, to every claim of the plebs, and the latter gained political equality with the Licinian Law of 367 B.C., by which one of the two consuls was to be a pleb. Before that they had succeeded in gaining the privilege of marriage into patrician families. The powerful office of Tribune was later established to give a representative of the plebeians power to veto any act of a magistrate which violated their rights.

As in the case of the Greek cities, the traditional law of the Twelve Tables applied only to citizens who cases came before the *praetor urbanus*. What law, then was the *praetor peregrinus* going to apply in the administration of cases involving foreigners of all nationalities? The problem which confronted him was by no means new. Long before Rome appeared on the scene of legal and political history there had existed a lively commerce in the Mediterranean carried on by ships from Egypt, Crete, Phoenicia and Carthage, as well as from Greece itself. Even where the traders came only on sufferance and without political rights, it was only natural that the mutual advantage of bargaining would develop agreements into contracts which, even if extra legal, would be recognized by the merchants of the various commercial centers. But the habits and customs of the foreigners not only differed from those of the Romans but they also differed among themselves. The Roman magistrates had therefore to decide any disputes where the relatively primitive stock of local law was not applicable and new principles of law had to be found which would furnish a satisfactory settlement for all concerned.

The body of law which was thus worked out in the practice of the courts received the name *jus gentium*, or the law of the peoples. The more common translation, the law of the nations, is confusing both because the ancient cities were not nations and because the Roman jurists never worked out a system of international law. That could happen only in an international society, a stage of political development never reached in the antique world. Nevertheless, the *jus gentium* became, in course of time, the best expression of the universality of Roman law, because it embodied elements proven, by comparison of the laws of different people, to have the general approval of mankind. Therefore, centuries later it became a vital factor in the formation of that international law which was to spring up in the fifteenth and sixteenth centuries. But the *gentes*, or peoples, to which the *jus gentium* referred, were any people, any single governmental unity, whether of city or tribe; they were not the territorial states which we think of as nations today.

Since the legislative body of the Roman state (the Roman populace acting in assembly) was such an unwieldy body, changes in law were left largely to the Senate, of whose powers in this regard we have already spoken, and to the praetors. The latter, while not legislating, nevertheless changed the law by interpretation and by the promulgation of edicts in which were set forth the way in which certain cases were to be decided for the next year, thereby getting rid of outworn laws that might still be on the statute books. Thus Roman law was to a large extent judge-made. But this creative process became less vigorous in the later empire. While the great code of Justinian in 533 A.D. was of tremendous advantage to later centuries in preserving in concrete form the collected thoughts of Roman jurists, the necessity for putting them into writing shows that during the years the vitality had gone from the Roman courts and Roman judges; they could no longer draw from the basic elements of the profession the law to fit the case but must have everything in black and white to follow by rote.

Meanwhile, the *jus gentium* was seen, as time went on, to be superior to the formal procedures and complexities of the law for citizens. Gradually it tended to take over parts of the sphere of the older law, and in the code of Justinian the two were finally used.

The result was a body of law without parallel in history, one of the three greatest gifts of the ancient world to Western civilization; the other two being Hellenism and Christianity. We should, therefore, pause a moment to examine it. Fortunately, we have in Rudolph Sohm's *Institutes of Roman Law,* a masterly summary of the main principles:

The *jus gentium* came to be regarded as a universal law, as a law common to all mankind, because based on the nature of things and the general sense of equity obtaining among all men — a sort of natural law, exacting recognition everywhere by virtue of its inherent reasonableness. It would, however, be erroneous to suppose that the Romans attempted to introduce a code of nature such as the philosophers had devised. The *jus gentium* was and never had been anything but a portion of *positive Roman law* which commercial usage and other sources of law had clothed in concrete form. Nor again must it be imagined that the Romans simply transferred a portion of foreign (Hellenic) law bodily into their own system. In the few exceptional cases where they did so, they never failed to stamp a national Roman character on the institutions which they borrowed. . . . The *jus gentium* was that part of the private law of Rome which in its fundamental conceptions was in accordance with the private law of other nations, more especially with that of the Greeks, which would naturally predominate along the seaboard of the Mediterranean. . . .

There is a moment in the history of every nation when the claims of a natural sense of justice assert themselves and revolt against the hard and fast austerities of ancient traditional forms. . . . The *jus gentium* did not come down like a hurricane and sweep away the *jus civile*. The slow and gradual elaboration of a system of equity alongside the older and stricter law was rather the work of a patient and uninterrupted development extending over a period of more than five hundred years. The reform of Roman law was the result of a vast series of small changes of detail. And it was only by painstaking care of this description, by scorning all appeals to vague general principles of equity, that the Romans, aided by that keen sense of form, moderation and legality, which with them was hereditary, could succeed in reducing the *jus aequum* to a body of principles lucidly conceived, minutely elaborated, and carefully weighed in all their details. By such a method alone could Roman law, while its contents were so freely developing over so vast a field, preserve intact throughout that artistic power which moulds and subdues its materials, and erects them into a firm harmonious structure. It is this power which has made Roman law what it is: a model for all times to come such as has never been equalled.

In working out the *jus gentium* — those rules of natural equity which regulate the dealings between man and man — and in reducing it to a system of marvelous transparency and lucidity, which carries irresistible conviction by its form as well as its matter to the mind of every observer — in doing this, Roman law has performed its mission in the world's history. And it was this achievement, successfully accomplished for all time to come, that not only fitted Roman law for becoming the general law of the Roman Empire, but also endowed it with the power, when once it had emerged from the oblivion of the centuries, to conquer the modern world.

So much on the history and nature of the law. As for the administration of justice, it remained without any radical change under the Empire, because of the fact that it was in the hands of a specialized group of officials. It continued to be separate from politics except that it paid tribute to the power of the Emperor who could hear appeals, a right unknown under the Republic. Politically the Roman citizen might have no voice in the government, but his property was secure. He "knew where he stood" in a way the subject of arbitrary rule never did. Private rights tended to become systematized throughout the Empire, as we have related above, giving a sense of universality and unity; and under Caracalla, in 212, the rights of Roman citizenship were extended to all free-born inhabitants of the empire. This culmination of the long process of the extension of citizenship marks an epoch in the history of freedom; yet it was not granted by the emperor from any noble motives. It was a way for filling the treasury of a needy monarch, because the taxes formerly falling heavily on Roman citizens alone could now be collected from those who as foreigners, had not been assessed for them before. The result, however, in the history of Roman law was that it developed still further as the safeguard of the individual's rights, while at the same time accepting the prince's will as supreme authority. These two principles were to be of great importance in the revival of Roman culture at the end of the Middle Ages.

It is in this connection that we come upon the place of Roman law in the history of freedom. Its two basic features were universality and the protection of the person and property of the citizen. In the primitive stages of its development the Romans certainly did not have a clear consciousness of individual rights in a social system so closely knit and interdependent as that of the clan or tribe. There, as everywhere else in the primitive beginnings of the ancient world, the individual did not exist by himself alone. But in a warring society like that of Rome where the sword was the oldest symbol of law, the individual established his right on the basis of his ability to exercise it. In the early days, property was what a man could take with his hands (*manu-captum, manicipium*). Thus, personal energy and individual ability were basic sources of the private law of Rome itself, a feature which left its impress on later developments of both law and custom.

But progress in the appreciation of human rights, which is the very essence of freedom, came less by the development of the law of the city than by that of the *jus gentium*. As citizenship was extended first to the plebs, then to all Italy, and then to the Mediterranean world, its privileges were even more appreciated by those who had newly acquired them than by the old Romans themselves. The law became for them a shield and a protection against arbitrary power as well as against the unlawful acts of fellow citizens. Thus the magistracy maintained, even under despotic rulers, the instruments of that impartial justice which is the only true basis of freedom. It was this fact more than the participation in a world empire which in time made even the conquered proud to claim Roman citizenship. The appeal of Paul of Tarsus to the courts at Rome was a single instance of what was going on throughout the whole Mediterranean world. It was a tribute to justice and a recognition that freedom is a function of the law.

So far we have traced the evolution of Roman law as a development arising from the actual history of the Roman state, meeting the needs of a growingly complex civilization by the same kind of realistic method which had been pursued in the transformation of the Republic from a local city state to an Empire. The keynote to that political development, as we have seen, was the dividing up of power, a process which even the Empire continued outwardly to respect. It was but natural, therefore, that the practice as well as the study of law should call forth a legal profession and that it should attract some of the best minds that Rome produced. The work of these jurists was more than that of advisers as to procedure, which was all they became at Athens. At Rome, as a consequence of the revolutionary process which we have traced in the secularization of the law, the interpretation and custody of the legal tradition became the monopoly of professional lawyers. Nevertheless, profiting from its purely secular character, it did not acquire until the close of Roman history anything resembling canonical writings embodying fixed conclusions. It continued to be hammered into shape by magistrates in the actual administration of justice and systematized by the jurists for equally practical purposes.

From this point of view the Roman law is a rich and varied literature embodying the experience not only of the Roman people but also of those with whom they had dealings throughout the rest of the world. But to this realistic and creative teaching of the needs of daily life there was added in the later Republic and under the Empire the influence of the two great streams of ethical teaching of the ancient world, Greek philosophy and Christian doctrine. Outwardly submerged by violence and ruthless power, the moral forces, which had found expression in Judaism, Christianity and Greek philosophy here moved again in an environment different from that of church or academy. Of the two influences the Greek was undoubtedly greater than the Christian throughout the formative period of the law, although by the time it was codified under Theodosius and Justinian the influence of the Church was sufficiently strong to make the final formulation a fitting parallel, in the secular world, to its theology.

The chief influence of Greek thinkers upon Roman law was neither the idealism of Plato nor the realism of Aristotle. It is true that at the close of his life Plato saw the need of having something more permanent in which to embody the principles of justice than the passing lives of men, and so emphasized the importance both of the law itself and of the legal profession. Those "commissioners" who were to be sent abroad to study comparative law and apply it in the city state would have been "jurists" in the full sense of the word; and Aristotle's way of approaching the study of politics was but a variant of this same method. But the aim of both Plato and Aristotle was rather political than legal owing to the intimacy of political life in the small confines of the Greek city state. Neither the intellectualized world of Plato as embodied in the *Republic* nor the actual facts which Aristotle assembled could furnish the practical program for the Roman jurists. Their problems and the devices for solving them were wholly different.

It was not the details of Greek thinking, therefore, from which the Romans profited most but the emphasis upon moral purpose, that sense of duty which gave the color to Greek and all other serious thinking in the antique world. It was, however, most fully developed in the philosophy of the Stoics who put so much accent upon duty in a world based upon moral law as to have made the word "stoic" a synonym for the rigid performance of duty and the unflinching acceptance of suffering and misfortune. Stoicism drew its first inspiration from Zeno, the Greek philosopher, but it appealed to thoughtful Romans in public life, like Cicero and Seneca, and finally became the consolation of the philosopher-emperor, Marcus Aurelius, who stayed the process of imperial decay for a few short years, sustained by an outlook in which the intellectualism of the Greek was fused with the Roman sense of reality and that latent emotional fire which kindles thought into religion.

The early Roman had needed no urging to make the sense of duty the most real incentive in life but, in the later Empire, law needed the support of religion to reinforce the forgotten virtue of citizenship. Thus while it served the business of the secular world it acquired ethical elevation as well. It would be hard to overestimate the importance of this. Although stemming from the home of Greek philosophy at Athens itself, Stoicism was the product of that wider Hellenic civilization which followed the conquests of Alexander, and it came to Rome with all the influence of a vast and cosmopolitan following. Tarsus, Rhodes and Alexandria were its university towns, but it found its real home in the cultured circles of Rome where for over two centuries its doctrine was accepted almost like a creed. For, in a time when the national character seemed to be losing the ancient virtues of self-discipline, and respect for the gods was dying out, it offered not a new theology but an ethical doctrine in which right reason became the standard of conduct. The Stoic, being profoundly skeptical, did not exalt reason (*Logos*) to be the voice of God, but we may well apply to him the phrase which Epictetus applied to his predecessors, the Cynics: they were the "athletes of righteousness."

The Cynics had taught that reason is the basic law for men, the Stoics went far beyond this and identified it with the law of the universe. Socrates, as we have seen, had some such idea, which Plato developed from the sphere of morals to embrace the reality of thought itself. But the Stoics were more definite. Virtue is the law which governs the universe and justice is therefore a law of nature. This is the real foundation of human laws as well. It follows that there can be no difference between Greek, barbarian, bond or free. All are equal insofar as they partake of reason. This doctrine, although noble in concept, enabled the Stoics to compromise with the greatest evil of antiquity, slavery; for if only the wise man is free, the slaves are the unwise. We therefore come upon the paradox that a slave like Epictetus had no argument against the permanent institution of slavery, and all that a high-minded Stoic statesman like Seneca tried to do was to insist that its conditions be alleviated. In spite of this failure in application, history has paid a lasting tribute to the high ideals of these stern moralists whose austere vision of divine and human law became one of the most ennobling influence upon the law of Rome.

No higher note was ever struck in all history of law than that which opens the manual of Roman law, the *Institutes* of Justinian: "Justice is the fixed and constant purposes that gives to every man his due," thus summarizing the thought in Plato's *Republic*. It was the same thought that Confucius expressed in terms of ethics, and Jesus in terms of religion. The measured concept of fair play in a world of miscellaneous business was phrased by Rome in terms of abstract relationships. In this setting it came at last to embody the spirit of Greek philosophy and Christian teaching. It is a sobering fact that Roman society was on a higher level when it went to pieces than when it conquered the world. The more recent studies of provincial life in the fifth century show a relatively high grade of morals. Earlier historians, however, were misled by taking the word of the Christian critics who were contemporaries of the pagan world, and the Christian critic was naturally not an impartial judge. He has left us a picture of Roman morals which was not fair and no picture at all of the Romans who conquered the world in the first instance. Nevertheless, the formal justice developed by jurists and administered by magistrates did not reach the fundamental evil in the structure of Roman society. The inheritance of war in booty and slaves made impossible that kind of economic justice which is the only basis for permanent health in the social as well as the political organization. The Roman Empire did not fall because of a decline in morals but because the war system by which it was created contained the slow but fatal poison of a false economy.

The Economics of Conquest and the Fall of Rome

War was the creator and destroyer of the antique world. It is only now, with the rise of the social sciences as allies of history, that we have begun to see clearly this central fact of the first civilization of the West. The greatest historian of the decline and fall of Rome, Edward Gibbon, did not see clearly this *leitmotiv* of the great drama he described. Writing from toward the end of the eighteenth century with the anti-Christian animus of a *philosophe,* to explain why bare-footed monks should be clambering over the ruins of imperial palaces, he found the reason for the downfall of Rome in the same philosophy that Polybius had advanced for its rise: the character of men and institutions and arbitrary fate. Gibbon's work was a rationalist's reaction against the scheme of history based on the writings of the Church Fathers as summed up for the West by Augustine, according to which disasters were a part of the providence of God, a punishment for sin and a discipline for the spirit.

The nineteenth century enriched our knowledge of both events and institutions by the introduction of scientific method in history, especially in Germany; but from Niebuhr, who recast the story of early Rome, to Mommsen, who described the Empire, they worked for the most part within the traditional limits of political history. The conception of the past was therefore one-sided. Towards the close of the nineteenth century, however, the new analysis of the modern world in terms of economics and the other social sciences began to throw their reflection back across the centuries and a new set of interests developed in the study of the ancient world. The religious basis of the city state, brought into clear light by Fustel de Coulanges, has been taken over by those familiar with similar data in primitive life and early civilizations all over the world. Anthropology, joined with archeology, is now regarded as a definite part of the training for ancient history.

Most important, however, was the contribution of economics, revealing the way in which the civilizations of the antique world were gutted by the war system as the economic basis shifted from agriculture and trade to the spoils of war, tribute to enrich both the state and its citizens and slaves to do the work.

In the history of freedom this opens one of the saddest chapters, one which was never finally closed until our own day, not only cruel in its inhumanity but economically wasteful and disastrous. There was little awareness in either Greece or Rome of the economic consequences of slavery, for, as we have seen, even Aristotle accepted it as an inevitable, inescapable element in society, and it was not until the moral regeneration of Stoicism and Christianity transformed the outlook of thoughtful Romans that the legitimacy of slavery was questioned.

So long as Rome was a small city of farmers and traders, the slaves were not numerous, as even the patricians worked along with the household slaves they owned. The situation did not change materially with the early conquests of neighboring tribes, for it was the unique characteristic of Rome that until it became militarized in the later years of the Republic, it did not enslave the peoples whom it conquered, but steadily if slowly and reluctantly incorporated them within the expanding state. This extension of the rights and privileges of Roman citizens was forced along by social war and by the heroic championship of reformers like the Gracchi, and ultimately constituted the abiding strength of the Roman State. But it was a process of the extension of political rights which did not reach down to those who had no rights to begin with, the slaves.

At first few in number, the slaves multiplied with the increase of the late Republic and Empire, especially as the conquests reached out beyond Italy. Then the economy of Rome changed from the healthy basis of independent free peasant owners — large and small — to that of slave labor on great estates. The two institutions of war and slavery were interlocked in a joint process which seemed at the time to mark the height of civilized living, but which proved to be the ultimate cause of the decline and fall of Rome, and with it of antique civilization which thus it both preserved and betrayed. With the extension of the conquests, the supply of slaves grew tremendously.

When Epirus, in the mountains of northern Greece, was conquered in 168 B.C., one hundred and fifty thousand of its inhabitants were carried off as slaves to Italy. Another hundred and fifty thousand were taken as captives from German invaders (the Teutons and Cimbri) in 102 B.C. The victories of Pompey over the pirates tapped another great source of supply. Under the Cilician pirates, according to Strabo, as many as ten thousand had been sold in one day. Julius Caesar added many thousands from Gaul, selling sixty-three thousand on a single occasion. They were dragged through Rome on every triumph, either to join the vast army of slaves in city and country or as gladiators to kill each other in the arena for a Roman holiday. At the height of the empire, Trajan brought ten thousand gladiators at one time all the way from distant Dalmatia beyond the Danube. The slave trade with Rome flourished in Spain, Gaul and Africa, but especially in Syria and the adjacent countries of Western Asia. The result was disastrous. Gibbon reckoned that under the Empire half of the population was servile. This may be excessive, but even at the ratio of three free men to one slave, which is a possible estimate, there would have been over twenty million slaves in the Empire at its height under the Antonines.

The treatment of the slaves by Romans, originally mild, grew progressively more cruel, due apparently to increasing apprehension of conspiracy or uprising. The uprising came in 73 B.C., when the gladiator Spartacus led a revolt, defeating for two years the army sent against him, and even menacing Rome itself. The utter crushing of this uprising did not quiet the fears of the slave owners. The inscription of Ancyra, that unique record of the deeds of Augustus, stated that he delivered back to their owners some thirty thousand runaway slaves who had armed against the state. Yet there seems to have been a stirring of popular disapproval when, on the death of a noble in the reign of Augustus, his four hundred slaves were put to death. Although the law under which this crime was committed was strengthened under Nero, yet a moderating tendency had already been evident under Augustus when the sale of slaves for fighting beasts in the arena was forbidden, while Claudius (41-54 A.D.) freed slaves whom their owners wished to get rid of on account of illness.

The new moral outlook bore fruit when the institution of slavery was challenged in high places. Dio Chrysostom, the adviser of Trajan, pronounced it to be contrary to the law of nature, but such ideas were by no means widely shared. Under Hadrian, the slave was brought definitely under the protection of the law by the provision which enacted that he should not be killed without judicial sanction, and abolished the subterranean prisons. A much greater step forward was taken by Antoninus Pius in the enactment of the principle that slaves could take complaints of ill treatment by their masters to the court of the local prefect, and that when an estate was sold the slaves that were nearly related should not be separated. None of this legislation conferred legal rights on the slaves; it limited the rights of slave ownership. Yet these and other humane provisions, all of which were incorporated in the Roman law, led naturally to the threshold of the rights of the person as set forth by Justinian in the rule that the position and employment of a slave should be taken into account in granting damages for injuries to him.

Still, a slave was only property. He could be bought and sold and own nothing of his own, although in practice he could accumulate savings toward the purchase of freedom. In Cato's day his slaves shared his food and much of the daily life on the estate which he farmed and the management of which he described for all other well-born farmers. But as the estates grew in size and were left to overseers to manage, the masses of slaves became more and more chattels, chained even during sleeping hours in the slave quarter (*ergastulum*). Even in the city houses, the porters were chained to prevent escape. Yet the slave's savings, while legally belonging to the owner, were held on a kind of contract constituting a "natural obligation" on the part of the owner. In course of time the provisions of this left-handed recognition of the property of the slave were worked out in great detail in the law, showing how the more highly-placed slaves could enter into business operations. Emancipation came along these lines, but there were also other ways, some of them without regard to an owner's possible objection.

Unless formally emancipated by legal ceremony, a freedman remained the client of his former master, taking his name and owing him obsequious deference, performing set services or paying money. Freedmen thus constituted a special class, subject to civil disabilities and ineligible to full citizenship until the third generation. Under the Empire, however, the freedman rose steadily to fill the gaps in the official classes caused by a declining population, some of them becoming senators, provincial governors or even heads of the imperial officialdom in actual charge of imperial affairs. The amelioration of conditions continued; the sale of children was forbidden; and Diocletian, who reorganized both government and society so as to wipe out all vestige of political freedom, forbade a free man to sell himself, although the slave trade continued to be permitted. Finally, Justinian provided that emancipation by any means gave the liberated slave the full rights of a citizen.

From the fourth century, slavery began to decline, chiefly, as Gibbon points out, because the Roman conquests were over and the supply of slaves was no longer available. In place of the slave came the "colonus," originally a renter of land on fixed tenure, but degenerating under the Empire to the status of serf. By the time of Justinian his condition was definitely declared to be servile; every freedman who cultivated a strip of land for thirty years was held to it. He was disqualified from both civil and military functions, but, while unfree, was better off than the slave.

So far we have been tracing in outline the institution of slavery in antiquity, without regard to the influences of Christianity, although it must be remembered that they were finally traceable in the code of Justinian. The impact of Christianity was meliorating but not revolutionary. Slavery was as much taken for granted by St. Paul as by Aristotle. The slave is to be contented with his lot (if that is what is meant by I Corinthians 7:21), serving his master with "goodwill and singleness of heart as unto Christ." (Ephesians 7:5) Paul admonished the master to give the slave "what is just and equal" (Colossians 4:1), and not to threaten him, "knowing that your Master is in heaven; neither is there any respect of persons with Him." (*Ibid.*:9) The first epistle of Peter (2:18, 19) goes further still: "Servants be subject to your masters with all fear, not only to the good and gentle, but also to the froward. For this is thankworthy, if a man for conscience toward God endure grief, suffering wrongfully."

These injunctions were repeated by the early Fathers, urging resignation with one's lot, however hard, because of the perfect freedom in the world to come. Ignatius warned the slave to serve his pagan master with greater zeal because he has no such prospect of future happiness as the Christian. The only voice raised in quiet dissent from this attitude toward slavery was that of Clement of Alexandria, the first of the Fathers to bring a full knowledge of Greek philosophy and culture to bear upon the interpretation of Christianity. There is a noted Stoicism in his insistence that "slaves are men like us" and are to be treated like Christians as they themselves would like to be treated — the Golden Rule in a new setting. Although he nowhere denounced slavery as an institution, he warned against maintaining too many in a household and insisted on their education and the oversight of morals as social obligations almost on a par with those of parents to children.

This high note was not maintained by the later Fathers, some of whom, like Gregory Nazianzen, while admitting equality among all partakers of the Lord's Supper, were slave owners themselves. The accent was upon compassion in human relationship; slavery in itself was to be accepted as any other natural calamity. Chrysostom added a new argument, that the more distinguished the slave the more it is encumbent upon him to continue in servitude, as it offers an excellent chance to influence the whole household in which he is held. It would be hard to find a more perfect example of sophistry twisted to false purpose; but Isidore of Pelusium surpassed it when he argued that slavery might be preferable to freedom if on the day of judgment the slave could argue that his sins were committed at the behest of his master. However, these extreme speculations of theologians were not in the minds of the practical clergy, who, from the fifth century on, even accepted recruits to their numbers from the servile class, although tending to limit this method of enfranchisement to those of outstanding qualities. A general emancipation of slaves was never thought of as a consequence of Christianity in the Roman world.

From this long excursus on slavery in the Roman world, we turn back to the more general effects of war economics. The vitality of the Mediterranean culture had come originally from the free, independent and intensely patriotic city states, whose energy and ingenuity had taken advantage of the natural opportunities of their surroundings for the purposes of trade and their own aggrandizement. Their conquest by Rome brought advantages which at first seemed to outweigh the costs which it imposed, but their gradual absorption into an autocratic empire seemed to rob them of much of their spirit, to which the chaos of the third century was as a death blow. Slowly but steadily the economics of war took its toll of the whole Western world. Tribute was no longer forthcoming and taxes could not be collected. The population declined. The miracle of Roman history was that the Empire could endure so long under these conditions; the explanation lies in the fact that, even in its decline, it maintained a greater degree of peace than any other state of the ancient world.

The reforms of Diocletian had much to do with keeping it from dissolution for another hundred years. His separation of the civil and military administration made the army more efficient, more dependent on the Emperors and less likely to take part in political intrigues.

His changes strengthened imperial authority for the moment, but the numerous officials and the large mercenary army were too great a drain on the financial resources of the state. There were no newly conquered territories to provide spoils, nor could the outlying provinces be relied on longer for tribute. Diocletian introduced a new system of taxation, efficient from the government's point of view, but deadly in its effect on the people. The Emperor decided once a year how much money would be needed. This sum was divided up, each municipality being assigned to a definite amount to pay. The city fathers in the municipal council were held directly responsible for its payment. If they could not collect from the lower classes, they had to pay the entire amount out of their own pockets. The system showed what an empty shell the Empire had become. The members of the councils often could not collect the taxes and went bankrupt as a result of paying the taxes personally. This, in many communities, left destitute that upper middle class which had been the backbone of the state.

The "restoration" of the Empire by Diocletian shows how impossible it was by mere administrative efficiency to cure the evils from which the Roman world was suffering. Taxation levied upon the citizens of the Empire had to take the place of tribute imposed upon the conquered, but the imperial income which had proved inadequate for Diocletian's predecessors could not be wrung from the impoverished Roman world by fiscal manipulation. What was needed was increased production of wealth and this was impossible of achievement because history had at last caught up with the consequences of the false economy of a civilization based upon conquest. The supply of booty could only continue so long as there were new worlds to conquer and while slave labor could be relied upon to till the fields or build the cities.

This deadly process of decay was for a time hidden by the "Orientalizing" of the Empire, accentuating the "divinity" of the Emperor and surrounding him with that majesty which continues to impose itself upon the imagination long after the realities of power are lost. It was in the richer East that this phase of the Empire retained its structure longest, ably served by a bureaucracy, the chief duty of which was to keep the mold of a static world, but which in reality became a hotbed of intrigue centering in the palace of the Emperor. Such a method of government becomes inevitably self-centered and blind to the true character of statesmanship, and it is sufficient comment on the character of this last phase of Roman administration that the name "Byzantinism" has ever since been given to the kind of government which places power in the hands of fawning courtiers and irresponsible bureaucrats.

And so, eventually, the barbarians on the frontier were able to break through, and in 410 the city of Rome was sacked. Gaul fell into their hands, and Spain and Roman Africa, and Italy. The Empire was left in the East. The capital had been transferred to Constantinople many years before, but soon Latin was no longer heard in its streets; the pressure of the Orient obliterated most of the Roman influence. The name remained, however, and even when the Byzantine Empire, as the Eastern Roman Empire is called, fell to the Ottoman Turks in 1453, the Sultans of Turkey still called themselves Emperors of Rome, until, after the first World War and as a result of the secularizing revolution of the Young Turks, the Sultanate itself was formally abolished.

In the Western world the conquering Franks under Charlemagne (768-814) and later Otto (936-973), tried to restore the Empire. The latter called his loose confederation of German states the Holy Roman Empire. Though it had little actual strength and no resemblance to its namesake, it kept alive the title of Roman Emperor in the West until 1806. Such was the awe with which Rome was regarded even by peoples who had never lived under her rule.

The Judgment of History

The judgments of history are never final. They change from generation to generation, from age to age, because they are the projection into the past of our outlook and interests in the world in which we live. In proportion as our own horizon is enriched with greater knowledge of ourselves and of the things which influence our action, we are enabled to improve our understanding of what has happened to other people in the past.

It was but natural, therefore, that the growth of the social sciences in our own time should lead to a recasting of the perspectives of ancient history by making us more aware of the economic and social forces of which the purely political historian was only partially aware; but the social sciences themselves have suffered from a limitation which prevented them from dealing with the most important single activity in the formation and in the ultimate destruction of the antique world, the war system. The social sciences have, down to our day, dealt almost exclusively with society at peace. They have continued the tradition of Plato and Aristotle, Cicero and Augustine, concerning themselves with the problems of human association and welfare, of "life, liberty and the pursuit of happiness" at home and wherever there was freedom for their development. The polity of war, which the Greeks neglected, has not yet been brought within the scope of the social sciences. As long as this is the case, history remains fundamentally unadjusted to these sciences because it must deal with war fully as much, and at times even more, than with the data of peace.

Nowhere is this inadequacy more evident than in the history of Rome. It is true that there have been many important studies of the effect of the war system upon the Roman Republic and Empire, and the main results of these studies have been incorporated in the commonest textbooks; but the continuing effects of the war system upon the system of government, as well as upon the economic system, still offer a challenging field for the historian.

We have just seen how the economy of the antique world was falsified by the exploitation of the conquered as they supplied tribute and slaves to the victors. But in the field of government itself we come upon the striking fact that the only creative period in the history of Roman politics was that when the Republic was organizing itself for better government at home, and applying its experience in the extension of its rule over its conquests. The specialization of the functions of government, which produced magistrates of different kinds to deal with justice, money, morals and the like, was a creative process similar to that in the constitution of Athens. Persistent realism marked the treatment of colonies and allies and the grant of citizenship, a progress held in check by prejudice and caution, and yet perhaps all the stronger on that account. In short, so long as the conquests of the Roman Kingdom or Republic were of neighbors living close at hand who could be brought within the orbit of the city state as it expanded to cover all the surrounding territory, there was progress in the interplay of human rights and in the functioning of government itself; but as the Roman state extended to cover distant lands, this process yielded to that of increased military control until at last the whole political evolution was denatured by its very success.

From the time that the Imperator was able to establish the undifferentiated control of sovereignty over the whole state, controlling all the magistracies, down to the close of Roman history — that is throughout the whole imperial period — there was no real progress made in the art and science of government. From Tiberius to Diocletian and Constantine the process is one of increasing regimentation with a continual growth of tyranny, until not only government lost its capacity for adjustment but society itself became almost castelike in its rigidity. There was nothing in all this stretch of Roman history for later generations to copy, because there was a constant process of degeneration instead of growth. It is apparently an iron law of history that despotism produces still greater despotism. When it attempts to relax its control as, for instance, in France in the closing years of the reign of Napoleon III, it runs the danger of increasing its inadequacy in administration through laxness of control.

The tendency is the other way — to increase control — as is so clearly seen in the transformation of the Roman Empire from a state still bearing the

131

outer marks of a republic to one accepting the oriental concept of divine monarchy. Byzantinism has become a synonym for unchanging routine in bureaucratic control. It is, or at least it seems to be, the one safest method of tyrannical government; because under its set forms of organization and administration there is no place for experiment, and experiment is always dangerous for autocratic powers.

In the two great fields of economics and government the history of Rome has lasting lessons for statesmanship, lessons never more pertinent than at the present time. Unfortunately, however, the basic fallacies of the Roman system, which ultimately undermined its strength and caused its downfall, were never clearly seen by the Romans themselves, although there were always thoughtful people who saw some of these consequences. The inability to see how militarized government ultimately leads toward disaster should not be charged up against the Romans as an indication of a lack of intelligence in the theory as well as in the practice of government; for it must be remembered that in the period of the Empire, Roman society bore all the marks of being less militarized than that of any other people in history before then. The *Pax Romana* which reigned inside the far-flung frontiers was a new experience for mankind. The splendor of this achievement was of a character to impose upon the imaginations of peoples who had once been its victims.

Not only was the soverignty of the Empire universal, that is to say, covering all the Mediterranean world of antique culture, but it bore the marks of seeming permanence. In reality, however, all that was left by the fifth century was a hard shell, one which was easily broken by the battle-axes of a few barbarian war bands. The Roman Empire fell because of its internal weakness, rather than because of any great strength in those who attacked it.

When one turns from this story of politics and government, with its bearing upon economics and social life, to that of the history of Roman law, it is like turning from a mausoleum to a structure charged with forces still vital in the world today. For Roman law, unlike Roman government, was the embodiment of the sense of justice in simple men and women working out their relations with each other on the basis of their own experience and of that of the jurists who knew the tradition of justice as it has been developed from other cases in the past. The Roman law was in essence like the English common law, an expression of reality in all its varied forms; but unlike the English law, it was generalized from sweeping concepts of high principles, for it was informed within the ethics of stoic philosophy and ultimately of Christian teaching. The real lasting inheritance of Rome was not the great creation of its military chieftains, but the body of the Roman law.

CHAPTER VI

THE CITY OF GOD

The Background of Paganism

WE HAVE FOLLOWED the fortunes of the ancient city state from its prehistoric beginnings through a history crowded with glorious achievement, but ending in the inescapable tragedy which awaits every society that lives by conquest and exploitation. Neither the penetrating intellect of Greece nor the conquering genius of Rome could ward off the fate of those whose imperfect justice does not extend to all mankind. The Romans came closer to this ideal than any other people down to modern times, when they granted the equal rights of citizenship to conquered peoples and embodied the principles of that association in the vast system of the Roman law.

But the sword which cleared away all opposing sovereignties that lay in the pathway of this one imperium continued to hang like that of Damocles over the very provinces which it had conquered and policed, and finally over Rome itself. The revolution which produced politics by supplanting the taboo organization of clan and tribe with the secular arm of a united citizenship had carried civilization into a new era in which thought was freer than ever before, and produced in the arts and letters a culture which for boldness in design and beauty of expression has never been surpassed. But in a civilization in which the day's work is done by slaves and one's livelihood comes easily from the tribute of distant lands, there is bound to be a fundamental lack in human sympathy, a hardness in the temper of thought which leaves it indifferent to human suffering.

It is here that the great religions have, as we have seen, played their beneficent part in the lives of men and nations, offering them compensations for their sufferings and even for their failures and thus linking morals with faith. But neither Greece nor Rome developed a great religion of its own. This was not because of any native indifference to religion; it might even

133

be because of the very intensity of their sense of its potency in mysterious presences lurking at every turn and its wayward influence with the best laid plans unless warded off by the proper ceremonies. The ancient West shared with the ancient East the primitive orthodoxy of the taboo, but, unlike the East, it faced this world of mystery with a realism which made polytheism a mirror of the known world, with divinities repeating the frailties and frustrations as well as the achievements of their worshippers. Their pantheon was not filled, like that of India, with strange imaginings, but with idealized forms for which human beings served as models. Theology lost out to the arts of poetry and sculpture, while philosophy, which began by questioning and discarding the myths of the Homeric age, came to grips with purely human experiences, as in those schools of thought, the Cynic, the Stoic and the Epicurean.

In the history of freedom this trend of antique philosophy constitutes a unique and splendid chapter, that of an intellectual revolution which liberated the mind from the shackles of the taboo and the distortions of myth. In the Latin West this movement of enlightenment varied from the practical trend and genial eclecticism of the cultured mind of Cicero, whom a St. Augustine could, reluctantly, accept as a mirror of the best in a bad world, to the pure intellectualism of Lucretius, which left the primitive world of pagan cult so far behind as to deny belief in a supernatural government of the world and of a future life. But this movement of radical thought, while it represented a secularizing trend that went much farther than that which we have traced in the field of politics, was limited to that relatively small number who could claim citizenship in the city of the mind. To the uncultured crowd it was either unknown, or, if forced on their attention by a reformer like Socrates, was held to be as dangerous to the commonweal as heresy to the Medieval church.

The history of freedom as a major interest of mankind is something quite different from freedom of thought, which a slave like the Stoic Epictetus could share with a Roman noble like Seneca. Interest in philosophy has never been widely shared, and even in the higher circles of Rome, the truly great poem of the free-thinker Lucretius, *On the Nature of the World,* in spite of its intellectual power was not able to compete with the genial story of myth and legend in which Virgil linked the Homeric world with that of Rome. It is true that Virgil's theme had the advantage over that of Lucretius because the fancy of the poet is closer to the waywardness of ordinary thinking and is warmed by those currents of sympathy which are lacking in the austere world of the atheist, however gallantly he may lead the forces of science against superstition. A purely negative attitude, even in the noblest minds, is not enough to meet the needs of the common man. Those who were unschooled in the tenets of philosophy and who lived and suffered in unprivileged lives, refused to be orphaned of their divinities, not so much those of the state, but rather those of the daily life. The result was that, at the very time that philosophy was developing towards scepticism, a new and intense spiritual awakening was taking place within the framework of the secular state.

This "religion of the mysteries," as the Greeks called it, began by a re-crudescence of primitive beliefs transformed by influences from Asia Minor. It had its churches like that of Eleusis, and Orphic rites, like those of the sacraments, which "purified from sin," or ritual dances, as in the cult of Dionysos, like those of dervishes where the consciousness becomes confused in whirling frenzy. It was a religion of ceremonial rather than of creed, for it tended to blend into one scattered movement the devotees of the Greek mysteries and those of the Egyptian Isis and the Persian Mithra.

But the one thing that linked them and gave strength to the movement was a new and vital belief in immortality, in which the worshippers found compensation for the sufferings of this world. In place of the vague outlines of a world after death which was all that the earlier religions had supplied, the mystery religions opened the vista of a life everlasting to all those puri-fied by the mystic ceremonies. This ecstatic vision, denied to the skeptical philosopher, was thus opened to the humble and the outcast.

The Origins of Christianity

This was the setting for that greatest of all revolutions in the history of Western thought, by which Christianity, disowned by an unimportant peo-ple, the Jews, became the inheritor of both Greek philosophy and Roman polity. Beginning as a religion of western Asia, it spread over peoples so utterly foreign to the land of its birth that its adoption was not the least of the miracles. But no other religion was at that time so comprehensive in its cult, so bold in its faith or so strong in its ethical content. These three aspects of Christianity — cult, faith and good works — were fitted into a richly varied whole by the church fathers who were the successors of the Greek philosophers. But the process of welding them into one had already begun in the later Hebrew prophets when they changed the emphasis of prophecy from the worship of a tribal god to the spiritual regeneration of the individual. When mercy and loving-kindness were proclaimed to be the attributes of the Deity, religion passed from the crude background of prim-itive life into the field of ethics.

The structure of the thought of these prophets, however, was cast in the mold of faith, for the God who prefers a contrite heart to burnt sacrifices is in much more intimate relationship with the worshiper than one who must be propitiated as though he were only a super-chieftain of the tribe. The keynote of reverence and love sounded clear above the lessening echo of primitive dread and awe. There was as yet no very strong assertion of the doctrine of immortality in the later prophets, intent as they were on reform-ing the lives of those around them; that over-emphasis on the speedy com-ing of the day of judgment which marked a phase of early Christianity was more in line with the religion of the mysteries.

It is significant that the texts of the New Testament which most insist upon and round out the teaching concerning immortality are those of Paul of Tarsus, in whose epistles are found constant references to the religion of Christ as a mystery, not in the sense of something one fails to understand,

135

but in the narrower sense of "mysteries" familiar to him and to the Christian converts in the cities to which he wrote. It is chiefly a matter of emphasis, but the contrast between the treatment of the after life by Paul with that of Jesus should not pass unnoticed. The calm, quiet insistence that the Kingdom of God is within us, while surpassing the prophets in spirituality and boldness, is nevertheless in the line of their precepts and the fulfillment of them. Their distinctive contribution had been to make the cultivation of the inner life the very essence of religion. But nowhere was this so applied to the homely affairs of daily life as in the teachings of Jesus.

It is true that all the great religious teachers have been moral leaders as well, but nowhere else was there such a revolutionary turning away from ceremonial to upright living. In most religions the favor of the divinity is sought chiefly by ceremonies that lie apart from the daily conduct of life. Sacrifice, the culmination of worship, was so much a thing apart that only the priests knew how to conduct it. In the later prophets and especially in the teachings of Jesus, this sacerdotalism, instead of being the heart of religion, tended to become an impediment to its full realization. Holiness was to be found by the way of the prophet and the mystic rather than by that of the priest, in the effort to live a "godly" life instead of simply participating in religious ceremonies. This implies a new conception of holiness, which originally meant the possession of a supernatural quality as over against purely human attributes. In the early times, even as applied to Yahweh, it was a negative rather than a positive conception, emphasizing the separation of divinity from normal things. Although this conception of holiness still continued, from now on it was a quality of the divinity which was to be attainable by perfection of the inner life and not by mere compliance with ritual.

This was the culmination of that progress in enlightenment which had been achieved slowly and partially by the prophets of the Old Testament. With penetrating insight it denounced the persistent traces of the primitive taboo of religion which continued to becloud even "the law of Moses," by treating the texts almost like magic formulae, the observations of which would have the same kind of automatic effect on the observer as in the cults of India. The protests of the prophets against this persistent aspect of early Judaism reached revolutionary power in the denunciation of the "scribes and Pharisees" by Jesus, not only because of the fearless vigor and directness of his denunciation, but also because of the clear and simple doctrine which he offered in place of theirs. For, if worship consists in the imitation of the loving kindness of God rather than in the effort to propitiate him by the strict compliance with priestly prescriptions, a way to escape from the enslavement of the taboo has been found within religion itself.

Stated in these terms, the teaching of Jesus was simplicity itself, but, as the succeeding centuries have all too clearly shown, the form of worship which consisted in imitating God's loving kindness proved to be too difficult to apply without the stimulus of formal worship which externally had many points of resemblance with the ritual of prehistoric superstitions. That is not to say that the forms of worship which Christianity adopted were necessarily the intrusion of elements foreign to the mind of Jesus, for it must not be forgotten that while he denounced the externalism of the Pharisees, as for example in his open violation of the laws of the Sabbath and in mingling with publicans and sinners, he nevertheless attended the synagogue and worshipped in the temple. His attack on taboo was therefore the opposite of that of the Greeks. Whereas they approached the problem as skeptics who ultimately came to deny the very existence of the gods, his attack on superstition was based on a stronger, not a weaker, sense of religion as an immanent element of life itself.

It is a striking fact that the apostle who most clearly appreciated the fact that a new religion had been created by the life and teachings of Jesus was the one who had never known him personally and who first came in contact with his followers as their persecutor, Paul the Mystic. After his conversion on the road to Damascus, he did not go up to Jerusalem to learn about the life of Jesus from his intimate associates who were still there, but sought the meaning of that life by meditation and prayer in the desert. The method of approach to the understanding of Jesus was not by listening to those who had so often misunderstood him in their daily contact with him but by way of faith in the divinity of Jesus and the efficacy of the crucifixion to serve as the culmination of the long history of sacrifice. That history was now closed by the slaying of the Son of God himself, but a wholly new chapter was begun by the ceremonial repetition of the Last Supper with its sacrificial ritual in the solemn formula "This bread is my body which is broken for you . . . This cup is the new testament in my blood . . ."

Paul knew only too well the resemblance which this ceremony bore to those of the mysteries, especially of Mithra, in which the devotee became one with the divinity through a similar sacrament. He therefore had to draw the line with the utmost firmness between these ceremonies and those of the Christians. Although the religions of the mysteries had ceremonies resembling those of the Christian sacrament, the new religion was not a part of them but wholly separate and unique. The admonition to the Corinthians, "Ye cannot drink the cup of the Lord and the cup of devils. Ye cannot be partakers of the Lord's table and of the tables of devils." (I Cor. 10:21) was implicit not only in all of Paul's other writings but in the rest of the literature of the early Church.

It is clear from Paul's description that the church at Corinth, that most cosmopolitan, commercial city of Greece, had taken on the character of a "mystery." From the evidence which he supplies, its meetings even bore some resemblance to those of the orgiastic cult of Dionysos. Nothing could be farther removed from the temper and outlook of the Sermon on the Mount, but Paul's admonitions were not based on a reference to the teaching of Jesus but on the homely everyday virtue of common sense. The Christians were not to allow themselves to become over-excited to the point of annoying their fellow-worshipers, for that would be a sign of self-indulgence contrary to the spirit of Christian charity. It was this practical need of correcting the extravagances of the Corinthians which led Paul to write that noble passage in praise of charity which, in its elevation and warmth of spirit, outrivals even the Psalms, culminating in a phrase of benediction: "And now abideth faith, hope, charity, these three; but the greatest of these is charity."

It is well to be reminded that it was Paul who wrote these words for, in spite of the glorification of charity as the chief of the Christian virtues, the emphasis in the Pauline doctrine in principally on faith. The reason for this is clear. It was only by faith that the Church could be kept linked with its founder. Without it, even the memorial ceremonies would, in time, have lost their meaning. On the other hand, by means of it the worshipper could feel the immanence of Christ, not only in ceremonies but in his whole life. This is that doctrine of the justification by faith which was to play so large a part in the history of the Catholic Church and ultimately to furnish the basis for Luther's revolt from it. To Paul, faith was an instrument by which Christianity could keep its course clear from both Jewish and pagan cult. Many passages could be cited to illustrate Paul's reliance on faith as the safeguard of the new religion. But we have already seen that it is a double-edged sword; it and it alone could ensure the purity of Christian teaching, but by this very fact it also held all the possibilities of intolerance.

Intolerance indeed, was the outstanding characteristic of Christianity in contrast with the other cults of the Roman world. It was on that account more than any other that it was persecuted — because it refused to accept the emperors as even quasi-divine, which was the test of patriotism or treason. In the realm of faith there can be no compromise. For those who "put on the whole armour of God" to "wrestle against princes, powers and rulers of the darkness of this world," their feet may be "shod with the preparation of the gospel of peace" but they must be armed with "the helmet of salvation and the sword of the spirit." It was inevitable, therefore, that tests of orthodoxy should develop even within the Church, and this along with the performance of the cult called forth, before a century had passed, a whole new organization for the officership of the churches, consisting of bishops, priests, deacons and other helpers, in short, a clergy.

These local leaders of the churches belong, however, to the second phase of the history of Christianity. The first phase was that of ardent spirituality, mirrored in the writings of the apostles who, for the most part, travelled from city to city as missionaries rather than settling down to govern a community. The meeting of the disciples and the adherents of Jesus, which took place at Jerusalem at the feast of the Pentecost fifty days after Easter, came to be looked on as the very birthday of the Church, but it was singularly unlike the reverent ritual of the worship of later days. "Suddenly there came a sound from heaven as of a rushing mighty wind, and it filled all the house where they were sitting. And there appeared unto them cloven tongues like as of fire, and it sat upon each of them. And they were all filled with the Holy Ghost, and began to speak with other tongues, as the Spirit gave them utterance."

138

It is hardly too much to say that Christianity in this earliest phase, began as a religion of the Holy Spirit rather than of the person of Jesus. It was not wholly clear to many of the worshippers whether the spirit was the spirit of Jesus or a third person in the Trinity. The heresies which long divided the church on the question of the trinity had their root in the earliest days. It was but natural that the disciples of Jesus, suddenly bereft of his presence, should recall with growing clearness of memory the promise which then seemed to be fulfilled, that his leadership would not cease with his death but would continue as a comforter and guide. It was, however, also natural that the emotional intensity of this concentration upon evidences of the immediate presence of the Divinity should result in such disorders as in the church at Corinth. Fortunately for the new religion, there was not only a Paul to correct the Corinthians but a Peter to give direction to the meeting at Pentecost.

There are few texts in the history of the origins of institutions more instructive than this second chapter of the Acts of the Apostles, which records, on such evidence as the writer was later to discover, the way in which Peter explained the "gift of tongues" as a fulfillment of the Jewish prophecies and began the process of institutionalizing what might have remained mere religiosity by inducing all present to accept the solemn and sober rite of baptism by which they were initiated into a new organization, that of the Church. In this way the company of believers acquired permanence; and as they came together, not on the Jewish Sabbath, but on the first day of the week which, whether because it had been the day of the sun god Mithra, or in spite of it, became "The Lord's Day," they found in the repetition of the Last Supper a constant link with the historic Jesus, as the drama of his sacrificial death was recalled to them in the sacrament of the Eucharist and the sacrifice of the mass. This transformation from the intense spirituality of a religion of the Holy Spirit to a religion of Christ took place under circumstances too obscure for history to have left an adequate record. But as time passed and the age of the apostles had given place to that of priests and bishops, the structure of the Catholic Church began to emerge, even during the era of persecution, as a vast repository of religious power strong enough to challenge the might of the Roman Empire.

Before we turn to the Church of history, however, there is one aspect of the religion of the spirit which is of special interest in the history of thought. For, in the minds of the more philosophical of the disciples of Jesus, the spirit was identified with the *Logos* of Greek philosophy. At first it would seem as though there were no connection between Plato or Aristotle and that mystic phrase at the opening of the Fourth Gospel, "In the beginning was the Word, and the Word was with God, and the Word was God," but this was after all, only the Neo-Platonic transformation of the concept of Divine reason as the basis of natural law which we have already seen to be the chief gift of Greek philosophy to the law of Rome. Inherited in part from the earlier supernaturalism of the Egyptians, Babylonians and Hebrews, Neo-Platonism was a mystic development of Platonic idealism making religion out of philosophy by way of the mysteries. The writer of the Fourth Gospel had evidently studied in its schools, whether at Alexandria or elsewhere is not known. But instead of directing Christian thinking away from its foundations into the Neo-Platonic mold, he used its highest concept, that of the spoken mind of God as the creative element in the universe, to furnish the universal setting for a religion which otherwise might seem to the Gentiles to smack too much of its Jewish origins. Again, as in the case of Paul and Peter noted above, the apostolic tradition keeps the teachings of the Church clear of the vagaries of contemporary thought, this time in the field of philosophy.

The Early Churches

Meanwhile, the structure of the Church had begun to take on its historic form of local bodies, each presided over by its clergy and linked to the others by both formal and informal ties. The more important of these churches looked back to the foundation by one or more of the apostles; others had been established by "evangelists" who were the associates and successors of the apostles but lacked the sanction of that intimate association with Jesus which all the apostles but Paul had shared. The leader of the local assembly (*ecclesia*) was the elder, presbyter or priest, using the Greek term, who may not have been the oldest in years but one of the first among the converts. The choice of this title is not without interest, because it was not associated in either Greek or Jewish history with the traditional sacred office of the priesthood. The elder was an official in the synagogue, not in the temple, which means that the Christian priesthood was that of a new and purely Christian office.

As membership grew, however, this more or less patriarchal beginning of the clergy gave way to a more functional one, as in the history of the secular communities which we have been tracing. An overseer, the bishop (*episcopos*), was needed to look after the growing details of business and administer not only the affairs of the Church but of the social and moral life of its members. Such officials were already in existence in the later years of the apostolic age, as is shown by the references to them in the New Testament. But their prerogatives as rulers over presbyters as well as laymen, which began to development even under the stress of persecution, had become so necessary and so important by the fourth century that, when the church received its freedom and Christianity became the established religion of the empire, the authority of the bishops over church members was recognized as parallel to that of the secular magistracy. There is no more interesting page in the history of politics than the way in which the secularizing process which we have been tracing throughout both Greek and Roman history was thus to a certain extent undone. The Christian hierarchy received a recognition that supplemented the secular realm and partially superseded it. It was not only the bishop of Rome who came to be recognized as possessing qualifications lacking in the secular realm, but the patriarchs and bishops of the other apostolic churches and even to a lesser extent the whole Christian clergy.

The respect paid to them by the people in the cities in which they lived was, in the first instance, the tribute paid to the moral leaders of the community, a respect for character as well as for office. Therefore, as the local civil administration progressively lost its vitality under the rigid bureaucratic rule of the later Empire, the formal recognition of the place of the clergy as partners in authority with the imperial officials was not a revival of the crude sacerdotalism of the past; the church was saved from that by the character of its religion. Even in the most degenerate days of Christendom, the constant reminder of the virtues of charity and the admonition to imitate the life of Jesus made the Church the embodiment of the social conscience and it was not only an asylum for the oppressed but also a citadel for justice.

It would be wrong, however, to trace the development of the Church in the Roman world wholly from the standpoint of its administration and relation to the secular power. The contemporary literature of the Church paid relatively little attention to its business affairs, although this occupied so much of the attention of the clergy and even made of the subordinate office of deacon or helper, a kind of business manager both for the administration of alms giving to the poor and for the upkeep of the worship. There is still less historical record of the way in which the office of bishop interplayed with that of secular rulers. The bishops, as a class, did not do much writing, at least of the kind that has been preserved in the literature of the Church. Good administrators are of too practical a bent to devote their lives to studying and writing. There was also another reason for the inadequacy of the records of the Church; the central ceremonies of worship, the sacraments, had become a matter of sacred doctrine, the "discipline of the secret," as it was called. There had been ample reason for this during the period of the persecutions, both for the sake of safety and also to prevent contamination with pagan ceremonials, but the effect was to strengthen immeasurably the control of the clergy over their congregations through their control of the sacraments.

It is not too much to say that the sacramental system is the basis of Catholicism, through the teaching that the grace of God, that is to say, the very power of the Divinity, can be conveyed to the worshiper through rites which only the priesthood can perform. The outward resemblance of some of these ceremonies to those of the pagan cults and even of primitive magic presented the greatest danger in that it made the acceptance of the worship by converts all the more easy and therefore tended to bring within the Church a pagan attitude of mind. The danger which Paul foresaw, that the churches of his day might compromise with quasi-magical practices, was a constant preoccupation of the Church Fathers. Their method, however, was indirect. Instead of multiplying treatises upon the administration of the sacraments — of which there are relatively few — they concentrated on theology, thus following the lead of Paul, who was the first of all the great theologians.

It is in this connection that the Church Fathers were the successors of the Greek philosophers; and in some ways they were not inferior to them in capacity for creative thinking. The structure which they built was of bolder design than even the philosophy of Aristotle, and it has had a profounder effect on the thought of the West. But it was the structure of faith, not of free inquiry, for it rested, or claimed to rest, on the highest of all authorities, that of the revealed truth, revealed by God himself. There had been no such deity among the Greeks; the theology of the religion of the Homeric age which corresponds to that of the Old Testament, had been beneath contempt as theology, however pleasing as myth; it was even beneath the contempt of the thoughtful Greeks themselves. The religion of the mysteries was based more on cult than myth.

But Christianity, rooted in its Jewish background, and forced to explain the divinity of the Christ to non-Jewish believers, made an appeal to the mind by argument and conviction of faith — an appeal which has been the chief interest of its intellectual leaders to the present day. Christian orthodoxy has not been a matter of the observation of its rites, but of belief in its doctrine, although in many cases the two tests are inseparable. Therefore, because Christian thought rests on faith, we have come to the all-important question for this survey, namely, to what extent Christian faith aided or impeded human reason as it grappled with the problems of this mysterious world.

The pure secularist has a ready answer and it is entirely negative. For him a religion of faith is an obstacle, not only to freedom of thought, but to reason itself, because for him reason is an instrument for the clarification of the problems of life and the world by what might be called the process of intellectual engineering. But from the standpoint of the historian, reason is more than logic. It is too conscious of the limitations of understanding to be wholly satisfied with its results. Our judgments, therefore, of the part played by faith in the history of Christian thought should take into account the conditions under which it was produced.

It would be a gross historical error, to base our estimates of the contribution of Paul on the attitude of the mind of the scientific world of today. With Paul, faith was an instrument by which he freed himself from that Jewish formalism which had become a superstition. His own experience had led him to a profound conviction that the pathway to the freedom of the spirit, not only for himself but for all mankind, lay in the acceptance of the divinity, sacrificial death and resurrection of Christ — an acceptance which could only come by the avenue of faith. When Paul talked of freedom, therefore, he had in mind the escape from "the yoke of bondage" which "entangled" the minds of those, both Jew and Gentile, who held to superstitious practices and beliefs. Such a faith was not an involved philosophy, for God has "made foolish the wisdom of this world" and "if any man think that he knows anything, he knows nothing yet as he ought to know." (I Cor. 8:2) This would be simple obscurantism if it were not connected with the teaching that charity, that is to say, the love of God and man, is the one perfect guide of life. There is little of the dogmatic theologian in that magnificent disclaimer, "If I speak with the tongues of men and of angels and have not charity, I am become as sounding brass or a tinkling cymbal." The faith which thus subordinates itself to Christian charity is not the enemy of freedom, but, as Paul clearly saw, it is its instrument.

There were those among the Fathers of the Church who appreciated and carried on this conception of a religion of faith which at the same time was a religion of social service. Nowhere was it better summed up than in the phrase of Gregory Nazianzen which became a part of the ritual of the church and from that passed into the prayer book of the English Church. It is the unqualified statement that "the service of Jesus is perfect freedom." The paradox which finds freedom in service is one that has been too little understood in the history of freedom itself. As we shall see, the other concept of freedom as escape from responsibility, invaded the church to a very dangerous degree. Had the theologians rested content with fundamentals such as this, there would have been little foundation for the charge that their influence was toward the enslavement rather than the liberation of the mind. But they had to meet the attack of pagan scholars who challenged both Jewish history and the evidences of Christianity. They were therefore led to build up a whole system of thought which linked the governance of God under the old dispensation with that of the new.

We cannot pause here to examine how this was done chiefly by explaining the texts of the Old Testament, not in a literal, but in a figurative sense. The result produced by the ingenious, scholarly Origen was a conception of the whole world's history in terms of a single plan like that of a divine empire. By the subtle analysis of text boldly transferred from narrative to allegory, theology was rescued from the dizzy maze of Neo-Platonism and carried over into the field of history. Fortunately, the historian was at hand to give this grandiose conception more definite form at the very moment when the Church celebrated its imperial triumph over Constantine. Eusebius, Constane's biographer, not only pieced together, by laborious research, documentary evidence of the history of the Church in his Ecclesiastical History, but traced its antecedents all the way back to creation by comparative study of chronology. The *Chronicle*, in which these mileposts were set, was destined to fix the mathematics of Western history to our day. None of the "apologies" written in justification of Christian teaching against the pagan cities, could surpass this proof of the mathematical perfection of God's plan, the final creation of which was the Christian Church.[1]

Augustine's City of God

It would be hard to overestimate the importance of this contribution of scholarship to theology, for it saved it from being lost in the subtleties of speculation by bringing into it the substance of human experience as recorded in history. Nevertheless, it was not the Greek scholars but a bishop

[1] For fuller treatment, see my *History of History*. Volume I, Chapter XXVI, XXVII and XXVIII. (New York: Columbia University Press, 1939).

of the Roman West, Augustine, who, at the very time that Rome was falling, in the early fifth century, described with prophetic vision, the structure of the spiritual rule which he believed would replace it, that of the City of God. The way to blend dogma and ecclesiasticism had already been indicated by his predecessors, but it was left for the greatest of the Latin fathers to shape these materials into a sacred edifice of doctrine so magnificent in proportion and so strongly defended against the profane world of antique culture in which it was set as to secure it against all other interests in the antique world in succeeding centuries. The rejection of paganism is so complete as to cover not only religion, and politics, but even science and art. The attack on everything outside the range of Christianity is more thoroughgoing and ruthless in the fields of thought than that of the Goths and Vandals in the material destruction of Roman cities. There could be no greater contrast than that between the narrow dogmatism of Augustine and the generous eclecticism of his former master, Cicero. It would never have occurred to Augustine to have used Virgil as a guide in the *Divina Comedia*.

The "earthly state" or city of this world, was the work of the devil and the embodiment of sin. This doctrine is carried to its extremist form in the denial of the legitimacy of the whole political development of the antique world which we have been tracing. The tables are completely turned on Aristotle, and political organization is presented as a violation of the law of nature instead of its fulfillment. But things which have a sinful origin develop beyond their original purpose and so, in the effort to secure justice, even the "earthly state" can acquire a moral purpose and character. This, according to Augustine, was a condition as yet unattained in the Roman world, but by the grace of God the forces of justice could make the transformation complete so that the *City of God* which hitherto had been the very opposite of the city of this world would ultimately govern the whole world. But this would not mean that all the rights of citizenship in it would be shared by everyone. On the contrary, some were predestined to damnation and only a fraction of humanity would be elected to the eternal enjoyment of heaven after the earthly world had passed away.

This is not the place to discuss the validity of Augustine's theology. We are interested here only in its effect on the history of the West. From that point of view, however, although not from that of his readers throughout succeeding centuries, his depiction of *The City of God* was marred by his refusal to follow the best traditions of pagan thought even in the popular literary form in which it had been stated by Cicero, whose guidance he otherwise had found so helpful. Instead of turning away from antique mythology to abstract conceptions of general law, he traced the conflict between paganism and Christianity in terms of personal conflict between the hosts of Hell and those of Heaven. So vivid is this picture of the devils as the cause of disasters and calamities that it is almost as if a Christian Livy were writing the origins of the Christian Republic. In both cases the pagan gods are living realities. Only the orthodoxy has changed and the religious rites and services which Livy regarded with religious piety have become impious and nefarious influences. The conception of a divine order of the world which gives the architectural form to Augustine's conception is so haunted by these diabolic presences of the pagan past as to obscure the grandeur and nobility of its design.

From this angle the *City of God* might almost be termed an encyclopaedia of superstition. Its human interest was heightened by the drama of these supernatural personalities. Had Augustine translated these powers into the abstractions of impersonal law, it is doubtful if his book would have had anything like the influence which it was to exercise on his own and subsequent times. The persistence of primitive belief in miracle, which created a new mythology around the lives of the saints and the defenders of Christianity, was not beyond the comprehension of those who modeled their sermons on the crudities of what Harnack, the great historian of Christianity, has called "Christianity of the second degree." Nevertheless, in intellectual grasp, the *City of God* fell short of the reach of Greek philosophy. Both Greek and Christian thinkers regarded the law of nature as a law of God; but the Greeks studied the world of phenomena — including man — while the Christians turned to the primal cause in the study of God himself. This difference in the direction of investigation involved a fundamental difference in method, for the nature of God was studied in "revealed truth" while that of phenomena called for observation and experiment. In judging the *City of God*, therefore, we are again brought face to face with the difference between the scientific method widening the field of knowledge tentatively but with unhampered freedom and the theological method that rests on authority.

Gregory the Great

With Augustine, we take leave of the great Church Fathers. Already the framework of the empire was breaking up in his day and with it the framework of constructive thinking. It was not long until the high discourse of the great days of antiquity gave way to a recrudescence of barbarism which reached even to the heart of the decadent empire. The demonology which found its place in the pages of the *City of God* turned out to have a vitality which defied denunciation and brought superstition within the confines of the Church itself. With the extinction of learning, civilization sank to a lower level than it had held for centuries, and it was inevitable that the Church should share fully in this catastrophe because uncultured minds could not understand or had no interest in a philosophical theology. What they demanded was a personal religion stated in terms of their own experience. This meant that it had to be increasingly a miraculous religion, because miracle, that is to say, the direct intervention of God in the affairs of man or nature, was the one clear sign to them of the presence of the supernatural. In this way a miraculous universe took the place of that of a divine order which had conceived of nature as the mirror of the mind of God.

Natural law gave way to the anarchy of miraculous interference by devils and angels and a whole set of presences so pervading the world as to haunt all but the commonplace activities of life. This was not Christianity as the Fathers of the Church conceived it; but it was the Christianity most widely accepted throughout the dark age.

By the latter half of the sixth century, this trend of Christianity backward to the most primitive forms of belief had so enveloped the Church that the greatest Pope of the period, Gregory I, became the link between the Graeco-Roman and the Romano-Germanic types of Christianity, as these two phases of its history have been termed. Although born into one of the proudest of Roman families and given the best education to be had at the time, this statesman in the See of Peter shared to the full what might perhaps be called the religion of the vernacular.

Augustine had been an intellectual leader, appealing to minds of the nobler sort; but Gregory, in spite of his aristocratic origin, had a more homely sense of the outlook of the common man. A great preacher, he invoked the aid of saints and angels and all the host of heaven on behalf of the Church and its members. Gregory's chief interest was the same as Paul's, and for that matter the same as that of all the other founders of the Church: the assurance of salvation. But it was no longer to be achieved through "justification by faith"; it could not be wholly assured except through the performance of rites which bore external resemblance to those of magic. There could be no greater index of the decline of Christian thought than the way in which this close student of Augustine had left the uplands of theology for the borderlands of superstition, in order to keep Christian teaching within the reach of his contemporaries; but it was also an index of the general decline of culture in the Western world. The Germanic nations which had overrun the empire were only partly civilized and it was Gregory himself whose missionary effort reached out, not only to the heathen English but widely throughout all western Europe, in a progress in the faith which was constantly aided by miracle.

It was not these missionary exploits alone, nor the successful administration of the See at Rome which secured for Gregory his unique place in Western history as the greatest of the Popes for a thousand years. It was fully as much the simplicity and — let us be frank — credulity, of his teaching. For the schoolmasters of medieval Europe were the preachers whose sermons furnished almost the only avenue of knowledge which the ordinary person had open to him; and there was no other source in all the literature of the Church that was so plundered by the sermon makers as the writings of Gregory. In this way Christianity had come down to the people, but it had also brought them part way up to it. For if, from our point of view, Gregory compromised with superstition, it must not be forgotten that he ennobled worship through the solemnity and beauty of music, which, as all the great religions have discovered, can elevate the lives of men fully as much as meditation or philosophy. Finally, in Gregory the moral force of the monastic movement reached to the head of the secular clergy. He was the first of the monks to become a Pope.

Persecuted and Persecutors

There is no more subtle distortion of history than that due to the strong convictions of good men. We have already seen this in the attitude of Augustine toward the pagan world. An attitude which was in reality quite unfair in its judgments on those pioneers of Western civilization to whose experiments in politics we owe so much, not to mention the contribution in the higher realms of thought. This distorted perspective of history lasted until the Renaissance, when the balances were swung too far in the other direction. In the age of the Church Fathers, the propaganda of a church militant seemed justified by the supreme issue at stake, which was the establishment of the City of God on earth. It was inevitable, therefore, that the first three centuries of the Christian era, those in which the Church was fighting with the "powers of darkness," should be regarded as a heroic age in which multitudes of Christians suffered persecution at the hands of ruthless oppressors.

While it is true that there were both sporadic and general persecutions, the terrors of which were far-reaching, it is no derogation of the splendor of spirit of the noble army of martyrs for historians to point out, as they have done in recent years, that in the eyes of the pagans it was the Christians who were intolerant in their refusal to give to Caesar what the State regarded as his due, burn incense to his statue as a recognition of his divinity. They were willing to pray for, but not to, him. For them any such compromise with polytheism was a surrender to the devil, involving the deadliest sin, the denial of Christ. Monotheism, if devoutly believed in, cannot be tolerant of the worship of other gods; and the Jewish background of Christianity with its description of Jehovah as a jealous god lost nothing of its sternness in what appeared to many pagans as a new and more zealous cult of the Jews.

To the non-Christian world, there was something anti-social in Christian intolerance. From the earliest times, as we have repeatedly seen, its pantheon had been open to other divinities. One need only recall Paul's visit to Athens, where he found the inscription "to the unknown God," a typical instance of religious syncretism. The history of religion has no more generous mood to record than that expressed in the prayer to Isis in the *Metamorphoses* of Apuleius, in which the Egyptian Goddess, who was worshiped in the temples of the Nile, is identified with the Greek Ceres of the Eleusinian Mysteries, "the original and motherly nurse of all fruitful things on earth, Venus, the Goddess of Love, and horrible Persephone," the protectress from the ghosts of the underworld, all of them manifestations of the divine majesty of the Queen of Heaven.

It was not within the spirit of such open-minded paganism to persecute anyone for his beliefs. But to the authorities in Rome the Christians seemed to be disloyal citizens as well as trouble makers. The refusal to acknowledge the divinity of the emperor was treasonable, and if persisted in brought the penalty of death. Individual cases multiplied with the steady increase of converts, and the result was a head-on-collision, not so much between two systems of religion, as between the established order and a revolutionary cult. Twice only, under Decius (230-251) and under Diocletian (303 ff.) did this test of strength between the unyielding temper of the Christians and the government reach the dimensions of a general, unrelenting persecution. The other persecutions, such as those under Nero, were for the most part either local or partial. While terrible enough, they must be measured against the other state crimes of an age that built coliseums in every city to allow the populace to witness the murder of countless victims. Mob violence, or efforts to placate it, like that of Pilate, were responsible for most of the pagan atrocities.

It is possible that the very innocence of Christianity, its unworldliness, its belief in a speedy end to all earthly things, made it more suspect to a world held together by military power and believing in its eternal destiny, than if the Gospel had been a *Koran* calling for the crusading spirit of Islam. The Romans would have known what to do with such a militant religion; they would probably have made it their military cult, as they did with Mithra. Such speculations, in any case, fit in with the fact that the first steps taken to end the persecutions were more in keeping with pagan than with Christian tradition. From his death bed in 311, the Emperor Galerius issued a proclamation of toleration which was followed in 313 by the most famous of all such grants, the Edict of Milan of the Emperors Constantine and Licinius, giving full freedom to all religions, including Christianity, which thereupon became a recognized legal religion for the empire. The clergy, who thus acquired official status, were naturally intent upon using their advantage to the full; but Constantine, although he presided at the first officially recognized Council of the Church, that of Nicea in 325, still remained the head of the other cults as well and he postponed baptism until the approach of his death in 337.

In spite of the fact that an unbaptized emperor presided over the Council of Nicea, it was one of the landmarks in the history of Christianity and, therefore, in the history of freedom. In it Catholicism took over the sovereignty of the City of God, surrounding it with a wall of creed as a defense against all attacks from either pagans or heretics. Of these two enemies of the Catholic faith, the assembled theologians showed themselves most concerned with heretics, leaving the opposition of the pagans largely to the maintenance of peace under the emperor. But the heretics were doubly feared because they had always found ways of infiltrating within the church, therefore each member of the church must take the test of loyalty in a creed to be recited as an integral part of Christian worship. In the pre-Nicene period the heretics were consistently and vehemently denounced, but there was no authority to impose penalties against them. From the Nicene period on, heresy became a legal fact and the heretics, therefore, could be legally punished. This process, however, did not develop as an imperial policy until toward the close of the fourth century when, in 380, the Catholic Church was recognized by the Emperor Theodosius the Great in terms which showed that the long religious revolution of the Roman Empire was officially ended.

Although much of paganism lasted on in popular cult and belief, it had lost its vitality, and the only vigorous variants from Catholicism were to be found in a few notable heresies, chief of which were the persistence of Arianism and Manichaeanism in certain sections of the West. It was to suppress these non-Catholic trends that Theodosius, in the name of the three emperors (himself, Gratian and Valentinian)[2] gave the full sanction of imperial authority to Catholic orthodoxy in the edict which he issued in 380, soon after his baptism. This document marks one of the most decisive events in the history of freedom, and the text is sufficiently short to be quoted in full:

We, the three emperors, will that all our subjects steadfastly adhere to the religion which was taught by St. Peter to the Romans, which has been faithfully preserved by tradition, and which is now professed by the pontiff Damasus of Rome, and Peter, Bishop of Alexandria, a man of apostolic holiness. According to the institution of the Apostles, and the doctrine of the Gospel, let us believe in the one Godhead of the Father, the Son, and the Holy Ghost of equal majesty in the Holy Trinity. We order that the adherents of this faith be called *Catholic Christians;* we brand all the senseless followers of the other religions with the infamous name of *heretics,* and forbid their conventicles assuming the name of churches. Besides the condemnation of divine justice, they must expect the heavy penalties which our authority, guided by heavenly wisdom, shall think proper to inflict.

Thus, while the official religion of the State became that of the Nicene creed, the Catholic Church and the Papacy were identified, and from now on what might be called the Church of Rome took over both functions and offices from the imperial organization to which it was to be in no small measure the inheritor.[3] A *Pontifex Maximus* had been established in the West.

It is striking that in the edict prescribing Catholicism "for all the nations," Theodosius said nothing about the discarded religion, paganism. This was left for a series of edicts in the years which followed, closing the temples, confiscating their property and abolishing the privileges of the priests. The temples themselves, the richest monuments of antique architecture and the statues of the gods, the pride of antique art, were objects of concern to some of the emperors, but were left by others to the destructive violence of mobs, often led by monks or local bishops, like St. Martin of Tours in Gaul. Although the imperial authorities were responsible for the failure to check excesses, the fact remains that the overthrow of paganism was largely a popular movement.

After a decade of this revolutionary history, however, Theodosius struck the final blow by his last edict, that of 388 A.D., which made the acts of sacrificing and divination high treason, with death as its penalty. There were to be no exceptions to this supreme law, which applied to all subjects

[2] Theodosius could speak in the name of the two other emperors because Gratian at that time was twenty-one years old, and Valentinian II was ten.

[3] It is impossible in this short sketch to trace the rise of the Papacy. For a complete collection of the documents bearing upon the opening centuries of its history, in the English translation, see Louise R. Loomis and James T. Shotwell, *The See of Peter* (New York: Columbia University Press, 1927).

of the emperor, "whether magistrates or private citizens, however exalted or however humble may be their rank and condition." For less serious ceremonies there were to be lesser penalties, such as fines or conscription of property.

From the text of this decree it would seem that there was some doubt in the imperial mind as to its actual enforcement throughout the empire. That it was more or less of a dead letter is further indicated by subsequent legislation and its incorporation in the sixteenth book of the Code of Theodosius II (438 A.D.), repeating the previous edicts. But we know enough of the social history of the fourth and fifth centuries to realize with what tenacity pagans, in the upper classes as well as among the poor, clung to their ceremonies. The college of pontiffs, membership in which had been one of the greatest honors to which distinguished Romans could aspire, was dissolved under Gratian about 375 A.D., but the statue and altar of victory, at which the senators were sworn, and to which solemn offerings of wine and incense were made at the opening of public sessions, was not removed until over a decade later. Even the statues of the gods remained, along with some four hundred temples or shrines throughout the city. Finally, in 394 A.D., the Senate, though still divided in membership between pagans and Christians, in a session presided over by the emperor, formally condemned the worship of Jupiter and accepted Christianity as the religion of Rome and the empire. But it was not by the act of either emperor or senate that Christianity triumphed. It was by the conversion of the people themselves who showed the zeal of proselytes in the destruction of temples. Christianity won its greatest fight by the surrender of the enemy.

The conclusion to be drawn from this is interesting. Evidently paganism continued to survive in spite of legislation against it, not only because of growing weakness — even anarchy — in the government, but also by reason of its very lack of coherent unitary organization and creed. It had always been a miscellany and, therefore, tolerant of many cults. The transfer of loyalty from one god to another made it adjustable to circumstances, and it had the strength of immemorial antiquity behind it. So, while it endured some persecutions, it passed away with less suffering than in any other religious revolution of this magnitude. Some parts of it, indeed, were preserved and sanctified for Christian use within the Church itself.

That this great religious revolution took place without a major, empire-wide persecution of the pagans to force their acceptance of Christianity, was not due to any spirit of compromise or toleration on the part of the church. The absence of any such spirit was clearly shown in the persecutions of the heretics, the only opponents of Catholicism whose fanatic zeal seemed truly dangerous. The onus of the edict of Theodosius I, of 380 A.D., referred to above, is entirely directed against heretics, imposing "the severe penalties which our authority, guided by heavenly wisdom, shall think proper to inflict upon them." These penalties were elaborated during the next fifteen years in some fifteen severe edicts against heretical ministers, assemblages and persons, adding to the anathemas of the church a civil brand of infamy, which invited popular insult and injury. There was a death penalty, not only for the Manichaeans, that puritanical religion of Persia which succeeded Mithraism as the competitor of Christianity, but even for such minor violations of orthodoxy as the refusal to accept its date for Easter.

The pathway was open to the inquisition of later centuries by the institution of the office of Inquisitors of the Faith. Yet, says Gibbon, "we are assured that the execution of these penal edicts was seldom enforced; and that the pious emperor appeared less desirous to punish than to reclaim, or terrify, his refractory subjects. The theory of persecution was established by Theodosius, whose justice and piety have been applauded by the saints, but the practice of it, in the fullest sense, was reserved for his rival and colleague, Maximus, the first, among the Christian princes, who shed the blood of his Christian subjects on account of their religious opinions."

The first *cause célèbre* in this history of persecution, based on the law of Theodosius, was that of the Spanish heretic Priscillian, the ascetic, who, with six of his followers, was tortured and burned alive at Trèves, by a sentence of the Praetorian prefect. The case is all the more notable in that it also offered a precedent for the method of the inquisition in charging the heretic with gross immoralities, even when, as with Priscillian, the victims were extreme ascetics. Torture was the key to confession, more often false than true.

Monasticism

By the twelfth century the City of God stood in triumph over the stricken and dying culture of the antique world; a vast literature buttressed its doctrines of orthodoxy, and in the basilicas and cathedrals worshipers were awed by a ritual of magnificence and beauty. But just at the time when this structure of ecclesiasticism was establishing itself with pontifical assurance, there was a movement within it which, for a time, threatened to become a movement of religious anarchy. This was the growth of Christian monasticism, one of the most important movements in the thought and social life of western Europe. In its early phase it had filled the deserts and lonely places of Egypt and Syria with hermits living alone (the word monk comes from the Greek *monos,* meaning alone), and inflicting upon themselves bodily suffering to the last degree of endurance to free the spirit from all worldly entanglements. The doctrine of the *City of God,* which pictured the pleasures of the world as the allurements of Satan, became, in the writings of Augustine's contemporary, Jerome, the justification for a flaming and impassioned appeal to escape from contamination from so foul a thing and to devote one's whole life to uninterrupted worship.

But worship could be of two kinds, the attendance upon the offices of the church or individual meditation and prayer. The monasticism of the hermit life concentrated on meditation and ignored the former and, therefore, had it not been checked it might have become a rival to the clergy. But the religion of the sacraments proved too strong for that of silence and isolation, and the monks began to form communities which, in the dark age which followed, literally saved the western world for Christianity.

The hermit or anchoretic phase of monasticism, with which the movement began, need not delay us here because it never played any large part in the history of Europe. The extreme asceticism which involved self-torture of the body after the manner of Hindu fakirs was too extravagant for the Greco-Roman world to accept, and remained an isolated phenomenon of the Nile Valley and Syria. Even extreme isolation was soon broken down as the monks found that by meeting together they could strengthen each other in their common purpose, which was to escape those entanglements of the world that stood in the way of an entire concentration on the religious life. A compromise was therefore made between solitude and social life by those who found companionship helpful, which left them alone most of the time but brought them together for worship and for meals in common. This brought about the formation of a new class of monks, the Cenobites, or those who live together. The community life thus began. It needed direction and found it in one of the group whom they termed their "father" or abbot, a title which lasted throughout the centuries from the Aramaic term *abba,* "father," used in the earliest days.

But communities of even like-minded men need direction and organization, and this led to codes or "rules" drawn up by a series of monastic lawgivers, Pachomius in Egypt in the early fourth century, Basil in northern Asia Minor at the end of that century, and the greatest of them all, the Italian, Benedict of Nursia, in the second and third decades of the following century. The "rules" of Eastern monasticism need not concern us here, but the life of Benedict was almost a history of Western monasticism in miniature.

Like his disciple, Gregory the Great, who left us the only account we have of Benedict's life, he was born of wealthy parents and was sent to Rome for his education. While still a young man he fled to the wilderness of the Apennines and in a lonely cave spent three years in prayer and meditation. Then disciples flocked around him, drawn by the exceptional austerity of his life, and he formed them into little monasteries with a dozen monks in each, keeping the general direction of them in his own hands. Already the practical Roman mind was asserting itself in the control of a movement which, even in that neighborhood, was becoming unruly. Driven from this first establishment by the jealousy of rival monks, he found on the hilltop of Monte Cassino, halfway between Rome and Naples, a perfect site for a monastery, high enough above the rich farm lowlands to be undisturbed by the workaday world, yet near enough to join it in recognition of the great liberating principle *laborare est orare,* work is a form of prayer. This recognition of the dignity and importance of labor was the greatest single contribution of Western monasticism to European civilization; for, along with the work in the fields, it included that in the scriptorium or writing room, where the literature of the past was preserved. Contrary to widespread misunderstanding, Benedict did not found an order of monks. Each monastic estab-

152

lishment, sometimes with dependencies, was a city state of its own under patriarchal rule of the abbot, whose authority was final. But in order to regularize this government and furnish guidance for the monks themselves, Benedict wrote his Rule which, although not enforceable by the secular power, has been more successful than most codes of law. It furnished the basic principles and much of the detail for all subsequent monastic regulations.

The Benedictine Rule, therefore, cannot be left out of any general survey of the history of government. It must be remembered that at first the monks were laymen from the standpoint of the administration of the sacraments, and that they were drawn from all classes of society. Nevertheless, they were all to be treated without distinction of persons: "A free-born man shall not be preferred to one coming from servitude, unless there be some other reasonable cause." However fine such a provision of the Rule may seem to us, it must have been hard to apply in an age in which such distinctions were an inherent part of secular society. When necessary, however, the abbot was to "mix blandishments with terrors and display the feeling of a severe yet devoted master, . . . rebuking the unruly and the turbulent" but limiting himself to exhortation with "the obedient, the gentle and the patient." With supreme practical sense, Benedict realized that if the monks could be kept busy according to a definite routine, there would be less likelihood of discontent and "murmuring." The Rule therefore prescribed minutely for the life of the monks day by day, throughout the entire year, telling them at what hours they should do this or that, how much time there would be for sleep, for reading, and even for eating.

Yet the routine of the life which the Rule prescribed was so well balanced between worship and work, life in common and by oneself, that the Rule was adopted with practically no modifications wherever the Black Monks of Benedict set up their monasteries. The abbot, although given full authority in the Rule, was to consult the monks on important matters, paying attention to the advice given of even the youngest, "because often it is to a younger person that God reveals what is best." On lesser matters, however, the abbot was to "employ the counsel of the elder members alone." As for the monks, Benedict took for granted that there would be sinners as well as saints among them, and to prevent pride and jealousy, prescribed not only the clothes they should wear (with due regard to the weather) but also their places in church or at table. Mere outward humility was not enough; when guests were greeted with the kiss of peace, a prayer should first be offered "on account of the wiles of the devil." One had to be constantly on one's guard.

With Benedict's Rule, monasticism became an organized force to help preserve the Christian virtues in the midst of the violence that accompanied the decline and fall of the Roman Empire. Based on the three-fold vow of poverty, chastity and obedience, the monastic movement had attempted the supreme paradox of trying to reform the world while withdrawing from it. On the one hand it was a movement of escape from responsibility, on the other hand the assumption of what might be termed a puritanical mode of life with due regard to Christian charity. Poverty meant escape from worry about property, chastity, escape from family ties, and obedience, escape from the sense of individual responsibility for the acts of daily life.

From the religious point of view, monasticism was therefore the most definite attempt of formal Christianity to find freedom under its auspices. In spite of its checkered history, with periods of decline when its ideals were forgotten and its practices debased, it has offered and still offers to the spiritually minded that sense of freedom which comes through sacrifice. For sacrifice exalts the spirit, and humility, by the refusal to assert one's individuality offers the basis of a tranquil life. In short, the meek can inherit the earth because they do not claim it as their inheritance.

If this were the complete summing up of the history of monasticism, it would bring us closer to the theme of this book than anywhere else in ancient or medieval history. But this kind of freedom, this escape from social responsibility was, in spite of all the services it rendered, and they were many and great, an unsocial mode of life, because of its implicit denial of the legitimacy of the two fundamental bases of society — property and parenthood. While monasticism offered for centuries an unparalleled opportunity for retirement from the care of making a livelihood, it demanded a scheme of life which could not be accepted by more than a fraction of humanity and therefore it did not solve the problem of freedom for the common man. Within its own structure, the vow of chastity was maintained, through the flaming zeal of reformers, whenever laxity threatened; but the problem of property was never wholly solved by the devices of corporate ownership. Time and again ascetic leaders, like St. Bernard, sought escape from the allurements of worldly life, but time and again the purpose of such monastic reforms was falsified by gifts of land or money in exchange for prayers or masses for the souls of the benefactors. The monks individually could keep the vow of poverty, but many of them could also share in the life of the wealthiest establishments of the Middle Ages.

The advantage of such a mode of life to those enjoying it and to the countryside in which the monastery flourished, and which flourished because of them, was great enough to prevent any serious questioning within the orders of such a mode of business management until the thirteenth century, when the more extreme followers of St. Francis of Assisi, that teacher of apostolic poverty, refused to accept any trustee, even the pope, as the owner of Franciscan property. Such a doctrine was then recognized as heresy and those monks professing it were burned at the stake. Evidently the monastic movement has to compromise with the world in which it lives, at least to the extent of maintaining itself.

The Church and the Sacraments

The life of Gregory I and the provisions of the Theodosian Code mirror the growth of a state church in the West, officered by a clergy with a hierarchical organization resembling that of the empire itself. As the structure of the empire weakened, the bishops in the principal cities were recognized more and more as successors of the civil authorities. Within the Church, their administration of the sacraments, through the priests, meant to the common man the control of his salvation. This was more important to him than theological disputes over matters of doctrine remote from his limited and troubled horizon. What was all important to him was that the Church held, in the sacraments, the key to eternal life. From the fourth to the twelfth century, the period of the Dark Age, there were no new major controversies over the doctrine of the Church. The system of theology which the Church Fathers had hammered out in the earlier days was again brought into debate by the schoolmen of the thirteenth century, but in the long interval the strength of the church lay less in its system of theology than in its sacramental system.

A sacrament is defined as "the outward and visible sign of an inward and invisible grace." In the early Latin church the term *sacramentum* was used loosely, corresponding to the still more vague Greek word *mysterion* or mystery. In both cases, however, the clue to the meaning lay in the belief, older than history, that material objects could acquire mysterious or sacred (that is, taboo) qualities either by ceremonies or by contact with other objects previously so "sanctified." To understand the basic principles one would have to analyze the vast and varied history of sacrifice (that is, making things sacred). Here it is only necessary to recall the fact that, from the beginning, the Church practiced two outstanding rites, baptism and the Eucharist (or Lord's Supper), which were tests of membership and of salvation. Other ceremonies were regarded as sacraments by different writers from time to time, but it was not until the twelfth century that the Catholic doctrine of seven sacraments took final shape in the writings of Hugo of St. Victor (c.1120) and Peter Lombard (c.1150). They are baptism, confirmation, ordination, the Eucharist, penance, marriage and extreme unction.

It was not the mystic number which fastened this system upon the church, but the fact that from birth to death it met every crisis, and that by the sacrament of penance, which included confession, it gave the clergy control over the laity in the conduct of their daily lives. Only those shriven by the priest after confession could partake of the Eucharist, and those thus excluded from the altar were excluded from salvation in the world to come. By the sacramental system, the priest was armed with weapons which slew the soul. Never was the scene set for theocracy with greater power in the hands of the priesthood, powers that could mean terrors as deep as hell, or rewards of eternal life in the very presence of God.

And yet, when we turn from the potentialities of the medieval Church to the actual history of those ages we see that theoretic criticism of what looks like theocratic tyranny has to be modified by the constant reminder that the secular world never yielded to ecclesiastical compulsion to the extent which seems implied in the doctrinal order of things. The national state was taking shape at that very time, as much in defiance of churchmen as by their help. The process of emancipation from war and anarchy was, on the whole, one of secularization as well; just as it had been in ancient Greece and Rome. And freedom fought its revolutionary fight for the recognition of the rights of the common man against entrenched authority, whether sanctioned by the Church or not. But the reason Europe escaped theocracy was to be found as much within the Christian religion as without it. The teachings of Jesus were as fitting a guide for the secular statesmen as for the ecclesiastic. The mistake that Augustine made was to regard the *civitas terrena,* the city of the world, as something diabolic and the *civitas Dei,* the city of God, as its eternal enemy. The history of civilization, with all its tragedy of suffering and death and its spiritual triumphs of faith and charity, is both the city of man and the city of God. There is no other on earth.

CHAPTER VII

THE FOUNDATIONS OF EUROPE

THE BARBARIAN invasions of the fifth century which broke up the structure of the Roman Empire were no new phenomena. Through all history and beyond it, in the dim, prehistoric past, which archeologists are at last revealing to us, hardy tribesmen from the Russian steppes of ancient Scythia to the forests of Germany and Gaul kept pressing southward in successive migrations. One of the chief reasons for the Persian invasion of Greece was the need of Darius to throw back the movement which threatened Asia Minor from the north. The war with Greece was but a flank attack on the main movement against Scythia. But for a thousand years before the Persians came, these northerners had been penetrating the eastern Mediterranean in repeated waves. The Greeks from beyond Homer's time were northerners, and Homer's warriors fought with iron from the Danube Valley. Similarly, the capture of Rome by the Gauls (390 B.C.) was also merely one of a number of movements from the north, the pressure of which was relieved only in the last days of the Republic by Marius, in his defeat of the Teuton and Helvetian tribes, in 102 B.C., and by Julius Caesar's conquest of Gaul.

Not all of the movements of these northern peoples was directed against Greece and Rome. There were also chronic tribal wars among themselves, so that when history opens, the Gauls, whose origins we can trace back to southern Germany, had made themselves masters of the native population west of the Rhine in the same way their cousins, the Franks, conquered them in the fifth century. Even the inhabitants of Britain, isolated by the sea, were a mixture of peoples from successive conquests.

This reminder of the long history of invasions of which those of the fifth century were the most destructive is necessary as a corrective for one of the greatest mistakes in the understanding of Western history, that which interprets it in terms of race. The conception of the Middle Ages as a period when a new and vigorous race, the Germans, overcame the effete Romans because of their native superiority in physical strength and morale and their undying love of liberty is one of the most misleading myths of history. Physical vigor, it is true, had been preserved by the struggle for existence in the north while it had been weakened in the south from the false economy that offered booty and slaves instead of encouraging native labor, and mercenary troops instead of military discipline. But this is not racial difference. It is cultural, the product of history and circumstances rather than of racial capacity. This is not theory. It could not be otherwise because, owing to the movement of these peoples, there was no "pure" stock except in isolated and, therefore, relatively unimportant cases not reached by those major forces of history that transformed both institutions and man himself.

Unfortunately we do not know much of the history of the peoples north of the Roman Empire. The references to them in the passages of Caesar and Tacitus, to which reference was made in the introduction to this study, were written over two centuries before the fatal fifth century in which they finally overran the empire. In that long interval much had happened beyond the Rhine and the Danube, much that has left almost no written record. But that it was a period of intertribal wars is proven by the fact that the Germans (Teutons, the generic term used by the Romans), now consisted mostly of tribes unknown to Tacitus, the Angles, Jutes and Saxons, the Vandals, Thuringians, Burgundians, Franks and Lombards, while the Goths move to the foreground of their history, both along the frontiers and within them. As these people pressed south and west into the Roman Empire, they also gathered up others on the line of march, as was the case with all nomadic movements, and as they moved and settled in their new homes the invaders intermarried with the conquered. The invasions struck a mortal blow at the old tribal organization through the rise of chieftains and adventurous bands of marauders planting themselves in the little sovereignties that furnished a basis for feudalism.

Naturally, there were differences in the extent to which the tribal structure of the invaders was broken down as they moved in on the collapsing empire. By a strange paradox, some of those who retained their primitive coherence to a surprising degree were the very ones who pushed farthest south and west — the Vandals who reached Africa, the Visigoths and Suabians (Suevi) who settled in Spain, and the Lombards who settled in the rich valley of the Po in northern Italy. On the other hand, the conquests of Gaul and Britain were less in the nature of movements of single tribes than in the mingling of peoples on the march and the absorption of the local population. The Franks furnished Clovis with the necessary war bands so that he could easily overrun the almost unresisting country from the Belgian marshes to the southern river valleys of Gaul. Compared with the existing population there were

157

only a few thousand invaders, perhaps two to five hundred thousand in all, from the lower Danube to the North Sea. The conquest of Britain was a wholly different process; an invasion by sea brought only hardy fighters and their immediate kin.

In spite of the stories of wholesale slaughter of the inhabitants of Britain there was intermarriage with the native stock. The English of today are not the pure Germanic people which historians of the nineteenth century made them out to be. Although there were sections of the country, especially in the north, where the marauding bands were particularly savage and merciless, there were other parts of the country in which the invasions were somewhat in the nature of mere settlement. Throughout all history England has preserved to a surprising degree these local differences in her people; the low-lying hills and the varied aspects of nature have left upon the inhabitants the impress of the centuries in spite of the fact that it was in England that the spirit of nationality found first and fullest expression in the creation of the national state.

This was the nature of the movements of the fifth century, but there were still other tribes farther north who postponed their raids and migrations until a later date although they were originally a part of the same general family of tribes, the Danes and the Norsemen, or Northmen. They had been moving up from the western Baltic into the Danish and Scandinavian peninsulas, where they stayed until, in the eighth century, their seamanship had progressed to the point where the great water barriers between them and other lands were no longer impassable obstacles — not even the Atlantic Ocean. These Norsemen were also known as Vikings, which means "inlet men," probably because they came from the region of the fjords.

The process of mixture among the invaders was especially true in the case of the Huns, the first of the Asiatic horsemen to sweep across southeastern and central Europe from the great plain that stretches, almost without interruption, from the North Sea to the mountains of Central Asia. While the leaders of these hordes were Mongolian horsemen, they were reinforced along their way by the wreckage of defeated tribes, so their incursions lacked the permanence of the more settled Germanic kingdoms.

Europe itself did not produce nomads; the country was too broken up by mountains and rivers and too widely covered with forest, while most of its valleys and open spaces were fertile land. The great plains of northern Asia, on the other hand, are not generally fitted for agriculture. They have temperatures varying from intense heat in summer to intense cold in the winter. Evaporation exceeds the rainfall and the Caspian and the Aral Seas are slowly shrinking. However, the salt steppes to the south make good pasturage in winter, though in summer they dry up, while far to the north there are the grassy steppes, which are covered with deep snow in winter. This combination of circumstances makes for a nomadic population which must be very mobile since it has to cover distances of hundreds of miles every year, back and forth, to feed the stock which provides their diet of milk and cheese.

The nomads have no history like that of settled peoples. Their incursions keep recurring throughout all the history of the East and most of that of the Middle Ages in Europe. They had been a constant menace to the Babylonians, Assyrians and Persians, descending on their cities to ravage and plunder and then disappearing again. But these people had been of Aryan stock, belonging to the white race. The Asiatic nomads who now appear in the story were yellow and mongoloid. Their original home had probably been in the Tarim Basin in the center of Asia, a region of lakes, rivers and swamps with no external drainage, and, in the old days, quite fertile. But the Chinese Empire was slowly gathering strength, and under the great Han Dynasty of the last two centuries before Christ and the first two of the Christian era, not only raised the Great Wall against the plunderings of the nomadic barbarians, but was itself pushing out steadily across eastern Turkestan with the relentlessness which marks the progress of a people, well established at home, in their contact with unsettled barbarians, no matter how savage the latter may be. Under this pressure the nomads spread out through western Turkestan, and by the first century, A.D., were established around the Caspian Sea and, in the north, as far west as the Baltic where a branch of them called Finns had settled.

Just as the Nordic tribes did not vary much from one another, so we have little reason to believe that the successive waves of Mongoloid nomads from the steppes of Asia, whether called Huns, Avars, Bulgars, Magyars, Finns, Lapps, Mongols, Tartars, Khazars, or Turks, differed greatly from one another or from the nomads that still occupy these regions. What made them such formidable enemies was their mastery of the horse, which had originated on the Asiatic steppes and ran wild there in droves. The uncertainties of nomad life, while producing only the lowest forms of political organization, schooled these Asiatic peoples in hardship and made them able to cope with the unexpected, giving them a shrewdness and independence lacking in those whose course of action had been mapped out by long-continued custom.

Their loosely knit tribal organizations were constantly being broken up and reformed. At times certain tribes would band together for a while under some great war chief, called a khan, and then separate after his death. Thus in the fourth and fifth centuries were formed the tribes known as the Huns. Later similar formations, the Avars, Bulgars, and Magyars, entered Europe at different times during the early Middle Ages. One branch of these Asiatic nomads, the Seljuk Turks, swept over Baghdad to the gates of Constantinople in 1087. It was against them that the Crusades were fought. Another branch formed the great Mongol Empires of Genghis Khan and Kublai Khan of the thirteenth and fourteenth centuries which far outranked any other land empire. It stretched from the eastern frontiers of Europe across all Asia to the China Sea. After the inevitable break-up of the Mongol Empire, the various sections were retained for a time under Mongol or Tartar control — the empire of the famous Golden Horde — who kept Russia in subjection during the later Middle Ages, and the Ilkhans in Persia, Mesopotamia and Syria who destroyed the irrigation system of the Tigris-Euphrates and made a desert of one of the oldest garden spots in the world. To another branch of the Mongols belongs the savage Timur (Tamerlane) whose conquests in the fourteenth century swept in a whirlwind of death and destruction from Delhi in northern India to the frontiers of Europe on the Mediterranean.

All these devastating wars lay inside the Moslem world, checking the possibility of stable progress in western Asia; although it should be noted that it was one of Tamerlane's descendants who established the Mogul (Mongol) dynasty in India, which lasted until the eighteenth century, and marked the most splendid and unified regime India had ever seen. Finally, to add one last item to this chronicle of wars, it was during the first onslaught of the Mongols under Genghis Khan that the Ottoman Turks, originally a little band of refugees began their warlike career in Asia Minor, which in the fifteenth century, through the conquest of Constantinople, made them the successors of the Roman Empire in the East.

The destiny of much of Europe, China, India and Mesopotamia was changed by the Asiatic nomads. Though to a great degree savage and destructive, their actions depended largely on their leaders. Like most nomadic peoples they had a contempt and feeling of disgust for the crowded and effeminate life of the city. Some of them probably felt that they were acting in a worthy cause by destroying as much of it as they could. In military matters they were often superior to their more civilized neighbors. The armies of Genghis Khan moved according to a strategy well worked out in advance and based on the findings of a carefully laid system of spies in enemy territory. But the organization of the "empires" they established was designed for little more than the gathering of taxes and tribute.

If they left few positive evidences of their conquests, there were many negative ones. How much they destroyed of flourishing civilizations we can hardly estimate even yet. Their ravages were more terrible than those of the barbarian invaders of the Western world. Not only did such material structures as the irrigation works of Mesopotamia go down before them, but also the promise of a new civilization in Russia.

In between the Teutonic tribes moving eastward from the Baltic in the last days of the Roman Empire, and the Asiatic nomads coming westward, were peoples whom we judge to have been largely Slavic from the persistence of the Slavic tongue in these regions even where they were repeatedly overrun by the invaders.. In the course of events they became very much mixed with the Mongoloid nomads and to some extent with the Germanic tribes. Later in history they emerged as the Russians, the Serbians, the Poles, the Czechs, the Slovaks, and other present day Slavic nationalities.

The Slavs were a "backward" people, not because of any inherent lack of intelligence or talents, but because they lived in a region open to invasion and were the victims of successive raids. From the thirteenth to the fifteenth century the Russians were under the overlordship of the Mongols, and from the fifteenth century to the nineteenth the Balkans, inhabited by Serbs and other Slavs, belonged to the Turks. During this time these Slavic peoples were largely cut off from Europe and overrun by Asiatic invaders of alien race and religion. When the invaders were finally pushed out, the inhabitants found themselves hopelessly far behind their Western neighbors and were living in lands despoiled by Tartar or Turk, where no attention had been paid to developing and maintaining the economic side of life. Thus they were looked down on by their more fortunate neighbors to the west, and feared for the same reason. The retreat of the Tartars and Turks left Europe with as many problems as had arisen from their invasions, and for few of them are there as yet any adequate solutions.

The Invasions of the Fourth and Fifth Centuries

Some time during the first two centuries of the Christian era the Goths had moved down from their homeland on the Baltic and invaded the district north of the Danube, including Dacia, which was finally abandoned to them by the Romans. They were perpetually making raids across the river, and they had also been taken into the Roman legions to fight against their own tribesmen; for it apparently made little difference to the barbarians on which side of a quarrel they were. Like the early Germans and their neighbors, they lived by plunder and chose the side which offered the richest rewards. Settlements of them had even been interspersed throughout the Empire, so that by the fourth century they were no novelty to the Romans, nor were the Romans to them. Nevertheless, until the fourth century, most of them were still north of the Danube and east of the Rhine, which, with the Roman engineering works, provided strong buttresses against their invasion.

But in the fourth century the Huns, or a section of them, either finding the grasses around the Caspian were not sufficient for their stock or for other reasons, suddenly picked up their scanty belongings and, together with neighboring tribes, swept over the plains to the north of the Black Sea and drove in upon the Goths. In terror the latter fled across the Danube, or as many did as had not been overwhelmed by the Huns. They were granted permission to settle on the south bank of the river; but no provision was made for their livelihood, and, joined by Huns who became their allies, they made common cause in raiding. One of the decisive battles of history was fought at Adrianople in 378 not far from Constantinople, in which the Goths were victorious. The city itself, with its prodigious walls and defensive works, remained unconquered, but the Goths and other tribesmen remained for the time within the Balkans, a wedge between the eastern and western parts of the empire.

Then the storm burst in the west. For, so the story runs, Stilicho, the heroic defender of the empire, called in the garrisons from Britain and the Rhine frontier to prevent the Goths from crossing over from the Balkans to Italy. There was nothing left to prevent the Picts and Scots from sweeping down on Britain or the Angles and Saxons from ravaging the towns and villages of the south. The federated (that is Germanic) troops along the Rhine were no match for the invaders, and even before Alaric with his Goths had reached Rome in 410, they were raiding the vineyards of the Moselle and the olive orchards of Acquitaine.

As in Italy, so in Gaul; the populace, having given over their defense to the mercenary troops who filled the Roman legions, could only watch, if their lives were spared, while their towns and villas lent their plunder to the raiders. But this first storm passed as the Vandals and Suabians were lured on by the spoil of Spain or were driven over the Pyrenees by the west Goths, who, following this same urge, left Italy to drive this vanguard of the invaders out of Gaul and then out of Spain itself, forcing them into Africa while they settled in what became, for the next four centuries, Visigothic Spain, until conquered by the Moslems. The Visigothic code of Roman law was long in use throughout the West.

This first great wave of invasion did not entirely blot out the Roman culture of Gaul. Fifteen years after it, the poet Ausonius is again singing of the vine-clad hills of the Moselle and the rich vintage. The noble Apollinaris Sidonius dines with the King Theodoric and is genially interested in his Burgundian neighbors, who have settled in the central eastern part. By the middle of the fifth century, unaided by the shadowy Roman emperors, this mixture of peoples unite to defeat the invading Huns at Chalons. But these are the very years in which the Angles and Saxons blot out Roman Britain, and a new, more barbarous people move into northern Gaul, the Franks. They are almost as different from the Visigoths, who had long been in touch with Mediterranean culture, as the Iroquois from the Norman crusaders. Continually recruited from the forests and swamps of the lower Rhine, they do not cut themselves off from their ancient home and lose themselves in the midst of civilization. They first break what is left of the Roman state north of the Loire and then crowd the Visigoths down further toward Spain. By the year 500, Gaul has become Frankland. Then they too, like all the invaders of the Empire, yield to the new spiritual force that emanated from Rome, and become Catholic Christians.

Even such a brief résumé of the major barbarian invasions during the fifth century indicates in what confusion Europe lived. The barbarians were few in number. They broke down the Roman defenses because the latter were weak and the leadership bad in many cases. There was no popular support for the Roman government. It had caused so many hardships in its later years that there was no longer that sense of patriotism or loyalty which marked the era of the Republic. The path of the barbarians was often not contested. The cities put up the best defense, and the barbarians usually went around them, not having implements for siege warfare.

The barbarians did not set out to destroy the empire. In fact they continually joined in to keep it alive, in their ineffectual way by putting up candidates of their own for emperor. They were just as inclined to fight one another as to fight the Romans and could often be played off against each other, or satisfied by gifts. An Emperor usually held a shadowy court in the west until 476, and a united Empire was revived for a few years under Justinian, when he recaptured Italy and parts of Spain and Roman Africa.

But after his death in 565, these provinces were lost forever to the Byzantine Empire. In the sixth century another Germanic tribe, the Lombards, settled as rulers of Italy.

The Last Invaders

But that was not the end of the invasions. In 570 Mohammed was born in Arabia. Before his death in 632 he had fired his followers with the zeal of fanaticism, intent upon conquering the world for Islam. By 855 they had succeeded in defeating the Byzantine fleet, and for centuries the Mediterranean was dominated by Moslems. Much of the Christian trade was cut off from the south and the coast of the Mediterranean, which had once formed a unit for trading purposes, was thenceforth divided. In 711 the Moslems entered Spain and their advance in this direction was not stopped until they had overrun all the southern lands of the Franks. To the east they had conquered Persia. However, the Arabs, not having had any particular form of organized government before the conquest of this great empire, were unable to hold it together. By the middle of the eighth century it had begun to crumble and form separate units under rival caliphs. It is interesting to speculate on what would have happened if, in their original fervor, the Arabs had attacked the decadent Byzantine Empire with all their force. It seems probable that they could have conquered it and entered Europe through the Balkans and the Danube Valley in the depth of the Dark Age instead of in the fourteenth century. That part of Europe was still suffering from the series of invasions by the Slavs and the Asiatic peoples from north of the Black Sea. It could have offered only a feeble resistance against the onrush of the Moslem armies.

But instead of concentrating on the supreme prize of Byzantium, the Arabs spent the first vigor of their conquest on Persia and northern Africa. By the time they turned seriously to the assault on the Byzantine Empire their strength was insufficient. The eastern empire still stood as a bulwark between the newly forming kingdoms of Europe and the Oriental cultures of Asia Minor. Nevertheless, the strength of Moslem fanaticism was such that it could weld the tribesmen of the desert and Morocco into conquering hordes which swept over Spain into the heart of Gaul to be thrown back only by the hammer blows of Charles Martel at the battle of Tours (732 A.D.). Although Charlemagne's paladins could hold the marches of the Pyrenees, the horn of Roland at Roncevalles echoed for centuries in feudal Europe as a reminder of the power of Islam.

Although the Byzantines could close the door of Europe from Asia Minor, there was no barrier to close the wide gap between the Ural Mountains and the Black Sea through which the Asiatic nomads still kept coming, moving into the region of the Volga and then on into the Hungarian plain. First there were the Avars, driven back from Germany by Charlemagne at the end of the eighth century, and then the Bulgars, who conquered most of the Balkans and became thoroughly mixed with the Slavs, and then, about 900, the

Magyars who moved into the Hungarian plain, where they have been ever since. All of these inroads were accompanied by warfare and plundering.

Meanwhile the Norsemen had begun to go out in every direction in their little dragon ships. They raided the shores of Britain and France, going up the rivers, and along the network of Russian rivers, to the Black Sea, where they threatened the fleet of the Byzantine Empire on several occasions. They formed a kingdom in Russia under Rurik, about 850, around the cities of Novgorod and Kiev, and gave their name to the country, *Russ* being the first Slavic term for a Swede. (The Byzantines called them Varangians and an imperial bodyguard was formed of them.) They also made permanent settlements in Britain, where their raids had the effect of uniting the warring Anglo-Saxon kingdoms under the leadership of Alfred the Great. He finally made a treaty with them in 886 recognizing the Danelaw, as their settlement was called. They settled in Normandy (Northmandy) where they paid nominal allegiance to the Frankish king, though they managed their own affairs at home to their own liking. But before long they lost all sense of their origin and became thoroughly French. It was from Normandy that William the Conqueror conquered England in 1066, taking advantage of internal quarrels to make the last successful invasion of the island to date. And from Normandy there went out adventurers who descended into the Mediterranean and settled in Sicily, from which they made such disastrous raids on the Italian coast that had the Crusades not provided another outlet for their energy, they might have taken Rome.

The conquests resulted in such a complete hodgepodge of peoples throughout Europe as to make still more ridiculous any claim to racial purity. They also, and this is very important for us today, left in their wake islands of peoples with cultures, language or points of view different from those of the people who had settled around them. Some of these human islands have survived in spite of all the pressures of the national states to eliminate from their midst all those who do not readily conform to the speech, thought and habits of living of the majority. These minorities offer a problem which has become increasingly more baffling and troublesome in recent years.

The citizens of the Roman Empire, until the fatal fifth century in which the structure of the world finally crashed under the impact of the invasions, do not seem to have realized that the time was coming when the splendor of the achievements of the antique world would be all but forgotten, as the Roman roads ceased to connect teeming cities of commerce and the wilderness covered again the vineyards of Gaul.

The war system on which that culture rested, after having nourished it with the spoils of alien peoples, had finally destroyed the prosperity of both town and countryside and left them a prey to any wandering bands of marauders who could get past the enfeebled garrisons on the frontiers. Thus the Dark Age came upon Europe not merely as a result of the invasions, but as an inevitable result of the system of government; a system in which the needs of war sapped the resources of the Empire in time of peace, through the continuing cost of the military establishment and ruined the financial structure by a false system of taxation.

There is an ominous warning for us in the fact, already seen in the survey of Roman history, that it was Rome itself which prepared the way for the Dark Age of Europe by the very processes which gained for it the conquest of the Western world. A society built on exploitation cannot last. It may postpone its ultimate collapse for such long centuries as to give it the outward semblance of unshakable strength, but neither the massive structure of the antique world nor the dynamic force of modern science can overcome the effects of the violation of the simplest of all the laws of human association, that which in the language of the Roman law itself would "give to every man his due." This is the fundamental basis of civilized life, a fact more potent than the world has yet realized, in spite of the teachings of philosophers and prophets and the constant admonitions of religion. Nothing is more certain in the world today than that, unless we can escape from the tyranny inherent in both war-and-peace-time exploitation, the Dark Age will come again. There is infinitely more capacity for destruction in scientific weapons today than in the horsemen of Attila. Fortunately, as the history of civilization proves, the ultimate defense is to be found, not so much in armed force as in the growth of the institutions of justice and freedom. Nevertheless, as we look back to those warring centuries of the early Middle Ages, it should bring a sobering sense of the dangers of the present day.

The Early Kingships

There is naturally little to say of the period which stretches from the fifth to the eleventh century except as one digs for the foundations of the institutions of later times. Life was isolated both in time and space; literature and history passed almost out of existence except in a few monasteries and monastic schools, while trade and commerce dwindled to almost nothing even on the shores of the Mediterranean. The darkest age was in the ninth and tenth centuries when the Norsemen raided the settlements of the earlier invaders and the Mohammedans held the trade routes of the Mediterranean. Movable wealth no longer played its vitalizing part in economic life. Cities and towns became villages or were blotted out of existence. Coined money was scarce, and without money commerce could not develop beyond the bartering of the market place. Thus that great system of roads that had been built by the Roman engineers fell into disuse and in place of them the winding lanes furnished ready ambush in an unpoliced countryside. Each district, therefore, lived more and more by itself as the path of the merchant became increasingly dangerous and the markets for his goods declined, since people were less and less able to pay.

These little settlements, however, held some of the vital germs of the political evolution of Europe. Unperceived then or for a thousand years later, the history of northern Europe was beginning to repeat the evolution of the ancient world. It is true that it did not follow the pattern of the city state, but it began with the same elements as those which we have found not only in the settlements of the Mediterranean, but in all early societies. As we have seen, all the peoples of northern Europe, Gauls and Britons as well as Germans, were in the tribal stage of society when the Romans came in contact with them, and those outside the Roman Empire had not advanced beyond this stage when they crossed the frontier in the fifth century.

The transformation of these tribal units into territorial sovereignties was a long and complex process. Sometimes it meant the triumph of a single tribal lordship, as for instance, in the case of the Franks; sometimes a fusion with one tribal leader dominant, as in the case of the West Saxons (Wessex) in England. Sometimes tribal forces remained too strong to accept any permanent sovereign above them, as was in many instances the case with the Germans who remained at home. In Spain they lived on in spite of the illusory externals of unity. But in Italy the paradox was complete, for in spite of the lingering influence of Roman traditions, the local elements remained fully as recalcitrant as in distant Germany.

Again, as in the ancient world, it was above all by war that the forces of law and order established themselves over feudal anarchy. It was undoubtedly a necessary instrument in the politics of kings without which the anarchy of the Middle Ages could not have been beaten down; and the evil consequences that spring from sovereignty based on war-power were checked by a new economic life when, in the fifteenth and sixteenth centuries, Europe ceased to exist solely by itself and became part of the world economy. Thus the Dark Age furnished a new starting point for an evolution of politics which reached more than Rome ever did over the whole *orbis terrarum*.

The leaders of the invading tribes could not readily take over the functions of the Roman administrators, although many adventurous chieftains rose high in the service of the declining empire and led its armies against the invaders. One such, for example, was Odoacer (Odovacar), a soldier of fortune from the country of the Middle Danube, who finally deposed his Emperor, Romulus Augustulus, in 476 A.D. He joined to the Roman title of patrician that of king, not as a restoration of the ancient kingship of Rome which had lapsed for a thousand years, but as a lesser dignity than that of the imperial office, which was formally recognized in the Emperor at Constantinople. Odoacer's leadership in the revolution which ended the empire in the west came to a swift close with his murder by Theodoric, King of the Ostrogoths, but Theodoric himself invaded Italy with the sanction of the Emperor at Constantinople.

These are but two outstanding examples of the way in which the barbarians paid tribute of respect to the still imposing fabric of the Roman Empire. Clovis, Frankish conqueror of Gaul, although much less touched by this than the chieftains who invaded Italy, was proud to accept from the Emperor the title of consul. The connotation of this title made it appropriate to his rule over Gaul by right of conquest, but for his own people he was still king of the Franks. He was king of his own tribe of Salian Franks by inheritance, and of the other Frankish tribes by kinship with their royal families or by choice of the warriors who raised him on their shields. Neither he nor his successors down to modern times ever bore the official title "King of France."

The personal relation of kingship persisted as a Germanic heritage. Even the emperors of the shadowy Roman Empire east of the Rhine bore the strange title "King of the Romans."

It would be a complete misreading of history to attempt to find all that aggregate of powers which we now call sovereignty in these early kingships that struck their roots into those communities which survived the conquest on the soil of the former empire. The power of government was never wholly embodied in the person of the ruler but was never wholly divided up as in the case of the city state. Under these conditions, as in the Orient, prestige was a necessary attribute of royalty. It could be acquired by achievement on the field of battle, by dominance of personality or by skill in diplomacy. But there was one basis for it which far out-stripped any reputation for courage or wisdom, and that was the religious sanction which marked off the dignity of kings from all other honors in the world. The patriarchal king had been priest, as well as warrior and leader of his clansmen. Anthropologists have traced this religious basis of royalty still farther back to the belief in his divinity — that same belief which in the later empire spread from Asia Minor, with its many cults, into the secularized west and brought the worship of the Emperor as the test of loyalty to the state.

We have already seen what part this belief in the divinity of royalty has played in the governmental structure of Asia in the past, and until recently in Japan. With the conversion of the Germans to Christianity, the kingship lost its priestly function, but a link was found between the old ideas and the new in the religious ceremonies which accompanied the rite of coronation. This was commonly connected in the churchly teaching of the time with the kingship of David and the divine sanction given by the prophets to the royal line of Judea. The anointing with oil marked out the king by something like an eighth sacrament of the Church. This was especially the case with the kings of the Franks, when, from the ninth century on, it was believed that the oil with which they were anointed by the archbishops of Rheims was miraculously preserved for this special purpose.

It was, however, chiefly as local warlords that the early kings played their part in the obscure beginnings of the state system of Europe. While there were some enlightened law givers like Alfred the Great of England, all of them were, Alfred included, warlords by profession. Allegiance to them was therefore personal, as it must be when the king leads in battle. Personal rule covering all phases of government is possible only in small states. It cannot be applied to the widely extending territories such as those which the kings of sixth-century Europe were taking for their own.

If progress during the Dark Age seems to us discouragingly slow in the light of history, it was all that could be expected. The change from tribal kingships to those set up on a territorial basis was a vast and difficult revolution in government. Its leaders were not experienced statesmen maintaining an established tradition as in ancient Rome, one which could be recognized and accepted by the people themselves. They were ignorant, if crudely able, war leaders, especially marked out by prowess or cunning or election from a

167

family of royal blood. Their problem was therefore never clearly seen. It was, as we know now, the shaping of a national state system which could be unified only through a complicated system of government. We have seen the inadequacy of personal rule for such a task in both China and Rome. In the Orient the monarch maintained a stable state by leaving the social structure untouched and so limiting his own sovereignty to little more — outside of war — than the collection of tribute or taxes and the maintenance of routine. The Romans had solved the problem in an entirely different way from the Oriental, by dividing up the attributes of sovereignty so that each specialized agency of government worked within its own field and these were coordinated into a consistent system. But even the experience and genius of Rome failed to prevent the personal rule of military leaders from denaturing the whole structure of government.

Now there was no such escape from anarchy in northern Europe as China found in a stable social system or Rome in a specialized administration. Instead, kingships gave way to further anarchy in the rise of feudalism. They were unable to make good the promise of their leadership of the people as a whole until the twelfth and thirteenth centuries, when territorial lordship took on a new meaning with the emergence of a money economy and the rise of a merchant class who could bring a new and more efficient aid to kingship.

In what is now France, the line of Clovis and his legendary ancestor Merovech, the Merovingian kings grew steadily weaker from the sixth to the close of the eighth century when the mayor of the palace, or the chief of the king's household, Pepin, assumed the kingship and passed it on to his son Charles the Great (Charlemagne). Few of the great figures of history have dominated the world in which they lived more completely than this king of the Franks, under whom it seemed for a time as though the law and order of the ancient world would be restored without waiting for the slow process of the centuries. By repeated wars against the German tribes on the east and campaigns against the Mohammedans of Spain, he began that transformation of a rudimentary Germanic military organization into a political structure which lay at the basis of the evolution of Rome.

It is straining the analogy too far to say that the levy that met at the Mayfield in the campaign against the Saxons was a Frankish counterpart of the Roman *comitia centuriata;* but the promise of a similar future development was for the time strengthened by the new administrative system, with the king's officials, the *missi dominici,* carrying from the royal court to the confines of the realm royal ordinances, the *capitularies.* The effort to restore some semblance of uniform civil government, even more than the conquest of Saxons and Lombards, justified the action of the Pope when on Christmas Day, 800, he placed the imperial crown upon the brow of Charlemagne. It was an act never to be forgotten in all the history of Europe, but the Germanic north was not ready and the conditions of the time were wholly adverse to the erection of a permanent and universal empire.

When the strong hand of Charlemagne was removed there began at once the process of decline and division. The three grandsons of Charlemagne divided the empire, in 843, by the Treaty of Verdun. The imperial dignity remained with the elder brother Lothair, whose Lotharingia, an enlarged Lorraine, extended over the area which stretched along the left bank of the Rhine, remaining a frontier of dispute for over a thousand years between the Germans and the French. To the west Charles the Bald took over most of ancient Gaul, while to Ludwig the German went the old ancestral Frankish lands on the right bank of the Rhine and, in general, the territory lying between the Rhine and the Elbe. This family compact was arranged without regard to national differences, but the bilingual oath of Strasbourg which the brothers took the year before (842) showed already the cleavage of two great language areas, French on the west and German on the east, the first sign of the origins of nationality on the Continent in the heart of the Dark Age.

The Carolingian line of kings lasted, with interruptions, for two centuries, from the anointing by the Pope of Pepin in 754 to the coronation of Hugh Capet in 987. But mere heredity is not an adequate claim to a throne, especially in time of crisis, for while it lessens the chances of rivalry developing into civil war, it offers no guarantee of competence. Thus the descendants of the mighty Charles became as impotent in the ninth century as those "do nothing" Merovingian kings who, in the picturesque phrases of Carlyle, had wended their way in their ox carts into eternity. The weakness of inherited monarchy had been partly checked in the case of the Germans, as well as that of other peoples at the same stage of political development, by the election of the most competent member of the ruling house. But this left the door open for other candidates, and as the German dynasties, one after another, died out, the election of the Germanic kings became a process by which to limit and check their sovereignty.

Fortunately in France, however, the royal house which succeeded the Carolingians, the Capetian dynasty, produced a unique line of rulers whose claims to the throne were never successfully set aside throughout all the history of royal France. Hugh Capet himself, if not the greatest feudal lord of his time in France, was at least the one most strategically placed, for he held the key to the valley of the Seine in the walls and bridges of Paris, and his territory extended over the country eastward through the Ile de France, westward to Normandy and northward to Flanders. By marriage, diplomacy, but above all by war, the Capetians made their kingship something more than the sovereignties of their great feudal neighbors; and yet the contests with these feudatories seemed at times desperate enough. It was made doubly difficult by the fact that the dukes of Normandy became the kings of England and that they subsequently laid claim not only to other large feudal holdings, but even to the throne of France itself. Hardly less dangerous and more persistent was the opposition of such nobles as the dukes of Burgundy and the counts of Champagne and Flanders on the east and north, the dukes of Brittany on the west, the counts of Anjou and Blois in the center, and of Toulouse in the south. The unification of France under these conditions was a vastly difficult task, but it was made more difficult by the complications of the feudal system which was to dominate France throughout all of the early Middle Ages.

Feudalism

Not only in France, but generally throughout Europe, the tribal kingships, instead of developing at once into the unities of national states, found their authority denied by local heads of war bands or chieftains who parcelled out the rule among themselves, in a crude relationship based on war and land tenure which bore the name of feudalism. Europe still bears the mark of the centuries-long encampments of these petty territorial chieftains in the castles whose ruins rise on almost every defensible hilltop and dominate every river or ancient roadway.

Feudalism supplied a necessary mixture of personal and territorial ties as a basis both for rule and for the whole social structure. The formations of fighting men were similar to the *comitatus* — a leader and his knights or comrades who fought together and shared the spoils. Their personal relationship was symbolized in the ceremony of homage by which the vassal admitted that he was his chieftain's "man" *(homo)*. But these personal followers had to be supported and maintained, and, in the absence of money, the one way to insure this was to grant them lands. If the relation between lord and vassal had lost all trace of kinship, this was the case still more in the relation of the lord to the peasant who tilled the soil. For, between the "noble" who followed the profession of arms and the non-noble worker, there developed a class distinction which in the course of time became almost a difference of caste.

Therefore, although feudalism ultimately became the chief impediment to the development of the national state, viewed in its own time and setting, it constituted an advance from the early tribal form of society. When a greater warlord could overthrow the rivalries of the feudal nobles the national state was no longer held back from full political development by the personal ties which continued to prevail in the Orient.

War was the profession of the feudal ruling class. Force governed. The nobles, or chief warriors, respected each other's rights only when they felt they had to. Treachery and violence made mockery of the so-called laws of chivalry. In fact the term "feudal system" is a misnomer. It was feudal anarchy so far as the relations went between the members of the ruling class. The king or chief feudal overlord was not allowed directly to administer justice or raise troops in the territory of his vassals. He could command them to attend court and give them his instructions as to what he wished done, but the vassals carried out the orders. The king ruled directly only in his personal domains.

The same rules were followed in respect to the chief vassals and their sub-vassals and knights. Each owed service and allegiance to the man directly above him. There were wars between the kings, wars between the vassals, and wars between the vassals and their own king. The inhabitants of a district were accustomed to look upon their lord as their ruler. They paid their taxes to him, were judged in his courts, assembled under his banner. Consequently, if a quarrel arose between the lord and the king, they usually supported the former. With the feudal system thus not to be depended on, feudal rulers concentrated on war both to maintain their territory and to extend it so that they would have more lands from which to draw man power for their armies. At times great vassals became more powerful than the king, and in the early days of feudalism they were usually strong enough to make sharp and effective protest when the king took to himself powers that were supposed to belong to them. It was in such a quarrel that the feudal vassals of John of England forced him to sign the Magna Carta (1215) which has been considered in modern times as the cornerstone of English liberties for the common man, but which in the eyes of the English barons was rather a return to earlier practices, for John was forced to declare that he would reign according to the rules then customary.

While in theory feudalism was a hierarchy of overlordship and vassalage reaching in a series of grades from the great lords down to almost landless knights, in reality it was complicated by the fact that an overlord might do homage to a vassal for some piece of land to which the latter held title, and this was even true of the kings. An example of the intricacy of the relationships is shown in the old feudal register of the Counts of Champagne. In 1172, for example, the Count of Champagne had 2017 vassals, of whom 158 also owed allegiance to some 85 other lords, while the Count himself held the 26 castellanies of his estate from 10 different suzerains — the King of the French, the Holy Roman Emperor, the Duke of Burgundy, two archbishops, four bishops and an abbot. Besides the feudal nobles there were also archbishops, bishops and abbots who had been granted land which brought them within the feudal system although as spiritual princes they could at the same time claim exemptions from certain services.

But the chief complication which developed for feudalism was in relation to the kingship, for although the kings were always something more than feudal lords, they had to maintain their state by the same means as those who acknowledged them as suzerain. The king had little money, never enough to maintain the officers of his court and therefore lived in no one capital. He moved from feudal demesne to demesne for the simple reason that he had to receive the feudal dues and eat up his revenues on the spot. Under these circumstances, it was but natural that his court should keep the local color of the life of the great feudatories and that the developing of an adequate central government should be long delayed.

Naturally feudalism, based on local military situations, varied from place to place. There could not be any one "feudal system"; the feudalism of France differed from that of England in certain ways and both had a history different from that of Germany. Feudalism did not flourish in Anglo-Saxon England. It was six hundred years from the time the Romans left until the Norman conquest, but while the tribal kingships had developed on a military basis to carry on their tribal wars and meet the invasions of the Danes, they had never wholly destroyed the local life of the little communities which furnished the war bands. These were no longer held together by patriarchal family and clan connections, but elected their headmen from reeve and ealderman and aldermen to shepherd and cowherd. Thus in the Anglo-Saxon *tún* (town) there was a miniature, almost microscopic copy of the Greek and Roman city state. This as we shall see later was of vital importance in the English institutions of freedom. The folk-ways for their administration furnished a basis for the common law.

But before "politics" could develop from these obscure beginnings, the feudal baronage of William the Conqueror took possession under the strong arm of the king. We shall see later on how the structure of the English state bore the impress of its early history.

The Roman Empire of the German Nation

In the lands to the east of the Rhine feudalism secured an added hold because of the persistence of the old tribal or stem duchies. These had deeper roots than the feudal states of western Europe. They, more than any other state in Europe, retained the old tribal basis and for the most part remained firmly fixed in their ancestral lands.[1] Thus, the Saxons on the north, the Swabians on the south, the Franconians of the Middle Rhine and the other great stem duchies and their modern successors, were able to check the growth of a central sovereignty until the day of Bismarck. The unity which Charlemagne imposed on the western Germans was short-lived, lasting for less than a century. By his wars against the Saxons in the north, he carried the frontiers of his empire eastward to cover the western portion of Prussia, and by his campaigns in the southeast against the Avars he held the line of the Danube, so that the Germany of his time was about two-thirds of the area of modern Germany. But within that territory the kingly power had little scope beyond the major task of assembling the war bands for the campaigns against the heathen on the east. Consequently, with the decline of the Carolingian dynasty, the tribal rulers fell back on the old Germanic custom of an elected kingship.

It was but natural therefore, that the first line of genuinely German monarchs in the Middle Ages should be of that strong and warlike Saxon tribe, whose head, Henry the Fowler, became king in 1019. The first elected tribal leader was Conrad of Franconia (911-918), and it was due to his efforts that the east Franks joined with the Saxons to elect as his successor the Saxon duke. With the support of the east Franks he was able to force the dukes of old Allemanis (Swabia) and Bavaria to acknowledge his supremacy and then to clear the frontier of the Magyar invaders on the south and east, the Danes on the north, and the Slavs and Wends on the northeast.

To hold this threatened frontier, lieutenants of the king were set up as counts of the march (*margraves*) along the Elbe and the Oder. These marches

---

[1] The persistence of the old tribal ties is mirrored in their title for the great chieftains. They never translated *Herzog*, "the leader of the army," into the Latin *duke*, of the later Roman Empire.

or marks were frontier districts established as military outposts with forts against the invaders, and their later history repeats, in varied form, that of the Roman proconsulates. For it was but natural, that they should acquire an importance and an independence in keeping with their military situation. Their fortresses built for defense against the barbarians made them strong enough to rank among the great feudatories. Thus the German monarchs were obliged to see the very machinery of government, which was set up for their protection, dissolve into the common mold of feudal states.

At first the Saxon kings gave promise of doing for the Germans what the Capetians ultimately did for the French, making it a strong and unified country. Henry's son, Otto I, the Great, (936-973) crushed feudal rebellions with an iron hand and freed Germany forever from the menace of invasion by the Hungarians. Not content with victory in the field (Battle of the Lechfeld, 955), he brought in settlers from the Rhineland and planted them along the Danube in upper Austria between the Alps and Vienna in the neighborhood of Salzburg. There they settled in stockaded houses like those they had built in the north; and today after a thousand years the homes of these Austrian farmers are modeled on the old stockade with their outer walls enclosing a hollow center. This is but one of the lasting evidences of the far reach of the Saxon kings.

During Otto's time the frontier of the German tribes, for they were still little else but tribes, ran down the map from east of Berlin to near Vienna, following the curving line of the mountains which, for about a thousand years, divided the Czechs from the Germans. West of this arc were the Germanies in which the Holy Roman Empire and feudalism were dominant from the barbarian invasions to the modern era. East of it was the Orient.

Unfortunately for Germany, Otto and his successors were lured by the mystic spell of Rome and crossed the Alps to make themselves successors of Charlemagne and Augustus. The coronation of Otto the Great in 962, as Roman Emperor, was the beginning of that strangely unreal fabric known, from the middle of the twelfth century, as the Holy Roman Empire. Like its great prototype, it claimed universal sovereignty, but the medieval Caesars lacked the legions of Augustus to enforce their claims for more than brief intervals, either in Italy or in Germany. And even if they had sufficient military power they did not have an adequate machinery for civil government like that which kept the Roman Empire intact. The more widely the sovereignty was extended the more inadequate it became; for the Holy Roman Empire was a feudal structure over a society still cast in the early mold of personal relationships.

The history of the Orient and ancient Rome shows us that there are only two ways to rule over great stretches of territory. One is not to attempt to interfere with local rulers beyond securing tribute and the maintenance of peace through a vague and general oversight. The other is to exercise authority by the use of money economy; for the sovereign must buy his services or delegate them to others. The absence of money in the early Middle Ages made genuine unity impossible in any country. And in Germany the situation was made still worse by the fact that, until the close of the Middle Ages, there was no real effort to centralize financial administration.

If the Holy Roman Empire lacked authority, it was able to maintain to an astonishing degree that one prerogative of sovereignty which marked it out from other sovereignties, the prestige which attached to the conception of empire and the continuing influence of the tradition of Rome. Unfortunately for the Empire, however, its claim to that tradition was shared with a rival with greater spiritual ascendency over the whole Western world. The Papacy became the outstanding challenger of the prerogatives which it had established by the coronation of Charlemagne and of Otto. From the standpoint of German history the Papacy was always foreign; if it had been German instead of Roman there might have been some chance of success for the Holy Roman Empire.

The Papacy was in some respects the most powerful and efficient monarchy of the Middle Ages; and already in the dark age of feudal anarchy it was laying the basis for the triumphs of later centuries. While it would be misleading and, indeed, impossible to treat its history purely in terms of politics — for the religious aspects of the Papacy always played their part, even in the assertion of its temporal claims — nevertheless the Popes, as rulers on their own account and as overlords of other sovereigns, enter fully into the secular political history of Europe. Perhaps this would not have happened if powerful Roman emperors had continued to rule in Rome. The *Pontifex Maximus* at such a court would probably not have stepped into the position of a temporal ruler any more than the primates of the different European courts whose moral or personal influence played a part in molding the history of kings, but who remained throughout the heads of a priesthood and not rivals of the temporal rulers. The fact that Rome had ceased to be the home of the Emperor was decisive for the Papacy, for its moral leadership, so important in a time when political institutions were feeble or untried, was lessened by its local preoccupations in the government of Rome and central Italy. It is not distorting the perspective to say that while the Papacy profited from the absence of the emperors to escape immediate and constant dictation at their hands, it sank at times, so far as its political history was concerned, to the position of a minor ruler on the level with a feudal lord. In the middle of the tenth century it even seemed for a time to be less than that, hardly more than the plaything of the great rival houses of Rome itself, the Orsini and the Colonna.

It was Otto the Great who lifted it out of this degradation; but by so doing he brought it temporarily under the Emperor's control by his interference in the election of the Pope. This subjection of the Papacy to the Empire was repeated from time to time throughout the Middle Ages, but it was only at the close of the eleventh century that this relationship was turned to the advantage of both Pope and Emperor. This was under the romantic figure Otto III who had the dream, nourished by his Greek mother, of reviving the Roman Empire as a universal sovereignty, and whose tutor, whom he had elected as Pope Sylvester II, shared the same high purpose. For a few years a

Roman Emperor, dressed in the imperial purple of the ancient days, mirrored the splendor of Byzantium in his palace on the Aventine. What would have happened had this visionary monarch lived to mature years will always remain an unsolved riddle of European history. In spite of the dream world in which he lived he could be extremely practical in dealing with the Italian factions and the mystic sense of empire was a spur to real deeds.

When he died at the early age of twenty-two, it was fitting that his body should be brought from Italy to rest beside that of Charlemagne under the dome of the Basilica at Aachen. "None save he," says Bryce, "desired to make the seven-hilled city again the seat of dominion, reducing Germany and Lombardy and Greece to their rightful place of subject provinces. No one else so forgot the present to live in the light of the ancient order; no other soul was so possessed by that fervid mysticism and that reverence for the glories of the past, whereon rested the idea of the medieval Empire."

The Franconian Emperors, who succeeded the Saxon line reached, under Henry III in the middle of the eleventh century, the height of imperial authority in Germany. But the prince bishops were also princes of the Church, and the effort to curb the feudal magnates and the extension of royal lands and revenues aroused the opposition, not only of the leading princes of Germany, but that of the Pope as well, before whom Henry IV was forced to humble himself at Canossa. The Papacy, profiting from the great puritan movement which was sweeping over Europe from the Abbey of Cluny, was able so to strengthen itself that it won its freedom not only from the local danger of Italian politics, but also from its imperial masters. This was the work of Gregory VII (the monk Hildebrand), in the great battle over investitures, waged to make the bishops the spiritual vassals of the papal monarchy, a battle repeatedly renewed and only finally won by the temporal powers with the rise of the national state in Catholic as well as Protestant countries.

But while the Popes of the Middle Ages won most of their contests with the Emperors, they could not so easily throw off the influence of the anarchy of Italy in which, as rulers of the papal estates, they found themselves rivals of petty feudal overlords and vitally involved in the anarchy of the city states. This temporal lordship, which in feudal times seemed to be a guarantee of papal resources, was in reality an element of weakness; for in the nature of the case, the papal monarchy could have no political future among the secular sovereignties. The only monarchs who could succeed were those who had national states behind them. These secular governments, therefore, came more and more to regard as a rival and potential enemy the power that in the early Middle Ages had symbolized the moral forces of Christendom. In their eyes it was less an ally than an interference in the advance and stabilization of law and order. Moreover, the effort of the Papacy to share in secular sovereignty was doubly unfortunate owing to the fact that Italy, in spite of the new wealth which began to stir the states into commercial life, remained as backward politically as Germany itself. This fact left a fateful influence on papal statesmanship throughout all of the Middle Ages.

So far, this survey of the early Middle Ages has mostly followed the familiar lines of political history, laying the foundations for the national states, which the later Middle Ages were to take over for the use of the modern world. But, if limited to that, it would leave a wholly false impression of the society that worked itself up from barbarism to civilization in the six slow centuries, from the fifth to the eleventh. For it was the most unpolitical of societies, in which — except for war and, even in spite of it — folkways counted for more than the rule of kings, and the Church was more important as the custodian of morals than as a rival with princes for political power. Time and again in the long road which we have been following, we have touched upon the fact that the history of freedom carries us back from ruler to ruled, from the structure of society to the lives of the individuals comprising it. But again we come to the disturbing fact that the individual in early societies counts for little and is often only the helpless victim of forces beyond his control.

The beginnings of the peoples of northern Europe reveal the same forces at work as in the ancient world. There we have traced the process of civilization, in the narrower sense of that word, as the secularizing of society, urging it along out of the background of primitive superstition and tribal formation by the need of greater safety or greater prowess in war — the first great revolution in human affairs. We have seen how, in the new regime of politics, the interests of security remade the structure of society, recasting citizenship to strengthen the army, and how, by the sheer logic of events, this involved social and political institutions which lie at the foundations of freedom. But, at the same time, war, the liberator from taboo, never wholly liberated, and became the outstanding obstacle to both freedom and welfare.

Although we have already dealt at length with this primitive background of law and morals, we need, even at the cost of repetition, to recall the fundamental facts that freedom is a function of justice, and that justice, as we understand it, is a relatively late product of history. There is little to record of it in the beginnings of civilization, for it is a secular concept; it has to do with the relations of man to man and not with those of man to supernatural powers. In all early societies, it is this later relationship which is of supreme importance.

We do not have to go back to Plato's definition of justice to find that the relations of mankind to the gods do not rest on the same principles as those which determine secular society. If his definition of justice holds and it means rendering to everyone his due, then the measurement of what is due cannot be the same with reference to a divinity as under the usual conditions of human contact. Hence theology moves in a different sphere from that of ethics. Theology calls for resignation where ethics demands protest. It makes a virtue of compliance with the blows of angered gods; and sacrifice, which is the epitome of suffering, is exalted as a center of religious ritual.

Even more important than the theologies of religion, however, in the effect upon conduct, is the still more primitive, subconscious overtone that lasts on, down into the heart of even modern civilization, from the rude wizardry of primitive life. In our survey of magic and religion, we have seen how completely the taboo, still with us in so many of our social sanctions, once dominated all of conduct that was not already set in the pattern of habit. The new, the strange, the unexplained, the not-understood, all the realms of mystery into which every unaccounted act carried the anxious nerves of our savage ancestors, called for some equally mysterious rite to avert the lurking evils of the unexplored.

When the laws of taboo govern the world of change, it is but common sense to have as little change as possible. So habit with its dull unconscious repetition takes over the rules of magic and superstition, and reduces them to commonplace in the everyday routine of life. Neither the taboo nor the habit that grows out of it is based on a conscious concept of justice. Yet because the things the gods prescribe are often but the expression of tribal experience, the taboo embodies, along with its magical incantations and its supernatural apparatus, most of those rules of conduct which bring order and organization out of the chaos of mere savagery. The priest is the earliest law-giver, and the fact that the gods ordain what he decrees gives his precepts the power to dominate where force and violence would otherwise be unchecked. Religion, therefore, although its task is to link mankind to the gods, not only supplies the rudimentary beginnings of the idea of justice, but protects it by those very supernatural forces which tend at the same time to distort it.

Now these are strange and contradictory facts, but their contradiction is as nothing compared with that which the historian finds when he turns from these prehistoric beginnings to the origins of the great religions of today. Both in the West and in the East these have been the work of revolutionary leaders in revolt against the religious heritage of that prehistoric past. They either made over the existing religious beliefs on an ethical basis, that is to say, on the basis of a frank interest in human welfare, or, leaving the creeds untouched, built a secular philosophy alongside them, which in turn a credulous world made over into a religious faith as its founder became divine. Thus Buddha taught his ethical concepts in a revolt against the overladen world of taboo in India, which, however, proved stronger than his moralizing and made his benign figure the center of the vastest system of organized taboo in the world today.

Still more secular was the thought of Confucius, as secular as the Greek's and as un-Asiatic. He taught philosophy, not theology, a philosophy in which the gods play almost no role. Mankind stands out at last with problems of its own, not those that the gods have given it, problems of human conduct, to be solved by rules that have no sanction of taboo behind them but embody experiences that are projected as an ideal. His precepts therefore are of universal application, and the principal ones were as strongly held by Sun-Yat-sen and those who joined with him in the Chinese revolution as by the scholars of so many centuries who learned by heart the Five Books of the Confucian classics. But alongside this secular teaching, Confucius taught a reverence for tradition which, by its very nature, helped to perpetuate those popular beliefs which, as in the case of Buddha, though in far less degree, tended to distort into a sacred canon the homely lessons of the sage.

When we turn back from the religions of the Orient, we find the same historic laws at work. If Confucius recalls the Greeks, the affinity between Buddha and the reforming prophets of Israel is too familiar to call for more than passing comment. The prophetic message was, of course, cast in the fullest terms of religion. Righteousness is exacted, according to Amos, not only of the Jews, but of all the world by the universal deity. Burnt offerings and all the paraphernalia of sacrifice are henceforth less than upright conduct and the cherishing of social ideals. The pure in heart are to be granted the ecstatic glimpse of the divinity, not because of prayers or ritual but by reason of their attitude toward other men. But again the religious background of this teaching grew stronger than the simple precepts of the prophets, stronger even than those of Christ himself. The chief concern was drawn away from the human element to the divine. Jewish teaching held to the half-mystical, half-magical lore of the Talmud, and as for Christianity, as its faith strengthened in the expectation of the world to come, the evils of the present world seemed insignificant and transitory. Christian morals had injected the most revolutionary concept that had yet been offered to the world in the demand for charity, not only to one's friends but to one's enemies; but no one, certainly not the Church, thought of building society on its model. It was too revolutionary for adaptation to the secular world. Those who sought to realize it therefore retired from the world into a purely religious organization, or became heretics.

From this analysis we see that although the concept of justice was at the heart of the doctrine of the founders of the great world religions, nevertheless, religion itself was not the proper field for its development. This fact alone supplies a clue to that great cleavage in the history of civilization which marks off the Orient from the West. The ethical teaching of Asiatic religions is almost identical with that which Europe borrowed from the Old and New Testaments.

But although the ethics of Oriental religions strike these high keys, they have been so submerged in the great tide of religious belief and ritual as to fail to secure for themselves the adequate instruments for their own application in the world of everyday. Oriental secular society made little or no formal provision for the further development of justice. This does not mean that there has been an absence, or even any weakness, of the sense of justice as between individuals and groups in the nations such as China; but their ethical teaching was never built up into a code of law like that which Rome produced, and which became the secular parallel to the ethics of Christianity.

Law was at first a part of religion because religion dominated all the affairs of life. Without going back again to the primitive world, so fruitfully explored by the anthropologists today, or even to the still richer fields of Egyptian, Babylonian and Jewish archeology, we find in the origins of

Europe itself that same kind of enveloping superstition as prevailed elsewhere in early society. The ancient codes of the city states were designed fully as much for the service of their divine as of their human members — collections of prayers, rites, liturgies and rules for sacrifice and burial of the dead — matters of strict taboo, along with provisions as to property and social conduct acceptable to the gods.

In Greece this all-pervading sense of religion was strongly intrenched in the popular mind, not merely the state religion, but family and local cults and mysteries. The laws of Solon were a mixture of ritual, code and constitution, with provisions for sacrifice and worship of the dead along with those for marriage rites and property ownership. The intellectual revolt from superstition which was the great achievement of the Greeks, especially the Ionians and the Athenians, was only for trained minds. As has also been held in modern days, the Greek rationalists believed that religion was good for the masses. Plato as much as admitted this when he said "to obey the law is to obey the gods." It was because Socrates refused to make this concession to superstition that he was put to death.

Even among the Romans, the most practical of people, the distinction between *fas* (what is permissible under religious law and practice) and *jus* (law made by human authorities) was not worked out until the office of praetor, the magistrate charged with the administration of justice, was established in the fourth century, well on in the history of the Republic. Even after the civil law *(jus civile)* was administered, apart from the sacred law of the pontifices, they still retained a relationship. Moreover, it was the rules of religion *(fas)* which were applied in the declaration and conduct of war and a special class of priests acted as envoys in the making of treaties. It has been said that there were more gods than citizens in early Rome. No wonder, therefore, when living in the presence of these uncanny beings the citizen regarded the state as practically omnipotent, and to it he belonged body and soul. It not only controlled education, but prescribed the kind of life to be lived and the conditions to be met. Liberty of the individual, such as we cherish today, simply did not exist in the ancient city state, except in the circumscribed area of old habitual things *(mores)* which the gods had long allowed in the routine of life. No one had any rights against the will of the gods; heresy and treason were one. This perhaps explains one of the outstanding facts in the history of freedom — that the penalty for treason was almost universally death, for it was the crime which violated both of the two great complexes of fear in early society, fear of the known and the unknown.

There are two ways of escape: by reform of the laws and of the structure of the state. These two interlocked. We have seen the effect of the political revolution ascribed to Servius Tullius, breaking down the religious barriers of patriarchal privilege. It was along this line of widening citizenship that the plebs won their long fight for equal rights with the patricians, and that finally Roman citizenship was extended to all Italy and then throughout the Roman world. But what did citizenship mean? It meant equality before the law, and was, therefore, a guarantee of freedom only so far as the law guaranteed it. Property ownership and family ties were on a common basis, the old religious ties yielding to secularized business and social relationships. But, as the religious limitations on freedom lessened, secular regulations developed in their place, not in the same way, but with the same purpose: to protect society — that is the state — from the anarchy of lawlessness or the individual from the loss of his fundamental rights as a partner in what was becoming a contractual relationship.

This reminder of what happened in the ancient world is important for the understanding of the Dark Age in northern Europe. The breaking down of heathen superstition was, in this case, not due to that widening intercourse of commerce or the need of protection in war which were responsible for the development of politics in Greece and Rome. It was the influence of the Church which, during the fifth and sixth centuries, more than anything else, remade Germanic society. Although, as in antique society, justice was administered in formal trials, Christian teaching was given a force as strong as the secular arm, if not stronger, in the development of the penitential system of the Church for the punishment of sin. The penalties for disobedience were graded according to the nature of the offense, from minor inconveniences or humiliations to extreme self-inflicted suffering, in order to escape the still more terrible penalty of eternal damnation. This penitential system was so carefully worked out that its provisions were taken by secular law-givers as well. It was the great civilizer of the barbarians.

The Cruel Inadequacies of Law and Order; Torture

The Christianizing of morals in the Western world, under the aegis of the Church, was paralleled by new developments in law, also borrowed largely from Rome. The simple life of the Germanic tribesmen as described by Tacitus had become complicated by conquest, involving new problems in the management of men and property. The way in which the political problems of government were met by the growth of the kingships and the hard road which this development had to follow through feudalism to the formation of national states has been noted. But the political structure of the state or the organization of the Church constitutes only the outer framework of society, within which practices may develop for good or ill.

Yet, while these structures stand out in all our histories, the actual impact on the individual of the sovereign power residing in them, is the other half of the story of freedom. Indeed, it is more than half; it is the central theme. Freedom is the balanced interplay of the interests of society and the individual, which is also the meaning of justice. The state, which undertook to safeguard and apply it, found here a baffling task. For in the name of justice the practices of primitive barbarism were still carried out in the effort to enforce the law; and this not only in the ancient city states, but in the *City of God* as well. Freedom had still to await the modern world before it could provide, even in theory, adequate legal procedure to ensure impartial trial of those accused of crimes, especially such crimes as treason or heresy.

180

Indeed, in the light of recent history, civilization has still a long way to go before that principle of justice is firmly established.

The problem is two-fold: the erection of proper procedures for getting evidence at trials and of inflicting fitting penalties for those convicted. These two procedures interlock in the history of criminal jurisprudence. If the method of trial is adequate, a convicted criminal has cut himself off from the privileges of a free society, to face a penalty weighted only by the extent of the violation of other people's rights. But this implies a society which feels that those rights are secure and a government which is not afraid of freedom. Wherever the methods for discerning the guilt or innocence of the accused were inadequate, the penalties inflicted on the accused were increasingly cruel. Resort to torture is the instinctive reaction to fear, not only of lawbreakers but of the capacity of the state to deal with them.

The great question in the history of criminal law has been, and still is, how to detect the guilty one, when no one knows who he is. Reform in the penal law is secondary to this fundamental problem of detection. If it baffles the courts today, it would seem to be quite beyond the competence of primitive man, even when, as was often the case, he was shrewd and well endowed with homely common sense. But he met it in his own way, and with the approval of his own people, by invoking the mysterious potencies of the world of taboo, witchcraft and magic spells to point out the culprit. These tests by fire, water, or magical ceremonies, developed into a system of ordeals that was practically universal, and as varied as human ingenuity could conceive. The unscathed or the least scathed were proved innocent by supernatural means. It was from this background that the oath acquired its terrifying potency of the curse for those who violated it, one of the steps by which taboo passed into law.

More limited, but greatly used by the warrior class of the Middle Ages was the ordeal by battle, which, when duly solemnized, was not regarded as a mere test of skill and strength, but as a judgment of God. In England after the Norman conquest it superseded all other forms of ordeal, which were abolished in the reign of Henry II. But it died out with feudalism, and had so completely disappeared that it was never formally forbidden in English law until, in 1818, a clever defender invoked it in a murder trial. Then Parliament outlawed it.

Much more important for our survey, however, was the use of torture. Its origins go back to primitive savagery, though less as a device for protecting society, by testing the strength or fortitude of those suspected of being its enemies, than mere savage blood lust against helpless victims. It would be misleading, however, to try to discriminate between these two purposes in the technique of cruelty. Its use as a method for extracting evidence is as old as history. It is described in the early records of Egypt. On the other hand, the Semites, especially the Assyrians, used it with terrible refinements on war prisoners, outrivalling the practices of the American Indians. This makes the absence of it in the Mosaic Code all the more remarkable and significant. But practice was not always on the same plane as precept. There was no place for torture in the Zoroastrian law, but the kings of the Medes and the Persians used it with brutal abandon. India seems to have been relatively free from it, but it was commonly practiced in China and Japan. In Greece slaves were tortured, but not freemen, except in exceptional cases or by despots. As a method of obtaining evidence, however, its use was justified by the most enlightened opinion. Even Aristotle held that "it appears to carry with it absolute credibility, because a kind of restraint is applied!"

In early Rome, as in Greece, the use of torture was, in general, limited to infliction upon slaves, but a great step backward was taken when it became the practice in trials for high treason under the Empire, as that crime changed from the impersonal basis of active disloyalty to the state to the personal disloyalty to the emperor (*crimen majestatis* or *lese majesté*). Under the early emperors this charge was used less as a procedure of law than as an instrument of tyranny. The orgies of cruelty practiced by Tiberius, like those of oriental tyrants, were equally outside the law, as were those of his successors like Nero, Caligula or Claudius, who, in sheer degeneracy, revelled in human agony. Nevertheless, the protection of the rights of the Roman citizen could be invoked on occasion. The most notable instance of this is that of St. Paul's protest to the tribune who rescued him from the mob. The incident is so illuminating that the few verses (Acts 23: 24-29) are quoted in full:

The tribune commanded him to be brought into the castle, and that he should be scourged and tortured: to know for what cause they did so cry out against him.
And when they had bound with thongs, Paul saith to the centurion that stood by him: Is it lawful for you to scourge a man that is a Roman and uncondemned?
Which the centurion hearing went to the tribune and told him, saying: What are thou about to do? For this man is a Roman citizen.
And the tribune coming, said to him: Tell me, art thou a Roman? But he said, Yea.
And the tribune answered: I obtained the being free of this city with a great sum. And Paul said: But I was born so.
Immediately therefore they departed from him that were about to torture him. The tribune also was afraid after he understood that he was a Roman citizen and because he had bound him.

It should be noted that Paul apparently acknowledged the right to use torture (scourging) on a condemned criminal, but not on a Roman citizen without trial or in a trial. The formalizing of torture under the law was a long process, however, with different provisions under various emperors,[2] and finally summed up in the Digest and the Code, to become the basis of medieval law on torture, when it was generally applied without the humane qualifications which allowed the Roman judges to use discretion in the interests of justice.

The one great exception in the acceptance of torture in the Roman world was the disapproval of it by the Catholic Church. This was inevitable during the period of the persecutions, but it remained in the practice of the epis-

[2] There is a good historical survey in the chapter on torture in H. C. Lea's *Superstition and Force* (Philadelphia: Lea Bros. & Co., 1870, 407 pp.), p. 333.

copal courts, as over against the secular procedure. The Roman synod of 378 called this fact to the attention of the Emperors Valentinian II and Gratian; that of 384 followed this up with the provision that no Christian could be a magistrate because he would have to apply torture and this was in violation of the teachings of the Church. This was only four years before the edict of Theodosius, referred to above,[3] imposing the sentence of death for high treason on any practitioner of heathen rites of sacrifice. The Church was reaching new decisions.

It was Augustine who voiced, in strongest terms, the responsibility of the state to prevent the disruption of the Church by heresies within, as well as to protect it against pagan attack from without. This appeal to the secular power by the greatest Church Father of the West was destined to be used for the punishment of heretics condemned by the Inquisition; but, in the era of the Reformation it became a buttress for toleration and ultimate freedom. Augustine's own opinions completely shifted, however, in the course of his troubled life, but on the question of the use of torture he wrote one of the strongest and best arraignments of that barbarous procedure to be found in any literature. The sixth chapter of the *City of God* is worth quoting at length:

What shall I say of these judgments which men pronounce on men, and which are necessary in communities, whatever outward peace they enjoy? Melancholy and lamentable judgments they are, since the judges are men who cannot discern the consciences of those at their bar, and are therefore frequently compelled to put innocent witnesses to the torture to ascertain the truth regarding the crimes of other men. What shall I say of torture applied to the accused himself? He is tortured to discover whether he is guilty, so that, though innocent, he suffers most undoubted punishment for crime that is still doubtful, not because it is proved that he committed it, but because it is not ascertained that he did not commit it. Thus the ignorance of the judge frequently involves an innocent person in suffering. And what is still more unendurable — a thing, indeed, to be bewailed, and, if that were possible, watered with fountains of tears, — is this, that when the judge puts the accused to the question, that he may not unwittingly put an innocent man to death, the result of this lamentable ignorance is that this very person, whom he tortured that he might not condemn him if innocent, is condemned to death both tortured and innocent. For if he has chosen, in obedience to the philosophical instructions to the wise man, to quit this life rather than endure any longer such tortures, he declares that he has committed the crime which in fact he has not committed. And when he has been condemned and put to death, the judge is still in ignorance whether he has put to death an innocent or a guilty person, though he put the accused to the torture for the very purpose of saving himself from condemning the innocent; and consequently he has both tortured an innocent man to discover his innocence and has put him to death without discovering it. If such darkness shrouds social life, will a wise judge take his seat on the bench or no? Beyond question he will. For human society which he thinks it a wickedness to abandon, constrains and compels him to this duty. And he thinks it no wickedness that innocent witnesses are tortured regarding the crimes of which other men are accused; or that the accused are put to the torture, so that they are often overcome with anguish, and, though innocent, make false confessions regarding themselves, and are punished; or that, though they be not condemned to die, they often die during or in consequence of the torture; or that sometimes the accusers,

[3] See Chapter V, *The City of God*.

who perhaps have been prompted by a desire to benefit society by bringing criminals to justice, are themselves condemned through the ignorance of the judge, because they are unable to prove the truth of their accusations though they are true, and because the witnesses lie, and the accused endures the torture without being moved to confession. These numerous and important evils he does not consider sins, for the wise judge does these things, not with any intention of doing harm, but because his ignorance compels him, and because human society claims him as a judge. But though we therefore acquit the judge of malice, we must nonetheless condemn human life as miserable. And if he is compelled to torture and punish the innocent because his office and his ignorance constrain him, is he a happy as well as a guiltless man? Surely it were proof of more profound considerateness and finer feeling were he to recognize the misery of these necessities, and shrink from his own implication in that misery; and had he any piety about him, he would cry to God, "From my necessities deliver Thou me."

It might be thought that so great a pronouncement by so great an authority would have determined the policy of the Church in the succeeding centuries. But when the Church became, or claimed to be, the one and infallible sovereign over the minds of men, it fell back on the practices of the Roman law and accepted, as far as it could, the use of torture. In a bull of Innocent IV in 1282 the civil power was called on to use torture on heretics as murderers of souls. The canon law forbade priests to inflict it with their own hands, using charity instead in their punishments, but it laid down the principle that there was no sin in resort to torture by the faithful. The Spanish Inquisitor Torquemada issued a detailed code of instructions in 1484 to make sure that no suspect denounced for heresy could escape the ordeal of suffering. But, in spite of this and other refinements in cruelty, the Church had ceased to endorse torture before the suppression of the Inquisition.

It was not until 1816, however, that a papal bull formally denounced torture, declaring at the same time that the accuser should be confronted with the accused, and that the proceedings should be in public — two points evaded by secular authorities in recent years when communism became the heresy of the state.

Of the national states, the one with the best record is England. In his magisterial exposition of the Common Law, Sir Edward Coke could assert with pride: "There is no law to warrant tortures in this land"; but he was careful not to say that there had been no torture, for it had been frequently practiced for some centuries and more frequently than ever under the Tudors. But it was resorted to under the royal prerogative, by order of the king or his council or some extraordinary tribunal like the Star Chamber. It was Coke's great thesis that this prerogative was limited by the Common Law. He could cite article 39 of the Magna Carta: "No freeman shall be arrested, or detained in prison or deprived of his freehold, or outlawed or banished, or in any way destroyed . . . except by the lawful judgment of his peers and by the law of the land."[4] Coke commented on this famous text that

---

[4] Note that it did not cover the unfree.

"no man destroyed . . . meant "forejudged of life or limb disinherited or put to torture or death."[5]

Nevertheless there were frequent cases of torture at trials under James I and Charles I, and although there was no instance of torture proper after the Commonwealth (1649), another practice continued until 1726, that of pressing weights on a prostrate prisoner who refused to testify. There were other cruelties in the courts until the reform of the criminal law in the nineteenth century.

It would carry us too far afield to trace the history of torture in the national state system of Europe. In France it does not seem to have been applied before the thirteenth century; but from the reign of St. Louis to the Revolution it was regulated by royal ordinance until it was abolished in 1789. The Declaration of the Rights of Man finally stated (Article VIII) that "the law should establish only such punishments as are strictly and obviously necessary," and (Article IX) that "every man is presumed innocent until he has been declared guilty . . . all harshness not essential to the securing of the prisoner's person shall be severely repressed by law."

In Italy there were many notable victims of torture, such as Savonarola, Machiavelli and Giordano Bruno. But it was an Italian, Beccaria, who, as spokesman for the conscience of Europe, was the outstanding figure in the movement for the abolition of torture. His epoch-making *On Crimes and Punishments* (1764) opened the new sciences of criminology and penology, which by prescribing for the administration of justice, safeguards freedom where it is most endangered.

Serfdom and Villenage

There are few documents more often referred to in the history of freedom than the *Germania* of Tacitus. Its content is worthy of its fame. But the contrast which it implied between the freedom-loving Germans and the Romans at the height of the Empire has been much overdrawn. The freedom of fighting men who found it humiliating to give ready answer to a summons to tribal council was merely the mark of political immaturity. Even the fact that the Germans had only a few slaves, in contrast with the millions in Italy, was chiefly due to the fact that the domestic needs of men living off the chase were few. Even what slaves they had were not organized, as on the estates of the Romans, but lived in separate households paying only the tributes of grain, cattle or clothes.

These conditions, more like those of serfs than slaves, are reflected in the collections of early laws. War and conquest did augment the number of slaves, but even in the dark age between the fall of the Roman Empire and the development of feudal kingdoms, slavery never developed to a dangerous degree, either as booty in war or as settlement of debt. The history of it is for the most part obscure, but one gets a glimpse of the English slave trade

[5] Coke's *Institutes*, 2, 48b.

at the opening of the twelfth century from this law of the Great Council at Westminster in 1102: "Let no man for the future presume to carry on the wicked trade of selling men in market like brute beasts which hitherto hath been the common custom of England." Yet the British slave market was glutted under Henry II, and the border wars with Scotland were regular sources of supply. In the feudal anarchy of the Continent the situation was worse. It was only in the later Middle Ages that slavery died out of western Europe, until in the age of discovery the vast supplies of the African slave trade opened a new history of oppression and tragedy.

The decline of slavery in the late Roman Empire and the Middle Ages had never been accompanied by any questioning of its validity. The Church continued to justify it by quoting the works of the Fathers. But a new economic situation arose, in the need for settled agricultural workers in the depleted population. Good farm lands were going to waste; therefore it was better to have "colonists" (coloni) working them on fixed tenure and held to the soil, than to have the uncertain help of household slaves. It was also better for the servile class. The result was the growth of serfdom as the normal condition of the agricultural laborer, especially when his lord practiced only the one productive industry, war.

In its lowest form, serfdom meant ownership by the lord except for the provision that the serf could not be alienated from his land. But in course of time, and certainly by the thirteenth century, serfdom began to make way for villenage, in which there were only certain well defined duties to be performed, and the "servile tenure" of the land was also a guarantee against being dispossessed. These conditions were only customary, however, and the serfs had no right to appeal to the king's courts against infringement of them by ruthless lords. On the other hand, in the long run, there was an inherent advantage in not having the relationship rigidly defined by law, for there was no legal barrier to commutation of services.

This movement for emancipation got well under way in England in the early fourteenth century. Then, just when the Black Death swept over the land, and so lessened the number of laborers, Parliament passed the infamous Statue of Laborers (1351), providing that "every man or woman of whatever condition, free or bond, able in body and within the age of three score years . . . and not having of his own whereof he may live, nor land of his own about the village of which he may occupy himself, and not serving any other, shall be bound to serve the employer who shall require him to do so, and shall take only the wages which were accustomed to be taken in the neighborhood where he is bound to serve." The rate of wages was set at what it had been two years before the Black Death had disorganized the labor market. This law was followed by others against "fugitives" seeking work, with penalties reaching all the way to branding on the forehead, like a runaway slave. Then, in 1381, Parliament, largely composed of representatives of the new monied class, in order to carry on the war with France, passed a new poll tax planned to shift much of the burden upon laborers and workmen. The poor were goaded to desperation and rose in revolt the next year.

The uprising was, at bottom, a popular movement of protest against intolerable wrongs and misgovernment. But it was also something more. For the first time in Europe a voice was raised for the equal rights of man in the economic, as well as in the political field. Never before had anyone so openly attacked the established social order as did the priest John Ball, whose arraignment of the tyranny of the propertied class reads today with the vibrant note of revolution:

Good people, things will never go well in England as long as goods be not in common, and so long as there be villeins and gentlemen. By what right are they whom we call lords greater folk than we? On what grounds have they deserved it? Why do they hold us in serfage? If we all came of the same father and mother, of Adam and Eve, how can they say or prove that they are better than we, if it be not that they make us gain for them by our toil what they spend in their pride? They are clothed in velvet, and warm in their furs and their ermines, while we are covered with rags. They have wine and spices and fair bread; and we oat-cake and straw, and water to drink. They have leisure and fine houses; we have pain and labour, the rain and the wind in the fields. And yet it is of us and of our toil that these men hold their state.

Protests like this rang through England, and the revolting peasants marched on London, and laid before the young king, Richard II, the following demands:

1. That all men should be free from servitude and bondage, so that henceforth there should be no bondmen.
2. That the king should pardon all men, of whatsoever state, all manner of actions and insurrections committed, and all manner of treasons, felonies, transgressions and extortions by any of them done, and should grant them peace.
3. That all men from henceforth might be enfranchised to buy and sell in every county, city, borough, town, fair and market or other place within the realm of England.
4. That no acre of land, holden in bondage or service should be holden but for four pence; and if it had been holden for less in former times, it should not hereafter be enhanced.

The king, a lad barely fifteen years old, met the rebels and granted their terms, but later, at his request, Parliament annulled his act, and the revolt was put down in blood. Thousands were killed, and the leaders endured the torture devised by a barbarous penal procedure. Ball was condemned to be drawn, hanged and quartered on the charge of high treason. He is said to have confessed to have been a follower of John Wyclife, whose "poor priests" or Lollards, were at that time bringing the gospel into the lives of simple people and carrying their attack on the moral evils of the lives of the clergy over into a denial of some of the central doctrines of the Church based on sacerdotalism. Wyclif himself was not involved. Moreover, his chief protector was John of Gaunt, Duke of Lancaster and uncle of the king, whom the peasants blamed for most of their troubles and whose London palace was the only one they burned. Therefore, while the religious protests of Lollardy paralleled and may have helped to stimulate the social and political revolt, the two movements remained apart.

Parliament continued its reactionary policy, but in spite of laws, villenage was rapidly disappearing. Economic forces were stronger than tyranny, and money economy cut into the outworn structure of society. Rent-paying farmers took the place of villeins, of whom hardly a trace was left in England by the time of the Tudors.

On the Continent, the conditions of serfdom varied greatly. In France, in spite of the terrible devastation of the Hundred Years War and the anarchy of the succeeding period, the peasantry made greater progress than in other continental countries through villenage to the ownership of their lands. They still had feudal dues to pay, some of them taken over from the nobles by the Crown but still regarded as servile in origin and, therefore, not paid by the privileged classes. These were the remnants of feudalism which were ultimately swept away in August, 1789 in the destruction of the whole social system of the Old Regime. By the eighteenth century, there were only a few serfs left, mostly in southeastern France. The emancipation of these was only a minor item in the program of the Revolution, which was primarily directed to securing the rights of the propertied middle class against exploitation by king or nobility. Yet the *philosophe* did not limit his theory of liberty to these practical problems. He led Western thought in the advocacy of the abolition of slavery as an institution, everywhere.

In Germany the absence of a national state left social and economic problems almost entirely in the hands of those least likely to deal intelligently with them, the local sovereignties and feudal magnates who profited most from the labor of the unfree and the unprivileged. It was not until the sixteenth century that the depths of suffering and privation of these serfs and villeins were stirred to revolt. Then, in what is known as the Peasants' Revolt in 1526, the whole dark underworld of oppression and exploitation came to light in an upheaval which, like that in England two centuries earlier, was linked in history with the religious movements of the time, Lollardy and Protestantism. This interpretation, widely shared, is wrong. Revolutions occur, not when things are at their worst, but when social or political forces are already on the upward path from conditions once commonly accepted. It is the upsurge which tends to overturn the routine of life and work. But the forces making for change have to be strong, for the resistance is bound to be as tenacious as the interests involved are deeply rooted. The Peasants' Revolt in Germany was a fierce uprising, but was put down with a ferocity which should have brought protest from Martin Luther, but, on the contrary, won his ardent approval. The Protestant Revolt was in his eyes a purely religious movement; and, like the Church Fathers, he stood for the established social order.

Serfdom continued in greater or lesser extent in the different parts of Germany. But the leaders of the Peasants' Revolt, and the greater portion of the peasantry were personally free, although still holding land subject to dues which reduced them to practical serfdom. We have only to recall that as enlightened a ruler as Frederick the Great refused to emancipate the serfs in Prussia, leaving that great reform for Stein in 1807. It was in Austria that the theories of the *philosophe* first bore fruit when Joseph II, influenced by the writings of Rousseau, carried out with persistent energy the policy of emancipation already begun by his mother, Maria Theresa. But it was not until the nineteenth century, after the storm of the French Revolution had swept over the land, that all remnants of the old feudal system with its servile base, were done away with.

Having carried our narrative into the nineteenth century, it is fitting to add a word here on the most notable emancipation of serfs, that in Russia. Strangely enough, it would seem that the subjection of the whole peasant class to servile status was not accomplished until the early seventeenth century, by the action of the Romanovs. It was Peter the Great who finally erected a comprehensive system based on a census of the rural population. The peasant tenures were fixed and the peasants subject to the landowners. The exploitation which ensued was ruthless and cruel.

Finally in the mid-nineteenth century, the Tsar responded to a wave of moral reform, following upon the disaster of the Crimean War, by a proclamation of emancipation (1861). Some fifteen million serfs were set free, but on terms that were hard to meet, for, while the state idemnified the former land owners, the peasants had to redeem the payment by installments over a number of years. The immediate effect was rather to increase than lessen the hard lot of the peasant, and a reactionary government failed to follow emancipation by the necessary social and political reforms to make freedom real.[6]

CHAPTER VIII

THE CHURCH OF THE MIDDLE AGES

The Church in the World

THE THEME of the chapter on the early history of Christianity was cast in the terms in which Paul had set it forth in Galatians 5, that the Christian's first duty was to "stand fast in the liberty wherewith God has made us free, and be not entangled again with the yoke of bondage." The

---

[6] The use of Siberia as a vast prison camp by imperial Russia, and the virtual continuance of the system by Soviet Russia in the "work camps" belong to another chapter of the history of freedom, that in which political crimes are treated by imprisonment or exile.

effort to realize emancipation from the quasi-magic formalism of Jewish scribes and Pharisees and of the pagan mysteries produced a "new freedom." This new freedom was to be found in the imitation of the life of Christ, and faith in his divinity, in place of the superstitions of the past.

A great intellectual effort was made by the fathers of the Church to understand and teach the fundamentals of this revolutionary concept and how it resulted in a system of thought and ritual which called forth an organization rivalling that of the greatest secular state that had ever been known, that of Rome. The more spiritually minded sought to make that religious freedom the sole guide of life by escape into monasticism, and the whole structure was drawn together again under the aegis of a theological authority in which obedience to hierarchal control became a basic duty. The assertion of individual religious liberties was checked by the fear of that heresy which was the equivalent of treason in the City of God. In uncultured minds the "yoke of bondage" of quasi-pagan beliefs and practices continued under other names and forms to haunt even the sacred precincts of the church.

The lesson of this history is surely that which modern psychology has so strongly emphasized, namely, that the true emancipation of the mind is less to be sought in the mind itself, in meditations and speculations, than in the conduct of life, which is the language of its everyday activities instead of its rare and isolated moments.

This means, in other words, that the City of God had to be established, not as a thing apart from the secular state, but as the practical and directing element of it. It also meant that the teaching of the gospel of Jesus should not overshadow one's attitude towards one's neighbor. The tendency of the theologians to harden ecclesiasticism into rigid systems of control had to be countered by Christian ethics which were fully as revolutionary as the faith which framed the content of belief. The basic element of Christian ethics was personal and individually rooted in the inner life. But conduct is more than an attribute of personality; it is also, through its effect upon others, social and political. Therefore, to judge the full effect of Christianity upon the Western world, we should have to deal fully as much with its social as with its doctrinal history.

Unfortunately, the history of morals is the most difficult of all the aspects of civilization to trace. Normal conduct seldom finds mention in historical records, being too commonplace to be interesting. The annals of history are chiefly devoted to those extraordinary events which disturb the even tenor of life and challenge or violate morality. Moreover the sources for the history of morals are chiefly those of the moralists and preachers, who denounce the evils which they would reform and therefore give an undue emphasis on them in their description of contemporary society. Fortunately the correction of these well-meant distortions of social history lies outside the confines of this study. But there was one aspect of the teaching of Jesus in which the ethics reached directly into politics, that of the attitude towards war. As it was primarily the organization of war which produced that of politics in the antique world, this was a fundamental test of the place of the new religion in the secular world, a test recognized not only by the Christian converts themselves but even more so by the Roman authorities. We must therefore turn to trace this problem of the relation of Christianity to war, beginning with the teachings of Jesus.

In dealing with the texts of the New Testament, it is essential to keep in mind the difficulties confronting the historian of morals. It would seem quite clear from the records as we have them that Jesus did not teach in terms of politics. The admonition to "render unto Caesar the things that are Caesar's" was a necessary condition for the freedom he needed to carry his gospel of brotherly love to the point reached in the Sermon on the Mount, the most challenging passage in all the world's literature. It is not enough to be merciful; forgiveness and reconciliation are to be extended to one's enemies, because it is only by such complete submission to the gospel of love that one can participate in the essence of divinity. This doctrine is implicit in all the acts of the life and teaching of Jesus, but is summed up in such unforgettable phrases as the following:

Ye have heard that it hath been said, An eye for an eye, and a tooth for a tooth: But I say unto you, That ye resist not evil: but whosoever shall smite thee on thy right cheek, turn to him the other also. And if any man will sue thee at the law, and take away thy coat, let him have thy cloak also. And whosoever shall compel thee to go a mile, go with him twain. Give to him that asketh thee, and from him that would borrow of thee turn thou not away. Ye have heard that it hath been said, Thou shalt love thy neighbour, and hate thine enemy. But I say unto you, Love your enemies, bless them that curse you, do good to them that hate you, and pray for them which despitefully use you, and persecute you; That ye may be the children of your Father which is in heaven: for he maketh his sun to rise on the evil and on the good, and sendeth rain on the just and on the unjust. For if ye love them which love you, what reward have ye? Do not even the publicans the same? And if you salute your brethren only, what do ye more than others? Do not even the publicans so? Be ye therefore perfect, even as your Father which is in heaven is perfect (Matthew 5: 38-48)

This sweeping assertion of Christian charity as the most perfect mirror of the divine mind at once carries us beyond domestic virtues to the relation of one people with another. It is not merely the official duties at home which are envisaged here, but also the problem of war and peace, that eternal problem which extends the field of ethics from the easy application of self-centered advantage at home to the application of justice in dealing with those who apparently have no inherent part in the well-being of the community. In the teaching of Jesus there is no longer any hesitation on this point. The stranger and the foreigner are to be viewed in the same light as the fellow citizen.

Scholars have suggested, in analyzing this aspect of the teaching of Jesus, that he preached the ideal of self-renunciation, instead of the warlike religious nationalism of Judea, knowing that only by such renunciation could the Jews preserve their spiritual heritage against the splendor and power of a warlike Rome, and that it was because of this revolutionary pacifism that the Jewish leaders and people had put him to death, looking forward as they did to deliverance by the sword. This outlook of the Jews was but natural, because their history had been one of almost constant fighting even after they had welded into a nation. The return from the Babylonian Captivity left them still in peril and the victims of recurring oppression. They were looking for a Messiah who would help them to triumph over their enemies and bring the peace of victory into that eternal strife which surrounded their little country. Latterly the national movement in Judea, always a precarious thing, had been bolstered up by the support of Jewish communities in other lands, especially in commercial centers like Alexandria; for the Jews, unlike the Greeks, helped one another wherever they were. But the Roman conquest swept over all of these. Therefore the real test of the pacifism of Jesus was his attitude toward the Roman Empire.

It was here that the Church was destined to find its chief difficulty in accommodating itself to the crude world of reality, for a whole series of other texts have been preserved, similar to those of the Sermon on the Mount, in apparent support of nonresistant pacifism. Were they the only texts of the sayings of Jesus bearing upon this most difficult of problems, Christianity would seem to be a denial of the whole process of history. But the record shows that Jesus was also a realist as he looked out upon the world, and did not teach that justice and mercy would triumph of themselves. The textual verity of some of these latter texts has been questioned by higher criticism, but we do not need to enter into that question here, for they were not questioned from the days of the early Church down to the nineteenth century.

Alongside the frequently quoted admonition to render unto Caesar what was due to him (Matthew 22:15-22) there were incidents in the life of Jesus which seemingly recognized the legitimacy of military service. There was especially the case of the Roman centurion whose servant Jesus cured and whom he praised without any indication of disapproval (Matthew 8:5-13). Moreover, there was apparently no thought of the speedy disappearance of war as the result of the new gospel. This comes out in the prophecy concerning Jerusalem: "For the days shall come upon thee, that thine enemies shall cast a trench about thee, and compass thee round, and keep thee in on every side, and shall lay thee even with the ground, and thy children within thee; and they shall not leave in thee one stone upon another; because thou knewest not the time of thy visitation." (Luke 19:43-44) Again there is the same realistic outlook into a troubled future in the text, "And when ye shall hear of wars and rumors of wars, be ye not troubled: for such things must needs be; but the end shall not be yet. For nation shall rise against nation, and kingdom against kingdom." (Mark 13:7-8) From the evidence of quotations like these it was possible to draw the conclusion that war was permitted under certain circumstances as a part of the moral order of the world. The important thing for the Christian was to know just what those circumstances were.

There were, therefore, two sets of texts which, on the surface at least, seemed to present contradictory statements of the ideals of Jesus. The Apostles had the task of harmonizing the acceptance of the Roman state as an embodiment of law and order with the deeper ethical teaching of the Sermon on the Mount, so that the latter could still remain the outstanding guide for the conduct of Christians as individuals. Loyalty to the state is a duty upon the part of all citizens, for the Christian must not let himself be open to the charge of being an enemy of society. This doctrine was never more frankly stated than in the first Epistle of Peter, written presumably in the reign of Domitian (81-96 A.D.), for it bears the marks of the experience of persecutions. Whatever its origin it is more Roman than Jewish in temper, filled with a sense of law and order, and therefore is an excellent witness as to how the teachings of the early Church were being accommodated to the secular world. The source of authority, it says, is God — an important text for the future. Then it proceeds to fit Christian ethics to the Roman scheme of things:

Submit yourselves to every ordinance of man for the Lord's sake: whether it be to the king as supreme, Or unto governors, as unto them that are sent by him for the punishment of evildoers and for the praise of them that do well. For so is the will of God, that with well doing ye may put to silence the ignorance of foolish men: As free and not using your liberty for a cloak of maliciousness, but as the servants of God. Honor all men. Love the brotherhood. Fear God. Honor the King. (I Peter 2: 13-17)

St. Paul had been even more explicit than this as to the duty of the citizen to help maintain law and order even by the use of force:

Let every soul be subject unto the higher powers. For there is no power but of God: the powers that are ordained of God. Whosoever therefore resisteth the power, resisteth the ordinance of God: and they that resist shall receive to themselves damnation. For rulers are not a terror to good works, but to the evil. Wilt thou then not be afraid of the power? Do that which is good, and thou shalt have praise of the same: For he is the minister of God to thee for good. But if thou do that which is evil, be afraid; for he beareth not the sword in vain: for he is the minister of God, a revenger to execute wrath upon him that doeth evil. Wherefore ye must be subject, not only for wrath, but also for conscience sake. For this cause pay ye tribute also: for they are God's ministers, attending continually upon this very thing. Render therefore to all their dues: tribute to whom tribute is due; custom to whom custom; fear to whom fear; honor to whom honor. (Romans 13: 1-7)

It would be misleading to quote this section of the great epistle — which has been termed the first philosophy of religion and history worthy of the name — apart from its context; for its ruling thought is the Jewish conception of the moral order of the world. The Christian shares a heritage of freedom, because freedom is of the spirit. "Ye have not received the spirit of bondage again to fear; but ye have received the spirit of adoption, whereby we cry, Abba Father, in the 'glorious liberty of the children of God.'" (Romans 8:15f.)

It is clear, however, that, as the flood-tide of early spirituality passed away, and the churches became definitely established, the question whether a Christian convert could follow the profession of arms became of ever-increasing importance. The bishops, who were not only priests but managers of the affairs of the little Christian communities, tended more and more to invoke the authority of the Apostles for a practical solution. As for the Roman magistrates, they had no doubts as to where the duties of the citizen lay; the persecutions of the Christians were due not merely to their worship of a new divinity but to their denial of the divinity of the emperor which implied as well a refusal to do military service. A steady development took place away from absolute pacifism and toward a distinction between war as violence and war as the instrument of imperial policy. The former only was to be rejected.

By the early fourth century this had become the acknowledged orthodox doctrine and those who held to absolute pacifism were ruled out as heretics by the authorities of the Church. This made it possible for the Emperor Constantine to accept Christianity as the state religion of Rome. Then service in the armies of the Emperor was service for the Christian faith as well. The old fundamental question, however, could not be disposed of through mere political exigency. There was no way of denying the fact that there had been a frankly pacifist trend in the teachings of Jesus.

The Church Fathers who faced this paradox and who solved it, so far as it has ever been solved, were Origen and Augustine. Without following the argument too deeply into the problems of divine governance, of war or of the sinful nature of man, we can sum up the result of their conclusion in the statement that it is a Christian's duty to fight in a just war, but that unjust wars are absolutely forbidden. But how can one distinguish a just war from an unjust one? This was the question of Christian theologians for the next thousand years and has been that of an increasing number of jurists and philosophers ever since.

Augustine, whose debt to Cicero was so great that he has been aptly termed the Christian Cicero, had little difficulty in accepting the Roman precept that a just war was one in support of the state because, although he viewed the processes of pagan history as diabolic, he recognized that law and order were part of a divine plan. He could therefore link together the best pagan thought on the subject with that set forth so forcibly by the Apostles Peter and Paul. The command, "Thou shalt not kill," was not applicable to those acting in obedience to lawful authority. The horror and cruelties of war are no argument against its use in the support of religion and society, but the responsibility for deciding whether it is necessary and just or not rests on the ruler, not on the soldier who carries out his command.

It was of great importance for the future thought of Europe that Augustine shaped the outlines of the *City of God* parallel to those of the city state, even when denouncing the latter as false to truth, for it followed that good citizenship in the church was consistent with good citizenship in the state. The ancient city state in producing the universal state of Rome had, said Augustine, ignorantly and in sin, furthered the realization of God's plan. Even though the agency by which it had been built was pagan, the spiritual empire which was its fitting successor and fulfillment would still need protection from the powers of darkness, and the support of the established order was therefore in the service of God.[1] As we have seen, there was nothing novel in this formulation by Augustine of the Christian attitude towards war and secular rule. But nowhere else in the vast literature of the Christian Fathers was there so compelling a statement as this which summed up, at least for the Latin West, the orthodox teaching of war and peace. There were, however, two fundamental difficulties still unsolved. Augustine's support of the established order could be used as an argument for the maintenance of any existing rule, including even tyranny. In the second place the simplicity of Augustine's fundamental conception depended upon the unity of the secular world under a single government. Yet, at the very time he was writing the *City of God*, Alaric and his barbarian hordes were at the gates of Rome.

Christianity in the Dark Age

Throughout the Dark Age in the anarchy which followed the downfall of the western half of the Roman Empire, the *City of God* shared the fate of its secular prototypes. From the fifth century on, after their conversion of the heathen, the priests of the Christian religion blessed the warriors of rival tribes or nations without regard to the moral issues of war and peace. The long evolution of Christian teaching from the days of the prophets to St. Augustine was then interrupted for almost eight hundred years.

Yet during that time the Church performed a great task, in fact a superlative one. It tamed the barbarians, curbing the instincts of savagery and teaching our ancestors the ethics of Moses while promising them the salvation of Christ. In an iron, all-embracing code of morals and worship it enforced obedience by the terrors of eternal punishment for violation. It opened to the sons of peasants a career that promised equality with the haughtiest seigneur, or even the dictation over kings. There was hardly a detail of daily life which did not come within the cognizance or under the control of the Church: questions of marriage and legitimacy, wills, oaths, even warfare came under its surveillance. The institution of auricular confession, developed from the early Church, was the indispensable way of salvation through the sacraments, for, to die unshriven meant eternal damnation. As only the priest could grant absolution, and he only on terms prescribed by the Church, the control of the sacraments became the basis of a control over mind and body which had no parallel in secular society. Nor was it solely a religious organization; it was also a nursery of culture. It helped to preserve the best things of antiquity, for when the barbarians destroyed what was of no use to them, it was the Church which, as Rashdall the historian of the universities has said, widened the sphere of utility. In a time when learning had all but perished, its schools were the only ones there were, its ideals the only challenge to violence and crime. It cherished art for

[1] Augustine's *City of God* was a favorite book of Charlemagne, who consciously tried to build his empire according to its tenets.

altar and shrine, built monastaries like palaces in the heart of forests, and when the young cities grew in the twelfth and thirteenth centuries, crowned them with the glory of cathedrals. The spirit of the Romanesque still broods in Durham and Caen as though unmindful of the Gothic spell of Mount St. Michel and Chartres.

Yet learning was as slight as it was practical. Labor in the fields brought prosperity to the monasteries, but the travellers who found hospitality in these hostels were generally even more ignorant than their hosts were; so at best the monks had little direct contact with the varied world of men and nations. Life within a monastery was the very opposite of life in an ancient city state, where the gossip of the market place stirred the curiosity of idle and busy alike. The monastic routine of work and worship bred a habit of mind which dulled the sense of criticism and readily accepted popular beliefs whenever they "edified."

This resulted in a multiplication of legends of the saints, in which the denouement was always escape by way of miracle from danger or temptation and also from another kind of danger in which the devil lurked and wrought evil with counter-miracles. So deeply did the monks sink themselves into this popular religion of miracle, that, in spite of their physical isolation from the "world" they never left it behind mentally. By a paradox without parallel, those ancient Greeks who sought reality in travel and discourse cut themselves off from the traditional credulous world of their day more than the monks who outwardly had renounced all worldly things. When faith becomes credulity, it finds kindred spirits in the untutored, and shares in their reliance on the taboo. The monasteries of the early Middle Ages were schools of this orthodoxy. But, as they were almost the only schools there were, they drew within their walls the thoughtful as well as the credulous, and intellectual leaders began, here and there, to enlarge their horizon by a study of the Church Fathers and then, venturing boldly, of the philosophy of the pagan world.

There was, however, another class of monks, neither of the common type of the credulous nor of the philosophically inclined, who played a major part in the history of the time. These were the born administrators — for good administrators are born not made. They combine strength of character and resolution with a keen sense of reality; they live in the world of the possible, even when their imaginations reach beyond it. Such leaders of men are found in every stage of society, from the primitive to the civilized; they are not limited to any one profession or station in society, soldier or priest, king or commoner, scholar or self-made man. But in the Dark Age, which settled down over Europe after the almost complete extinction of antique culture, the monasteries were not only schools for credulity on the one hand or scholarship on the other; they were also schools for statesmanship. The apprenticeship in the art of government was in the management of the monasteries themselves. The duties of the abbot, as set forth in the Benedictine Rule, were those of the sovereign of a small state.

Naturally such a training brought to the fore men of great capacity, whose experience stood them in good stead when they were called upon to advise a secular ruler, whose only other advisers were feudal warriors, unaccustomed to any of the hard rigors of consecutive thinking. But the mitred abbots who stood alongside the armored knights in the presence of their suzerain, were not called to council as representatives of a religion of peace. They, too, were feudal lords like their warrior neighbors, and ranked with the wealthiest and most powerful of the nobility. Their politics, therefore, were often less ecclesiastical than feudal, based less upon meditation and prayer than upon the use of war as a means of achieving their ends.

The trend we have just been describing in the monastic or "regular" clergy, as it was termed, because it lived under a "rule" (latin *regula*), also shared by the "secular" clergy, those who lived "in the world" (*seculum*), the bishops, priests and lesser clergy of the churches. They, too, were often deeply influenced by ideals of asceticism, sometimes to the extent of joining the regular clergy, and always to the more limited extent of accepting outward signs which marked them off from the laity.

By the fourth century the practice of celibacy on the part of the secular clergy had already become widespread. But as their flocks, living in the midst of a work-a-day world, were not isolated in monastic foundations, their administrative duties as heads of the local churches involved them, as we have seen, almost from the first days of the Church, in questions of local politics. The guardianship of morals and the administration of charity called for the same kind of leadership in church affairs as was the case in the history of monasticism. But, within the political framework of the Roman Empire, and so long as it functioned, the bishops and priests could become impartial officials without being called upon to officer a militant religion; their functions never included leading the faithful to battle. The teachings of Jesus on peace might be open to discussion and more or less explained away, but no one as yet, as long as the Empire lasted, dared to dream of making a Califate of the Papacy or Emirates of the Partiarchates of the Eastern Church.The secular clergy resembled only the civil magistracy of Rome and not that military officialdom which culminated in the imperator. Thus the Roman principle of government, the division of powers among magistrates and administrators, which had developed under the Republic both to safeguard liberty and to increase efficiency, continued to be applicable to church officials, even under the growing crystallization of the great imperial bureaucracy.

The Church of the Sacraments, therefore, offered a school for statesmanship which outrivalled the monasteries, because it trained the moral leaders of the secular world in that kind of leadership most needed when the political structure of the Empire began to fall in ruins under the barbarian attack. The authority of the bishops continued to be recognized after that of their civil colleagues had disappeared. This was not merely a tribute to the moral force of an organized religion, it was also a recognition of the fact that the religion of peace had also its arsenal for spiritual warfare in the control of the sacraments. The legions of Caesar were no longer in garrisons in the cities from Britain to the Mediterranean, but the lightning of excommunication by the Roman pontiff was seldom defied, and still more seldom defied successfully. Thus the Church, even in its weakest hour of contamination with superstition, met the evils of the Dark Age in their own terms and forced respect for its pontificate, not only in its spiritual office but also at the courts or in the trains of rulers and chieftains, over whose shrewd but ignorant minds, the churchmen established increasing sway.

The qualification for the office of bishop was, therefore, not saintly unworldliness, but, as in the case of the abbots, capacity for leadership. The result was the same in both cases, the interests of the great game of politics tended to dominate those of theology, and power in this world overshadowed salvation in the next. As power, in the conditions of anarchy then prevailing, was maintained by the ready use of violence in both attack and defense, the bishops entered into the practices of the feudal system or the service of kings, even more than the abbots. Although it was not considered fitting for them to accompany war-bands on forays, they could join in major expeditions, as when Bishop Odo of Bayeux accompanied his half-brother, William the Conqueror, on what was perhaps the most successful marauding expedition of the Middle Ages. The Bayeux tapestry, that unique historical document which the Norman ladies embroidered for his cathedral, shows the doughty bishop wielding his battle-mace in the midst of the charging cavalry. The mace was the weapon of the fighting clergy because it avoided the spilling of blood; for, with nice distinction, they could use it to smash the enemies' skulls instead of piercing their bodies with the sword.

Such warrior princes of the church were bound to increase in numbers if the appointment to bishoprics or abbacies were to get wholly into the hands of the secular rulers. Fortunately for the church, this danger to its independence as well as to its spiritual life was averted by movements of reform, the greatest of which spread from the Burgundian monastery of Cluny in the tenth and eleventh centuries. Ultimately, under the leadership of a stern monk, Hildebrand, who, as Gregory VII, became pope in 1073, it struck back at the growing feudalism of the upper clergy, with terrifying effect. The triumph of Gregory over the Emperor, Henry IV, who knelt in penitential sackcloth and ashes in the snows of Canossa in Tuscany while he sought audience with the Pope, was a dramatic episode in the efforts to protect the clergy from the sin of simony, that is, traffic in church offices by secular patrons. The struggle over preferment was by no means ended by this dramatic blow nor by agreements (concordats) which followed, for the "war of investiture" between papacy and monarchs continued with varying success throughout the whole Middle Ages. But the moral standard, which had been raised in the heart of the Dark Age by the joint influence of monastic and papal reformers, remained as a lasting bulwark against the further feudalism, that is to say militarization, of the Church.

The Cluniac reform did not stop here, however. In one of the most daring protests of all history, at the very time when force and violence dominated Europe, it struck at the war system itself. In the closing decade of the tenth century, spurred by the Cluny monks, aided by the greatest noble of southern France, the Duke of Aquitaine, church councils in central France, followed by similar action a little later in northern France and Burgundy, opened a new chapter in the history of law, in an effort to lessen if not in fact to put an end to private warfare — the one kind of war that was most prevalent and disastrous in feudal Europe. Bishops and counts were called upon to enforce within their territories peace decrees drawn up to protect the defenseless and unarmed, not only members of the clergy and church property, but also the merchants, the pilgrims, the women, the peasants, and even the cattle and tools for farming. The ban of excommunication was the weapon to be used against violation of what was termed the Peace of the Church *(pax ecclesiae)* or the Peace of God *(pax Dei)*.

Less sweeping but more practical in those iron times, was the Truce of God *(treuga* or *treva Dei)*, which forbade all acts of war during certain days of the week. It began (1027) as a glorified week-end, from Saturday noon until Monday morning, but by the middle of the eleventh century covered a full half of the week, beginning Wednesday evening, and in many areas extended over Lent and the greatest of the feast days of the Church. About three-quarters of the year was thus to be reserved for peaceful life. Nursed by Cluny, the movement soon spread over France and Flanders, and thence throughout Germany as a result of the action of a synod held in Mainz in 1085, in the presence of the Emperor Henry IV. In England, where the strong arm of the king was the chief guarantee of peace, the Truce of God was of less importance, but in the formative period of English law-making in the middle of the twelfth century, its principles were embodied in the laws of the land. In course of time, this was also true of the movement in the land of its origin. The strong line of the Capetian kings, who prepared the way for the prerogatives of the thirteenth-century kings, Philip Augustus, Saint Louis and Philip IV, by their suppression of rival feudal lords, achieved what the Church had failed to establish through the use of its spiritual weapons.

For the Truce of God, like the Peace of God which preceded it, was a failure. That is the universal judgment of historians. Even the support of Popes and Church Councils, from that at Clermont in 1095 to those of the Lateran in the twelfth century, was not enough to make the great reform effective. Neither excommunication nor the prescription of oaths of adherence to leagues of peace held back the tide of war, whenever the prize was high enough or the chance good for spoils of victory. The only prevention of war that was really effective was the resort to force by sovereigns or peoples strong enough to suppress anarchy. Peace within the state and peace between states has no sure footing in self-abnegation. It awaits the coming of justice; and justice, at least in warlike societies, wears a sword.

The lesson from the Dark Age should not pass unnoticed now. The moral outlawry of war was tried once, with all the terrors of excommunication behind it, promising violators eternal punishment in hell. But even in that credulous age, when no one doubted that such realities lay behind the ban of the Church, the lust of war could not be suppressed by moral appeals or the threat of consequences hereafter. It is true that the churchmen of the tenth and eleventh centuries had to deal with a society given over to constant war, but they had a stronger ally in the unquestioning faith of their flocks. It was only as the processes of daily life grew more and more dependent upon peace, and as this dominant fact became embodied in institutions capable of defending themselves against force and violence that the Dark Age, with its iron law of war, gave way to an era in which the ideals of Christianity began to be realized in slow but certain progress.

In spite of the feudal and local character of much of the history of the Church through the Dark Age, it kept alive a sense of the spiritual unity of the Christian peoples. In fact in all the confusing elements of the medieval world it was the one really unifying agency both by the influence of its creed and of its organization. The Bishop of Rome had the prestige of spiritual succession to the Emperors, bearing the title of Pontifex Maximus, inherited from the head priest of the old pagan regime[2]. The retention of Latin as the language of its worship even among people who could not understand it was also a unifying element, linking its worship with the city in which it was believed that Peter the "Prince of Apostles" had established the Episcopate.

The connection with the East, however, had never been strong, and in 1054 there was a formal separation of the Roman Catholic Church from the Greek Orthodox, a schism never wholly healed. In the West, however, the Church carried on the heritage of Rome in its structure, copying the administrative divisions of the Empire in its ecclesiastical organization. That it could successfully take over to a great degree the Roman structure of government was partly due to the fact that the Church could tap a new source of income in the tribute paid it by its members. Unlike the temporal powers, it could count upon the free gifts of those who received spiritual benefits in return for material contributions. Thus it was able to build its churches, and its schools were enabled to furnish the rudiments of education. It encouraged travel both by the hostels which the monks maintained for wayfarers and by its provisions for moving the clergy from place to place. In many cases it substituted its law for the crude justice of king or tribal leader. Though canon law was religious rather than secular, this had no reactionary consequences in the early Middle Ages, since the Church served as an instrument for the revival of some of the secular influences of antique law.

Finally all of these trends towards the unity of the Christian West were fused into a new concept of Christendom as a result of the Crusades. In the

[2] A few words of explanation may be pertinent here. The Pontifex Maximus under the Roman Republic took over the functions of the king in the administration of religious law and resided in the *regia*, "the house of the king." The sacrificial duties of the king were carried out by a *rex sacrorum*, a designation not used in the hierarchy of the church; for, in the administration of the sacraments, there is no higher title than bishop; the Pope is only *Bishop of Rome* in the hierarchy of holy orders (*hierarchia ordinis*). He holds his more exalted status, as do the cardinals and archbishops, as administrators, in the *hierarchia jurisdictionis*.

eleventh century, there was a revival of Islam, much of which had fallen into the hands of the Seljuk Turks, a tribe of Asiatic nomads who took up the Crescent with the vigor of converts. They lacked the tolerance of the earlier Moslems and closed the Holy Places in Jerusalem to Christian pilgrims. They also constituted a new menace to the still surviving Eastern Roman, or Byzantine, Empire. The Pope Urban II (1087-99) saw great possibilities in this sequence of events. If the Church could take the Holy Land out of the hands of the Moslems, its prestige would be increased at home and perhaps abroad to the extent that East and West might be united again. No one knows all that Urban may have dreamed. In 1095 he summoned the first Crusade against the infidel. The response to that call was tremendous. From all stations of life and all nations the crusaders came. But as crusade succeeded crusade for about two hundred years, the influence of this movement upon Christianity was to make it more like that of the Mohammedanism which it combated, a religion of militarism, promising eternal salvation for those who killed the enemies of the true faith.

The early crusades were justified by both clergy and warriors alike as pilgrimages of penance, in keeping with that penitential system by which the Church sought to enforce the moral law in the rude society of the early middle ages. Under the influence of the Clunaic reform in the tenth century, pilgrimages to holy places increased, and the first crusade was a pilgrimage in arms, to ensure safety both on the way to the Holy Land against the Saracen there. As time went on the military character tended to dominate. But, fortunately, by a natural evolution, the commercial and purely worldly interests came to the fore, and the crusaders brought about a great growth of trade, especially throughout the Mediterranean. The need of money for campaigns at such a long distance from home made the feudal rulers more concerned with the prosperity of their domains than with the wars of the countryside. Thus, the very movement which gave expression to the idea of Christendom ended by strengthening the elements of secular politics in the national state.

The Papacy

Before national kingships could develop, however, the Bishops of Rome had extended their spiritual empire over all Western Europe and had asserted claims of sovereignty superior to those of any other ruler. This was not merely the consequence of moral prestige in a world that offered little to rival moral leadership; nor is it to be explained being simply due to the fact that the Roman organization was the only one which had inherited the efficient structure of the old Roman Empire. In the absence of developed secular government the sphere of religion extended over many things which are now regarded as purely matters of worldly concern. The Church was the pioneer in agriculture as well as in education; and by its control of the crises of life through the sacramental system it gave the sanction to what was proper in society. But over and above all this, in a world which with unquestioning faith regarded this life as but the preparation for the life to come, the officials of a divinely ordained organization directing the pathway of mankind to these eternal ends were bound to translate influence into power, and for the interest of the common man, persuasion into coercion.

The development of the Papacy from the Bishopric of Rome to the papal monarchy of the Middle Ages was at first slow and uncertain. But by the latter part of the fifth century its prestige was already powerful enough for Leo the Great to turn back the invasion of Rome by the Huns. A notable step towards securing its independence from secular interference was taken in 1059 under Nicholas II, who issued a decree which definitely and for all time took the election of the Pope out of the hands of the Emperor and the people of Rome and placed it in those of the cardinals, or clergy of his own court. A few years later the claim of papal sovereignty was clearly set forth by Pope Gregory VII.

In his brief document called the *Dictatus*, he asserted the absolute sovereignty of the Pope within the Church and his supremacy over all princes; no one could pass judgment upon his acts nor annul his decrees; he could depose emperors and "absolve subjects from allegiance to an unjust ruler." To William the Conqueror of England he laid down the theory that the papal and kingly powers are like the sun and moon among the heavenly bodies, the kingly being responsible to the papal authority. But his most dramatic triumph was over Henry IV at Canossa, when the emperor was forced to accept the Pope's terms under the most humiliating conditions. Henry gained a strategic advantage from it in his struggle with German feudalism, but the stigma of penance was a warning to secular rulers.

For the next two centuries the struggle for supremacy between Popes and Emperors was the outstanding theme of European history. But its familiar outlines, traced in the pages of every school textbook, need not be detailed here, because the political issues with which it dealt, the claims of theocracy or empire, were not permanent in the history of Europe. The papal prerogatives rested upon the protection of the rights of the Church at a time when the secular state was too weak or immature to perform more than the most elementary functions of government. Under these conditions moral leadership could never hope for complete victory, but it could at least hold in check the cruder forms of violence and anarchy and ultimately provide the secular rulers with trained and intelligent ministers who could take their place alongside those who had risen in the rough school of war. From the Norman Lanfranc to Richelieu a long line of ecclesiastical statesmen had helped their sovereigns to impose upon Europe the discipline of law and order.

Meanwhile the Papacy pursued its great career. The most powerful monarch of the Middle Ages was Pope Innocent III (1198-1216) to whom all the rulers of Europe offered their obedience or yielded to the threat of excommunication and interdict. But already the tide was turning, and the national states began to show a capacity for government which by the end of the century enabled them to prevent for all time the establishment of anything resembling a califate of the Western world.

Of the great fields of medieval government, war, justice, and taxation, the Church was by its very nature withheld from war — except insofar as it became involved in feudalism or could justify it as a just war for the defense of the faith or the established order. Now it was to see both the administration of justice and of money fall into the hands of the national state. In the administration of justice the Church courts had never held more than a fraction of the field, mainly that concerned with the lives of the clergy themselves. Now even this was to be taken from them, although the process was a long and slow one.

In the control of the purse, however, though there was destined to be a compromise which permitted the continuing of offerings to Rome, the power of Papal taxation was soon disputed and overthrown. The Popes themselves naturally refused to recognize this historic trend and thus claims to supremacy were never more extreme than those formulated by Pope Boniface VIII in the opening years of the fourteenth century. He forbade all churchmen to pay any part of the Church's revenues to a king without Papal consent and threatened with excommunication any ruler who attempted to exact payments of this kind. Although he later modified these claims, the treasure that flowed to Rome was far greater than that of any other monarch. In the jubilee year of 1300 more than a million pilgrims thronged to the city of Peter, filling the papal coffers with their offerings so overwhelmingly that the keepers are said to have had to collect the piles of money with garden rakes. But three years later this last of the great medieval Popes died in exile forced upon him by the king of France.

The Canon Law

The medieval Church was more than the organization of religion; it was the guardian of morals, and therefore played a major role in the history of freedom in an age when secular institutions had by no means so strong an influence on human conduct. It was a state as well, with laws of its own, a vast and complicated administrative system, and a supreme executive. There is nothing in all the history of politics that parallels the development of this institution, which survived Roman persecution to share the power of the Caesars and which arose through feudal anarchy to assert its leadership over Christendom.

It is only the historian, however, who shares with the theologian the interest in this unique assertion of the moral order throughout long centuries of European anarchy. The process of secularization embodied in the national state was destined to deny the claims of ecclesiastical sovereignty with the result that the polity of the Church has been largely ignored by those who study politics with an eye to its practical bearing upon the lives and fortunes of their contemporaries. This process of lessening interest in ecclesiastical institutions had already begun when the medieval lawyers revived the study of Roman law in the eleventh, twelfth and thirteenth centuries.

But to understand the history of Europe when the national state was taking shape, it is necessary to keep in mind the fact that the Church was something more than an agency of salvation; it was also a government ruling the conduct of large sections of the population and in this latter regard was a political organization paralleling those of the secular world. The two functions required two different hierarchies in the Church, the "heirarchy of jurisdiction," as it was called, for the administration of the affairs of the Church, especially its finances and its relations with the secular powers and, on the other hand, the "hierarchy of holy orders" for the guidance of man's relation to God. The latter function falls within the sphere of theology, the former of law and politics. The sacramental system has been observed by devout Catholics who at the same time have asserted their opposition to the claims of bishops, archbishops or the Popes themselves in the management of the Church and its relations to other sovereignties.

The principles upon which the hierarchy of jurisdiction rests are drawn chiefly from the legislation of Church councils and the decrees of the Popes. From the sixth century on, collections were made of these, but in course of time seeming contraditions crept in where a council or a Pope was evidently in disagreement with previous pronouncements. If the medieval Church was to have a systematic body of law supporting its claim and assisting its administration, the jurists of the Canon Law had to codify it in the manner of the Roman law. This task was undertaken in the twelfth century and by brilliant scholarship was embodied in a volume which became the manual for Church courts throughout the Middle Ages, the *Decretum* of Gratian.

Gratian's task as he defined it was to make a "harmony of the discords," *concordantia discordantium canonum,* and he achieved his purpose by scholastic methods applied to the whole wide reach of Church history and theology. Although he did not solve all the questions in a way wholly satisfactory to the theologians and his manual was never made the authoritative law book of the Church, its influence remained unabated and the text later received additions at the hands of popes themselves. But throughout the Middle Ages there was no authoritative acceptance of the body of the canon law. That had to await the Council of Trent in the storm and stress of the religious controversy of the sixteenth century. Then finally the teachings of the Church were defined in both matters of faith and discipline.

It is a striking fact that there is no special treatment of peace or war in the canon law. Gratian's great collection of citations of the Church Fathers here fell back upon Augustine and quoted a few familiar extracts on the two points of the profession of arms and the defense of just war. The just war is one that is waged in support of existing order; unjust war is war in support of irresponsible anarchy. Between established governments, however, war is just when after formal declaration it is waged to regain what has been stolen, or to repel attack. As for the profession of arms, the soldier who fights in obedience to authority is not guilty of murder in killing his enemies; on the contrary, the performance of his duty calls for the highest praise when it is carried out in the interests of the common good. This is indeed a slight treatment of so vital a subject, but it is perhaps all that might be expected from one writing in the midst of the feudal age.

The chief interest of the canon law and by far the greater part of Gratian's manual dealt with the punishment for sin, whether in violation of the rules of society or those of the Church. As war itself was not a function of the Church but of the secular power, the prescription for its use did not lie within the field that might be called the public law of the Church, a field which was narrowed progressively by the rise of the national states. The law of the Church was chiefly in the field which we would call private law today, having to do with the conduct and morals of the individual. But whatever the reason, the fact remains that ecclesiastical law never came clearly to grips with the application of those general principles which were laid down by Augustine.

St. Thomas Aquinas

In the later Middle Ages, as the national state developed and assumed an ever-increasing role in the suppression of feudal wars, it was not the lawyers but the theologians who carried on the discussion as to the nature of just and unjust war. For, as the lawyers were more and more recognized as functionaries serving the secular rulers, practical politics tended to supplant interest in theory. The contribution of the theologians, however, was not wholly theoretic, for it was based on a treatment of the nature of law which the jurists could in turn apply to the practices of government. It therefore emerged in full force in the seventeenth century with the new and challenging advent of international law.

It was while St. Louis was king of France in the middle of the thirteenth century that Thomas Aquinas, the greatest of the medieval theologians, built upon the foundations laid down by Augustine the system of scholastic thought with reference to war and peace which still remains for Catholic thinkers the classic formulation of the place of war in civilized society. It should be said, however, that neither Aquinas nor any other of the great scholastic philosophers took up the problem of war and peace as a major section of their system of thought. Nor did they make any great advance upon the teaching of Augustine. They systematized and adapted it to an age in which the national kingdoms were arising to dispute the prerogatives of any other sovereignty, whether of Pope or Emperor. Therefore, the single tenet of Augustine's day, that a just war might be fought for the maintenance of a single established order mirroring the moral order of the world — like that of the Roman Empire of which the Church was a part — was less and less applicable to the realities of politics.

The result was that the teachings of the medieval theologians became more abstract. Going back to the pagan philosophers of Greece and Rome they proclaimed again that there was a natural society of man and upon this fact the rights and duties relative to the morality of war were based. The same high moral note is to be found in the statement that peace by conciliation is to be preferred over the exercise of force and that there is greater merit in preventing war than in vindicating one's rights by bloodshed. But when the scholastic turned from these moral exhortations to the more realistic question of just how conciliation and pacific settlement should take the place of war, they had to recognize that the absence of a superior tribunal before which a prince could seek redress might justify him in making war even when he was not the victim of attack.

Upon the whole, Aquinas' treatment of war and peace is hardly more than a refinement upon Augustine's, although for both of them the pioneering work had been done by the early Church Fathers. Both of them were eclectic systematizers rather than bold explorers in the realm of thought like the greatest of the Greeks. The reason was to be found in the fact that religion based upon faith is bound by its very nature to set limits to free inquiry. To recognize this fact is not to disparage religion but to seek new frontiers for thought outside the field of theology. This is what has happened in the modern world which still finds a place for scholastic learning and theology while greatly extending the areas of secular thought.

The measure of advance between the fifth and the thirteenth centuries is registered in the fact that while Augustine used Cicero as his chief guide to antique thought Aquinas had at his disposal translations of Aristotle made by fellow Dominicans under his own direction. This was of the greatest importance because he was able to draw upon the most comprehensive and systematic thinkers of the pagan world. If his treatment of war and peace was somewhat sketchy, this was compensated for by his masterly survey of the nature of law and of government in which the thought of Aristotle was sharpened through a definite application to Christian teaching, and the "natural law" which governs the universe became "divine reason." Human reason being a mirror of the divine is capable of distinguishing between good and evil. The knowledge of the truth which is shared by all men in varying degrees is therefore a perception of eternal law, which in essence is as unchangeable as the Deity. Since the nature of God is revealed to us in the Scriptures, the performance of Christian duty is the test of good citizenship as well as of good government. Nowhere does he cut through the close-knit fabric of his logic to reach the conclusion, implicit in it, in any such powerful phrase as that of Jesus, that the fulfillment of the "law of the prophets" lay in the single command to love God and one's neighbors; and yet the conclusion of the whole vast system of scholastic thought summed up by Aquinas is simply this, that charity should be the guiding principle of men and governments. But he is careful to add that charity does not exclude the idea and practice of the correction of evil by compulsion. Peace is not anarchy based upon individual goodwill but an ordered relationship for the purpose of establishing or strengthening control, a thought which was continually recurring in the Canon Law. But concord does not mean uniformity; in this way the political philosophy of Aquinas reached out and beyond either the unity of church or empire to furnish guidance for the new political system of the national state which was only then beginning to show its outlines, in the days when Aquinas taught[3].

[3] As in Hooker's *Ecclesiastical Polity*. See below.

The political philosophy of Aquinas was much more than that of a churchman. His great *Summa Theologica,* designed to weld Christian thought with that of the best of antiquity, especially as developed in Aristotle, distinguishes between the theological virtues founded on faith and the natural virtues founded on reason. Faith looks for guidance to revelation, reason to natural law. By reason Aquinas did not mean individual reasoning, but the whole rational process or idea, a scholastic phrasing which veiled the historic importance of this revival of the central idea of Stoic and Christian ethics as embodied in Roman law. It is a long way from this philosophical discussion of Aquinas to the American Declaration of Independence, almost five centuries later, but in Aquinas we have the basic principle set forth in Jefferson's appeal to the "Law of Nature and of Nature's God." This is not the only modern touch in the great *Summa.* Lord Acton[4] has pointed out that the monk of Cassino was one of the pioneers in the theory of the sovereignty of the people, and summarizes two texts of Aquinas in support of this claim:

The whole nation ought to have a share in governing itself; the Constitution ought to combine a limited and elective monarchy, with an aristocracy of merit, and such an admixture of democracy as shall admit all classes to office, by popular election. No government has a right to levy taxes beyond the limit determined by the people. All political authority is derived from poular suffrage, and all laws must be made by the people of their representatives. There is no security for us as long as we depend on the will of another man.

"It is worth while to observe," says Acton, "that Aquinas wrote at the very moment when Simon de Montfort summoned the Commons, and that the political vision of the Neopolitan friar was centuries in advance of the English statesman's." It must be added, however, that as Acton himself admits, Aquinas "would have made the Papacy control all Christian governments."

The Heresy of Pacifism

Before turning from this current of religious thought we must pause for a moment to recall the fate of that trend of Christian faith and practice which was based on the Sermon on the Mount and the nonresistant element in the teaching of Jesus. We have seen how the Church even in the Apostolic age had refused to allow the doctrine of Christian charity to be exaggerated to the point of weakening the moral fibre or disturbing normal social obligations. The apostles and the bishops who followed after them were conscious of the need of preventing the new religion from becoming an Oriental orgiastic cult like those other religions of Asia Minor which were at that time penetrating the Empire. St. Paul's admonitions to the Corinthians and the Romans were those of a wise administrator and law-giver when he warned the Christian converts not to exaggerate "the freedom which is in Christ" but to accept the duties of Roman citizenship wherever they did not run contrary to the fundamental principles of the new religion.

[4] *Cf. Essays on Freedom and Liberty,* p. 64.

The Church thus took its stand upon the side of law and order, but this did not hush the consciences of many in the early days of Christianity who took literally and without qualification Christ's admonition to return evil with good and to turn the other cheek to the agressor. This unqualified acceptance of the doctrine of nonresistance is the denial of the legitimacy of war altogether. It was not long, however, until these followers of the gospel of meekness passed out of the orthodox fold into heresies. They were the uncompromising puritans of the early Church.

This spirit of nonresistance never wholly died out in Christendom. In their refusal to admit the legitimacy of one of the oldest duties of citizenship, that of bearing arms, the Christians opened themselves to the charge that they were the enemies of society. As the Church became more and more responsible for the maintenance of the social structure in the anarchy that followed upon the break-up of the Empire it had no place for those extremists who could not accept a compromise which might force them to become the spiritual accomplices of secular warriors. It could and did provide a way of escape from the dilemma for the more moderately minded by enabling them to become members of the clergy which did not itself bear arms. But the secular clergy of bishops and priests were still much closer to the stern rulers of a world so largely given over to violence than the monks who sought escape from all contamination from the world.

For a time, in the opening of the fifth century, it almost seemed as though the new religion were becoming primarily a monastic movement, for the deserts were filled with thousands of hermits and the monasteries began to multiply. The ardent call to the monastic life by Augustine's contemporary, St. Jerome, found a strong echo in the more spiritually minded; but this did not wholly satisfy the ardor of those to whom the Sermon on the Mount remained the vital guide of Christian conduct. Citing the words of Jesus, these became the heretics of pacifism, and in one movement after another they kept reappearing throughout the Middle Ages. They had no influence, however, upon authority until after the Protestant Reformation. Then in sects and movements of which the Anabaptists and the Quakers are perhaps the most important they continued to maintain the spirit of nonresistance which neither persecution nor the failure to win the world to their conviction has ever shaken, much less destroyed. There is no greater witness to the power of the moral ideal in history than the fact that this relatively small group of those who in the eyes of the law and the Church were in fact moral anarchists has profoundly affected public opinion in all civilized countries in the world today.

Faith, Its Great Adventures and Its Crimes

The Church of the Middle Ages presents two contrasting chapters of history: the one illumined by the high adventure of philosophic thought on eternal problems and by poetic vision or saintly life; the other, the dark, cruel and terrible chapter of persecution and the Inquisition. The history of freedom must keep both of these aspects of medieval religion and society in mind.

It was inevitable that the medieval mind should be dominated by the one institution that offered it a home. Slowly but steadily through the Dark Age the monastic schools extended their influence, producing from time to time intellectual leaders whose teachings challenged the Church to movements of reform. Then the cathedral schools developed under the sponsorship of the bishops, to become the nurseries of universities at centers like Paris and Oxford. The one great subject, of superlative intellectual interest, was then what it still is, an inquiry into the nature of life and the world.

But having in the Church his source of knowledge, outside of the limited experiences of daily life, the medieval thinker was naturally held to it as the guide to truth. This, however, did not prevent Scholasticism from reaching boldly into the realm of mystery over which theology asserted sovereign rights. It ventured the bold claim for reason, that it could apprehend absolute, objective truth, and thus rethink the thoughts of God; that philosophy could even extend beyond theology to learn from Aristotle what was not to be found in the scriptures or in the doctrines of the Church, and finally set about working out to its logical conclusion all the assumptions upon which is built its vast edifice of thought.

At its best, as in Abelard, Scholasticism was an adventure in freedom, questioning the authorities by listing and then showing up their opposing principles. But this method of the critic was taken over by the systematizer, as when, in *The Sentences* of Peter Lombard, the sacramental system is woven together out of authorities that fit the plan, or as in Aquinas, the greatest of them all, when the whole system of theology is rounded out by superlative logic. Both in method and subject matter, it might have been expected that Scholasticism would breed heresies; but speculation was not heresy if it were not designed to question the practices of the Church or destroy the loyalty of believers. The limits of Scholastic thought were not set by ecclesiastical courts or inquisition so much as by the inherent limits of its own method, that of deduction from authorities instead of questioning their validity. There is nothing here of the bold, critical method of the Greek thinkers, which is that of science today.

But the greatest of the Scholastics could build freely on the accepted foundations of faith an intellectual structure of enduring strength. Unfortunately, philosophy also attracts the dilletantes, and they brought Scholasticism into disrepute, and properly so when the problems became trivial mental puzzles from which serious people were bound to turn away. Attacked by both humanist scholars and Protestant theologians, Scholasticism became an object of ridicule; but neither of these opponents had found the basis for a substitute method so long as they held to authorities, biblical or pagan, as the basis of their ideas or opinions. The humanist critics were skeptical, but not constructive beyond the scope of antique thought. It was only with the rise of science that the real intellectual emancipation from medievalism began. There had been isolated examples of it long before, in

Roger Bacon, Gallileo and others; but the scientific revolution, which is the real beginning of our age, did not get under way until the eighteenth century.

As we turn from this high plane of speculative thought to the history of heresy and persecution, it is as if the very shadow of the prison closes in on our spirits as it did on those of the victims of the most terrible of oppressions in medieval history. It is important to realize that the Inquisition, as the authorized instrument for the suppression of heresy, was not founded until the thirteenth century, paralleling in the Church the new policing of kingdoms by royal officialdom. The Dark Age bothered little over distinctions in matters of creed, when superstition thrived on ignorance and credulity. Although heathen myth had been disowned and forgotten in the conversion to Christianity, its world of taboo lived on.

There are no better manuals on it than in the lives of the saints of those times, especially that of Gregory of Tours[5]. Demons and angels had replaced the heathen spirit world but carried on in much the same way, to be placated by magic spells, or ceremonies performed by the priests, who were often not less superstitious than their flock. The Church sought to reform the cruder of these superstitions, but became contaminated in the process, a fact which produced the great monastic reforms and was also a cause of heresy in the protests that reached beyond demands for reform to rebellion.

There were two reasons why heresy played no important part in the history of the Dark Age: the first is traceable to the credulity and ignorance of the clergy as well as the laity; the second was that monasticism, especially in movements like the reforms of Cluny and Clairvaux, offered within the church a favored place for the spiritually minded. The church councils continued to denounce heresy, for that was part of their traditional functions, but no major heresy threatened the life of the church in the early Middle Ages, even in the new centers of learning, for they had to await more vital stimulus to faith than was to be found in the wrangling of schoolmen. It came where men of stern moral character challenged a church whose officers trafficked with evil and in their eyes were the betrayers instead of servants of Christ.

Although the history of heresy is, as we have seen throughout this study, an essential — and often a central — chapter in the history of freedom, we are interested here only in the treatment of variant beliefs, not in their content, except as they bear upon their treatment in church and state. Viewed from this point of view, we may divide the heretics into three classes. First there were those spiritually minded men and women whose protests against worldliness in the church led to a denial of its control of salvation through the priesthood of the sacraments, a deadly heresy in the eyes of those who were at that time building the structure of clerical power into the magnificent proportions of the papal monarchy. Of such evangelical heresies the one which was widest spread was that of the Waldenses, described below.

[5] There is an illuminating treatise on this in Ernest Brehaut's *Gregory of Tours* (New York: Columbia University Press, 1916), 284 pp.

The second class of heretics had nothing in common with those who believed themselves to be more Christian than the Church, for they were frankly non-Christian, professing a new kind of paganism, not unlike that cult of Mithra which five centuries earier had been a rival to Christianity in the Roman Empire. This was the heresy of the Cathari, better known in our histories as that of the Albigenses in southern France, its chief home. The third class of heretics were those theological leaders capable of framing systems of belief whose followers either separated themselves from the church or were driven out of it, except insofar as they recanted. Of these the outstanding figures were John Wyclif in fourteenth century England, John Huss, in fifteenth century Bohemia, and finally Martin Luther and the other heads of Protestantism. So closely indeed are they related to Protestantism that we shall deal with their movements there instead of as part of medieval history.

The story of the Waldenses is one of the most humanly touching and tragic in the history of persecutions. The name comes from Peter Waldo, a rich merchant of Lyons, who in 1170 sold or gave away his possessions, part to his family and the rest to the poor, to whom he dedicated the rest of his life, preaching from New Testament texts which he had learned by heart, simple sermons for ignorant people who shared his high dream of a restoration of primitive Christianity. "The Poor Men of Lyons" (*Pauperes Spiritu,* the Poor in Spirit) as they called themselves, or simply *Pauperes,* had a message for the slum-dwellers of the medieval cities which, in its religious appeal, was in fact not unlike that which fed the flame of Christian faith in the working quarters of the Roman Empire. It was also much the same impulse which led the Franciscans in the thirteenth century to preach their gospel of apostolic poverty. The success of Waldo's Poor Men was immediate. Missionaries travelled from city to city, working their way as cobblers or common laborers, entering the homes of the poor and spreading doctrines which struck at the root of Catholicism: that sinful priests cannot have the "power to bind and loose," that central doctrine of the sacraments; that masses or prayers for the dead are of no avail; that laymen can preach and hear confession; that prayers are as efficacious from a stable as from an altar.

Waldo and his followers showed once more what the history of Christianity made clear from its beginning: that simple minded men can penetrate farther into the confused processes of history than the philosophers of the schools. The heresies in the Waldensian doctrines were absolute rebellion against sacerdotalism and were at once recognized as such. But four centuries later most of them were embraced by half of Christendom, for the Waldenses, or what was left of them, after enduring the cruelest of persecutions, finally were merged into Protestantism.

The story of these persecutions is as noble a record of indomitable courage and unyielding moral stamina of the victims as it is a witness to the inhuman cruelty of the persecutors. In the history of freedom those who suffered and died for their beliefs — whether they were right or wrong, and many were wrong — were as truly heroes as the martyrs of the early church.

They were murdered by the thousands in Spain, in France, in Italy and Germany, yet they maintained a great, a fundamental principle, the right to worship God in their own way. And with this they denied any right to enforce their beliefs upon others because, like the Quakers of a later day, they would not take an oath and held that all homicide, even in the execution of a sentence, was a mortal sin. The history of freedom has no more inspiring chapter than that of the Waldenses, whose last massacre in the Apline valleys of Savoy roused Protestant England and stirred Milton to write immortal verse on their behalf.

Utterly different was the history of the other, and greatest of all medieval heresies, which lies across the pathway of freedom, the Cathari.

The Cathari (from the Greek word *Katharos,* pure), were the most widely spread of medieval heretical sects. We know them best as Albigenses, citizens of Albi in southern France, although their greatest center there was Toulouse. However, they were but the Western offshoots of Eastern sects known as Bogomils, Bulgari or Paulicians, named after Paul of Samosata, the Patriarch of Antioch, who was deposed by the pagan emperor Aurelian in 272 A.D., because he taught the humanity of Jesus instead the doctrine of his merging with the *Logos,* which was then developing into the orthodox creed. The influence of this Paulician doctrine extended throughout the East, where it still lasts on in Russian sects. In Europe it survived such persecutions of those as the Empress Theodora, who is alleged to have murdered a hundred thousand in the Balkans; and in the tenth century new settlements were made by immigrants from Asia Minor.

The movement of this obscure heresy, henceforth known as Bulgar or Bogomil, spread along the mountain ranges of Central Europe, into Milan and the West. Then, in southern France, it linked up with the similar heresy of Adoptionism — that Jesus was adopted as the Son of God in his baptism by John — which had lingered on in Spain at least until the ninth century. Finally, in the eleventh century, the Catharists carried these heresies to an extreme by tying them in with the greatest theological rival of the early church, Manichaeanism, that Persian system of dualism in which Satan, the power of Darkness, continues the age-long battle against the God of Light. The Cathari, according to one manual of the sect which has escaped destruction, can escape from the devil only by destroying the flesh, and the "pure" by a spiritual baptism may receive the true and only resurrection, that of the spirit. Asceticism is carried to the complete renunciation of family ties and the rule of absolute chastity.

Never was there a sterner code nor one less worthy of acceptance as a guide to civilized life. But the suppression of the Albigenses was carried to the bitter end of their complete annihilation by a crusade and the erection of the Inquisition of the Middle Ages. It therefore marks the opening of a new era, that of the systematic effort of both church and state to suppress heresy — efforts so prodigious as to denature for a while, the central purposes of both, as even the state took over from the Inquisition some of its most barbarous procedures. Persecution tends to spread like a contagion, and the era of the Inquisition was a prelude to conspiracy and religious wars. But history also makes sudden turns, and the red glare of those years of persecution and war proved to be the dawn of a larger freedom than the world had ever known.

The Inquisition of the Middle Ages

Although the recognition of Christianity as the state religion of the Roman Empire at the close of the fourth century was marked by intolerance, religious persecution was not efficiently organized until almost nine centuries later, in the erection of the Papal Inquisition. In this long interval, the suppression of heresy was sporadic, but failure to inflict punishment was due to the lack of competent tribunals and the relative weakness of heresy itself rather than to any hesitation to punish the greatest of all crimes, treason against God. The crusade against the Manichaean Cathari of Languedoc in the early part of the twelfth century, which was the terrible curtain-raiser to the Inquisition, was an episode apart and belongs with the unification of the French monarchy as well as with the history of persecution. Popular violence against those charged with heresy could generally be counted upon by bishops when they took action either by themselves or in concert with the secular power. But the most extensive measures were those of the free-thinking Emperor Frederick II, and good kings like St. Louis supported and applied the cruelest of procedures in the service of Catholic orthodoxy.

Within the Church the case for persecution was clear to both canon lawyers and theologians. With the growth of law the canonists could fall back on the authority of the Roman codes, not only that of Theodosius, which we have noted in an earlier chapter, but that of Justinian, prescribing death for Manichaeans. Gratian's *Decretum* has a passage that reads like an incitation to violence that seems almost incoherent. "Cut off the decayed flesh, expel the mangy sheep from the fold, lest the whole house, the whole body, the whole flock, burn, perish, rot, die. Arius was but one spark in Alexandria, but as that spark was not at once put out, the whole earth was laid waste by its flame."[6] As for the theologians, the greatest of them, Aquinas, stated the case with merciless clarity and a deceptive appearance of humanity. The heretics "deserve not only to be separated from the Church by excommunication, but also to be severed from the world by death." The Church, however, is merciful, and "looks to the conversion of the wanderer; therefore she condemns not at once but after the first and second admonition. After that, if he is yet stubborn, the Church, no longer hoping for his conversion, looks to the salvation of others by excommunicating him from the Church, and furthermore delivers him to the secular tribunal to be exterminated from the world by death." Aquinas dwells, in the next section, on the charity of the Church in receiving back a penitent heretic, but with due imposition of penance. But with the relapsed, the case is hopeless and "they are not delivered from the pain of death."

[6] Gratian, *Decretum*, II, Causa XXIV, Q. 3, can. 16.

In God's tribunal, those who return are always received, because God is a searcher of hearts, and knows those who return in sincerity. But the Church cannot imitate God in this, for she presumes that those who relapse after being once received, are not sincere in their return; hence she does not debar them from the way of salvation, but neither does she protect them from the sentence of death.[7]

In the light of history, few texts are more misleading than this last sentence. If the Church "did not debar [the relapsed heretic] from salvation," it made sure of his death by turning him over to the secular arm for execution.

To deal effectively with the heresies of the thirteenth century, the Church needed something more efficient than the bishops' courts, a tribunal under papal control, officered by specially qualified experts. The rise of the Mendicant Orders, especially the Dominicans, or preaching friars, supplied inquisitors who, moving from place to place, generally from monastery to monastery, had no local ties and only one allegiance, that to the Pope.

In 1252, two years after the death of Emperor Frederick II had removed the last Hohenstaufen rival of the Papacy, Pope Innocent IV promulgated the bull *Ad extirpanda* in which the whole framework of the Inquisition was set up. In every city and state of Italy, heretics were to be denounced by citizens nominated by bishops or inquisitors who delivered them for trial, while seizing their goods. There were elaborate provisions for ensuring that the State should hold all accused in prison and, when they would not confess, inflict torture on them. The expenses of the Inquisition were borne by the State. The fines and proceeds of confiscation were divided between the city and the bishop and inquisitors. There is a suggestion of possible opposition to this stupendous law in the instructions issued by Innocent to inquisitors to enforce it by excommunicating those failing to apply it. Yet there are only a few isolated instances of recalcitrance by the local authorities.

This Papal Inquisition as set up in Italy was not recognized north of the Alps where episcopal courts were more to the fore. But the system developed in France in the suppression of the Cathari and the "Poor Men of Lyons" or Waldenses. In England the inquisitors were not well received until Wyclif's time, when with the rise of the Lollards, Parliament taking alarm, passed the article *De haeretico comburendo* in a statute of 1401, which imposed the penalty of death for heresy. The law had a chequered history in Tudor times, being invoked in numerous burnings, and was finally abrogated under Charles II.

The procedures of the Inquisition were designed not to weigh evidence with impartial tests but to secure conviction of those brought before it, accepting the mere fact of their accusation as the presumption of guilt. The accused were not allowed to know who had accused them or what was the evidence on which they were held. They had to meet their judges in secret, faced with the dread uncertainties — and certainties — which they had no way of countering but by denials which were not believed. The chief pur-

[7] *Summa Theologica*, Part II of Second Part, Q. 11, art. 3 and 4.

pose of the Inquisition was to extract confession, and the inquisitor had ample means at his disposal to secure it.

First of all, with fellow inquisitors at his side, he could browbeat the victim by reminding him of the fearful fate in store for him unless he complied with what was expected of him, confession and penance. If this terroristic seance failed to shake the resolution — or the integrity — of the accused, the next stage in the procedure of the Inquisition was solitary imprisonment on starvation fare, from which the accused could be brought back into court weakened in body and, it was hoped, weakened in spirit as well. This was the session to which the clever inquisitor could look forward with satisfaction, for, if he could confuse the victim by tricky questions against which a tired mind had no sure defense, he then achieved a legalistic success in his infamous profession.

The inquisitor was also the judge and was not held down by any formal rules of legal procedure. His actions were wholly arbitrary and could not be questioned without endangering the case of the accused by arousing the inquisitor's vindictive enmity. The accused was forbidden to have advocates or lawyers present to advise him and support his case, having usually to meet his judges alone. In all the literature on the Inquisition there is almost no mention of witnesses for the defence; it would have been a dangerous thing to testify for an alleged heretic.

If all these devices failed, the accused was taken into the torture chamber to scare him, if possible, by the threats of the torturer, or to subject him to the most refined instruments for the most terrible of bodily suffering. Finally, there was the sentence of death, camouflaged under the formula "release to the secular arm," as the Church itself did not shed blood. The actual number of executions due to the Inquisition has been much exaggerated. There were relatively few compared with the many heretics actually tried. For most of them the terrifying procedures of the trials themselves were apparently sufficiently effective. With heavy penances and sentences reaching as far as life imprisonment, it would not seem reasonable to expect that many should be sent to the stake. But no ruler could refuse to carry out the sentence without becoming a party to the crime of heresy, and both governments and people joined readily in putting to death those who were adjudged guilty of the greatest of all crimes, treason against God by the denial of the authority of His representative on earth, the Catholic Church.[8]

To most people the word Inquisition applies only to Spain. The Papal Inquisition of the Middle Ages, which we have been examining, has been forgotten by all but students of the history of those far-off centuries. But the flames of the Spanish auto-da-fe flickered across the seas after America was discovered and when Europe was stirring with the new day of the Renaissance. It differed from the medieval institution in one fundamental respect:

---

[8] The analogy between heresy and treason was established by Innocent III in a bull of March 25, 1199, (*Decretals* V, VII, 10) before the founding of the Inquisition, but it was used by it to punish heretics after death by dishonoring their remains or taking over whatever property they might have left.

it was wholly Spanish and royal, an instrument of national unification as well as of orthodoxy.[9] Although there were persecutions and massacres, especially of the Jews, in the thirteenth and fourteenth centuries, it was not until 1480 that the Inquisition was finally established in Castile by Ferdinand and Isabella, and a few years later in Aragon.

From the first, therefore, it had the great advantage of strong central control over local tribunals throughout the country, with an elaborate, well articulated spy system, thus ensuring rapid action and unquestioned authority. The advantage to the monarchs was financial as well as political, as they shared in the confiscations of the property of all those convicted by the Inquisition. Under the monarch the inquisitor was supreme. He could try clerics as well as laymen, and the dread procedure of his tribunal was systematized torture, greatly refined from even the terrible methods of the Middle Ages. Moreover, unlike the Medieval Inquisition, death was the penalty paid by thousands. The inquisitor who wielded this malign power with the greatest or at least the most effective zeal was the Dominican Torquemada, under whose direction alone over two thousand victims are said to have been burned at the stake. It was he and fanatics like him who forced almost a million Jews to leave Spain. By confiscating their property, a regular proceeding of the Inquisition, and driving out the most alert and enterprising part of the population, Moors as well as Jews, Torquemada forced the reluctant Ferdinand and Isabella to ruin the land they had united. The commercial decay of Spain was a direct consequence of this blind bigotry, while the temper of the Spanish people took on the sharp edge of intolerance which it had notably lacked in the early Middle Ages.

So great an institution as the regimentation of belief calls for a larger survey than is possible here. It marks a distinct stage in the history of European thought. While it was only one manifestation of intolerance, and was followed by others equally cruel, in the wars of religion and the tyranny of despots, yet it is more than an incident in the history of freedom. It lies sinister and menacing across the pathway of justice, with the denial of even the most elementary safeguards of human rights. Fortunately, the fact that it dealt so largely in controversial matters has not prevented either Catholic or Protestant historians from dealing objectively with it. The greatest of these, Henry C. Lea, raised American historiography to new levels by contributions to the history of law and religion in the Middle Ages. His *History of the Inquisition of the Middle Ages*[10] has become a classic, but, like so

[9] Lea, the historian of the Spanish Inquisition, makes the point that this use of it as an agency of the monarchy was a coincidence rather than a deeply conceived political scheme.

[10] The work of Henry C. Lea as one of the greatest historians America has produced has never been adequately recognized outside of the field of scholarship. In addition to the three-volume *History of the Inquisition of the Middle Ages,* he wrote *A History of the Inquisition in Spain* in four volumes, *Superstition and Force,* dealing with the antecedents of the Inquisition in the institutions or ordeal and torture, a *History of Auricular Confession and Indulgences in the Latin Church,* in three volumes, *Sacerdotal Celibacy in the Christian Church,* and other studies in Church history.

many classics, is seldom read. It is fitting, therefore, to quote here the eloquent and moving conclusion of this work:

When we consider the simple earnestness with which multitudes of humble heretics endured the extremity of outrage and the most cruel of deaths, in the endeavour to ascertain and obey the will of God in the fashioning of their lives, we recognize what material existed for the development of true Christianity, and for the improvement of the race, far down in the obscurer ranks of society. We can see now how greatly advanced might be the condition of humanity had that leaven been allowed to penetrate the whole mass in place of being burned out with fire. Unorganized and unresisting, the heretics were unable to withstand the overwhelming forces arrayed against them. Power and place and wealth were threatened by their practical interpretation of the teachings of Christ. The pride of opinion in the vast and laboriously constructed theories of scholastic theology, the conscientious belief in the exclusive salvation obtainable through the Church alone, the recognized duty of exterminating the infected sheep and preserving the vineyard of the Lord from the ravages of heretical foxes, all united to form a conservatism against which even the heroic endurance of the sectaries was unavailing. Yet there are few pages in the history of humanity more touching, few records of self-sacrifice more inspiring, few examples more instructive of the height to which the soul can rise above the weakness of the flesh, than those which we may glean from the fragmentary documents of the Inquisition and the scanty references of the chroniclers to the abhorred heretics so industriously tracked and so pitilessly despatched. Ignorant and toiling men and women — peasants, mechanics, and the like — dimly conscious that the system of society was wrong, that the commands of God were perverted or neglected, that humanity was capable of higher development, if it could but find and follow the Divine Will; striving each in his humble sphere to solve the inscrutable and awful problems of existence, to secure in tribulation his own salvation, and to help his fellows in the arduous task — these forgotten martyrs of the truth drew from themselves alone the strength which enabled them to dare and to endure martyrdom. No prizes of ambition lay before them to tempt their departure from the safe and beaten track, no sympathizing crowds surrounded the piles of fagots and strengthened them in the fearful trial; but scorn and hatred and loathing were their portion to the last. Save in cases of relapse, life could always be saved by recantation and return to the bosom of the Church, which recognized that even from a worldly point of view a converted heretic was more valuable than a martyred one, yet the steadfast resolution, which the orthodox characterized as satanic hardening of the heart, was too common to excite surprise. . . .[11]

A few words will suffice to summarize the career of the medieval Inquisition. It introduced a system of jurisprudence which infected the criminal law of all the lands subject to its influence, and rendered the administration of penal justice a cruel mockery for centuries. . . . In its long career of blood and fire, the only credit which it can claim is the suppresion of the pernicious dogmas of the Cathari, and in this its agency may be regarded as superfluous, for those dogmas carried in themselves the seeds of self-destruction, and higher wisdom might have trusted to their self-extinction. Thus the judgment of impartial history must be that the Inquisition was the monstrous offspring of mistaken zeal, utilized by selfish greed and lust of power to smother the higher aspirations of humanity and stimulate its baser appetites.[12]

[11] Henry C. Lea, *History of the Inquisition* (New York: Harpers, 1888), Vol. III, pp. 645-646.

[12] *Ibid.*, pp. 649-650.

CHAPTER IX

THE BEGINNINGS OF THE NATIONAL STATE

The Origin of the National State

NO OTHER single theme in medieval or modern times can compare in importance with that of the history of the National State, for it is the upbuilding of the varied structure within which the peoples of the civilized world have until now worked out their destiny. The process by which it developed from simple beginnings to the vast and complicated institutions of today cannot be described in terms of politics alone, for politics is but the register of an infinite number of other things, the needs and impulses of man pushing forever against the inertia that clings to immemorial habits of thought and action. Viewed in this light, the national state is not a structure of set design to be analyzed according to the laws of logic; it is rather a thing of mystery because it partakes of the mystery of life itself. This means that the social sciences can never reduce it to formulae; the plotted curves of the statistician are forever breaking down, as unforeseen forces spring surprises on the intelligence.

Indeed the work of the social scientists is, strangely, not unlike that of their far-distant predecessors, the prophets and the law-givers, who once canalized mystery from magic to religion, attempting, like St. Paul, to control and direct for the benefit of society those forces which have power to sway the life of men and nations, while recognizing that the things of mystery with which they dealt lay in another world from that of rational control. Politics in the secularizing West took on the task begun by those pioneers who first charted the course from barbarism to ordered life.

The fact that the Western world had to begin almost over again with the decline and fall of the Roman empire did not change the nature of the problem confronting civilization; it only varied the terms. In the open stretches of the north there could be no such neatly planned reconstructions of the body politic as in the little city states of the ancient world. In both space and time the drama widened out. The northern peoples had to wait almost eight hundred years after the Germanic migrations — from the fifth to the thirteenth century — before they found their counterparts to Cleisthenes and Servius Tullius. Even then, when law courts had been established and parliaments begun, no one could well foresee the kind of a state system which was taking shape for the nations of the modern world. It grew out of the soil of tribal and feudal Europe, forced by need and shaped by circumstance. So varied was the development that what happened in England and France in the thirteenth century did not take place in sections of central and eastern Europe until the nineteenth or even the twentieth century, although some of these areas of backward political evolution were as far advanced in culture, in arts and in letters as the peoples of western Europe.

It would carry us too far afield to trace all the elements which have gone into the making of this most complicated of all political creations, in which the nations of the modern world sought to achieve for themselves in one way or another the equivalent of what the American national state set forth as its ideal of freedom, in the Declaration of Independence — the right to life, liberty and the pursuit of happiness. Our survey covers only the major elements in the history of politics within the different countries with which it deals and the final results of political evolution as shown in the forms of government and the interrelations of the national states with one another. But our understanding of either the domestic or the foreign policies of governments depends upon the degree to which we understand their heritage and outlook in the past, their characteristics as shown in their history, and their relative equipment for the battle of life in resources and in strategic situations in the world.

The history of the state is the largest chapter in the history of freedom.

Nationality and the National State

Little is to be gained from attempting at this point to define what we mean either by "nation" or "national state." We have already seen that the nations of Europe are not racial unities in the anthropological sense. In course of time, however, the long association of those who lived under like circumstances produced characteristics which other people did not share and which were therefore considered to be typical of a nation as a whole. Although these differences are chiefly in externals, such as manners, modes of speech and ways of living, it is the externals which always impress the traveler and literary observer and even, to a great extent, the people themselves. Although there are nations of fairly pure racial stock, there may be other nations alongside them of the same stock, but fully conscious of a different national life. The thing that makes a nation is its sense of its own identity, and this is more a cultural than a racial fact.

There is no need to elaborate this point for any American reader; the crowd at a baseball game may be drawn from all corners of the earth, but it responds differently to the excitement of the sport from the way the individuals or their ancestors would have done in the lands of their origin. One of the greatest American scientists, Professor Pupin, who had been a Serbian shepherd boy in his youth, used to tell how he first became aware that he was an American; it was not in the classroom where the science of government was being taught, but on the college campus where he received the accolade of comradeship from his fellows. These are processes which far outrun the scope of politics, but political history and experience give them a final expression in the conscious life of that great historic entity which we call a nation.

The national state is this nation organized. It is therefore both the people and their government. It is well to bear this distinction in mind because in the final analysis government is not all. There is the "sphere of freedom" in which the individual holds his own against the tendency of government to overreach itself. Pushed to the extreme, freedom becomes anarchy. When it is denied, the state becomes a tyranny. These are commonplace axioms when formulated in such general terms, but the supreme issue of politics today is this very question of how the national state can, at one and the same time, make the state efficient and yet do justice to the claims of the individual.

It goes without saying that there was little if any consciousness of these high themes in the Orient or Russia or in the governments which were laying the foundations of the national state of Europe in the heart of the Dark Age. The processes of fusion, which were at work through those long centuries of the early Middle Ages, did not all point in the direction which history subsequently followed. The unity of the church presented a rival ideal to that of the secular ruler and one which might well have seemed to be the embodiment of the forces of civilization because of its championship of the oral order. Feudal rulers held their estates with little regard to national frontiers, and kings as well as emperors conquered foreign territory solely for the wealth and power it brought them. These were the cross currents of history before the national state got fully under way.

They even swept across the language frontiers, although language is perhaps, in spite of certain exceptions in commerce, the most distinctive mark of nationality. It was not until modern times, however, that the language frontiers largely coincided with the boundaries of states. Under the feudal regime, French was long the language of the English court — Richard the Lion-Hearted, the hero of English legend, did not speak English — half of France was held by the English kings, and Burgundian lands lay along the language frontier to the east of France with roots in Flanders, part of which owed allegiance to both the King of the French and the Holy Roman Emperor. The various parts of France, Germany or Italy were almost as different from one another as the nations of the present day. Indeed, some of the languages and cultures of Europe were blotted out in the formation of the modern nations, as was the case with the culture of Toulouse in the southwest and the language of Brittany in the northwest of France. While differences of speech have lasted within each nation, they have been subordinated into dialects which, however, have a remarkable tenacity.

Symbols of Nationality

The self-conscious effort of nationalist leaders in the world today has by a strange paradox made nationalism seem more artificial than it really is. For the teachers of nationalism would make little headway if they could not invoke as allies the pride and prejudice which spring from a sense of par-·ticipation in great achievements by the nation of which they are a part. Those of us who live in the hurry of a busy world are apt to forget how much the past lives on in both the conscious and the subconscious mind. The flag is not just the symbol of present loyalties, but the principal expression of all the history that a people cherishes. Bugle notes are stirring, not merely because of their music, but because men's feet have marched to those notes in battle. Nationalism is history seen emotionally, and when the emotions take command, only that history is listened to which repeats the well-worn orthodoxies, no matter how their romances may violate the actual facts. For example, it does not matter to an Englishman that the flag that "braved a thousand years the battle and the breezes" has only been in existence since the seventeenth century when the Cross of St. Andrew was joined to that of St. George. The Tricolor had no such past behind it, but Lamartine could quell a revolution by appealing to the pride of Frenchmen, saying that it had made the circle of the world when in reality it was the symbol of but a minority of Frenchmen.

The flag, however, merely stands witness to that mythical kind of history which exalts the emotions of a people as it used to do when the blind bard wove it out of the deeds of gods as well as of men. From the eagles of the Roman legions to the Stars and Stripes in the American schoolroom there has always been some emblem or device to evoke loyalty to both past and present. But the outstanding symbols in the history of European nationalism were not the standards of kings but the kings themselves. The oriflamme of France would have meant little without such personalities as St. Louis who embodied the finest ideals of the thirteenth century, or such efficient organization as that of Philip IV, "the lawyer's king" at the opening of the fourteenth century. The anointing of kings with sacred oil was already an old ceremony before the days of Saul of Judah, but in the middle ages it became almost an eighth sacrament. The one constitutional document produced by the Holy Roman Empire, the Golden Bull, was mostly concerned with insuring proper ceremonial at the coronation of the emperors. Court protocol still lasts on in Europe, but only a shadow remains of the dominant place it once occupied as a symbol of royal power. It was not only Confucius who recognized that ceremonial is an inherent element in government, but the people as well as the rulers of Europe. Royalty has been the greatest institution of developing nationalism, for under its protecting aegis warriors and statesmen have hammered out the framework of the state. Even where the kings no longer rule, the state itself retains some flavor of that personal devotion to Majesty which played so great a part in the history of European nations.

The nationalism of today is not in essence different from that of past centuries. It is wholly wrong to think of it as the mere product of a make-believe kind of history which pretends, falsely, that primitive tribalism can be revived as a permanent factor in the modern world. But, however fallacious the theory of racial unity, nationalism can create a kinship of the spirit for those who share, or whose ancestors have shared, common dangers and have participated in great events. This kinship finds expression in art and literature as well as in the upbuilding of the state, but it is created above all by the enforced solidarity in times of crisis, when everyone is more or less dependent on everyone else. This is one reason why war is the common motif of the history of nationalism; the drama of battle is also an intense school of discipline. Practically all nations have fought their way to freedom or to secure and maintain their right to live. But war carried a double-edged sword and the security which it sought by force of arms created insecurity in the relations of one nation with another by the inevitable resistance of one nation to politics of power.

This is the supreme lesson of the Nazi and Fascist revolutions of our time. But it also has been the clue to the history of Europe from the thirteenth century to the present. Just as in the ancient city state war furnished a framework of politics, so it was destined to do in the countries of northern Europe; but it was ultimately to prove as deadly for them as for the states of the antique world. We have seen that war was not only an instrument of policy in the dealings of one state with another, but that it was also the instrument of statecraft by which the structure of government in Greece and Rome was recast from primitive beginnings into the world of politics.

The same was true, in varied terms, of the history of the northern countries of Europe. The time came when the needs of war could not be met either by feudal levies or royal levies, and then politics began to take shape in the institutions of representative government and systematic legal procedure. But, as in antiquity, each state developed government for itself alone, and — at least at first — left to war or haphazard diplomacy the interrelations of the states among themselves. The result of this partial evolution of government, which so largely limited its institutions to domestic affairs, was that the national state system of Europe grew to resemble, in fatal if enlarged outlines, the world of ancient Greece, a world of separate sovereignties in which the war system remains as the one great force in human affairs still uncontrolled and filled with infinite capacity for good or ill. It is that world which is today at grips with destiny.

Growth of Territorial Sovereignty

Feudal politics, if one may so dignify the intrigues and wars of the early Middle Ages, was very different from the complex relationships of the modern world, so much so indeed that in literature as in history feudalism has remained a more or less unreal romantic episode in the history of Europe rather than what it really was, an age-long impediment to the progress of civilization. So far as it had organization — for upon the whole it resembled anarchy more than the settled processes of law and order — its organization was that of immobility rather than of continuing adjustment to changing circumstances. The reason for this was that the circumstances changed seldom or only slowly, for a system based on land is by its very nature repetitive like the seasons, whose recurring routine governs the habits of those dependent upon the soil for their livelihood.

This very inertia, however, tends to strengthen old and familiar folkways because the only safe rule of life is to repeat year after year what has been necessary or profitable the year before. Local customs, therefore, while they differed from one countryside to another, offered a rude kind of fundamental law, which even chivalry hesitated to break and which gave a certain strength to even the hopeless and sordid world of serfdom and villenage. This is partly the reason why feudalism in Asia as well as in Europe maintained its institutions, slight as they were, through long centuries, rivalling if not surpassing the stability of those of the tribal organizations of the society which preceded it. A landed society tends to take on the immobility of the land itself. There are but two ways to change it; by war or by the use of money. Feudalism did not differentiate between ownership and sovereignty; and it was only slowly through the twelfth and thirteenth centuries that the dynamics of war began to make way for the more elusive dynamics of money.

In one regard, however, the feudal rulers were like modern governments, for territorial sovereignty has remained the chief interest of national states. It is a paradoxical but ineluctable fact, that, in spite of the growth of capitalism, nations cling to their lands much more than to their investments. The land is the visible symbol of a nation, a home just as it was that of the feudal domain. But the fact that in feudal times the land was almost the sole basis of subsistence explains to some extent the prevalence of war, because the lack of important wealth in either goods or money forced the feudal rulers to rely upon the produce of their estates. The extension of their power, therefore, could only come by increasing their lands at the expense of their neighbors.

It was this linking of landed wealth with military power which determined the character of the first stage of the evolution of the national state. For the business of kings was first of all to become the greatest feudal lords by incorporating more and more feudal territories under their sovereignty. Insofar as feudalism was organized anarchy, the only escape from it was by the extension of single units of power over the heterogeneous mass of lesser rulers. It was but natural, therefore, that the war system should produce the war lord as supreme ruler; thus we come upon the first task of kingship, the incorporation of multiple ownerships into a single sovereignty.

But even within feudalism, war by no means covered all the activities or interests of either ruler or ruled. Though the feudal magnates concentrated upon war as the basis — or assurance — of their power, within their own states they administered justice and collected the feudal dues or levies according to customary rules. These differed more or less from one feudal court to another, but, like the differences in language and customs, they changed relatively little, reflecting as they did the static nature of a society based upon agriculture and the primitive arts of warfare. Progress in law and order came where the trickle of trade through forest pathways broadened out to commerce in the market places of rising towns and cities. This change in western Europe took place about the same time as the Crusades and has often been attributed to them; but it is also possible that it would have taken place, and perhaps even more rapidly if the feudal leadership of western Europe had not been diverted from the growth of industry and trade at home to far off adventure in the Holy Land.

Even as it was, those rulers who became the most powerful were the ones on whose territories the market towns were situated and who were shrewd enough to see the advantage that must accrue to them from defending and protecting the merchants while profiting from their increase in wealth. With money they could buy services and employ mercenary troops who would always be at their command, instead of the feudal levies of vassals of uncertain and divided allegiance.

Towns and Cities

There is no more obscure movement of emancipation in the history of freedom than that of the communal revolution which broke through the rigid framework of a landed society, with war as its corollary, to the dynamics of a money economy, with its stimulus of rivalry within and between nations. The road to economic freedom has still a long way to go, but it began when the traders of the early Middle Ages, threading their way with their packs on the forest pathways along the estates of robber barons, gave way to caravans under military protection, and the market towns grew into cities. The extension of royal policing helped to end this long era of isolation; but more important were the effects of the Crusades, opening the markets of the Levant to Italian adventurers who sold their goods on both sides of the Alps.

The settlements which began in the Dark Age were of various kinds. The townless Germans were naturally most impressed by the mighty walls with which the Romans had protected their cities, calling them fortresses or burhs (*bourges* in Gothic, *boroughs* in English) and their inhabitants "burgesses." Rebuilding the walls of the cities along the Rhine and the Danube, under the rule of prince bishops, they enjoyed a special peace, with heavier penalties against violence than elsewhere and the right to be sued only in the town court — a protection also extended to the traders in the new towns in the interior of Germany. The attempt of bishops and princes to treat newcomers as serfs was countered by the Emperor Henry V in charters for Spires and Worms, which forbade this practice; and the saying ran "Stadtluft macht frei," "The air of the city makes one free." The result was a rapid growth of the German cities in population and in self-government, which spread even first among the merchants, then among the workers in craft-guilds regulating on the own account much of the social as well as the economic life.

This development of industrial democracy in the early days of capitalism worked out badly, however; for the craft-guilds, although subordinate to the town-council (*Rat*), made up of the richer merchant class, succeeded in getting a narrow, local protectionist policy accepted which restricted the trade with strangers. This isolationizing trend of the German cities had fatal consequences for the country as a whole. No strong middle class became nationally self-conscious, ensuring political freedom for the common man. The city leagues of the Rhine and the Hansa, were, as we shall see, sufficient proof of German capacity for politics in the new capitalist era. Unfortunately the political disunity of the country offered the middle class no inducement for more than temporary alliance with either king or nobles, that left-handed way in which the English institutions of freedom secured a footing.

In France the dawn of the new era of business came in the reign of Philip II at the opening of the thirteenth century, and reached high noon by the century's end. The first step toward freedom in that feudal age was for the towns to demand a place in the feudal system itself, insisting on freedom from outside interference, and excluding clergy and nobles from membership. The movement to establish these communes was favored by the king as a check on feudalism and spread in something like a revolution in northern France. There were more towns, however, the most of them in central France, which contented themselves with charters limiting the services to be paid to their lord but not granting them political rights. Paris, like other larger cities, still remained largely subject to seignorial exploitation, with a complex of officials which enabled the king to keep his hand in. This he did through the provost of Paris, appointed by him, leaving less and less for the leading representative of the citizens, the provost of the merchant guild. Yet Paris proved to have a vitality to rival that of royalty when, in the dark days of the Hundred Years' War the Provost of the Merchants, Etienne Marcel, became for a short and tragic interlude, the voice of commercial France. Unfortunately, the other cities refused to respond to his call, for no middle-class conscience developed in a France devastated by war and nerveless from oppression and misrule.

Turning from the Continent to England, we find an entirely different history. From the earliest days, the *tun*, even if only a village, sometimes took on the character of a minute city state, electing its own officials and holding its own in the conduct of most purely local affairs, while the boroughs (*burhs*), strongholds or places of refuge, were more subject to lord or king, except when given privileges by royal charter. But even this had its advantages, for the fact that the burgesses paid military and court dues to the sheriff, the king's officer, was the reason that they sat with the knights of the shire in the House of Commons, when Parliament was organized in the thirteenth century. Seldom has so important an event depended on what

225

looks at first sight to be a mere technicality. For it was the Commons which made Parliament the voice of English freedom, and, ultimately, by its control of the purse the sovereign power in the government. It was more than a technicality, however, which widened the base of the Commons by including the lesser gentry, it was a practical device for dealing with national problems, which showed how far the feudal system was sinking into the background of English life.

There was no one pattern for the English towns, each one fitting into its local setting:

> There were many distinct elements which were combined in each of the complex groups which we call a town. London was not improbably a combination of Hundreds (divisions of a county), and Norwich of leets (a kind of limited baronial court); while others were more like an aggregation of separate manors. The mere analysis of the surviving officers shows how complete each separate structure was — in some instances the agricultural element is strong; in some the old royal officer, the portreeve, maintained his position through many changes: in some a manorial officer, the bailiff, continued to hold sway; in others we find a constitution of the Norman type, or at least with Norman nomenclature, in which the mayor, who was an elected official, held the reins of government.[1]

London still reflects in its quaint customs of Lord Mayor's Show and Guildhall ceremonies the varied origins of its liberties.

The King's Justice

The advantage which the greater sovereigns had over the lesser feudal lords in military matters was paralleled by an equal advantage in peacetime government. For the king could provide a more experienced administration of justice than the cruder feudal courts. There were two main sources of law in the Middle Ages: local custom and the vestiges of Roman law and administration. The former was chiefly handed down by tradition and varied greatly throughout the feudal world; but it was systematized and improved by both ecclesiastical and temporal rulers. The Church as we have seen, tried to impose morality by its system of "penitentials" which graded penance for sins according to their nature and by the legislation of its councils and the decrees of the Popes.

The secular rulers in the early Middle Ages played a less important role, but even shortly after the invasions, some of the "barbarians" codified their tribal law when they had settled down upon the territory of the Empire. The outstanding examples of this process were the Salic law of the Franks and various collections of Anglo-Saxon laws, especially of Ine and Alfred. Some of these helped to construct the framework of a national law out of the varying pattern of still earlier days. Merely to write down the law was to bring more system into it and give it permanence.

Alongside this dual development of ecclesiastical and Germanic law the

---

[1] W. Cunningham, *Growth of English Industry and Commerce during the Early and Middle Ages*, 4th edition (New York: Cambridge, 1905), 998 pp.

Roman law itself persisted in a fragmentary form in those sections of the Continent where the Roman population was strongest. This was made possible by the Germanic principle of the personality of the law, that is to say, that each individual carried his own law with him. This sense of the personality of the law was common to all primitive peoples. We have spoken above of the attempt of the Roman praetors to judge foreigners according to their own law and how the development of the *jus gentium* (mistakenly referred to as the law of nations) eventually influenced the law for Roman citizens. The Code of Justinian was unknown in the West outside Italy and was too vast a structure for ready use in the simplified life of the early Middle Ages. But other collections, such as the Code of Theodosius and "epitomes" were available, and their use never wholly died out even in the heart of the Dark Age. Nevertheless, the anarchy of feudal days offered little opportunity for the development of any systematic organs of government and it was not until the end of the twelfth century that the study and practice of law became a profession. This was largely due to the recovery of a good text of Justinian and to its study especially at the University of Bologna, which became the first great university of the Middle Ages. Teachers and students alike had to translate technicalities of the old Roman procedure in terms that would make them applicable to or at least intelligible under medieval conditions. They therefore wrote "glosses" upon the texts, sometimes merely verbal definitions, sometimes historical and legal comment.

It was not so much this profession of scholarship, however, which drew the thousands who thronged from over the Alps to the lecture rooms of Bologna as the promise of a secular alternative to a career in the Church which previously had been the only profession open to those who did not wish to become either soldiers or merchants. For the practice of the law was becoming a new adjunct of politics, as the jurists returned from the classroom to advise rulers how to set up courts of law as well as how to run them. It was in this way that Rome exercised such a decisive influence on the structure of the new states in continental Europe, an influence more real though less obvious than that of the shadowy prestige which it conferred upon the medieval empire.

While the lawyers were available for the service of any ruler intelligent enough to see how they could be used to strengthen his grasp upon his subjects, they were mostly to be found at those larger courts where the business of governing was becoming more and more complex with the rise of money economy. Of these the court of the Kings of the French was the busiest and most important, as Paris in the thirteenth century was the metropolis of western Europe. While the university taught philosophy and theology on the hill of St. Geneviève where it still stands, the lawyers concentrated around the royal palace on the island on the Seine, where in the middle of the century Louis IX (St. Louis) made over a portion of the palace to them for the central law courts administering royal justice. There was still a touch of the earlier day when St. Louis held his court under an oak tree in the Park of Vincennes to the east of the city, as the earlier Germanic kings had done.

But by the end of the century the lawyers had so established themselves as the servants of royalty that Philip the Fair, who defied and overthrew the pretensions of the last great papal monarch, Boniface VIII, was known as the "lawyers' king."

Although in France the members of the new lawyer class were on the whole upon the side of the king against the feudal nobility, in Germany they upheld the authority of the duke or prince over against the claims of the emperor. They were sagacious and unscrupulous enemies of feudalism, the Papacy, the empire or any other power that threatened the rights of the princes on whom they were directly dependent for their livelihood and for their position in society. From the Roman law of the late imperial period they developed the principle that the will of the prince shall be law, the last resort of appeal. This was a principle which became very important in the early modern era, when it was applied to the authority of royalty as the basis of absolutism of the seventeenth and eighteenth centuries — the theory of the divine right of kings. Later it was applied to the authority of the national state, as had been the case in Republican Rome before sovereignty was concentrated in the hands of a monarch. It is an interesting fact that when the absolutism of the kings was overthrown by the revolutionary movements of the seventeenth and eighteenth centuries, the national state system went back again to the doctrine of Republican Rome, asserting absolute sovereignty for each state.

In England the strong rule of William the Conqueror had made possible the more extreme forms of feudal disorganization by preventing the growth of any great feudatories sufficiently powerful to challenge royalty itself. But Domesday Book, that unique mirror of medieval life at the height of feudalism, shows that the claims of the Norman conquerors who established their lordship throughout the country were largely conditioned by old English law, which was never abrogated or supplanted by a comprehensive enactment after the Conquest. Although French laws and customs were imported wholesale, local justice, that is, to say, the maintenance of ordinary law and order among the people themselves, continued in most of the old-time ways.

The "King's justice" profited from the practice, begun by William, of using sworn "juries" and itinerant "justices" for the administration of royal decrees, and for ascertaining property valuation in the collection of taxes. In course of time, that is to say by the end of the twelfth century, these juries had become the basis for the institution of trial by jury; and the financial duties of the traveling justices had so far given way to judicial functions that they constituted in effect circuit courts. It was in these courts, where cases were settled in the name of the king, that there developed the famous Common Law of the English — "common" because it was the same for the whole country, unlike the hodge-podge of traditions, laws and arbitrary decrees of feudal justice which, as on the Continent, differed in each community. Because it was more efficient, royal justice, administered in the twelfth and thirteenth centuries by the professional lawyers of the king, became more popular and was used as a decisive tool to weld the nation into a strong state.

The decisions of these royal justices were, in course of time, influenced by the canon law administered in the church courts and by treatises on the Roman law; in this latter connection two names stand out in the history of English law — Glanville, the justiciar of Henry II (1154-1189), and Bracton, the jurist of the middle of the thirteenth century whose treatise was to furnish an arsenal of precedent and argument for the lawyers who opposed the Stuart despotism four centuries later. Both of these, especially Bracton, were conscious of the fact that they were to some extent repeating the experience of Republican Rome, and while they exalted the power of the king over against feudal anarchy, they held to the principle of the earlier Roman jurists that the supreme authority resided in the state rather than in an absolute monarchy.

The great point about the Common Law was that it preserved the Anglo-Saxon right of the free man to be tried only after indictment by a jury of his peers. This was a fundamental principle of English criminal procedure; in the phrase of the lawyer it was "accusatory, not inquisitorial." This principle, undoubtedly borrowed from old English custom, was established in the King's courts after 1200; for the Norman and Plantagenet kings, being eminently practical rulers, built upon native institutions as a matter of convenience and efficiency. The Normans had brought little if any written law, while the realm which they had conquered was rich in experience in lawmaking, an experience which had strengthened instead of lessened the sense of individual rights and personal freedom. Therefore, the resort to Anglo-Saxon methods after the conquest ultimately proved of value not only to the king and the commonalty but also to those of the Norman feudatories who stood out against the Crown. In this way the principles and procedure of the Common Law helped to check that trend toward tyranny which prevailed on the Continent.

Unfortunately for the historian who wishes to produce a single clear-cut picture of the past, the Common Law was never codified. It was a recognized principle that its application and content were governed by local circumstances and followed precedent in such detail that the "king's justice" was not unified by any single hard and fast set of rules. Thus it served as a living vehicle for the expression of the common life and interest of both great and small in a country that took advantage of the king's protection to make the law work for the well-being of the community.

With the overthrow of feudalism, the king was regarded as the source of all law and of all justice — as is still the legal fiction today in England. Thus there grew up two sets of laws which it was the business of the courts to apply, the Common Law whose composite origin and make-up we have just described, and the edicts of the kings. The latter would seem to open the pathway to tyranny in spite of the institutions of liberty preserved from the past and might conceivably have done so under a strong line of rulers if the kings had not needed money for their wars, conducted for the most part in France and therefore less easily fought by feudal levies. They were thus obliged to turn for help to those who could fill the empty coffers of the royal treasury. This brings us to the origins of Parliament, one of the greatest chapters in the long history of government. With its advent the history of European politics opens its modern era. It is true that we are still in the thirteenth century, but that was when the institutions of the national state assumed the outlines which are recognizable today.

The Rise of Parliament in England

Along with the courts came parliaments, but with slower pace, for there was no such insistent need for the making of new laws as for the proper administration of the existing law and customs of a community. The evolution of the legislative branch of the government had, therefore, to await emergencies either in the affairs of the people or the ruler, because it was not in the nature of early societies to make changes in the laws except under the spur of immediate need. There could be little growth in the legislative organs of government in a society that was predominantly static.

The growth of legislation is in direct proportion to the transfer of social relations from a landed to a moneyed basis. It is primarily the effort to interpret and control changing relationships based on shifting rights, especially those arising from industry and trade. Thus we have seen in the ancient city state how the economic revolution that was disrupting the landed society changed both the structure of the state and the nature of citizenship. The same kind of revolutionary movement which recast the institutions of Greece and Rome swept with insistent if slower pace over western Europe from Denmark to Spain in the twelfth and thirteenth centuries, creating or developing an organ of government called parliament. It was, however, by no means so clear-cut a development as in the case of the city state, for it varied from a mere shadow of formal meetings, as in some of the feudal states of France and Germany, to a real organ of government in England, and, for a short time, in France as well.

The origins of these legislative bodies are almost as obscure as those of their juristic counterparts, the courts, and they reach to an equally remote antiquity. The councils of the elders who advised tribal chieftains in times of war or crisis furnished their primitive prototype, but in northern Europe these were more like feudal gatherings of the heads of tribes, such as that which met at the will of Agamemnon, than like the council of a single city state. The Assembly of Clovis' warriors, for example, was such a meeting of petty "kings." It is true that Charlemagne's Mayfield was more of a general meeting of his leading warriors, but the king-emperor summoned it to assent to his acts rather than as an embryo legislative body. The Reichstag of the Holy Roman Empire, which was in a sense its successor, reverted to the feudal type of a meeting of sovereigns for consultation and not of the representatives of a state, meeting to establish new laws in the common interest. Now and again the strong hand of an Emperor could give it more the semblance of a legislative body, and at the close of the Middle Ages, when the money power of the state was able to make itself felt, there was again the appearance of a parliamentary government in Germany. But the central story of the evolution of national law-making through representatives of the people is not to be found in the Empire. It was in England, and to a lesser degree in France, that the national state took the form which became the universal model for the nineteenth century, by developing under the aegis of royalty a body which was destined to take over the actual control of government.

The Anglo-Saxons, as we have seen, for some inexplicable reason, more than any other section of the Germanic peoples, kept alive that sense of personal rights and liberty which Tacitus described as characteristic of the early Germans. Just how much of its Germanic inheritance was retained by the Anglo-Saxon people has never been fully agreed upon by historians because the record is so slight. More than five centuries stretch between the Anglo-Saxon and Norman conquest, only a century short of the whole period from Magna Carta to the reign of Queen Victoria. There was much warring between the English tribes among themselves and between them and the Vikings and Danes who invaded them; and the only sources for the history of this period are some laws, charters and monastic annals.

Yet, from a close study of these records and of the traces of early institutions still showing in the structure of later times, historians have established the fact that alongside of and within the militaristic framework of feudalism and Norman kingship, the English people maintained some at least of the fundamentals of self-government. The feudal manorial system never wholly blotted out the self-government of the villages with their elected "reeves" and assembly "moots," for the oversight of local affairs, and "shire moots" which were left over from the tribal kingdoms. The National Assembly — composed of the leading dignatories of the realm; both clerical and lay — the "Moot of the Wise men," or *Witanagemot*, had at one time the outer marks at least of the later parliament. In theory, its powers were vast. It "could elect or depose the king, and it was only through its consent that the king could publish laws, impose taxes, decide on peace and war and form a tribunal of last resort for causes criminal and civil."[2] But actually it played no such sovereign role through most of its history, except in the one unhappy function of levying taxes or tribute money for the Danes. The tradition of the Witanagemot — or Witan as it continued to be called long after the conquest — was not lost, however. The Norman kings' great council *(Magnum Concilium)* which met from time to time, carried it on, although for advice in the daily tasks of government the Norman kings used the smaller personal council, or *curia regis*, which became more and more a judicial body — a court of law in the modern sense of the word.

The history of the welding of old English institutions with those which the Norman introduced is as rich as it is challenging. "From the eleventh century, most of the great forces of English history — royalty, the landed gentry, the Church, local institutions — proceed in their course of development through many a momentous crisis, but without substantial break. Be-

[2] F. W. Maitland, *Constitutional History of England* (Cambridge: The University Press, 1926. 548 pp.), p. 58.

fore the eleventh century, we witness the stunted growth of a Teutonic state which might have resulted in something more akin to the formation of Denmark or Norway than to that of England as it came to be. The eleventh century may be truly called the watershed in the development of English society."[3] But the sources for the history of this epochal development are also inadequate. The Norman kings were administrators rather than lawgivers. The laws of William I are few; there is no trace of a Norman law book until the very last years of the twelfth century, and both William and Henry I acceded to the demand for the "laws of Edward," which was really a demand for the old English law.

The origin of Parliament is obscured by the shifting meaning and indefiniteness of the terms used in contemporary records. It is only in the thirteenth century that it emerges as a national institution. In medieval Latin, *parliamentum* meant a *colloquium*, a discussion, such as the monks had in their monasteries on theological and other questions, or a conference between rulers or dignitaries. It finally came to be applied to the *concilium*, which had the right to "talk things over" with the king or his representatives. It was not to be expected that the king would readily bring questions of policy to this kind of assembly, which slowly acquired not only a name but a claim to share in the king's sovereignty. What the medieval kings wanted was support to carry out the policies which they had already decided upon. In earlier days and under feudalism this support would consist of men-at-arms, but as money economy began to make possible the hiring of mercenary troops, the chief object of discussion would not be how many soldiers were needed for war, but how much money could be raised to meet the expenses of the king. Fortunately for England the Plantagenet monarchs persisted in carrying on expensive wars on the Continent. The so-called Angevin Empire, which for long threatened the unity of France, and especially the wasteful crusades and wars of Richard I, by impoverishing the kingdom, created a situation of great embarrassment for the kings, of which the baronage, as the leaders of public opinion at that time, was quick to take advantage. The results were Magna Carta and Parliament.

Magna Carta was both a feudal and a national document. Insofar as it reasserted the rights and privileges of feudal barons it was, as we have said before, distinctly feudal; but it also set forth the fundamental principle that neither king nor baronage but the law of the land should be supreme in the realm. We have seen how the Norman and Plantagenet kings resorted to native English institutions; now the Norman barons were doing the same thing in a different setting: they borrowed from Anglo-Saxon customs to protect themselves from the Crown, and coupled baronial rights with those of the general rights of Englishmen. This meant that the institutions of English freedom were recognized and respected in a "law of the land," *(lex terrae)* instead of merely in the old Germanic idea of the personality of the law. The enduring value of this fundamental formulation of the suprem-

[3] Sir Paul Vinogradoff, *English Society in the Eleventh Century* (Oxford: The Clarendon Press, 1908), p. 1.

acy of law was more than an incident in medieval society; it was a permanent gain in the evolution of government, and in the history of freedom. This was evident when, four centuries later, the battle against the Stuart tyranny repeated in no small measure the issues of the time of King John, and Magna Carta appeared once more in a new and splendid reincarnation as the palladium of English liberation, a role which has never been denied it since, at least in the opinion of the English people.

The development of Parliament in thirteenth century England was a national growth, not the creation of any one statesman or king. History properly accords to Edward I the chief credit for the Model Parliament of 1295, but for half a century before it, the elements had been taking shape. As John's misrule had been the prime cause of Magna Carta, the incompetence of his son, Henry III made possible the first constitutional steps toward limited monarchy. This was the celebrated charter called the Provisions of Oxford of 1258, in which the barons set up a committee as a check on the misgovernment of the king.

But rule by an oligarchy proved to be a poor substitute for autocracy, and encouraged by the moral support of the Pope and the saintly Louis IX of France, Henry resorted to war on the hostile baronage. The rebel forces were joined by recruits from the cities and universities untrained in war but inspired by the thought (expressed in prose and verse at the time) that they were fighting for the rights of Englishmen. Welded into an army by the patriot soldier Simon de Montfort, they defeated and captured Henry and his son Edward (battle of Lewes, 1264), and then summoned a meeting of the great council to which, for the first time, representatives of the towns were called. This "Parliament" of 1265 was not representative of the whole nation, however, but only of the section of it which had fought the battle of freedom. Only twenty-three barons met in this packed session of the great council, and they had no thought of sharing their political power with the commoners — a thought still foreign to reactionaries for at least six hundred years of English parliamentary history.

The new device of representative government was not as new, however, as it might seem at first. For in the shire courts the juries had long been chosen to deal with the conduct of local affairs, chiefly juristic but also in part administrative. Moreover, although the ordinary meetings of the King's Council, (concilium regis) were attended by relatively few, others than the great magnates were sometimes called in.[4] Therefore it was not a departure from precedent but a definitely English use of it which Edward I fell back upon, when, in the "Model Parliament," he summoned the representatives of shire and borough to meet and "talk things over" with the Great Council.

This parliament was still not a law-making body, the legislative branch of the government which it is today. Its prime purpose was not to make laws,

[4] For example, in 1254, in order to meet the expenses of war in Gascony, Henry III summoned two knights of the shire by royal writ. This recognition of the minor gentry furnished a precedent for their representation in the parliament of 1265, when two burgesses were also summoned from every borough.

which remained the prerogative of the monarch, but to discuss questions of policy, some of which might be set forth in statutes bearing the king's signature, and, more especially, to help him by supplying him with funds. This last was certainly its chief purpose in the eyes of the kings; for as feudalism declined, the business of government began to cost more than the feudal dues could supply, and when there were added to the routine expenses of court and office, added to this the extraordinary expenses for war the representatives of the nation could take advantage of the hard-pressed monarch to insist that he follow their advice in matters affecting their welfare. The opportunity was therefore at hand to present petitions to the monarch at the time the money was voted, and it was this opportune pecuniary advantage, which the well-to-do citizens enjoyed, that enabled them in the course of time to transform the right of petition into the august process of law-making.

It is impossible, and unnecessary, to trace English history through all the vicissitudes of the fourteenth and fifteenth centuries. The pattern of constitutionalism was at times obscured but never lost in the long struggle between rival factions which followed the culmination of the Plantagenet dynasty in the great reign of Edward I at the close of the thirteenth century. At times the barons appeared again as the champions of liberty as they had under John and Henry III, and thus they helped prevent their own feudalism from developing into sheer anarchy, as was so largely the tendency on the Continent. It would be a misreading of history to accord to them the distinction of having championed the cause of English liberties in the sense in which we use that phrase today.

But it is equally wrong to think of them in the thirteenth century as a mere Norman nobility of the continental type. They managed their own sub-sovereignties largely by Anglo-Saxon custom; and, as we have said above, in those customs were certain individual rights which they respected and which, conversely, they made good against the king. Just as at the opening of the thirteenth century, it was they and not the kings of England who first saw the value and importance of having as their allies a representation of those interested in the country's welfare, so a hundred years later they continued to find parliament a useful instrument for checking the pretensions of the monarchy. From time to time they invoked this aid to reaffirm the claims they had set forth, as for example in the Provisions of Oxford, passed by the "Mad Parliament" of 1258 to establish a baronial regency over the weak king Henry III. It was the great work of Henry's son, Edward I, "the English Justinian," to take over parliament from the feudal opposition to the king and make it an instrument of royal government.

In the light of later history the most important part of the Model Parliament of 1295 was that in the summons of two knights of the shire, to represent the minor gentry, and two burgesses from every borough to represent the rising business class, it pointed the way to the one unique body which marked it off from the Estates General of the Continent. But in those early days there was little hint of the subsequent power of the Commons by its control of the purse. The knights of the shire at first were naturally drawn by social ties toward the upper baronage, and it was not until the first year of the reign of Edward III, 1340, that they met with the burgesses in a House of Commons. As for the representatives of the towns, they were at first by no means happy at being summoned to parliament; for they knew that the summons was for the purpose of taxing them and their fellow townsmen. Attendance was doubly irksome, for it meant interrupting their business and the cost of the journey was begrudged by those whom they represented. Moreover, there was little likelihood that their petitions would have much influence with either the Crown or the earls, barons and the high dignitaries, whose very presence overawed them.

Yet, at the very time that the House of Commons was taking shape, the principle was established that new taxes, those not arising from feudal and other levies, required Parliament's approval. The needs of the king in this case arose not from a contest with his barons, but from the far greater demands imposed upon him by the Hundred Years' War. It was the year of the naval victory of Sluys (1340) by which England achieved the mastery of the Channel. Six years later Crecy was fought, and Calais was taken the year after that. Although the war threw the rich cities of Flanders open to the English markets, expenses kept mounting, and with them the opportunities of Parliament increased, to such an extent that in the next decisive struggle with a misgoverning king, Richard II (son of the Black Prince), the challenger, Henry of Lancaster, had himself elected King Henry IV, by Parliament, thus virtually — if unconsciously — falling back upon the ancient custom of Germanic kingship.

Henry IV, the first of the House of Lancaster, thus began his reign more definitely under the aegis of Parliament than had been the case before. Under his son, Henry V, the Hundred Years' War, which had lapsed for a long interval, was resumed, and the needs of the king were again the opportunity of Parliament. The Commons then (1414) took the important step of drawing up their petitions in the exact terms in which they wished to have them granted, that is, they outlined in a "bill" of Parliament the "act" which the king should make law by his signature. Henry V, in giving in to this demand reserved only "his royal prerogative to graunts and denys what him lust of their petitions and askynges aforesaid." This formal acknowledgement of the right of the Parliament to frame legislation in its own language, must not be taken literally, however. It was not until Henry VI that it became an accepted fact.

From this sketch of the formation of the national state in England it is apparent that we are following the same kind of development as that which determined the constitutions of the city states. The needs of war and the new means of meeting those needs owing to the influx of money raised problems which could not be solved by the simple personal rule of either tribal or feudal life. Law-making became more and more an operation in which the ruled insisted upon having their share alongside the rulers. But in addition to the development of the technique of legislation, the technique of the judicial and administrative functions of government also developed as had been the case in Rome. The officers of the king's household became the officers for the conduct of national affairs. This was a century-long process, for even by the time of Edward the Confessor the chief of the royal chaplains had become the king's chancellor, that is to say, his secretary and the custodian of the royal seal. In this growing complexity the courts also profited, but that is too technical a subject for us to pursue here. The situation may be summed up by saying that by the fifteenth century the outlines of the constitution are already clearly visible.

This is more than the background of the history of freedom; it is one of its important chapters. Unique among the nations, the England of the Middle Ages created instruments for freedom which as the nation developed could voice the conscience and involve the participation of the citizen. The principle was established that the laws were of his making, or by his consent; justice was to be what he thought it should be, and it was to be applied by his equals. The schooling in these "rights of Englishmen" was long, and at times — under Tudors and Stuarts — they were lost sight of, but because they were so widely shared they were never lost. While other nations developed patriotism, the English went beyond them to develop public spirit, the one absolutely essential qualification for leadership in freedom.

The National State in France

No one in the thirteenth century could guess that the contemporary history of England could possibly match in importance that of the country which was in more ways than one an acknowledged leader in medieval civilization — France. The University of Paris was the center of learning for all Europe. The art of the Gothic cathedrals was at the height of its miracle. French cities were growing to rival in both size and splendor the older centers of the Mediterranean. This rapidly expanding society still lacked, however, an adequate political framework, and the political experience of the English. There was no such inheritance of native institutions to draw upon.

It is true that a line of strong kings had for a time at least extended the sovereignty of the Capetian house for over most of France. But feudalism had created such a universal anarchy that the task of the French kings was primarily a military one. The Capetian family had to add to its domains by conquest or inheritance duchies and counties here and there throughout the country. The French kingship succeeded in this extension of the royal power because of the strategic position of its own domains, the rich farming lands of the Ile de France controlling the arteries of trade which concentrated at Paris itself. The suppression of the great feudatories, which William the Conqueror achieved for England at a single stroke, was rendered doubly difficult for the kings of France by the fact that the greatest French feudatories were the kings of England themselves and that there was at least one other great feudal house which divided its allegiance between France and Germany, that of Burgundy. By the middle of the thirteenth century, however, this process of territorial unification had been crowned by a sufficient measure of success to enable the kings to turn to the other half of their problem, that of reforming and systematizing the administration.

It was then that the lawyers began to play that important role in the evolution of the French state to which we have referred above, for even when the feudal states became provinces of the realm they retained a large amount of local autonomy. Business and administrative relationships were becoming more complex than in the relatively simplified national state of England. By its very nature, therefore, French society lent itself to the more stable relationships of law rather than to the relatively shifting force of politics. It was not because the Roman law was taught and applied more commonly in France than in England that the French state tended to take on a more legalistic character. It was partly due to the fact that there was an incipient federalism in the disunity of medieval France. There was therefore the same tendency to fall back upon contracts or the dicta of the lawyers, which one can detect today in the United States, as over against the purely political trend of English government; for the more complex the relationships in a society the greater the opportunity — or the need — for the lawyer.

The symbol of the evolution of the medieval state in France was, as we have said, the fact that Louis IX lodged the law courts in his own palace at Paris — where they still are. So effective was their work that by the end of the century the problem of the territorial unification of the country had taken second place to that of the control of finances. This was a task for which the feudal nobles were ill-fitted, and the kings fell back upon the skill and cunning of lawyers and business men.

The richest, or at least the most accessible, source of revenue was not the feudal nobility nor even the new wealth of commerce but the Church, more especially the Papacy, which, as we have already noted, gathered in more money in the jubilee year 1300 than any medieval monarch had ever had in its treasury. The legal battle between Boniface VIII, the last of the great line of papal monarchs of the Middle Ages, and the law courts of Philip, who had forbidden the export of precious metals to Rome, culminated in the personal attack upon the Pope in the castle of Anagni (1303), one of the most famous dramas of medieval history, after which the Papacy was held in its "Babylonian captivity" at Avignon for the next seventy years, (1303-1377).

It was primarily to mobilize support for his defiance of the Papacy that Philip IV called the Estates General of 1303, the one body which even in slight degree resembled the parliament then taking shape in England. It was not an organ of government. Representatives of the three estates, clergy, nobility and a "third estate" of the wealthier citizens, met in the cathedral of Notre Dame in Paris not to assert their political claims against an increasingly bureaucratic royalty, but to strengthen their king's hand in his struggle with the Pope. They met separately, each estate concerned with its own interests rather than with those of the nation as a whole, and no provision was made for its reassembling. Yet its moral — or political — influence was sufficient to lead the king to summon it again in 1308 to endorse his seizure of the rich treasure of the Knights Templar.

There was no difficulty in getting popular support for these measures of the hard-pressed king, faced with the ever-increasing cost of government; but when he called a third Estates General in 1314 for supplies for a war in Flanders, it suddenly gave signs of becoming more than a weapon in the financial wars against the papal treasury or the corrupt, foreign banking practices of the Templars. This time the Estates were called upon to tax themselves, and refused. Nobles and townsmen joined together in protest against the proposed levy. But the Estates General had no national prestige behind it, like the Parliament of England, and French feudalism never produced a statesman like Simon de Montfort, capable of turning an emergency into an institution representative of the whole nation.

Only once, when the French king was taken prisoner in the disastrous defeat at Poitiers, did the Estates General claim to act as an independent and permanent deliberative assembly. This was in the *Grande Ordonnance* of 1357. But hardly a year had passed, when, with the country in anarchy, the burgesses of the important cities withdrew their support from the reformers led by the Provost of the Merchants of Paris, Etienne Marcel, whose defeat and execution by the royalist forces marked the end of the one brief episode of promise for political liberty founded on the control of taxation by the citizens. What the country wanted, devastated by a century of war and decimated by plague, was a strong hand at the helm; and the path toward national organization led more and more toward irresponsible monarchy.

The explanation of the failure of the French nobles to help realize the unity of the nation lay in the fact that this was just what they were fighting to prevent. Even when, by the devotion of Jeanne d'Arc, France was freed from the English menace, the king whom she had had crowned, Charles VII, had to face rebellion by the great nobles when he tried to suppress the anarchy which reached its climax in the atrocities of the bands of unemployed mercenary soldiers (*écorcheurs*, who flayed their victims). The greatest need of France in the fifteenth century remained what it had been throughout the Hundred Years' War, security, and that could only be established if the king had a standing army to act as a police force. This was granted Charles VII by the only Estates General which met in his reign, when it agreed to a permanent annual direct tax, or *taille*, which enabled the king to disband the mercenary troops left over from the war and create an army that would be both disciplined and loyal.

A great step had been taken to establish law and order under the king, but it was taken in violation of the first principles of constitutional liberty, equality before the law. For the tax was not to be levied on the clergy, the nobles, most of the royal officials and soldiers and the citizens of self-governing cities. This meant that the nation was divided into the privileged and the nonprivileged classes, and the *taille*, became, therefore, a symbol of subjection — increasingly so until its hated imposition was abolished in the French Revolution.

With the king as supreme war-lord, opposition to him by the nobles turned more and more to plotting with rival factions, Burgundian or Armagnac, carrying on desultory, if ruinous, civil strife. The final weapon was counter-plotting, in which the cunning and unscrupulous Louis XI had an easy advantage. Such was the path to the royal triumph, embodied in national institutions under the iron hand of Richelieu. The opportunity had been lost for all time for the nobles to become the leaders of French nationalism. Instead they became courtiers, dependent upon royal favor, absentee landlords losing contact with and interest in the people in the provinces from which they drew their support. Thus the feudal dues became more irritating than the royal taxes, because they were spent not for the purposes of government but for extravagant and licentious living by the irresponsible satellites of the king.

The effect of the political eclipse of the French nobility, which left them only social prestige, was to leave the middle class without its proper support against the pretensions of royalty. The Estates General of Philip the Fair remained almost like a signpost along a pathway which was never traveled by the footsteps of the nation as a whole until 1789, almost five centuries later.

The National State in Spain

Alongside the two national states, England and France, which developed through the storm and stress of the Middle Ages, there was only one other large territorial sovereignty which had achieved unity, or at least external signs of unity, by the close of the feudal period, Spain. But while there are resemblances and parallels between Spanish history and that of France, the more one examines them in detail the less the parallels hold. For the history of Spain is unique, not simply because of the Moorish conquest, but also because national unity of the French or English kind has never been attained in the Iberian Peninsula even down to the present day. The invasion by the Moors did not impose a unity upon the Christians as might have been the case elsewhere. It was typical of the confusion of feudal days that the *Cid*, the legendary hero of the eleventh century, could transfer his services not only from one sovereign to another but even serve the Moslem king of Saragossa. The little Christian kingdoms of the north which fought against the Moors represented real division of the Spanish people, the most individualistic of any of the nations of Europe.

In a sense Spanish disunity has been a replica of that of ancient Greece on a larger scale and for apparently much the same reason. Nowhere else is the "mirage of the map" more misleading than in the representation of the Iberian Peninsula as a solid mass resembling the unity of France. On the contrary it is the most varied of all the countries of Europe, with a wide range of climate, soil and natural resources, shut in between high mountain ranges which divide the different parts of the country. In a penetrating study Professor Castillejo pointed out how the varying Spanish types have persisted through all history; in the central north the Basques, the Aragonese and the Navarrese have maintained the tough mental rigidity and inflexible obstinacy which foreigners have often mistaken for the characteristics of Spaniards as a whole; in Galicia of the north-west "self-confidence takes the form of mistrust of others" and defends itself by flexibility and reserve; in the south the passionate, imaginative Andalusian recognizes "no ties material or logical," has no memory of the past, but a supreme sense of freedom; Leon and Castile in the center hold a balance between these extremes; the only part of Spain which marches with the mainland of Europe is Catalonia on the northeast, fringing France. It is important to keep these differences in mind in dealing with the history of Spain because they, more than the institutions of the national state, explain what Spain has been and still is.

The miracle of Spanish history was that it was not the Spaniards themselves but the Moslem invaders who gave Spain its Golden Age. The miracle is made all the more challenging by the fact that the Moors themselves have no other great creation to their credit, and their descendants, driven back to Africa, have reverted to type and shown none of that capacity for culture and statesmanship which marked the Emirate of Cordova. This interlude of semi-Oriental culture is not properly a part of European history, but it is something more than a reminder of romance, for it poses the question whether the Christian civilization of Spain was ever wholly cast in the right mold to realize its potentialities. The organizing and engineering skill which built not only palaces and mosques but watered a vast countryside by a great system of irrigation canals was something that the Christian rulers of Spain were never able to repeat. Was it because the Moors were less blindly tyrannical? Like the califs of Damascus or Bagdad, and like those other great Moslem rulers, the Turks, they knew how to employ tolerance as an instrument of tyranny, using the subject population as resources of wealth and power by stimulating their capacities, a policy applied to Christian as well as to Jew.

Whatever the explanation, the fact remains that it is not even the massive Gothic cathedrals of Burgos or Toledo which stand today as the monuments of Spain's medieval culture, but the forest of pillars of the Mosque of Cordova, the golden portal of the palace of Seville and the wizardry of the Alhambra at Granada where the nightingales still haunt the gardens of the last of the emirs. The contrast between these witnesses of departed splendor and the vast prison-like enclosure of the Escorial which symbolized the Spain of Philip II has somewhere in it a lesson for the statesman which has not yet been learned by the Christian masters of Spain.

To return to our European story, we must remember that in a land so varied as Spain, it was inevitable that territorial unification would not carry along with it national institutions to embody the principles of self-government and liberty as was the case north of the Pyrenees. It bore the impress of the military history of the Peninsula, the long series of crusades which the kingdoms of the north carried on for some seven centuries with varying success. The institutions of civil liberties, while sturdily defended, could not prosper under such conditions. Although in Spain the thirteenth century had begun with the greatest victory in the reconquest of the Peninsula, that of *Las Navas de Toloso* in 1212, which was followed by the decline of the Moorish power in both Spain and Africa, the promise of the century, which was so great in the annals of England and France, was not fulfilled in Spain because of local wars and feudal anarchy. Moreover the preaching of crusades was no school for liberty; on the contrary it led to that development of intolerant fanaticism which was to culminate in the Spanish Inquisition.

Great military orders like that of Santiago rivaled the feudal nobility in wealth and power. But the city life continued as a potential ally of the kings. Those of Castile granted charters of self-government to the towns, and called the burghers to the Cortes or parliaments which continued to meet and maintain their place in the state in spite of the decline of the towns, throughout the fourteenth and fifteenth centuries. In Aragon there was a movement not unlike that of Simon de Montfort in England in which the nobility forced the King, in the Cortes of 1283, not only to grant the privileges of the nobles but also accept the principle of annual meetings of the Cortes and the safeguard of the rights of the citizen in courts of law. In Castile, on the other hand, the fact that the nobles were free from royal taxation left them no incentive to work together with the towns against royal tyranny. Their position, as in France, was purely that of the selfish assertion of the privileges of the feudal class. And their anarchy reached its height in Castile in the years just before Isabella succeeded to the throne.

It was left for Isabella and her husband, Ferdinand of Aragon, to lift Spain out of this medieval background into the semblance of a modern State; but it remained semblance only, for unification brought with it a tyranny of Church and State in which the forces of freedom never wholly won out, in spite of temporary successes by those who sought to establish regimes of liberty.

The Holy Roman Empire

It was difficult and indeed impossible for the Emperors of the early Middle Ages to erect the structure of a state on the basis of feudal anarchy. In the middle of the twelfth century this futile theme of the history of Saxon and Franconian Emperors was carried to its conclusion by the Hohenstaufen Emperors, the last of the great medieval dynasties, the splendor of whose courts and whose exploits over the Alps left a note of high romance in the annals of both literature and history. The fabulous circle of King Arthur was far outdone by that new German knighthood, the "Free Lords" *(Freiherren),* who owed to the Emperor their small domains and castles on the hilltops where their men-at-arms could check the ambitions of the greater noblemen and courtly life found voice in the lyrics of the Minnesingers.

For a time it seemed as though the German kings had solved the problem of government by creating one feudalism to wage war upon another. But within the vast orbit of medieval empire, it was not in the Germanic north, but south of the Alps in the Italian states that the forces of progress were mobilizing, as the commerce and industry of the Mediterranean centered in busy cities like Venice, Florence and Milan. The last of the Hohenstaufens, Frederick II, lived in Italy, observing this new trend of history and studying the interplay of Saracen and Christian culture. More fortunate than the last of Hohenzollerns, he was able to impress his versatility upon his contemporaries and to acquire a title which, in more critical times, would have brought ridicule rather than admiration, that of the "Wonder of the World" (*Stupormundi*). The personalities of Frederick I (Barbarossa) and II still haunt the imagination of the German youth, but in spite of all that they attempted and achieved, they failed in the one great task which challenges the profession of kingship, that of government.

If a strong empire could have been organized on the basis of feudalism it would have been achieved by men like these, powerful and intelligent personalities, alert to the problems of statecraft as they existed in their time. Yet their very efforts to consolidate their power prepared the way for the downfall of the Empire. Though Frederick Barbarossa planted throughout Germany the lesser nobility of imperial knights bound directly to the Emperor, many of these Freiherren, established as a check upon the anarchy of the magnates, became themselves robber barons whose strongholds tended to escape all law and order as the monarchy itself declined. Still more deceptive in the long run was Barbarossa's effort to maintain the Emperor's authority over the two greatest fiefs of the Empire, Saxony and Bavaria, by the creation of the Duchy of Austria on the south and the Mark of Brandenburg on the north; for these were destined to become the nurseries of the two rival imperial houses of Hapsburg and Hohenzollern.

The disruption of the Empire in northern Italy was a chapter of history by itself. In the eleventh century a communal movement had spread from the Alps to the center of the peninsula, by which the city states under their bishops had checked and then absorbed the feudal nobles. For a time it seemed as though something resembling the ancient Greek city-state system might be repeated in disguised form. But rival factions and internecine wars proved the undoing of these local sovereignties even more than in Greece. For it was but natural that the rival factions should appeal on the one hand to the Pope and on the other to the Emperor, and the division which lasted all through the later Middle Ages as between Guelfs, partisans of the Papacy, and Ghibellines, supporting the claims of the Empire, prevented any healthy growth of civil liberties.

The pretensions of the Emperor were set forth by the professors of Roman law in the University of Bologna, citing the precept of Justinian that the will of the prince has the force of law. Applying these principles in northern Italy, Barbarossa placed imperial agents (*podestàs*) over the cities. The result was insurrection and the ultimate triumph of the League of the Cities in the battle of Legnano (1176). From that day on northern Italy was left to work out its own destiny. For a while, however, the conquest of southern Italy compensated for the loss of the north; and then Frederick II, the son of a Sicilian mother, set forth to recover by cunning what had been lost by arms. In the struggle with the cities and the Papacy which followed, Italy suffered such dreadful carnage that the way was opened to rule by the strongest in every little principality and city. From the death of Frederick in 1250 it maintained its independence of the Empire.

After the Hohenstaufens came the Great Interregnum (1254-1273), in which law in Germany descended to the nadir of anarchy. *Faustrecht,* the law of the fist, was countered by vigilantes and secret tribunals to preserve the semblance of law and order. The influx of money and the general if slow advance of trade and commerce throughout Europe both increased the widespread disorder and brought the apparent chance of escape from it. While there were feudal lords who fell back upon pure robbery and plundering to secure gold, treasure or goods from the hard-pressed merchants on the routes of trade, there were others more enlightened who saw the advantage to be gained by the encouragement of fairs, markets and towns. At the courts of some of these, from the days of Frederick Barbarossa, German students of the Roman law were available as judges and administrators, although the circumstances of the time did not permit any nation-wide acceptance of a consistent system of justice. The real centers in the fourteenth century were less the courts of princes than the cities along the avenues of trade, which grew steadily in wealth and influence behind the shelter of their fortifications.

Within the feudal structure and as rivals to it, these became political factors, especially in the two leagues which they formed, one in the Rhine country and southern Germany and the other linking the cities of the Baltic and North Sea in the more powerful confederation known as the Hanseatic League. Feudalism was too strong for cities to play their full part in the creation of the German national state, however, and without a powerful burgher class aware of their common interests in such a union, that structure could never be realized. The tragic consequences of this retarded development were not fully appreciated in the governing circles of Germany until our own day, for the militarism of Clausewitz and Bismarck was feudalism clothed in modern dress, a military order of society denaturing the internal as well as the external politics of the nation.

The full measure of the backwardness of Germany's political development can be seen in the provisions of the Golden Bull, the one effort to write a formal constitution for medieval Germany. Issued with a great flourish of imposing ceremonial by the Emperor Charles IV in 1356, it prescribed the conditions of the election of the Emperor in the firm but delusive hope that there would be less likelihood of strife and disorder if the election was carefully limited to seven Electors, three ecclesiastical and four lay. Instead of achieving this result, however, it strengthened rather than lessened German disunity by elevating the office of Elector to that of a separate class of princes ranking above all others, and it ensured the continuance of their power by providing that their territories could not be divided.

The seventh elector, the King of Bohemia, regarded as a foreignor, was not permitted to participate in any electoral function other than that of the actual choice of the King of the Romans. Feudal privileges were formally recognized including that which was becoming so important, the right of mining and coinage. In the words of Bryce, Charles IV "legalized anarchy and called it a constitution." No greater contrast could be found than that between the scheme of government accepted in this document and that which was being worked out in the evolution of the national state in England and France. The contrast lies upon the surface as well. Long and trivial directions prescribe in great detail not only the way in which imperial elections are to be carried out but also the etiquette to be observed in all ceremonies attending it, the order of the seating of the bishops and the princes' electors and all other matters of courtly procedure.

There is something reminiscent of the monarchies of Asia in these provisions which sought to elevate majesty by the outward trappings of power; still more does it bring to mind the hollow splendor of the contemporary Byzantine court where imperial power was already lost. At a time when the Emperor could no longer command the princes to march under his colors in war, he at least could prescribe the order of their marching in the imperial processions. On this point, typical of many others, the Golden Bull provides:

... by perpetual imperial edict that as often as, in an assembly of the Emperor or King of the Romans and of the aforesaid princes, the Emperor or King of the Romans shall be walking, and it shall happen that the insignia are carried in front of him, the archbishop of Treves shall walk in a direct diametrical line in front of the Emperor or King, and those alone shall walk in the middle space between them, who shall happen to carry the imperial or royal insignia. When, however, the Emperor or King shall advance without those same insignia, then that same archbishop shall precede the Emperor or King in the aforesaid manner, but so that no one at all shall be in the middle between them; the other two archepiscopal electors always keeping their places — as with regard to the seating above explained, so that regard to walking — according to the privilege of their provinces.

Provisions such as these are to be found where government by prestige seeks to impose upon the imaginations of even those who are intent upon escaping from its restrictions. For prestige after all plays a very considerable part in maintaining such fragments of authority as can still be asserted in the name of ancient and proud tradition.

To the greatest Italian of the Middle Ages — or of all time — Dante, the Empire, in spite of its inadequacy, was more than a tradition; it was a monarchy above all others, the embodiment of that supremacy in the secular world which God had granted to the Roman people. The treatise, *De Monarchia* in which this theme is expounded was written in Latin to make its appeal to all the world. It was written sometime between 1311 and 1313 while the Emperor Henry VII was in Italy, fighting to re-establish his sovereignty and when the claims of the other rival for universal rule, the Papacy, were also being challenged by the national states of France and England. But Henry's failure and Dante's exile from Florence silenced this strong voice for the restoration of the Empire in Italy, except for the echoes of it in the *Divina Commedia*.

Though Dante was silenced, another and even more powerful voice was raised for the Empire in the *Defenser Pacis,* or Defence of Peace, of Marsilius of Padua, published in 1324, two years after Dante's death. This was much more than political pamphleteering; it was a work of profound scholarship, marshalling the evidence of all antiquity, pagan and Christian, to build the secular parallel to the City of God, the State. Only the historian or philosopher is interested now in following this massive text, but in its day it was a secular parallel to the *Summa* of Aquinas, drawing on the same sources but for an opposite purpose. Although the great debates of Scholastic philosophy on the nature of the universe were over, the University of Paris, of which Marsilius was made rector in 1313 and where he lectured in later years, was responding to the new challenge in law and politics.

The Middle Ages had rounded out its system of theology, but the pioneers of modern thought were already heralding a new intellectual outlook, and among the pioneering moderns Marsilius ranks high. His argument, weighted heavily with quotations from authorities, is based upon the premise that reason and revelation — in short, Aristotle and the New Testament — do not support the papal claim that "order" and "unity" rest upon submission to the Papacy, or for that matter to the priesthood. On the contrary the papacy and the clergy have been the chief obstacles to unity; and therefore to peace, which is defined as "the embodiment of the good life," or as Marsilius terms it, following Aristotle, "the sufficient life."

The book consists of two parts or "discourses" and a summary of conclusions. In the first, which deals with the nature of the state, its need for internal peace and the strife that frustrates its beneficent designs, Marsilius brings his anti-clerical artillery into place, but it is in the second discourse that he opens fire on the papal pretensions to universal rule. Here the Paduan speaks, in the accent of his former neighbor Dante, stirred by the busy secular life of a north Italian city state holding its own against the reactionary clericalism centered in the papacy. There is a parallel with Machiavelli in this patriotic zeal, but by Machiavelli's time the Papacy itself, under the Borgias, had become secularized in its politics. The contest between the two greatest political theorists of medieval Italy lay deeper, however; for while Machiavelli's aim was to increase the power of the prince, Marsilius kept always in the forefront the "sufficient life" of the people. Although their ultimate aims were the same, the creation of an efficient secular state, the *Defenser Pacis* differs fundamentally from *The Prince,* in its emphasis on humane and moral principles of action.

Unlike Dante, Marsilius had the opportunity to play a very temporary part in the theatre of imperial politics. He became the political adviser of Ludwig of Bavaria when that prince claimed, and won for a short time, the imperial crown. It was probably Marsilius who wrote the imperial proclamation when citizens of Rome acclaimed Ludwig as emperor. But the fickle mob soon turned against him and he, with Marsilius in his train, went back to Germany, while Italy embarked on another way to modern times than that by a revival of the Holy Roman Empire.

The impact of the *Defenser Pacis* reverberated during the following centuries, both from hearsay description of its conclusions and from the actual reading of it. It was a book at which solid men of the age shuddered. When popes, cardinals, and writers simply concerned with preserving the social order wished to condemn heretics — Wyclif, Hus, Luther, among others — they charged them with having gotten their ideas from the "accursed Marsilius." To be a Marsilian was regarded as subversive in a way similar to that which, centuries later, attached to being a Marxist. The analogy between Marsilius and Marx is not entirely without point, in this crucial respect, both men set themselves in opposition to dominant institutions and ideas of their respective eras, and both gave expression to forces which wrecked havoc with those institutions.[5]

Switzerland

In the outline of the rise of the national state in Western Europe, it would have been a distortion of history to have limited it to the central theme of this book, freedom. It was a confused and varied history of the many interests which fuse into the political unity of the state. When war was endemic, security, the sense of survival, was more vital than the assertion of human rights; and when despotism prevailed, the ways to recovery of those rights were often long and devious. But there was one little country where freedom itself was the one theme of history, Switzerland.

Measured in terms of the great issues of kingdoms and empires, Switzerland's history is slight enough; at first just three small tribes of mountaineers in the very heart of the Alps, holding their own against the attempts of the Austrian Hapsburgs to rule and exploit them; then, having driven out the aggressors, joining with other Alpine districts, sometimes peacefully, sometimes by local wars, into the first — and only — federal state of Europe, reaching out from its German origins to include French-speaking cantons on the north and west and Italian-speaking cantons south of the great mountain range. It bears the marks of an artificial creation, and certainly some of its frontiers seem artificial, as when suburbs of Geneva, with their market gardens, are in France. But, in reality, it is the least artificial of nations, for it is held together by a common tie — freedom. The spirit of independence of mountain peoples is an axiom in history, but too often, as in the Highlands of Scotland, they have abused their freedom by wars among the clans. The Swiss, too, have had their dissensions and wars, but the vital force of a free nation proved unconquerable, from the Middle Ages to today.

It was fitting that Swiss history should begin with a myth. The story of William Tell's exploits of the thirteenth century goes back no further than the fifteenth century, and historical research has completely rejected it. The same is probably true of the second great legendary hero, Arnold of Winkelried, who was credited with having won the battle of Sempach by gather-

---

[5] Marsilius of Padua, *The Defender of the Peace*, translation by Alan Gewirth (New York: Columbia University Press, 1956), Vol. II, p. xix. Volume I, a critical study, was published in 1951. Strangely enough this is the first translation of the whole work into English, and text, notes and extensive commentary constitute a product of American scholarship of the first order.

ing into his own breast the spears of the Hapsburg front line so that the Swiss could break through it, and disrupt the whole enemy formation. Though this heroic sacrifice for freedom must apparently go the way of William Tell's exploit, into the limbo of legend, the battle of Sempach of 1385 repeated the miracle of that at Mortgarten in 1315, when with only 1,300 to 1,500 men, the Swiss utterly routed a Hapsburg army of 15,000. At Sempach the odds were not quite so great, for while the Swiss had only about 6,000, the Hapsburg forces were about the same number. Yet the victory was final; the Archduke himself was killed; and the little Swiss confederation was relieved from the Hapsburg overlordship.

This confederation, the foundation of the Swiss republic, grew out of the League of the men from the three forest cantons — the very name suggests their isolation — of the valleys of Uri, Schweig and the lower valley of Nidwalden, and formed an Everlasting League for defense against the rising power of the Hapsburgs, who had just acquired the duchy of Austria. The first of August, 1291, when this league was formed, is one of the decisive dates in history. In contrast with the growing centralization of the great states of Europe, the union of the three cantons, which grew into eight in the fourteenth century and into twelve by the end of the Middle Ages, achieved the double purpose of mutual protection against outsiders and against their own Swiss neighbors by the one device which could secure both national and local freedom — confederation.

The character of the union was not determined by political theorizing. It reflected the differences of the men of the three valleys in their relations to the lords or great monasteries, from whom many held their tenancy. Nowhere were feudal rights more varied, and the league in throwing them off kept to the old ways of living, limiting itself to the maintenance of peace by a citizen soldiery and domestic tranquility, for which local magistrates bore the first responsibility. This primitive model was never changed in fundamentals, although in the nineteenth century the trend set in from a confederacy, with its central government practically limited to foreign affairs, to a federal union in which its powers extend over such matters of national concern as education and economic policies. The cantons still jealously cherish the right to run their own affairs, preserving, as the very soul of liberty, the local peculiarities of a people divided by the varied histories of their mountain valleys, yet holding the mountain ramparts of freedom with a common sense of patriotism that has grown with the centuries.

CHAPTER X

THE RISE OF CAPITALISM

The Slow Beginnings

WE HAVE WATCHED the unfolding of the drama of mankind, which began on the ill-lighted stage of the prehistoric world, to the dawn of modern times. How the dominant forces of religion and war played their awesome and awful part in moulding the structure of society and in the conduct of daily life; how the reactions to the dangers of the unknown and the known became creative even before they ceased to be dangerous, as superstition grew into religion, and brute force into politics, has been seen. But we have noted only in passing a third force, more subtle and elusive yet, in the long run, even more decisive than the other two, the influence on history of that all-pervading network of human relations which today passes under the inadequate name of economics. There is a dogma prevailing in the communist world, that this is the one and only determining force in the evolution of society. But Marx's economic theory of history far overstates the case, leaving out of account not only the responses of life to all of its environment, the infinitely varied influences of circumstances, differences in nature and climate, and in the native capacity of man. But, while the perspectives of history are distorted if seen only through doctrinal economics, they are equally misleading if they do not cover the chief interest of most people most of the time, which is their work and welfare.

This has been touched upon slightly in the primitive and ancient world, where the comforts or luxuries were produced chiefly by slaves, or gathered in as the prize of war and commerce was often hardly distinguishable from piracy. We have seen how law and order developed to deal with property in things as well as in land, as early as the days of Hammurabi, and we have touched in passing on the influence of commerce on the development of law. But the prevalence of slavery in the production of goods both delayed invention and prevented sound thinking on economic problems.

Ownership of land and the management of an estate remained the mark of wealth and respectability. This was the opinion of Aristotle, reflecting the limitation of Greek thought on economics.

The same point of view was repeated literally by Cicero in *De Officiis*, where he develops at some length the thesis that merchants cannot be honest in buying and selling, but may become respectable if they retire to landed estates brought by their gains in trade. In the late empire, however, the monied class was practically wiped out by taxes and war, and the Middle Ages started over again with only the ruins of Roman cities — if even the ruins remained. In Italy Moslem raids from the sea added to the anarchy on land. Of the five hundred cities of modern France, hardly eighty go back to Roman times, while London, which had been a prosperous, if relatively small city, so far declined that the Anglo-Saxon chronicle does not mention it for over a century and a half. The entry for the year 418 is typical of that age: "The Romans collected all the treasures that were in Britain and hid some of them in the earth that no man might afterwards find them and took some of them into Gaul."

From the breakdown of the Roman Empire in the fifth century, almost eight hundred years passed before western Europe had re-established a civilization which could rival — and eventually surpass — that of the antique world. By the twelfth century feudal anarchy, which had succeeded to that of tribal kingdoms, was yielding to the strong arms of kings. But the process only reached its full strength in the thirteenth century, when the rise of the cities reflected the dawn of a new era, that of monied economy.

We have traced the rise of the towns in the feudal times, the communes of northern France dealing as corporate units with lords or kings, the boroughs which were fortresses against lawless lords, and the more complicated systems of government in the larger cities like London and Paris. But the townsman was not interested in the long range of these arrangements. What he wanted was to get rid of dues and obligations and make as good a bargain as he could with the military overlords, lay or clerical, who could afford him police protection. He had no idea that in easing his lot from feudal or royal exactions he was sharing in a movement toward an ideal abstraction, liberty. He was a practical man dealing with practical problems. Sovereignty and property were confused; jurisdiction meant revenue or service. Even the text of *Magna Carta* is partly a business document; at least twenty of its sixty-three provisions deal with money or other dues or exactions. The significance of this economic fact should not escape us. The national state was taking shape for the protection of property, as well as of personal liberty.

"Property and Liberty." They were linked together all through the rise of the national state, including that of the United States of America. The phrase of John Locke, which was the inspiration of George Mason and Thomas Jefferson was — "life, liberty and property" — changed by Jefferson to the less mundane but also less economic idea of a pursuit of happiness. It was the new form of property in the form of money or goods, instead of land only, as in feudal times, which helped royalty by centralizing the collection of taxes and so relieved the king from dependence on feudal dues. Moreover, those busied with moveable wealth, living mostly in the towns, needed more than mere local policing for their commerce.

As this web was woven by the traders, the markets they tied it into needed a common law of the realm and a sound national coinage against both local variants and royal debasement. In England this was already recognized before the end of the thirteenth century. Under Edward I, the law *De Mercatoribus* of 1283 provided for the recovery of debts in terms that give a graphic picture of the problems confronting the thirteenth century merchants: "For as much as merchants which heretofore have lent their goods to divers persons be greatly impoverished because there is no speedy law provided for them to have recovery of their debts at the day of payments assigned, and by reason hereof many merchants have withdrawn to come [from coming] into this realm with their merchandises to the damage as well of the merchants as of the whole realm, the King by himself and by his council ordains that when the debt is acknowledged before royal officers in specified towns, they should be empowered under the King's seal for debt in default of payment."

This legislation was further developed in 1303 with reference to foreign traders in the sweeping provisions of *Carta Mercatoria* "for the peace and security of merchants coming to England from Germany, France, Spain, Portugal, Navarre, Lombardy, Tuscany, Provence, Catalonia, Aquitaine, Toulouse, Quercy, Flanders, Brabant and other foreign lands." This law opened English markets to foreign merchants to sell almost all kinds of goods, free from the special tolls and payments ordinarily exacted previously and allowed them as well to sell to strangers as well as townsmen, retail or wholesale, with a royal judge to sit for appeals of any violation of the law. Had this great "law merchant" been fully enforced, it would have made of Medieval England the free market for the world which it later developed in the course of the nineteenth century. But local feeling in the towns was too strong for adequate royal enforcement of the charter and foreign merchants met consistent hostility from the closely knit corporations of the townsmen, who even carried on a kind of licensed private warfare with the merchants of northern Europe during the fourteenth and fifteenth centuries. Although there was very little English shipping at the time, a Navigation Act was passed under Richard II, directed against the Gascon merchants, while an export trade was beginning to develop in the hands of Merchant Adventurers, pioneers of the new era of capitalism.

These economic interests played a larger and larger part in England in the fourteenth and fifteenth centuries, in spite of the disasters of war and plague, as the feudal system broke down and the new middle class emerged as the ally and dependent of royalty. But the tie that bound them was not so much a common interest — for what merchant could share the interest of a king — but rather property: the demands of the king's treasury and the protection of the merchant's money chest. There were also the non-economic rights of freedom of the person, trial by jury and all the legal and political rights of citizens, but these we deal with elsewhere. Here we are concerned only with the rights of livelihood and welfare, which, after all, were the chief concern of most people in peace times, except under tyranny.

Money Becomes a Power

It was money in the hands of kings which finally dissolved the feudal structure, built on the immutable foundations of land and personal service. For centuries wars were waged and battles fought for dominion over lands and peoples, but they would only have substituted one form of feudal rule for another if money power had not substituted for the age-old way of settled life the dynamic force of capitalism. The leverage, which ultimately broke down the walls of feudal castles — little capitals of little states — was already beginning to work when hired mercenary troops or free men from town and country began to take their place alongside feudal levies and then replace them by armies paid from royal exchequers. Government became systematized when the king could maintain his court in one place and not have to travel with his many retainers from castle to castle to consume the royal revenue (paid largely in kind) in the neighborhoods where it could be found.

The slowness of progress in this transformation was not solely due to the fact that the ruling class had only one profession and that not a productive one, the profession of arms; but also to the fact that in the dark ages, precious metals, the medium of exchange had become very rare. The rich store of money that had financed the Roman Empire at its height — estimated at as much as one or two billion dollars' worth in present currency — had disappeared almost entirely, until by Charlemagne's time it was probably less than a tenth as much. One of the most valued feudal privileges was, therefore, the right to coin money, a right which became the monopoly of kings only in the twelfth and thirteenth centuries, through the rise of trade, due partly to the crusades and partly to the growth of handicrafts.

It was not only the scarcity of metals which delayed the rise of money economy, however. Its use as a medium of exchange or payment for services spread naturally; but to charge money for its use — an entirely different thing than employing it as a medium for exchange — opened up the whole question of usury, which, from the beginning of history, had been an open door to slavery. This has been touched on slightly in the description of the reforms of Solon in ancient Greece, where small proprietors had become so indebted to the rich as to be practically their slaves. Solon's cancelling of these debts was like an act of emancipation and a foundation for the strength of the Athenian state. In Rome the early laws of the Twelve Tables (c. 500 B.C.) fixed a maximum rate of interest but no change was made in the law of debt, and in two or three centuries the small farmers were wiped out. When Cato, a landowner, was asked what he thought about usury, he replied by asking his questioner what he thought about murder.

Provisions against usury run widely through other early law-making.

That in Deuteronomy (23:19-20) is especially thought provoking: "Thou shalt not lend upon usury to thy brother; usury of money, usury of victuals, usury of anything that is lent upon usury. Unto a stranger thou mayest lend on usury; but unto thy brother thou shalt not lend upon usury, that the Lord thy God may bless thee in all that thou settest thine hand to in the land whither thou goest to possess it." How this partial denunciation of usury was abused is graphically shown in the account of the rebuilding of the temple after the return from Babylon (Nehemiah 5). "Some said . . . we have mortgaged our lands, vineyards and houses that we might buy corn because of the drought. There were also those that said, we have borrowed money for the king's tribute, upon our lands and vineyards . . . And lo, we bring into bondage our sons and our daughters to be servants and some of our daughters are brought into bondage already; neither is it in our power to redeem them, for other men have our lands and vineyards." Fortunately Nehemiah was equal to the emergency and both by his own example and by forcing the priests to do likewise, ended the usury and the slavery to which it led.

When the Church took over the morals of the West, it profited from the lessons of antiquity, especially the later Roman law in which unjust exaction had been distinguished from interest on profitable enterprises. (Justinian had set the rate at 6 per cent except for mercantile transactions where it was 8 per cent). But in the early Middle Ages the texts of Justinian were unknown, and it was a text in Luke 6:35 which read in the Vulgate: *"Mutuum date, nihil inde sperantes,"* "lend hoping for nothing in return," that furnished the basis for the Church's denunciation of usury and its refusal of burial to "usurers" (1179), a position which it strongly held and which resulted in turning the usurers over to the Inquisition (1311). The result was that banking passed into the hands of the Jews, who were considered already damned.

But already in the twelfth century, Lombards, that is to say, Italians from commercial cities of northern Italy, backed by the teaching of Roman Law, began to lend money "gratuitously" for a given period, but to demand payments for each period payment was retarded. This idea of a loan office soon spread over Europe. There were Lombard Streets as the financial center of more cities than London. In France, Philip the Fair (1283-1314) used men trained in the Roman Law and business to battle with feudal privileges and papal exactions. Money was becoming so vital an issue that both Philip and the Papacy used Lombard bankers as their agents. It was also the underlying cause of the persecution of the Order of Knights Templar, which had gained immense wealth by financial operations in the crusades. The French king and a vacillating Pope used the Inquisition to torture and then to burn the leaders of the Order as heretics, while their wealth was confiscated.

The short supply of money was especially felt in centers for more distant commerce. The earliest of these to develop were those along the Mediterranean. Even through the period of the invasions, the ships of the fishermen who lived in the reedy marshes at the head of the Adriatic reached out to trade with the harbors of the eastern coast and were able to maintain their freedom against those who ruled the mainland. From these beginnings they built for themselves the trading empire of Venice. By the time of the crusades other Italian cities, particularly Genoa and Pisa, which had never lost touch with the Byzantine Empire, were rivaling the Queen of the Adriatic, and they all turned to advantage the transport of the troops or the commerce of the crusaders.

For those who could deal in luxuries there was an advantage in having ports in the Levant in the hands of the Christians. After the first crusade there was a clearer road to the East and a new freedom of movement. People traveled. New comodities appeared in the market place. Credit, which had hardly been known before, began to be used in business transactions, although throughout all the Middle Ages it was hampered by the prohibitions of the Church upon the taking of interest on loans. This tendency to prohibit instead of regulating banking had the unfortunate effect which always follows when capital is insecure: money lending became usury. Bills of exchange came into use as the Templars helped to finance the crusades. Kings as well as nobles mortgaged both past and future rights for the great adventure, and the shrewdly provident found another way to power than by feudal warfare.

The revival of commerce led to the renaissance of city life. The early development of trade in the north took place chiefly at periodic fairs under the protection of the local rulers. To these came individual merchants, peddlers, as we would call them, who exchanged their wares for those of the local artisans. The traveling merchants, however, could not always be on the road; they had to stay overnight where they could be protected and to show their wares where they could attract the most people. Outside trade, therefore, stimulated local trade. Where this trade took place cities grew up. This process once begun was bound to grow and by the thirteenth and fourteenth centuries the cities of the north were beginning to rival those of the Mediterranean. Towns along the larger rivers grew into cities. The ports of Flanders, fortunately situated on the estuaries where the Rhine, the Scheldt and the Meuse flow into the North Sea, became a set of focal points for trade which gradually spread inland. Then, over the narrow seas in England and along the Baltic, cities sought and obtained special privileges to enable them to carry on their business with the south and with one another.

Feudalism, based as it was on landed society, offered no place for this new class that was rapidly taking its position in society, the merchants. So they formed their own associations, the merchant guilds, partly social, partly for collective action in dealing with the officers of the king or with feudal rulers. Only those who had won their way by apprenticeship and business capacity reached the higher grades of membership in the guilds. Therefore, while they steadily asserted and developed the rights of property, they formed a conservative, not a revolutionary element in the medieval cities in which their wealth and social standing gave them a dominant position. The craft guilds, on the other hand, in which the skilled workers organized according to the pattern of the merchant guilds, were never as important or as influential.

Thus, in the medieval cities there was the same relation of importance between the monied trading class and the artisans which has been the characteristic of the whole capitalistic enterprise of modern times. But it was not until the national state was organized that the problems arising from the growth of capital became serious in the field of politics. The medieval rulers who protected the "middle class," as these tradesmen began to be called in the thirteenth century, did so not from a humanitarian point of view, which would have seemed utterly unreal and altruistic in the Middle Ages, but because they needed the money which the wealthier members of the middle classes could supply. Thus royalty, which began as territorial overlordship, found a new hope of power in its alliance with capital, as the thirteenth century dawned.

The money of the cities even reached out over the countryside, although in very slight amounts. The more fortunate peasants, marketing their produce outside the feudal domain on which they lived, were enabled to gain a little money with which to commute their service to their lord. The more clever of the feudal barons soon found an advantage in this for they could have mercenaries like the king and luxuries like their wealthier neighbors. Wasteland was cleared and cultivated. Serfdom was lessened, and by the close of the Middle Ages had wholly disappeared in England.

Progress in the country, however, was slow compared with that of the towns, which grew into cities under the protection of a neighboring friendly castle or monastery, by river fords or harbors. The larger ones, like Paris, crowded an evergrowing population within the confines of their walls and then spread over into new suburbs. Castles that had been crude stockades in the Dark Age had already been rebuilt in stone in the feudal days, but now they became, if still severely military structures, centers of little courts rivalling each other in extravagance.

But the real magnificence in which the creative art of the Middle Ages showed its great capacity was in the erection of Romanesque and Gothic cathedrals which were the pride of the cities fully as much as of the clergy. There was nothing here of the poise of the antique temples, held in perfect equilibrium, nor the realism of antique art as a mirror of life. But the ancient world produced no such daring creations as the high-flung Gothic arch and vault, which symbolized not only the religion of the people in its shadowy, mysterious strength, but also their sense of power to challenge the static world of routine in which their lives were spent. The message of the cathedral had a double appeal. It meant both an effort to better the world and to escape from it.

It was left for the City of Man to handle with singleness of purpose the problems of the work-a-day world, a secular task alongside the spiritual one. At the very height of the power of the Church, in the twelfth and thirteenth centuries, the national state had begun — but only begun — to take the form we recognize today. The traders needed protection and were willing to pay for it. On the other hand, the king or the richest noble could assemble a more reliable army than the old feudal levy by paying for mercenaries.

And so it was but natural that a bargain was struck between those most needing protection and those best able to supply it. The kings furnished the army, the burghers the money. This took place first and developed furthest in England and France, not because the British and French had more political capacity than the Germans (as even the Germans used to say), but because of the two impediments to German political development, which we have noted above — the revival of the Roman Empire which distracted the German kingship by the lure of Italy, and more important still, the continuously unsettled conditions along the eastern frontier. This was a frontier not between petty states which could easily be absorbed by royalty, but between Teuton and Slav, and the war organization which was called forth by its needs, kept back the political evolution of the rest of Germany even in modern times. When one whole section of a country remains backward it holds back the development of the rest. And so the transformation from military leadership to civil administration proceeded more rapidly west of the Rhine country than east of it. But whatever the reason for the backwardness of Germany's political development, it became one of the most tragic facts in the history of Europe.

We are now beginning to see that what was true of the internal history of Germany is true of the world as a whole — that we cannot safely make progress in the civilization of one section and leave the rest backward and undeveloped.

Economic Tyranny

The progress of the middle class in the late Middle Ages was far from a general movement of emancipation. Although it broke through the mold of feudalism, it retained the rigidity of medieval society. The merchant guilds were exclusive, narrow oligarchies. The craft guilds, where one might have expected to find the germ of democracy, held apprentices to minor servitudes for as much as seven years. By the fifteenth century, the new capitalists began to set up looms in country hamlets for the thriving cloth trade, where vagrant agricultural laborers would work for starvation wages. The result was a system of national regulation, setting up government officials, not municipal officers, to oversee the most minute details of manufacture.

We have seen how in the realm of religion the poor and unlettered stand with the rich and learned in suffering and persecution. The economic parallel to the revolutionary movement against the medieval church was that which broke down the medieval system of land tenure by the increased use of money; and it revealed an equally implacable temper to prevent, by a tight corporate control over commerce and industry, the growth of economic heresy of a free economy in which wage earners could sell their services for what they could get. In England, the issue came to a crisis as a result of the Black Death of 1348, when nearly half of the working class perished. The resultant rise in wages was checked by the Statute of Labourers (1357), designed to force the laborers into accepting a set, low wage on pain of imprisonment for refusal. Later statutes added whipping and branding to terrorize the recalcitrant. Act after act of Parliament, each more stringent than the last, registered a continuing failure to deal with so great a grievance. And finally the levy of a poll tax on rich and poor alike brought the great revolt of 1381, when armed uprisings took place in many parts of the country and bands one hundred thousand strong invaded London.

In the merciless repression which followed, Parliament took occasion to try to turn back the wheels of progress by enacting legislation to secure the continuance of villenage. For example, it provided that if any youth should have worked behind a plough or cart until twelve years old, he or she must not be taught any other "mystery" or handicraft. In spite of all efforts to suppress it, however, the economic revolution continued, and even the landowners became parties to it, as the market for wool in Flanders led them to turn to sheep farming, enclosing larger areas, on parts of which the agricultural laborers had once had rights as villeins. As a result, the migration of laborers to the towns became a national problem. Measures against this migration were increasingly ineffective in the face of this major change in English agriculture; but then it was the turn of the towns to oppose the threatened breakdown of their tightly built economic structure. This time it was not manorial rights which were at stake, but the jealously guarded class distinctions of guilds and corporations. The propertyless "vagrant" worker was already the chief problem of domestic politics at the very dawn of modern capitalism.

Here we come upon one of the most significant chapters in the history of freedom. For two or three centuries the founders of capitalism held to the same kind of narrow, rigid control in the world of commerce and money which had prevailed in the ownership of manors in landed economy. At first it seems like a contradiction, that the owners of the vastly expansive power of commerce, enlarging old markets and creating new ones, ranging both sea and land for profits, should repeat the medieval exclusiveness against outsiders. But that is what happened in both home affairs and foreign commerce. At home the aim was monopoly; abroad it was at best a limited peace in a warlike world. Modern business began in the harness of medieval thought.

In the world of commerce, the war system of the Middle Ages had been broken through to a limited extent in the grant of safe conduct or market rights to foreigners. But there was no thought of freedom outside of these special grants, and when the local interests of trading centers merged into a national economy, the idea of maintaining barriers against foreigners became a national policy, the "Mercantile System," which lasted from the fourteenth century to the nineteenth. It was based on the age-old idea of protecting markets or wealth against foreigners, who were set upon getting the better of one. We have seen that in the ancient world so openminded a man as Cicero regarded trade as a method for exploiting customers. The Latin adage *caveat emptor*, "let the buyer beware," was witness to the anti-social conception of commerce, which is prevalent in all early societies, and indeed lives on still in much of the rest of the world. Bartering, to get better bargains by the battle of wits, is the peaceful substitute for the more primitive seizure by force, and European trade was beginning to reach this level of economic development when the opening of world trade intensified national rivalries by the vast increase in goods and precious metals of the Commercial Revolution. The chief aim of that trade was not just to acquire objects specially desired, but to get a balance in money (or treasure) for that was regarded as the supreme embodiment of wealth. The mines of the new world added greatly to the store of precious metals in Europe, the strategy of trade was to sell so as to increase one's store of money.

It was natural therefore that the measures against outsiders should be increased as the accepted way for dealing with the elusive problem of national wealth. A weapon short of war, yet on the border of it, was the control of shipping through the "Navigation Acts" of the English Parliament in the seventeenth century. That of 1651 provided that no goods or commodities from Asia, Africa or America or any part thereof could be imported into England, Ireland or any part of the empire except in ships of which the master and a majority of the crew were English, under penalty of forfeiture of the goods and the ship. Ten years later another act permitted the use of ships built in the plantations, thus stimulating New England shipbuilding. The effect of this legislation was almost the equivalent of a victory at sea over the Dutch, whose carrying trade was struck so heavy a blow that war followed — with one result of lasting importance, the Dutch colonies of New York, New Jersey and Delaware became British. The wars with France, in which England took over a world empire had other roots than economic rivalry, but it made the English that "nation of shopkeepers" whose hidden sources of power Napoleon could not understand.

We have concentrated on the growth of capital and commerce in England rather than on the Continent, for it is more directly along the line we are following, the forces which played most strongly on the development of freedom. The economic development of France and the Continent generally was less significant until the French Revolution swept away most of the framework of the old regime which had impeded freedom for trade and industry, so that the ground was cleared there, is it had been in England, for the newest and greatest force in history, the Industrial Revolution.

So much on the world of commerce. The rise of money economy had an equally profound effect on English industry. The common law made it a crime, as a conspiracy against the peace and tranquility of the realm, for wage earners to combine — even a few of them — to deal collectively with their masters, who not only had the right to combine in guilds or corporations but were held to do so. Between thirty and forty acts of Parliament, from Edward I in the thirteenth century, to George IV in the nineteenth, attempted to apply and strengthen by statute the iron, reactionary trend of the common law in industry, until it was forced to make way for the trade union movements, after the Industrial Revolution had created a wholly new situation by the rise of the factory system — when freedom itself went on trial.

In another context, in the section on the history of slavery, we refer to money as the great emancipator. But the early history of capitalism reveals its equal capacity for tyranny. The fifteenth and sixteenth centuries, the "age of the despots" produced a series of laws in Tudor England which, taken as a whole, come closest to anything resembling a code in English history. So comprehensive and detailed was this legislation that it is impossible to do more than illustrate it by the one act which attempted to do most, the "Act touching diverse orders of artificers, labourers, servants of industry and apprentices." This Statute of Apprentices, taking over the regulation of industry and labor from local authorities, tried, by cruel penalties of corporal punishment, to prevent emigration of workers from country to town, and obliged them to accept the wages set by local justices of the peace.

Suppression of freedom in labor brought increased hardships, as the land proprietors enclosed the common lands which the villagers had formerly used for pastures; and there were constantly recurring disorders from "valiant and lusty beggars" who were to be stripped and beaten "until his or her body be bloody." This law of 1563 was not repealed until 1815. It was based on the established belief that all the able-bodied should be made to work — agricultural laborers until the age of sixty but others only to thirty or marriage. The working day was from five in the morning "until seven and eight of the clock at night," but with time out for meals, "and all the said artificers and labourers between the midst of September and the midst of March shall be at their work from the spring of the day in the morning until the night of the same day, except it be in time appointed for breakfast and dinner, upon pain to forfeit one penny for every hour's absence to be deducted out of his wages. If a servant leaves a master without a testimonial from him he is to be subject to imprisonment or whipping, and anyone hiring him is to be fined £ 5."

Although the Statute of Apprentices, as it is known, was a bulwark of reaction in English social history, nevertheless it should be noted that its drafters were not wholly blind to progress, for, contrary to the earlier Statute of Labourers, it did not attempt to hold down the rate of wages to previous conditions, but allowed a rise owing to the general rise in prices. The Poor Laws (also in force for two centuries) committed the "lame, old, blind and not able to work" to "work houses" — the name is expressive — and their children over to be apprentices. We have thus, in this, a good example of the conservative way in which the English middle class approached its responsibilities. On the whole, the propertyless class suffered less restraint from the owning class in the economy of money than they had endured in the landed economy of the Middle Ages. It was not too discouraging an omen for the years ahead.

If in England "the lower classes" were held down by law, while the new monied class pushed its way upward, their condition was worse in France. For the destruction of the political power of the nobility by the kings had left the social structure of feudalism intact, or nearly so. Although serfdom had all but disappeared, the peasants had to pay onerous dues and perform services for the landowners, while in the cities the journeymen struggled long and unsuccessfully against the supervision and control of the masters, a struggle which, it should be mentioned here, was even more intense in Germany.

The economic devastation of France by the Hundred Years' War and the ravages of the Black Death were followed by factional wars and disorders, for which the only remedy was a strong, centralized monarchy. From Louis XI to Richelieu and Louis XIV, France developed the only system by which despots can rule, bureaucracy. The social system, rooted in feudal privilege, was left almost untouched, until it was swept away in the opening days of the Revolution; but the economic life of the country was increasingly a concern for the king and his ministers. Some of these were statesmen of great capacity, like Sully under Henry IV and Colbert under Louis XIV, but the final result of their organizing genius was the destruction of municipal liberties, the erection of a protective system for industry, which proved a barrier to national development, the nursing of colonies for profit while prohibiting their commerce with foreigners, and hampering domestic industry with countless other regulations. All of this was so much in defiance of both economics and politics that France lost its world empire in 1763 and went bankrupt twenty years later. The economic tyrannies of the Old Regime in France, perpetuating an outworn social system and straight-jacketing the new capitalism, could end only in revolution.

The Modern City States

While in England and France the political evolution of Europe overtook the economic, and the national state took shape in disregard of the freedom of the working class in town or country, the law and order it provided rendered local liberties less and less important to the nation as a whole. But there were three or four important exceptions to this trend from local economic interests to national unity, where the economic interests were so great and the local ties so strong that, instead of fitting into the mold of the national state they tended to become like the ancient Greek city states, cherishing sovereignty each for itself, uniting only to meet common dangers in a world where war was endemic. These were the cities of northern Italy, of Flanders and the Rhine; to which should be added the Hansa cities of the north, although they developed a greater sense of unity.

Unique among all cities was Venice, "the gift of the sea" as Egypt was "the gift of the Nile." Begun as an asylum for war refugees fleeing from the Huns, the wattled huts in the marshes became, as the centuries passed, palaces for merchant princes. Although its doge or duke was forced, in the twelfth century, to yield to the control of an oligarchy of leading families, this one republic of the Middle Ages never developed beyond this to anything resembling a free democracy. A patrician caste voted for the great council for domestic policies, while foreign affairs were in the hands of the senate. The famous, or infamous, Council of Ten acted as a police committee of public safety, acting in secret and on anonymous accusations. To crown this elaborate system, the *collegio* or cabinet had all powers of initiative; only it could send matters to the senate, while at the apex of this hierarchy sat the doge and his council.

The whole machinery of government in this first modern republic was devised to prevent the development of freedom. Its economic policies were similarly limited. As it cleared the Adriatic of Dalmatian pirates in the year 1,000 — an event commemorated in the "wedding of the Adriatic" when the doge dropped a ring into the sea — and planted its colonies along the sea route to Constantinople, it gathered in the spoils that created the splendor of St. Marks and the palaces on its Grand Canal. It could hardly be expected, therefore, that its economic policies would be anything but grossly self-centered, refusing to recognize the rights of any other traders with the Levant. The result was century-long war with the great rival, Genoa, with merciless butcheries on land and sea.

But worse than this was the treacherous turning of the Fourth Crusade by Venice against Constantinople — Christian in name at least, though a citadel of bureaucratic oppression and corruption — and finally, the fact that Venice was the first Christian state to make terms with the Turks after their conquest of Constantinople in 1453, although it was a bulwark against them in the next century. Then Venice had its golden age of the Renaissance. It had become a land power in northern Italy as well, with a population of over three and a half million, almost the equal of the England of that time in size and certainly its superior in trade, with merchant ambassadors at every court and at all great markets. Then, suddenly, came the downfall — the Portuguese and then the Dutch and other sea powers opened the seaways to India and undercut the caravan trade which had fed Alexandria and Constantinople.

This, however, is the story of a later chapter. The point of our narrative here is that the greatest economic state of the Middle Ages prospered in spite of the violation of liberty at home or of good faith abroad. The point must be clearly made, and the meaning of it must be equally clear. It is not that the forces of economics are strongest when freed from all moral restraint, but when wars are the determining forces of history the strategy of war will cover economics as well as politics; and the strategy of war is governed not by morals but by military needs. In short, the history of Venice furnishes an outstanding example of the war system applied to both economics and politics. It has no lesson for the world today. Instead of standing out as a bright example on the long road to freedom, it is a dark, ominous prelude to the despotisms that developed in the modern state system.

The other cities of northern Italy belong more with the age of the despots than in a history of economics, although they all owed their prosperity to trade or banking. The Milanese prospered by both trade and money lending, as did the Florentines, whose Medici were among the wealthiest traders of the late Middle Ages. But everywhere there was danger of war. The watch-towers against assaults rose higher and higher above grim fortresses with dungeons below. They could play with danger, as when alongside its leaning tower, Pisa was decked with the garlands of its art galleries. They were proudly patriotic, but only of their city, like the ancient Greeks. Within these limits, they cherished freedom with an ardor that was never cooled by the recognition of those greater issues that are involved in nationhood. In other words, freedom was so local that it was anarchy. The wistful call of a Dante or the reasoned politics of a Marsiglio of Padua for peace through the Emperor, was as futile as the ruthless realism of Machiavelli. But while Italy failed to realize political freedom, it gained, in the liberalizing forces of the Renaissance, an intellectual freedom for scholarship and for art that remains its chief glory.

The cluster of north Italian cities was matched by a similar group in Flanders, linking the low-lying dunes along the North Sea, Ghent, Bruges, Ypres, Lille, Douai and others, stretching over to Brussels and Antwerp. Flanders was borderland between the German Empire and France, and its counts, while maintaining sovereignty, encouraged the growth of communes and "free towns," relatively free from interference by emperor or French king. Like the cities of Italy, they built with pride and magnificence. The castle and cathedral were even surpassed in daring architecture by such belfries as that of the town hall of Bruges, the "city of Bridges," two hundred and fifty feet high, with its everlasting clatter of chiming bells; and, for a short but golden era, Flemish art rivalled that of the Italian masters. Prosperity came partly from trade, Bruges being the Dutch port of the Hansa, but also it came from industry, from hard work. Ypres, at the opening of the thirteenth century, is said to have had four thousand looms and over two hundred thousand inhabitants, as many as Bruges. The chief output was cloth; and, as the chief source of wool was England, the ties between the two countries were close.

But the economic history, unique as it is, is less significant than the sturdy character of the people. Already, at the dawn of history, Caesar had said that the "Belgae" were the bravest of the Gauls, and they have sustained their reputation for courage in many wars. In the fourteenth century, Jacob Van Artwelde of Ghent formed a federation of Bruges, Ghent and Ypres, treating on equal terms with kings; but rivalry between Bruges and Ghent broke the alliance, to the profit of the dukes of Burgundy, and through them to the house of Hapsburg.

The Flemish cities stand high in the annals of freedom, matching the chivalry on the battlefield of Courtray and holding their own in domestic rights. But again, freedom was a local privilege and there was no welding it into the patriotism of a national state like that which took shape in the Dutch provinces to the north. The rise of Antwerp was at the cost of the commerce of Bruges. Its eclipse until the nineteenth century was due to Spanish tyranny — including massacre and persecution — and then to the rivalry of the Dutch and English, closing the harbor by European treaties.

While the cities of Italy fought each other, not only on the distant shores of Asia but at their very doors — neighbor against neighbor, Genoa against Pisa, Florence and Milan against each and all — the cities of Germany drew together into two leagues which, with varying fortunes lasted throughout the later Middle Ages: the cities of South Germany and the Rhine from Basle to the North Sea; and the Hanseatic League of the Baltic and north seaports. Nowhere else did purely economic union show what inherent power it had to win and hold from feudal or ecclesiastical lords the freedom to regulate their own way of life, even in the anarchy of the feudal Middle Ages. The prince bishops of the Rhine found cities like Cologne hotbeds of heresy as well as of stubborn assertion of economic and civic rights, building their walls to protect themselves against their lord protectors. Their league varied with the fortunes of war, but with Mainz as its head city counted over a hundred cities at one time among its members. It was powerful enough for its cities to win a place in the Diet of the Empire, but never a political union capable of playing its part in the formation of a national state.

The Hansa, on the other hand, "the Venetians of the North," began as a league of frontier traders, settled at harbors, like Visby and Lübeck when the Slavs were driven back along the Baltic in the tenth century. For two centuries the navy of this merchant league policed the northern waters. It had begun as a fishing fleet, but when the Baltic herrings, for some unknown reason, moved into the North Sea to the benefit of the Dutch and English, it turned to trade. The Baltic became a German lake as the Hansas forced Norway and Denmark to give the league control over the straits and special trading privileges. Sweden was dependent on its trade and it tapped that of Russia at Novgorod. On the west it included Hamburg and Bremen and reached through the Netherlands to Cologne. There were seventy-seven cities in it in the late fifteenth century. It had the English carrying trade of wool to Flanders, of Russian furs, and traded for Venetian goods in German cities. Special privileges were enjoyed in foreign ports, as in the London "steelyard," where the money of these "easterlings" was so much the standard that it still bears the name, corrupted into "sterling."

But the diet of the League at Lübeck was never a government, and the privileges their merchants enjoyed in foreign countries could not stand out against the rise of rival commercialism in the national states which took over their trade — Holland and England. The decline of the sixteenth century, which came to a close in the seventeenth, was due to the Commercial Revolution, which was also ending the great career of Venice. By 1776 Adam Smith could write: "no vestige now remains of the great wealth said to have been possessed by the greater part of the Hansa towns."

The Dutch in their mud flats of the northern Netherlands were well situated for trade by both river and sea, but their greatest asset in the Middle Ages came from the shift of the herring shoal from the Baltic, which influenced the Hansa to turn from fishing to commerce. Then a single invention brought fortune to Holland when a new way was found for curing fish — so important a commodity in Catholic Europe that it drew Basque and French fishermen to Newfoundland Banks before America was explored. From fishers to traders the step was inevitable; and the Dutch leaving the Hansa became the leading commercial nation of Europe, with trade in the

Mediterranean as well as in north Europe to contend for the mastery of the seas with Spanish and Portuguese, and then with England and France.

It was in this busy Netherlands that the dual struggle for freedom, political and religious, won first to a victorious close, a struggle unique in the annals of Europe, matching the heroism of the Greeks in the wars against the Persians by as brave and desperate and as successful a defense against the might of the Hapsburgs. With freedom came the Golden Age of the Netherlands as it became for a half a century the intellectual and artistic capital of Europe. This was partly due to the upsurge of economic life which combined banking with commerce and placed both at the service of a new, vigorous nation. But not all the credit should go to the Dutch themselves, for, in furnishing asylum for refugees from persecution in other lands, they were the beneficiaries of a great influx of talent and energy: Flemings and Walloons from their neighboring cities under Hapsburg tyranny, French Huguenots, Spanish, Portuguese, Jews and English exiles from political or religious oppression. The professorial chairs of the newly established University of Leyden were filled with the most famous scholars of the century, making it for a few short years what the University of Paris had been to the Middle Ages. Amsterdam and the Hague, where most of the free literature of Europe was printed to escape censorship in the native country of the author, had learned academies with rival bodies in other cities challenging their scholarship. There, in the midst of a world still largely blanketed by bigotry and ignorance, intellectual freedom won its first unquestioned triumph in the history of a nation.

The Commercial Revolution

Nowhere else in Europe do the Middle Ages live on as in Venice. Rome tunnels the hill for street cars to pass the Campus Martius to the Capitoline Hill; Paris was modernized by Napoleon III; London is also of the nineteenth century, but the Queen of the Adriatic preserves almost untouched the palaces of its merchant princes built over five centuries ago. It is more than a museum of the past, however; it is the best vantage point from which to watch the pageantry of modern history. For it was the emporium of Europe when London was a provincial town and the great Dutch ports but fishing harbors. The contrast now between the unspoiled medieval pageantry of the rialto and the busy life of London Bridge is the measure of the greatest change in the direction of European history, when the Commercial Revolution moved the lines of trade from the Mediterranean to the seaways of the world which lay open to the ports of the north.

It was this Commercial Revolution, more than the Renaissance or Reformation which set the terms of the problem of freedom for modern times. For, of the three great forces with which this study deals, religion, war and economics, it was economics which was destined to be the one most powerful lever in lifting civilization out of its medieval setting. We have seen its feeble beginnings in the early Middle Ages, the way in which it was held under local and then national rigid control. Now we are to see it escape from the fetters of landed economy and local interests and open the world to Europe and Europe to the world. The fact that discovery widened the horizon of Europe was less important than that it changed the economic and political life of Europe, remaking its geography by transferring the routes of commerce from the Mediterranean and to the ocean ports on the west and north and creating a new world of politics through the rise of the middle class in western Europe to replace kingship as the soverign power of the state.

Never has history been more touched by romance than in this epoch-making change from the medieval to the modern world. It began in an effort to revive that most medieval of all movements, the Crusades, when Henry "the Navigator," prince of Portugal, undertook to outflank the Turks by sailing down the coast of Africa and then turning east to join forces with the legendary Christian monarch of Abyssinia, "Prester John," for a final victory over the Moslems. Prince Henry's geography was wrong, and his initiative had as a terrible consequence the opening of the modern African slave trade; but by 1488 Bartholomew Diaz had rounded the Cape of Good Hope and by 1499 Vasco de Gama reached India.

Meanwhile Columbus, who had studied in Portugal and talked with Portuguese seamen, set out to find India by the western sea route. Asia was the magnet that drew them all, as it had been for traders from the beginning of history. Then America, which was an unwelcome barrier on the way to the Orient, and which for a century or more the explorers did their best to break through, even after the era of colonization began, surprised Europe by its silver and gold and so furnished the counterpart to the commerce of Asia.

The key to this story is the cheapness of sea freight. When the two or three little Portuguese caravels arrived in Calicut, there were still caravans on the old routes that had fed Babylon and Bagdad. Ships on the Indian Ocean headed for the Red Sea had already cut in on the costly travel by land, but Arabia was still a barrier to the Syrian ports. The Portuguese had no such problem of trans-shipment. Each caravel could carry more than several caravans; yet the cost of Vasco da Gama's third expedition was less (by rough calculation) than two hundred thousand ducats, and brought in a cargo valued at a million ducats, or some twenty million dollars.

The first to feel the impact of the Commercial Revolution were the cities of Italy. Although they continued for a while their primacy in culture, the Renaissance which they had nourished soon ceased to be their monopoly, as art and scholarship found new centers in the nations of northern Europe, which, taking over the command of the sea from Spain and Portugal, were soon to rival the glory of Venice, Florence and Milan at their height. Venice was ruined in a few years after the opening of the sixteenth century. The wares which its merchants had bought at Alexandria and Beirut were no longer to be had after the Portuguese captured the Arabian Sea route to India and then reached the spice islands beyond. Only a few bales of pepper and spices, the prize items of trade, and of other items of imported luxuries reached Venice, so the merchants of northern Europe turned to Lisbon as the new center of trade. From now on Venice was less a commercial capital of Europe than a museum of medieval and Renaissance splendor, with the trophies of its past conquests in its many pillared cathedral and the colorful lacework facades of its palaces, once the dwellings of its merchant princes, lining its canals. Its great age in culture was that of its political and commercial decline. The masters of art were rivalled by the leaders of the new learning as the workship and house of Aldus the printer became the rendezvous of scholars from all Europe.

The rich prize of ocean domination was now to be fought over by the sea powers of the Atlantic and the North Sea as savagely as the Italian cities had fought each other in the Middle Ages. The first to turn on Portugal were the Dutch. Their revolt against Spain in 1568 and Philip II's acquisition of Portugal in 1580 left them with only an illicit trade with Portugal. And when Philip seized fifty Dutch ships in Lisbon harbor, the Dutch built better and stronger ships than the Portuguese had had and took over all but two small Portuguese harbors in Asia. It was their possession of the Spice Islands and of Java and Sumatra which was the foundation of their power in Europe. The Dutch East Indies Company, founded in 1602, was the first joint stock company, as shares were bought and sold from hand to hand. With the clove and nutmeg islands under their control they could destroy what they were unable to sell and so maintain a monopoly in the spice trade. Soon the dividends reached 60 per cent. Philip II seized the crews that fell into his hands and flung them into the dungeons of the Inquisition, but the result was only better ships and larger crews.

When Portugal became independent of Spain in 1640 it was too late to recover its Asiatic empire. At the height of Dutch power, about the middle of the seventeenth century, Colbert, Louis XIV's Minister, estimated that the Dutch had 16,000 vessels of the 20,000 then sailing the northern seas, while Captain Mahan, the naval authority, says that the Dutch navy at that time was about the equal of both the French and British navies combined.

If the economic interpretation of history were to stand, the country which ought to have dominated the commercial revolution was France. It was the greatest national state, rivalling the conglomerate monarchy of the Hapsburgs in a long duel for power. In spite of its disasters of war, plague and feudal sedition from the fourteenth to the middle of the sixteenth century, it grew in wealth of agriculture and industry. Its feudal castles were rebuilt for the luxuries of the Renaissance, and its cities, especially Paris, burst their walls even more than they had done in the great cathedral-building thirteenth century. No wonder that Colbert should look with envy at the great fleet of twenty thousand ships in the commerce of the upstart cities on the mud flats of the Netherlands, when, according to his reckoning, there were only six hundred French merchant ships. In the statesmanship of that time, such a supremacy in sea power was a challenge to war, especially as the Dutch were natural enemies of Colbert's master, Louis XIV, being republicans and heretics. Colbert, therefore, founded the French marine and encouraged merchant shipping.

But the kings of France had no vision of the new era of economic power initiated by the Commercial Revolution. With blind persistence they continued to extend their power over western Europe the same way they had established it within France, by territorial conquests. Thus, from the more or less chivalric contest between Francis I and Charles V to the closing years of the eighteenth century, they concentrated on dynastic wars which brought only a few miles of conquered land and the bankruptcy which ended in the Revolution. Only half-hearted support was given to the enterprises overseas, to the French pioneers in America and traders in India. In 1664 a French East India Company was founded and popular investment enlisted by a prospectus too alluring to escape partial quotation: "From those fertile countries comes what is most precious and contributes most to the comfort of life or to grandeur and magnificence . . . Without exaggeration, Madagascar has so much gold that when it rains the veins lie open along the mountain sides." But French thrift was not to be won over by even such Gasconade and the enterprise had a troubled history. The government of an absolutism, like that of France in the Old Regime, is a poor guarantee for business; and at the very time when world trade was remaking the economy of nations, that of France did not keep pace with the others. The leaders in it were free Holland and free England, especially England.

There are myths to clear away as one turns to the history of England as a sea power. The royal navy dates, not from the time of Alfred, but from that of Elizabeth. At times in the Middle Ages there was a fleet at sea, as in the victory at Sluys in 1340, when the French navy was destroyed by Edward III. But a few years later, being out of money, he opened the English ports to the Easterlings and Flemish, to the destruction of the English merchant marine; and for a full century these rivals and not England were the trading powers of the northern seas. Foreign trade was itself a kind of cold war, waged under strict rules for protection against foreigners or interlopers, by monopolies such as that of the staplers in wool and the Merchant Adventurers in cloth. In the narrow confines of medieval society, England was a backward country on the fringe of the Continent; then, in less than two centuries, it was swept by the Commercial Revolution to a position of supremacy in sea power and commerce, and, by the revolution of the middle class thus created, became the leader in the new era of freedom.

The most revolutionary chapter in the Commercial Revolution has still to be traced — the sudden increase of silver and gold. By the time of the discovery of America the total value of the precious metals in Europe was about a hundred and fifty million dollars in today's currency. By the end of the next century it was almost ten times as much, and it kept on increasing. Most of this flood of gold and silver came in the galleons of Spain, even after the English freebooters had taken their heavy toll. But Philip II hoarded the treasure instead of investing it in either trade or industry. Moreover, in addition to his expulsion of Jews and Moslems, he repudiated his debts, destroying his credit and ruining his Italian and German bankers. The result was that Amsterdam, in the free and prosperous Netherlands, became for a while the monetary center of Europe.

The increase in money brought an increase in prices. The wage earner had been the first to feel it in the purchase of his few necessities by the few pence of his earnings. But by the sixteenth century he had been forced by suppression of uprisings to accept his lot in the capitalist era, with inadequate relief from the poor laws. But the owners of money and credit, bankers, merchants and landowners now rise to power. Property must have its day. Economics becomes politics. The first revolution for political freedom is before us.

CHAPTER XI

THE AGE OF THE DESPOTS

The Path to a New Dark Age

OF ALL THE POPULAR misconceptions of history there is no distortion of perspective more misleading than that of the "Middle Ages."[1] From the days of the humanists who had a distaste for everything since the great age of Greek and Latin literature, to those of modern scientists, who have an instinctive reaction against a nonscientific period, the thousand years between the overthrow of the Roman Empire and the Italian Renaissance has been viewed as an era of stagnation, a level plain lost in the shadows of two sunlit summits of achievement. For five hundred years following the break-up of the Roman Empire, from the fifth to the tenth or eleventh centuries, the lights of culture were dim in the Dark Age of primitive tribal life and feudal society, illumined only by the Church as the nursery of art and learning.

But, as we have seen in tracing the beginnings of the national state in England and France the static world of landed society was breaking its mold with almost revolutionary speed by the thirteenth century. Similar developments were taking place in the Spanish Peninsula, Italy, Germany and Northern Europe. The pulsation of a new life was evident in varying degrees throughout the whole of European society so that, by the opening of the fourteenth century, we seem to be almost on the brink of modern times. But then, however, came a check to progress so great as to threaten Europe with a new Dark Age. Again, and with greater capacity for destruction, wars ravaged country and town. Pestilence swept its Black Death over the impoverished lands and social disorders followed, as both the product of

[1] Cf. James T. Shotwell, "The Middle Ages," article in *Encyclopaedia Britannica*, 11th ed.

267

disaster and the sign of approaching change. The result was that whole sections of Europe suffered almost, if not quite, as much as when the Germanic invaders poured over the fragments of the Roman Empire.

Fortunately, however, life in town and country of the thirteenth century had an inherent vigor which was lacking in the Roman Empire of the fifth. Although war was endemic, it was only rarely of that thoroughly destructive character which the Romans used in Carthage and the Germans in Poland in World War II. Feudalism was bad enough as the exploiter of villein and serf, but the owner of the feudal domain, unlike the Roman tax-collector, found it to his interest to make it pay. There were, of course, stupid ruffians who did not understand their own advantage and followed the wasteful profession of arms to the exhaustion of their resources. But in the crude competition of feudal society, these dull-witted leaders lost out to those who farmed their estates well and encouraged the growth of towns. There had been little or nothing of all of this in the militarization and bureaucracy of the later Roman Empire; and accordingly Europe came out of feudalism with a fund of economic resources which Rome lacked, and which was all the more effective in that it was not concentrated under any one control but maintained its spontaneity in market place and countryside.

It was undoubtedly this greater vitality of the Europe of the early fourteenth century which prevented its complete collapse under the stress and strain of the feudal and dynastic wars. As it was, however, the rising structure of the national state with its promising organs of representative government, courts of justice and safeguards against oppression could only partially stand up against the almost constant wars, and for a while, especially in the fifteenth and sixteenth centuries, seemed on the point of crumbling into a system of tyrannies. As it mimicked the chivalry and the more romantic aspects of the Middle Ages, it tended to repeat in the larger arena of national affairs the anarchy which had marked the relations between rulers of the feudal era.

The prime cause of this period of reaction in western Europe was war, especially the Hundred Years War. It it true, as the nineteenth century historians pointed out, that both English and French nationalism became more definitely self-conscious during this long struggle. The English yeomen at Agincourt on the one side and the inspiration of Jeanne d'Arc on the other are symbolic of movements beyond the reach of the feudal period. But this creative power in the cohesive forces of militarism, which laid the basis for the later development of the national state, was, at first, more than balanced by misrule in England and by the murderous pillage of the Black Prince and in southern and central France. The Jacquerie, and its suppression in blood, and the parallel movement of the Peasants' Revolt in England were more disturbing symbols of disorder than the dynastic and feudal wars such as those between the Houses of York and Lancaster in England, and those of Orleans and Burgundy in France.

In Spain the continuance of crusading movements against the Moors impressed a military character upon political institutions which left its mark on succeeding generations down to our own time. In Germany and Italy feudal anarchy and local wars continued to block political unity in spite of the increasing wealth. The dream of a mighty empire which seemed almost realized under the Hohenstaufens of the thirteenth century passed away forever as the local rulers and cities, taking law and order into their own hands, fought each other without so much as trying to establish a permanent state of peace as the prime basis of political unity. It was not until the closing years of the fifteenth century that the idea of a universal peace within the German nation *(Landesfriede)* was advanced by a statesman living long before his time, but, as we shall see, the Emperor himself continued to invoke the war system against any such far-reaching reform as this. The result was that the political evolution of both Germany and Italy was falsified, distorted and delayed so that when they finally achieved unity in the latter half of the nineteenth century, they brought with them into the modern state the political heritage of feudalism and the tyrannies which overcame it. The policy of "blood and iron" which Bismarck fell back upon for the unification of Germany was the same kind of ruthless force which had been used in France by Louis XI and Richelieu, and by the Tudors in England, and which the Sforzas and Borgias used to extend their power through the chaos of the Italian Renaissance.

Thus the trend of the new Dark Age, which seemed opening before large sections of western Europe in the fourteenth and fifteenth centuries, was turned aside, but not into the path of freedom. There was often little or no difference between the methods used by the kings to assert their authority and those persisted in by the recalcitrant nobility; for both resorted to violence to achieve their ends. But in proportion as royalty ceased to be merely an enlarged feudal sovereignty and grew more and more to stand for the safety of the state, the right of warfare, as it became illegitimate in private hands, remained the supreme prerogative of the monarchs. Thus its use within the state tended to become the equivalent of the police power and its use between nations the guarantee of national security. Here again, Germany and Italy were at a disadvantage as compared with the new development of coordinated power of the kings of England, France and Spain.

But a still greater disadvantage was to befall Central Europe when the theatre of history suddenly widened in the closing years of the fifteenth century and the early years of the sixteenth with the opening of the sea routes and the discovery of both America and Asia. The countries which were ultimately to take the largest share of this new wealth were those which had already proceeded furthest in their political evolution. Nevertheless, the stimulus of the new age had hardly begun to reach into the heart of Europe when the "wars of religion" again checked progress in both France and Germany. In France these were not only wars of creed, but a series of fights by factions under feudal as well as royal leadership, the last of their kind in French history. But while they ended in the triumph of the French kings and the unity of the country, in Germany they "consolidated the anarchy" in princely units and all but extinguished the last flickering spark of vitality in the Holy Roman Empire.

England Under the Tudors

Although England was not ravaged by wars throughout the fourteenth century as was the case on the Continent, progress in self-government was slowed down by the factional struggles in the nobility and the slow growth of prosperity in a country still predominantly agricultural. But, as we have already seen, the economic drain in both manpower and supplies for the war in France, especially in its renewal in the fifteenth century, forced the king to acknowledge the right of parliament to vote — or veto — his requests for money with which to carry on his government. Thus, the needs of foreign war forced the development of the constitution from its crude beginnings, reinforcing it with the sinewy strength which lies in the control of money. The result was that, as occasion offered, the baronage and royalty outbid each other for the support of the yeomanry of the countryside and the burghers of the towns.

This happy state of affairs was, however, not destined to fulfill its promise until two centuries later, when the power of the purse overthrew all rivals in the Great Revolution of 1688. For, unfortunately for English liberties, the Wars of the Roses, between the houses of Lancaster and York, rivals for the throne, coming after the Hundred Years' War, decimated the feudal nobility and this left royalty in a stronger position than it had held since the days of William the Conqueror. The result was an interval of tyranny which for almost a century brought English history into a clear parallel with that of the Continent. The parallel, however, was incomplete, for the pattern of English history never wholly lost its unique design, that of ordered liberty under the reign of law.

This was fully recognized by the founder of the House of Tudor, Henry VII. He had acquired caution in the perils of his youth, in exile as the last Lancastrian claimant to the throne, and he set about buttressing the royal power. Realizing that the weakness of monarchy lay in the need for money, especially for carrying on wars, he turned from war to diplomacy, winning concessions for English commerce in the countries around the Baltic Sea, while in domestic politics he forced the baronage, weakened by the Wars of the Roses, to accept the authority of the Star Chamber Court with special jurisdiction, powerful enough to deal with the most powerful offender. In addition to imposing forced loans he found an easier way of taxing the people by debasing the coinage and so was able to leave a full treasury and a united kingdom to his son, Henry VIII.

Henry VIII inherited all of the deftness if not the self-restraint of his father. Circumstances seemed all in his favor. The new prosperity which was to develop into the "spacious times" of his daughter, Elizabeth, had already

begun. The increased wealth of the nation, which was due to an unprecedented era of peace and which would have filled the coffers of Henry VII to
overflowing, was however, not enough for the spendthrift son whose court
was aping the splendors of the France and Italy of the Renaissance. When
monarchs dazzle each other on a "field of the cloth of gold," some one else
than the king has to pay the cost. The needs of the royal purse were ultimately satisfied by the plunder of the wealth of the monasteries and the treasure
of the church. By means of this act of spoliation, Henry VIII was able to
reward the followers of the Tudor House. The change from monasteries to
great country houses left its mark on the governing classes of England for
the next three hundred years; few of the "stately homes of England" date
from before the Tudor period.

Neither Henry, however, nor his equally strong-willed daughters ever for
a moment allowed these new soldiers of fortune to become a ruling oligarchy or even to have enough importance to be able to make that kind of
alliance with Parliament which had checked the prerogatives of the king in
earlier days. The Tudors were sure of themselves to the point that they could
use the institutions of English self-government for their own advantage.
Although for a while Henry VIII was tempted to assert personal rule without
regard to the traditional forms of the constitution, he ultimately found it more
to his advantage to rule through them, dominating and even falsifying their
purpose. Thus, those institutions of government which had become part of
the pattern of English life survived. Parliament was not destroyed, the courts
still functioned and in spite of many instances of arbitrary power, the Tower
of London was never quite the symbol of despotism to the English that the
Bastille was to the French.

In the perspective of the history of freedom, the tyranny of Henry VIII
stands out as something un-English, more like that of an oriental despot than
of the successor of such statesman-like kings as Henry II or Edward I, under
whom royal power was strengthened by the institutions of national justice
and legislation. It was a much more ruthless despotism than the Stuart kings
ever dreamed of, and certainly far more than they ever attained. The reasons
that this strange interlude happened do not lie in the character of Henry
VIII, although that explains much. They are rather to be found in the fact
that his reign lay between two eras: the medieval, in which the feudal
baronage had checked the royal power, as in Magna Carta and many another
test of power, and the modern, in which the middle class rose to power. This
new force of English nationalism was just beginning to change the temper
of England in Henry's day, but not enough to assume the political role of a
protector of the liberties of the people, which it accepted with stern resolve
under the Stuarts.

More confusing still, as a basis for the despotism of Henry VIII were the
questions raised by the rise of Protestantism. Leaving for a later chapter the
religious issues involved in it, we find here, as in other countries in varying
degrees, that the undoing of the structure of the medieval church involved

the structure of society as well, and that the transfer of oversight from ecclesiastical to secular rulers opened the door to new problems in politics. It was a door which ultimately led to freedom, but not at first. For the religious revolution happened at just that interval in European history referred to above, in which the political, as well as the religious, systems of the Middle Ages had not been replaced by that of modern times. The national state system was being hammered into shape by the same forces which were welding the new religious polity, but in the days of Henry VIII, in England and for a long time afterwards on the Continent, the hammer was in the hands of the king.

With no one to check him, Henry VIII was a perfect example of the truth of Lord Acton's aphorism that "all power tends to corrupt and absolute power corrupts absolutely." All opposition was ruthlessly suppressed as the king made himself head of the church, while protesting orthodoxy. Both Catholics and Protestants were persecuted if they refused obedience to this sword which cut both ways. No other European ruler (unless we include Russia with its Ivan the Terrible and Peter the Great) ever used murder more vindictively as an instrument of power than did this wilful tyrant, under whom England left the Middle Ages behind.[2]

After Henry's death the reign of terror was tried only once, by Mary, as a system of royal policy, and then for purely religious persecution. Elizabeth, although by no means guiltless, had been schooled as her grandfather Henry VII had been, by the adversities and dangers of a perilous youth, and had acquired an uncanny gift of knowing just how far she could go in asserting her authority, which is the first qualification of successful tyranny. Skilled advisers continued and almost completed the process already begun, by which the court became more like an office for the transaction of the business of government than an assemblage of dignitaries. A competent executive thus left less for the Legislature to do, and had the time been one of quiet peace and stagnation the Queen could have enjoyed to the full the pleasures of ruling by the exercise of her womanly intuition. Her greatness lay in the fact that in a period of social change and external danger she envisaged the role of the English monarch, not as an arbitrary embodiment of personal power, but as the symbol of that new England which was becoming self-conscious as its ships began to sweep the seven seas and its art and literature to reflect not only the new learning of the Renaissance but the universal scope of the free spirit of mankind at grips with its destiny. Pericles too had known how to manage the Athens of his day, and while Elizabeth had no such intimate share in the creation of the immortal works which began to make their appearance in the closing years of her reign, she not only steered the ship of state with consummate skill but made it a thing which all Englishmen were, and still are, proud to look upon.

[2] The list of Henry's victims (not checked by the author) has been drawn up as follows: 2 queens, 2 cardinals, 3 archbishops, 18 bishops, 13 abbots, 500 priors or monks, 60 canons, over 50 doctors, 12 dukes, marquises or earls, 29 barons, 335 nobles, 110 women of rank; in all some 72,000 capital punishments.

The persistent and unconquerable vitality of the French people is one of the most outstanding but least understood of the elements of the history of Europe. It carried the culture of the Middle Ages to such supreme expressions as those of Gothic art and the learning of the universities, and at the opening of the fourteenth century the nation had seemingly become organized, with a king recognizing the reign of law. How far this process would have gone on had there been no Hundred Years' War is a riddle of history that can never be solved, but even in the midst of this discouraging task of clearing away the debris of that vast disaster, the king, Charles V, could utilize a period of truce to reconstruct finances and establish a royal police force in the shape of permanent companies of soldiery.

However, contrary to what happened in England, the Estates, as representatives of the nation, were not strong enough to assert their financial control over the monarch, which became a function of the royal bureaucracy (Chambre des Comptes) in Paris. When the war began again France reached the depth of impotence and anarchy, yet then the national spirit found voice, not in parliamentary debate, but in the military leadership of a Lorraine shepherd girl whose mystic vision has remained the inspiration of French patriotism from that day to this. The coronation of the king (Charles VII, 1429) with the sacred oil of Rheims marked the turning point in the fortunes of Capetian (Valois) kings, and although the disorders of the time continued, with famine, pestilence and widespread ravages of the countryside, the king whom Jeanne had crowned continued to build his police into a royal army, and his son Louis XI built on this apparently fragile foundation the structure of a royal tyranny which was to reach its culmination in the splendors of Louis XIV.

While the evolution of the national state in France owes more to its kings than does that of England — in France the problems of police and territorial unity were more insistent than that of finance — nevertheless the towns and cities played their parts as well. The steady stream of trade, especially from the Mediterranean, was producing allies of royalty in the growing middle class although it was not strong enough to ensure that the Estates General should be a really national legislature as was becoming the case in England. The lawyers, too, continued their work, but also rather as tools of the king than as an expression of national life. In the middle of the seventeenth century, the law courts of Paris, profiting from their long history, were strong enough to offer a rallying point against the monarch in the wars of the Fronde; but during this earlier period, in which the French kingship established itself on the ruins of the feudal structure, they played no such part in the preservation of the liberties of the citizen as they continued to do throughout the realm of England.

One reason why in France the national state was concentrated more and more in the person of the monarch was that the task of national unification was as yet far from complete. Not only were the outlying provinces practically independent, as in the duchy of Brittany, but there was especially the great rival house of Burgundy on the east which thrust its holdings into the very heart of the realm. It was rich from its connection with the busy cities of Flanders, and also did homage for some of its lands to the imperial House of Hapsburg. Under Charles the Bold it seemed for a while to be on the point of realizing the old lost kingdom of Lothair, Charlemagne's grandson, which in the ninth century had held, for a fleeting moment, the promise of becoming the middle kingdom between France and Germany — a Lorraine which should be the central power in Europe. The threat of Burgundy, never absent from the statecraft of the kings of France was now real and imminent. It was as though a wealthier and more powerful Scotland were holding the English Midlands, for the Flemish frontier came almost to Amiens on the north, and on the south Dijon was more important to Paris than York was to London. The circumstances under which Louis XI ruled France therefore called for less of constitutionalism than of militarism. But the militarism he employed was of a new type, one less of fighting than of diplomacy, or at least of fighting long-range duels by plot and assassination rather than by arms in the field.

Statesmanship, therefore, took on the character of cunning and unscrupulous disregard for anything except the ultimate triumph of the king. The despot not only had to have superior forces against emergencies but he had constantly to be on guard to check opposition before it could become dangerous. As the power and resources of the French king grew with the overthrow of more dangerous rivals and the extension of his own domains to the far corners of the country he was led to apply as an increased exercise of police action the royal monopoly of the right of warfare, which was the result of the suppression of feudalism.

The function of the police within the state is the most elusive and difficult to define of all the elements of politics. Indeed, even today and in countries so jealous of personal liberty as the United States, it has never been defined with precision. It is here that the courts play their role as the protectors of the rights of the citizen and at this point we see the fundamental contrast between the French and the English despotisms. The fact that the King's justice in England owed its vitality less to the jurists of the King than to the fundamental principles of freemen expressed in the Common Law and to the sense of local self-government in the shires, kept alive the sense of the rights of Englishmen and set a boundary to the royal power which was never wholly obliterated.

On the Continent, on the other hand, the growth of royal justice was, as we have pointed out, very largely an adaptation to royal needs of the principles of imperial Roman law. In other words, it was stronger in the field of public law than in private law. The obscure and complicated processes of the English courts by which the king's writ was made to run were foreign to the spirit of continental jurisprudence, which had not been built up out of the homely interests of the humble citizen as was the case with the Common Law, but was an instrument and organ of government from the standpoint of

ment produced no new and efficient tyranny in Germany like that of the Tudors or Capetians. German despotism was of another kind. It was the maintenance of arbitrary power upon the part of the princes and princelings, each with his dungeon underneath the keep of his castle. The more enlightened of them employed jurists trained in the Roman law to systematize their rule while justifying the exercise of irresponsible power. Thus, as in Italy, the intelligentsia looked to the nobility for support and now and again found it in a benevolent prince. There were even those among the imperial knights, like Ulrich von Hutten, who could match their scholarship with the humanists of the Renaissance and express themselves in the vernacular which was then shaping itself to become the universal literary language of Germany.

But, as a class, the German nobility was ill prepared to give enlightened leadership to the German people; the uncertain truce of feudal warriors is no more peace than the petty intrigues of rival courts is statesmanship. The rule of force was symbolized in the men-at-arms who thronged the castles and plundered the countryside. In spite of reform movements here and there, cruelty and oppression remained characteristic of government, as it had been throughout the Middle Ages. In the absence of a national state anarchy triumphed.

This was the condition of Germany when on the thirty-first day of October, 1517, Martin Luther nailed his ninety-five theses on the door of the university at Wittenberg. We shall deal later with the revolution in religion and in the history of thought which followed upon that daring challenge to the theory of salvation. But we have already pointed out that the Catholic Church has a two-fold organization, that which serves as the intermediary between man and God through the sacraments and that which has to do with management of the Church itself; the former is in the field of theology, the latter in that of government. Luther's first protest was purely theological, drawn from the emphasis placed by St. Paul and St. Augustine upon justification for salvation by the faith of the individual rather than by reliance upon the sacraments controlled by a priesthood. So far he was merely following in the steps of the great disputations of the Church Fathers; but when the authorities of the Church challenged his doctrine, he turned from theology to ecclesiastical revolt and denied the legitimacy of the papal claims not only in Germany of his day but throughout all the past. From this point on the movement took on secular as well as a religious character.

Then in 1521, at the Diet of Worms, the case came before the Emperor Charles V, then only twenty-one years old, who had succeeded to the Empire two years before on the death of his grandfather Maximilian. He had, however since 1516, been King of Spain, which he inherited through his mother, and he came to Germany for the first time to attend the Diet. He had, therefore, been brought up in an atmosphere utterly foreign to that of the Monk of Wittenberg. The result was that he lost for himself and for the Empire the one great chance to make the common cause of the Germany princes against the Papacy a truly national movement. We must remember, of course, that the Lutheran movement seemed to the conservatively minded to be little more than a carrying of the prevailing anarchy of German individualism into the field of religion, and it was only natural that Charles should take this point of view.

One wonders, however, what would have happened if the Emperor had been less well schooled in orthodoxy and had been a wholly secularly minded prince instead of a conscientious and devout member of the Church. What a strange page of history it would have been if, for example, Charles had been like the Emperor Henry IV, who could rise from the snow at Canossa to mobilize even a rebellious nobility against the imponderable forces at the disposal of the greatest of the Popes, Gregory VII; or if there had presided at the Diet of Worms a cosmopolitan free-thinker like Frederick II, the last of the Hohenstaufens.

It was the most fateful moment in German history. At a time when the national state was taking shape as the predominant form of government in Europe, the protest against papal exactions furnished a basis for unified action which would have been to the material benefit of the German nobility as well as to the cities. Moreover, it was just at this time that the Sultan of the Turks was advancing upon Vienna supported by the power of the Moslem world. Had a Richelieu or a Bismarck been at the side of Charles V one can imagine how he would have taken advantage of this combination of circumstances to make the imperial leadership of Germany a reality recognized throughout the world. Here was a foreign enemy against whom could be rallied under the imperial insignia any recalcitrant elements in the country. It was one crusading army against another, for before the decree of Worms, outlawing Luther, could be put into operation, the Turk had overrun Hungary and was besieging Vienna itself. The common danger broke in upon the religious and princely feuds to impose a temporary truce, but Charles failed to capitalize upon it, subordinating the national interests of Germany for those of his own house. As Hapsburg ruler rather than as Emperor he began, in the war with Francis I, the century-long rivalry with the Bourbon kings of France, a policy forced upon him by his far-flung territories in Spain and the Netherlands and his dynastic interests in Italy.

The German princes, left largely to themselves, fought their religious war to a standstill in the Peace of Augsburg (1555) which established freedom of worship for the Protestant princes and free cities. But the implied challenge of the Protestant League brought to the fore the opposition of a new and vital force in the Counter Reformation which had its doctrinal origin in the Council of Trent (1545-1563) and its missionaries in the Society of Jesus, a religious order exacting absolute obedience under the direct control of the Papacy.

The result was a division of Germany into Protestant and Catholic states. South Germany, which was predominantly Catholic, ultimately found two strong leaders in the Emperor Ferdinand II and the head of the Catholic League, Maximilian, Duke of Bavaria. The lists were prepared for the Thirty Years War, the most awful civil war in the history of Europe. Fought out with mercenary soldiers and the aid of the foreigner, Swedish, Danish and French, its horrors eclipsed the Hundred Years War in France. This was the last futile effort of the Roman Empire of the Middle Ages to establish itself as the champion of the Catholic world. The Treaty of Westphalia (1648) registered this failure for all time.

Unfortunately, in its final phase the Empire had become not the embodiment of law and order under which free institutions could be nourished, but the symbol of a complete and efficient tyranny which threatened to dominate the whole intellectual as well as the economic and political life of the country. It is true that religious tolerance was as yet a feeble and almost untried experiment in government and that the Protestant leaders were by no means engaged in a crusade to establish that ideal throughout Germany; but the singleness of purpose which animated the Counter Reformation did not leave the door open to compromise as was the case with the princes of northern Germany. It is therefore not too much to say that in their ultimate triumph the Protestant leaders achieved more than they had been fighting for, a world in which the religious issue was definitely forced to take a second place and the secular organization freed from the worst of all despotism, that of bigotry in the seat of power.

Italy and Machiavelli

The age of the Despots had its one great apologist in the Italy of the Renaissance, Machiavelli. That unique figure was destined to become the more or less conscious guide of despotic rulers down to our own day, and because of the influence he has exerted through the succeeding centuries and the interest which all students of politics have found in his political philosophy he is generally classed among the first of the moderns in the field of political theory.

But Machiavelli was really the exponent, not of the general laws of the evolution of government, but of that period of European history which we have just been examining. It was an age of transition when that technique of government which had been applied through the warring centuries of feudalism was still resorted to, although it was becoming inapplicable to the new society then emerging under the stimulus of rising but still unemancipated capitalism. One might have expected that the political problems of this age of change would have been solved first and best in Italy, that part of Europe which throughout the later Middle Ages was the recognized leader in commerce and industry as well as in culture.

The fourteenth and fifteenth centuries were the Golden Age of the Italian city states. The splendor of the court of the Visconti at Milan far outshone that of any other ruler in Europe. When the English nobles slept on straw and the cavalcades of the kings of France splashed through unpaved streets to royal castles, Milan, Venice and Florence were centers of wealth and luxury unparalleled since the great days of Rome. Nowhere else was intelligence more keenly spurred by mutual rivalries to a competition in economic progress. Moreover, from the days of the Hohenstaufens, these cities were free from interference, left to themselves to work out their own destiny. It is a sufficient commentary on the extreme difficulty of mastering the art of government that these highly endowed people failed to lead Europe in the development of the state.

There was, it is true, the unique example of Venice, the richest republic of the Middle Ages, but its complicated constitution was a facade for the tyranny of the Council of Ten, a committee of public safety which ruled the Republic from the early fourteenth century. In fact, tyranny was intimate and all-pervading and was brought within the constitution of the state when an unknown accuser could send a man to secret trial and lasting imprisonment. Compare this with the provisions of the English system of justice in which the accusation must be made by a jury of one's neighbors! The dungeons in the prison behind the Bridge of Sighs were as much a function of the government of Venice as the palace on the waterfront from which it leads.

But the tyrannical control of the Venetian Republic was only a refinement upon the despotism which characterized the government of every state of northern Italy. The promise of the communal movement of the eleventh and twelfth centuries had long since passed away. In the continued disorders of the time the military leaders could more than hold their own against the merchants, and the nobility crowded their castellated strongholds within city walls rivalling each other in high-reaching watch towers and in bands of retainers. It is unnecessary to follow here the fortunes of the families which rose to power under these conditions, the Viscontis and the Sforzas, the Medici, the Estes and the Borgias. Italy became the theatre for disorder in which the rival factions used every weapon of intrigue and unmitigated cruelty. Assassins lurked in the shadows while their masters plotted in this swift game of life and death. The deft fingers of Cellini were equally skillful with the dagger and the sculptor's chisel. The fine art of poisoning, that accompaniment of despotism both as weapon and defense, was never more practiced since the days of imperial Rome. So deep was the hold upon society which these methods of the Age of the Despots had gained that they involved the Papacy as well, and placed upon the chair of St. Peter men who if qualified to rule the Papal States on the basis of the Italian politics of the time were utterly unworthy to meet the spiritual responsibility of the head of the Church.

There was only one reform movement which for a short time cut into the heart of this moral and social degeneracy. The Black Friars of the order of St. Dominic had all through the Middle Ages been "the preaching friars" and the puritans militant of the medieval Church. In 1494, the prior of the monastery of San Marco, Savonarola, after twelve years of preaching against the corruption which he witnessed around him, established for three short years a theocratic republican government in the city of Florence. With the zeal of a visionary and a prophet he sought, by realizing the City of God on earth, to prepare against the approaching Day of Judgment. But the Pope, Alexander VI, was less interested in the plans to meet the Judgment Day than in forming a league of Italian Princes to drive the French king, Charles VIII, out of Italy; and Savonarola was excommunicated, not for errors of doctrine — for the Church has never accounted him a heretic — but because he stood in the way of papal plans in Italian politics. It was the government of Florence, however, and not the Papacy which brought about his execution, the fickle populace making it clear that politics could not be dominated by religion if the aims of the state were as worldly and as unchristian as those of the warring cities of northern Italy.

It was this society which set the problem for the Florentine Machiavelli. As we have indicated above, he stood at the crossroads between feudalism and the national state. Of neither of these was he fully conscious. He was a humanist, and as such was not historically minded except as he found lessons for the practical politics of his day in those of ancient Rome. Although his thought had little resemblance to that of the Middle Ages, being pagan rather than Christian, and the France of St. Louis and Jeanne d'Arc seemed far away, yet the medieval elements in the structure of society and government as applied to the Italy of Machiavelli's time determined the character of his thought more than he was aware. This is as evident in the things he leaves out of his survey as it is in the things which interest him. He had no interest, for example, in the one element in the history of Europe which was even then transforming it more completely than any military power was able to do, the economic impulse inherent in the rise of industry and trade.

Indeed the aim he had was similar to that which had animated the English and French kings of an earlier day — he wanted to see Italy under the government of one prince who would be powerful enough to keep law and order at home and defend his country from outside invasion. The means by which the unification was to be carried out were those which these kings had made familiar, namely, ruthless suppression of one's enemies through intrigues and murder, and, if need be, by deceit and war wherever the opportunity offered itself to enhance power or increase territory. To regard this analysis as marking a turning point from the Middle Ages to modern times is a misreading of European history, for while it is modern enough in the starkness of its realism, the principles it advocates were much more practiced in the Middle Ages than in modern times. A Richard III in England or a Louis XI in France would have had little to learn from Machiavelli's *The Prince*. On the other hand, in the modern world there has been a growing sense of the heavy price which Machiavellian politics must pay, because sooner or later duplicity destroys confidence, and confidence in the integrity of a government is, even more than armed force, a guarantee of its stability. This lesson of history has still to be learned by the totalitarian tyrannies; but it is inescapable.

The short monograph by which Machiavelli is most widely known, *The Prince* (1514), was not his most serious work, which was in the field of history, especially an analysis of Livy's account of the rise of the Roman Republic, and a history of Florence. *The Prince*, however, was so crystal clear a presentation of the methods of despotism and its uses as to reach the dignity of a classic in political history. Dedicated to Lorenzo de Medici, it was an appeal that the new Medici Pope of that day, Leo X, should support his nephews in Florence in the way the Borgia Pope, Alexander VI, had supported his nephew a few years earlier, to the end that northern Italy might be united and the everlasting internal warfare between the city states be suppressed by efficient despotism.

But in stating the case for his Italian Prince, Machiavelli wrote in general terms an apology for unscrupulous politics which has not been equalled in the literature of any country. The man whose career is held up as a model was none other than Caesare Borgia, whose crimes and treachery have marked him as one of the most sinister figures in European history. Though Caesare was not a successful prince and his policy of deceit was largely responsible for his failure, this fact did not lessen the influence of Machiavelli's manual of statecraft, which stripped hypocrisy from a world given over to the politics of power.

Naturally in this manual war is the outstanding instrument of politics. The whole question of the just and unjust war is disposed of without any moral scruples. The argument can best be followed in his own words (the translation is that of C. E. Detmold): "War is just when there is no hope in doing anything else. . . . No one should ever submit to evil for the sake of avoiding war. For a war is never avoided, but is only deferred to one's own disadvantage." The use of war as the supreme instrument of politics determines the nature of peace-time rule. "A Prince, then, should have no other thought or object so much at heart, and make no other things so much his special study, as the art of war and the organization and discipline of his army; for that is the only art that is expected of him who commands." Since the welfare of the state depends on the uncertain balance of power, "a sagacious prince . . . cannot and should not fulfill his pledges when their observance is contrary to his interest, and when the causes that induced him to pledge his faith no longer exist." This maxim is not a mere apologia for duplicity; it is sound statesmanship, recognized in international law on the principle of *rebus sic stantibus*, that the validity of a treaty depends upon the continuance of conditions which it registered. In this setting, Machiavelli goes on to assert that honesty is more praiseworthy in the prince than craft or deceit, "and yet the experience of our own time has shown that those princes have achieved great things who made small account of good faith, and who understood by cunning to circumvent the intelligence of others; and that in the end they got the better of those whose actions were dictated by loyalty and good faith." "It is much more safe to be feared than to be loved . . . for it may be said of men in general that they are ungrateful and fickle, dissemblers, avoiding of danger and greedy of gain."

This denial of the restraints of Christian morals in the philosophy of Machiavelli is reduced to the single maxim that "right and wrong have nothing to do with government." The state as he viewed it was creation of power held in the hands of the ruler and not a republic held together by the common interests of the citizens. A realist in politics, he was blind to all but the exercise of political power. Looking back to the Roman Republic as a model of government (as we see better from his *Discourses* on the first ten books of Livy than from *The Prince*), he attributed its success not to the specialization of functions, as we have described it, but to efficient organization for the purpose of conquest.

The advice which he gave to the representatives of the richest banking family in Florence, the Medici, showed no glimmer of the business side of politics. Money, he says, is not the sinews of war. "Every one may begin a war at his pleasure, but cannot so finish it. A prince, therefore, before engaging in any enterprise should well measure his strength, and govern himself accordingly; and he must be very careful not to deceive himself in the estimate of his strength, which he will assuredly do if he measures it by his money, or by the situation of his country, or the good disposition of his people unless he has at the same time an armed force of his own. For although the above things will increase his strength, yet they will not give it to him, and of themselves are nothing, and will be of no use without a devoted army. Neither abundance of money nor natural strength of the country will suffice, nor will the loyalty and good will of his subjects endure, for these cannot remain faithful to a prince who is incapable of defending them. . . . And money alone, so far from being a means of defense, will only render a prince more liable to be plundered. . . . There cannot, therefore, be a more erroneous opinion than that money is the sinews of war. . . . I maintain, then, contrary to the general opinion, that the sinews of war are not gold, but good soldiers; for gold alone will not procure good soldiers, but good soldiers will always procure gold." Numerous examples from history are produced to prove this point. The whole argument looks backward and as the history of our time was to show, is increasingly inapplicable in a world that is developing industrialized warfare. There is, of course, an element of permanent truth in the statement that "gold alone will not procure good soldiers." But neither can there be soldiers without it — except under feudalism.

This discounting of the economic factor in the politics of power implied as well a discounting of it in politics generally. He left out of his calculations the nation itself, the people and their fundamental interests and activities. The task of government is the safeguarding of the welfare of the state, which means the people within the state. Once this is seen, it is not possible to maintain that politics is by its nature divorced from morals. Welfare is a social fact, depending on the interaction of individuals, whose lives are passed in activities that affect others as well as themselves. Economic facts are thus bonds of interdependence; and the threefold categories of producer, distributor and consumer form a community in which the interest of one is, in the last analysis, involved in the interest of the others. The recognition of this fact is the basis of social and economic justice. Thus ethical factors are inseparable from any sound theory of economics.

It was Adam Smith the economist rather than politicians and publicists who challenged the fundamental basis of Machiavelli's philosophies with his clear demonstration that the wealth of any one nation is conditioned by the wealth of others with which it deals and that as capital and industry increase the mechanism of their control of nature, there is increased opportunity for social welfare. The economic world is an interdependent world, and that means it lies within the moral law.

But Machiavelli wrote before the rise of the middle class. Popular government was still remote. The Commercial Revolution had only just begun. If he was blind to the fact that in the revolutionary movements to come the common people would contest with the military the rule of the state, it was a blindness that darkened the vision of Europe for years. Indeed it is a blindness that mocks the intelligence of many people still. Thus throughout the centuries the baleful philosophy of Machiavelli has maintained its place openly or disguised in the councils of more than one government down to our day. It is a philosophy which is particularly current at those times when order is threatened. While men of property have hated tyranny and interference by government, they have hated even more disorder, anarchy, uncertainty. The organization of safety through military power was the first concern; it was the first concern in the days of Machiavelli, it still comes first.

And yet, though property and culture can mean little if we do not have some modicum of safety in which to enjoy them, it is equally true that security alone, mere existence, is not worth much. Safety and welfare go hand in hand. One without the other is insufficient. Without protection, we cannot live; without law to secure our private rights and an opportunity to work out our destiny, we are the slaves of tyranny. It has ever been the problem of mankind to have enough of the one without endangering the possession of the other.

Unfortunately we cannot dispose of Machiavellianism merely by pointing out that Machiavelli wrote as an apologist for despots in an age of despotism, seeking to use the dominant political force of his day as an agency to relieve Italy of the prevailing anarchy of factional disputes. For the challenge to morals in his writings, however local its origin and application, was flung in the face of all the moralists, Greek and Roman as well as Christian. It is this unlimited denial of ethical standards implied in Machiavelli's manual which makes it unique in the literature of politics.

There would have been nothing extraordinary in a humanist ignoring or discounting the teachings of theologians, especially the Scholastics of an age which they despised. But it was a wholly different thing for him to ignore practically the universal outlook of the thinkers of pagan antiquity including such dominant figures as Aristotle and Cicero. And yet, once committed to his theory of government by the unscrupulous use of despotic power, Machiavelli had no other choice than to proceed as though philosophy were as nonexistent for him as theology. For the ethical system of the Church Fathers had been so welded to that of the Greeks that by the time of Aquinas they were fitted into one great system, natural law and revelation buttressing each other in one harmonious whole. It was this supreme structure of religion and history which Machiavelli denied, in the interest of practical politics.

If Machiavellianism was more than an episode in Italian history, it was also more than an episode in the history of European thought. So bold a disregard of morals in the practice of government was bound to appeal to ambitious rulers and to those — perhaps the majority of mankind — who, conscious of the legitimacy of their purposes, are eager to believe that in their cases at least, the end justifies the means. Many of the latter are quite unaware that there is anything Machiavellian in their outlook, and they would be utterly shocked to learn that this was the case; for the "idealists" have been as susceptible to this argument as the "realists."

It might seem to be stretching the concept of Machiavellianism too far to include such attenuated or negative politics along with that of the robust and positive sort represented by despots. But Machiavelli had all of this in mind; for his approach to his problem was historical as well as practical. The historian of government who is intent upon reform is aware that the deliberate acts of the evil-minded constitute upon the whole no greater obstacle to progress than the connivance or indifference of the worthy, who throughout the ages have offered a full complement of hypocrisy. For hypocrisy takes many forms, the commonest of which is cherishing high ideals without a willingness to accept the responsibilities involved in realizing them. That type of extreme pacifist, for example, who would accept tyranny as the price of peace is not only an unconscious ally of the tyrant, but also an unconscious supporter of the war system, because, as all thoughtful people now recognize, peace is a function of justice. The reason Machiavelli did not treat this part of his problem in detail was that he took it for granted that the negative element in despotism, popular acquiescence, could be counted upon if the despot were sufficiently adept in the great art of government.

In any case, it has been these apt pupils who have won for themselves the doubtful honor of being the real Machiavellists of modern history. All of them are despots; for, in spite of their belief in the feebleness of both the intelligence and the moral calibre of the average citizen, which they attempted to control by specious propaganda, they never dared to leave to popular opinion decision of their right to rule. Mussolini's tirades against liberty ("the stinking corpse of liberty") and his Fascist henchmen securing "unity" by terror, were but the cruder expressions of Machiavellian policies. The Germans, having had a longer schooling in war and bureaucracy, did things better. As the Gestapo outdid the Inquisition, so Hitler outdid the "Prince" with guns instead of butter and the enslavement of other nations while trampling upon the liberty of his own. Also, the more one compares the policies of the Kremlin with Machiavelli's precepts, the more one sees in them the one great example of that ruthless trickery which falsifies justice while invoking its name and utterly ignores freedom. There can, therefore, be no more important issue before the world than the analysis of this doctrine in the light of history.

Only two years after the appearance of *The Prince*, the most famous scholar of the Renaissance, Erasmus, wrote for the greatest monarch of his day, the Emperor Charles V, a manual which was in effect, though not in form, a reply to Machiavelli. *The Education of a Christian Prince* bears in the title the antithesis to the Italian statecraft.

"The duty of the Christian Prince," says Erasmus, "is to keep the peace and remember that a mere promise from him is more sacred than an oath from anyone else"; that "it is base not to live up to agreements made in solemn treaty"; and that "the prince should never go to war until every other means has been tried to avoid it." Here we have the emphasis upon the pacific means of settlement so often repeated in our day: "Some princes deceive themselves that any war is certainly a just one and that they have a just cause for going to war. We will not attempt to discuss whether war is ever just; but who does not think his own cause just? Among such great and changing vicissitudes of human events, among so many treaties and agreements which are now entered into, now rescinded, who can lack a pretext — if there is any real excuse for going to war."

But Erasmus goes beyond the Scholastics with a challenging statement which sounds like a text from the writings of today: "War is always disastrous. From war comes the shipwreck of all that is good and from it the sea of all calamities pours out. Then too no other misfortune clings so steadfastly. War is sown from war; from the smallest comes the greatest; from one come two; from a jesting one comes a fierce and bloody one, and the plague arising in one place spreads to the nearest peoples and is ever carried into the most distant places."[4]

The same year, a statesman who was also a scholar of distinction, Sir Thomas More, published a little book in Latin to describe an imaginary country of his ideals. It bore the title *Utopia* (Nowhere). No one knew better than the author that he was writing of an unreal world, one that had never existed and most likely never would. Unlike Plato he framed his ideal commonwealth in terms so far removed from human frailties, or at least from the age-long trend of history, that it was not to be thought of as more than a vision of immaterial thinking. It is a sad commentary on human affairs that one who heralded the coming of modern times and whose thought was ripened in devout acceptance of Christian doctrine should have to recognize that the realities of his time lay not with such humane conceptions of peace and justice but with injustice rampant in a world still held in the iron fetters of an inescapable war system. One needed an unyielding faith in God's providence to see in this conclusion anything else than the failure of morals throughout history; and this was the point of view from which the most realistic of all political writers viewed the evolution of the state.

Utopia reflects the age of discovery. Three years before it was written, Balboa had discovered the Pacific Ocean, and More, in imagination was its first navigator, in a romance which has never lost its charm or failed to challenge the inadequacies of our civilization. A companion of Vespucci on his last voyage keeps going west over land and sea until he circumnavigates the globe, and finds an island where the evils and absurdities of Western civilization are unknown. The laws are so simple and straightforward that lawyers are not needed. There is tolerance in religion. War is held in detestation, but

[4] Translation by L. K. Born in *Records of Civilization*, No. 27 (New York: Columbia University Press, 1936), p. 239.

the state is armed and the citizens fight bravely when necessary, though they prefer to have others fight for them. Everyone cultivates the soil, for that is the source of life and comfort. There is no coinage; gold and silver are not even valued as ornaments; private property is unknown, each person leasing from the community what he especially wants. Everyone must work, drones being driven from the hive; but there are slaves, not held by individuals, but owned in common. This acceptance of slavery as an institution in Utopia is in its way as significant as the idealistic dream of a society otherwise freed from most of the practices which have hampered its advance. Such are the main lines of the civilization of "Nowhere."

Both Erasmus and More built out of the protest against violence a system of international ethics. And yet it must be admitted that the influence of these writers was very slight indeed. Their precepts were little practiced by the princes whose authority they strengthened or whom they served. The actual facts of history ran counter for the most part to these dictates of justice and mercy. The national states of Europe, like those of ancient times and like the feudal states which they supplanted, were welded together by blood and iron, and statecraft employed deceit and trickery alongside force to achieve its ends. Thus history supplies the cynic with the argument against the ethical teachers; and the world today has still to choose which of these two irreconcilable philosophies it shall follow, the technique of peace that looks to developing justice by withholding support to arbitrary force, or that of force itself applied to secure the triumph of the cause in which it is enlisted. Over against Augustine stands Machiavelli.

The Divine Right of Kings

Machiavellianism was an out-spoken, unqualified challenge to Christian ethics — or for that matter to the best political thought of pagan antiquity. Although based on history, it was a denial of morals. So great a reversal of Western thought denied all that philosophy had taught from the days of Plato and Aristotle, or jurists had incorporated in law, or philosophy in the system of medieval thought. No wonder its claim to be the real lesson of history had so strong and lasting an effect on realistic minds that there is a tendency to attribute to it the ruthless disregard of honor and right on the part of rulers who never studied *The Prince*.

One of the first of these was Henry VIII's most efficient and unscrupulous agent, Thomas Cromwell. His Catholic enemies accused this most vigorous of the supporters of Protestantism of having been a close student of Machiavelli, but, like many another unscrupulous ruler, including his master Henry, he needed no prompting from Machiavelli to establish or strengthen autocracy. For there was another doctrine to fall back upon, which supported despotism to the full and had greater authority than that of a private citizen behind it. It was the precept set forth in the Institutes of Justinian that "the will of the prince has the force of law."[5] No wonder that in the revival of Roman law the legists who applied such principles as this to support the claims of kings or princes were popular at the courts. Their influence was mostly limited to the Continent, however, and it was not until the Tudor tyranny that the ancient safeguards of English liberty gave way before such a reactionary type of government. We must also be on our guard against attributing any great influence of legal principles on the practical politics of those men of action who were the successful rulers in the transition from feudal anarchy to the national state. Yet it was something to be able to invoke the great name of Rome in support of absolutism, and the lawyers were useful alongside the men-at-arms.

The one justification for tyranny in the ruler of the national state was that referred to above, the need for the suppression of anarchy and civil wars, which by their very nature inflicted more terrible evils on the citizen than the forces of the crown. The two best examples of this were the success of the ruthless measures of the French kings in ultimately welding a nation into a condition of internal peace, and the equally instructive lesson of the emperors in failing to achieve this in Germany.

It was the problem of the suppression of anarchy — especially the wars of religion in France in the sixteenth century which was the background of the first scholarly treatise on the State and its government, the work of Jean Bodin[6] which, in spite of its reactionary conclusions, is regarded as the most important study of political science from the days of Aristotle to modern times. The starting point is the famous definition of the state as the sovereign power *(maiestas)* which is inalienable and absolute. The wielder of this power is its embodiment, and owes no responsibility to anyone but God. "The prince or people [note this concession] in whom this sovereign power resides, cannot be forced to give an account for their deeds to any but Immortal God." Here we have two absolutes in one, the sovereign state and the sovereign ruler. The latter took shape in the divine right of kings, the former in the absolute state which still blocks the pathway to international peace.

We are, therefore, at a turning point here, not merely in the history of thought, but in the history of politics. The opening chapter of the modern era is not towards freedom but towards despotism. The chief concern was security, and all history shows that when security is uppermost in men's minds, freedom is in danger. That this should be so was admitted by the most cosmopolitan of Romans, Cicero, in his famous doctrine "The safety of the people is the supreme law" *(Salus populi suprema lex)*. Today again this

---

[5] "Quod principe placuit habet vigorem" (*Institutes*, 2.6) It is interesting to note that this precept embodies late Roman and Byzantine ideas, such as those we have described in treating of the system on Rome. Machiavelli drew his ideas mainly from the study of Republican Rome. There was almost no discussion on sovereignty during the formative period of Roman history.

[6] *Six Livres da la République*. Bodin himself later published a Latin edition (1586). An English translation appeared in 1606.

issue is to the fore. Never was it more clearly shown than in the alarm felt by the countries that have treasured freedom when confronted with the threat of Communist aggression. The same kind of thinking lay in the work of Bodin, although personally he was so advanced in liberal thought as to be an advocate of freedom of conscience in religion, indeed one of its earliest advocates.

Like Aquinas, Bodin drew on Aristotle, but his ethical content was no longer dominant, or a new ethics took its place, that of successful practical politics under competent guidance. While Bodin admitted that the prince should rule with due regard to the constitution of the state, he is the source of power in the body politic. The practical politician who made this principle of government supreme in France, Richelieu, found time in the midst of plotting and counter-plotting at home and wars abroad to set forth his principles of statecraft in his *Political Testament,* a manual for a despot based on his own experience. It cannot be said that it is very encouraging to aspirants for power, however, for the tasks of the ruler are extremely hard, "depriving them of all manner of rest and contentment, except that which they receive in seeing many sleep quietly in reliance on their watchings and live happily by their misery." By such good government the ruler is assured "that it is impossible for a people not to love a prince when they are sensible that reason is the guide of his actions."

It was Richelieu the implacable minister rather than Richelieu the moralizer, who laid the basis of that absolutism of the divine right of kingship which found its classical expression in the claim of Louis XIV, "I myself am the State" (*l'Etat c'est moi*). Bossuet, the tutor of the dauphin who became Louis XV, drew the same lesson from history in his *Histoire Universelle,* the first of all textbooks on world history: "The whole state resides in the person of the prince." Machiavelli would have had some reserves on so sweeping a generalization of the history of politics.

The history of the divine right of kings in England is the tragic story of the Stuarts. There could hardly be a worse school for kingship than in the Scotland where James I, son of Mary, Queen of Scots, had to win his way in the midst of murderous plots by rival nobles and to submit to a galling tutelage of Presbyterian divines. Therefore he went to extremes in asserting his sovereign rights as king of England. "As it is atheism and blasphemy to dispute what God can do, so it is presumption and a high contempt in a subject to dispute what a king can do, or to say that a king cannot do this or that." Fortunately for England, this claim was never accepted by the nation at large, stirred to a new sense of pride in the great era of Elizabeth and of new wealth from the Commercial Revolution. The Stuarts failed to make good the majesty of kings by any such magnificence as the splendor of Louis XIV, which overawed Europe and exalted France while ruining it. But neither James nor his son Charles I had any appreciation of the strength of the opposition to their claims.

This same failure to appreciate the temper of Puritanism and the importance of the Commercial Revolution in the transformation of the State and in the creation of new and irrepressible forces working for freedom, was shared by the one English writer who wrote the strongest argument in English literature in support of the absolute authority of the sovereign, whether king or Assembly. This was Thomas Hobbes, whose *Leviathan* mirrored the new rationalism of the dawning era of science in its indifference to religious issues, but insisted that the rights of men came from an original contract with society. This social contract created "that great Leviathan called the Commonwealth or the State, which is but an artificial man, though of greater stature and strength than the natural, for whose protection and defense it was intended."

Here we have an extended analysis of the "social contract" which was to mean so much to Rousseau. It dealt a fatal blow to the divine right of kings, but offered despotism a stronger base in what was regarded as a rational scheme: namely that the body of the governed had made over to the ruler all rights but that of self-preservation. The ruler was therefore absolute, for to oppose him would be like opposing one's self. Moreover, this contract is inalienable and binds future generations. The prevention of tyranny lies, not in constitutional provisions, but in general education and enlightenment.[7]

This most un-English work is a strange expression of the England which at that time was fighting the first European revolutionary war for freedom. Its theory of the social contract was by no means new, having been developed at great length by Richard Hooker in his *Ecclesiastical Polity* in 1593, but based on the thought that all men really deserve a happy life and find it in the increase of their general welfare. Thirty years after Hobbes, John Locke, in line with Hooker, held that government was a moral trust and is therefore forfeit if the trust is not fulfilled. We are already at the doctrine of the American Revolution and may forget Hobbes and Divine Right.

The age of the despots and that of divine right of kings were brought to a close in Great Britain and France by three revolutions for freedom — the Great Revolution of 1688, the American Revolution of 1776 and the French Revolution of 1789, which open the era of modern politics. East of the Rhine, despotism tried to make good by those who aspired to the title of "benevolent despots," the Kings of Prussia, the Hapsburgs and even, in a more limited degree, the Romanovs; and it became the fashion for lesser princes to follow this "enlightened" example. But this trend toward good government never reached the hidden springs of freedom; the people were the ruled and their first duty was obedience to "law and order," both dictated from above. The result was to leave most of Europe east of the Rhine unschooled in the responsibilities of self-government, a lack which they felt less the better they were ruled.

[7] There is a good analysis, although not on these lines, in John Bowle, *Western Political Thought*. (New York: Oxford University Press, 1948). 472 pp.

CHAPTER XII

THE TROUBLED DAWN OF MODERN TIMES

Renaissance and Reformation

FOR A THOUSAND years after the fall of the Roman Empire the forces that make for civilization were moving toward the light, slowly, almost imperceptibly at first, then, from the twelfth century, with increasing momentum. Progress was neither constant nor uniform, hindered by war, persisting anarchy or plague. But finally, in the fifteenth and sixteenth centuries, the boundaries of the Middle Ages were burst by three revolutionary movements: the Renaissance of humanism and art; the Protestant Reformation; and the Commercial Revolution that followed upon the age of discovery.

Although diverse, all three movements had one thing in common: their interests lay outside the Middle Ages, from which they sought and found avenues of escape. It is true that medieval society and thought progressed toward new and better creations, yet these were mostly for a world in which life repeated itself within known and familiar confines. The weight of repetition is heavy on the mind, the mere fact that the same things are done in the same way creates an iron law of habit from which escape is difficult and rare. The greatest theatre of repetition is agricultural life, with its enforced routine of the seasons; seed-time and harvest dominate the calendar in unvarying routine. It was natural, therefore, that medieval society, being predominantly landed, should remain largely within the framework of familiar things, and, as in all such societies, reforms were presented and accepted as a recovery of the ancient customs embodying the wisdom of the fathers. Politics was an adjustment to a known world, not an adventure into a new one. Medieval thought was capable of noble creations, but it was masonry like that of the cathedrals, finely carved and set logically in order or design that did not yield readily to change.

Then the horizon widened to include a past that had been forgotten and a new world offering in gold and silver and foreign goods the dynamics of change from land to commerce, with an immediate impact on the structure of religion as well as of politics. In confusion and conflict, but with imperious might, came the new era of Modern Times.

The name was not new. Cicero had used it to distinguish his age from that which had already become ancient history. It was natural, therefore, that the humanist scholars, looking back to Greek and pagan antiquity, should feel strongly the much greater contrast between their times and those of the Scholastics. The consciousness of escape from the rigid disciplines of disputatious logic and the opportunity to range the wide fields of antique thought were paralleled by the revolutionary zeal of rebels from the medieval church, while the navigators and discoverers had a wholly new world to explore. Yet history could not be cast aside like a worn-out garment. The structure of society, in church and state, continued to harbor the institutions which were essential for the very existence of civilization, into which the new forces had to be fitted whenever possible. If the old and the new could not be made to work together, one or the other must go. This meant a troubled period of history, out of which came the world of today.

The shape of things to come was apparent in the royal tyrannies that developed in Tudor England and Bourbon France, and in the age of the despots in Italy. The new structure of the state system of modern times was not based directly upon the solid framework which was slowly building through the Middle Ages, but upon the shifting ground of conflicting interests and politics of power, responding to new economic forces in the rise of capitalism. Dynastic wars still further confused the historical perspective, but just when politics seemed almost meaningless, the meaning of life itself took on new dimensions in "the new learning," as humanism came to be known, in art, religion and discovery. Even this widened horizon would not be enough, for not only were these movements distinct from each other in technique, they touched only the fringe of the greatest revolutionary movement of all, science.

Through this period of change and turmoil the history of freedom runs such a tortuous course that it is almost impossible to trace it. The growth of enlightenment was paralleled by the growth of persecution, the blind acceptance of authority by new insistence on doctrine, by new movements of social revolt put down in blood; and yet, through it all, men fought for their rights both old and new and finally won them in three great revolutions in England, in America and in France.

Before we turn to these great chapters in the advance of freedom, however, we must pause for a while on the threshold of this new era, if only to remind ourselves that the story is only half told in the political annals of the nations. For freedom is more than the granting of charters or the guarantee of laws. It is the expression of the spirit of man as it reaches furthest away from the self-centered cruelties of the animal world. It is the test of intelligence. *"Tout comprendre, c'est tout pardonner"* is the final judgment on mankind. It is more than a conclusion drawn from the history of morals. The accent is not on pardoning but on understanding. We are only now beginning to see what a revolution this calls for, not only in the ways of man with man, but in government and criminology. The history of freedom thus merges with that of civilization — as civilization matures.

Nowhere in the long stretch of the centuries which we have been traversing is the merging of the history of freedom with that of civilization more evident than in that period which humanist historians proudly name the "Renaissance." The name itself was a challenge to the Middle Ages, and not quite a fair one, for the devotees of the new learning of classical scholarship of the fifteenth century were not wholly free of the insistence on authority which had dulled the adventurous spirit of medieval thought. But they made good their challenge by offering in the study of Greece and Rome a rival to the study of theology, remaking the curricula of the universities of Oxford and Cambridge, and erecting their Collège de France alongside the Sorbonne at Paris.

The Renaissance was a much more vital thing than scholarship, however. New wealth was accumulating in the cities where merchants rivalled kings in the magnificence of new palaces. And instead of only illiterate men-at-arms clanking along their corridors, a new class of retainers was maintained by the newly rich aristocracy, artists, sculptors and architects along with the humanist scholars. The change came first in Italy, where the canals of Venice were lined with the most luxurious homes of Europe. Venetian merchant envoys, accustomed to a cultured environment, reported a lamentable crudeness in the conditions of life north of the Alps, especially in England; but already a new wind was blowing over France, down the Rhine Valley and over the Thames. The age of the despots was also one in which fresh energies were opening and holding open opportunities never before within reach of the common man.

With the Renaissance, history loses the simple lines of medieval annals. The subject is no longer that of a massive structure bearing the long, slow stress of national policy and meditating on eternal verities. It becomes as varied as the new interests in literature and art as well as in the new problems of religion and of politics in a world of rival nations. The history of freedom covers all this heritage; for the fullness of life is not gauged by politics alone.

We now turn, therefore, to the two contributions of the Renaissance, Scholarship and Art, and then after a survey of the revolt of Protestantism against Catholicism and of science against humanism, reach modern times by way of the Commercial Revolution which leaves the medieval world behind. The long road then passes by revolution and war to the era of applied science, with freedom ever gaining and ever faced with new dangers. The theme is too great for history; but it holds the clue to the meaning of the world today.

Humanism and Science

Humanism is a common word now-a-days, but it was a declaration of independence in the fifteenth century. The term was taken over by the classical scholars as the symbol of revolt from the dominance of theology and scholastic philosophy. While most gave at least outward conformity to the Church, their supreme interest was mankind as such, in its own world, here and now. But humanism meant to them much more than mere scholarship. It implied what Cicero had meant in the use of it: liberal education, elegance of manners or language, cultivated tastes, refinement. The perfect humanist was supposed to have all of these qualities, although it is highly doubtful, judging from their capacity for vituperative controversy, if more than a very small fraction of those who took *litterae humaniores* instead of divinity at Oxford were better gentlemen than the theologians.

Humanism as a technique was scholarship recovering the lost treasures of Greek and Roman literature. But while critical of texts, it was not sufficiently critical of the thoughts they contained. With some notable exceptions, there was much the same attitude towards the pagan masters of thought and style as the Scholastics had shown in their discussions on the writings of the church fathers or Aristotle. The exceptions were outstanding, like Valla, denying the authenticity of the Donation of Constantine; Machiavelli, building his statecraft out of Livy; or Erasmus, with his comprehensive learning concerning antiquity and knowledge of his modern world. But, although we owe the basis of our scholarship to the humanists, the point that stands out in this history of freedom is that they never fully emancipated the mind from the dominance of classical authority; and, in the years and centuries that followed, their disciples fastened upon education a rigid system with disciplines not wholly unlike those of the medieval universities.

Yet, although some of the grammarians, working on texts, were as narrow in their interests as they were keen in their microscopic search for words and phrases scattered haphazardly in the blurred palimpsests preserving antique texts in the manuscripts of rituals or lives of saints, they were pioneers in a new era of freedom, opening up a world so diverse from that of the Middle Ages that the very contrast stung thoughtful minds to new energy. While the academic tradition in school and university later reached out its unimaginative control over humanists as it had done over Scholastics, the bolder spirits that were stimulated by the Renaissance carried the thought of Europe into ever new adventures.

Unfortunately, these leaders of freedom were so disdainful of the Middle Ages as to create a wholly false perspective of European history, one in which the thousand years between the fall of Rome and the Renaissance were viewed as a long era of stagnation, with mankind absorbed in wars or in philosophical and theological quibbles. Thus, while history was enriched by the rediscovery of the golden ages of Greece and Rome, it was robbed of its medieval heritage. The theologians fought over the history of the church, but there was no one among the humanists to do for the national state what Dante and Marsiglius of Padua did for the Medieval Empire — point out the possibility of its service to peace and justice by its own inherent capacity to deal with its problems on its own terms — problems beyond the reach of antique experience.

The long story of the creation of a new framework for Europe in which freedom could develop was never written by the scholars of the Renaissance. Yet, compared with the obscure process of the spread of the king's justice along the highways and through the forest lands of the twelfth and thirteenth centuries, and the slow but sure enhancement of the people's rights, the history of the ancient world, which interested the humanists, remained academic. Here and there a ruler or a statesman attempted to apply the political lessons of Greece and Rome, but in the wholly different world of the sixteenth century there was very little they could apply. The chivalry of Germany or France, pouring through the Alpine passes for a coronation or a campaign left little trace in history but its political futility. Only in the arts and letters and new intellectual interests of polite society did the impact of the Italian Renaissance reach nothern Europe; it had no political message — except the distorted theories of Machiavelli, because Italy was as backward in politics as it was advanced in culture.

This absence of political feeling, which had been so strong in Dante, was especially notable in the man who is often termed the father of the Italian Renaissance, Petrarch. Dante's patriotic zeal is quite lacking in the poet of the sonnets, whose political views were so unsettled as to hail with passionate enthusiasm the Roman Republic of the visionary revolutionist Cola di Rienzi, and yet treasure the friendship of tyrants like the head of the noble houses of the Visconti of Milan, the d'Este of Ferrara, the Gonzaga of Mantua, the Malatesta of Rimini, or the Carrara of Padua. It was as a self-centered individualist that Petrarch lived and wrote, saved only from being a dilettante by the beauty of his verse in the Italian vernacular, the richness of his Latin scholarship (he had almost no Greek), and his love of nature. A modern man in all but politics, Petrarch was a leader in both aspects of the Italian Renaissance, an artist in words, and a humanist scholar. No one else, neither Boccaccio, Petrarch's friend, the immortal story teller, nor Ariosto, the "perfect poet" of a century later, holds quite his place among the pioneers of modern times, "the first among the poets to climb a hill for the sake of the view."

While the Italian humanists gloried in their escape from "the prison house of Scholasticism," the revolt from Aristotle did not open the doors to freedom of thought for that galaxy of intellectuals who formed the Platonic Academy of Florence. For their chief interest remained that of the Scholastics whom they despised, metaphysical speculation; only, instead of following Aristotle, they followed Plato at second hand; that is to say, they became devotees of neo-Platonism, that last effort of the antique world to find in mysticism a harmony between the universe of Plato and the teachings of the Church. The result was not the sunrise of reason over against the dusk of Scholasticism. It was the romanticism of Plato and Plotinus (the founder of neo-Platonism) supplanting the scientific analysis of Aristotle and Aquinas. The great thing was not the change in the body of thought but the freedom to have such a change. The humanist leaders in the new movement used a method that obscured Greek history, rather than interpreting it, because the speculative philosophy they revived had been an escape from reality in the latter age of Greece. This trend in humanism was not important in itself, but needs to be recalled here, because it shows that there were humanists of the Renaissance who were still medieval at heart. Others, however, as we shall see, turned from it to the founders of modern science.

The great contribution of humanism to the history of intellectual freedom was of much the same kind as that of its development in early Greece, the rise of criticism. Uninhibited questioning of the sources bred an independent habit of thinking, only now the questioner had a wider world than that of the Ionian cities, one which, by more than happy chance, kept forever widening with discovery and the new world of science, both of which were far more important in the drama of modern times than humanism. But the field of interest of the Italian humanists was not the same as that of those north of the Alps. In Italy the past that was recovered was its own, that of a world as magnificent as it was pagan, the Hellenistic world which for a thousand years had lain in the dark shadow cast by Augustine's shining City of God. The German humanists, among whom we should place Erasmus, had no such ancestral share in the antique pagan heritage as the Italian, and, therefore, turned also to the Christian antiquities, the early history of Christianity and the Jewish scriptures.

At the beginning of "the new learning" German scholars went to Italy, but soon Greek, Latin and Hebrew scholars were teaching or setting up academies in German cities. The list is as long as that of Italian Humanists. The greatest name is, of course, Erasmus, the uncrowned king of the learned world. Believing in a reform instead of a revolution in the Church, he held back from Luther, but in both controversies with obscurantists and in the translation of the New Testament, he threw the weight of his great influence on the side of enlightenment. Reuchlin the Hebraist, second only to Erasmus in renown, fought a long fight with the Inquisition and finally won as other humanists poured ridicule in the famous "Letters of Obscure Men" on the suppression of scholarship. But the Lutheran movement absorbed the interest of scholars like Melanchthon (Graecized from Schwartzerd, black earth), the outstanding humanist among the theologians. Cities like Augsburg, Basel, Nuremburg and Strasburg had become humanist centers and Vienna, under the sympathetic emperor Maximilian, had an academy like that of Heidelberg. A generation of distinguished scholars maintained the traditions of scholarship, while artists like Dürer and Holbein rivalled in their German idiom the drawings of the Italians.

In France the output of both art and letters was even greater. In the field of letters, two outstanding names must be mentioned, Rabelais, the humorist, and Montaigne, the essayist, both of the first rank. But parallel with the output of individuals was that of two institutions for critical scholarship. The Collège de France was established as a home for humanist learning alongside the University of Paris, with its traditional interest in philosophy; and clerical scholars raised history to a science in the critical exploration of the sources of church history. This dawn of scientific history-writing centered in the Benedictine Monastery of St. Maur in Paris. It was as great a service to the historical study of Europe as the recovery of antique texts had been to that of Greece and Rome.

Steadily, irresistibly, the new freedom of scholarship and thought made its way into the mind of Europe. Strongholds of reaction continued and still continue, but wholly new horizons opened up, world-wide in geography and limitless in science; and the narrow confines of the Middle Ages were left behind in less than a century. At the same time that the humanists were recovering antique thought, navigators were exploring America and Asia, and Copernicus and Galileo were discovering the nature of the universe. The primitive, medieval world of repetition and miracle was making way for one of laws which were growingly comprehended in the new world of science.

Again it was Greece which gave the clues that Copernicus followed, working on them in the very years that Luther was launching his revolt. Copernicus himself stated that it was the Pythagorean theory of the earth as a globe, suspended in space with the other planets revolving around it, that first gave him the clue to his "system." The Greek of the sixth century B.C. had not placed the sun at the centre and explained its light like that of the moon as a reflection from another central fire. But Copernicus, for all his originality of mathematical proof, began in the school of the humanists. It was by experimentation, however, that his system was brought to conclusion, testing observation by instruments, crude and inadequate, but sufficient to justify the new hypothesis.

Next to Copernicus stands Galilei Galileo, the Abelard of modern science, who drew more than two thousand of the intellectual flower of Europe to his lectures on physics at the university of Padua. Making, himself, a telescope, by improving on that of a spectacle maker, he was the first human being to see the "mountains and seas" on the moon, the spots on the sun and the phases of Venus. He also established mechanics as a science by his researches on the laws of motion. But the Copernican system which Galileo could not but accept had to be renounced at the threat of the Inquisition. History has treasured the legend that when forced to deny the movement of the earth he muttered "Eppur si muove" (yet it does move), but unfortunately the story is apocryphal. Had he not yielded, the Holy Office might have been obliged, even against the feelings of the learned Cardinal Bellarmin, in charge of the proceedings, to punish him for heresy. Such at least had been the fate only sixteen years earlier (1600) of the uncompromising skeptical scientist Giordano Bruno, whose statue now stands in the flower market of Rome (Campt di Fiori), where he was burned in 1600.

The currents of scientific thought in the Italian Renaissance touched art at a number of points, most notably in the prodigy of genius, Leonardo da Vinci. Architecture was a testing ground for mechanics, and a new type of building spread from Italy over northern Europe, especially France. Appropriate setting had to be created for the new wealth and splendor; and the sense of a new era was mirrored in vernacular literatures.

Science, too, pursued its austere way. From Denmark and Germany, Tycho Brahe and Kepler followed the work of Copernicus, enlarging the horizon of the heavens and measuring the movements of the stars by the inescapable laws of mathematics; while, in England, Francis Bacon, in an encyclopaedic survey of knowledge, denounced the old philosophy to make way for a sounder technique of inductive science than even the Greeks had had. Bacon's method of collecting and observing facts to find the laws of nature was for a completely different purpose than that of medieval or even of Greek philosophy. The "Advancement of Learning" was "for the happiness of mankind," and not for the great adventure of exploring the ultimate truth about God and the universe. Natural science was no speculative philosophy, but a function ministering to human welfare. The yoke of Scholastic authority was shaken off in order that knowledge might be useful in the daily life of man. Bacon not only discounted medieval philosophy, he also criticized the Humanists for their acceptance of antique authorities as being more worthy of respect because of their antiquity. In this regard one might think of him as the first outspoken modern man, for he gloried in the discoveries of the explorers who were then remaking the map of the world and the pioneering astronomers who were exploring the universe. "It may truly be affirmed to the honor of these times and in a virtuous emulation with antiquity that this great building of the world had never through-lights made in it till the age of us and our fathers . . . To circle the earth as the heavenly bodies do was not done nor enterprized until these later times . . . And this proficience in navigation and discoveries may plant also an expectation of the further proficience and augmentation of all science."[1]

More important than Bacon was Descartes in the breakdown of humanist tyranny of thought which had threatened to supersede that of medieval Scholasticism. While Bacon revered the classics, Descartes broke completely with the past, and based the advancement of knowledge on a method of his own, insisting that doubt should range through all our accustomed thought as the basis for true freedom of the mind. He did not develop the implications of this method as applied to the ever-widening horizons of knowledge, but the theory of progress which it implied became the inspiration for a whole school of thought, Cartesianism. The world was to become God's open stage for the play of mechanics and geometry.

With the Cartesian theory to spur him, Newton then went on to measure the universe. No greater tribute was ever paid to a man of science than that by Leibnitz, the greatest figure in German intellectual life in the early eighteenth century, that Newton's contribution to mathematics was greater than that of the whole of history until his time.[2]

[1] *Novum Organum*, 129, cf. J. B. Bury *The Idea of Progress* (London: Macmillan and Co., 1920), p. 55.

[2] *The Living Past*, by F. S. Marvin (Oxford: Clarendon Press, 1913) has this arresting comment on Newton's *Principles*: "It was essentially the same human mind which had once counted fingers and marched pebbles in the primeval cave, and was now reaching to the stars measuring the speed of light and reading its own riddles in the unfathomed depths of space. On the one hand, the savage, struggling to five as the limit of his number; on the other, the astronomer studying stars so distant from us that our whole solar system, if seen at all, would be but a speck, and finding in their motion fresh illustrations of the conic curves of which Appollonius, Descartes and Newton expressed the law."

The age of mathematics was also that of scientific discoveries, especially in physics and chemistry; and all this new knowledge was stirring a new critical spirit about a political system as out of date as scholasticism. In Spinoza, the philosopher, the Cartesian critique reaches over from geometry to a treatise on ethics, which contains an eloquent defense of freedom of thought and speech in the whole field of speculative inquiry.

Nowhere did the new scientific spirit breed a stronger skepticism than in France. The whole philosophe movement of the eighteenth century was its off-shoot. The Encyclopaedists were the popularizing apostles of the new learning. But there, more than elsewhere, this intellectual freedom turned from pure science to ally itself with reformers, impelled thereto by the backwardness of the whole social and political system. We shall, therefore, leave them here, to meet them again in the old regime on the eve of the French Revolution.

Art

The outlines of ancient and medieval history which we have followed in this history of freedom have concentrated upon two main themes: religion and politics, building the structure of society as a defense against the ever-haunting evils of superstition and war, with human welfare as the final goal. But the achievements in these fields are not the full measure of man. His mastery over dangers and obstacles is registered not only in the safeguards of society but in the growing power of freedom of the mind, in the history of thought upon which we have touched too lightly here, and in the field of art, which we have not explored at all. The slightness of our reference to freedom of thought may be partly excused by the fact that this is the subject most developed in the literature of freedom.

But art has seemed to be a distraction from the steady march of politics, law or economics; and, having a technique of its own (the Greek word for art was techne) did not fit readily into the stern prose of history. Yet the Renaissance showed how much of the life of the time was reflected in its art creations, and by initiating the search for the treasures of Greek and Roman art, paralleled the work of the humanists in the recovery of texts. But, like the humanists, the creators as well as the patrons of Renaissance art were blind to the importance of art as a source of history and were interested only in its great creations. In the history of freedom, however, the limitations of art are as significant as its achievements; in both respects it mirrors the minds of its creators.

From the dim, prehistoric background of primitive life, there had always been another escape from the enslaving reach of the taboo than that which we have traced in the institutions of society and government. As the mysterious potencies in places and things became presences to be placated by ceremonies, the heaps of stones or piles of earth became altars (literally "high places"), to be ornamented or inscribed. It was a long way from the imitative magic in these ceremonies, with its mimicry, to the ritual of religious worship, but the arts that later developed into the drama marked almost every step of it. Crossing the gulf between the fetish and the divinity, between sticks and stones and images, was a triumph of art as well as of belief. For, throughout all history, in its growing mastery of form and line, art has been the language of freedom.

Begun as a defense against supernatural evils, art passed from prophylaxis against the dangers of a magical world to joy in creation, finding a growing sense of wonder and beauty in line, color and form. From the drawings in the caves of neolithic man and the ornamented pot-sherds that became vases in Cretan palaces, from altars that were crowned with temples as homes of the gods and goddesses, whose sculptured forms were idealized human beings, the theme is one of growing mastery. As art progressed it reflected an ever greater interest in the secular world, in men building homes for themselves both in the mind and in the environing world of daily affairs.

The parallel in art to the story of the secular revolution, which we have traced in the politics of the ancient world, is the record richly illustrated by the statues of the pharaohs, still god-like but human, and by the monuments and tombs of rulers, massive like the Egyptian pyramids, Babylonian temples or palaces on the line of Alexander's march, vainly challenging time the destroyer. They are the reminders of human achievements, even when recorded with due deference to supernatural aid. They are uncensored texts that tell of cruelty and oppression, faithfully transcribed by art. Yet, even from the days of Hammurabi, this pictorial or monumental history of warriors records as well a dawning pride of the rulers in their work as lawgivers.

All this, however, is still so primitive that its roads to freedom ended in blind alleys; and, however fascinating the theme, we cannot carry it here through those far off days of Babylonia, Assyria and Persia, where military monarchs slowly gained secular controls through the long, confused and uncertain evolution toward politics. Moreover, the theme suddenly became clear in the history of Hellas, where, in art as in literature and politics, freedom spoke freely for the first time.

It is perilous to generalize upon so large and varied a subject as Greek art. But there is one characteristic upon which there can be no disagreement. Beginning in stilted, traditional forms, it became intensely, magnificently human. The gods are there, but at the height of Greek art they are distinguishable from the heroes only by a certain stateliness of bearing. The line between the epic heroes like Achilles and the mythic deities like Heracles is a thin one. Critics have been divided in opinion whether the life-like figure on the pediment of the Parthenon was Dionysus, the god, or Theseus the legendary founder of constitutional government in Athens. Pallas Athene still wore the helmet as she sprang full armored from the head of Zeus, but the bust of this protectress of the city came to portray womanhood in its noblest aspect of contemplation on the problems of life. And all this is the expression of a warrior people, as the pediments of Agina and so much else of Greek art show, athletes at war, fighting with deadly skill, but not in the mechanical, assembly-line of death of the enslaved soldiers of the Assyrian kings. The other theme of Greek art that ranked alongside war was sport.

The statues of the winners of athletic contests were almost as common as those of the heroes of war. Steadily, the religious motive lost its compelling power in official art, while it went underground in the mysteries in the ways we have already traced in the section on religion.

Art in Rome reflected, as it does everywhere, the spirit of the people. It was the voice not of freedom but of power, with the magnificence of engineering triumphs in domes or bridges and the roads and fortresses for its greatest art, that of war. When the power was gone, its monuments were mostly left in ruins, except where a church could be made out of a temple or basilica. Only in Byzantium was the art of the engineer kept alive in vaults that impressed the Orient as far as India, where centuries later the soaring vault of Santa Sophia was reflected in the dome of the Taj Mahal, and where the illumination of books or missals rivalled the jewel-like miniatures of Persia. But this Byzantine art reflected in its stylistic rigidity the outlook of a bureaucratic society, and, however delicately the medieval artists copied it, it was foreign to the new spirit of Italy to which Giotto gave voice.

In spite of all its varied interests and the far reach of its speculative thought, the medieval mind was not free to see the world as it is. From the days of Gregory I and beyond, allegory was a constant device to reconcile the Old Testament with the New, and allegory was a misleading theme in art. It seldom grappled with reality by the objective study of detail, when dealing with the fanciful ornaments of cathedrals; for the details of griffons did not matter, and the saints and apostles were imaginary or traditional. There were exceptions to this in sculptures, like those at Chartres and Rheims, and in effigies on tombs, but it was in Italy in the fourteenth century that both sculpture and painting emerged from the limitations which Byzantine taste had fastened upon early medieval art. Giotto, who brought the new technique to art expression still chose religious subjects, in the church of St. Francis of Assisi and the chapel at Padua, where Dante visited him; but the figures are no longer stilted images; they are real people drawn by a master untrammeled by formula. Freedom in art had come.

The Renaissance in art had this advantage over the Renaissance in literature that, in escaping from the trammels of the Middle Ages, it did not, like humanism, go to the other extreme and yield to stylistic imitation of Greek or Roman models. "It is not so much an outcome of studies in antiquity as an exhibition of emancipated modern genius, fired and illuminated by the masterpieces of the past . . . Its religion is joyous, sensuous, dramatic, terrible, but strictly human . . . The art of the Renaissance was an apocalypse of the beauty of the world and man in unaffected spontaneity, without any side thoughts for piety or erudition, inspired by pure delight in loveliness and harmony for their own sakes."[3]

The pioneering figure in this new chapter of art, Giotto, was the contemporary and friend of Dante, whose portrait he drew. Escaping from the Byzantine formalism, which had lent majesty to but hampered the freedom of

[3] John Addington Symonds, in the article "Renaissance," Encyclopedia Britannica, 11th ed.

his master Cimabue, he acquired in painting the freedom of a vernacular, in which to tell a human story, whether of the Holy Family or of Francis of Assisi. There is a new note of "homely gracefulness" in his work. "Almost single handed he had made Italian painting which his style dominated for at least a century."[4] Yet the great masters were still to come. The first was Leonardo da Vinci, surpassing in intellectual power Botticelli's vision of beauty, and linking art to science, as had never been done before or since. Then came the golden age of Raphael and Michelangelo, the one a sensitive soul, responsive to beauty in everything; the other proudly intellectual, a colossal figure by any measurements. This was the judgment of their time, and has never been challenged by those competent to judge.

The further history of Renaissance art lies outside the scope of this survey; but it opens up some of the questions that are hardest to answer in the history of freedom. The most puzzling paradox is that art, which demands freedom for its full expression, flourished under despots, often with apparent indifference to anything but art itself. For that matter, some of its grandest creations in ancient Greece had been under the tyrannies of Peisistratus and his successors at Athens. The point to remember is that politics in both the ancient city states and in the national states which were being fashioned in the Middle Ages was politics of power. It was this point which Machiavelli drove home in his insistence that the chief aim of the state should be efficiency and that the most efficient would be a ruthless despotism. The modern issue of freedom as a concern of the state did not develop until a century later when the middle class acquired in money a new weapon of power, through the rise of commerce and the influx of New World gold and silver. Under the conditions of the fifteenth century, the artists found freedom either in avoiding political and social questions or in frankly separating aesthetics from morals.

This may seem like an unsatisfactory conclusion, but perhaps it was the best that could be reached until new social and political horizons were opened by the Commercial Revolution. For in Greece, as in Renaissance Italy, there never had been any clear understanding of freedom as a function of the state. It had been an escape from responsibility rather than an assertion of the right to participate in power. The extremes of such individualism were held down by regimes like the Spartan or Roman discipline, so that Tacitus could be shocked by the action of the German levies, when the soldiery purposely came late to assert their independence. But it was this same spirit of personal liberty which made for the fatal anarchy of Greece and the rivalries of Italian states so much deplored by Machiavelli; and its one positive result was art. Nowhere else, neither in philosophy nor law, the other great legacies of civilization, does the individual stand alone. Art has its limitations, too, as the artist reflects the interests and capacities of his time. It is that fact which gives art its place in the history of freedom; but it

---

[4] *The History of Italian Painting* by Frank Jewett Mather, Jr., a masterpiece of criticism. He adds: "The Cavemen would have understood Giotto and so would the post-impressionists of today." (New York: Henry Holt and Co., 1948.) *Cf.* pp. 28 and 40.

is not a major part, for it reaches its highest achievement when it is free from other preoccupations — the very preoccupations with which the rest of this narrative mostly deals.

The Religious Revolution

The long history of heresies, which we have traced through the early church and the Middle Ages, came to a climax in Protestantism, when revolt became revolution. It was long a tenet of Protestant writers that this successful challenge to the Catholic Church — successful in part, at least — was the opening chapter of religious freedom, and so, in the long run, it proved to be. But the immediate effect was the very opposite, an intensification of religious fanaticism and persecution, the fires of which lasted on through some of the most savage wars in European history.

No one has done more to correct the perspective than Lord Acton, the most learned of modern historians, whose *History of Liberty* has been termed the greatest history that never was written! Only three fragments of his researches have been published, *The History of Freedom in Antiquity; The History of Freedom in Christianity;* and *The Protestant Theory of Persecution.*[5] These chapters are as devastating in their implications as they are scholarly. The thoughtful reader will note the judicious restraint of the historian in not stressing the point that at the beginning of the sixteenth century, "the most visible sign of the times was the decline of religious influence that had reigned so long," for the implication would seem to be that but for the Protestant movement the religiosity of the Middle Ages might quietly have died out, yielding to the new worldly interest in economics and politics, in which case there would have been no religious persecutions. Yet Acton warns that the indifference to religion was also an indifference to liberty. The age of the despots and that of the royal tyrannies which followed witnessed as cruel and inhuman oppression as that of the Inquisition; indeed, the Spanish Inquisition was part of it. One generation beheld the change all over Europe from the anarchy of the Wars of the Roses to the ready submission, the gratified acquiescence in tyranny that marked the reign of Henry VIII and the kings of his time.[6] Moreover, the decline in morale was also a decline in Christian morals, all of which brought a decided lull in religious persecution until the war of creeds in the middle of the sixteenth century.

It was into this current of reaction that the Protestant movement was launched, reviving both religion and morals by an intense concentration upon the problems of belief and conduct. At first, as in the case of most heresies, it seemed to be an assertion of the right of the individual to freedom of belief and therefore a step forward on the long road toward religious freedom generally. Luther's protest at the Diet of Worms, *"Hier stehe Ich; Ich kann nicht anders"* (Here I stand; I cannot do otherwise) was at least a

---

[5] *Cf.* Lord Acton, *Essays on Freedom and Power* (Boston: Beacon Press, 1948).
[6] *Ibid.*

declaration of religious independence. But the reason he "could not do otherwise" than reject the emperor's demand to recant was not a refusal to accept authority in religion; it was the acceptance of authority other than that of the Catholic church. He had set this forth the year before in his Treatise on the *Liberty of the Christian Man,* which stated in language that all could understand, the theory of justification by faith. In this profoundly spiritual document Luther proclaimed the doctrine of the priesthood of the common man under the immediate sovereignty of Christ, instead of by way of a complicated system of sacraments under sacerdotal control.

But justification by faith was a dogma just as firmly held as the Catholic dogma of justification by works and priestly sacramentalism. In the mind of Luther and the other Protestant leaders, conscience ruled in place of ecclesiasticism. But the more intense the belief the less it is ready to yield to others, and no belief could be more intense than that of a conviction of personal, direct access to God. Slight variants in creed or cult, if they expressed the same fundamental beliefs could be treated as substantially the same, but in the development of the major churches of Protestantism, to suppress or war against those in extreme disagreement, Catholic or Anabaptist, was much a duty to God as it had been in the medieval inquisitions. Thus, what looked at first like a new chapter of freedom, became one of the darkest eras of persecution, in which both Catholics and Protestants were persecutors.

Like all the great movements in religion, Protestantism owes much of its success to its founders, especially Martin Luther, whose volcanic energy stirred the dormant conscience of his time and country as it had never been stirred before. But also, like all great movements, the vital elements which responded to his call were already present, although until then obscure and inarticulate: German national opposition to Papal exactions, and a spirituality of which the people themselves were not wholly aware. The first of these, the political situation, presented the paradox at which we have already looked, in the life of the Emperor, Charles V. A foreigner in Germany, bred at the court of Spain, he reversed the politics of past emperors and joined with the Pope against the German nobles and the rising nationalist feeling voiced by Luther. The result was disaster for the Holy Roman Empire, registered finally in its disintegration at the Treaty of Westphalia in 1648. As for the other element which woke to life at Luther's call, religious revolt, it also had origins in history, which Luther himself at first disowned, for they lay outside Germany and he had thought of them as foreign heresies to be shunned as mortal sins. They were the movements of Wyclif in England and Huss in Bohemia.

Of all the heroes in the history of religious freedom few names rank higher than that of John Wyclif, master of Balliol College, Oxford, and founder of the one distinctly English heresy of the Middle Ages. His life is an almost exact prototype of that of Luther, even in the protection of a prince against persecution, John of Gaunt, Duke of Lancaster, as over against Frederic, Elector of Saxony. His doctrine of anti-sacerdotalism in his great work, *Kingdom of God (De Dominio Divino),* is almost an exact parallel to that of Luther's justification by faith, in its insistence on the direct responsibility of everyone to divine authority, with the individual conscience as the guide in obedience to either church or state. Then, like Luther, Wyclif turned from scholastic Latin to the vernacular and became the father of English prose, both in numerous tracts and in the translation of the "Wyclif Bible," part of which is his own text. The parallel continues through the denial of transubstantiation in the Eucharist ceremony, the suppression of religious vows, and, indeed, practically the whole Lutheran ecclesiastical policy.

Meanwhile, one of the rare romances in the history of heresy had taken place. Anne of Bohemia, first Queen of Richard II, had helped to send Wyclif's tracts and his translation of the Bible to Prague, where their influence may be measured by the fact that in 1410, over 200 volumes of Wyclif's writings were burned in the Bishop's courtyard. More important, however, was the fact that they found a voice in the vernacular sermons of the most eloquent Bohemian preacher, John Huss, who was also more than once rector of the university. At first, Huss limited himself, as Luther did a century later, to attacks against abuses in the church: but, like Luther, this led to attacks against its doctrines. When excommunicated, he stated the case for religious freedom in absolute terms: "In the things which pertain to salvation, God is to be obeyed rather than man." The rising spirit of Bohemian nationalism was deeply stirred by his sermons in Bethlehem chapel, Prague;[7] and, when, betrayed by King Sigismund at the Council of Constance, he was burned at the stake as a heretic, his name became a rallying cry for freedom, both religious and secular. His heroic death overshadowed the events in Bohemia in the unhappy years of war and disorder which followed.

Hussite Protestantism, at first successful in securing religious freedom, was finally crushed by the army of the Hapsburg emperor Ferdinand in 1620, and the Jesuit counter-reformation won control. Yet it never wholly succeeded. Those who had learned to read, cherished their hidden bibles, copies of which are now on exhibition in libraries and museums in Czechoslovakia, whose President-Liberator, Thomas G. Masaryk, chose to become a Protestant.

When, in 1517, Luther nailed his ninety-five theses against abuses in indulgences on the church door at Wittenberg, his protest, in his mind, had no connection whatever with Hussite doctrines. But, when forced to defend his views at a disputation with Dr. Eck at Leipzig in 1519, he found himself to his surprise practically on the same footing with Wyclif and Huss, because the doctrine of justification by faith was in reality a denial of the whole system of salvation through the sacraments. It was when Eck went to Rome to secure the bull of excommunication, that Luther prepared his challenge to papal authority by writing the three primary treatises which became the manifesto of revolution.

The pamphlet *On the Liberty of a Christian Man* swept away the com-

[7] Taken over by the Communists as a propaganda center.

plications of medieval theology by the one revolutionary principle that made salvation depend on the individual's own relation to God. The *Address to the Christian Nobility of the German Nation* called upon the secular power to help reform the church, in which "The Romanists" had intrenched themselves as "thieves and robbers" on the false theory that the "spiritual estate" of pope and clergy has a higher calling than that of the common man who works for the common good. *The Babylonian Captivity of the Church* carried these attacks to their definite conclusion. "I must begin by denying that there are seven sacraments and must lay down for the time being that there are only three, baptism, penance and the bread, and that by the court of Rome all three have been brought into miserable bondage and the church despoiled of her liberty." By 1521, when Luther was summoned to appear before the Emperor, he was a more dangerous heretic than Wyclif or Huss had ever been; for the German nation was being deeply stirred by this proclamation of revolt.

The appeal from the clerical to the civil power did not mean, however, a complete surrender of the conscience to the temporal rulers. "Princes are not to be obeyed when they command submission to superstitious error, but their aid is to be invoked in support of the word of God." Luther still held, in these opening years of his heresy, that heretics should not be put to death because "when there was a statute for the killing of false prophets and heretics, in time it came about that only the most saintly were killed . . . I cannot admit that these false teachers are to be put to death. It is enough to banish them."

But this temperate attitude changed as a result of the rise of the Anabaptists and the Peasants' Revolt in 1525. During Luther's seclusion in Warburg castle, where he worked on the translation of the Bible, things got out of hand in Wittenberg, where his colleague Carlstadt preached so violently against church practices as to cause rioting. At the risk of his life, Luther returned, and by his moral authority restored order, much as St. Paul had done by his letters to the Corinthians, when he admonished them that in matters of worship, as of morals, one should keep in mind the golden rule of moderation. Much more serious, however, were the extravagances of the Anabaptists, to whom such ecclesiastical reforms were wholly insufficient, especially in the rejection of infant baptism, but also in their repudiation of force and in reliance on the practice of loving kindness, with attempts to revive communism of goods referred to in the scriptures. Unlike the Waldenses, they did not accept the doctrine of apostolic poverty, although they mostly belonged to the poorer classes in town and country. When the Peasants' Revolt broke out, the Anabaptist preacher Münzer became one of its leaders, and in its murderous suppression, the simple, nonresistant sectaries suffered indiscriminately with the victims of social revolt.

This was an important turning point in Luther's teaching on religious freedom. Luther's savage advice to the forces of law and order is quoted in all anthologies of reaction: "Let all who can smite, slay and stab, secretly or openly, remembering that nothing can be more poisonous, hurtful or devilish than a rebel." Such a statement deserves the obloquy which it has received, but it has unfortunately been quoted too often as though it represented an inherent tendency in Luther to violence and persecution. Such a conclusion is wholly wrong. He was an ardent conservative who believed he was repairing, not tearing down the structure of Christian society, which was what he believed the peasant leaders were trying to do. He saw in their movement nothing but anarchy against both church and state, and spoke out with all the uncurbed vitriolic vehemence of a peasant's son who had, on this occasion, reverted to type. It must be admitted that the provocation was great, for the anarchy knew no bounds, when churches as well as monasteries were burned and pillaged, and the movement spread beyond Germany into the Netherlands. The issue, therefore, was not merely one of liberty of conscience; it called for some counter action against violence. But, as so often happens when there is no strong police power at hand, the suppression of disorder became an unrestrained convulsion, resulting in the slaughter of thousands of peasants and the sectaries in the towns. Therefore, horrible as it was, the suppression of the revolt does not belong in the same category of persecution as the judicial murders of the Inquisition, inflicting death upon harmless people who suffered merely for conscience sake.

Not the same can be said for Calvin, however. There was something of Torquemada in the stern ruler of Geneva, who brought to trial and execution one of the intellectual leaders of his day, Servetus, because of his denial of the doctrine of the Trinity. It is true that he opposed burning at the stake, which was the method actually used, because burning was "an atrocity," but upheld death by beheading. He held with the Inquisition that the state should be the preserver of church purity, which meant in practice the denial of religious freedom.

As the new heresies of Protestantism began to challenge the medieval church — which meant challenging the structure of society — the leaders in their war of creeds still kept to the idea of the unity of religious belief, if not in a universal church, at least that of their creation or choice. Thus the Lutherans drew up their "Confession of Augsburg" in 1530 and Calvin published his "Christian Institutes" in 1535. The Church of England, after thirty years of evolution, finally settled upon its Thirty-Nine Articles in 1562. The alignment crystalized the molten forces of Protestant belief, but it did not, at first, make for tolerance. Calvin's crime, the execution of Servetus, has been execrated by subsequent generations, but was condoned at the time by the Swiss church, by such a conciliatory spirit as Melanchthon, the author of the Augsburg Confession, and by public opinion generally in Protestant countries. The Calvinist Presbyterians of Scotland could be as cruel persecutors as their Catholic opponents. The English Puritans were intolerant in both church and state. The stern stuff of the Huguenots is shown by their survival during fifty years of persecution and civil war with an unshaken church of their own, and this in spite of the horrors of St. Bartholomew in 1572. Meanwhile the counter-revolution was carrying on with persecution and war in all the Hapsburg realms. No wonder Protestantism felt that it was in danger and was slow to grant toleration to those whom it feared. All in all, Europe from the middle of the sixteenth century to the middle of the seventeenth was so stained with religious persecution and war as to obscure its great creative history in the modernization of politics.

Secular Control

The Peasants' Revolt of 1525 and Luther's reaction against it were, as we have seen, more than incidents in history. They marked the opening of a new chapter, not in the history of the revolt or of the Anabaptists, but in the trend towards secular control over religion. In the opinion of Catholic appraisers of the Lutheran movement, this was, in itself, the cause or condition of a wider anarchy, creating divisions not only between Catholic and Protestant, but between Protestant sects. In the opinion of Protestants, it was the path towards ultimate religious liberty. So great an issue calls for further analysis.

The issue was not new; it had much history behind it. In a certain sense the struggle between Papacy and Empire through the Middle Ages was the one long prelude to its revolutionary phase in Lutheranism. The almost equally long movement for Gallicism in the French clergy and state was also, in a sense, parallel, not to mention the overt acts of Philip IV against Boniface and the "Babylonian Captivity" of the Popes at Avignon. But by far the strongest claims of national and royal rights against "Rome" were those in England, with its statutes of Praemunire and Provisors against papal control of finances or clergy. For the most part, however, these are instances of opposition to papal prerogatives without reference to religious practices. Thus, as we have seen, The Ghibelline Dante, in *De Monarchia*, while insisting that the imperial power comes from God, through the Roman people, leaves the whole spiritual sphere to the Papacy. Only Marsilius of Padua, the most modern voice of the Middle Ages, left to the secular powers the treatment of heretics.[8]

This history of the division of the powers must be clearly distinguished from that in the organization of the church itself. There it is inherent in the Canon Law, with its hierarchy of jurisdiction, as we have already seen, for the government of the church over against its hierarchy of holy orders for the administration of the sacraments. In the sacramental hierarchy, the Pope is only a bishop; there is no higher rank. It was in the hierarchy of jurisdiction that the Papacy claimed its supreme power. There the only possible rival was an ecumenical council to which appeal was repeatedly made by leaders of reform movements or other opponents of the Pope and his Curia. This conciliar movement was called into action by the threat of the Protestant schism, and it was at a council, that of Trent (1545-1563) that the Catholic creed was given its first full formulation.[9] This time the Papacy triumphed, for it was at Trent that the medieval church became

[8] Cf. Chapter IX.

[9] The medieval church, based on the great principles of the Council of Nicaea, avoided definition of creed. It is only from the Council of Trent that it has stressed such definition.

definitely and finally Roman Catholic, thus completing the long evolution from the decree of Theodosius at the end of the fourth century. Finally, it was at the Vatican Council of 1870 that the proclamation of papal infallibility drew the two hierarchies together in a single rigid organization, the spiritual monarchy of the Papacy.

When Luther denied the authority of the Council as well as of the Pope, there was only one other authority to turn to: that of the secular power. This step, already implied in his revolutionary tract *Address to the Nobles of the German Nation,* was destined to be one of the most important events in the history of freedom. It is also a complicated and obscure chapter. For here, at last, mankind was getting rid of the dangers first apprehended in the taboo and the inhuman way of dealing with them, even in the most humane of religions, supported by the opinions of enlightened men and by almost every government. Just how the change finally came about which ended the age of persecution in Europe will always remain a matter of dispute among historians, for the influences making for toleration and then for full religious freedom were varied and the source material not easy to evaluate. But in the course of a little over a century after Luther's revolt, the fires of persecution which had burned with unparalleled fury, died down to a few embers which were ultimately extinguished in the nineteenth century.

There was no other country in which the jealous assertion of secular power against clerical privilege or papal interference had been more strongly supported by public opinion than in England. This helps to explain how Henry VIII could become head of a national church. The Parliament of 1532, recalling the statutes of Praemunire and Provisors, declared that the king was supreme over all his subjects, clergy as well as laity, and in 1534, by the Act of Supremacy, proclaimed him "the only supreme head of the Church of England," enjoying all the rights and profits appertaining to this office. But then the Act of Supremacy went on to revolutionary ground in allowing to the king authority over the realm of belief, "with full power to visit, repress, redress, reform and amend all such errors, heresies, abuses, contempts, and enormities, which by any manner of spiritual authority or jurisdiction might or may be lawfully reformed."

This over-stepping of the Canon Law was followed later by the Articles of Religion, drawn up by Henry himself and accepted without protest by a submissive convocation of the clergy. These were only half way toward Protestantism, for transubstantiation and the confession were kept, although the sacraments were reduced to three: Baptism, the Lord's Supper and Penance. Parliament then enforced the Articles by threat of the penalty of death for violation. These Acts, combined with the suppression of the monasteries, the chief economic revolution of the Reformation, executed ruthlessly under Henry's Machiavellian minister, Thomas Cromwell, carried the conflict with Rome completely beyond the initial stages of a dispute over Henry's divorce from Catherine of Aragon.

There are few chapters on the history of freedom more difficult to explain than the way the people of England allowed itself to be trampled under foot by the most despicable of tyrants. The explanation generally given for Tudor despotism, and the one touched on here, was the destruction in the Wars of the Roses of the old nobility which had served as a check on absolutism. But the deterioration in national outlook was also due to the impact of war and plague on a society already in transition from the set framework of medieval life to the uncertainties of a new era which was to culminate in the Renaissance and the Reformation, both of them denying the old loyalties. In such a world personality counted for much; and, whatever one may think of Henry VIII, he was not lacking in personality. He began his reign as a prince charming, alert to the new intellectual interests of which humanists like Erasmus were spokesmen. Yet he remained typically English; for, although the record of his reign is sanguinary enough, he never engaged in general slaughter but had practical reasons for each execution.

Under this tyrant, wilful and capricious as it was, Protestantism made progress in England. The English bible, Tyndale's version, smuggled into England from his refuge on the Continent, had apparently somewhat the same effect as Luther's translation had in Germany; but, although Thomas Cromwell, who succeeded Cardinal Wolsey as Henry's minister, favored the Protestants, the king's own creed remained substantially Catholic and his persecutions were directed only against those who refused to acknowledge his headship of the church as a national instead of a papal institution — with whatever implications that involved. A clue to the changing religious outlook may be found in the fact that the one rebellion in Henry's reign, the "Pilgrimage of Grace" was a pro-Catholic movement, while, the uprising of peasants under his successor, the boy-king Edward VI was definitely a secular movement due to the enclosure of common lands by the nobility.

Upon the accession of Henry's young son Edward, persecution ceased in England, as Parliament, under the regency of the Duke of Somerset, repealed the acts which had sanctioned Henry's tyranny. Edward himself was devoutly Protestant, having been brought up under the tutelage of Archbishop Cranmer. In 1549 the Act of Uniformity established the national Church of England with services and prayer-book bearing the stamp of Cranmer's Protestantism. But neither Somerset nor his successor, the Duke of Northumberland had the stern religious convictions of a persecutor, and the country enjoyed an interlude of toleration which was to make the record of the next reign, that of Mary, the daughter of Catherine of Aragon, all the blacker by contrast. Controversy still continues to rage over the character of "bloody Mary," for she began her reign with kindliness and generosity and only became a persecutor for conscience sake and for what she believed to be the welfare of her subjects. But, though personally far from cruel, she sanctioned the burning of some three hundred victims at the stake; and, instead of bringing her kingdom back into the Catholic fold, caused a national revulsion against Catholicism which lasted on through all its subsequent history.

In passing judgment on her we must bear in mind that it was not only Catholics who supported the theory of persecution; for Calvin — not to mention John Knox, who called the murder of Cardinal Beaton "a goodly deed"

— rivalled Aquinas in regarding heresy as treason against God, and therefore doubly calling for the supreme penalty of death. Persecution was warfare for the faith, a warfare sanctioned most by the most devout. Mary's reign was less bloody than that of her husband Philip II in the Netherlands or of the equally well-meaning Charles IX of France, the organizer of the massacre of St. Bartholomew, in which it is estimated that some 72,000 Huguenots perished. The horrors of the Thirty Years War in Germany were due less to religious differences than to the political breakdown of the State, but religion was a cloak for princely ambition and for the most ruthless slaughter since the Hundred Years War. Remembering the background of history and the foreground of murder by assassination and war, we must judge Mary Tudor by the standards of her age.

Fortunately for England, Elizabeth was no fanatic and had no sympathy with extremists, either Catholic or Puritan. She was a child of the Renaissance rather than of the Reformation. Her interests were secular, a Tudor love of pomp and ceremony — her court knelt when she appeared — and a genuinely patriotic love of her country and a desire to bask in the sunshine of popular approval. Her own inclination was, happily for her, in line with the trend of public opinion, away from Mary's religious despotism. Parliament readily responded to the cue, and restored and strengthened the pro-Protestant legislation of Edward VI, which it had nullified under Mary. This is significant of the growing change in the national outlook; but it is a sad index of the weakness of Parliament under the Tudors that it never once made itself the mouthpiece of independent public opinion, but mirrored, instead the policy of the throne. It should be added that the final articles of faith, for the national church, were drawn up neither by monarch nor parliament but by the church itself.

Elizabeth's attitude toward religious toleration was clearly expressed by her in the proclamation which she issued when the Pope excommunicated her. She stated that she would not disturb men's consciences so long as they did not violate her laws by deeds. This distinction was both politically sound and historically justified by the Church's own practice in the days of its plenitude of power. The medieval church, as we have pointed out, indulged constantly in theological disputations, and the title of the text-book on Canon law, Gratian's Decretum, was *The Harmony of Discordant Canons*. The heretic was less the man of thought than the man of action or the inciter to action, the rebel intent on destroying the institution which he had come to regard as the embodiment or agent of evil. Under Elizabeth this issue ceased to dominate, for the mounting spirit of nationalism — especially called out by the menace of the Spanish Armada — tended to give assurance to the queen that religious plotting was not the serious danger it had once been.

In the acceptance of justification by faith as its fundamental principle, Anglicanism and Lutheranism were at one in regarding the control of the church as a function of secular power. But while this was accepted in states with monarchical forms of rule, it was going too far for the republican organization of Calvinism, which insisted that its clergy should share the rule with the laymen, and much too far for the dissenters or nonconformists who developed varying theories of democratic church control. The total result was a trend toward religious anarchy among Protestants. The solution in Germany, that the religion of a state should be that of the prince (*cujus regio, ejus religio*) was substantially that attempted with considerable success in England by the Acts of Supremacy and Uniformity, and in Sweden under Gustavus Vasa; indeed it may be regarded as the type of settlement for most of northern Europe. The result of this injection of secular authority was to place the power to persecute in the hands of those whose interest in religion was increasingly submerged in the worldly affairs of politics.

This trend away from religion to politics is true even of the country which was guilty of the last great religious persecution, France. The massacre of St. Bartholomew was the culmination of a long series of persecutions, some of which like the massacre of three thousand Waldenses in 1548, had little or no political significance; but the Huguenots grew in spite of repeated attempts to suppress them, and anarchic "wars of religion" developed from political factional fights. Finally it seemed as though religious peace was won, when Henry of Navarre, a Huguenot prince, became Henry IV on renouncing Protestantism, "Paris is worth a mass," and granted a charter of religious and political freedom in the Edict of Nantes (1598). It gave liberty of conscience throughout all France, full civil rights to Protestants whose pastors were to be paid by the state on practically the same terms as the Catholic clergy. Protestant worship was limited to centers (outside Paris) where people had the right to worship previously and a hundred places of safety were assigned to them for eight years. This was too much like a state within a state for Richelieu, one of whose first acts of power was the siege and capture of the Huguenot stronghold, La Rochelle, after which the Huguenots ceased to be a political force in France.

Limited toleration was continued in the early years of the reign of Louis XIV, who declared in 1652 that the Edict of Nantes should be maintained in full, and in 1660 it was estimated that there were some 630 Huguenot churches with over a million members. The Catholic clergy never ceased, however, to urge action against the "odious edict," and over-zealous officials, like the Intendant of Poitou, in order to send to the court a long list of converts, placed soldiers in the homes of the "reformed," *missionaires bottés*.

This was the mild beginning of what became a brutal persecution in the *dragonnades* of the soldiery, begun even before the king had repealed the Edict of Nantes in 1685. In strongly Huguenot districts, like Bearn, the inhabitants were given eight days to become Protestants or receive the troops, and those who left town were ordered to return within three days under penalty of death. The soldiers refined their tortures so successfully that, as the courtly chronicler St. Simon recorded, "from the torture to the communion there was often less than twenty-four hours, and their torturers were their witnesses." Couriers arrived day after day at the court telling of the conversion of whole churches. With the repeal of the Edict, the measures of repression only speeded the flight of the Huguenots from France, in a migration of almost half a million of the finest citizens of France to other countries for safety. In London there were over thirty congregations; the crypt of Canterbury Cathedral still has its Huguenot chapel.

The persecution, coming as it did, after the religious war and massacre of the previous century, seemed at the time to be a success. But although Huguenotism had suffered terrible losses, it was never entirely destroyed. Louis could be His Most Catholic Majesty; but the cost to France was incalculable, England, the Netherlands and Prussia were the gainers, and the New World as well, where leading Dutch settlers have French names.[10] It was both a crime and a blunder, the kind of thing that can be done by a king by divine right, if there is no hardheaded Richelieu alongside to guide him. Not all the Huguenots fled, however. Braving death or the galleys, they re-established their worship and continued to struggle for freedom of conscience, until, partly owing to the zeal of Lafayette, an edict of 1787 renewed the civil rights of the Huguenots. Finally, the French Revolution in its Declaration of the Rights of Man, affirmed the liberty of religion. The way was open for a Huguenot, Guizot, to become prime minister of France, in which religion has been progressively divorced from politics.

We have concentrated upon Huguenotism because of its importance as a force in the national and international life of modern times. But Calvinism, its creed, offers one of the most puzzling paradoxes in history: the most rigid, intolerant of Protestant sects, it nevertheless furnished the religion most adaptable to the new wealth, which was just then beginning to make the middle class a power in Europe. The form of government set up by Calvin for his church was a mixture of clerical and lay, with elders (presbyters) presiding alongside ministers, but all of them accepting the Calvinistic creed of justification by faith of those whom God had "elected" for salvation. The manner of life, as well as of worship was to be puritanical, a protest against "worldliness" in all forms.

Asceticism has always been a proper soil for intolerance, being a self-imposed suffering, imposed by denial of what one wants or wants to do. While Presbyterianism is commonly thought to have had the monopoly of puritanism, there was a strong element of it in the established Church of England, and it was also strong in the reform movements inside Catholicism. Yet nowhere was the tone of life more puritanical than when the Calvinists were in power. Sternly repressing worldly enjoyment by themselves or others, these "elect" in the providence of God were not the kind to surrender their rights, religious or political, to kings. And yet, it was in a Calvinist country, the Netherlands, that religious liberty found its first national home.

This involved a revolution in the outlook of the Dutch people. Nowhere

[10] The writer recalls a striking and significant incident that throws a curious light on this chapter of history. In 1919, after World War I, the only Hohenzollern statue in Berlin to have a wreath at Christmas was that of the Great Elector inscribed: *"In ewiger Dankbarkeit, das Consistorium der Französischen Kirche."* He had given asylum to the persecuted Huguenots.

else in Europe had religion been a more intimate guide to life than in the Dutch cities at the very time when their hard won freedom and independence opened their great career in commerce and industry. Yet, in ways that history does not fully explain, the sternly Huguenot Dutch — and there were none sterner — allowed their homeland, and especially their metropolitan port, Amsterdam, to become the outstanding center of freedom of thought and expression in the new era which was taking shape.

It was in the Netherlands that Protestantism and Catholicism were first brought under a common guarantee of religious freedom and liberty of worship, when, in 1572, William of Orange accepted on these terms the leadership of the league against Philip II. Five years later, the northern provinces in their Union of Utrecht, repeated this provision. But as the Dutch became increasingly Calvinised, the inherent persecuting ardor of religious bigotry showed itself in the Synod of Dort, 1619, the formative event in the history of the Dutch Reformed Church. The issue was that of the strict Calvinist creed of predestination, held by the majority and the "heretical" doctrine of "conditional" predestination, which had been taught some years before by Arminius, the theologian of Leyden, and had been maintained in a "remonstrance" against Synod action. In 1618 the "Remonstrants" were crushed by Prince Maurice of Orange, their chief advocate, Hugo de Groot (Grotius) imprisoned and after an adventurous escape forced to take refuge in France.

But the persecutions sanctioned by Maurice gave way to the tolerant statesmanship of Prince Frederick Henry in 1625, when the Netherlands tered upon its great career, holding its own in the midst of European wars, enriched by the commerce of Asia, and, above all, paralleling her achievements in art by those in science and philosophy. The hotbed of rival sects became the nursery of intellectual freedom. The change came in a single generation.

The history of intellectual freedom has larger dimensions, however, than that of the Netherlands. It was largely due to the fact that Protestantism attacked established authority in the realm of belief as well as of priestly control over salvation. The new emphasis placed upon the Bible and its translation into the language of common speech made for popular education, so that all could read "the book," and equally called for infinite sermonizing to guide the unwary through its inspired text. Unfortunately this combination of inspiration in the text and sectarian doctrines in its exposition lessened the value of Bible study as an instrument for freedom of thought. It was only in the nineteenth century that higher criticism of the Bible — primarily of Protestant origin — squared Bible study with the methods of scientific study of history. A long and tortuous path led to a truer concept of religion — and intellectual freedom.

Protestantism also brought — in course of time — freedom to choose among various forms of church government: by bishops or presbyters and laymen. The conservatives kept to the episcopal form, omitting only the Papacy; all other churches are based, in varying degrees, on democratic principles, choosing their ministers and administering their own affairs. In this democratization, Calvinism played a major role. In his *Institutes,* Calvin set forth a plan which has proved as stable as that of the episcopate. The members of each congregation elect its officers, duly ordained by the laying on of hands by the pastors (presbyters), to preside over the discipline of the church and administer its sacraments, alongside whom are certain pious, grave and holy men, to advise the minister, and deacons to care for the poor. It was also their duty to lessen the allurements of a sinful world — an ascetic ideal which always limits man's freedom of enjoyment, especially of beauty in art or nature. The puritan was a sturdy defender of freedom against oppression; but his conception of freedom was narrow. The appeal was to sober intelligence, and it was not in vain; only too sober for many, who, it was feared, might not be foreordained to be saved.

Religious Tolerance and Freedom

At the dawn of the new day of religious toleration and freedom it is fitting to pay a tribute to those who so largely shaped the thought of an emancipation which is now so taken for granted that its epochal importance becomes clear only in the light of history. Some of the leaders were outstanding figures in the intellectual history of Europe, but others have long been forgotten; all of them deserve the everlasting gratitude of every beneficiary of freedom.

The list begins with the Christian humanists, especially Erasmus; but however forthright their thought, their humanism kept them from stirring passionate revolt against the persecution they abhorred. [11] The first bold challenge — though even it had its qualifications — was the work of a professor of Greek at Basle, Switzerland, Sebastian Castellio, whose protest against the burning of Servetus as a heretic by Calvin rang through the theological world, in which that crime against freedom of conscience had been a matter of wide and deep concern. Castellio's work on heretics *(De Hereticis)* reflects the fundamental humanism of Erasmus and the German mystic, Sebastian Franck: man is inherently good and, as all are children of God, there is no danger in their freedom. "Where the spirit of God is, there is freedom — no constraints or tyranny, partisanship or compulsion, that He should drag anyone to heaven by the hair or push anyone into hell and deprive him of the grace that is extended to all men. Man alone deprives himself of it."[12]

Castellio shared this view of man's perfectability but joined to it the conclusion that no one is good enough to persecute. Atheism and blasphemy

[11] On the other hand, Sir Thomas More, whose *Utopia* was a challenge to a worn-out social system, carried out far more persecution for heresy during his three years as Chancellor than Cardinal Wolsey in his twenty years of power.

[12] Quoted in R. H. Brinton, *Concerning Heretics,* an anonymous work attributed to Sébastian Castellio (1935), p. 98, an authoritative work of textual criticism and scholarly translation; Cf. also the study, *Sébastien Castellio,* in *Persecution and Liberty* (New York: Columbia University Press, 1931), pp. 183-209. Records of Civilization: Sources and Studies, No. 22, 1935.

might be suppressed, but no one should be put to death for heresy. Basing his teaching on the New Testament instead of the Old Testament, which had furnished Calvin with his strongest arguments for persecution, he concentrated upon the Golden Rule. In his *Advice to Ruined France,* written in the midst of the wars of religion, he asks of the Catholics: "Would you like to have this done to you? Would you like to be persecuted for not having believed or confessed something against your conscience?" and of the militant Protestants of that time, "Here are the three remedies you employ: to shed blood, to force conscience, and to condemn as infidels those who do not agree with your doctrine." To both Catholic and Protestant the one rule applies: "Do not unto others what you would not that they do unto you.[13] A rule so true, so just, so natural, and so written by the finger of God in the hearts of all men that there is no one so degenerate, so estranged from discipline and enlightenment, but that he will confess this rule to be right and reasonable, the moment it is proposed to him."

From Basle we turn to Poland, the home for many years of the Italian scholar Lelio Sozzini (or Socinus), and his nephew Fausto Socinus, the founder of Socinianism, later termed Unitarianism. The strong stand taken by the leaders of the new sect against persecution can partly be traced to the continuing reaction against the burning of the Unitarian Servetus. But toleration was also an integral part of the teaching of a doctrine that repudiated a set creed and fell back upon a historical view of early Christianity, before either the Pauline or the Petrine trend toward ecclesiasticism. There was no more subtle way to undercut the whole Augustinian theology than to assert man's inherent goodness, as had already been sensed by the enemies of Castellio. But there was one Calvinist theologian who found the way to link this optimistic view of man's capacity for good with trinitarian orthodoxy, by insisting on conditional, not absolute, orthodoxy. Ths was Arminius of Leyden, whose influence was to prove so important in England and America, through John Locke and Roger Williams.

In England there were two lines to follow, that of leaders like Hooker, Milton and Locke and that of dissenting pamphleteers who flooded the country with tracts in support of the Puritan revolution. The fusing of these two currents into a national attitude of limited tolerance was urged along by the political forces let loose in the struggle with the Stuarts; indeed the political and religious are practically inseparable.

The intellectual leader who raised the whole tone of religious controversy to a new level was Richard Hooker, whose *Laws of Ecclesiastical Polity,* published in 1593,[14] marks an epic in English prose and thought; it is Elizabethan England at its best. The whole book is an exaltation of the role of law "whose seat is the bosom of God; whose voice is the harmony of the world." Law is the expression of the fundamental principle seen in na-

[13] This negative form of the Golden Rule is the way in which the practical Confucius phrased it.

[14] In eight books, only five of which were published in his lifetime. The most recent edition is in Everyman's Library, 2 vols., New York, 1907.

ture and man and in all social formation, including nations and governments. Although he draws a distinction between natural and positive laws, he leaves it to human reason to determine what is eternal and what is temporal, and therefore places ecclesiastical rule on the same human basis as civil government. Since, according to Hooker, that basis is the agreement of the community itself, or at least its acceptance of the inheritance of ancestors, it follows that the nation is the real sovereign in both church and state.

It was this theory of government which John Locke took over,[15] changing it in ways that Hooker might not have liked, to emphasize the supremacy of the secular power. The church is limited to moral authority, a free association of its members. "Nobody is born a member of any church: otherwise the religion of parents would descend unto their children by the same right of inheritance as their temporal estates, and everyone would hold his faith by the same tenure as he does his land, than which nothing could be more absurd." Therefore, "no man is by nature bound to any particular church or sect," but is free to choose the one he prefers. This leads to the ultimate conclusion to be drawn from the secular control of the church for which Protestantism has stood: that "the civil government can give no new right to the Church" which would impair its rights as a voluntary organization. "Will any man say that any right can be derived unto a Christian church over its brethren from a Turkish emperor? . . . The civil power is the same in every place. Nor can that power, in the hands of a Christian prince, confer any greater authority upon the church than in the hands of a heathen; which is to say, just none at all."

In powerful passages Locke then calls for the abolition of all physical penalties for differences of religious belief. The persecutors are really violators of the fundamental basis of Christianity, charity. "It will be very difficult to persuade men of sense that he, who with dry eyes and satisfaction of mind, can deliver his brother to the executioner to be burnt alive, does sincerely and heartily concern himself to save that brother from the flames of hell in the world to come." Magistrates as well as clerics have no right to punish dissidents. "The care of every man's soul belongs to himself. But what if he neglects the care of his soul? I answer: What if he neglects the care of his health or his estate, which things are much nearlier related to the government of the magistrate than the other? Will the magistrate provide by an express law that such a one shall not become poor or sick?"

One is tempted to continue the quotations from this rounded treatise on religious toleration, but the issue shifts to include civil liberties as well, and we must leave this issue for a later chapter. Locke's ideas on religious toleration were apparently molded by his exile in Holland, where he came under the influence of Arminius, the advocate of toleration as against Dutch Calvinism. The argument of his book, *The Reasonableness of Christianity,* bears further evidence of this in its assertion that there is nothing in revelation contrary to human reason; but a national church must not rest on sub-

[15] In his *Letter on Toleration* (there were three letters written at different times. The first, originally in Latin, in 1689).

tleties of intolerant theologies. All in all, a tolerant Church of England, with individual liberty of thought would be a reasonable solution. A final comment on Locke's ideas on toleration might, therefore, be that he anticipated what actually was to take place, just as in his political philosophy he was to be the master spirit of the American Revolution. For the Anglican church, reflecting the changing temper of England, became in course of time one of the most tolerant and open-minded of churches.

Behind Locke lay Puritan England. Here we are concerned only with its Puritanism, but we must not forget that it was also the theatre of the first great drama of political liberty, and that the tyranny it fought, and got into its veins as well, was partly responsible for that stern, uncompromising mood which we associate with its religious character. For the early Puritans, those of Shakespeare's day, were not the gloomy fanatics of the days of Cromwell. Milton, their noblest spokesman, wrote gay as well as serious verse. "The temper of the Puritan gentleman," says historian Green, whose account of Puritan England has never been surpassed, "was just, noble and self-controlled . . . The gorgeous colors and jewels of the Renaissance disappeared. Colonel Hutchinson left off very early the wearing of anything that was costly, yet in his plainest negligent habit appeared very much a gentleman."

With the new sobriety went better taste. It was to this England that Hooker addressed his solid, well-balanced arguments against narrow dogmatism. But as time went on and the Stuarts attempted to enforce the high church clericalism of Archbishop Laud, with its "Romish" ceremonials and its effort at the suppression of private worship, the temper of the country changed. Separatists and Dissenters developed into what later became Congregationalists and Baptists, while Presbyterianism gained powerfully in the middle classes. The civil war cut in across this religious development, but the reaction against it after the Restoration of Charles II seems to indicate that it was a temporary, if very significant, phase of English history. However that may be, the literature of protest against tyranny was enriched by some of the finest documents in the history of freedom.[16]

It is not, however, in the high level of the arguments of Hooker or Locke, nor in the splendor of Milton's prose, that the outlook of Puritan England is most clearly revealed. It was rather in the tracts of the Dissenters, mostly unlearned in the great models of antique eloquence which gave the gleam of elegance to those intellectuals who had ranged in the literature opened up by the Renaissance. There was a compelling simplicity of speech in those men of the common life, who could quote only from the Bible and *Magna Carta*, but who knew how to use their texts with driving force. Whenever they rose to eloquence, and it was not seldom, it was largely due to the influence of the "authorized" or "King James" edition of the Bible (1611), one of the greatest products of English scholarship. Puritan England, says Green, became the people of one book and that was the Bible. The Dis-

[16] It will be recalled that Luther's translation of the Bible had an even greater formative effect upon the German language and literature.

senters, those who refused to accept the national church, with its episcopal rule and ritual, broke into a number of sects; but, upon the whole, they showed the typical English character of moderation and, with few and unimportant exceptions, indulged in no such orgiastic rites as the extremists on the Continent.

But the battle "for conscience sake" was fought out among the sectaries in as unyielding a spirit as in the courts of justice or in Parliament or in the civil war. Coke and Hampton had their counterparts in the pamphleteers who fought the battle of dissent in what became almost a kind of journalism.[17] The memories of past persecutions and atrocities stirred the fires of fanaticism; and yet, although some Puritans still suffered imprisonment, the tables were turned by the rebellion against the Stuarts, and it was the leaders of despotism, Archbishop Laud and the tyrant Strafford who suffered death, to be followed by Charles I himself.

Three figures stand out before us in this decisive struggle for religious rights in England: John Milton, George Fox, the founder of the Society of Friends (Quakers), and Roger Williams, the founder of a free commonwealth.

Had John Milton never written a line of poetry, he would have had a memorable place in the history of English literature and thought. His prose writings began with a series of pamphlets against "papacy and prelacy," in which his powerful invective is softened by a statement of his reluctance to leave "the calm and pleasing solitariness of poetry to embark on a troubled sea of noises and harsh disputes." But in the years that followed, no voice was stronger, no eloquence more moving than Milton's plea for freedom of speech as well as of conscience.

In the light of Milton's own description of the world of turmoil in which he lived, one wonders if without the affliction of blindness he could have turned to poetry again. His description in *Areopagitica*, of London in 1644, is also a reflection of his own interests: "Behold now this vast City: a city of refuge, the mansion house of liberty encompassed and surrounded with His protection; the shop of war hath not there more anvils and hammers waking, to fashion out the plates and instruments of armed Justice in defence of beleaguered Truth, than there be pens and heads there, sitting by their studious lamps, musing, searching, revolving new notions and ideas wherewith to present, as with their homage and their fealty, the approaching Reformation: others as fast reading, trying all things, assenting to the force of reason and convincement. What could a man require more from a Nation so pliant and so prone to seek after knowledge? What wants there to such a towardly and pregnant soil, but wise and faithful labourers, to make a knowing people, a Nation of Prophets, of Sages and of Worthies? We reckon more than five months yet to harvest; there need not be five weeks; had we but eyes to lift up, the fields are white already."

[17] This literature has proved to be a rich mine for the historian. Cf. William Haller, *Treatise on Liberty and Reformation in the Puritan Revolution*, 3 vols. (New York: Columbia University Press, 1934.)

The scene is confusing; but the spirit is strong, and the hopes are high.

The situation here so graphically described is perhaps the chief reason why Milton's plea for moderation had no effect at the time. Although himself a partisan, he was too intellectual and scholarly to have popular appeal, and his immortal prose poem on freedom of speech, *Areopagitica*, seems to have been but little noticed at the time.

Before Milton had turned to Puritan pamphleteering and while he was still writing the glorious poetry of his youth, another young man, Roger Williams, across the seas in Massachusetts was starting up the first successful establishment for complete religious freedom in all history. He had had a dual training in the politics of freedom, under the tutelage of the greatest legal champion of the rights of Englishmen under the common law, Sir Edward Coke, and was deeply impressed by the Arminian Baptists, whose influence had reached over from Holland to England. He thought to find an asylum for religious dissidents in New England, to which he sailed in 1631; but instead of freedom he found the most iron-bound of theocracies.

The transfer of authority to the secular power, which in the long run turned out to be the greatest step towards religious freedom, had in New England resulted in the violation of every principle of toleration; for the Puritans, Presbyterians and Congregationalists were using their democratic form of church government to reach farther into the private lives of the colonists than the medieval church had even tried to do. All "freemen" had to be church members over whom the government had "full and absolute power and authority to correct, punish and rule."[18] The fierceness of Puritan intolerance was given free range in the brutal persecution of Baptists and Quakers, including cutting off ears, boring tongues, scourging, or even death, a systematic cruelty quite different from the hysterical hanging of witches thirty years later, but based on the same fanaticism. As a pastor in Salem, Williams attacked not only the religious intolerance of the church but the action of the state in carrying out the persecution. For the state, in enforcing uniformity violated the fundamental freedom of the Christian man to choose the church of his belief. The argument resembles that of Locke, as Williams set it forth in his controversial pamphlets and in his *Bloudy Tenent of Persecution for the Cause of Conscience*, addressed to Parliament, which has been termed "perhaps the most extreme statement of natural rights which had yet appeared."[19] "It is the will and command of God, that a permission of the most paganish, Jewish, Turkish or Anti-Christian consciences and worships bee granted to all men in all nations and countries, and they are only to bee fought against with that sword which is only (in soule matters) able to conquer, to wit, the Sword of God's Spirit, the Word of God." "True civility and Christianity may both flourish in a

---

[18] This test was not applied to Plymouth Colony nor to the new colony at New Haven, Connecticut, which, however, had laid down its fundamental orders that the government must in all things accept the Bible as its guide.

[19] Cf. Haller, *op. cit.*, p. 60. Although *Bloudy Tenent* was not written until 1644, it embodies his views from the first of his ministry.

state or kingdome, notwithstanding the permission of divers and contrary consciences, either of Jew or Gentile."

It was in 1635 that Williams escaped from the intolerance of Massachusetts and founded the colony of Rhode Island as "a shelter for persons distressed of conscience," where everyone professing any kind of Christian belief could have the full enjoyment of political rights, "as long as he does not violate peace and quietness and does not abuse this liberty in a licentious and profane manner." On these terms Parliament granted the charter that created the first government in the world devoted to the assertion of religious freedom. The freedom was soon made complete by the admission of Jews to all the rights of citizens, although apparently few came.

The stage was also set in the New World for two other acts in the steadily developing drama of toleration. Two years before Roger Williams founded Rhode Island, Charles I granted the barony of Maryland to George Calvert, Lord Baltimore, with the one proviso that the proprietor was not to do anything contrary to "the true Christian religion." The Calverts, being Catholics in a Protestant country, carefully avoided defining what was the true religion, and Maryland was open to Protestant as well as to Catholic colonists. The same freedom was established in the colony to the north, by William Penn in the charter which, under the title "Concessions" became the constitution for Pennsylvania. Here, for the first time, the Quakers had the responsibility of adjusting the difficult art of government to the most extreme form of individualism in the Christian religion.

The history of the Quakers is the most fitting close to this long and confused era of persecution and the ultimate triumph of religious freedom; for in both England and America it offered the last terrible example of suffering for conscience sake and the most complete emancipation of religion from its own intolerance. No teaching of the Dissenters was farther from the established church, whether Episcopal or Presbyterian than the teaching of George Fox which denied all sacerdotalism, substituting for it direct spiritual inspiration, "the inner light," of the common man. No priests were needed where there were no sacraments. In reality, however, Quaker worship did have a sacrament of its own: silence. Instead of the magnificence of ritual at the altar or the organ music of cathedral choirs, which throughout the centuries had raised the aspirations of worshippers, the Quaker meetings waited silently for inspiration to touch the spirit, and discovered what seems to have escaped religious leaders before, that the silence can speak with supreme authority when it is shared by others. There is no more profoundly moving ceremony in the world today than the two minute silence of the thousands who gather on Armistice Day at the Cenotaph to the dead, in London.

The Quaker silence was sure to be broken by those whom it most deeply touched; no clergy were needed. But it soon began to be clear that, as in the early days of Christianity, there was danger that highly emotional outbursts might go to extremes. It was apparently some such extremes that led to the name of Quaker for those whom Fox called simply by the nonecclesiastical term, Friends. They had no regular meeting places and no systematic organization until after the Restoration. Indeed it was after that — at the same time as the Massacre of St. Bartholomew in France — that the worst of the Quaker persecutions in England were endured, prior to the Act of Toleration in 1685. It has been estimated that in all some four hundred died in prison and at least one hundred more from violence. In 1662 there were four thousand, five hundred in prison.[20] In Massachusetts the worst persecutions were earlier; the hangings stopped on a word from that very unChristian king, Charles II.

We cannot leave this story, so slight a sketch of so poignant yet inspiring a theme, without calling attention to the statesmanship which prevented freedom from becoming anarchy by raising morals to the height of law. The Monthly or Quarterly meeting of the Quaker community — it should not be called a church — backed by the authority of the national Annual Meeting, has an oversight of morals which reaches from the home life to business, and its rulings are seldom questioned or disobeyed. The same moral code which regulates the private life stands without any equivocation or qualification against the two greatest evils which have lasted on from savagery, slavery and war. But the history of the Quakers rises above these negative prohibitions. The unyielding democracy that would not doff a hat to a king because all men were equal in the sight of God, led in the reform of the prisons and asylums for the insane, those last remnants of barbarism in both England and America, and the Quakers were the first in England to take practical action against the slave trade, denying membership to any involved in it. In place of military services they offered social service, nursing and the furnishing of supplies even to enemies; until this smallest of sects (170,000 in all) became a symbol of Christian charity throughout the world. When we add to this the freedom of religion, we place the Religious Society of Friends in the forefront of Civilization.

[20] Even twenty years later, 1,200 Quakers were released from prison at one time by Charles II at the instance of William Penn.

CHAPTER XIII

THREE REVOLUTIONS FOR FREEDOM

The English Revolution

THERE IS NO chapter in the history of freedom more difficult to trace than that in which England finally made good the promise of its thirteenth century and became a model of freedom for the modern world. That it did achieve this unique distinction among the Western nations is without question. But from the cowed acceptance of the tyranny of Henry VII, at the opening of the fifteenth century, to the supremacy of Parliament and the rule of law almost two centuries later, the ship of state kept tacking on an irregular course, blown by contrary winds and drifting with contrary tides. The story of how it ultimately reached a harborage, where all the freedoms — civil, political and religious — could become the possession of the nation at large, reflects the confusion and contradictions of the time; but it is as inspiring as it is challenging.

The prelude lies in Tudor England, when Parliament, weakened by the decimation of the great nobles in the Wars of the Roses — the heroes of Magna Carta and the pioneers of Parliament — gave the monarch a rare opportunity for personal rule. But already under Henry VIII the nation was changing, becoming more business-minded as the Commercial Revolution got under way and the Reformation transferred so much of the landed wealth of the country to secular owners, constituting a new aristocracy. Elizabeth, the last of the Tudors, with superb — if instinctive — statesmanship, identified herself with these forces which were creating a new, self-conscious England, accepting gifts from the spoil brought home by her buccaneering sea-captains, while the country prospered from the wealth flowing from cities to countryside. The defeat of the Spanish Armada, one of the decisive victories of history, not only made England a great sea power, it awakened a new sense of national solidarity, which, while it meant loyalty to the Queen, meant also a growing awareness of the rights of the citizens, at least those owning property.

Medieval England was fast being left behind in the "spacious days" of Queen Elizabeth. But the new culture and the new criticism of the Renaissance, while making the worldly minded more worldly, also made the religiously minded more religious. Steadily the temper of the nation turned from the enjoyment of this life to the contemplation of that to come. The stately ritual and episcopal government of the established church seemed too much like that of Rome to satisfy those who believed that eternal salvation was a personal matter between the individual and God. While all Protestantism was based essentially on this belief, in Puritanism it became a social as well as a religious revolution, creating a sobriety in conduct and a sternness of temper which refused compromise with opponents. It thus became a force for freedom in the assertion of the religious rights of the individual against efforts to suppress it, while at the same time it remained intolerant on its own behalf, especially in its most uncompromising form, Calvinism.

At the very time that English nationalism was taking on the sterner qualities of Puritanism, rigidly unyielding in its assertion of human rights and carrying with it an implicit denial of absolute monarchy and the divine right of kings, Elizabeth died and the throne was left by right of succession to James I, son of Mary Queen of Scots, and therefore a distant cousin of Elizabeth. As James VI of Scotland, he came with a wholly un-English background in education and experience. Scotland, in self-protection against England, had been closely linked to France, and James had absorbed to the full the theory of the divine right of kings, then accepted on the continent as the orthodox doctrine of sovereignty. The issue between him and Puritan England was one that could not be solved by compromise, and the result was that England in the seventeenth century fought it out by civil war and revolution.

Fortunately for England and the world, James I was as inept and unwise as Elizabeth had been deft and clever, for if the Stuarts had shown even a fraction of her capacity for yielding to Parliament when public opinion was with it, or wheedling reluctant ministers to gain her way, the great revolution, which made England the leader in political freedom, might have been long delayed. But the kind of efficiency by which the Hohenzollerns established and maintained their bureaucratic rule in Prussia was utterly lacking in the Stuarts, and they had no iron-but-competent Richelieu or wily Mazarin by their side, like the Bourbons of France, to fasten on England the divine right of kings in which they believed. Besides, their Scottish background denied them that sense of English patriotism which Elizabeth not only shared but embodied, the pride in its great traditions and the regard for its institutions of self-government, Parliament and Law Courts.

The ineptness of James and the stubbornness of Charles should not blind us to the fact, however, that the problem of government was more difficult than it had ever been in the past. Coming from poverty-stricken Scotland,

James had the vision of a prosperous England, of rich farming land and richer cities garnering in the wealth of a new world commerce. But the revolution in prices due to the influx of silver from America, raising the cost of goods and services, had made the country business-conscious and quickly critical of extravagance by the king and his ministers. James' claim to rule by divine right might be more or less ignored in theory, for it was widely shared at the time on the Continent; but it was entirely another thing to attempt to put it into practice in raising money to fill a bankrupt treasury, and even worse to affront Puritan England by insisting on "high church" forms of worship, for the Puritans, who included many country gentry as well as city dwellers, were prepared to fight to the bitter end against any trend toward "popery." Never since thirteenth-century England produced Magna Carta and Parliament, had there been so stern a mood of national protest against absolutism in church and state.

It was the religious problem which confronted James first. Even before he reached London he was presented with a petition signed by some eight hundred Puritan members of the clergy — the Millenary Petition, claiming a thousand signatures — requesting that all "Romish" forms and ceremonies be abolished. James, although the son of the Catholic Mary, Queen of Scots, had been brought up a Calvinist, but had reacted against the browbeating by Presbyterian ministers who insisted that all men were equal in the sight of God and that the Church should be independent of state control. It was no wonder that he preferred the Anglican state church system and came out strongly for it at the Hampton Court Conference of both the Presbyterians and Anglicans over which he presided (1604).[1] Angered by the stiff-necked Puritans, he determined to make them conform, and deprived of their livings some three hundred of the nonconforming clergy. Some fled to the Netherlands and then to Massachusetts to found Plymouth colony; but compared with the earlier persecutions and those which followed under Charles, the measures against the Puritans, while they aroused passionate opposition to the king, were relatively humane.

Much more serious was the problem of the Catholics. Misinterpreting his early tolerance of them as he made peace with Spain, deserting the cause of the Dutch, they began to gain ground so rapidly that he became alarmed for fear they might attempt a counter reformation in England, and signed an act of Parliament restoring and extending the penal laws of Elizabeth against them. To be treated this way by the son of Mary Stuart brought bitter disappointment to the Catholics, and a small band of them conspired to blow up the House of Parliament when the king, his sons and his ministers were there to open a session. The Gunpowder Plot was discovered just in time; but it had a profound effect on the nation. Though the Catholics were upon the whole loyal to the king, they were popularly believed to be capable of any crime, and Parliament passed acts denying them the right to

[1] The one positive result of the Conference was the new "King James" translation of the Bible, one of the great monuments of English literature as well as of religious guidance for the English-speaking world.

travel more than five miles from home, to hold any public office or practice any of the learned professions. Although James did not enforce still more cruel disabilities voted by Parliament, the Catholics of England never recovered their full liberties until the nineteenth century.

Even in Puritan England, however, these religious issues were of less importance than the violation of personal and political rights by the Stuart kings. It must be admitted that the business of government had been made extremely difficult for them by the rise of capital, not only in the creation of a new monied class growing impatient in the assertion of its rights, but also in the increased complexity and scope of government, changing from what had been little more than an enlarged household economy under the medieval kings to a complicated and far-reaching relationship of men and property, both at home and abroad. As the scope of government increased, new sources of income were needed, and the only avenue open to the king was in the more or less disputed control of customs duties in the foreign trade. But this aroused the opposition of the trading and financial circles which they voiced in parliament. To meet this opposition both James and Charles fell back upon personal rule. While the result was disastrous for them, it marked the dawn of a new political era. The struggle for freedom begun in the parliaments and law courts of James I and in the Civil War culminated in the Great Revolution of 1688, which furnished the model for the American Revolution; and its principles have inspired liberal movements in Europe ever since.

The dawn of so great a day in the history of freedom was, however, long in breaking and became clear only after almost a century of confusion and conflict. What no one at that time could fully appreciate, the "power of the purse" on which parliament's sovereignty rests, was being extended by the Commercial and Monetary Revolution to cover far more of the national life than when it was first invoked in the parliaments of the past. The treasure that had been captured by the free booters who plundered the galleons of Spain had not been left in the hands of rulers to accumulate in hoards for the payment of soldiery or the extravagance of courts. The seamen of the northern nations were backed not only by the adventurous element of the country gentry, but by the business men, who speedily learned how to use capital in productive enterprise. Merchant adventurers all, whether members of the body bearing that name or not, they introduced into the economic life of Northern Europe — and also of America — a different sense of property than that which formerly concentrated upon territorial holdings, although not a little of the investment came from landed proprietors.

Fluid property to the extent of these new millions in gold and silver coins had never before presented such a temptation to monarchs, and never before had its owners been sufficiently strong or united to maintain their rights against the needy, or greedy, rulers. It was now clear that the only political framework of government which would be valid for England or the Netherlands would have to provide safeguards for property if the monied class was to maintain its place within the state. But it could not have been clear to

James I, for the argument that Parliament should have the power of the purse was based on English precedent, in a history which he, a Scot, had had no share.

It is a paradox that the political theorist who under Elizabeth had fought the same kind of religious battle as James did later, Richard Hooker, in opposition to the Puritans and in support of the episcopacy, had as we have seen, fallen back upon the concept of the law of nature as the embodiment of reason, and that therefore laws must harmonize with this fundamental test and be upheld as long as they are fitted to that end. In the effort to show the Puritans that they were wrong in their objection to what the majority desire, "the judicious Hooker," as Locke termed him, in his *Ecclesiastical Polity*, argued that reason calls for adjustment with realities, which for him meant episcopalianism.

This brings Hooker and Locke once more into our story, this time not for their contributions to religious freedom, but for their pioneering thought in the freedoms of the secular state. Naturally, the two themes overlap, but they both belong in this narrative. Hooker's contribution to politics rested on the same basis as that of his *Ecclesiastical Polity* — the law of nature. This borrowing from Aquinas was in his eyes equally applicable to secular society, because, in the pursuit of happiness (the phrase had not yet acquired currency) the interplay of interests lead men to agree upon some form of government to harmonize their varying desires.

There is nothing new in all of this, for it is the old debate familiar to Cicero, long before the Scholastics. But it was to lead also to the fundamental thought of Rousseau, that of a social compact as the basis of society. Hooker's wording, however, is very unlike Rousseau: "By the natural law whereunto God hath made all subject, the lawful power of making laws to command whole politic societies of men belongeth so properly unto the same entire societies, that for any prince or potentate of what kind soever upon earth to exercise the same of himself, and not either by express commission immediately and personally received from God, or else by authority derived at the first from their consent upon whose persons they impose the laws, it is no better than mere tyranny." Thus Hooker's contribution to English political thought leads to the conclusion that a test of the validity of laws is the consent of the governed. It is a paradox which was bound to be noticed that in this way, while arguing for the support of the Tudor Queen in her ecclesiastical policy, he enunciated a theory quite at variance with the earlier trend of Tudor despotism.

Hooker's influence, however, was limited by the fact that he was writing a treatise against the Puritans, and they, in their struggle for power, found support in the more practical mind of Chief Justice Sir Edward Coke. The real battle against the Stuarts was to be fought out on more definitely English terms. Coke, as the protagonist of the common law, drew his arsenal of arguments from English experience. There was an advantage in his argument with the sovereign in his not being held down to a single set of principles like those which the king was fond of reciting from the Roman law in support of his claims of absolute kingship. In building upon the English past, Coke went so far as to strain historic truth in the support of freedom. Maitland's remark that Coke "invented Magna Carta" is but another way of saying that he used it to the full and for perhaps a little more than it was worth. For it was a mighty buttress for defence against royalist exactions. Yet, while refusing to follow the lead of the Roman jurists, he fell back upon much the same method in his insistence upon a fundamental law — the common law — rather than parliamentary statutes.

James I met the claims of the English jurist by reiterating the precepts of late Roman law in which the will of the monarch was recognized as supreme. Over against this basic citation in support of Divine Right, Coke, as McKechnie puts it, "read into Magna Carta the entire body of the common law of the seventeenth century, of which he was admittedly a master," and did it so effectively that it assumed substantially the character of a statement of natural law. Thus he and Hooker were approaching from opposite angles that theory of human rights which had played so large a part in the theory of the Stoics. The law of nature could evidently be reached by the experimental processes of English justice as well as by the philosophic deductions of Aquinas.[2]

Of these two streams of history, the English and the Continental, the latter runs with limpid current between banks that were opened and made straight by the logic of Roman legal engineering, while the former meanders obscurely and at times is almost lost to view as it sinks in the soil of English life. But the green meadows of the common law, which it refreshes, spreading out by village and countryside, are a more vital symbol of freedom than the prouder creations of the Roman jurists at the court of rulers. Let us take an example of this vitality. The United States Bill of Rights of 1791 thunders "nor shall any person be deprived of life, liberty or property without due process of law." Behind this, of course, lies the classic phrase of Article 39 of Magna Carta,[3] but the very terms of the United States law, clad in the quaint Norman French of 1354, were enacted by the Parliament of Westminster in the twenty-eighth year of Edward III, six years after the battle of Crecy.[4] The gap between the two texts is four hundred and thirty-seven years, but the intervening centuries are not the only gap: the phrase "due process of law" took on new meaning, not only in the substance of the laws but in the "process" or procedure of its administration.

As the biographer of Coke points out, "England had as yet no rules of evidence. Anything was accepted — hearsay, opinion, garbled recitation of gossip years old. And on the presentation of evidence the prisoner's fate

[2] Cf. *The Lion and the Throne, the Life and Times of Edward Coke (1552-1634)*, by Catherine Drinker Bowen (1956), an exhaustive survey of the role of Coke as Chief Justice and in Parliament, and all the issues involved. (Boston: Little, Brown & Co., 652 pp.)

[3] "No freeman shall be arrested . . . unless by the lawful judgment of his peers and by the law of the land."

[4] The text of this statute read as follows: "Que nul home soit oste de terre ne de tenement ne pris nemprisone ne desherite ne mis a mort saunz mesne en response par dues proces de lei."

depends: what is allowed, what overruled. 'Strike it from the record.' No prisoner of Coke's day heard these words in his defence. Three centuries must pass before the law — and custom — evolved them, and the public could demand the protection therefrom afforded."[5] This comment on the unfinished task of perfecting legal procedure in safeguarding human rights must not be taken as a depreciation, in any way, of the great work of Coke and the jurists who followed him, for it was largely under their leadership that England was saved from becoming a land where the king could imprison people on *lettres de cachet* such as those which filled the Bastille, and from the levy of arbitrary taxes.

In the subsequent civil war the free rights of Englishmen to dispose of both person and property were sealed in blood; but, as the forces engaged in the conflict were ranged under banners of political faith, it was the protection of property which took precedence over personal liberty, as the very names of the opposing forces indicate. It was a war of parliament against king; not of law courts against illegality, although the two principles were united in their fundamental opposition to rule by Divine Right. The contrast with what happened in France is interesting at this point; for there it was the law courts which led in the civil disturbances of the Fronde. In England it is true that Coke regarded parliament as a court, and the phrase "High Court of Parliament" had a mystical strength against royal encroachment on or disregard of its rights. Before long, however, in the struggle with the Stuarts, the propertied classes went beyond juristic to political liberty as the fundamental principle of their Constitution.

The temper of parliament under James was embittered by his failure to give adequate support to the cause of Protestantism, then seriously endangered by the Counter-Reformation, and when he refused their petition that England join in its defense, they protested "that the liberties, franchises, privileges and jurisdictions of parliament are the ancient right and inheritance of the subjects of England . . . and that in the handling and proceeding of those businesses every member of the House hath, and of right ought to have, freedom of speech to propound, treat, reason and bring to conclusion the same." The king tore this protestation out of the Journals of the House, dissolved Parliament and only called it back three years later when forced to do so by lack of money.

From the very first of his reign, Charles I defied Parliament, but was forced to accept the Petition of Right (1628), which recited and reenacted the statutes against arbitrary taxation, punishment except by the lawful judgment of one's peers, arbitrary imprisonment without stated charge, and other established rights of Englishmen. When, the next year, Charles dissolved Parliament, Sir John Eliot replied in a challenge which history was to make good: "None have gone about to break Parliaments, but in the end Parliaments have broken them." And Parliament went on to state that any minister endorsing a levy of supplies not granted by Parliament was "a capital enemy to the kingdom and commonwealth," and anyone voluntarily

[5] *Cf.* Catherine Drinker Bowen, *op. cit.*, p. 113.

complying "a betrayer of the liberty of England and an enemy of the same."

For the next eleven years (1629-1640) Charles ruled without Parliament. The warning of Parliament was partly taken to heart, however. Expenses were cut and peace policies followed, but the Court of Star Chamber, comprised mostly of the king's privy councillors, had wide scope, acting on charges brought by the king's attorney. The very name became odious as an instrument of tyranny. Finally, resistance to royal exactions that stirred the whole country came in the refusal of John Hampden,[6] a leading Puritan member of Parliament, to pay "ship money" — a tax on English ports for defense, which the king tried to collect from inland counties as well.

But, however stern the temper of the Puritans was in defense of their civil rights, it was much sterner in defense of their religion. When Charles chose to enforce the High Church worship prescribed by Archbishop Land, not only by expelling nonconforming clergy but by the mutilation of their outspoken advocates, the temper of revolt needed but an incident to set the nation in flames. This happened in Scotland, when Charles attempted to force bishops and a liturgy on the Presbyterian Scots. In St. Giles Church, Edinburgh, when a great ceremony was under way attended by two Scottish archbishops, bishops, Lords of the Council and other dignitaries "to give solemnity" to the inauguration of the High Church regime, a riot broke out, led, it is said, by a woman, Jenny Geddes, hurling her stool at the officiating bishop. The popular uprising against the new episcopacy spread, and when Charles issued a proclamation declaring all meetings and protests treasonable, the Scottish leaders drew up a National Covenant, pledging the signers to resist in defense of the true religion. The Covenant was signed almost everywhere, either with enthusiasm or under threats by its promoters, and the General Assembly of the Church, meeting at Glasgow, refused to obey Charles' order to dissolve, deposed the bishops and denounced the prayer book.

Charles accepted the challenge and two years later (1639) advanced with an army to the Scottish border to face that of the Scots. But he had no money and had to call a Parliament after eleven years of personal rule. Parliament, reflecting the national temper, called first for a redress of grievances, and Charles quickly dissolved it. But the army of the Scots was now invading England and Charles was forced to turn again to Parliament. This was destined to be the most important and longest Parliament in history, lasting through a civil war on to a republic. It began to assert its sovereignty by forcing Charles to sign the warrant for execution of the two chief leaders of his despotism in state and church, the Earl of Stratford and Archbishop Land.

But although it was unyielding against the king, it was not at first revolutionary. It looked back to the role played by Parliament in the past. It was Charles, not Parliament, who forced the issue, fatal to himself, by person-

[6] Hampden's tax was assessed at only 20 shillings, which was almost nothing for so wealthy a man to pay; but it was the principle which was at stake. Hampden was a cousin of Oliver Cromwell.

ally going to Parliament to arrest five members — who escaped. London was jubilant at the king's failure. He left it in high dudgeon never to return until his execution, seven years later. In November 1642, Charles raised the royal standard at Nottingham. The Civil War which followed lies like a red stain on the history of freedom. Civil wars always tend to be cruel, but this one has the added ferocity of a religious war as well. The soul of the revolt was Puritanism. The sturdy sense of the rights of Englishmen animated men like Coke, Eliot, Pym and Hampden, when it was a political question of royal prerogative, but the sterner mood of Puritan England — nurtured as much on the Old Testament as on the New — was touched into life when, alongside Strafford's violation of the rights of Parliament, Archbishop Land outraged Puritanism by his High Church episcopacy, with its resemblance to Catholic ceremonial. The Civil War thus became a war of religion as well.

Nowhere is this more clearly seen than in the letters of the country squire who rose in the course of the war to be the commander-in-chief of the army of Parliament, Oliver Cromwell. For him the war was a crusade against the forces of evil. His letters, many of them written from the field of battle to the Speaker of the House of Commons, are superlative historical sources. One passage has become a classic in its revelation of the temper of the Puritan in battle. In the letter written the day after the battle of Marston Moor, the bloodiest of the whole war, won by his strictly disciplined "hymn singing" troops and his own superior generalship, while thousands of the dead were being buried, Cromwell wrote: "Truly England and the Church of God hath had great favour from the Lord in this great Victory given unto us, such as the like never was seen since this war began. It had all the evidences of an absolute Victory obtained by the Lord's blessing upon the Godly Party. . . . God made them as stubble to our swords. We charged this regiment of foot with our horse and routed all we charged. . . . I believe of the twenty-thousand the Prince [Rupert] had, not four thousand left. Give glory, all glory to God."[7]

While this extract leaves only the impression of fanaticism, other letters of Cromwell uphold the liberty of conscience for the Protestant extremists — Fifth Monarchy men, Baptists and Levelers — against the measures taken against them by a Presbyterian parliament. There was an added reason for this; that the "new model" army was largely drawn from these sectarians; but there was also a place for toleration in the mind of the greatest Puritan soldier. If Puritanism was primarily a religion, rare spirits like Milton saw in it a manifestation of freedom, and so did Cromwell.

The overthrow of absolutism in England brought with it the death of the king. It is a tribute to the majesty that enshrines the kingship that this execution still casts a shadow on the pathway of freedom. But it should be remembered that in the judgment of Parliament Charles was guilty of treason against the state, and that in the war the blood of the best of England's manhood was shed because a monarch refused to compromise with those

[7] In *Letters and Speeches of Oliver Cromwell* (New York: George H. Doran Co. 1924), 382 pp.

who were the chosen representatives of the nation. There is more than a fanciful likeness between the aristocratic cavaliers and the French chivalry at Crécy or Agincourt faced with the solid body of English yeomanry. Cromwell's "new model" army was equally a forecast of the nation in arms. But it was also a danger to the freedom it safeguarded, as it showed when the fighting in England was over and Charles a prisoner. Then to ensure a verdict against the king, the army turned on Parliament, purging it of all opposition to its will — and Charles' fate was sealed.

There was still war in Ireland, where Cromwell was guilty of terrible massacres, and then with the Scots whose defeat was his "crowning mercy," bringing all three kingdoms under a military dictatorship. When the "rump" parliament, as the purged parliament was termed, proposed to perpetuate its inefficient and corrupt rule which threatened anarchy, Cromwell went down to Westminster, expelled the members and ordered his soldiers to take away the mace, "that bauble" (the term for a jester's baton) which was the symbol of the legality of Parliament.

But Cromwell was too solidly English to want to rule by the army alone, and as "captain general" summoned a parliament of notables chosen by a council of officers, the "Nominated Parliament" of 1653. Designed as a constituent assembly to draw up a new constitution, it was largely composed of radical reformers who proceeded at once to plan to end imprisonment for debt, abolish the Court of Chancery — where over twenty thousand cases had lain undecided for years — make the judges independent, abolish titles and even to consider lessening the size of the army. Some extremists, pointing out how far short even this fell of the ideals of the New Testament, had a vision of a genuine Christian society, which alarmed the sober sense of the most practical of nations. The moderate members, therefore, although a minority, held an early session without the knowledge of their opponents, and passed a resolution which declared the parliament dissolved and resigned their powers to Cromwell.

The army now took over, and its council of officers drew up the first written constitution for a nation and the only one in English history. This "Instrument of Government," as it was called, vested the supreme power in a Protector, Oliver Cromwell. The republic, or Commonwealth, was to have a Council of State instead of the House of Lords, and a Parliament free from the veto of the Head of State, although he might delay legislation for a short time.

On the surface, the struggle for English freedom had produced a military dictatorship, disguised but more effective than that of the Stuarts, and that was the judgment of later generations as they looked back to Cromwell's England. But the history of those years of crisis was more complicated than the superficial reading of it indicates. Cromwell's sense of his mission, distorted like that of all benevolent despots, was that of a defender of freedom. He dissolved the Long Parliament for the same reasons that he had struck at Strafford and Laud, the agents of Charles' political and religious tyranny, when the Long Parliament tried to make itself a permanent, irresponsible oligarchy, and its Presbyterian fanaticism denied religious freedom to the other Protestant sects. The Nominated Parliament was too visionary for him, upsetting the whole social order, while he was for a "settlement" which would disturb the life of the nation as little as possible.

In his address to the first Parliament of the Protectorate,[8] Cromwell laid down his program as one of "Healing and Settling," ridding the land of discord, especially of the mistaken "notion" of the Fifth Monarchy[9] — with its threat to abolish Law and Property, and maintaining true "liberty of the conscience and liberty of the subject — two of the most glorious things to be contended for as any that God has given us." His speech, a long one, ended with the admonition "I do therefore persuade you to a sweet, gracious and holy understanding of one another and your business."

But there was no sweet agreement either in this or any other of Cromwell's parliaments. The reason for this, apart from the inherent troubles of a bitterly divided nation, lay in a disagreement over the form of government. Parliament insisted on a supremacy which would make the executive merely its agents, to carry out its will; Cromwell held that the government of the Commonwealth was not completely lodged in Parliament, but that it shared it with "a single person," whose legal title to administer the affairs of the nation rested upon the consent of the nation itself.

This claim was developed in his address to his second Parliament, a detailed justification for his rule. It had been accepted not only by the army but by the city of London, the country gentry and the judges, declaring "that they could not administer justice to the satisfaction of their consciences until they had received commissions from me. . . . This being so, though I told you in my last speech that you were a free parliament yet I thought you understood withal that I was the Protector and the Authority that called you; that I was in possession of the Government by a good right from God and men. . . . I do not know why I may not balance the Providence in the sight of God with any hereditary interest. . . . It is true that there are some things in the Establishment (the Instrument of Government) which are Fundamental, so there are others which are not, but are Circumstantial . . . Fundamentals are somewhat like a Magna Carta, which should be standing, be unalterable. . . . Is not liberty of conscience in religion a Fundamental? . . . Liberty of conscience is a natural right, and he that would have it ought to give it. . . . Every sect saith, 'Oh, give me liberty'; but give it to him, and to his power he will not yield it to anybody else. . . . All the money of this nation would not have tempted me to fight upon such an account as they have been engaged in, if they had not had hopes of liberty of conscience

[8] John Richard Green [*History of the English People* (New York, Harpers, 1903, Book VII, Chapter XII)] says of this Parliament of 1654, "Few Parliaments have ever been more memorable or more truly representative of the English people. It was the first Parliament in our history whose members from Scotland and Ireland sat side by side with those from England. The members from rotten boroughs had disappeared. In spite of the exclusion of royalists and Catholics from the voting booths and the arbitrary erasure of the names of a few ultra-republican members by the Council, the house had a better claim to the name of a 'free Parliament' than any which had sat before."

[9] That of Christ, after the four monarchies of Babylonia, Persia, Alexander and Rome.

better than Episcopacy granted them or than would have been afforded by a Scots Presbytery. . . . This I say is a Fundamental. If there be an absoluteness in the imposer without fitting allowances and exceptions from the rule, we shall have the people driven into the wilderness; as they were when those poor and afflicted people, who forsook their estates and inheritances here, where they lived, plentifully and comfortably, were necessitated, for the enjoyment of their liberty, to go into a waste howling wilderness in New England, where they have, for liberty's sake, stript themselves of all comfort, embracing rather loss of friends and want than be so ensnared, and in bondage."

This address to Parliament, which continued at great length, is a unique document in the history of England; for in support of the ideal of freedom it offers a political philosophy which would undermine the powers of the one body which had championed freedom through the centuries, Parliament. The constitution of the republic, as expounded here, placed the "Fundamentals" of government in the hands of an Executive chosen by an informal plebiscite or vote of confidence, with the army standing by. The distinction which Cromwell drew between the "unalterable" Fundamentals and the Circumstantials or day-to-day concerns of the business of government was inherently false to the theory of parliamentary rule in the unwritten constitution of England.

The first application of Cromwell's political philosophy was the dissolution of Parliament, followed by his personal rule supported by the army. Even the control over taxation was taken over, on the plea of emergency in case of a possible uprising of royalists. Cromwell's excuse for this was the same as has served despotism elsewhere: "The people will prefer their real security to forms."[10] But these "forms," so lightly rejected, were those of freedom — the safeguards of self-government for which Cromwell himself once fought a tyranny not unlike his own.

The temptation to linger over the England that led — along with little Holland — in the struggle for freedom must be resisted, for after the death of Cromwell, whose strong hand held the divided nation together, it began to fall apart — Presbyterians coming back, the Long Parliament revived, Independents lessening in the politics of the army, and Royalists plotting the return of monarchy. Above all, the country was tired of conflict and of the Puritan intolerance of "worldly" pleasures; and the restoration of the monarchy was a natural way of escape. Before Charles II "came back from his travels," however, he issued a declaration (from Breda in Holland) which registered the end of absolutism: a general amnesty for all, so far as Parliament chose to apply it; liberty of conscience, as Parliament might define it; security for property acquired during the war and Commonwealth, as Parliament might determine; and full arrears of payment to the soldiers, as Parliament might enact. The Revolution was not undone. When Charles II reached London he gave his royal assent to Magna Carta, the Petition of

[10] Green's comment on this is that the Protector's words might have been used by Strafford.

Right, and other measures upholding the ancient rights of the citizen against usurpation by the Crown. The absolute monarchy was gone, never to be revived.

It was the new Parliament of the Restoration, nine-tenths of its members Cavaliers, and not the easy-going indolent king, which executed the regicides (thirteen of them) and had Cromwell's body dug up from Westminster Abbey to hang in chains at Tyburn. At heart, Charles was as merciless as his Parliament, going to watch the executions; but it was the Cavaliers' hatred of Puritanism which found expression in a series of vindictive laws against them. Not only was the Puritan clergy expelled, but private worship attended by more than five persons outside the family was forbidden, and the jails were filled with Nonconformists —— such men as George Fox, the founder of the Society of Friends (Quakers), and John Bunyan, whose *Pilgrim's Progress*, telling the story of Christian journeying from the City of Destruction to the City of God, became, next to the Bible, the most widely read book in the English language.

Religion played little part in the life of the licentious Charles, but it was still vital in the life of his nation. Ready credence was given to an alleged "Popish plot" to burn London, massacre the Protestants and murder the king, and Charles' ill-timed effort to quiet the panic by a Declaration of Indulgence giving Nonconformists ·liberty of worship, which but heightened the suspicion that his chief interest was to shield the Catholics, resulted in the Test Act of 1673. This bulwark of intolerance, until its repeal in 1828, obliged all officeholders to make a declaration against the Catholic doctrine of transubstantiation, and to take the sacrament according to the rules of the Church of England. James, Duke of York, heir to the throne, gave up his offices and left England, but returned just before the death of Charles to be at hand for the succession.

Out of the confusion of these years two important gains were registered. The first was the development of the party system of government, as Parliament divided between the Whigs, supporters of its prerogatives, and the supporters of Charles, soon to be known as Tories. The ministers of the Crown were not yet organized into a cabinet system acting as a unit under their own Prime Minister. But the germ of the bi-party system lay in the Parliament of Charles II.

The other important gain was the Habeas Corpus Act of 1679. *Habeas corpus* (literally, "you may have the body") is the one Latin phrase which holds its own in common English usage. It was the opening phrase of the writ issued to test the legality of imprisonment. The Act was the formal enactment by Parliament of a procedure known to English law even before the Magna Carta, where the insistence on the right of a free man to a fair trial is already established. The Petition of Right had restated this principle, but both Charles I and Charles II violated it by delaying or otherwise avoiding trials, while keeping their victims in prison. The one point about the Habeas Corpus Act was that it called for a specified trial at a specified time, and so its writ was the most definite safeguard against illegal imprisonment.[11] No other single document has so often been invoked to prevent unlawful imprisonment.

The reign of James II brought to an end the long paradox of Stuart history, in which the liberties of Englishmen were won in a struggle fought fully as much in the field of religion as in that of politics. By his very first act, James stirred the fires of religious opposition by an open violation of the Test Act, attending a mass in St. James Palace celebrated with solemn pomp, which turned the bishops of the Established Church against him. The year, 1685, was that of the Revocation of the Edict of Nantes in France, and English Protestantism, deeply affected by the persecution of the Huguenots, was still more disturbed when James admitted Catholics to the Privy Council and issued two Declarations of Indulgence designed to help the cause of Catholicism. The failure of a jury to convict seven bishops for having protested against the second declaration brought great popular demonstrations, but the birth of a son and heir to perpetuate the Stuart dynasty brought revolution. William, Prince of Orange, husband of James' daughter Mary, was invited over to England to become King, and James fled to France.

A Convention, meeting in January 1689, declared "that King James, having endeavoured to subvert the Constitution of the Kingdom by breaking the original contract between King and People, and, by the advice of Jesuits and other wicked persons, having violated the fundamental laws and having withdrawn himself out of the kingdom," had abdicated the Government, and that the Throne had thereby become vacant. But, before settling the crown upon William and Mary, it obliged them to sign a Declaration — which then became a Bill of Rights — which marked the end of an era and the beginning of a new. The "Glorious Revolution" of 1688 had become law.

The Bill of Rights gives not only a guarantee of the freedom of the citizen, but also a definite limitation on English sovereigns; for William and Mary were forced to sign it before Parliament accepted them as King and Queen of England. More than any other document, therefore, it is the fundamental basis of England's unwritten Constitution, for it furnishes in a detailed but comprehensive review a restatement of the principles of English freedom as set forth from time to time in Magna Carta and since. The main points in its thirteen provisions were:

1. That the pretended power of suspending laws, or the execution of laws, by regal authority, without consent of Parilament, is illiegal. . . .
4. That levying money for or to the use of the Crown by pretense of prerogative, without grant of Parliament, for longer time or in other manner than the same is or shall be granted, is illegal.
5. That it is the right of the subjects to petition the king, and all commitments and prosecutions for such petitioning are illegal.
6. That the raising or keeping of a standing army within the kingdom in time of peace, unless it be with the consent of Parliament, is against law.

[11] The wrongful denial of the writ in the American colonies was one of the causes of the Revolution, and the Constitution of the United States and those of most states provide that it shall not be suspended except if peace is endangered. By an accident of history, the writ is unknown to Scottish law, because the Habeas Corpus Act took place before the union of Scotland and England. The Scottish procedure is different.

7.   That the subjects which are Protestants may have arms for their defense suitable to their condition, and as allowed by law.

8.   That election of members of Parliament ought to be free.

9.   That the freedom of speech, and debates or proceedings in Parliament, ought not to be impeached or questioned in any court or place out of Parliament.

10.   That excessive bail ought not to be required, nor excessive fines imposed, nor cruel and unusual punishment inflicted.

11.   That jurors ought to be duly impaneled and returned, and jurors which pass upon men in trials for high treason ought to be freeholders.

12.   That all grants and promises of fines and forfeitures of particular persons before conviction are illegal and void.

13.   And that for redress of all grievances, and for the amending, strengthening, and preserving of the laws, Parliament ought to be held frequently.

The provision that Parliament ought to be held frequently was made more definite by the needs of the King and the state, which called for yearly voting of supplies, and there has, therefore, been a yearly meeting of Parliament since 1690. The power of the purse has proved decisive in the long struggle for English freedom, although the full import of this fact was obscured by the absence of any symbol of the final transfer of sovereignty from King to people. He is still, in title if not in fact, "King of England by the Grace of God," a phrase seemingly left untouched in medieval splendor. "King and Country" continued to be the theme of patriotism; loyalty to the Crown was loyalty to England, a tie that was doubly strong because of the fusion of two sentiments in one. History and literature have woven around it the glamor of romance, from Shakespeare's tribute, "This royal throne of Kings, this sceptered isle. . . . This blessed plot, this earth, this realm, this England," to Winston Churchill's vibrant call to the historic spirit of England in the Second World War.

The sentiment attached to the homeland of a people could never be transferred to a possession like money, shifting and illusive in ownership. Yet, it was the lordship over capital which made the little island of Britain the theater of one of the greatest achievements in the history of politics: freedom under the law — the creation of the liberal state through the supremacy of Parliament, the protection of civil liberty through the Bill of Rights and the supremacy of civil over military authority through the Mutiny Act. To these should be added the final recognition of the Dissenters in the Toleration Act.

The philosopher of the English Revolution was John Locke. This advocate of religious toleration was also the exponent of the rule of law in the world of business. Without reverting again to the religious issue — although it was on it that James II lost his throne — we find in Locke's *Two Treatises on Government*, published in 1691, the classic statement of the principles of "government by the consent of the governed" established by the Revolution for the protection of life and property. "Political power" he defines as "the right of making laws with penalties of death, and consequently all the penalties for the regulating and preserving of property." All men are equal in the state of nature, which "has a law of nature to govern it. . . . Men are

God's property, made to last during His, not another's pleasure." Here we have the law of nature or reason insisted on by Hooker, and the refutation of the ideas of Hobbes on absolute monarchy. Civil society (Locke calls it the Commonwealth) is established the better to safeguard the inherent rights of liberty and property which are unsure in the state of nature; therefore, it rests on an original compact providing for rule by the majority. The right to govern is a moral trust forfeited when its terms are violated by the ruler. Since the purpose of the compact is the common good, the Commonwealth has no power to take away anyone's property without his consent and under a law equally applicable to all. This applies to taxes, which the Commonwealth alone can levy.

When we come to think about it, there is nothing strange in the fact that the Revolution should put the protection of property to the forefront. But it was a *tour de force* for the English philosophers of that period to read this fundamental interest of theirs into the law of nature so completely as to make the identification seem axiomatic. It is true that there was a hint of the possibilities in Greek and Roman literature, but those possibilities were not developed and applied to the conditions of the modern world until Locke wrote his famous *Treatises on Government*.

Locke's interest in the protection of property carried him far afield: to accept labor as its origin — the principle which Karl Marx was later to take over from Adam Smith. But perhaps even more striking is Locke's relatively slight treatment of personal liberty. While this is not lacking — as is evidenced by his advocacy of the right of revolution — it is not the chief issue, as it would have been in France, under the shadow of the Bastille. Yet a whole area of freedom was left with inadequate protection in the backward state of criminal law and penology in England — a condition not reformed until the nineteenth century, when England at last awoke to the fact that its protection of the "life and liberty" of its citizens had not kept pace with that of their property.

Locke's influence was immense, not only in England and America, where it was to guide the thought of a new revolution, but also in France, where its democratic principles were stimulating to critical *philosophe* thinkers. Although in its theory of the contractual origin of government, it bears the mark of its time and of his forerunners, this touch of anachronism is completely overbalanced by his forward looking treatment of a world of capitalistic politics.

The English Revolution opened a new era in the history of freedom. As we have shown, although its dynamic force was largely economic, the sense of nationality was also based on history and greatly strengthened by religious ideals. The Marxian interpretation of history does not explain as complex a movement as we have traced here. Moreover, both here and in what follows, we must not lose sight of the all-important political fact that the new capitalists were not limited to merchants and bankers. The wealthiest element remained the landowners, noble or non-noble, who, while the actual conduct of business was not in their hands, had the foresight to supplement

340

the income from their estates or farms by investments in commerce and banking. While London, Bristol and the other seaports grew in size and importance, it was from the country gentry that most of the leaders in politics were drawn.

From the seventeenth century to the eighteen-thirties, when the first Reform Bill brought businessmen to power, the great affairs of state were almost entirely in the hands of the aristocracy, whose country estates, graced with stately homes, were the pride of the whole country. The practical sense which linked the most alert of this landed gentry in business with merchants and bankers was not only responsible for their alliance in the struggle against the Stuarts, it also found expression in the Whig party, which remained, like an oligarchy, in power during most of the eighteenth century. Socially, the structure of privilege was taken for granted; but with the industrial revolution of the nineteenth century, the way was cleared for political equality and economic reform. This belongs, however, to a later chapter of our survey which deals with the further development of British freedom.

The final assertion of the sovereignty of parliament was made in the Act of Settlement (1701) when, upon the death of Anne's heir, the crown was settled upon Sophia, Electress of Hanover, granddaughter of James I, and her descendants. It added one immensely important provision, that judges should hold office for life and be removed only upon an address from both houses. Thus the administration of justice achieved the same freedom as Parliament. The Crown could never again appoint judges to implement tyranny, as had been the case under the first two Stuarts; and, since by the writ of *habeas corpus* the judges could review, hamper or even veto an action by the executive, the liberties of the subject were finally and fully safeguarded, except only in times of national crisis when Parliament, and only Parliament, could suspend the Habeas Corpus Act in the interest of national safety.

The American Revolution

The American Revolution, like that of England, was not the beginning but the culmination of a history of freedom. The forces which disrupted the Empire in 1776 drew their strength from the same sources as those which overthrew the Stuart despotism over a century earlier. The link between the two revolutions was personal and direct — so far as New England was concerned, for John Winthrop belonged to the same stock of country gentry as John Hampden, and the settlers in Massachusetts, had they stayed in England, would have been soldiers under Cromwell. This had not been true of the earlier settlers, those of Virginia, who went there simply to make their fortunes, but the instruction issued by the Virginia Company to the governor, ordering him to introduce the common law of England, with due process of law, would have gladdened the heart of Chief Justice Coke. It was also to summon a representative assembly, although its by-laws were subject to the company's consent. "Democracy made her American debut on 30 July, 1619, when twenty-two 'burgesses,' two from each settled district, elected by the vote of all men aged seventeen and upward, met with the governor's council in the church at Jamestown. . . . From that time forth government of the people, however limited and thwarted, has been a fundamental principle of the English colonies and of the United States. No colony of any other nation obtained representative institutions before the nineteenth century, except Iceland."[11]

In November of that same year the Mayflower pilgrims landed at Plymouth, an exploit of courage and high purpose the reminder of which has never failed to stir the heart of America. The expedition, small as it was, took on the solid tone of history when, shortly after landing, their leaders drew up the famous Mayflower Compact, which served as a constitution for the isolated colony. Few texts in the history of freedom are clothed with more glowing sense of the innate sovereignty of the Christian man. It was not a royal charter, but by covenant of its signers it assumed authority over the community.

In the Name of God, Amen. We whose names are underwritten, the Loyal Subjects of our dread Sovereign, Lord King *James,* by the Grace of God, of *Great Britain, France* and *Ireland,* King, *Defender of the Faith,* etc. Having undertaken for the Glory of God and the Advancement of the Christian Faith, and the Honour of our King and Country, a Voyage to plant the first colony in the northern Parts of Virginia; Do by these Presents, solemnly and mutually in the Presence of God and one another, covenant and combine ourselves together into a civil Body Politik, for our better Ordering and Preservation, and furtherance of the Ends aforesaid; and by Virtue hereof do enact, constitute, and frame, such just and equal Laws, Ordinances, Acts, Constitutions and Offices from time to time, as shall be thought most meet and convenient for the general Good of the Colony. In Witness whereof we have hereunto subscribed our names at *Cape Cod* the eleventh of *November* in the Reign of our Sovereign Lord King *James* of *England, France* and *Ireland,* the eighteenth and of *Scotland* the fifty-fourth, *Anno Domini* 1620.

The Mayflower Compact bore only forty-one signatures and the colony remained only a village, slight and poor and hardly able to maintain itself. They were the radicals of Protestantism, the Separatists or Independents who were not satisfied, like the other Nonconformists, with merely reforming the ritual of the Church of England, but held to the absolute separation of the spiritual and temporal commonwealths. The repressive measures of Elizabeth bore especially on these uncompromising Puritans. Yet of all those persecuted they were the only ones who believed in toleration for others. Their belief in a personal religion, which held that all life was sacred — not merely that devoted to church services with sacraments and priesthood — might have gone to the extremes like some of the medieval heresies, but, while there were exceptions, the body of the Separatists remained in all other matters than their beliefs law-abiding citizens.

[11]S. E. Morison and H. S. Commager, *The Growth of the American Republic* (New York: Oxford University Press, 1937), vol. I, p. 41.

Men like William Bradford of the Mayflower and William Penn, the Quaker, succeeded in holding their fellow members to the precepts of Paul in admonishing the Corinthians to make their personal religion a basis for sounder citizenship instead of an excuse for the anarchy of unrestrained emotional spirituality, as had been the case with the Anabaptists of Germany. The little colony of Plymouth did not lack practical guidance any more than the Quakers of Pennsylvania. "The liberty wherewith Christ hath made us free" did not mean license.

After the death of Elizabeth the repression of the Separatists was more and more extended to the moderate Nonconformists, who sought to reform the national church from within, by "purifying" its ritual and eliminating an episcopate that, to them, seemed too much like that of the Roman Catholic church. It was the persecution of these Nonconformists under Charles I and Archbishop Laud that brought the migration of Puritans to New England in 1629. At the same time that Pym, Eliot and Hampden were fighting the battle of freedom at home, another country gentleman of the same sturdy stock, John Winthrop, sailed in a fleet of seventeen vessels with a thousand Puritans for Massachusetts Bay, settling at and around Salem and founding Boston and towns nearby.

In the preceding year, in March 1628, the New England Council — established in 1620 but failing for lack of capital and popular support — had granted to John Endicott and five associates a large grant extending westward from the Atlantic to the South Sea, and the Nonconformist members of the moribund Council were persuaded to secure from the king a charter authorizing them as "The Governor and Company of Massachusetts Bay" to colonize the territory. With political finesse Winthrop got a provision which transferred the seat of the company to New England, so the commercial corporation became a self-governing colony.

The quaint English of this vital document in the history of American freedom runs partly as follows.

There shalbe one Governor, one Deputy Governor and eighteene Assistants of the same Company, to be from tyme to tyme constituted, elected and chosen out of the Freemen of the saide Company. . . .

And Further . . . That the Governor of the saide Company . . . shall have Authoritie from tyme to tyme . . . to give order for the assembling of the saide Company, and . . . saide Company . . . maie once every Moneth or oftener at their Pleasure, assemble and houlde and keep a Courte or Assemblie of themselves, for the better ordering of their Affaires . . . and wee Doe . . . give and graunte . . . that the Governor . . . and six of the Assistants at the least to be seaven shall (elect officers and) make laws and Ordinances for the Good and Welfare of the saide Company, and for the Government and ordering of the saide Landes and Plantacon and the People inhabiting them, as to them from tyme to tyme shalbe thought meete.

AND . . . We doe graunte to the saide Governor and Company . . . That all and every Subiets of Vs . . . which shall inhabite within the saide Landes . . . shall have and enjoy all the privileges and Immunities of free and naturall subiets within any of the Domynions of Vs.[12]

12 The excisions are mostly those in the text as printed in Henry Steele Commager's *Documents of American History* (5th ed.) (New York: Appleton-Century-Crofts, 1949, 759 pp.), pp. 16-18.

Under this charter of freedom for the Puritan Nonconformists New England grew rapidly. By the time of the Civil War in England, some twenty thousand people had found refuge in it from Laud's persecution. Village by village — each with its town meeting, its church and school — they pushed into wilderness. Life on the ever-extending frontier was a continual school for freedom; as not only security from Indian raids, but the very means of livelihood depended on the courage, energy and foresight of each man or each family in a self-sufficient community.

We have concentrated upon New England in this reminder of colonial history, but, with the exception of New York, where the reactionary feudalism of the Dutch settlements on the Hudson River left its mark even after the English conquest, every colony responded early to the impact of the frontier. Proprietary governments and rule by aristocratic landowners gave way to representative assemblies and, as the wilderness was opened up, new local governments of towns and counties spread a network of self-reliant communities, forced by the hardships of pioneer life to be mindful of their rights. "British subjects," wrote Franklin in 1755, "by removing to America, cultivating a wilderness, extending the wealth, commerce and power of the mother country, at the hazard of their lives and fortunes, ought not, and in fact do not thereby lose their native rights."

This brief for the colonists, valid as it was, left out of account the protection which the British troops had offered in a century of intermittent warfare with the French. The English colonists held only a coastal belt reaching back to the Appalachian mountains, while the French claimed all the continent north and west of them; and, although bad British generalship resulted in disastrous defeats, the French were held at bay. All this changed when, following their defeat at Quebec, the French lost their American empire in 1763. The English colonists had taken their full part in the war, having raised twenty thousand troops and incurring heavy debts, but they reaped great benefits from it, while the English landowner saw no such gains for himself, having to pay an unheard-of amount of tax — four shillings on every pound. Parliament took it for granted that it both could and should impose new taxes on the colonies, increased the duties on their imports, which threatened to ruin the trade with the West Indies, and then, almost without debate, passed the Stamp Act designed to bring in revenue from all business transactions.

There is no more instructive lesson in the history of politics than the complete misunderstanding in Parliament of the colonial reaction to an act that roused resentment in every town and countryside, for the British were completely surprised at the resistance to what seemed to them a just sharing of the cost of government. The real issue was the imposition of a tax without the consent of the governed. It seemed to the colonists to be a fundamental violation of the unwritten but vital principles of the constitution. The Massachusetts House wrote to leading English statesmen, reminding them that "There are fundamental rules of the constitution, which it is humbly presumed, neither the supreme legislature nor the supreme executive can alter.

344

In all free states, the constitution is fixed; it is from thence that the legislature derives its authority; therefore it cannot change the constitution without destroying its own foundation."

In a circular letter to the other colonies a month later, the House repeated this theory of the constitution in even stronger terms: "The constitution ascertains and limits both sovereignty and allegiance, and therefore his Majesty's American subjects, who acknowledge themselves bound by the Ties of Allegiance, have an equitable Claim to the full enjoyment of the fundamental Rules of the British Constitution." The circular letter ended, however, on a note of loyalty, which reflected the moderating influence of men like John Adams: "This House cannot conclude without expressing their firm Confidence in the King our common head and further, that the united and dutifull Supplications of his distressed American Subjects will meet with his Royal and favorable Acceptance."

But more effective than protests was the action of the merchants of Boston, followed later by other parts, agreeing not to import goods from England, so long as the mother country imposed duties on them. Then came the British monopoly of East India Tea and the Boston "Tea Party" and after it the "intolerable acts" of 1774, closing the port of Boston until the damage done by the loss of the tea was repaid; the Massachusetts Government Act suspending colonial and local governments to "purge the [colonial] government of all its crudities," and an act transferring the administration of justice to another province or Great Britain.

In June, "a very large and respectable" meeting of the freeholders and freemen of Philadelphia, resolved: "That the act of parliament for shutting up the port of Boston, is unconstitutional, oppressive to the inhabitants of that town, dangerous to the liberties of the British colonies, and that therefore, considering our brethren at Boston, as suffering in a common cause of America. Second, that a congress of deputies from the several colonies in North America is the probable and proper method of procuring relief for our suffering brethren, obtaining redress of American grievances, securing our rights and liberties, and re-establishing peace and harmony between Great Britain and these colonies on a constitutional foundation." The meeting went on to organize a committee to carry this resolution into effect. Even New York had its meeting of protest and support of the idea of a "Congress of American" deputies to be held in Philadelphia, "and that an engagement to this effect be immediately entered into and sent to the Congress, to evince to them our readiness and determination to cooperate with our sister colonies for the relief of our distressed brethren of Boston as well as the security of our common rights and privileges. . . ."

The action of Virginia was especially important, for in a meeting of eighty one burgesses held at Raleigh Tavern in Williamsburg it was resolved to instruct the delegates to the Continental Congress that, while strongly supporting the constitutional connection with Great Britain, they regarded the proclamation of General Gage, the British commander in Boston in declaring it to be treason for citizens to assemble and protest against his military

345

rule to be "the most alarming process that ever appeared in a British government. . . . If the said General Gage conceives he is impowered to act in this manner, as the commander in chief of his majesty's forces in America, this *odious* and *illegal* proclamation must be considered as a plain and full declaration that this *despotic viceroy* will be bound by *no law,* nor regard the rights of his majesty's subjects, whenever they interfere with the plan he has formed for oppressing the good people of Massachusetts-Bay, and therefore that the *executing* or *attempting to execute* such proclamation will justify *resistance* and *reprisal.*"

The first Continental Congress met in September and at once set about drafting its Declaration and Resolves, giving full backing to the protests of the colonies against the violation of the fundamental constitution which guaranteed their rights. Yet, while charging the British government with "tyranny" they stated "we have for the present only resolved to pursue the following peaceful measures; 1st To enter into a non-importation, non-consumption and non-exportation agreement or association. 2. To prepare an address to the people of Great Britain, and a memorial to the inhabitants of British America, and to prepare a loyal address to his Majesty, agreeable to resolutions already entered into." To give validity and force to these resolutions, the Congress adopted an Association which was in a sense, the beginning of the American Union.

There was still time for parleying, but not for surrender of fundamental liberties, for the country was being covered by a network of "committees of correspondence" and there were strong speeches at Liberty-pole celebrations, while raw recruits were being drilled. The issue was now clearly peace or war, and the English command at Boston took the final step in the march on Concord — to meet the "embattled farmers" at Lexington, April 19, 1775. On May 10, the second Continental Congress, now an openly rebellious body, named George Washington commander of a colonial army which was yet to be organized. But already the patriots organized themselves locally. The strong fortress of Ticonderoga was captured by the Green Mountain Boys, and on June 16-17 the battle of Bunker Hill was fought. Finally, on July 6, 1775, the second Continental Congress laid bare the whole tragic situation in a Declaration of the *Causes and Necessity of Taking Up Arms.* While not yet a declaration of independence, its ringing sentences match in tone if not in full content that other Declaration of a year later, for Jefferson had a hand in shaping this one too. Its opening sentences are especially Jeffersonian:

If it were possible for men, who exercise their reason, to believe that the divine Author of our existence intended a part of the human race to hold an absolute property in, and an unbounded power over others, marked out by his infinite goodness and wisdom, as the objects of a legal domination never rightfully resistable, however severe and oppressive, the inhabitants of these colonies might at least require from the parliament of Great-Britain some evidence that this dreadful authority over them had been granted to that body. But a reverence for our great Creator, principles of humanity and the dictates of common sense, must convince all those who reflect upon the subject, that government was constituted to promote the welfare of mankind and ought to be administered for the attainment of that end. The legislature of Great-Britain, however, stimulated by an inordinate passion for a power not only unjustifiable, but which they know to be peculiarly reprobated by the very constitution of that kingdom . . . have attempted to effect their cruel and impolitic purpose of enslaving these colonies by violence, and have therefore rendered it necessary for us to close with their last appeal from reason to arms. Yet, however blinded that assembly may be, by their intemperate rage for unlimited domination, so to slight justice and the opinion of mankind, we esteem ourselves bound by obligations of respect to the rest of the world, to make known the justice of our cause.

The Declaration of Independence said it again, but its summary of the misrule of the king lacks the appeal to history of this protest to Parliament, which contrasts the despotism of the last eleven years — since the end of the Seven Years' War — with the founding of the colonies when "societies or governments, vested with perfect legislatures, were formed under charters from the crown and an harmonious intercourse was established between the colonies and the kingdom from which they derived their origin. The mutual benefits of this union became in a short time so extraordinary as to excite astonishment." But now all was changed; the iniquities attributed to George III in the Declaration of Independence were here attributed to Parliament, to whom the Congress issued this defiance.

We most solemnly, before God and the World, declare that, exerting the utmost energy of those powers, which our beneficent Creator had graciously bestowed upon us, the arms we have been compelled by our enemies to assume, we will, in defiance of every hazard, with unabating firmness and perseverance, employ for the preservation of our liberties; being with one mind resolved to die freemen rather than to live slaves.

The white heat of this defiance was somewhat cooled by the sentences following it:

Lest this declaration should disquiet the minds of our friends and fellow-subjects in any part of the empire, we assure them that we mean not to dissolve that union which has so long and so happily subsisted between us and which we wish to see restored. . . . We have not raised arms with ambitious designs of separating from Great-Britain and establishing independent states.

There was no backing away from the opposition to the action of Parliament in its interference with colonial trade and self-government, enforcing its acts by armed force; but, while refusing to accept the authority of Parliament, the colonists still could claim their place within the empire. Their case had been stated in 1770 by Franklin[13] in the following terms.

That the colonies originally were constituted distinct States, and intended to be continued such, is clear to me from a thorough consideration of their original Charters, and the whole conduct of the Crown and nation towards them until the Restoration. Since that period, the Parliament here has usurped an authority of

[13] He had reached this conclusion in 1768, only five years after the end of the Seven Years' War which had given the British world empire for which they were not politically prepared. The two extracts from Franklin's works referred to here are quoted in Carl Becker's *The Declaration of Independence* (New York: Alfred A. Knopf, 1948, 286 pp.), pp. 101-104.

making laws for them, which before it had not. We have for some time submitted to that usurpation, partly through ignorance and inattention, and partly from our weakness and inability to contend: I hope, when our rights are better understood here [in Great Britain] we shall, by prudent and proper conduct, be able to obtain from the equity of this nation a restoration of them. And in the meantime, I could wish, that such expressions as the supreme authority of Parliament: the subordinancy of our Assemblies to the Parliament, and the like . . . were no more seen in our publick pieces. They are too strong for compliment, and tend to confirm a claim of subjects in one part of the king's dominions to be sovereigns over their fellow subjects in another part of his dominions, when in truth they have no such right, and their claim is founded only in usurpation, the several states having equal rights and liberties, and being only connected, as England and Scotland were before the union, by having one common sovereign, the King.

This line of thought that, in Franklin's words, "the only bond of union is the king" envisaged a political framework for the empire which over a century later was realized in the British Commonwealth of nations. It did not mean an extension of royal prerogatives; for the kingship as Franklin conceived it was that limited monarchy which had been created in the Revolution of 1688. There would have to be adjustments to meet overseas problems in defense and trade. But the legislatures of the American colonies would otherwise be on a par with that of Great Britain itself. This line of argument was especially developed by James Wilson of Pennsylvania and John Adams. As a lawyer, Adams fell back upon Coke's distinction between allegiance to the person of the king and allegiance to the crown as limited by the constitution. This really left the crown as a symbol of unity, not an irresponsible ruler of empire. The twentieth century was to see this theory realized in the Commonwealth, but it had no chance of acceptance under a monarch like George III.

Wrestling with this problem, James Wilson of Pennsylvania found the answer in Locke and even in Blackstone, that "all lawful government is founded on the consent of those subject to it: such consent was given with a view to ensure and to increase the happiness of the governed, above what they would enjoy in an independent and unconnected state of nature. The consequence is that the happiness of the society is the first law of every government." The "fundamental rules of the constitution" were thus already identified in principle with the "law of nature," and the argument could rest on a universal basis instead of on English precedents alone. The colonists could then place their case before the tribunal of "the public opinions" of the world.

The history of the Revolutionary War in which these issues were fought out is too well known to be repeated here, although this vital chapter of the history of freedom would be sadly incomplete which failed to pay tribute to the nobility of Washington's character and the courage and endurance of the soldiers. Our theme, however, is not the fighting but the reasons for it. We can best review these in the following luminous passage by Carl Becker:

The issue between England and America is not to be resolved by computing the value of a penny tax, or by exposing the sordid motives of British merchants and

348

Boston smugglers, still less by coming "armed at all points with law cases and acts of Parliament, with the statute book doubled down in dog's ears" to defend either the cause of liberty or authority. The issue, shot through and through, as all great issues are, by innumerable sordid motives and personal enmities and private ambitions, was yet one between differing ideals of justice and human welfare; one of those issues which, touching the emotional springs of conduct, are never composed by an appeal to reason, which formal argument the most correct, or the most skilled dialectic serve only to render more irreconcilable. . . . Few Englishmen could imagine an empire of free states; few Americans could understand a nation bound against its will.[14]

The one great fact to which parliament was as blind as the king was that, while the sense of freedom had been dulled in eighteenth century England by the absence of any serious challenge from the throne, in the New World the colonists not only continued to treasure the heritage of English history, but strove to build responsible and representative colonial government. The tie which linked the colonies together, more than their formal loyalty to the Crown, was the sense of liberties dearly won in the past and now shared alike, though in different ways, by sternly puritanical New England, tolerant Rhode Island, Pennsylvania and Maryland, and Virginia with its landed aristocracy and back-country farmers. The conditions of life on the frontier made for both personal freedom and local community action for safety and welfare, not wholly unlike conditions in Anglo-Saxon England, which had so largely set the model for English self-government over a thousand years before. The settlers were still mostly self-reliant adventurers, of sturdy moral fibre — the least inclined of all people to allow even the Mother of Parliaments to tell them how much or how to pay taxes, still less to bow to royalist governors, the immediate symbols of despotism. Indeed for them, as for the leaders of the English Revolution, the issue was a moral one on which there could be no compromise short of the liberties they claimed as a right.

But if parliament forced the issue in the great dispute, why did the Declaration of Independence concentrate its attacks upon George III? Because, as the Executive, he not only attempted to enforce the law, but, with excessive zeal, set aside the most unyielding of colonial governments and replaced them with royal officials under military protection. In anger, the now rebellious colonists saw in George III a new, less courtly successor to the Stuarts, having parliament behind him. Their allegiance, however, was to him and not to parliament, and so it was his tyranny they denounced.

No one then, and few since gave thought to the fact that until the united colonies became a nation, the experiment of federal government, with its division of powers between central and local bodies, had never been tried on a large scale. Had the demands of the colonists been accepted in London, the unwritten constitution of Great Britain would not have sufficed. There would have had to be a formal statement of clearly defined limits of sovereign and subordinate governments, such as that finally worked out in the Constitution of the United States, and recently in the British Common-

[14] Carl L. Becker, *The Beginnings of the American People* (Boston and New York: Houghton-Mifflin Co., 1915, 279 pp.), p. 203.

wealth. Such a creation was difficult enough among the colonies alone, as the Constitutional Convention was to show. To have it extend over a continent and an ocean and to deal with world affairs from a European capital would have been utter unreality. Therefore, the choice was independence, and with independence, freedom.

This ultimate, inescapable conclusion only became clear as the rebellion grew into revolution, which then became a two-fold movement, military and political. Victory in the war only opened the door to the real test of the new nation, its ability to organize a government which would safeguard its own freedoms. Fortunately the principles at stake were not in doubt, they were those which it regarded as its English inheritance, accepted almost as a gospel in the political philosophy of John Locke. This found expression in the very first of the permanent instruments of government of the new republic, the Constitution of the State of Virginia, shaped in Williamsburg in June 1776.

This document preceded the Declaration of Independence, although by only a short space of time. As we read the text of the Bill of Rights drafted by George Mason, and inserted in this pioneer document of the liberties of America, we see at once how natural such a statement would be from so close a student of Locke. "All men are created equally free and independent and have certain inherent natural rights of which they cannot by any Compact deprive or divest their posterity; among which are the enjoyment of Life and Liberty, with the Means of acquiring and possessing property, and pursuing and obtaining happiness and safety." The second article continues the same theme in the same universal terms, "that all Power is by God and Nature,[15] vested, and consequently derived from the people; that magistrates are their Trustees and Servants and at all times amenable to them."

Bills of Rights, such as that to which these ringing sentences furnish the prelude, were incorporated in the constitutions of seven of the revolting colonies. This undoubtedly was not due to any tendency to copy the formulations of Virginia, but to a widespread trend in colonial thinking of the same ideas as those which emanated from Mason and his associates.[16] Later on, when the substance of this Bill of Rights was incorporated in the Federal Constitution, this action by the various states was lost sight of except to the eye of the researching historian.

Nevertheless, it is a peculiar fact that it was one of the influences of the American Revolution upon that of France which left a definite trace for the historian. The Convention which was drawing up the Constitution of the French Republic ordered a translation to be made of the Constitution of Virginia, thus having at hand for comparison with the Declaration of the Rights of Man and the Citizen, the Virginia Bill of Rights of George

[15] The phrase "by God and Nature" of Mason's draft was stricken out of the Virginia Declaration of Rights, which, it should be said, was not strictly a part of the Consitution.

[16] The Massachusetts Declaration shows a very different tone, and while the Pennsylvania Declaration contains much that is practically identical with the Virginia formulation, it also shows some significant differences. New York had no such formal declaration at all.

Mason. It is of much greater interest to us, however, to compare the latter document with the Declaration of Independence drafted by a different hand but drawn from the same creative source whose fountain-head was the College of William and Mary.

Mason's enumeration of "inherent natural rights" is longer but more precise. The great phrase of the Declaration, "Life. Liberty and the Pursuit of Happiness," has become so much a part of American history that we seldom pause to think of the swift sweep of the trilogy as needing any further definition. Yet the longer phrase of Mason's text is a more careful statement, if less effective, than the headlining which Jefferson gave to it. The inherent "natural Rights" which Mason enumerated, are enjoyment of Life and Liberty, not Life itself, nor even Liberty. And parallel with this is the opportunity for acquiring and possessing property, enabling the citizen to pursue and obtain happiness and safety. Here we have Locke's *Treatise on Government* paraphrased in a single clause, but with a significant accent upon a phrase lacking in the *Treatise on Government,* "the pursuit of happiness." Locke was no Puritan to whom this world was merely a stern school fitting the soul for the life to come by an austere denial of present enjoyments. On the contrary, he emphasized the right which men have to "enjoy their goods and possessions" as a fundamental condition of organized society. But this ideal of the good life suffered a sea-change when the Virginians, Mason and Jefferson, gave it voice in the New World; it was not the possession but the pursuit of happiness which was set before the American people as the thing to be desired. Never was prevision more justified, for it is surely the peculiar quality of American life that it does find happiness in the pursuit of it. Forever following its star, it is forever stirred with a sense of aspiration and endeavor. Thus Jefferson, by the deft use of this single phrase, added a whole new province to the field of natural law, carrying it over from the static world of ancient times and the Middle Ages to that of the tumultous pressures of today.

One wonders just what the New England Puritans thought of this pursuit of happiness as an ideal for America. It must have sounded strange in the ears of those for whom life in this world was but a preparation for that in the world to come. It is certainly an added reason for rejoicing that the Declaration of Independence was turned over to be written by a Virginian, because otherwise it is doubtful if it would ever have cheered, as it has, the prospect of so many generations. Whether George Mason's Cavalier ancestry predisposed him toward the acceptance of this genial idea of pursuing happiness while acquiring and possessing property, or whether he was simply giving homely expression to the more sober thought of Aristotle that the ultimate end of society was the furtherance of the good life is a point which can never be settled. It has been surmised that perhaps the influence of the Swiss writer Burlamaqui, an author exceedingly popular in America at that time, was responsible for the linking of ideas of happiness and prosperity. Although almost forgotten now, he was one of the most widely read of the political theorists of that time. His work was a textbook in the classes of the

College of William and Mary, and was used by George Wythe, who had so great an influence upon the intellectual development of Jefferson. The evidence of Jefferson's Commonplace Book, however, seems to point to James Wilson as the medium through which the influence of Burlamaqui's thought was transmitted. However this may be, the fact remains that Mason's reference to property disappeared from the Declaration of Independence. It was a bolder challenge to the future, that the new nation was to pursue happiness.

The happiness of a nation is no careless rapture but a condition of life, for, as Mill pointed out, "all that makes existence valuable to anyone depends on the enforcement of restraints upon the actions of other people." The nation that was dedicated to the pursuit of happiness had, therefore, to organize liberty so as to give it lasting and efficient life; but constitution-making had to await military victory. The "United Colonies" fought the War of Independence before they were organized as a nation. The Declaration was but the prelude to that second act in the great drama which culminated in the Constitution. The Revolution was already over; the United States was responsible only to itself as it framed its instrument of government; but while this was taking shape, the French Revolution had begun.

The French Revolution

The history of freedom shows that it manifests itself in two ways: in the minds and acts of its leaders or its beneficiaries, and in the institutions which embody and express the nation's will. Nowhere is this dual aspect of its history more evident than in eighteenth century France, with its "era of enlightenment" enlightening Europe, and its Revolution recasting its institutions. The sovereignty of reason was asserting itself in the intellectual world, while the political sovereignty, outwardly so much more magnificent, was verging towards collapse. A hurried survey of both fields is essential to the understanding of the Europe of the nineteenth century and today.

Throughout the eighteenth century, French political and philosophical writings led the world in boldness of thought, and the criticism of existing society was all the more effective because of the failure of the political regime to adjust itself to modern conditions. To Montesquieu, Voltaire, Diderot, and their *"philosophe"* associates, the sovereignty of reason was supreme over the historical orthodoxies of either Church or State. Their negative criticism cleared the ground for the revolutionary thought of Rousseau, who was not a rationalist but an impassioned prophet of revolutionary doctrines.

Never before or since have the intellectual leaders of a nation struck more telling blows against authority. The latter half of the eighteenth century was a period of outspoken and acrid criticism of outworn social and governmental systems. Leaders of public opinion openly and eloquently challenged the persistence of feudal privileges and inequalities which had lasted on from the Middle Ages and the lack of those institutions of self-government which gave form and substance to English and American freedom.

Of the leaders of this attack upon the "old regime" in France, Montesquieu's pioneering contribution in *Lettres Persanes* and *l'Esprit des Lois* laid the basis and supplied the model for much of the political criticism which followed. We shall later deal with his influence upon American thinking, but naturally it was still stronger in France, where works of erudition are doubly appreciated if they are cast in brilliant literary phrase and especially when they play with ready wit upon the point of attack. The comparison with oriental or antique nations where things are done better than in France was a device commonly used throughout the eighteenth century, and by no one better than by Montesquieu's great successor, Voltaire.

For over a century the name of Voltaire remained the most controversial among the leaders of thought, and even today the smoke of battle still blurs his lustre in many eyes, because his chief campaign for freedom of thought was waged against the church, and he fought it, not with respect for an institution that offered the richness of faith and the solace of hope to mankind, but with ridicule for the obscurantism which it shielded; and ridicule is never forgiven.

In spite of his barbs of cynical wit, however, and his seeming disregard of the good which even the ignorant may do, Voltaire was not merely a negative force in the history of Europe. Early in his career he had studied England and the English at first hand, having chosen exile to imprisonment in the Bastille, where he had been sent for his attack on a member of the great and noble house of Rohan. A bourgeois had no right to attack an aristocrat, but Voltaire's exile brought important results, for his *Lettres sur les Anglais* opened the eyes of the rather self-centered French intellectuals to the contrast between arbitrary government and the restraints of limited monarchy; and also, even more, to the English practice of toleration and the safeguards of personal freedom.

Voltaire's chief work, however, was as a protagonist of rationalism. His *Essai sur les Moeurs* (*moeurs* is what men do, as well as what they think) was a revolutionary recasting of history, freeing it from the theological framework, which from the days of Eusebius and Augustine had explained events by divine intervention in human affairs. Voltaire's history of mankind was an essay in rationalism, emphasizing natural phenomena and rejecting miracle in the theory of creation. Such an outlook was mirrored in all, or nearly all, of Voltaire's writings, although he was too true an artist to belabor his readers with heavy blows of doctrine. Without reserve, however, he struck at ignorance, bigotry and oppression in a crusade which lasted throughout his whole life, and his influence reached out wherever the new conceptions of science touched the mind of Europe.

The satirist of religion and manners was also one of the most devoted apostles of the reform of the criminal law in France, which still used torture to extract evidence and lacked the safeguards for the accused which had developed in England. In this, one of Voltaire's greatest crusades and one of his truest claims to lasting renown, he was stirred to action by the work of the pioneer in criminal law reform, the Italian Beccaria, whose name should have more than this adventitious mention as one of the greatest benefactors of mankind. For it was Beccaria who led in replacing the savage, inhuman treatment of prisoners by a study of criminology and penology as sciences which he may be said to have created.

The case which Voltaire fought, in the forum of an awakened public opinion, was that of Calas, a Huguenot victim of mob hysteria and ecclesiastical bigotry, who suffered torture and death on the charge that he had murdered his son to prevent his becoming a Catholic. The eloquence and sincerity of Voltaire's plea, showing the falseness of the charge, made history in France. The sentence was reversed, too late. But another case, that of Sirven, revealed the same bigotry and intolerance and called for another effort by Voltaire to meet it. The fact that the higher magistracy responded in both cases to the appeal to reason was not only a tribute to Voltaire; it was a sign of the awakening of the era of enlightenment on the uplands of justice.

This short sketch of a great life may best be concluded by the tribute to Voltaire by John Morley, the most un-Voltaire-like of rationalists: "When the right sense of historical perspective is more fully developed in men's minds, the name of Voltaire will stand out like the names of the great decisive movements in the European advance, like the Revival of Learning or the Reformation. The existence, character and career of this extraordinary person constituted in themselves a new and prodigious era. . . . A new type of belief, and its shadow, disbelief, was stamped by the impression of his character and thought into the intelligence and feeling of his own and the following times. We may think of Voltairism in France somewhat as we think of Catholicism or the Renaissance or Calvinism. It was one of the cardinal liberations of the growing race. . . . Voltairism may stand for the name of the Renaissance of the eighteenth century, for that name takes in all the serious shortcomings of this strange movement as well as all its terrible fire, swiftness, sincerity and strength. The rays from Voltaire's burning and far-shining spirit no sooner struck upon the genius of his time, seated dark and dead like the black stone of Memnon's statue, than the clang of the breaking chord was heard throughout Europe, and men awoke in a new day and more spacious air."

The name of Jean Jacques Rousseau is commonly linked with that of Voltaire, but no two men could be more unlike. While Rousseau had contact with the *philosophes*, chiefly through Diderot, he was not one of them, for the intellectual and social freedom which he sought was not the rationalism of science, but a romantic return to "nature." The eloquence of his appeal rang throught the hollow formalism of his time, passionate in protest against the artificiality of society and the tyranny of government. "Man is born free and is everywhere in chains," the opening words of the *Social Contract*, sound an ominous note of rebellion, very unlike the philosophic tones of Hobbes or Locke, and the book itself outranked any other in influence on politics until the days of Karl Marx and Hitler. For it bears out as a whole the challenge with which it begins, so that it became the gospel of the republicans of the French Revolution who, organizing Rousseau's concept of "the general will" under Jacobin discipline, rang the tocsin for the reign of terror. The critic of today finds the text faulty in both logic and history; but the power to sway men's minds is often greater in proportion as the writer is less impeded by having to be sound in his thinking and correct in his facts. Rousseau was neither. He was frankly a demagogue, and the fact that he was sincere in his convictions gave urgency to his conclusions.

The personal note, which gives such a human appeal to Rousseau's writings, is struck in the introduction: "As I was born a citizen of a free State (Geneva), and a member of the Sovereign, I feel that, however feeble the influence my voice can have on public affairs, the right of voting on them makes it my duty to study them; and I am happy, when I reflect upon governments, to find my inquiries always furnish me with new reasons for loving that of my own country." This nostalgic reference to Geneva was justified so far as it stood for political freedom, but his sentimentality went farther than that, for it was on his support of Genevan censorship of Voltaire's plays, as disturbing to religion and morals that Rousseau came to an open break with the *philosophes*. When, in his *Emile*, he attacked the educational methods of his day, both Geneva and the *philosophes* turned on him and Rousseau solemnly renounced his Genevan citizenship. Yet it was in the field of education that Rousseau's influence was most lasting. For here he applied, with happy results, the return to nature in developing the inherent capacities of the child. Here, at least, the gospel of freedom had positive results — provided always that, as in the political world, it was not carried to extremes. Unfortunately, that is what happened in both cases.

So unique a figure as Rousseau escapes analysis; as is always the case with genius. But the full measure of his influence in France may be gathered from the comment of the one French historian who was least in sympathy with his political philosophy, Taine, the conservative historian of the French Revolution, who has this comment on Rousseau: "All accumulated dissatisfactions, weariness of the world, *ennui*, vague distrust, a multitude of suppressed desires gush forth like subterranean waters, under the sounding-line that for the first time brings them to light. Rousseau with his soundings struck deep and true through his own trials and through genius. In a wholly artificial society, where people are drawing-room puppets, and where life consists in a graceful parade according to a recognized model, he preaches a return to nature, independence, earnestness, a manly, active, ardent and happy existence in the open air and sunshine. . . . It is through these contrasts that Rousseau is strong. He revealed the dawn to people who never got up till noon, the landscape to eyes that thus far rested only on palaces and drawing-rooms."

Turning from these leaders of the new thought of France to the political structure of the State, we find at once a complete contrast to English history. Above all, there was no real parallel to the English Parliament. The "States

General," which had, in the fourteenth century, given promise of becoming a national legislature, was called only at rare intervals, until the reign of Louis XIV and then had ceased to be called. Not only was there no bill of rights to safeguard the citizens against arbitrary arrest and imprisonment, but the king, or nobles having influence with him, could secure the imprisonment of their enemies by the notorious sealed *lettres de cachet,* which were a constant threat against the free expression of opinion, sending victims to prison without trial.

The only institutional check lay in the law courts *(parlements),* especially the *parlement* of Paris, which registered the edicts of the king and which could venture to "protest" in case it disapproved of the edict. The formula which it used was one which did not directly deny the king's right to govern as he pleased, but which threw upon the king's ministers blame for having abused his confidence. To strengthen its case the *parlement* sometimes printed and sold its protest for one or two pennies a copy so that public opinion could be mobilized against the oppressive measures of the "King's Ministers." When the king received one of these protests he might either act on it or summon the *parlement* before him and in a solemn session *(lit de justice)* command it personally to register the law. This was final, although as the Revolution approached, the law courts began to claim that a decree registered against their will was not valid. More and more mention was made of principles of government or "fundamental laws" which, although never defined in definite terms, were regarded as embodying the national will.

Even though in this way public opinion was becoming more articulate, it had no recognized political organ of expression. The great age of Louis XIV built a magnificent facade for this incomplete structure of the national state within which medieval conditions lasted on because of the lack of any institutional way of remedying them. Even territorially, the country was not united, different provinces maintaining their own laws and systems of government. Although the Roman law had long been used in the practice of the law courts throughout France, there were no less than two hundred and eighty-five different legal codes of law in existence, so that people moving from one town to another might find themselves in a wholly unfamiliar legal system. Commercially the situation was even worse, for customs lines cut off the central provinces about Paris from the outlying ones as from a foreign land, and taxes varied with the locality.

More important than these obstacles to unity, however, was the fact that the nobility and the clergy were privileged orders, which left the heaviest of all taxes to be paid by the rest of the nation, the Third Estate. Although serfdom had almost entirely disappeared, the privileges of the nobles were bitterly resented, especially when they left their estates to live at the Court of Versailles, and the peasant could no longer look up to his absentee lord as a ruler and protector, but regarded him rather as an exploiter engaged in a sort of legalized robbery of his precious harvest. The heaviest of the taxes, the hated *taille,* from which the privileged classes were exempt, supplied one-sixth of the entire revenue of the State, but the amount collected was kept secret, and no distinction was made between the king's private funds and the state treasury, whereas in Great Britain, the monarch was given a stated allowance. The royal officials asked no questions when the king issued drafts to bearer, and Louis XIV is said to have spent no less than the equivalent of over a hundred million dollars in present day currency in this irresponsible fashion in a single year.

It was the threat of bankruptcy which finally brought this confused and antiquated Old Regime to a close in the greatest revolution Europe had yet witnessed. In the autumn of 1787, the *parlement* of Paris, the highest court of the realm, refused to register a great loan needed to carry on the government unless the king would pledge himself to assemble the States General within five years. When, in May of the following year, it decided that the king's ministers were set upon evading this provision, *parlement* drew up a sort of declaration of rights, among which were: the right of the nation to grant all taxes voluntarily through its representatives in the States General; the right of the judges to retain their offices in spite of the opposition of the king; and the right of every citizen, if arrested, to be brought immediately before a competent court and to be tried only by regular judges. This was less of a sketch of a constitution than a protest against absolute and despotic power, but public opinion had been stirred so deeply that there was no longer any possibility of evading the calling of the States General, which held its first session at Versailles on May 5, 1789.

At once it was clear that both feudalism and absolute monarchy were doomed. The Third Estate had been allowed as many deputies as both the other Orders put together, namely 600. It now claimed that it really represented the whole nation, or at least 96 per cent of it, and declared itself a National Assembly. So far the revolution moved peaceably, but the court party, supported by Queen Marie Antoinette, persuaded the king to summon troops, mostly Swiss and German mercenaries, to disperse the States General. When the news of this reached Paris, revolutionary leaders called upon "the people" to arm and defend themselves and the National Assembly from betrayal by the Court. All night mobs surged about the streets seeking arms in the shops of the gunsmiths and in the Bastille, the royal fortress at the eastern gate of Paris, in whose dungeons many notable prisoners had been held without trial, and which was therefore the symbol of despotism, although at the time there were only some seven prisoners in it. The poorly defended Bastille was quickly taken. Although in itself a case of mob violence, this unexpected triumph was speedily acclaimed as the first act of a revolution, and its anniversary on July 14 is still celebrated in France as the chief national holiday, presaging the regime of "liberty, equality and fraternity." King Louis XVI entered in his diary for that day, that "nothing had happened," *"rien aujourd'hui,"* for he had not had a good day's hunting in the palace park.

To prevent the spread of violence, a "National Guard" was organized, made up of volunteers of well-to-do citizens. General Lafayette, as a leader of the liberal-minded among the nobles, was put in command. The governments of Paris and other cities were reorganized under municipal regimes bearing the old medieval name of Commune. These measures were not enough, however, to prevent uprisings throughout the country, the burning of chateaux, and the obstinate refusal of country people to pay their taxes, rents and feudal dues. The result was that on the night of August 4-5, amid great excitement, the privileged Orders formally surrendered their ancient privileges in a memorable session of the National Assembly. It should be said, however, that the law embodying this renunciation, passed a few days later, was by no means so sweeping. However, it was decreed that "taxes shall be collected from all citizens and from all property in the same manner and in the same form" and that "all citizens, without distinction of birth, are eligible to any office or dignity." At the same time, the different provinces, principalities, districts, cantons, cities, and communes of France surrendered their special privileges in order to create an "intimate unity of all parts of the realm," an act which resulted in making for France a highly centralized government. A few months later, the whole country was divided into administrative districts of convenient size called *departments*. Thus the last remains of feudal disunion were obliterated from the map.

This tremendous upheaval of August, 1789, culminated in one of the most notable documents in the history of freedom, the Declaration of the Rights of Man. It not only aroused general enthusiasm when it was passed by the National Assembly, but it appeared over and over again, in a modified form, in the succeeding French constitutions down to 1848, and has been the model for similar declarations in many other Continental States. Behind each article there was some crying evil of long standing against which the people wished to be protected: *lettres de cachet*, religious persecution, censorship of the press, and despotism in general. The text of the Declaration follows:

Article 1. Men are born and remain free and equal in rights. Social distinctions may be founded only upon common utility.

Article 2. The aim of all political association is the conservation of the natural and imprescriptible rights of man. These rights are liberty, property, security, and resistance to oppression.

Article 3. The principle of all sovereignty resides essentially in the nation. No body, no individual, can exercise authority which does not expressly emanate from it.

Article 4. Liberty consists in freedom to do all that does not injure others; hence the exercise of the natural rights of each man has no limits [except those] which assure other members of society the enjoyment of the same rights. These limits can be determined only by law.

Article 5. The law has the right to prohibit only those actions harmful to society. All that is not prohibited by law, cannot be forbidden, and no one can be forced to do anything that it does not ordain.

Article 6. Law is the expression of the general will. All the citizens have the right to assist personally, or by their representatives, in its formation.

All citizens, being equal in the eyes of the law, are equally admissible to all dignities, places and public employment according to their capacity, and without distinction other than of their virtue and talents.

Article 7. No one can be accused, arrested or imprisoned except in the cases determined by law. . . . Every citizen, when summoned or arrested by virtue of the law ought to obey instantly as resistance constitutes an offense.

Article 8. The law should establish only such punishments as are strictly and obviously necessary; and no one can be punished except it be legally inflicted by virtue of a law passed and promulgated before the commission of the offence.

Article 9. As every man is presumed innocent until he has been declared guilty, if arrest shall be deemed indispensable, all harshness not essential to the securing of the prisoner's person shall be severely repressed by law.

Article 10. No one shall be disturbed because of his opinions, including religious views, provided their manifestation does not disturb public order as established by law.

Article 11. The free communication of thoughts and opinions is one of the most precious rights of man. Every citizen may accordingly speak, write, and print with freedom, but shall be responsible for such abuses of this freedom as shall be defined by law.

Article 12. The security of the rights of man and of the citizen requires public military forces. These forces are, therefore, established for the good of all and not for the personal advantage of those to whom they shall be entrusted.

Article 13. A common contribution is essential for the maintenance of the public forces and for the cost of administration. It ought to be equally distributed among all citizens according to their means.

Article 14. All citizens have the right to decide, either personally, or through their representatives, as to the necessity of the public contribution, to grant it freely, to know to what use it is put, and to fix the quota, mode of assessment, and of collection, and the duration of the taxes.

Article 15. Society has the right to demand from every public agent an account of his administration.

Article 16. A society in which the observance of the law is not assured, nor the separation of powers defined, has no constitution at all.

Article 17. Since property is a sacred and inviolable right, no one shall be deprived thereof except where public necessity, legally determined, clearly demands it, and then only on condition of a just and previous indemnification.

In the Declaration of the Rights of Man, the National Assembly proudly claimed that it was closing the door on the whole era of European history in which "the rights of man had been misconceived and insulted for centuries," and that they were now "re-established for all humanity in this Declaration, which shall serve as an everlasting war cry against oppressors. Some say that it is impossible to regenerate an old and corrupt nation. Let such objectors learn that there is nothing corrupt but those who wish to perpetuate the corrupting abuses and that a nation becomes young again the moment it resolves to be born anew in liberty."

The king, however, hesitated to ratify the Declaration of the Rights of Man, and rumors spread that under the influence of the courtiers he was again calling together troops for another attempt to end the revolution. It was said that the new national colors, blue, white, and red (the tricolor), had been insulted at a banquet at Versailles. These things, along with the scarcity of food, aroused the Paris populace and a mob of several thousand marched out to Versailles and brought the king and queen back with them to the Palace of The Tuileries in Paris, to be followed a few days later by the National Assembly itself. Constitution-making went on in spite of the opposition of the Court and the attempted flight of the royal family, and on October 1, 1791, a limited monarchy came into existence with an elected National Assembly.

But Queen Marie Antoinette's brother, the Emperor Leopold II, in conjunction with the King of Prussia, issued a declaration that they were ready to join the other European rulers to restore to the King of France his "sovereign rights." This act inflamed public opinion and strengthened the opposition to the monarchy led by two political factions, the Girondists and the Jacobins. The Legislative Assembly forced Louis XVI to declare war on Austria (April 20, 1792) — a war which was to last almost continuously for twenty-three years and ultimately to cover every country from Ireland to Turkey and from Norway to Naples. Prussia joined Austria immediately, bringing in the veteran troops of Frederick the Great to assist in the invasion of France. The French Army was in no condition for war, since many of its officers, who according to law were nobles, had deserted to join the enemy. The Assembly thereupon declared the country "in danger" and the revolutionary commune of Paris organized the second revolution which overthrew the monarchy on the 22nd of September, 1792, a date reckoned by the French Republic as the first day of the Year One of Liberty.

This first French Revolution, in less than two years, carried out a tremendous task in the modernization of France. Never before had so great a transformation of the society as well as the politics of a nation been carried out in so short a time. Neither the English Parliament during its five hundred years of history, nor the benevolent despots of the Continent had ever attempted to make such far-reaching changes as those permanently achieved by the first French Assembly. No wonder observers in other lands were amazed. The most English of English poets, Wordsworth, wrote: "Bliss was it in that dawn to be alive, but to be young was very heaven."

The social revolution, which ended feudal and other privileges, was the permanent revolution when it ended the Old Regime in August, 1789. But before the "Convention" called to draft the constitution of the republic could complete its task, the golden dawn of freedom lost its lustre in the darkness of "the terror," that crime which did irreparable damage to freedom because it was committed in its name. Just how this happened is, therefore, a matter of first importance, especially as there are indications in the world today of a capacity for the same "blind fury" of fanaticism as that which gained the upper hand in France in 1793.

The explanation lies in both the treason to the Republic by the court party in league with enemies across the Rhine and in the confusion of inexperienced politicians trying to make a constitution without precedent or French history behind it. The danger of invasion to restore autocracy was real, as the enemy was soon on French soil, the veterans of Frederick the Great and Austria marching to what looked like certain victory over the raw recruits called to the colors by the first national mobilization in history, the "levée en masse" of all Frenchmen capable of fighting.

Then the miracle happened; the disciplined grenadiers of Prussia, most of them serfs, gave way before the fiery onslaught of crusaders singing the new battle hymn, the *Marseillaise*. But as the danger of war and courtly treason diminished, that of confusion of council grew, and subtly took the place of monarchical intrigue. The fatal flaw in republican politics was that the country had no precedents to offer, no experience to profit from. The orators fell back upon the history of Greece and Rome, and a cult of admiration for antiquity gave a quaint tone not only to the political debate, but even to French art through the whole revolutionary era. Nothing, however, could stifle the new patriotism of an awakened nation, a vibrant passion which was destined to have a lasting influence for good and evil on the spirit of France.

The great debate on the nature of the Republic was carried on outside the hall of the Convention in every town and city of France, but especially in political clubs and the local communal councils. The most effective of these organs of discussion was the Jacobin club, taking its name from the disused Dominican, or Jacobin, monastery where it met in Paris. The history of this body, the way in which it changed from an organ of discussion to an instrument of terror, is of the first importance in the understanding of the history of freedom in the new era of democracy. The *liberté* in the name of which the Jacobins took over the French Revolution was almost the exact opposite of the freedom of the Puritan Revolution in England, and still more of the fundamental principles of the American Revolution. Both in England and the United States, the issue was personal freedom, the individualism that accepted differences of opinion on political matters as a matter of course. In France — and the same was true of the Continent generally — *liberté* meant the acceptance of a new authoritarian regime, in which individual rights must yield to the sovereign will of the majority. The disciples of Rousseau dreamed of a religion of humanity almost like a secular parallel to Catholicism, and applied to it the same doctrines of intolerance as had been accepted by the universal church of the Middle Ages. From this point of view, at least, the "new democracy" of Stalin, intolerant and persecutory, was by no means new.

The Jacobin club in Paris, begun as a meeting of provincial deputies getting their bearings in the new profession of law-making, soon expanded and admitted as associates similar bodies throughout France, and kept up a regular correspondence with them. The American Revolution has had its Committees of Correspondence, but no such network of over four hundred clubs, the first highly organized national propaganda body. At first moderate in its demands as representative of the middle class, it made the fatal mistake[17] of admitting the public to its sittings, thus giving the demagogues the encouragement of the Paris mob, the middle class *sans-culottes* (dressed in everyday business clothes with trousers instead of knee breeches), the out-of-work and starving poor. Under these influences the generalities of the philosophes gave way to attacks on "traitors" and a nation-wide suspicion of all not in agreement with the philosophy of Rousseau as interpreted by Robespierre.

The terror was supported by Robespierre, who ultimately became completely identified with it, but it was Danton who made its Committee of Public Safety the general staff of a fanatic republicanism, and Carnot, the "organizer of victory," who mobilized the armaments and armies of the Republic for the conquest of Europe under a young artillery officer who knew how to combine the Jacobin crusade for "liberty, equality and fraternity" with the age-old prize of war booty. But Napoleon's imperialism was not without lasting reforms. In France, the Code of Napoleon rivals that of Justinian in the greatness of its reform of the outworn system of law; and his system of government, while far too much like a military system of centralized control, remained the basis of the political structure under Empire and Republic.

The impact of the Revolution, carried across Europe by the armies of Napoleon, ended the structure of the Middle Ages there, although less completely than in France. Military genius was not the only reason for the strangest episode in European history, the Napoleonic Empire. The Revolution had not only produced armies filled with a new sense of national mission, but it had also revealed how much genius may lie concealed until freedom opens the doors to talent or genius. A whole galaxy of great army chieftains was at Napoleon's command. Never was democracy more justified than in the discovery of so many gifted men in the new empire of France, in civilian as well as in military service. Unfortunately, their services were all held within the authoritarian groove of the soldier-emperor.

Whatever strictures history has to pass upon Napoleon, he was more modern than his continental enemies and against their medievalism was a crusader for freedom, for the first effect of his conquests was to carry the ideals of the French Revolution over the Alps and across the Rhine. The congeries of little states which had persisted under the Holy Roman Empire, ruled by petty princelings and dukes, was swept away, and with them the empire which dated from Charlemagne. Serfdom was blotted out in the wake of the French armies. In Prussia this was accompanied by a removal of feudal restrictions on the buying and selling of land; but the regenera-

[17] The same mistake of admitting unruly auditors was responsible for the extremes in the Communes and the Convention.

tion of Prussia was less an acceptance of French ideology than a reaction against it, and its statesmen, Stein and Hardenberg, were more influenced by the doctrine of economic freedom of Adam Smith. The deepest impress of France in Germany was in Bavaria, where the Code Napoléon became the basis of law reform.

The French revolution was a vast and complicated movement, many revolutions in one. For a quarter of a century, from the summoning of the Estates General in 1789 to the battle of Waterloo in 1815, the center of European history was France. Republic and empire were both embodiments of the politics of revolution. But that revolution, in spite of its prodigious strength, its capacity for uprooting age-old institutions and remaking the structure of society, ultimately proved to be less complete than either the English or the American revolution. The English revolution was shared in by the nation as a whole, as was still more the case in the United States. The French revolution was different; owing to the sudden violent overthrow of ancient privileges the upper class remained hostile to the regime that had cost them those privileges. This was true also in other countries on the Continent over which the tide of French revolutionary Jacobinism swept and receded.

The result was to be a fundamental difference between the attitude toward the government in England and the United States on the one hand and the Continental European countries on the other. The key to the understanding of this is not to be found in the revolutions themselves, for the resort to force and violence differed only in degree; the Puritan Ironsides of Cromwell were as ruthless as the Jacobins and left as bitter personal memories in the families that suffered at their hands. But it is a law of revolutions that they do not destroy but rather reveal the fundamentals of a nation's life; and the history of England reflected a national solidarity that had never been realized in the France of the old regime. It was an alliance of the country gentry with the well-to-do citizens of the towns which overthrew the despotism of the Stuart kings, and together they continued to rule Great Britain as a parliamentary oligarchy as the inheritors of the "Great Revolution" of 1688.

It was the lack of this alliance of nobility with the third estate in France which made the revolution there incomplete in spite of the prodigious changes which it wrought. There was a stability in English political life due to the fact that, except for the disastrous interlude of George III's interference, Parliament continued to act for the nation as a whole, by a recognition of that check on the government known and recognized officially as "His Majesty's loyal opposition," a device never fully developed on the Continent. In both the making and the application of the laws, freedom broadened out "from precedent to precedent." Revolution was replaced by reform — reform in the law courts as well as in parliament, until finally the oligarchy of the eighteenth and early nineteenth centuries yielded to democracy, not willingly, but with the good manners of British self-control.

Although, as we have seen, the American Revolution resembled the English Revolution, and the issues which it solved were much the same as those of English history, geography soon cut in upon history. The struggle of the colonists to secure "the rights of Englishmen" to "life, liberty and property," to use the formula of Locke and Mason, was replaced by a growing preoccupation with the adjustment of these rights to the varied needs of the far-flung settlements. The histories of thirteen colonies had been geared into that of the common English heritage; but while all shared in the inspiration of the revolution, the great experiment of federalism raised new issues which after long debate produced the tragedy of the Civil War. Still, even in the darkest hour of conflict, both sides invoked the principles of the founding fathers of the Revolution. They continue to be invoked in the world crisis of today.

But while the foundations of politics in Great Britain and the United States are basically similar, the English parliamentary system works differently from that of the federal government of the United States, with a corresponding difference in national political outlook. The British parliamentary system, working through debate toward a common goal, the welfare of the people as a whole, tends to produce compromise from conflict, and British political theorists recognize this as one of their greatest achievements in the art of government. On the other hand, as Bryce pointed out in his monumental work, *The American Commonwealth,* the federal system rests more upon legal contracts in the relation between the state and federal government, and even in the law-making of the federal government itself. European observers find in the American system a degree of reliance upon legal safeguards which seems to be inherent in so complicated a system as that forced upon the American people by all the varied differences of geography as well as racial backgrounds of the citizens. This is a point given greater consideration elsewhere, but it should not escape our attention in measuring the impact of the revolutions in Great Britain and the United States and comparing them with that of the French Revolution in Europe.

The French Revolution did not maintain its hold on the subsequent history of Europe, or even of France, as consistently as was the case in the post-revolutionary politics of England and the United States, because history was not ready for it. The freedom it proclaimed had never been experienced on the Continent, outside the Netherlands and Switzerland, which were like islands in it; and experience is the only sure school for freedom. It must be earned the hard way by sharing in the responsibilities of government "by and for the people." This was unthinkable wherever princes claimed to rule by divine right, or thinkable only by an intellectual elite, as had been the case in pre-revolutionary France and Germany. It was therefore inevitable that the excesses of the Jacobin revolutionaries who attempted to apply altruistic principles by forcing them on nations unprepared for them, should be followed by an equally extreme reaction, and that the freedom so hardly won should have to be won over again.

Here we touch upon a basic difference between the nations of Continental Europe and the British — a difference which also applies to those trained in the British tradition. In the continental nations, always excepting the Netherlands, Switzerland and the Scandinavian countries, the nobility continued to be class conscious rather than public spirited, which was the characteristic of English patriotism. The British never talked about equality and did not practice it in social life, but they applied it where it counted most, in the world of business and ultimately in politics. In France and more especially in Germany, the descendants of the old aristocracy never fused with the nation in the British way.

CHAPTER XIV

GOVERNMENTS UNDER FREEDOM

The British Way

REVOLUTIONS do not solve the problems of government; they only make possible new solutions by clearing away the outworn structures of the past. The national state system, the origins of which we have traced through the slow processes of the Middle Ages, emerged at the dawn of Modern Times more like a system of dynasties than of nations. The claim of the monarch to be the sovereign state as well as its divinely appointed ruler — "L'état c'est moi" — had a historical justification not only in the fact that his coronation was a sacred ceremony which gave the sanction of a sacrament to his high office, but also that it had been the sword of the king which had ended the anarchy of feudalism. But when, as in the late Middle Ages, and in the Commercial Revolution, kingdoms became less like mere substitutes for feudal lordships and more like the management of a national economy, on which the increase of wealth and the welfare of the nation largely depended, the time had come for the nation to take it over. But that meant not merely getting freedom from a system of government no longer appropriate for its task, but also the creation of a new one in which the problems of freedom could be worked out on their own terms.

It was fortunate for England and for the other countries that profited from the Glorious Revolution that the Parliaments of the Restoration reflected the still-divided political opinions of the nation. The two parties which had fought each other over Stuart attempts at absolution were forced by the temper of the nation — especially in reaction to Cromwell's military rule — to lessen their antagonisms to peaceful if still at time acrimonious debate, the Cavaliers merging into a less militant Court party known as the Tories, and the Roundheads into a party called the Whigs. The English people were too politically minded to hold either party to a rigid doctrine; although the Tories upon the whole supported the royal prerogative, on occasion they, and their successors, the Conservatives of the nineteenth century, were responsible for great reform measures, while the Reformers or Liberals, successors of the Whigs, at times stood firmly for the established order. The important point is that each needed the other to check or spur its action when in power.

When Labor added a third party, this fundamental fact of the English constitution, the existence of a "loyal opposition," did not change; for in course of time the old Liberal Party made way for the Labor Party as the second member of the bi-party system. While the Conservatives have, upon the whole, ceased to be the party of Tory reactionaries which once repressed social movements as sedition, it has remained the advocate of economic protection and political imperialism. The Liberals equally have changed from the crusaders for Reform who brought the Middle Class into power in 1832 to an essentially conservative outlook in maintaining the best of all possible worlds, anti-imperialist abroad and anti-radical at home.

Slight as is this sketch of the development of the bi-party system, it opens up a central issue in the history of freedom. Government by an assembly must provide for free debate or it becomes a tool of despotism, as the one-party system has shown in Communism, Fascism and Nazism. The recognition of the right of the minority to present variant views is as essential as that of the majority to act. But unless it is systemized and held within bounds, opposition may become a kind of negative tyranny or at most the confusion of uncertainty. It was the achievement of England to work this out in two centuries of trial and error, from the days of Pym, Eliot and Hampden to those of Gladstone and Disraeli. The solution lay in linking the bi-party system of the legislature with the executive, through a cabinet depending upon the support of at least the majority party in Parliament.

On so fundamental a matter as the bi-party system two comments may be quoted, one from John Stuart Mill's essay *On Liberty*, the other from Gilbert Murray's *Liberality and Civilization*. Mill, writing in 1859 said:

In politics it is almost a commonplace that a party of order or stability, and a party of progress or reform, are both necessary elements of a healthy state of political life; until the one or the other shall have so enlarged its mental grasp as to be a party equally of order and of progress, knowing and distinguishing what is fit to be preserved from what ought to be swept away. Each of these modes of thinking derives its utility from the deficiencies of the others but it is in a great measure the opposition of the other that keeps it within the bounds of reason and sanity. Unless opinions favorable to democracy and to aristocracy, to property and equality, to cooperation and to competition, to luxury and to abstinence, to sociality and individuality, to liberty and discipline, and all the other standing antagonisms of practical life, are expressed with equal freedom and enforced and defended with equal talent and energy, there is no chance of both elements obtaining their due, one scale is sure to go up and the other down. Truth, in the great practical concerns of life is so much a question of reconciling and combining opposites that very few have minds sufficiently capacious and impartial to make the adjustment with an approach to correctness and it has to be made by the rough process of a struggle between combatants fighting under hostile banners.[1]

The comment by Gilbert Murray is an eloquent justification for the freedom of judgment:

There is no real substitute for truth any more than for justice. Therefore we should understand that "liberality" [which is Murray's name for Liberalism] and Conservatism are not contrary principles; they are complementary; neither is complete without the other. Neither is absolute or fanatical. Conservatism is an immensely important principle. It is based upon the truth that mankind in the civilized nations has by centuries of trial and error, experiment and struggle, built up a social order which is extremely precious and whose destruction would mean the loss of all that has been painfully won by the great reforms of the past. The object of Conservatism is to save the social order. The object of Liberality is to bring that order a little nearer to what the reformers aimed at and to what the judgment of a freeman — free from selfishness, free from passion, free from prejudice — would require, and by that very change to save it more effectively. The Conservative sees the importance of maintaining the strength and authority of his country, with the existing religion, social structure, and organs of government. He stresses the point that a faulty system which people like and understand often works better than a superior one which they do not want. The Liberal does not disagree, but feels more strongly that, if he wants to find what is really just he must be on his guard against the delusive powers of custom, prejudice, inertia, and the unconscious sleepless all-embracing egoism of his class and nation.[2]

Neither John Stuart Mill nor Gilbert Murray make the point that the success of party government in Great Britain is the nearest to a miracle in politics that history records. The ancient world failed to develop it; the Greeks outlawing or murdering political critics when they were considered by the party in power to be a danger to the state, and the Romans finally denying power to even so illustrous a body as the Senate, largely composed of ex-magistrates. The British parliament was saved from such a fate by the fact that from the Great Revolution to the nineteenth century there was nothing else to take its place. The incompetence of kings forced the nation itself to become politically minded and to make parliament both more responsible to public opinion and more competent to rule. This it did largely through the influence of great personalities, the development of the bi-party system in parliament and the country, and then through the extension of the suffrage, which by the twentieth century had become universal.

Of these, the most novel was the bi-party system reflected in even the structure of the House of Commons which places the party in power on one side of its center aisle[3] and the opposition across from it. The significance of this grows when one looks closely at it in action, as described by the best of authorities, Walter Bogehot in the following terms[4]:

[1] *On Liberty*, Chap. 2, first published in 1859. It has been reprinted many times.

[2] Gilbert Murray, *Liberality and Civilization*, The Hibbert Lectures (London: G. Allen & Unwin Ltd., 1938), p. 38.

[3] A member who changes sides is said to "cross the aisle."

[4] In the *English Constitution*, 2nd ed. (Oxford University Press, 1873), p. 201. Though written in the eighteen seventies this description holds today.

Of all forms of government, the oddest really is government by a *public meeting*. Here are six hundred and fifty-eight persons collected from all parts of England, different in nature, different in interests, different in look and language. If we think what an empire the English is, how various are its components, how incessant its concerns, how immersed in history its philosophy: if we think what a vast information, what a nice discretion, what a consistent will ought to mark the rulers of that empire, — we shall be surprised when we see them. We see a changing body of miscellaneous persons, sometimes few, sometimes many, never the same for an hour; sometimes excited but mostly dull and half weary, — impatient of eloquence, catching at any joke as an alleviation. These are the persons who rule the British empire.

It was not merely by perfecting party organization, however, that the British people developed government under freedom. The Crown was still sovereign in theory, and that meant that its influence, and even its interference continued intermittently, as circumstances offered and personality played its part either in the open stage of politics or behind the curtain of intrigue. The unwritten constitution of England verified the dictum of Aristotle that "royalty is preserved by the limitation of its power," for the practically-minded English, in transferring power from the Crown to Parliament left the symbols of royalty almost untouched. Fortunately for a hundred years the monarchs were of too limited intelligence to take full advantage of the ambiguity, and by the time of Victoria the executive as well as the legislative branch of the government was firmly in the hands of Parliament. The device which secured this was two-fold; a Prime Minister and his Cabinet.

The Cabinet system shaped slowly — avoiding any repetition of revolution — out of the Privy Council of the king, with a Prime Minister presiding over it and responsible for it and with it to Parliament. "The Prime Minister" said John Morley, "is the Keystone of the Cabinet." In theory, he is still merely the first servant of the king or queen, if not like the medieval Justiciar or Chancellor, at least in line with Wolsey under Henry VIII or Cecil under Elizabeth; but his dependence upon the House of Commons steadily grew, being more constant and real than personal intervention by the Monarch, and by the time of Victoria, Gladstone could say to her, in protest against her reminder "Sir, I am the Queen of England," "But Madam, I am the people of England."

Disraeli, without yielding his prerogatives as the voice of Parliament, managed her better by wheedling and diplomacy. But no Prime Minister could have taken over the functions of sovereignty on his own authority. While he spoke in the name of the majority party in the House of Commons, he did not represent them as an individual but as the authorized spokesman for a Cabinet which was neither the privy council of the monarch nor a committee of parliament but of the Prime Minister's own choosing. This subtle device the Mother of Parliaments passed on to her children, the parliaments of the commonwealths, as they developed constitutions of their own; but no other nations ever learned to use it in the same way. The Founding Fathers made no mention of it in the United States Constitution; the President's Cabinet is not recognized by Congress.

This subtle but powerful instrument of government was a private meeting of ministers of the Crown for an informal exchange of information and discussion of policy. Until 1916 it had no secretary and kept no minutes.

It was Lloyd George who instituted a Cabinet Secretariat to organize the business of the War Cabinet.[5] The Cabinet meetings still are secret, and the taking of votes is exceptional. The debate continues until agreement is reached, for the solidarity of the Cabinet is a fundamental principle. The Prime Minister cannot speak with the necessary authority if his cabinet is not wholly with him. When differences arise on matters of principle, the disagreeing member resigns, but upon the whole everyone agrees — even the opposition — that factional dispute must never endanger the stability of government.

If the Constitution of Great Britain took its present shape only during the last hundred years, the same is true of practical politics, both domestic and foreign. The eighteenth century presents incredible contrasts between a backwardness in morals and politics at home and the establishment of a world empire by brilliant statesmanship abroad. We shall deal later with the problem of colonial rule, but here we must pause to look at the homeland of the eighteenth and early nineteenth centuries.

First of all, Parliament did not represent the nation as a whole; it was more like a club of oligarchs. The great Whig families, the inheritors of the Revolution, were careless of their inheritance. Aristocratic or intriguing owners of "pocket boroughs" or "rotten boroughs" used them like private property to place their nominees in the House of Commons. Elections were largely farcical, rowdy, drinking affairs. In the army and navy commissions were bought and sold, and military expenses were open sources of corruption. There was almost universal drunkenness and gambling in the upper as well as in the lower classes. Reform in criminal law was long overdue; there were merciless floggings and executions for minor offences, and prisons that were schools for crime mixed criminals with debtors and the insane.

These conditions were common in other countries as well, and it is to the credit of England that it led in a movement, which became a crusade against this moral degradation. The religious revival of the Methodists in the eighteenth century was more than a sectarian movement, it was a re-awakening of the spiritual force of the Dissenters of the seventeenth century, and the inspiration of what later became known as the "nonconformist conscience" of England — a movement which has embodied the moral purpose of the people and continues to do so, one of its real elements of greatness.

There were heroes and heroines as well in the movements for social reform, which redeemed Great Britain from its inhumanities. There were among others, Elizabeth Fry, the Quaker crusader for prison reform — that marginal chapter of the history of freedom; Francis Place, the champion of the trade unions, membership in which had been made a crime by act of

---

[5] The War Cabinet even published a Report for 1917 and a second Report of Imperial War Cabinet, 1918, which, while prepared for war time are invaluable sources of history. It all grew out of the excellent work of the Secretary of the Committee on Imperial Defence, Sir Maurice (later Lord) Hankey, who became first secretary of the Cabinet.

parliament in 1806; Wilberforce, "the emancipator" whose anti-slavery crusade showed that a Tory could lead in a great humane effort; and the Earl of Shaftsbury, who went to live in the slums in order to gather facts for his advocacy of factory legislation. In the annals of freedom these moral leaders stand high.

Why could writers as well as politicians of England and Scotland be so little moved by the conditions of their time that Sir Walter Scott, kindly and humane by temper, shared with the Duke of Wellington — who, when the first Reform Bill was passed (1832) said, "We can never hope to be so happy or prosperous again" — the feeling that change would make things worse? The answer has been given by one of the greatest liberals of our time, Professor Gilbert Murray, who, while shocked by the statement of the Iron Duke that the system of rotten boroughs almost surpassed the limits of human wisdom (". . . indeed I should almost call it an emanation of a higher mind"), explained that such a sentiment had really little or nothing to do with political reform. The Duke "was certainly not thinking of his economic interest, perhaps not even thinking very exclusively of the rotten boroughs; he was thinking of the days and scenes, the memories, the persons, that he loved in England, all that he had fought for and striven for throughout his life, and then transferring his emotions to something quite different: the constitution of English society. He felt towards England rather as Lord Baldwin does. It hurt him to think of altering a thing so beautiful."

Such was largely the temper of the upper and middle class in the years following the French Revolution, the period of romanticism in literature and art, a reaction of tired minds against both the stiff intellectual challenge of the "era of enlightenment of eighteenth century thought and the jacobinism of the Revolutionary era. The escape from crude reality was made by a mental excursion into the Middle Ages, when knighthood was in flower and chivalry a poem. Serious historians were already beginning to reveal how unhistorical these creations of fantasy really were, that Richard the Lion-hearted, hero of a whole series of English sagas could not speak English and was only a few months in the country at most, that King Arthur's knights were creations of writers centuries later who knew nothing of ancient Britain and that the *Chanson de Roland* was mostly a glorious invention. But romanticism was an escape from history as well as from the hard facts of life, and the new middle class drowned responsibility in sentiment.

There is, of course, a freedom in escape; but it lacks the fullness of life by the very fact of its unreality. It is at best an episode in the life of men and nations. True freedom, as all the great religions and philosophies showed, lies in participation in the interests of the society of which each is a part.

It is in this setting that we come upon the ethical movement away from the false, self-centered sentimentalism of the romanticists, Jeremy Bentham's political philosophy of "the greatest happiness of the greatest number." For over half a century this "utilitarian" creed exerted a great influence on English thought, civil and criminal law and the machinery of government. While it all bore on the major problems of freedom, its direct application was made by John Stuart Mill in an essay that is still unsurpassed in its scope and clarity of analysis:

The object of this essay is to assert one very simple principle, as entitled to govern absolutely the dealings of society with the individual in the way of compulsion and control, whether the means used be physical force in the form of legal penalties, or the moral coercion of public opinion. That principle is, that the sole end for which mankind are warranted, individually or collectively, in interfering with the liberty of action of any of their members, is self-protection. That the only purpose for which power can be rightfully exercised over any member of a civilized community against his will, is to prevent harm to others. His own good, either physical or moral, is not a sufficient warrant. . . . The only part of the conduct of anyone, for which he is amenable to society, is that which concerns himself his independence is, of right, absolute. Over himself, over his own body and mind, the individual is sovereign.[6].

Having stated his doctrine in these general terms, Mill at once limited its application. He dissociated himself from the traditional discussion of abstract rights, which had been the battle ground of debate from the Greeks through the Middle Ages to the French Revolution. Without mentioning Bentham he goes no farther back.

I regard utility as the ultimate appeal on all ethical questions; but it must be utility in the largest sense, grounded on the permanent interests of a man as a progressive being. Those interests, I contend, authorize the subjection of individual spontaneity to external control, only in respect to those actions of each, which concern the interest of other people. . . .

This, then, is the appropriate region of human liberty. It comprises, first, the inward domain of consciousness; demanding liberty of conscience in the most comprehensive sense; liberty of thought and feelings absolute freedom of opinion and sentiment in all subjects, practical or speculative, scientific, moral or theological . . . Liberty of tastes and pursuits; and . . . freedom to unite for any purpose not involving harm to others. . . .

The ancient commonwealths thought themselves entitled to practice, and the ancient philosophers countenanced the regulation of every part of private conduct by public authority, on the ground that the State had a deep interest in the whole bodily and mental discipline of its citizens; a mode of thinking which may have been permissible in small republics, surrounded by powerful enemies, in constant peril of being subverted by foreign attack or internal commotion, and to which even a short interval of relaxed energy and self-command might so easily be fatal that they could not afford to wait for the salutary parliament effects of freedom. In the modern world, the greater size of political communities and above all the separation between spiritual and temporal authority (which placed the direction of men's consciences in other hands than those which controlled their worldly affairs), prevented so great an interference by law in the details of private life.[7]

If some of these thoughts seem now so self-evident as to be commonplace, it is partly due to the fact that here, as in his other writings, he was building up a logical system every part of which fitted into the whole. That makes it all the stranger that the essay *On Liberty* is weakest where one might have expected it to be most enlightening, in the field of economics; where he was

[6] John Stuart Mill, *On Liberty*, Chap. 1.
[7] *Ibid.*

an accepted authority and where freedom took an opposite course from that of the movement for social and political reform in which Mill was so deeply interested. The dominant doctrine, that there should be as little an interference by governments as possible in economic affairs remained untranslated from its French original "Laissez faire" — let governments leave things alone, their interference with the operation of economic laws will only make matters worse. Although checked and modified from time to time this negative principle of politics remained for over a century the most widely accepted theory of politics in practically every country.

Its origin was not devoid of drama. Its pioneering exponent was Francis Quesnay, physician to Louis XV, who, starting from the *philosophe* conception that society is a union of individuals all of whom have natural rights, came to the conclusion that government is a necessary evil, which should interfere as little as possible with individual freedom. This philosophic doctrine, the one revolutionary product of the palace of Versailles, was applied to an economic theory which need not concern us here, that agriculture is the one real source of wealth, manufacture only changing its form and commercial its ownership.

Laissez faire became a doctrine of freedom against the shackles of the "mercantilist" system of bureaucratic controls. The pioneering thought of Quesnay, that there was a natural law in the world of business making for the general welfare and that governments should not interfere with it, was developed into one of the most powerful doctrines in the history of ideas by Adam Smith, Professor of Moral Philosophy at the University of Glasgow, whose work *The Wealth of Nations* became the gospel of "the system of national liberty" of the next century of European and American thought.

Familiar with the works of Quesnay and Turgot, and the English Hume, Smith built a more solid basis for his attack on government interference with business by his bold assertion that the source of a nation's wealth is — not land as the physiocrats held — but labor. Labor, he said, is the "real measure of the exchangeable value of all commodities . . . it is their real price; money is their nominal value only." The increase in a nation's wealth depends, therefore, on making labor more efficient by organizing it, dividing it so as to cheapen production, which, in turn is stimulated by a division of trade and the whole complex furthered by the extended use of capital. To give full play to this complicated but natural and vital operation it must be freed from the artificial restrictions of government.

The *Wealth of Nations* was published in 1776 and it is no exaggeration to say that this philosophy of economic freedom ranks well up with that other great Declaration of political freedom of that same year. For, by the time the French Revolution was over and Europe had once more turned to the arts of peace, the era of the Industrial Revolution had begun and *laissez faire* passed from economic theory — where it dominated — to politics, in both domestic and foreign affairs. In the latter field it advocated a lessening of tariff and other barriers to trade, winning support for its policies not only in Great Britain's ultimate acceptance of free trade, but France and even

Prussia in the first half of the nineteenth century. This was a movement in which everyone shared; but in domestic matters the new freedom from government control in industry resulted in an economic and social tyranny, the record of which is one of the darkest pages in the history of freedom — that of the wage-slavery of the early industrial period, when the factory system began to change the work of the world, and the worker had no protection against its irresistible power.

Before dealing with this greatest of all changes in our long story from the ice age in our own time, we must return to the theme of this chapter, for this slight sketch of British government under freedom would be doubly inadequate if it ended on the negative note of *laissez faire*. In spite of the economists the scope of government widened. The first to profit were, naturally, the middle class owners of the new wealth in the Reform Bill of 1832. But the fact that Parliament was no longer the preserve of an oligarchy of aristocrats as in the eighteenth century made it so much more a national institution that the working class demanded representation in it as more important than legislation on their behalf, however well meant. Their platform, set forth in a Charter, for which they claimed six million signatures included universal suffrage and secret ballots in elections, but the year 1848 in which the movement reached its climax was a year of revolution in the Continent, and the propertied class, in panic fear, assembled a great army of special constables under the Duke of Wellington to prevent riots. Nothing happened, however, neither riot nor concession, and the working class did not get the right to vote until the Reform Bill of 1867. Two more reform acts were needed before Great Britain became a complete democracy. Gladstone's Reform Bill of 1884, which enfranchised the agricultural laborers and the various measures which by 1924 had extended the franchise to women.

It had taken over six hundred years for Parliament to become representative of the whole nation. There was even a pride in the slowness of the process. England in the eyes of its poet laureate was:

> A land of settled government,
> A land of old and just renown
> Where Freedom slowly broadens down
> From precedent to precedent.
>
> Where faction seldom gathers head
> But by degrees to fulness wrought
> The strength of some diffusive thought,
> Hath time and space to work and spread.

In these lines, and many others Tennyson voiced the sense of contentment of the Middle Class in the great days of Victorian England, when even in a losing cause, the conservative could hold his own in debate with the reformer in the bi-party system of government. Convictions were strong on both sides of the argument for extending all the rights and privileges of citizenship to all the people. The despair of the Duke of Wellington over the first Reform Bill was matched by that of Lecky, the historian of rationalism, over the second one in 1867, sadly commenting that it was folly to expect a better government from the least informed part of the nation. The answer of history to this doubt was clear; the legislation after each reform act was much more vigorous and wiser than in the preceding years. The explanation apparently lies in the fact that a ruling minority, however well-meaning, interprets the welfare of the nation in the light of his own interests whereas in a democracy there is a larger area of experience to draw upon.

While the most consistent leader of British liberalism in the second half of the nineteenth century was Gladstone, his rival, Disraeli, the architect of empire,[8] tried to turn the Conservatives from being a Tory "clique of nobles" to a national party supported by and supporting labor. *Laissez faire,* to which the Liberals, as the representatives of the Middle Class, were devoted, was attacked in the strongest terms. The Liberals were led "by a combination of oligarchs and philosophers who practice on the sectarian prejudices of a portion of the people." Public opinion, Disraeli continued, had not awakened to the seriousness of the situation. The country was really composed of "two nations, between whom there is no intercourse and no sympathy; who are as ignorant of each other's habits, thoughts, and feelings as if they were dwellers in different zones or inhabitants of different planets; who are formed by a different breeding and fed by a different food, are ordered by different manners, and are not governed by the same laws — the Rich and the Poor."[9] With subtle political instinct, Disraeli discerned that in England the two extremes, aristocrats and working class, had a common interest against the middle class, the creation of the new capitalism with its monopolist ownership of the means of production. "Tory democracy" gave radicalism the sanction of history.

The Liberals could only meet this strategem of the Conservatives by outbidding them. Gladstone, back in power, granted freedom to labor to create and belong to trade unions, and established a national educational system, a reform long overdue. The secret ballot was introduced and religious tests were abolished at the Universities.

The test of the British system, slowing broadening out "from precedent to precedent" came from World War I, not from the war itself, for the self-imposed restrictions and discipline of defense are merely temporary interruptions of the peacetime process, but from the disruption of world trade and loss of over-seas capital — a devastation less visible but as real as that of northern France. Instead of Britain becoming a fitting "home for heroes" as Lloyd George had promised the returning soldiers, factories closed as the world market declined and the unemployed lived largely on the "dole" of government support; a condition which grew worse instead of better until in September 1931 — the very time Japan started World War II in Manchuria — Britain went off the gold standard, which had long been the emblem of its financial empire.

[8] See Chapter XXI.

[9] Benjamin Disraeli, *Sybil or The Two Nations,* 1845,

Then the test of a free people held. For while discontent burst into the fury of revolution in Russia and tore down the safeguards of normal peaceful life in central Europe, the British strengthened Parliament by making it the architect of the "Welfare State," the farthest possible opposite of *laissez faire*. The Labor Party, drawing support from all who lived by working instead of by "owning," stood for policies of nonviolent socialism, "to secure for the producers by hand or by brain the full fruits of their industry and the most equitable distribution thereof that may be possible, upon the basis of the common ownership of the means of production and the best obtainable system of popular administration and control of each industry and service."

The claim of the "right to work or maintenance" remained more a slogan than a program, but the socialist measures included nationalization of mines, land, railways and electric power and a national minimum-wage law. Some of these were dropped by the Conservative government of 1957; but the welfare state continued for a generation to curtail fortunes by taxation and to better the living conditions and health of the working class. Its strength, however, lies not in its achievements so much as in the constant testing by its critics, both in parliament and out of it. The safety of this, as of all other creations of democracy lies in the vigilance and intelligence of those who maintain their independence of judgment. But, in Britain, the long road to freedom is at last on the uplands of social justice for all.

The American Way

A month before the Declaration of Independence, Richard Henry Lee of Virginia moved in the Continental Congress that a committee be appointed to draw up Articles of Confederation, but it was not until 1781 that the Articles went into effect by the consent of all the colonies. The failure of this league of sovereign states is so outstanding a chapter of history that we may leave it to the historians; but a new chapter begins with the making of the Constitution.

The debates in the Constitutional Convention which met in Philadelphia in 1787, and the speeches and pamphleteering throughout the country went back to fundamental principles. There were no models to go by in creating a federal state of this magnitude, and even for the gifted men who worked at it the going was hard. History was to show, by long controversies and the tragedy of civil war, that the problem of government under freedom could be adjusted to a changing world. The safeguards in the Constitution were two: the Bill of Rights, subsequently added in amendments, and the separation of the powers of the government itself.

It was natural that, the Revolution having been won, the chief concern of those who issued the call for the Constitutional Convention, was not freedom but property rights. There was every reason for concern. Property was imperilled, both by popular state legislation and the fear of widespread popular uprisings. But the only voice raised in the Convention in sincere concern for the rights of personal liberty was that of George Mason, who proposed that a bill enumerating the inalienable rights of the people, like that of his Virginia Declaration of Rights, should be inserted in the Constitution. When Gerry moved that a committee be appointed to draw up such a declaration, the Convention voted unanimously against it. Jefferson, who was absent as Minister to France, showed his concern over this drift of affairs. When, after the Constitution was drafted, Madison sent him a copy, he wrote back that "a Bill of Rights is what the people are entitled to against every government on earth, general or particular, and what no just government should refuse, or rest on inference."

The argument of the Federalists, Hamilton, Madison and Jay, on the other hand, was that a strong government would overcome the defect of a lack of specific guarantees of liberty by "that prompt and salutary execution of the laws which enters into the very definition of good government." It was not, however, uitil the 84th number of their serial publication, the *Federalist Papers,* that classic in American political theory, that they came squarely upon the issue stating "that the Constitution is itself in every rational sense and to every useful purpose A Bill of Rights," in the same way as "the several bills of rights in Great Britain form its constitution." The heavy artillery of the Federalists, however, could not prevail against the deep feeling of the people that a formal guarantee was called for against the possible development of tyranny in the newly-formed government. This protest was not what Hamilton would have called "the voice of the rabble." Its most powerful backer was still George Mason, to whom Jefferson in his old age paid tribute as one of the wisest among the statesmen of the time. Madison, the Father of the Constitution, apparently won over by the arguments of his Virginian friends, changed his Federalist standpoint for that of Mason, and finally, on June 8, 1789, he rose in Congress to propose the first Ten Amendments to the great document which had been so largely his creation.

It is not the purpose here to attempt to trace the history of the Bill of Rights throughout the nineteenth century. That is a task for the specialist in the history of law. It is not a theme which has played any large part in American history as taught in the schools. Even in recent years the widely read volume on *The Rise of American Civilization* by Charles and Mary Beard, while giving a good account of the making of the Constitution itself, passes over the first Ten Amendments without any mention of the Bill of Rights contained in them. Indeed, the term "Bill of Rights" does not appear in the Index of that volume. The explanation for this is perhaps partly to be found in the fact that there was another safeguard of freedom, both of person and of property, in the Constitution, provided in the independence of the judiciary.

The architect of that tripartite edifice of government which rests upon a separation of the Powers was not John Locke, but Montesquieu. The manual of the French jurist which was destined to play so great a part in our history, *The Spirit of the Laws,* was primarily drawn from a study of the way in which the Romans of the Republican period had broken up the universal powers of kingship into the appropriate divisions of government with especial reference to the evolution of Roman law. Montesquieu thought he discovered in the English Constitution a similar separation of powers. This was not Locke's point of view because he regarded the legislature as supreme. Nevertheless, the principle of the independence of the English judiciary as a bulwark against the extension of royal prerogative was one of the decisive gains of the English Revolution. There was therefore both French and English precedent behind the creation of a Supreme Court, the members of which were appointed for life, although it was left for John Marshall, by a broad interpretation of the Constitution, to give that court the place which it has come to occupy, not only in juristic theory, but in the public opinion of the country, as the safeguard of the Constitution against the violation of it by either the Legislative or Executive branches of the government. The extent to which the court has become "a palladium of liberty" in popular opinion was shown in the complete overthrow of a recent Executive effort, that of President Franklin Roosevelt, to weaken it.

The shape in which problems appear to each new generation is ever changing. The fundamental principles by which those problems must be tested remain the same but need to be re-stated from age to age in terms of the present. As this country filled up and its last frontiers were reached, new questions of social justice arose to challenge the conscience of men. The Bill of Rights, which had been a revolutionary product, now showed, in its new formulation in the Fourteenth Amendment, that it had also a conservative aspect. The question which arose, therefore and which even yet is by no means settled, was whether it would be possible to retain those liberties for which the Founding Fathers had mutually pledged their lives, their fortunes and their sacred honor, and at the same time to provide for the economically submerged of our nation the material basis without which, as George Mason may have meant to show in linking it with property, the pursuit of happiness may be but an illusion.

Not only because it is the clue to so much of the history of the United States, but also because it is so vital — if still unsolved — an issue in the politics of today, the text of the Bill of Rights, in the first Ten Amendments to the Constitution, follows:

Article I

Congress shall make no law respecting an establishment of religion, or prohibiting the free exercise thereof; or abridging the freedom of speech, or of the press; or the right of people peaceably to assemble, and to petition the government for a redress of grievances.

Article II

A well regulated Militia, being necessary to the security of a free State, the right of the people to keep and bear Arms, shall not be infringed.

Article III

No soldier shall, in time of peace be quartered in any house, without the consent of the Owner, nor in time of war, but in a manner prescribed by law.

Article IV

The right of the people to be secure in their persons, houses, papers, and effects, against unreasonable searches and seizures, shall not be violated, and no Warrants shall issue, but upon probable cause, supported by Oath or affirmation, and particularly describing the place to be searched, and the persons or things to be seized.

Article V

No person shall be held to answer for a capital, or otherwise infamous crime, unless on a presentment of indictment of a Grand Jury, except in cases arising in the land or naval forces, or in the Militia, when in actual service in time of war or public danger; nor shall any person be subject for the same offence to be twice put in jeopardy of life or limb; nor shall be compelled in any criminal case to be a witness against himself, nor be deprived of life, liberty, or property, without due process of law; nor shall private property be taken for public use, without just compensation.

Article VI

In all criminal prosecutions, the accused shall enjoy the right to a speedy and public trial, by an impartial jury of the State and district wherein the crime shall have been committed, which district shall have been previously ascertained by law, and to be informed of the nature and cause of the accusation; to be confronted with the witnesses against him; to have compulsory process for obtaining witnesses in his favor, and to have the Assistance of Counsel for his defence.

Article VII

In Suits at common law, where the value in controversy shall exceed twenty dollars, the right of trial by jury shall be preserved, and no fact tried by a jury, shall be otherwise re-examined in any Court of the United States, than according to the rules of the common law.

Article VIII

Excessive bail shall not be required, nor excessive fines imposed, nor cruel and unusual punishments inflicted.

Article IX

The enumeration in the Constitution, of certain rights, shall not be construed to deny or disparage others retained by the people.

Article X

The powers not delegated to the United States by the Constitution, nor prohibited by it to the States, are reserved to the States respectively or to the people.

These guarantees of personal freedom stand out with ever increasing clearness in the history of recent years, but the greatest guarantee of all lies neither in such instruments of government as the Constitution, nor even in the Bill of Rights. It lies in the capacity of the nation to make of them a "living Constitution," to use the words of a great jurist. On the hundred and fiftieth anniversary of the founding of the Constitution in 1939, Chief Justice Hughes, in an historic address to both Houses of Congress reminded the members that though the institutions of democratic government exist to interpret the will of the people, it is the demand of the citizen for individual freedom which gives it meaning.

Our guarantees of fair trial, of due process in the protection of life, liberty and property, which stands between the citizen and arbitrary power; our guarantees of religious freedom, of free press, free speech, and free assembly — these are the safeguards which have been erected against the abuses, which from time to time threaten, or gusts of passion and prejudice which in misguided zeal would destroy the very basis of democracy. But the firmest ground for confidence in the future is more than ever we realize that, while democracy must have its organization and its control, the vital breath is individual liberty.

There was an echo in this of de Tocqueville's *Democracy in America*, when, with uncanny insight, that first analyst of American institutions placed the vital strength of liberty not in the structure of the national government or even of the state government, but in the people themselves:

A sovereign power exists above these institutions and beyond these character-istic features which may destroy or modify them at its pleasure — I mean that of the people. . . . In America the people appoints the legislative and the executive power, and furnishes the jurors who punish all offences against the laws. The American institutions are democratic, not only in their principle but in all their consequences; and the people elects its representatives directly, and for the most part annually, in order to insure their dependence. The people is therefore the real directing power; and although the form of government is representative, it is evi-dent that the opinions, the prejudices, the interests, and even the passions of the community are hindered by no durable obstacles from exercising a perpetual influ-ence on society. In the United States the majority governs in the name of the people, as is the case in all the countries in which the people is supreme. This majority is principally composed of peaceable citizens, who, either by inclination or by interest, are sincerely desirous of the welfare of their country.[10]

Here, then, we come to the vital force in United States politics, the party system, through which the governments, national, state and local, act. In all free countries, it provides a check upon the party in power by the recognition of a party, or parties, of opposition, the absence of which in communist countries makes them the most serious, and dangerous, enemies of freedom. Where freedom of debate is treason, the fundamental conception of freedom is lacking.

The origin of the two great political parties in the United States goes back to colonial days, reflecting much the same outlooks as those of the English Tories and Whigs. The Revolution wiped out colonial Toryism, but the inherent differences between conservatives and radicals began to develop on a national scale under the presidency of Washington — Hamilton champion-ing the Federalists and Jefferson the Republicans. Washington's last adminis-tration was embittered by this growth of party conflict, which he deplored and tried to prevent. The Farewell Address, so often quoted only for its warning against entangling alliances, argued at greater length and with deep concern against the danger of factional passions destroying the unity of the nation. But Washington's high-minded conception of a free government without party lines was not destined to stand the test of practical politics. Indeed, there is a certain irony in it when we learn that the draft of the text

[10] Alexis de Tocqueville, *Democracy in America* (New York and London: Oxford Univer-sity Press, 1947), p. 110.

on which Washington relied was written by Hamilton, himself a leader of faction.

The Federalists, forming an oligarchy of wealth and talent, lost out in the election of 1800 and Jeffersonian democracy began almost a half century of political power, reaching its culmination in the eighteen thirties under Andrew Jackson, the hero of the frontiersmen, the small farmer, the poor and the shopkeeping classes. Against them the Whig leaders Clay and Webster, championed conservative policies. But already economic issues were yielding to the graver issue of slavery. The party of the Jeffersonian tradition, now known as the Democrats, came more under pro-slavery influence while the northern opposition organized a new party under the name Republican. The fact that both parties not only survived the Civil War but became still more the living embodiment of politics is the outstanding tribute to the inherent strength of a bi-party system which provides for a loyal opposition.

It was when party government was showing its most unlovely aspects in the spoils system under Jackson that de Tocqueville (anticipating John Stuart Mill) described it as something like a law of nature:

When the War of Independence was terminated, and the foundations of the new Government were to be laid down, the nation was divided between two opinions — two opinions which are as old as the world, and which are perpetually to be met with under all the forms and all the names which have ever obtained in free communities — the one tending to limit, the other to extend indefinitely, the power of the people. . . . All the domestic controversies of the Americans at first appear to a stranger to be so incomprehensible and so puerile that he is at a loss whether to pity a people which takes such arrant trifles in good earnest, or to envy the happiness which enables it to discuss them. But when he comes to study the secret propensities which govern the factions of America, he easily perceives that the greater part of them are more or less connected with one or the other of the two divisions which have always existed in free communities.[11]

De Tocqueville's survey was but the prelude to an ever-growing literature on the history and institutions of the United States, surveys which would have satisfied the surveyor who became the Father of his country, historically and politically sound, not the rhetorical assertion of principles in terms of sentiment or even of ideals, but an examination of the extent to which those principles were actually realized or capable of being realized along existing lines of action. Such a survey reveals an underlying unity in American life, in spite of conflicting interests and even war. Until toward the close of the nineteenth century there had always been a frontier to conquer; not a frontier as Europe had known it, with potential powerful enemies or competitive states beyond, but the frontier of wilderness and mountain barriers. While the influence of "the westward movement" lessened as the East and Middle West filled up, for most of their history the American people continued to be engaged in the same great enterprise which had occupied them as colonists. There were at least enough of the original conditions left to secure a con-

[11] *Ibid.* pp. 111 and 114.

tinuity and an almost unquestioned acceptance of the original theories of government.

It was not merely that the material conditions of life tended to repeat themselves in a long process of settlement; these settlements themselves repeated the original mould. Throughout the whole period of territorial growth, no community, however peculiar its social or religious tenets — as, for instance, Mormonism — was able to inject its incongruities into the political framework of statehood. The pattern laid down in the original states was spread across the continent.

At first sight this looks too rigid a scheme, too unadjustable to change in time and circumstance. The external resemblances which proudly bear the stamp of Washington, Madison, Jefferson or other Fathers of the Republic, conceal internal differences and modifications due to the exigencies of practical politics. There is mobility within the framework. The lessons learned by one State are taken on by another when a situation demands it, and these repercussions sooner or later reach through the whole Federal structure to the national government itself. The American system of government is, as Lord Bryce pointed out, a whole group of laboratories in the science of government, where tests can be made upon single sections of the country without involving the nation as a whole, until the previous results justify our trying it.

The uniform pattern of the commonwealth has, therefore, been something more than repeated outline; it is also of varied color in material setting and varied richness in human experience. But while the process of adaptation is continually going on in both local and national governments, the very existence of this formal mould, so wide-spread, so uniform, so apparently inevitable, makes more and more necessary the contribution of the historian. It is his duty to point out that the purpose in the minds of the creators of this system of politics was not that it should be used as a second-hand garment by a poverty-stricken political world or worn threadbare by generations too indolent to weave the fabric needed for their own protection, still less that it should be regarded as something sacred in itself, to be preserved from any questioning or any effort to adapt it to new situations and new demands. There would be no surer way to lose the heritage of freedom than to conceive of it in terms of its external mould. The validity of that mould depends upon its continuing effectiveness as the means for expressing the matured judgment of the people themselves; and those elements in either original design or copied pattern which stand in the way of free expression of this kind of critical thought imperil the heritage much more than the criticisms which may be directed against them.

This leads us to an important point. Fortunately it was a part of the philosophy of those English and French thinkers who furnished the basic political doctrines of the Fathers of the country that over against government itself there is a sphere of liberty which is to be preserved even as against the government itself. Montesquieu's theory of the separation of powers of government was adopted in the American Constitution in the separation of the executive, legislative and judicial functions. But there is a further separation still, which marks off the freedom of the individual over against the totality of government. This has been safeguarded in the United States, not only by the Bill of Rights and the courts, but by a kind of social contract, like that which made the unwritten English constitution a guarantee of freedom, but with the added strength that came from the self-reliance of a nation that was conquering a continent. The spirit of the frontier lasted on after the continent was won for settlement, but its task was confused by the development and the suppression of slavery and then by the rise of a new industrial era and the influx of a vast new immigration of workers in the closing years of the nineteenth century. As the nineteenth century moved along, the nation, strengthened by trial and matured in experience, held with unyielding persistence to its heritage of freedom. How this worked out in past centuries and how it determines action in the twentieth are dealt with in later chapters.

The Ways of Western Europe

Throughout the first half of the nineteenth century, Great Britain, in spite of its inadequacies, furnished the model of the national state for national state planners on the Continent who sought to safeguard freedom from reaction or revolution by framing national constitutions for representative governments. There was nothing new in this interest of European intellectuals and reformers in the English political system. It began in the early eighteenth century with Montesquieu and Voltaire and the Philosophes. But the French Revolution cut across this trend because both France and the other countries of the Continent lacked that long, slow education in politics from which the English had profited from the time of the Tudors and beyond.

The France of the old regime had not been a completely organized national state, in spite of the ruthlessness of Richelieu, the political finesse of Mazarin or the statesmanship of Turgot. It remained, for the most part, a congeries of provinces which had been acquired at different times by kings who did not weld them into a single unity, but left them their local systems, maintaining customs barriers between them almost as though they were foreign countries. The larger provinces had their local estates (parliaments), while the legal systems varied throughout the country. As the nobles were exempt from direct taxes, it was hardly an exaggeration for the taxpaying middle class to say, or have Siéyès say it for them in the National Assembly of 1789, that the third estate was the nation. In any case, the one lasting result of the Revolution was the creation of this new nationality, clothed with power.

But freedom also brought new responsibilities, and unfortunately the one responsibility on which all governments finally depend was not fully appreciated — the payment of taxes. It was all very well to make the nobility pay by abolishing their privileges, but the costs of government kept mounting with imperialist wars and increased domestic expenditures: buildings, roads, bridges and the like. So the propertied class has continued, even until today, to maintain some of that feeling against the tax collector which his ancestors had had before the Revolution. The result is that French liberalism has tended to be more a negative political force safeguarding the Republic against reaction than a positive force uniting the nation under it. The slogan of the Revolution, "liberty, equality, fraternity," is still emblazoned on the buildings of the government, but it means little more than it did in 1789 — the elimination of privilege rather than the full and free participation in the obligations of citizenship, which translates freedom into public spirit by eliminating the narrow selfishness of pure individualism.

In "the Germanies," as Madame de Stael properly termed the possessions of kings or princelings within the orbit of the old Holy Roman Empire, the national state system began to take shape when the shadowy sovereignty of the Empire came to an end by a resolution of its Diet in 1806 at the behest of Napoleon. While the Hapsburg monarchy, made up of many nationalities, did not fit into the new state structure, the reaction to the French Revolution in the rest of Germany was profound. The little principalities and prince bishoprics of the Middle Ages disappeared, leaving only Prussia, Saxony and Bavaria and a few other states grouped together in a loose confederation, which still acknowledged the presidency of Austria in its Diet at Frankfort. But more important than this new group of German states were two continuing influences of the French Revolution on their life and thought: nationalism and militarism. These, linked together, were to dominate the history of Western Europe in the nineteenth century, and bring ultimate disaster in the twentieth.

The prophet of nationalism whose influence on Germany in the nineteenth century was almost as profound and as perverse as that of Rousseau on France was the philosopher Fichte, who, in 1806-1807, the year after the disastrous Prussian defeat at Jena, delivered in Berlin his *Addresses to the German People,* which became a sort of classic to be read in time of victory as well as of national adversity. In the darkest hour of German history, shortly after Napoleon had used Berlin as a secondary capital from which to launch his decrees of continental blockade against Great Britain, Fichte spoke the language of the unconquered — and unconquerable.

Turning away from the noble universal concepts of the greatest of German philosophers, Emmanuel Kant, "the Copernicus of Philosophy," whose essay *Perpetual Peace,* like his *Critique of Pure Reason,* was addressed to all mankind, Fichte spoke in these lectures only to Germans, telling them what they wanted to hear. The future, he said, belonged to the Germans, the one superior race in the whole world, speaking a purer and more virile tongue than any decadent language that bore traces of enslavement under ancient Rome. As an inspiration to recovery from the contemporary enslavement under Napoleon, this weirdly unscientific rhapsody had the power to stir to martial prowess like the bards in the tribal wars of ancient times. But, coming from a renowned philosopher, it did irreparable damage to the world outlook of the German people.

A greater philosopher than Fichte, Hegel, did even greater damage by building a more imposing creation of a philosophy of history which carried conviction by its apparent realism as an interpretation of the past and present. World history was divided into three main periods: the oriental, the classical and the Germanic; the first that of single despots; the second of a dominant class; the third that of a regime of freedom. The theme of the whole human drama was freedom, and its last stage was, for Hegel, none other than the Prussia which Fichte had glorified. Many times, before and since, freedom has been identified with bureaucracy and militarism, but it is not to be forgotten that it was a student of Hegel, Karl Marx, who, by "turning the Hegelian system on end," as he said of it, produced the dialectic of socialism.

Nationalism was more than a philosophy in Germany; it was a reaction against defeat by France, shared widely and effecting the whole academic life, especially at the newly established University of Berlin. Student movements, even in athletics, kept alive the fires of patriotism, but in the intellectual sphere it was the historians who supplied the fuel for the fires. A new pride in the achievements of the German past began to replace the sense of present failures. The great collection of documents of medieval history, the *Monumenta Germaniae Historica,* offered a rich store of material, and German historical scholarship rose to primacy in Europe. But while the greatest of the historians, especially Leopold von Ranke, held to the disciplines of science, seeking only to reproduce the past as it actually had been, the most popular were those who made it the reflection of their own interests in nineteenth century Germany.

This nationalist trend of history culminated in the lectures and writings of Heinrich von Treitschke, whose *History of Germany in the Nineteenth Century* was a major influence on the generation of Bismarck's time. With winning frankness he stated his confession of faith: "The narrator of German history fulfills but half his task when he indicates the connection of events and expresses his views with frankness; he should also himself feel and should know how to awaken in the hearts of his readers what many of his countrymen have forgotten in the disputes and vexations of the moment, — a delight in the fatherland." Treitschke wasted no time in his history to prove that the German people had been and still were morally superior to the rest of mankind. By the mid-nineteenth century, his readers took that for granted. Nationalism had completely permeated German education.

The other nation which had not yet achieved unity, Italy, also produced its literature of protest and of hope. Indeed, more alluring than any poet of this poetry of the human spirit was Mazzini. The narrow intolerance of the German nationalism was entirely lacking in the intellectual leader of the *Risorgimento,* nor was there any trace of the cruel truculence of that other tutor of Italian patriotism, Machiavelli. Italy, which was still only what Metternich cynically called "a geographical expression," was for Mazzini "the home which God has given us, the home of those we love and are loved by, with whom we have a more intimate and quicker community of feeling and thought than with others. . . . In laboring truly for our country we are laboring for humanity. . . . But before associating ourselves with the nations which compose humanity, we must exist as a nation." Forced in his weakness to resort to conspiracy as the only weapon against the Austrian oppressor, Mazzini never accepted militarism as a system of safety and left for his country a heritage of democratic thought which, persisting through Fascism and reaction, still remains an inspiration.

At first thought it may seem strange that the greatest prophets of nationalism were in the nations of Europe that had not yet realized their destiny as national states — Germany and Italy. But this was also true of Asia, where, a century later, Sun Yat-sen in China and Ghandi in India awakened a new life in these ancient civilizations. The explanation is the same as in the prophets and founders of religions — the projection of great ideals to stir people who had never risen to their height before. In countries where nationalism could be taken for granted, as in historic England or isolated America working out destinies already charted by time and circumstances, patriotism was already an established creed. This did not prevent its recital on every possible occasion, but it was less a creative than a preservative faith in a political system accepted and familiar.

It is as the repository of independence, however, that nationalism comes into this history of freedom; and this opens up the greatest and still unsolved paradox that the supreme danger of the state has been met by a resort to it — war. The history of militarism has lain like an underlying motif in the whole epic of man, from the age of stone to that of the atom. At times it ushered in new eras of progress, as in the revolution of the ancient world when taboos made way for secular government, or in the Middle Ages, when the more powerful warlords established kingdoms in place of feudal anarchy. But the instrument of progress was also an instrument of disaster. And this lesson of history had to be learned all over again in the national state of the nineteenth century.

While militarism is as old as history, in its modern form it dates from the French Revolution, when the victories of the "nation in arms" led to a new era in military history, that of national conscript armies. In this development Prussia led. The utter humiliation of its defeat by Napolean never blotted out the memory of Frederick the Great; but even that enlightened monarch of the eighteenth century could never have conceived of the conscript army surreptitiously prepared by Scharnhorst under the very eyes of Napoleon's agents. Officership was no longer reserved for the young men of noble birth, although a military caste soon developed again, preserving the old tradition. As an institution, the army of Prussia was accepted generally as its outstanding manifestation of patriotism.

Already, at the opening of the nineteenth century, Prussia made its own the two doctrines of disaster in the twentieth century: that of German racial superiority and the absolute sovereignty of the state, with "blood and iron" as the final argument with other nations. There was no trace of that Jacobin nationalism which the French Revolution had once spread through central

Europe. After Waterloo, the dynastic age returned, with Tsar Alexander attempting to replace Napoleon as master of the fate of Europe, with Metternich from the unreconstructed court of Vienna directing for thirty years the forces of reaction, and with the Hohenzollerns in Prussia, and the Bourbons in France. Only Great Britain among the great powers, although tory in sympathy, held back from cooperating in the effort to blot out all traces of the revolution.

The era of reaction that set in ranged all the way from ruthless repression by police action to romanticism in literature — an escape not only from the realities of revolution but still more from the stern realism of eighteenth century critical thought. Fancy played with creative art and the Middle Ages lived again, not only in history and novels, but in the recovered texts of the *Nibelungenlied,* the *Chanson de Roland,* and *Morte d'Artur.* From Siegfried to Franz von Sickingen (the Götz von Berlichingen of Goethe) a thousand years of knighthood flowered, beguiled with the songs of troubadors and minnesingers, Bertrand de Born and Walter von der Vogelweide. The cultured circles of Europe turned to the same kind of escapism as that which replaced Puritan England with the uninhibited pleasures of the Restoration under Charles II. There were, of course, a few great figures who rose above both trends, revolutionary and reactionary, to see life whole — a Goethe at the little court of Weimar, a Beethoven at Vienna and sensitive souls like Wordsworth, who swayed with the storm and then sought peace in nature and the philosophic mind. But in their various ways, from the austere philosophy of Kant to the knight errantry of Byron, the voices of Europe carried echoes of the call to freedom, even when the great crusade itself died down at the courts of restored reaction.

The political scene had no such alluring human quality. The Congress of Vienna held by the Allied Powers on the abdication of Napoleon, had paid at least a left-handed tribute to the moral force of freedom by agreeing that the slave trade should be abolished as soon as possible, but in the Europe which they parcelled out among themselves they restored the old regime of privilege and oppression by police action at home and military action in such helpless countries as Italy and Spain. The decisions of the Congress were to be enforced by a Quadruple Alliance of Austria, Russia, Prussia and Great Britain, agreeing to hold meetings from time to time and to take such measures as might seem necessary to preserve order in Europe. This secret treaty was to become the basis for the "Concert of Europe," which, under Metternich's guidance, upheld the principle of rule by divine right of the "legitimate" sovereigns.

This practical program, ruthlessly applied, lasted in Central Europe until the second wave of revolutions in 1848. It should not be confused with the Holy Alliance, the contribution of the idealist Tsar Alexander. This was a pious document published in September, 1815, in which the monarchs, ruling as "delegates of Providence" over various branches of the human family, promised to base their policy on "the sublime truths which are taught by the eternal religion of God our Saviour." The Tsar and the King of Prussia were the only monarchs who took this alliance seriously; Metternich used it with cynical but deft diplomacy; but the English statesmen, with the same sense of practical expediency, discarded it utterly because the policies it shielded were building up an European system like that of Philip II of Spain or Louis XIV of France, designed to destroy the balance of power, which was the English formula for peace with freedom among nations.

The era of reaction which followed the French Revolution is often referred to as the era of Metternich; but that gives him too much credit, or discredit, for it was also the era of Alexander I and the unalleviated despotism of his successor Nicholas I, of a stupid Hohenzollern Frederick William III in Prussia — where the Junkers were to find a reactionary but far-sighted leader in Bismarck — and of all the lesser princes and princelings of Germany and Italy. In France the revolution had so completely remade the country that there was no "old regime" left to return to, and the restored king, Louis XVIII, brother of Louis XVI, not only left the administrative structure of Napoleon intact, but granted a constitution in the form of a *Charter*, reaffirming the essential freedoms, personal and religious. All citizens were declared to be equal before the law and eligible to civil or military positions; and all, without distinction of rank, were required to pay taxes in proportion to their means. In short, all the greater reforms proclaimed by the Declaration of the Rights of Man were guaranteed in this document, issued by a "king by the grace of God."

But the forces of reaction, mobilized in the returning *émigré* nobility, soon began to override the mild liberalism of Louis XVIII, and when he died, in 1824, his brother Charles X carried reaction to the extreme in enormous subsidies to the émigrés and finally in decrees forbidding the publication of any journal without royal permission and providing that in future all new laws were to be made by the king. The day after the edict was published (July 26, 1830), Paris was again in the throes of revolution. The street fighting lasted only three days, for the republicans who led in the revolt were joined by the middle class, whose leaders forced the abdication of Charles by choosing another king, his cousin Louis Philippe. The new king was himself bourgeois by temperament and after the revolutionary wars had lived two years in the United States, seven years in England, and then had come quietly back to Paris, keeping out of politics during the reaction.

Thus the middle class came back to power in France, with a king who really accepted constitutional limitations. The easy victory over reaction in Paris was repeated a month later in Brussels when the Belgians broke loose from the kingdom of the Netherlands to form one of their own. It seemed for a while as though the fires of revolution would spread over the Continent repeating the great conflagration of 1792, but the French bourgeois had no thought of repeating the republican excesses of the Jacobins at home or joining in crusades abroad. The middle class wanted to run things by and for itself, but it wanted to run them peacefully and not suffer from interruption or loss of trade. So, while there were some revolts in the Germanies and in Italy in 1830, the absence of French aid prevented major revolutions. Lesser

German States, Hanover, Saxony and Brunswick, won limited constitutional government, but Prussia and Austria remained bastions of reaction, and Metternich was able to send an Austrian army into Italy, to quell revolts there with ruthless cruelty. Still more tragic was the fate of the Polish patriots who revolted and for months withstood the might of the Tsar's armies, but who finally had to give up the dream of a restored Poland. The Grand Duchy of Warsaw, Napoleon's device which had been accepted at the Congress of Vienna, became Russian Poland.

Appropriately enough it was Greece, the ancient home of liberty, which was the first to rebel successfully against the tyranny of the Concert of Europe and establish its independence. It was a war without quarter on both sides, with revolting massacres; but the issue stirred liberals in Western Europe and Byron was not the only one to volunteer in the struggle for freedom. But the Greeks themselves had never learned that freedom given over to factional fights is only anarchy, and after eight years of the same kind of anarchy as had ruled ancient Greece, the Powers had to face the fact that Islam was establishing itself over the war-torn land and its islands, this time with Egypt in command.

This was more than the rulers of the Holy Alliance could stand, and the Tory government of Great Britain also, while it was as little inclined as they were to a renewal of the crusades, was forced by public opinion to join with Russia and Austria in a naval demonstration, which turned out to be a sea fight and victory, that of Navarino. More or less blunderingly and not in full agreement among themselves, the governments of the reactionary Powers had won the first victory for freedom after Waterloo, by establishing the kingdom of Greece (1829).

The other permanent gain for freedom from the dark chapter of the reaction was the episode which brought America into it: the suppression of revolution in Spain, which planned to suppress it as well in the Spanish colonies in America. These had thrown off the Spanish yoke in a series of revolutionary movements under the inspiration of leaders like Bolivar and San Martin. Metternich had secured the use of French troops to crush a rebellion against the restored Bourbon king, Ferdinand of Spain, which resulted in a repression so brutal that it horrified Europe. When it was proposed to use the same means to restore the rule of Spain in the colonies, Canning, the British Foreign Minister, proposed to the American Ambassador that Great Britain and the United States make a joint *demarch* against this extension of the Continental system to the New World.[12] President Monroe chose to take action alone, and in his message to Congress in December, 1823, stated clearly what has become known as the Monroe Doctrine, that the United States would consider any attempt on the part of the European Powers to extend their system to any part of the western hemisphere as dangerous to the peace and safety of the United States and as an unfriendly act.

[12] It was also a warning to Russia not to attempt to extend its foothold on the Pacific coast.

This pronouncement was one of the most important gains in the history of political freedom of the first half of the nineteenth century. The fact that it had an English background does not in any way lessen its significance in American history; nor the added fact, too little realized in the United States, that throughout that century, it was the British navy, in the absence of adequate United States seapower, which was the guarantee of Spanish American freedom. The doctrine was sincerely meant and would undoubtedly have been upheld if the test had come; for when, in the twentieth century, it actually did come, there was no hesitation in American opinion on the question of war with Spain. In any case, United States history can register the fact that the one principle of its foreign policy which it cherished as its own was a doctrine of freedom.

In France, although the reactionary rule of King and nobles had been swept away in the revolution of 1830, the promise of that revolution, liberty under constitutional government was made good only for a short time. (Louis-Philipe in his youth had been a Jacobin, but all trace of that doctrine had been wiped away in twenty-two years of exile, spent partly in the United States and in England.) Great Britain was then at the height of its prestige and its constitution therefore became the model, not only for France, but for all liberals on the Continent. But it was the England of the unreformed parliament, of rotten boroughs and oligarchic rule; and its chief appeal to a wartorn continent was not that it was perfect in theory but that it worked, and that under it the British people had not only fought the greatest war in history, but were becoming rapidly wealthier by their mastery of the Industrial Revolution.

The French copy had all the defects of the English model. Although Louis-Philippe began by a gesture of liberalism, restoring the tricolor of the Revolution instead of the Fleur de Lys of the old regime, granting freedom of the press and assembly and a cabinet responsible to parliament instead of to the king, yet liberalism in France was — and still remains — conservative, utterly unlike that of the liberals who led the Reform movement in England. For five years the new privileged conservative middle class watched with apprehension the growth of discontent, expressed with that forthrightness which is the birthright of the Gaul, in meetings, journalism and such satirical cartoons as those of Daumier, "the Michelangelo of caricature"; then all pretense of liberalism was thrown aside in the famous "September Laws" of 1835. Republican journals were suppressed, their editors fined or imprisoned; it was made a crime to criticize the king, who now began personal rule, choosing his cabinet without consulting parliament.

The evil genius of this middle class reactionary rule, which became as corrupt as it was irresponsible, was Francois Guizot the historian of the English Revolution and of the Civilization of Europe, whose works are still among the classics of history. Personally incorruptible, this Huguenot successor of Richelieu, while professing liberalism, never understood the saving quality of the parliamentary system, the provision for a loyal opposition ready to take over the government when the party in power loses the confidence of the nation. The alternative to an unyielding government is revolution, as France and the other Continental countries learned by sad experience when the long stagnation of the Concert of Europe was broken by the revolution of 1848. Guizot failed to see that the surest safeguard for national stability is in party government, responsive to the will of the people at all times.

There was no parliamentary reform in France as in England, and the suffrage was limited to two hundred thousand in a population of some thirty-five million, in which the industrial revolution had begun to create a new rich bourgeoisie, discontented at its exclusion from politics, and a growing proletariat ready to link up with the elements of Jacobin republicanism which still persisted. But France was largely a peasant country, in spite of the growth of industrialism in the cities, and for eighteen years Louis-Philippe was able to hold the country in political stagnation. This surface calm was broken by eloquent protests from writers and speakers, from the republicanism of Lamartine to the socialism of Louis Blanc and Ledru-Rollin, or the mordant wit of the artist Daumier and the poet Heine. But neither Guizot nor his king took warning, and were taken by surprise when the populace of Paris rose on the afternoon of February 24, 1848, and, invading the Tuileries, in a few hours overthrew the monarchy and proclaimed a republic on the site of the Bastille and at the Hotel de Ville.

The tricolor remained its symbol instead of the red flag of socialism, but "national workshops" were established for the unemployed. This concession to the socialists was carried out by those who connived in its failure, but the extent of the sufferings of the workers due to the industrial revolution in France can be measured by the fact that, in their desperate need, over a hundred thousand thronged for a pay of two francs a day to do what they knew was unproductive work, the building of fortifications around Paris. When in the elections of April the conservatives returned to power and the national workshops were abolished, the barricades went up in the streets in a futile uprising which was ruthlessly suppressed by the army, drawn from the middle class and the peasantry. Over ten thousand men were killed or wounded, and great numbers more were imprisoned or deported. The "days of June" 1848 were never forgotten or forgiven by the working class. They opened a chasm between it and the bourgeoisie in France which, widened still more by the similar rise and repression of the Commune in 1871, has never been wholly closed.

In every capital of Europe the news of the February revolution spread dismay among the reactionary rulers. Metternich declared that "Europe finds herself today in the presence of a second 1793." This seemed at first to be the case. In March, the populace of Vienna rose and Metternich fled. The Austrian emperor accepted constitutions for the kingdoms of Hungary and Bohemia as well as for the Austrian provinces, with all the guarantees of personal freedom. In Italy there were movements for freedom and constitutions in Naples, Rome, Tuscany and Piedmont, and Italy began its first war for independence against Austria. In Germany, reform movements swept over Baden, Wurtemberg, Bavaria and Saxony, but in Prussia the situation was more confused. Frederick William IV was an unbalanced eccentric who, when the Prussian Diet attempted to claim oversight over the budget, stated the Hohenzollern thesis in the classic phrase that he would never allow "to come between Almighty God in Heaven and this land a blotted parchment, to rule us with paragraphs, and to replace the ancient bond of loyalty." Yet when news reached Berlin that Metternich had fallen, and rioting broke out, the king in his fear of riots and his love for histrionics headed a procession around the streets of the city wrapped in a German flag. For a short interval the Prussian autocracy seemed not only to accept the new liberalism, but to lead it. But the end was as in France. By 1849 the constitution of Prussia was recast to meet the wishes of the reactionary Junkers and the Hohenzollern monarchy of the old tradition.

The end of the dream of 1848 came soon in Austria as well. Young Francis Joseph ascended the throne, which he was to occupy for sixty-eight years. The Hungarian patriot Kossuth was defeated, fleeing to the United States, and the Tsar joined his forces to those of Austria to suppress Hungarian liberty, taking terrible vengeance in a reign of terror in which thousands were hanged, shot or imprisoned. The uprisings in Italy were also put down in blood, leaving only the little territory of Piedmont, which a young king, Victor Emmanuel, was later to make the basis of a kingdom of Italy.

The climax of the 1848 movements in Germany was the attempt of liberals to revive the medieval empire in modern dress as a parliamentary federation. Frankfurt, the old city of imperial coronations, saw a representative assembly draw up plans for unification without resort to arms. But the revolutionary movement was divided between moderate liberals and radicals, and while the Frankfurt assembly debated on theories of political reform, the forces of reaction, recovering their ground in Vienna and Berlin and in the lesser German states, turned on the revolutionary parliament and swept it away, leaving only disillusionment in liberal circles.

In France, the Second Republic, born in disaster, continued in political incompetence. It placed all executive powers in the hands of a president elected by popular vote, and placed in this office one of the great adventurers of history, Louis Napoleon, nephew of the Emperor. The Legislative Assembly, monarchist and reactionary, played into his hands and he dissolved it by a *coup d'état* "To save the country and the Republic from harm" on December 2, 1851, the anniversary of Austerlitz. He then ordered a referendum or "plebiscite," asking the nation if it supported his act. The vote was a majority of almost seven million in his favor. It was a clever device, for no alternative course was offered the nation, and a year later it ratified his assumption of the title "Emperor of the French."

The Second Empire began with a regime of absolutism, controlling the elections and the press and dismissing university professors who refused to comply with it, including such distinguished men as Michelet, the historian, and others. But the Emperor was genuinely concerned with the welfare of the working class. He arranged for arbitration in industrial disputes, granted subsidies for old age and sickness insurance and, from 1859 on, began progressively to liberalize his regime, allowing political exiles to return, relaxing control of the press, and finally (1867-69) turning to a former Republican, Emile Ollivier, to establish a "liberal Empire," one "crowned with liberty . . . equally removed from reaction and revolutionary theories."

These concessions, far from winning over the Republican opposition, merely made it more vocal. Leadership of these irreconcilables was won by a young lawyer, Léon Gambetta, who charged the Second Empire with being criminal in origin and tyrannical in rule. His oratory rang throughout France. "On the second of December there grouped themselves around a pretender men whom France had never known, men without talent, without honor, without position; men of the type who at all times have been the organizers of conspiracies. . . . And these men had the audacity to pretend that they were the saviors of France. . . . The time will come when the country will impose upon you a great national expiation in the name of Liberty, Equality and Fraternity."

The time came after Sedan, when this same Gambetta proclaimed the fall of the Emperor at the Legislative Assembly, and the establishment of a republic at the Hotel de Ville. A Third Republic was by no means certain, however. Royalists dominated the National Assembly, and Paris suffered the terrors of the Commune and its merciless suppression in which thousands were shot down in a slaughter worse than that of 1848. It was only because the royalists could not agree among themselves, and because the pretender to the throne, the Comte de Chambord, insisted on replacing the tricolor with the lily flag of the old regime, that a provisional settlement was reached in a series of "organic laws" which avoided using the term "Republic." But finally, by a majority of one, the National Assembly designated the head of the state "President of the Republic." The first election went overwhelmingly Republican and the President, MacMahon, though a royalist, was forced to accept a Republican ministry. The Catholic church was strongly on the side of the royalists, and Gambetta gave the Republicans the rallying cry "Le clericalisme, voilà l'ennemi" — which remained a slogan of the Republic until the separation of church and state in 1905. The other danger to Republicanism was militarism, and this was ended by the strong republican government after the Dreyfus case.

The history of the Third and Fourth Republics is one of the anomalies of the history of freedom. Judged by the frequency of changes of ministries, it seems to be an utter condemnation of democratic government. But the French parliament, fragmented by faction and personal loyalties, had a more consistent record in domestic reforms than that of either Great Britain or the United States, where the bi-party system prevails. But this record, little known abroad, was blurred by partisan antagonisms at home which cast increasing discredit upon the Republic. Then, to the catastrophic losses in two world wars was added the loss of the colonial empire in Asia and the threat of its entire loss in Africa. As, in times of crisis, the Roman republic had entrusted its liberties to a dictator, so France listened to the man who had led the resistance in World War II, General de Gaulle, and in a peaceful revolution went back to the type of government which Louis Napoleon had established by plebiscite in 1851. All executive powers are left to the President, unimpeded by a quarreling Chamber of Deputies. Apparently the history of political freedom in France had gone the full circle. But this may prove not to have been the case. There is no monarchist plotting against the state and no Imperial tradition behind de Gaulle. Whatever the future may hold, there is no doubt that only a dictator — for he acted like one — could preside over the transformation of the French colonial empire into a commonwealth. But of that we have more to say later.

It would be misleading, however, to judge the contributions of France by its politics. Just as in the old regime, the chief glory of France now lies in its intellectual and cultural achievements, in literature, philosophy, art and science; nor has there been any lack of appreciation for the leaders in these nonpolitical fields. A single incident is revealing. Some years ago a Parisian newspaper had a national poll on the greatest Frenchman of the nineteenth century. Napoleon was not even second on a list which Pasteur led by an immense majority. In the light of national attitudes like this, the tragedy of a proud but thrice-smitten nation can be understood.

CHAPTER XV

A NEW AGE IN PEACE AND WAR

The Meaning of Invention

GREAT AS WERE the effects of the political revolution which made the national state the instrument for freedom and justice, the eighteenth and nineteenth centuries were to witness an even greater revolution, greater than any other in all history, one which opened up a wholly new horizon for civilized living — the rise of modern science and its application to take over the day's work of the common man. This is not only the greatest event in our time; it is the greatest in all time. It is the one underlying fact which gives the final meaning to all the rest, for it is the measure of the control of power both by individuals and by nations. And power is sovereignty whether it is applied to the relations of men in society or to the lonely fields of philosophic thought. Freedom to think is therefore the key to all freedoms.

Throughout all the centuries of the past, power was man-power. This was equally true of the individual worker and of the ruler who mobilized men for that other form of labor which registered power most directly — war. Either in working or in fighting, the tools men used were little more than aids to their brute strength. This meant that power in the last analysis was strength of muscle, individual strength or that of the mass. Political power was measured by the amount of physical strength it could control, and economic welfare was based upon the same fundamental application of strength or expertness to labor. To be sure, the mind that controlled these forces gave them direction and purpose, but all the techniques of peace or war were but the extension of the animal capacity of man to win his way and hold his own against the contending forces of nature.

The claws which became our hands a million years ago, the nerves which became our brains, the physical habits which we must still satisfy, all of the attributes of mankind whose rudiments lie as far the other side of the ice age as we do this side — this inheritance of our evolution has been the key to our history down to our own day. And there is still more in each of us from the other side of the ice age than from this side. But at last, just in the world of today, we are turning from this animal inheritance to something new. The nerves in our brain cells are apprehending the world differently from anything that could be called knowledge in the distant past. There have been, it is true, pre-visions of these possibilities in the minds of oriental and medieval philosophers, and especially in the pioneering science of Ancient Greece. But never before our day did science attempt to take over the conduct of daily life as has been the case wherever machines have been set to work.

The significance of the rise of modern science can be seen only in the light of this long perspective of human evolution. Almost overnight we are suddenly launched upon the second million years. We have no clear idea and can have none as to the kind of world which lies ahead, except for one fundamental fact, that mind will more and more take the place of muscle, that intelligence will more and more not only rule brute strength but replace it by other powers and forces. This means that the society of the future, at whose portals we stand today, will have basis other than that of the groping animal past; and yet the thing with which it will have to deal, man himself, will continue to hold as in a fusing reservoir the appetites, desires and passions that come from the fact, from which there is no escape, that he himself is after all an animal.

When science invented the machine it created a substitute for man to do his work for him. This was something wholly different from the tool which helps the man to do his work but leaves him still the worker. The machine supplies power to the tool so that man as the worker needs only to step aside and make the machine take his place, supplying it with power and fitting it to its appointed task. But he cannot do this without disturbing both his own routine of life and that of the society in which he lives. For the machine has unlimited capacity for production and unlimited strength of endurance in its iron and steel. Thus there grows up alongside mankind another population in the world, driven by steel or electricity or the power of combustion, and making all kinds of things, great and small, with infinitely more precision than the most skillful hand and infinitely vaster than all the energy of all past ages put together.

This new scientific era is not a mere passing interlude in human affairs like the splendor of Greece or the beauty of the Renaissance. It provides for its own continuance and will never stop. Every new invention creates a displacement in society which in turn calls for other discoveries; if it breaks down, it stimulates further invention to meet the social needs. So we pass from the quiet centuries where habit and routine perpetuate the past into an era of perpetual change, of continual increase in the control of nature and continual added need of social readjustments.

The past presents a fundamentally different picture from this. In it men mostly did the things their fathers had done generation after generation under similar conditions. The farmer's life was one of repetition, bound by the iron routine of the calendar. Seed-time and harvest brought their accustomed tasks at the same time year after year, century after century, and the self-contained economy of the isolated farm or manor changed but little. George Washington's estate at Mount Vernon was almost exactly what Aristotle described in Ancient Greece; the household economy for which he used the word "economics." Now there are no Mount Vernons in any highly industrialized nation. It is not only slaves that are gone but the independence of its economy. From dawn until dark the world outside is drawn upon for what the household needs; most of the produce of the estate is consumed in distant cities, and the owner maintains his luxuries by investments in stocks that are on all the money markets of the world.

But the new industrial era cannot escape from the two fundamental laws of economics — those of supply and demand. The raw materials must be available and there must be markets for the finished articles. And here we come upon the central problem of international relations, for the world has been settled by peoples and nations wholly without regard to the economy of science. The frontiers that have been traced, behind which nations have been attempting to work out their national prosperity, were drawn without any relation to the distribution of raw materials or their natural markets. The reason for this was that they were drawn mostly by farmers or those who lived from the products of the soil, and by merchants seeking either to barter goods or exploit the resources of weaker people. Above all, military power determined where the frontiers should run, and it was the surface of the earth and not the riches that lay beneath it which soldiers and statesmen had in mind when settling where the boundaries should run. Today a wholly new world of natural resources has come to our knowledge, and the relationship between it and the centers of industry is one of the most pressing of all international problems.

But marketing is equally as important, for the old boundaries block the path to natural centers of distribution, and the old conception of trade as a technique for getting the better of the customer makes the political frontiers effective economic barriers as well.

The result is that the whole mechanism of international trade is held back by a system of society which has no proper relationship to the real needs of the peoples composing it. The countries of today are the creations of the pre-scientific era. This applies to those that have been created most recently as well as to those with a longer past; because the forces which called them into existence were not those of science or engineering but an entirely different set of causes. The modern nation needs raw materials and markets as the very condition of its existence, but it is the expression of something wholly different from either science or economics. It is the embodiment of all the attitudes of mind that come from common habits of work and of living together. This reservoir of like-minded attitudes is strongest where society repeats the immemorial things with the least amount of change. The sense of nationality is therefore fundamentally at variance with the rational processes of science, but statesmanship consists in making just such discordant elements fit into a harmonious whole, and the supreme task of statesmanship today is to secure for science a *modus vivendi* with nationalism, recognizing the sovereignty which it exercises in the minds of men, but providing at the same time for the potent forces of the future which will not be denied because they hold the key to prosperity.

Thus the revolution in science and industry has brought about a fundamental change in the two most important things in all of man's experience: work and thought — the day's labor and the inquiring mind. Until our own time these two activities seldom met. It seems incredible now that this greatest event in secular history should not have been appreciated in its full magnitude until over a century from that fateful year in 1776 when the steam engine began to replace hand and water power. The name "Industrial Revolution" was not given it until, at the turn of the nineteenth century, Arnold Toynbee (uncle of the famous historian) wrote a book with that title, after he, an Oxford scholar, had gone to live in the London slums among the wage slaves of the industrial system. The problems of labor and capital had been, in the English manner, treated as practical matters of political strategy between the new monopolists of freedom, a capitalist class growing rich from ownership of the means of production, and a working class to whom the word freedom was a mockery. England was turned to an industrial battlefield, in which coal and iron, the source and the embodiment of power, covered the sky and earth of the smiling central countryside with black smoke and slag. The same was true, a little later, of the German Ruhr, the French Pas de Calais and the industrial areas of the United States.

Yet there was more than wage slavery, or the new ugliness of country and city slums; it was the dawn of a new way of life. The full significance of it escaped the intellectual world, concentrating on the economics of it and the problems of *laissez faire*, radicalism and socialism. The first philosopher to see it whole as a complete revolution, not only in industry but in the history of thought, was Henri Bergson, whose challenge to classical philosophy in his *Creative Evolution* was the sensation of fifty years ago. His eloquent tribute to the Industrial Revolution implies a new approach to the problem of freedom, not merely in the economic and political spheres but in every aspect of life:

A century has elapsed since the invention of the steam-engine, and we are only just beginning to feel the depths of the shock it gave us. But the revolution it has effected in industry has nevertheless upset human relations altogether. New ideas are arising, new feelings are on the way to flower. In thousands of years, when, seen from the distance, only broad lines of the present age will still be visible, our wars and our revolutions will count for little, but the steam-engine, and the procession of inventions that accompanied it, will perhaps be spoken of as we speak of the bronze or chipped stone of pre-historic times: it will serve to define an age. If we could rid ourselves of all pride, if, to define our species, we kept strictly to what the historic and pre-historic periods show us to be the constant characteristics of man and of intelligence, we should perhaps not say Homo Sapiens, but Homo Faber.

History has justified this vision. Art, literature and philosophy had pursued their ideals with little regard for the conditions of the life of the common man; at last they were brought together in a new process, that of the machine. The machine is thought in action, the perpetuation of the thought of the inventor. Its operations replace those of the workman whose job it is simply to make sure that the machine keeps working at full capacity. This capacity changes with each new invention, so that, instead of the continual repetition of hand-labor, we have continued change in both methods of work and output. The past and future were once alike; now they are forever and increasingly different.

Scientific discovery remakes time and space, and invention enables man to asume the mastery of the material world. For the future it holds promise of ever-increasing betterment and of man's ultimate release from unremitting toil as well as from want and poverty. And yet, if we consider the past, the present and the immediate future, we must admit that the first effects of this still-young revolution are by no means reassuring. The emergence of this new power, by disturbing the accustomed ways of living, brings new problems of adjustment, and will continue to do so throughout the future, because the force for change — intelligence in action — has started upon a career which will never cease.

The Factory System

The new industrial era began in one of the oldest of all industries, the spinning of thread and the weaving of cloth. In the very years of the American Revolution, an obscure revolution was taking place in the cottages of England where wool was being spun and woven into cloth. The spinning jenny, invented in 1764, was a frame of spinning wheels fitted with upright spindles, all working together, so that one spinner could do the work of several. Only five years later this was elaborated into the "mule," which could be run by water power. Then, in 1785, the power loom was invented, which could weave automatically. The hand spinners and hand weavers became factory employees.

Both machines and power were owned by capitalists, whose wealth kept increasing with the vastly increased output, while the condition of the workers grew steadily worse — their labor, the only thing they had to live on, being steadily lessened in value by the competition of the machine and by their own competition in the labor market. The greatest distress was among the hand weavers, unable to earn a living wage and forced by starvation to move from their village homes to the crowded tenements of factory towns, where the over-supply of labor gave the factory owner the opportunity to employ them at low wages for long hours.[1] Since the labor in textiles was largely confined to watching the machines, piecing broken threads and working levers, women and children could be as useful as men and be paid even less. The result was social demoralization as well as economic hardship.

The first effect of the factory system belongs in the history of freedom because it was the first chapter in the unrestricted freedom of the middle class, and because it denied freedom to the working class, which was to struggle for sovereignty in many a movement of reform and revolution down to today. There is another reason for pausing to take evidence on the tyranny of the capitalist in this first era of his economic sovereignty: the record shows how evil a thing freedom can be when it is not shared by all. The industrial revolution had no such reign of terror as that of the Jacobins, but, instead of the guillotine, its victims faced wage slavery from childhood to early death. Medical evidence in the Report of the Factory Commission of 1834 stated that in the Lancashire mills 60 per cent of the workers were under sixteen years of age, and only 6 per cent were above forty.

The most poignant stories are those of the children, many of them brought from the "work houses" and all of them without previous education. The Factory Act of 1834 (in full force by 1836), revealing the evils it sought to correct, provided that no child under nine should be employed in any except silk mills, and none under thirteen should work more than nine hours a day. The children were mostly scavengers, employed to keep the machinery in good running condition, and therefore had to be at work all the time. Every moment they had to spare they were stretched at full length on the floor and strapped by the factory operatives, who had to keep the children at their heart-breaking work, especially toward the end of the nine or ten hour day, when they were so tired that they were likely to have accidents. "When the children are at work in the evening, the very first thing they ask is 'What o'clock is it?' and if it is only seven they say, 'Only seven; it is a great while to ten, but we mustn't give up till then!' "[2]

Such was the life of a child in the mills, but even worse was that of the children and women in mines, as the need for coal drove the shafts deeper and farther along tunnels so low that the carriers could not stand upright. In a supplement to the Report of 1834, we read: "They have found out where children are beaten with straps and sticks; but not where they were beaten with pick-axes. They have found out where they work in tempera-

[1] A parliamentary Report on the handloom weavers in 1834 supplied evidence that weekly earnings ran as low as 10 shillings a week, with a working day of 13 hours — until 10, 11 or 12 at night. Yet the commissioners had no recommendations to make, and only asked that the inquiry should be continued. There were over 800,000 dependent upon the industry.

[2] From Sadler's Commission, 1831-32, vol. XV, pp. 74, 79 ff.

tures between seventy and eighty, but not where they work in 112, and where it is hot enough to melt tallow candles. They have found out where they are imperilled from carelessness at machinery, but not where their lives are never safe. . . . They have found out where they sometimes have to work at night amid the glare and heat of lamps, but not where they never work otherwise, even by day. They have found out their places of work are eight or nine feet high, but not where they are eighteen inches. . . . In a word, they have found out where their labors, though hard, are comparatively light and easy, and have disregarded those occupations in which infant slavery is so severe as would seem to make life a torment and death a mercy."

The comments on these conditions by defenders of the factory system seem now to be singularly naive, if not callous. A Doctor Aiken, in his *Description of Manchester*, writing in 1795, begins his account with the reminder that "the invention and improvements of machines to shorten labor has a surprising influence to extend our trade and to call in hands from all parts, especially children, for the cotton mills. It is the wise plan of Providence that in this life there is no good without its attendant inconveniences."

More important than these reactionaries was the prevalent doctrine of *laissez faire* which, embraced by the reformers of the Reform Bill of 1832, made most of them as rigid opponents of government interference in business as their Tory predecessors had been. They, as well as the factory owners and the leading economists, maintained that the government should not attempt to regulate the price of goods or their quality. Neither should it interfere with the employer and his workmen, except to protect them from violence. Nor should it fix the hours of work, or try to remedy the conditions in the factories. Prices, they maintained, should be kept down by competition among the manufacturers, and wages could be fixed by supply and demand. The government, in fact, should not attempt to interfere in any way with this new economic life. To tamper with the iron law of economics would only make matters worse.

The chief trouble with this political and economic theory was that it did not work well in practice. On the contrary, the great manufacturing cities, instead of being filled with happy and prosperous people, became filled with multitudes of poor working people who had to compete with each other in an oversupplied market, and who often did not earn enough to keep their families above the starvation level. In other words, economic freedom carried to the extreme resulted in economic slavery, just as political freedom carried to the extreme creates anarchy. In both cases society needs protection against arbitrary action, whether the tyranny be that of kings, or capitalists, or mobs.

Much less easy to explain is the attitude of religion, not merely that of the established church, but even of the Methodist revival and the new growth of nonconformist chapels. There was a new moral outlook as the result of the movement, but the facts of economics were rigidly applied as they were accepted, and it was part of a Christian's duty to accept the lot which God had assigned to him. There was no disparity between *laissez faire* liberalism and the teachings of the Sunday School. Sometimes the result was an indifference to social questions, while concentrating upon the supreme issue of salvation. There was nothing new in this. The medieval motto, *miser est res sacra,* is still to be seen inscribed on religious establishments, meaning that poverty may be a discipline for the life of the spirit. But even the Franciscans, while embracing this doctrine, were led by human sympathy to minister to the needs of the poor. In England, the religious fervor of the Methodist revival also developed its social counterpart in the "nonconformist conscience" which ultimately became a guiding monitor for the nation, becoming a chief agent it its reform.

While the debates in Parliament and more especially the reports of its commissions of investigation remain the prime sources of our history of the period, it is also mirrored in literature. The change in the life and interests of England during the industrial revolution is marked by the distance between Sir Walter Scott's romantic revival of the Middle Ages and the works of Charles Kingsley and the young Disraeli, both of them depicting the England of the early forties, in which the oppressed working class was becoming restive. But more soul-searching than these theories of reform disguised as novels was a single poem by Elizabeth Barrett Browning, *The Cry of the Children.* Even today it wrings the heart of any sensitive reader:

> Do you hear the children weeping, O my brothers. . . .
> They are weeping in the play time of the others,
> In the country of the free. . . .
> They look up with their pale and sunken faces
> And their look is dread to see. . . .

No indictment of *laissez faire* capitalism could be stronger than this poem by the sheltered daughter of a rich London banker.

Reform or Revolution

To redress the evils created by the industrial revolution, three movements developed: a reform movement in politics; the rise of the trade unions among the workingmen; and a new doctrine known as socialism. It would carry us too far into the internal history of each country to trace the origins of these movements in detail, but the central issue in world politics today — the divisions between "free" nations and those under communist rule — cannot be understood without a short survey of their background.

The movement for reform by legislation began in England in the "Factory Acts," which in the course of twelve years from 1833 to 1845 limited the hours of work of children under eleven years of age to nine a day and that of women to twelve. These acts prohibited the employment of children in mines, and, for the first time, provided general rules for the health and safety of the workers. Ways were found, however, to postpone or evade many of these legal safeguards, and the working class began to demand not merely the protection of laws but the right to share in their making. Their program was set forth in a Charter, first drafted in 1839, then recast in a great national Chartist movement in 1848, which was the British parallel of the revolution of that year on the Continent. The Reform Bill of 1832, which brought the middle class to power, still excluded workingmen and farm hands from the vote, yet so great was the prestige of Parliament, that the Charter, drafted by the workers, concentrated on the suffrage instead of remedial legislation. Its six points were: universal suffrage, secret voting, equal electoral districts, no property qualifications for members, payment of members and annual elections. The Chartist demands were set forth in a petition which was alleged to have three million signatures, and the procession presenting it to Parliament was two miles long.

But this first great demonstration of British democracy did not shake the resolution of the defenders of middle-class rule. Reformers or Liberals were as bitterly opposed to it as was the Duke of Wellington, under whom a quarter of a million special constables kept law and order at the height of the crisis in 1848. Lord John Russell, the sponsor of the Reform Bill, said that "even to discuss such demands would bring into question the ancient and venerable institutions of the country," and Macaulay, the historian of the English Revolution, said "universal suffrage would be fatal to all purposes for which government exists. . . . I conceive that civilization rests upon the security of property." Although the Chartists continued to draw up petitions, Parliament refused to accept them, and the movement ended in fiasco. They were not revolutionists at heart, as their regard for Parliament showed, and Parliament ultimately granted all their demands but one, that of annual parliaments.

The trade-unions, which were formed by workingmen in the various trades and industries to protect themselves against their employers, were quite different from the medieval guilds, which had included both capitalists and laborers. At first the English law forbade these unions, but by 1824 Parliament permitted them to exist although hampered by various restrictions. The method of the trade-unions was that of direct action, using the strike either to force employers to grant their demands or to influence the government to push labor legislation. Throughout the nineteenth century, the unions were at a disadvantage because they were divided among the different industries, and thus lacked national unity. At the end of the century, however, a General Federation of British Trade Unions was founded which established friendly relations with the unions that had already been taking shape in Germany and other Continental countries. The labor unions of the United States were organized into the American Federation of Labor in 1886. Nonrevolutionary in character, but class-conscious, the trade unions formed an important element in the political as well as in the economic structure of nineteenth century Europe.

Of far greater political significance than the trade union movement was the development of socialism. The pioneers of socialism in the first half of the nineteenth century were idealists who agreed with Saint-Simon, the founder of French socialism, that "the whole of society ought to strive toward the amelioration of the moral and physical existence of the poorest class; society ought to organize itself in the best way adapted for attaining this end." He shared with Robert Owen, the mill-owner who became the founder of British socialism, the belief that the heads of industrial enterprises were the best fitted to bring about a new spiritual direction of society, which would not only bring social justice, but would even abolish war. Robert Owen exemplified this high ideal in his own industry, and actually set up cooperative communities in which, under careful supervision, families could share in work and the enjoyment of its products. Like Saint-Simon, Owen based his project on the belief in the innate goodness and perfectability of mankind. The appeal was to the awakened conscience of the upper classes rather than to the workers themselves. Owen applied his principles in his own factory, but such benevolent despotism was not to the liking of other mill-owners won over to the comfortable doctrine of *laisssez faire,* that matters were only made worse if one interfered with the "iron laws" of economics.

But, alongside this temperate, kindly socialism of moral reforms, a new and utterly different attack upon the whole problem was made by a young refugee from Germany, studying the parliamentary papers in the library of the British Museum, Karl Marx. He was the first economist to study the reports of parliamentary commissions on the effects of the industrial revolution, from which we have quoted above, and from his long and scholarly researches he came to the conclusion that the only solution for the evils disclosed by the documents was the socialization of the means of production, in other words, the absolute antithesis of *laissez faire,* the abolition of the rule of the capitalist and the transfer of his power to the hitherto powerless proletariat. Marx's theory was further elaborated by his friend, Friedrich Engels, and together they stand as the creators of militant socialism. It was a revolutionary challenge not only to the capitalists but to the national state system. Not content with its practical bearing upon the problems of the day, it reached back to the whole development of civilization in the economic theory of history, which traced all the great movements of the past to economic causes. For the next half century socialism remained more a threat than a political or economic reality; but in the twentieth century in the more militant form of Communism, it moved out in power on the state of world history.[3] But the national state system had still more than one page of history on which the middle class could inscribe its achievements and its ideals.

Science and War

We have seen how militarism was linked with nationalism in increasing measure after the French Revolution, and how Prussia became the leader of this joint movement. But it was not philosophers or historians who masterminded the theory of war as the instrument of national policy; it was the Prussian general, Karl von Clausewitz, whose masterpiece, *On War (vom Kriege),* remains today the unrivalled exposition of the philosophy of war. The kernel of this philosophy is that "war is not merely a political act but a

[3] *Cf.* Chapter XVI.

real political instrument, a combination of political intercourse, a carrying out of the same by other means." It is "an act of force to compel our adversary to do our will," and theoretically there must be no limit to the force, no "artistic way of disarming and overthrowing an adversary without too much bloodshed."

To Clausewitz and to the soldiers for whom his manual was written, the main thing was military strategy. The political implications were taken for granted. But no sooner was Prussia ready to accept Bismarck's policy of unifying Germany by "blood and iron" — Clausewitz's way — than the major question arose, who was to have the final control of this instrument of politics, the soldier or the statesman. The issue came to the fore in the Seven Weeks' War between Prussia and Austria, with the decisive defeat of Austria at the battle of Königgrätz. The Prussian army had opened the way to Vienna, and its leaders, von Roon, the Minister of War, and von Moltke, Commander-in-chief, were determined to reap the full fruits of victory. There is nothing more emphatic in Clausewitz than that the purpose of war is to break the will of the enemy by making victory complete. But Bismarck wanted only a partial victory, so that he could win over Austria later to remain neutral while Prussia turned on the next victim, France. None of the far implications of this torturous, Machiavellian policy were matters for soldiers, intent only on immediate success in fighting; yet Bismarck told later what a really terrible struggle it was to hold back the military "instrument" from running away with policy. The Iron Prime Minister (he was not yet Chancellor) was reduced to tears and near-hysteria after denying the army leaders the control of policy in their hour of triumph.

In France there was little left of the military tradition of Napoleon after the humiliating defeat at Sedan. But from time to time there were incidents which the republicans won, but which kept them on guard: the attempted *coup d'état* of the president, Marshal MacMahon; the theatrical demagogy of General Boulanger, "the man on horseback"; and, above all, the Dreyfus case, which ended military intrigue in high places. The "pin-prick" policy of the Kaiser kept the nerves of Frenchmen on edge, but the anti-clericalists were determined not to allow the German menace to create the rise of a military class in France. There must be security against domestic as well as foreign attack on the rights of the common man. The program of this double safeguard of freedom was set forth by the socialist statesman, Jean Juares, in *L'Armée Nouvelle*, one of the great works in military literature, and in the defense of democracy.

Here we have the heart of the problem as far as it comes within this survey — an issue not yet settled, nor likely to be settled as long as war is the admitted final instrument of policy. The question is as old as politics itself. The whole history of Rome furnished one answer, as the *imperator*, master of the legions, took over the task of statesmanship, and ultimately failed — in spite of, or rather because of, the power of his military command. The one state that first established civilian control was England, which did away with a standing army — at least of any size likely to endanger the liberties of the State — and placed the control of the army in Parliament by the simple, perhaps unpremeditated, device of voting supplies for only a year at a time. This Mutiny Act of 1689, voted for an emergency to suppress a mutiny, was recast from time to time, and is still the bulwark of civilian control over the military.

It takes more than a legal device, however, to assure the subordination of the military to the civilian branches of the government. Tradition and national character molded by circumstances play their part as well. A sea power like Great Britain is not so presently aware of its protecting navy as is a land power like France, with garrisons in every border-land city for defense against invasion, of its army. Still less aware of militarism was the United States in its isolation from Europe. At the outbreak of the Civil War in 1861, the total nominal strength of the United States army was only 17,113 — officers and men — and many of these were scattered throughout the West policing the garrisons against possible Indian uprisings. The nominal strength of the navy was 90 vessels, but only 42 were actually in commission. Wars with other countries during the nineteenth century had raised no constitutional problems; in both the war of 1812 and that with Mexico, civilian control of policy remained supreme, as was also the case in the Spanish war at the end of the century, when the issue of imperialism which it raised was fought out in Congress. The outstanding instance of what looked like a military decision in the political field was General Grant's offer to General Lee at Appomattox to let the Confederate soldiers take their horses home for the spring plowing, but this was only carrying out the policy outlined in Lincoln's Second Inaugural, calling for "charity for all." In spite of the dark days of reconstruction after the war, the country cherished in later years the proud memory of this rejection of militarism and, even while not pacifist in temper — as shown by the honor paid to military heroes — regarded war as a nightmarish episode, to be ended and forgotten as soon as possible.

There was no American Clausewitz to correct this altogether too casual view of the nature and place of war in the shaping of a nation's life. Strangely enough, however, there was a naval strategist, Captain Mahan, whose work on the influence of sea power on history was as great a classic in its field as that of Clausewitz in land warfare. But, as we have noticed in the case of England, sea power does not create so great a danger to civilian government as does the army; and the question which faced Bismarck and the statesmen of France did not arise.

Safe in its isolation, the United States began the twentieth century with only a small skeleton army, and the military tradition was so weak that, when in World War I conscription was enacted in 1917, there was grave doubt that there would be loyal response in certain sections of the country. This fear proved to be unfounded; but as soon as the fighting in Europe was over, there was an irresistible national demand to "bring the boys back home" and leave Europe to the Europeans. War, even a world war, was but an interlude or interruption in the affairs of peace; it was not and apparently could not be what it was for Europeans, the instrument of their national policies, for the United States had then only one policy in dealing with Europe: to stay out of it as much as possible. This policy, or lack of it, was again dominant in the counsels of Franklin Roosevelt and his generals at the end of World War II, when, against the protest of Winston Churchill, they planned a strategy which, by concentrating solely on immediate military aims, left Soviet Russia in possession of all of Eastern Europe.

Meanwhile an industrial revolution was taking place in the technique of warfare parallel to that which had re-made the arts of peace, and even more far-reaching in scope. More important than the growth of conscript armies was the development of military science. The dictum of Napoleon, and of other conquerors before him, that the God of battles was on the side of the strongest armies, was constantly in the minds of those who led in the race in armaments at the end of the nineteenth century and the opening of the twentieth. The efforts of the Hague Convention to stop that race proved futile. Mechanization first became a part of active strategy in the American Civil War; it then was used to advantage when World War I suddenly opened the new day of scientific warfare. It still took two years for the revolution to reveal its full meaning, but by the end of 1916 France and England had followed the example of Germany and made the whole country into a vast munitions industry. Most important of all, neutrals were drawn in and the commerce of the seven seas diverted to the one aim of winning victory. When it finally came, it was due to the blockade of munitions and war supplies more than to victories on the battlefield, and its ultimate effect was shared by all in the Great Depression ten years after the war was over.

The conclusion to be drawn from this stupendous fact is that the nations of Western Europe, which had used war as the instrument of their policy through all history, could no longer count upon it, for it had got out of control, and was bound to do so in any future war. The interdependence of the warring nations was greater than their differences. The direction of strategy was no longer determined by that of marching troops, but by the command of resources from far-off lands. In short, war had changed in fundamentals, and science had ended its ancient use as an instrument of policy.[4]

Before we proceed, however, to develop in detail the proof for so great a generalization on the effect of science on warfare, we must retrace our steps to deal with the revolutionary movements of socialism and communism, the origins of which have been given previously.

---

[4] The first to see the fallacy of militarism under the conditions of today was Norman Angel, whose work, *The Great Illusion* (1910), remains a classic in its field.

CHAPTER XVI

COMMUNISM

Marx and the Communist Manifesto

THE THREE revolutions which opened modern history had one common aim: freedom. But it was freedom organized for the politically emancipated, those who in the old regime had not shared — or had not fully shared — in the great business of government. That new freedom belonged only to those who had a stake in it, and that stake was property. The original slogan, drawn from the philosophic analysis of John Locke, "life, liberty and property," was much nearer reality than Jefferson's more inclusive and more alluring phrase, "life, liberty and the pursuit of happiness." How could a nation pursue happiness except by the enhancement of those conditions which enriched life by relief from want and the assurance of leisure for the enjoyment of culture and the arts? Locke was right. Property was the basis of freedom; but it could also be the basis of oppression, for its ownership was power. Failure to appreciate this fully had been the fallacy of *laissez faire*. The revolutions for freedom were incomplete if they excluded those whose only property was life itself. If, as Adam Smith had said, the basis of property was labor, then not merely those who owned property, but also those who labored, had a right to a just share of the product.

Property ownership played its increasing part in the long, slow development of the Middle Ages from slavery to serfdom and villeinage; but the growth of yeomanry in England and of private ownership of farming land in France still left a propertyless substratum of those who depended for their livelihood on their daily labor. The introduction of machinery swept together as in a glacial drift all of these poor people into a new propertyless class, the proletariat. The name was as old as the origins of ancient Rome, when King Servius Tullius listed as the lowest class those who served the State not with property, but with their children *(proles)*. Two thousand years of history had intervened, and a new era was opening, with the promise of greatness that would far outshine that of ancient Rome; yet the modern proletariat had little, if any, share in this new wealth and power. The problem of freedom had taken on new dimensions.

There were two lines of approach: that of reforms within each national state by the extension of social legislation, and that of an international movement working through revolution. The history of what might be called the democratization of economic control is touched upon in many parts of this general survey. It covers such diverse procedures as the social legislation of both Tories and Liberals in England, culminating in the "welfare state" of the Labour Party; the "state socialism" of Bismarck adjusting the traditions of Hohenzollern paternalism to the new economy; the rise of the "popular front" in France; and above all, the new political outlook in the United States, which began at the turn of the century with the writings of the "Muckrakers" against corrupt practices in politics and business, and found expression in the measures of successive presidents — the "Square Deal" of Theodore Roosevelt, the "Fair Deal" of Woodrow Wilson and the "New Deal" of Franklin Roosevelt.[1]

The one unifying principle in all these varied measures of different countries was the attack on *laissez faire* and the acceptance of government oversight or control of those economic activities which most affect the lives of most people. But, however far-reaching these reforms, they failed to satisfy the communistic socialists, because they did not change the economic basis of society. To them, the emancipation of the workers was neither secure nor complete until they took over the ownership of the means of production.

The classic statement of this revolutionary principle was the *Communist Manifesto*, issued by Karl Marx and Frederich Engels in December, 1847, just in time for the revolutionary movement of the next spring, although it played no great part in shaping the early ideas of communism at that time. The text of a document which was to become the testament of the religion of communism is too long to quote in full, although all of it belongs in this survey. The opening words, "A spectre is haunting Europe," were not intended to alert the bourgeoisie, but rather to stir the revolutionary communists to action. Yet it did both:

A spectre is haunting Europe, the spectre of Communism. All the powers of old Europe have entered into a holy alliance to exorcise this spectre: Pope and Czar, Metternich and Guizot, French radicals and German police-spies. . . .

The modern bourgeois society that has sprouted from the ruins of feudal society, has not done away with class antagonisms. It has but established new classes, new conditions of oppression, new forms of struggle in place of the old ones. . . .

In proportion as the bourgeoisie, i.e., capital, is developed, in the same proportion is the proletariat, the modern working class, developed — a class of laborers who live only so long as they find work, and who find work only so long as their labor increases capital. . . .

[1] *Cf.* Chapter XXII.

Of all the classes that stand face to face with the bourgeoisie today, the proletariat alone is really a revolutionary class. The other classes decay and finally disappear in the face of modern industry; the proletariat is its special and essential product. . . .

The social conditions of the old society no longer exist for the proletariat. The proletarian is without property; his relation to his wife and children has no longer anything in common with bourgeois family relations; modern industrial labour, modern subjection to capital, the same in England as in France, in America as in Germany, has stripped him of every trace of national character. Law, morality, religion, are to him so many bourgeois prejudices, behind which lurk in ambush just as many bourgeois interests. . . .

All previous historical movements were movements of minorities, or in the interest of minorities. The proletarian movement is the self-conscious, independent movement of the immense majority. The proletariat, the lowest stratum of our present society, cannot stir, cannot raise itself up, without the whole superincumbent strata of official society being sprung into the air.

Though not in substance, yet in form, the struggle of the proletariat with the bourgeoisie is at first a national struggle. The proletariat of each country must, first of all, settle matters with its own bourgeoisie. . . .

The workingmen have no country. We cannot take from them what they have not got. . . .

The Communists disdain to conceal their views and aims. They openly declare that their ends can be attained only by the forceful overthrow of all existing social conditions. Let the ruling classes tremble at a Communist revolution. The proletarians have nothing to lose but their chains. They have a world to win.

Workingmen of all countries, unite!

This is not the first time that the evils endured by long-suffering humanity brought a revolutionary concept of history to the fore.[2] St. Augustine's *City of God* was projected against the background of a denunciation of antique society as the work of Satan, its institutions the creation of devils. But Christian teaching offered escape by moral regeneration and the practice of the Golden Rule, a guide held out in varying degrees by all the great religions, Jewish, Buddhist, Confucian and Islamic. The spiritual element of charity, which Roman law fused into "the fixed and constant purpose to give to every man his due," was discarded by materialist communists as the means to their goal. Like Machiavelli, they held that force is the only sure instrument of achievement. The contrast of the two ideals is the supreme fact in the world today, for the self-discipline of charity makes for freedom, while the insistence on force creates despotism.

The *Communist Manifesto*, like much of the Marxist literature, is compounded of two elements: a theory of history and a call to revolution. The capitalists or "bourgeois" are the last of a long series of exploiters — last because the communist revolution will for the first time establish power in the hands of the great mass of the people, the workers, who, once they achieve their freedom, will no longer form a class but become part of a classless

[2] Plato's *Republic*, the most revolutionary theory of antiquity, lies outside this survey, as it remained nothing more than a daring excursion in political philosophy.

society. The state will "wither away" and a system of complete freedom dawn for mankind. To reach this shining goal, there must be no compromise with the capitalist exploiters. The first stage in the revolution must be a dictatorship of the proletariat, which has to be accepted as it is the last of all class conflicts. The strategy of the revolution is not to be checked by regard for bourgeois ethics, for it must not stop short of the overthrow of "law, morality, religion . . . behind which lurk in ambush . . . bourgeois interests." Instead of them, communism will achieve peace and happiness in a world of social justice.

While the inhumanity of ruthlessness lies like a red smear across some of Marx's pages, he never fully envisaged the nature of the revolutionary process. Trained in German philosophy and tinged with German liberalism, then in revolt against the system of Metternich, he lacked the practical bent of a man of action, and, as a rigid doctrinaire, was chiefly interested in the maintenance of his doctrine. It was left for Lenin to change the accent, when the hour for action had come, and thus to give a new, less humane, meaning to communism. There was to be no "withering away" of the state, (as Marx had prophesied), once it had taken over the dictatorship of the proletariat. For dictators must govern; and they must not be swayed by the voice of the multitude, but sway it. The one nation best fitted to give Lenin's uncompromising tyranny a trial was Russia, steeped in Byzantine bureaucracy and autocratic rule. Tyranny is the worst of all schools for freedom; for its blight extends even beyond the limits of Lord Acton's saying that "absolute power corrupts absolutely those who would wield it"; it corrupts the victims equally, for they tend to use the same remorseless methods in the name of freedom.

None of the problems of communist politics were in the minds of the authors of the *Communist Manifesto*. Marx, in his later works, concentrated on the economic problems of capitalism and collectivism. There was even a touch of the prevalent doctrine of *laissez faire* in his belief in the "withering away of the state." The structure of society would, according to his theory, respond of itself to a new sense of social and economic justice. But neither Marx's economic theory nor Lenin's mastery of revolutionary technique could wholly undo history or wholly overcome the current trend toward free democracy. It was therefore natural that the leaders of the two great communist empires, Russia and China, should play up the forms of democratic government while attempting to nullify them in practice by the dictatorship of the Party and its leaders. In China, the Confucian background of a conservative social order was transmuted as far as possible along Marxian lines. In Russia, a blending of popular and dictatorial institutions was used to fool the public by such devices as elections, trade unions, cooperative associations, parliament, local self-government and courts of law, all of them, however, under the control of the dictatorship of the Party and its leaders.[3]

Even from this short listing of the problems of communism, it is clear that

[3] The points noted here are summarized in Chapter XIII of *The Soviet System of Government* by Professor John N. Hazard (Chicago University Press, 1957), p. 186 f.

it is not the solid monolithic power which it seems to be when contrasted with the varied and often contradictory elements of politics in the countries of freedom. Throughout communist states, there runs a political cleavage which is frankly acknowledged by the leaders; the autocracy, which they outwardly disguise by popular institutions without real power, acts almost like the priesthood of a cult which the common people must accept but cannot understand. The Marxian economic theory of history is treated as infallible in its analysis, which culminates so daringly in the year one of the new dispensation, that of the communist revolution. But this doctrine has to be taken on faith by the proletariat, for only the high priests of the new cult fully understand it. Here lies the fundamental weakness of the system, for the leaders must rely on the unquestioning adherence of the Party and the loyalty of bureaucracy to keep conditions from getting out of control of the dictators.

This means that politics must not touch in any controversial way on issues defined by the communist creed, either in the press or in public discussion; the judiciary is an arm of party policy, the police is permitted to make arrests and to try those whom it has arrested in its own tribunals without reference to the courts. The phrase, so important in free societies, "due process of law," is meaningless here. It is only fair to the founding fathers of communism, however, to recall that the old regimes in eastern Europe and Asia which they overthrew had also lacked anything like the safeguard of freedom in the English common law, and that their only share in the heritage of Rome was in the mummified bureaucratic system of Byzantium. The new imperialism, which they planned to apply to every nation everywhere, took an opposite course from that of the Roman empire. Instead of drawing the principles of universal law from the varied experiences of other peoples, as the Romans had done, they undertook to escape from history and to begin civilization over again on new lines. From the standpoint of history itself, this was both grandiose and naif.

It was also self-deception, for the idyllic vision of Marx — shared in at first by Lenin — of a world freed from exploitation by providing that everyone should have a share in the means of production, far from creating a more perfect freedom than that of the society of individual choice and initiative, established a new dictatorship, with controls widened to include almost everything in the life of the common man, and treating every violation of its rules on thought or action as treason against the state. The communists still repeat the creed of the *Communist Manifesto* that the workers of the world should unite, having "nothing to lose but their chains," but what they were really doing was forging other chains to bind their followers to their own autocracy. The issue was no longer the emancipation from the overlordship of the middle class, but of emancipation from its alleged emancipators.

But this issue, perhaps the greatest single issue in the history of freedom, is little understood in the communist countries of eastern Europe and Asia. All of them are countries which have never had the great experience or borne the responsibilities of constitutional and representative, much less democratic, government. They cannot improvise freedom on the background of a history of autocracy or bureaucratic rule, for they do not know what it means, what safeguards it must have against abuse by even its devotees, what dangers lie in resort to police action to achieve designs of state or in the imperialism of threats or conquests of power.

Russian Communism

The supreme example of this autocracy is, of course, Russian communism. Fortunately, in spite of a prodigious effort to keep us in the dark, there is no mystery about the fundamental nature and purpose of Soviet policy. There is also no mystery about the realistic politics of the Kremlin, especially when faced with crises, and it is the crises which are our chief concern. In short, the iron curtain, while it bars the way to intercourse, does not completely prevent our understanding of what is going on behind it.

The outstanding fact in Soviet policy, domestic and foreign, is that Lenin and Stalin reversed the classic definition of war by Clausewitz, that "war is the continuation of [peaceful] policy by other means," putting it roundabout, that "peace is the continuation of war by other means." To the Bolshevists the communist revolution is still going on. It may be held up temporarily here or there, and held back temporarily from parts of the world, but its movement is inevitable and its triumph beyond question. Therefore, its adherents are forever enlisted in a holy war against the enemy, capitalism. But ideology is not strategy; it can inspire, but not guide in the actual conduct of a revolution. This is what Lenin, at heart the most doctrinaire of communists, clearly saw in 1917. While strongly and persistently proclaiming the Marxian doctrine of universal communism based on the economic theory of history, he led a national uprising in a country where capitalism had never established its rule. His revolutionary call was to a dispirited and beaten army in a war which had become, so he insisted, the meaningless struggle of two imperialisms. To the soldiers and the country he offered peace; to the peasants he offered land. With these slogans to win the masses, the Bolshevists, the left wing of the Social-Democratic Party, seized power in the disordered politics of Petrograd for a "Council of Workers and Soldiers," the Soviet, which was to become the general staff of the revolution, fight civil wars (1918-1921), and finally create a government which assumed supreme power in Moscow.

The structure of Bolshevist society as planned by Lenin was the blueprint for communist organization everywhere, and its guiding principles still guide. Lenin's idea, as summarized by Trotsky, who disagreed with him, was that the organization of the party should take the place of the party itself, the Central Committee take the place of the organization, and finally the dictator take the place of the Central Committee. Lenin himself began this process by having all urgent matters decided in the Politburo (the Political Bureau of the Central Committee) or the Orgburo, charged with the direction of all the organizational work of the Party, or in informal meetings of leaders who were available when problems arose. But, to ensure harmony and efficiency, all decisions were to be carried out by the Secretary of the Central Party.

This organization of communism under the Party, accepted by the Ninth Congress of the Party in 1919, proved to be an effective, ready instrument for despotic rule when, at the Tenth Congress, in 1921, the Workers Opposition was outlawed and critical discussions of the Party forbidden. The next year Stalin emerged as Party Secretary, and it was soon evident that the Congress had surrendered its powers to the leader of the Party. From this time on, the path to power was bathed in blood, not of reactionaries as in the Civil War, but of dissident communists; every Party Congress was prepared by a prior purge, and this was continued even after Stalin had the unanimous support of the Congress. The great purge of 1934 eliminated all but twenty of the hundred and twenty-four Central Committee members and candidates, and from 1939 Stalin never even called a Congress for thirteen years, until 1952, shortly before his death.

From this short sketch of the development of Russian Communism, it is evident that Stalinism was the legitimate offspring of Leninism, and that when the collective leadership (of Khrushchev, Bulganin and their associates) proclaimed that Lenin's greatest service to Marxism and to mankind was the creation of a party of a new type, and when they launched the slogan "Back to the Leninist form of party leadership," this is the kind of party they have in mind.

What Karl Marx would have thought of this development of communism is a problem for theorists. The pathway to collectivism was one that no Western thinker could ever have imagined. The Union of Soviet Socialist Republics became the inheritor of Muscovite imperialism, and this in spite of the fact that the real power lies in the Communist Party, whose Secretary, Stalin, became, after Lenin's death, the successor of the Tsars. As the accepted guardian of doctrine, the Party is panoplied in inviolability and this gives it a political power not set forth in the constitution. But the doctrine is in the hands of practical men, and orthodoxy does not stand in the way of either nationalism or expediency. The hold which Stalin had up his people cannot be understood by studying "economic determinism" or communist "dialectic." While these are important elements in Soviet policy, holding the promise of a golden age sometime in the future and justifying sacrifices to attain it, the strategy of the Kremlin is never chained to its ideology. Russian communism is an instrument of policy and power, the armor bearer of imperialism.

The mixture of nationalism and communism was brought out in the early days of the revolution by Stalin who, as a Georgian from the Caucasus, stressed the national cultures in the vast regions of the Tsar and the need for some degree of federal autonomy. But, however varied the peoples of the U.S.S.R., the dominant characteristic was Slavic. And the Slavic attitude toward life and the world was moulded by influences other than those which produced the culture and policies of Western Europe. There was nearly always something of an iron curtain shadowing the realm of the Tsars. Throughout the centuries in which England and France worked out the institutions of freedom, Russia was isolated from all the benign influences of Western culture. The symbols of law and order were the bureaucrats and the police of a heavy-handed, obscurantist autocracy. The mass of the people, as is usual in a servile population, resorted to secretiveness as a defense against exploitation and tyranny, while a small body of intelligentsia gave voice to a growing awareness that their world was out of joint.

This was the society mirrored in the masterpieces of Russian literature in the nineteenth century, subtle, penetrating and poignant analyses of human motives, the counterpart in the realm of creative imagination to the ideas of the political revolutionists, with whom some of the writers were personally associated. The impact of Tartar rule, which for centuries linked to Asia the richer areas of the country, and the effects of the feudal anarchy of the Boyars were never fully erased even by the most ruthless of the Tsars, while no sturdy middle class developed, as in Western Europe, to assert its rights against the new tyranny of Tsardom. Antiquity spoke through Byzantium, not Rome, in both Church and State, in reactionary clericalism and bureaucracy. Political freedom had no chance to develop the institutions of responsible government when the economic life of the country was so backward, and there was no tradition to build upon.

This had been the school for revolution of Lenin, Trotsky and Stalin. Bolshevism sprang from the same roots as had produced the nineteenth century Russian anarchists, although its ultimate idea of a controlled society was the opposite of anarchy. All of them had one common enemy, autocratic Tsardom, a despotism with which there could be no compromise. The only weapon against the despot was conspiracy, and it was used unrelentingly. For both police and revolutionists it was a war without quarter. The prisons were filled with those suspected of complicity or sympathy with the terrorists, and Siberia was a vast land of exiles. The more fortunate leaders escaped to the two havens of safety, England or Switzerland. Among these was Lenin himself, re-introduced into Russia from Switzerland in 1917 by the Germans to undermine their Russian enemy.

Such was the Russia in which Lenin and Stalin grew up. So far as the strategy of their revolution was concerned, it was determined fully as much by this background as by Marxian socialism. The scruples which kept West European socialists to the use of parliamentary debate and trade union action were not shared by the Russian communists. For them, the revolution was war, and no humane consideration should stand in the way of total victory. The Russian-led communists carried their program of violence into the European socialist movement, and tried, with the aid of extremists in other countries, to capture it. It had been set up in London in 1864 as the International Workingmen's Association, with Marx in fact, though not in name, the head of its general council. A second "International" was founded in 1875, as the Social Democratic Workingman's Party. But in spite of its appeal to all workers in every country to unite, as in the *Communist Manifesto,* the moderate, law-abiding socialists retained their established places in political life in the Western countries. The extremists alone bore the title "communists," to link up definitely with the most revolutionary utterances of Marx. The split between the two factions came to the fore after the first World War in the communist uprisings in Berlin, Vienna and Budapest and, under Lenin's leadership, the Communist "Third International" was formed in 1919, with the violent overthrow of capitalism as the acknowledged aim. Russian ruthlessness had won the day.

Failing to dominate the socialists who were not in their own extremist camp, the communists transferred their bitterest enmity to those who, as in Great Britain, not only refused to join in the forceful overthrow of their governments, but actually and vigorously upheld them. This constitutes a chapter of European history of great importance for us and for our understanding of the cold war. Socialism, in contrast with communism, is an ally, and a devoted ally, against violent revolution. It believes that social justice can best be attained through governments that are democratic and responsible, acting through parliaments and supported by the courts. On the other hand, communism is the ruthless embodiment of revolutionary movements that have been born, like those of Russia, in conditions where freedom has never established institutions to safeguard the rights of the citizen. Communism has never won more than a small, if disturbing, minority in the countries of Magna Carta or the Bill of Rights and has never been dominant anywhere in Western Europe. In spite of the Marxist theory that it is the inevitable creation of the Industrial Revolution, its home is along the fringe of the Orient or in the Orient itself, where, until now, governments have been instruments of tyranny. Unfortunately that fringe reaches over half the world, a portentious fact. For these are the lands that never knew freedom, and the fact that they are behind an iron curtain means less to them than to us. Such isolation existed for centuries in China and Japan. The danger in the situation lies in the stirring of imperialist ambitions to reach out for the control of other peoples and in the expansive forces of modern industry, seeking vital source materials or markets for its goods.

Although the crisis reaches out over the whole world, it still centers in the Kremlin (as even Mao Tse-tung insisted), and the only solution is one which includes it. The Soviet formula "peaceful co-existence" is meaningless, however, if compromise is surrender; and it is unreal if each side still distrusts the other. The attacks on Stalin by his former accomplices in the Bolshevist regime of terror, instead of inspiring confidence in the good faith of his successors, seemed to point to a continuing Machiavellianism; and Machiavelli had no scruples in misleading those whom his Prince (in this case, the Kremlin) had marked for destruction. What had been so sinisterly unique in Stalin's case was not so much the ruthlessness of his orgy of persecution, but the fact that the victims, his former colleagues, so consistently confessed their guilt. The Christian martyrs never admitted that they had been wrong in denying divinity to Caesar. The admission of guilt was sometimes wrung from heretics by the torturers of the Inquisition, but seldom from their leaders. But the associates of Lenin and Stalin confessed heresy in thought or deed, and accepted death as a just penalty. Fanaticism may explain some of the confessions, but it still leaves much to be explained — perhaps by the sufferings of mental tortures even more than physical, in a procedure which had been justified by the victims themselves when used against the enemies of communism.

A lurid light was thrown on the Stalinite terror by his successor as Party Secretary, Khrushchev, in a dramatic attack upon his former leader, delivered with passion and in tears before the Twentieth Congress of the Party. The whole world, communist and free, was startled by what looked like a revolution in the Party; but it soon looked more like a palace revolution within the Kremlin. The men who cast all the blame upon Stalin had been his creatures and accomplices. "Malenkov ran the card index and dossiers of the purges. Khrushchev carried them out in the Ukraine, where they raged with unexampled fury. Bulganin was the eyes and ears of Stalin in the army. Mikoyan, Kaganovich and Khrushchev worked together to purge Moscow and each took his turn in the two-decade holocaust in the Ukraine."[4]

It seemed too much to expect that men like these, who had shared in Stalin's paranoic cruelty, should now renounce terror as an instrument of power. Yet this is what they did. They executed only one of their number, Beria, not for his past crimes as head of the secret police, but on the charge that he was plotting a counter-revolution against the new masters of the Kremlin. It soon became clear that there had been no change in the theory of government; the real power still lay in the Party, where Lenin placed it, and the head of the Party was the head of the state. The use of this post by Stalin to establish a personal despotism (a "cult of personality") was the point of attack by Khrushchev and his associates in that incredible session of the Congress which seemed to be washing out the stain of Stalinite tyranny in a flood of emotion. But though the new regime began by a renunciation of terror, the structure of the government was unchanged. The Party remained the real power and its new head, Khrushchev, deftly ousted his colleagues one by one, having them assigned to minor and widely isolated posts, until his own position as head of the state was unquestioned.

Moderation in tyranny is the most difficult form of government and also the most difficult to appraise. "If the dictator is willing to base himself, as Stalin did, predominantly upon force and upon an evergrowing use of force, terror, the police, exile and execution, if the dictator has the will and the strength to carry out such a policy relentlessly and if his machinery of force is well founded, he can defy public sentiment for a long time and successfully. But if a dictatorship seeks to steer a middle course, as has been the

[4] February 24, 1956. *Cf.* Bertram D. Wolfe, "Stalin's Ghost at the Party Congress," *Foreign Affairs* (July, 1956), p. 566.

case since Stalin's death, then this course is powerfully influenced by the currents of public sentiment and opinion."[5] The writer of this comment goes on to point out that "the most profound sentiment now affecting Soviet men and women is a deep, emotional attachment to peace which stems from the horror and sacrifice of World War II. . . . It is this mood of the Soviet public which is reflected in the ceaseless flow of peace propaganda from Moscow. What is seldom perceived is that the greatest weight of this propaganda is directed to the home audience — to convince the Soviet people that their Government is as dedicated as themselves to the cause of peace."

But how can this be reconciled with the major thesis of Russian communism, the inevitable conflict with the capitalist world in establishing communism the world over? At least lip service must from time to time be paid to Lenin, to the confusion and concern of the noncommunist world. But observers in Russia note a growing apathy there toward appeals to doctrinaire goals and an equally growing demand for not only more material comforts but for a freer system of life, with fewer restrictions and more security of personal rights. "Any attempt to reimpose the harsh *diktat* of Stalin upon the Soviet people would be fraught with danger. Stalin required many years, many purges, many trials, many victims, many executions to perfect his rule. With his acute sense of political realism, Mr. Khrushchev may well have deduced that he himself would be the most likely first victim of any attempt to revive the terror in Russia."[6]

It would carry us too far afield to trace the way in which Khrushchev turned these domestic problems to his profit in his deft diplomacy with Washington and the West, taking advantage of disorders, conflicts and Western blunders in the Middle East to reach farther than Imperial Russia had ever done, and, backed by outstanding achievements of Russian scientists, keeping the West guessing as to his real policy on disarmament. Upon the whole, the chief field of operations for Soviet strategy was shifted more and more into the practical fields of politics and economics rather than in the risk of war with the great Powers of the West. The communist and socialist parties in Western Europe have been very much in the mind of Khrushchev, although he has had little success in drawing them together into closer ties with the Kremlin. The "heresy" of Tito — that there are more ways than one to communism (meaning more ways than by submitting to the dictates of Moscow) — which successfully defied excommunication by Stalin was followed by a similar but less pronounced movement in Poland, tending in the same direction of national opposition to Russian domination. The age-long national antagonism of the Poles to encroachments by Russia, which showed itself in riots in Poznan, proved strong enough to overthrow the pro-Russian clique in the Polish Government and cause the Kremlin to recognize (at least outwardly and for the time being) the same kind of autonomy for Polish communism as Tito had won for Yugoslavia. These

[5] From a thoughtful appraisal of Khrushchev's regime by Harrison E. Salisbury in *The New York Times Magazine*, August 24, 1958.
[6] *Ibid.*

concessions might never have been given were it not that just at this time the protest against Moscow's imperialism burst into flames in Hungary — flames which were quenched in blood by the very men who had accused Stalin of inhumanity. The free world was aghast, but intervention would have meant a third world war, and the successors of Stalin had a murderous triumph. The United Nations protested in a blistering resolution, and kept the protest against continued Soviet intervention in Hungary on its agenda. But that was all.

In Asia and Africa the U.S.S.R. is moving strongly, exploiting the long-standing grievances against the former colonialism of the capitalist Powers of the West, grievances which have left resentments even after the causes have been removed by recent reforms in commercial and political relations. Thus, even where the charge of colonialism no longer stands, the consequences of past history endure. And these are embedded in a racial antagonism against the white Europeans which plays directly into Soviet hands.

As Soviet Russia leaned more and more toward Asia, some gains were made in countries where political experience was lacking or limited. In India, Burma and Indonesia, where the reaction against European colonialism had been strong, communism made headway among the socialist parties and the exploited masses, but never achieved power. In China, on the other hand, it swept over the country in what may yet prove to be the greatest of all revolutions, challenging the oldest of all civilizations and changing the folkways of over six hundred million people. The impact of this tremendous fact upon the rest of Asia leads to one conclusion: that the strategy of militant communism in its attack upon the capitalist West will be more and more by way of the flank movement through Asia. This will be described in the chapter on the "New Asia and Africa" below.

The New Class

The rise of communism to power in Russia and its challenge to capitalism has produced a controversial literature which almost outreaches that of the era of the Protestant Reformation. But it was left for a Marxist to write the most powerful critique of the system of communism as it developed under Lenin and Stalin in a volume which critics have measured in importance with John Locke's *Of Civil Government* in the clarification of a new era of political thought. This is *The New Class* by Milovan Djilas,[7] once the comrade-in-arms of Marshall Tito in the war against the Nazi, and Vice-President of communist Yugoslavia, now a prisoner of his former colleague for his outspoken attack upon the new ruling class, the Members of the Communist Party and Bureaucracy, which he denounces as an instrument of tyranny.

Djilas is a Montenegran by birth. Perhaps that partly explains the firmness and frankness with which he denounces the new privileged order of the

[7] English translation, Frederick A. Praeger (New York). The following extracts are quoted by permission of the publisher.

regime of communism, for the Montenegrans, in their eagle's nest behind the Black Mountain (*Monte Negro*), held their bastion of freedom through the centuries, when even the stubborn Serbs were forced to yield to the Turk. Only a small and isolated tribe, they remained in spirit and in fact unconquerable, and the tradition of courage is their heritage. In the war against the Nazi, they furnished guerrilla soldiers alongside the Serbs and Croats, and it was there that Djilas became the right-hand comrade of Tito, whose rebellion against the high-handed autocracy of Moscow he strongly supported. When, however, Tito as a practical politician halted halfway in his opposition to the Kremlin, Djilas went on to deny the legitimacy of the monolithic structure of the new oligarchy which had developed under Stalin.

The body of the book deals with the history of this new class. Instead of summarizing it, for the general lines of that history have been touched on above, we may better savor the sting of Djilas' attack by quotations from his text.

In Communism the state machinery is not the instrument which really determines social and property relationships; it is only the instrument by which these relationships are protected. In truth, everything is accomplished in the name of the state and through its regulations. The Communist Party, including the professional party bureaucracy, stands above the regulations and behind every single one of the state's acts.

It is the bureaucracy which formally uses, administers, and controls both nationalized and socialized property as well as the entire life of society. The role of the bureaucracy in society, i.e., monopolistic administration and control of national income and national goods, consigns it to a special privileged position. Social relations resemble state capitalism. The more so, because the carrying out of industrialization is effected not with the help of capitalists but with the help of the state machine. In fact, this privileged class performs that function, using the state machine as a cover and as an instrument.

Ownership is nothing other than the right of profit and control. If one defines class benefits by this right, the Communist states have seen, in the final analysis, the origin of a new form of ownership or of a new ruling and exploiting class.

In reality, the Communists were unable to act differently from any ruling class that preceded them. Believing that they were building a new and ideal society, they built it for themselves in the only way they could. Their revolution and their society do not appear either accidental or unnatural, but appear as a matter of course for a particular country and for prescribed periods of its development. Because of this, no matter how extensive and inhuman Communist tyranny has been, society, in the course of a certain period — as long as industrialization lasts — has to and is able to endure this tyranny. Furthermore, this tyranny no longer appears as something inevitable, but exclusively as an assurance of the depredations and privileges of a new class.

In contrast to earlier revolutions, the Communist revolution, conducted in the name of doing away with classes, has resulted in the most complete authority of any single new class. Everything else is sham and an illusion. . . .

The greatest illusion was that industrialization and collectivization in the U.S.S.R., and destruction of capitalist ownership, would result in a classless society. In 1936, when the new Constitution was promulgated, Stalin announced that the "exploiting class" had ceased to exist. The capitalist and other classes of ancient origin had in fact been destroyed, but a new class, previously unknown to history, had been formed. . . .[8]

[8] *Ibid.*, pp. 35-37.

Behind Lenin, who was all passion and thought, stands the dull, gray figure of Joseph Stalin, the symbol of the difficult, cruel and unscrupulous ascent of the new class to its final power.

After Lenin and Stalin came what had to come; namely, mediocrity in the form of collective leadership. And also there came the apparently sincere, kind-hearted, non-intellectual "man of the people" — Nikita Khrushchev. The new class no longer needs the revolutionaries or dogmatists it once required; it is satisfied with simple personalities, such as Khrushchev, Malenkov, Bulganin, and Shepilov, whose every word reflects the average man. The new class itself is tired of dogmatic purges and training sessions. It would like to live quietly. It must protect itself even from its own authorized leader now that it has been adequately strengthened. Stalin remained the same as he was when the class was weak, when cruel measures were necessary against even those in its own ranks who threatened to deviate. Today this is all unnecessary. Without relinquishing anything it created under Stalin's leadership, the new class appears to be renouncing his authority for the past few years. But it is not really renouncing that authority — only Stalin's methods which, according to Khrushchev, hurt "good Communists."[9]

The heroic era of Communism is past. The epoch of its great leaders has ended. The epoch of practical men has set in. The new class has been created. It is at the height of its power and wealth, but it is without new ideas. It has nothing more to tell the people. The only thing that remains is for it to justify itself.[10]

While the new class accomplished one of its greatest successes in the revolution, its method of control is one of the most shameful pages in human history. Men will marvel at the grandiose ventures it accomplished, and will be ashamed of the means it used to accomplish them.

When the new class leaves the historical scene — and this must happen — there will be less sorrow over its passing than there was for any other class before it. Smothering everything except what suited its ego, it has condemned itself to failure and shameful ruin.[11]

The mechanism of Communist power is perhaps the simplest which can be conceived, although it leads to the most refined tyranny and the most brutal exploitation. The simplicity of this mechanism originates from the fact that one party alone, the Communist Party, is the backbone of the entire political, economic, and ideological activity. The entire public life is at a standstill or moves ahead, falls behind or turns around according to what happens in the party forums.

Under the Communist systems the people realize quickly what they are and what they are not permitted to do. Laws and regulations do not have an essential importance for them. The actual and unwritten rules concerning the relationship between the government and its subjects do. Regardless of laws, everyone knows that the government is in the hands of the party committees and the secret police. Nowhere is "the directing role" of the party prescribed, but its authority is established in all organizations and sectors. No law provides that the secret police has the right to control citizens, but the police is all-powerful. No law prescribes that the judiciary and the prosecutors should be controlled by the secret police and the party committee, but they are. Most people know that this is the case.[12]

. . . There is a constant tendency to transform an oligarchic dictatorship into a personal dictatorship. Ideological unity, the inevitable struggle at the top of the party, and the needs of the system as a whole tend toward personal dictatorship. The leader who succeeds in getting to the top, along with his assistants, is the one who succeeds in most logically expressing and protecting the interests of the new

---

[9] *Ibid.*, p. 52.
[10] *Ibid.*, pp. 53-54.

[11] *Ibid.*, p. 69.
[12] *Ibid.*, p. 70.

class at any given time. . . . The thirst for power is insatiable and irresistible among Communists. Victory in the struggle for power is equal to being raised to a divinity; failure means the deepest mortification and disgrace.[13]

Few pages in the literature of history are more lucid than this negative criticism of the development of the communist system. But when Djilas turns, at the close of the book, to the positive problems of the present and future, he is by no means so sure of himself. He admits, but does not develop the thesis, that "atomic energy is already leading to changes in individual countries and in the world as a whole" which "do not point toward that communism and socialism which the Communist 'theoreticians' desire. . . . The effect of atomic energy will tend toward the further unification of the world. On the way, it will shatter inexorably all inherited obstacles — ownership relations and social relations, but above all exclusive and isolated systems and ideologies, such as Communism both before and after Stalin's death." Ruling out war as the means for world unification, because "it would inevitably leave behind it the sparks of new conflagrations, discord and injustice," unification by peaceful means is "the only steady, wholesome and just way"; but "the process will take a long time, since it would be the fruit of the organized efforts of the economic and other leading powers of humanity, and because complete unity of production cannot be achieved. The earlier unities were never attained as something final; this unity too is being established only as a tendency, as something toward which production, at least that of the most developed countries, aspires."[14]

This sounds more like the "functional" union of British Commonwealth type, but Djilas soon recognizes how foreign it is to Russian communist thinking:

In the West, economic means which operate toward world unification have become dominant. In the East, on the Communist side, political means for such unification have always been predominant. The U.S.S.R. is capable of "uniting" only that which it conquers. From this point of view not even the new regime could change anything essentially. According to its ideas, oppressed peoples are only those on whom some other government, not the Soviet one, is inflicting its rule. The Soviet government subordinates its aid to others, even in the case of loans, to its political requirements.

The Soviet economy has not yet reached the point which would drive it to world unification of production. Its contradictions and difficulties stem mainly from internal sources. The system itself can still survive despite its isolation from the outside world. This is enormously expensive, but it is achieved by the widespread use of force. But this situation cannot last long; the limit must be reached. And this will be the beginning of the end of unlimited domination by the political bureaucracy, or by the new class.

Contemporary Communism could help achieve the goal of world unification most of all by political means — by internal democratization and by becoming more accessible to the outside world. However, it is still remote from this.[15]

Here we come upon the doubt of a Marxist, dealing in a puzzled way with Western democracy. Yet the book ends on a note of hope. Someday the communist leaders will find out that the capitalism which "they rant about no

[13] *Ibid.*, p. 81.   [14] *Ibid.*, pp. 194-197.   [15] *Ibid.*, pp. 210-211.

longer exists," and, "in rating the modern Western countries as blind instruments of monopolies," they are just as wrong as they are in interpreting their own system as a classless society." The solution lies in freedom from dogma. "If the Communists interpreted the world realistically, they might lose, but they would gain as human beings, as part of the human race. In any case, the world will change and will go on in the direction in which it has been moving and must go on — toward greater unity, progress, and freedom. The power of reality and the power of life have always been stronger than any kind of brute force and more real than any theory."

These are the closing words of this remarkable book. With them we bring to an end this long analysis of Russian communism and turn back to the narrative which it has interrupted.

CHAPTER XVII

WORLD WAR I AND THE LEAGUE OF NATIONS

Revolution in Warfare

IT IS INEVITABLE that the mobilization of communism should dominate discussion of freedom in the world today. But there is an approach to this problem other than that of the economics of production. It was not by way of the factory system that Lenin set up the first communist government. It was by war: first the disasters of Russia in World War I, and then the civil war. And the point needs repeating, that the cold war which followed was only a truce on the pathway of revolution. With this in mind, we need to remember that the issues of war and peace are central to the history of freedom; that war is the most terrible of tyrannies, more terrible than persecution, because it lures as well as forces its victims to disaster or destruction in indiscriminate mass massacre. We have traced its history into the modern era, through its extension in the French Revolution by the *levée en masse* to cover all citizens, to the theoretical refinements of Clausewitz and Bismarck, and to the revolution in armaments caused by modern science. But it was left for World War I to demonstrate that it had finally changed its very nature and had ceased to be an instrument of policy because it had ceased to be controllable.

So great a change in the basic relations of power is a major fact in this history of the new dimensions of power, through new conceptions of freedom. We, therefore, turn from the theme of peacetime development to examine the nature of modern war as revealed in World War I; for World War I was much more revolutionary in its effects than World War II.

World War I

After two world wars it is impossible to appreciate the impact which the coming of the first World War had on the mind of western Europe and America in the opening week of August, 1914. In spite of the fact that it was preceded by a series of ominous crises, when peace seemed almost to hang by a thread, the actual outbreak struck with a tragic force unparalleled by any event in Western history, at least since the wars of the French Revolution. From the first, all the belligerent governments recognized that the national state system which had been maturing since the Treaty of Westphalia in the mid-seventeenth century was now faced with a vastly different test than that of limited wars of rival sovereignties.

It is true that there had been four major wars after the peace settlement of the Congress of Vienna — the Crimean War, the War of Italian Liberation, the Franco-Prussian War, and the Civil War in the United States — and that with the emergence of the German Empire there had been a threatening development in the race of armaments which neither diplomacy nor the Hague Conference could check. The balance of power, which was achieved primarily through British diplomacy, had been recognized even during Bismarck's day as a basic principle of peace, but when Wilhelm II dismissed his pilot from the ship of state and began to challenge Britain on the sea as well as France and Russia on the land, the balance ceased to be a guarantee of peace and became instead a preoccupation of those who were planning the strategy of a future war.

Nevertheless, although there was a growing sense of danger in Europe, the conditions of life remained almost unchanged by these apprehensions in the chancelleries of governments. The intercourse between nations developed with speed and freedom. One could travel all over Europe without a passport. The prevalent political philosophy was based on the theory of progress which, while admitting the obstacles in the path of civilization, registered a serene confidence in the triumph of the moral order. Nor was this a mere theory. Steadily the horizons of life had been widening with the development of the arts and sciences and of education. The time had long passed when sovereigns could go to war without regard to the sentiments of their subjects.

No one knew this better than Bismarck; he used all the devices of publicity to win public opinion for the war which he was preparing. But Bismarck's use of deceptive diplomacy and the "reptile press" was a slight affair compared with the mobilization of propaganda in July and August, 1914, when the Foreign Offices of the warring nations published the documents that covered the diplomatic history bearing upon the outbreak of war. The British Blue Book, the French Yellow Book and the Russian Orange Book were matched in what was properly known as the Rainbow Series, by the White and Red Books of Germany and Austria. Never had there been such an appeal to public opinion by governments that felt obliged to justify themselves not only to their own people, but to all the world. On the surface, it looked like a recognition of that very moral order which was being violated by the act of war, and to a great degree this was the case, but the flood of documents which the Foreign Offices published to prove the justice of their case was also designed and accepted as part of or parallel to military strategy. The enemy nations refused to listen or replied with opposing and hostile claims. It was a war for the conscience of mankind as well as for the political mastery of Europe.

Perhaps the most incredible thing is that up to the last fateful days of July, 1914, the outbreak of war was so little expected. At least in England and France and in the United States it seemed as though the structure of civilization had suddenly been shaken by an earthquake. There had been so many warnings of wars that did not materialize, that people had got into the habit of believing in the continuity of the processes of peace in spite of the growing tensions of national rivalries. The last great war had not taken place in the lifetime of the rank and file who were to fight in the first World War. The European State System had grown up in a coordination of purpose and interest to preserve the peace in spite of all the preparations for war or the actual menace of it.

The murder of the Archduke Ferdinand at the end of June gave a shock for the moment to popular confidence, but it seemed as though war might be avoided. In Austria the Archduke had never been very popular, and Viennese society, never politically-minded, seemed relatively little troubled by the tragedy. It was in the middle of the holiday season in Germany as well. Kaiser Wilhelm II left rather ostentatiously on July 5th for a cruise on the Baltic. The German Minister of War purposely continued his holiday in the mountains. International meetings that had been scheduled were duly held. One of them bears directly upon this story, for it was a conference called by the Carnegie Endowment for International Peace to plan its studies and researches for an understanding of the conditions upon which an enduring peace could finally be built. The organizer of this conference was Professor John Bates Clark of Columbia University, Director of Economics and History of the Carnegie Endowment, who had a world-wide reputation as an economist. Under his direction leading economists from many countries had accepted the call to meet in Berne, Switzerland, and were already on their way when stopped by the outbreak of war.

Equally earnest efforts in the cause of peace were made by leaders of labor and business, especially in England and France, who had been deeply disturbed by the series of ominous incidents in Germany's diplomatic campaign against the policies of England and France in the Near East and Africa, for the action of the Kaiser had taken the form of threats, as when his gunboat sailed into the Moroccan harbor of Agadir. The French Socialists who had opposed their own government's foreign policy, sought to link up with the leaders of the German labor unions to give a sense of reality to the claims of international Socialism. These movements of labor to lessen the international tension were paralleled by similar efforts in the world of finance and business, built as it was upon the confidence of continuing peace. A leader in this movement was Sir Thomas Barclay who, in 1914, had been one of the chief architects of the *Entente Cordiale* between England and France, by clearing away the misunderstandings which had kept these nations at enmity intermittently since the Hundred Years' War. It seemed to him that the same common-sense methods of intercourse and education would clear away the barriers between Germany and her western neighbors. But, while these efforts to bolster peace were under way the decisions had been taken which brought war.

Suddenly the Austrian ultimatum filled the headlines of the papers. A day and a night were left for the decisions of peace or war; which meant that there was no chance of peace. Although the deadly timetable of the General Staffs had begun to tick off the hours before mobilization, it hardly seemed possible that the quarrel between Austria and Serbia should become the cause of universal war, but the feverish activity of the Foreign Offices to check the on-coming flood proved futile, and on August 3 the German army marched into Belgium for its invasion of Northern France with ruthless disregard of Belgium's neutrality which Germany had guaranteed.[1]

Germany was carrying out the Schlieffen Plan, drawn up a decade previously, for the invasion of France through its unprotected northern frontier where neutral Belgium had been relied upon by the French as a barrier against attack. The great fortresses of Verdun and Sedan and the heavily defended escarpments of the Vosges along the eastern frontier were to be outflanked by this northern invasion. From the military point of view, it was the grand strategy which was to bring swift victory to Germany. But the neutrality of Belgium was almost as vital to England's safety as it was to that of France. Long before Napoleon proposed to use Antwerp as a dagger pointed at the heart of Britain, the question of the control of the Scheldt had been a major interest in Britain's foreign policy. Now it was evident that in the opening hours of the war the guarantees of internation law were being swept aside by the German General Staff — a fact which Bethmann-Hollweg, the German Chancellor, sadly admitted in a feeble apology for what had been done. The full import of that opening act in the drama of the war was in the mind of Sir Edward Grey, Britain's Foreign Secretary, when on the evening of August 3 he looked out from his room in the Foreign Office at the twilight gathering over the London streets and said "the lights are going out all over Europe. We shall not see them lit again in our life." The next day England declared war.

Sir Edward Grey's premonition of disaster was realized to the full in the years that followed, but in the opening weeks and months of the war it was apparently not widely shared in Britain. In the country that had escaped

[1] The conclusion to be drawn from recent researches is that Austria was primarily to blame but was led to believe that Germany was solidly behind it.

the dangers of the Spanish Armada and Napoleon's threat of invasion, it seemed to the ordinary citizen as if this were another continental war in which Britain would play its traditional role of sending an expeditionary force, as it had done in the days of Marlborough and Wellington, while remaining safe at home behind the bulwark of the British Fleet. With imperturbable confidence in the outcome, shopkeepers and businessmen began to hand out the sign "business as usual" and the slogan was widely lived up to.

In France, however, the sense of universal tragedy dominated public opinion as the German invasion swept nearer and nearer to Paris in the attempt — which almost succeeded — to encircle and destroy the armies of Joffre. Although this fate was averted by the "Miracle of the Marne," and the little English expeditionary force grew to an army sufficiently strong to hold the western flank from the Aisne to the Channel, the war in the trenches which followed maintained a perpetual horror for four long years, with no apparent way of escape from its malignant tragedy. On the eastern front there was equal victory and stalemate for the Central Powers when the Russian armies were overrun at Tannenberg, but the slow-moving might of Russia denied ultimate victory to the invaders.

To the military mind, as developed in the iron clamp of Prussian history, there was something supremely inspiring in this spectacle of men marching to a rendezvous with death; but the death that was waiting for them and which they sought to inflict upon their enemies was not that of the high drama of war, but of multiple assassination in the sordid, vermin-infested setting of trench warfare. The world was aghast at such a spectacle, which seemed to revive the worst horrors of barbarism. Nor was this progressive degeneration merely physical. Both at the front and at home the fighting nations became steadily more callous and less responsive to the ideals of peace-time. The impact of the war reached to the innermost recesses of the mind of everyone involved in it, and this meant practically everyone in the world.

The fact of this universal involvement made the struggle in Europe a world war even while the actual combatants were limited to the two European alliances. Not only were there moral issues involved which affected deeply all right-minded men, but the war itself revealed the fact that the political boundaries of nations were by no means their true frontiers. The commercial and industrial revolutions had created economic ties and dependencies which extended all over the world. Raw materials for clothes or weapons had to be sought in Asia or America, to supplement the small supplies of the European homeland. War industries sprang up on neutral soil to meet this new imperious demand. And so the area of conflict widened over the seven seas.

Although the full extent of the revolution in warfare due to science was not at first clearly sensed, the appalling cost in life and property began to stir deeply even the uneasy consciences of those — and they were in the great majority — who had accepted as an axiom of history the inevitability of recurring war as the "final argument of nations" and an indispensable instrument in the polity of sovereign states. The failure of the peace movements of the nineteenth century to affect practical politics had been climaxed by the futility of the Hague Conferences of 1899 and 1907 to lessen the scope of the horrors of war. It was evident that the whole problem of the nature of war needed re-studying.

Sensing this situation, Professor Clark as head of the Research Division of the Carnegie Endowment for International Peace, convinced the President of the Endowment, Elihu Root, of the need for a thoroughly objective, scientific study of the war, not from the military standpoint of strategy, but as a vast, disturbing phenomenon. This idea of dealing with the impact of war on economic and social life seemed to be a more realistic approach to the problem of international peace than the academic program which had been prepared for the Conference the preceding summer, which had dealt primarily with the remoter causes of war. The re-casting of the research program of the Endowment resulted in the *Economic and Social History of the War,* which, before the completion of its hundred and fifty volumes, ten years after the end of the war, had drawn upon the war-time experience of sixteen countries.

The magnitude of this undertaking was commensurate with the theme, and the credit for making it possible should go to Elihu Root who, as President of both the Carnegie Endowment for International Peace and the still greater Carnegie Corporation, was able to inspire their policies with the same kind of imaginative statesmanship as he had evidenced in public affairs. Conservative by temper and training, his convictions were based solidly upon long experience, but with stability of purpose went a rare breadth of vision and a boldness in initiative — qualities which evidently had endeared him to the heart of the creator of these foundations, Andrew Carnegie. Root had at first no thought of a comprehensive history of the European war, for no one in those opening months of the conflict imagined that it could endure through years of exhaustion and suffering. The point of exhaustion seemed always to be near, as the daily cost of the war in the destruction of life and property reached staggering proportions.

Here, so it seemed, was an argument for peace more compelling than the slow processes of reform in international law.[2] But it had to be studied as a problem, not treated as an accepted basis for pacifism. The fact that, from its very beginning, the war had cut so deeply into the life of the nations was due not only to the vast changes wrought by science in military technique, but also to the changed nature of industrialized society at peace. The days of hand industry, however backward and limited in achievement they seemed from the standpoint of the twentieth century, were at least equally limited in the capacity for destruction. Evidently the Western world, by testing that capacity in the autumn of 1914, was also raising the question of

[2] The cost and devastation of World War I did not prove to be a preventive of the resort to war. It did, however, prove that war under the aegis of science cannot be used as an instrument of policy between highly developed nations because of the impossibility of controlling and directing it to achieve original purposes.

the validity of international war, not by the pacifist refusal to fight, but by the consequences of the very acceptance of the principle that war is an instrument of national policy.

These fundamental issues, however, lay quite outside the range of those responsible for the conduct of the war, who, in the effort to destroy the resources of their enemies, were forced to exhaust their own. The one solution for such a universal disaster, which was shared at the time by military and political leaders alike, was that the war should be a short one. The sooner it was over, the greater the chance of recovery. But when the war in the west sank into the nightmare of the trenches and the stubborn courage of the Russian mujiks was making victories meaningless in the east, the hopes of an early end to the carnage faded away.

Wars of peoples are not as easy to stop as those waged by princes or governments, as was already shown in the first war of nations, that of the French Revolution. But even Napoleon had known when to stop — as at Leoben — if only to gain an interval before a renewal of the struggle, and Bismarck could call a halt to his policy of blood and iron when, for the purposes of statecraft, he held the army of von Moltke, after its victory at Königgrätz, from marching into Vienna. But there were no Bismarcks or Napoleons in 1914. The deadly drama had escaped control, a fact already apparent before the end of the year. Evidently it was becoming a test, not merely of the endurance of the warring nations, but of war itself.

It cannot be said that these ideas were either clearly seen or widely held in these first months of the war. On the contrary, the greater the demands of the war the more it became the duty of the warring governments to maintain morale by obscuring costs or offering a glowing, imaginary balance sheet of the prize of victory. The fallacies of war economics are familiar now, but in war-time when everyone is employed and wages are high, the coming day of reckoning is ignored. More fundamental, however, is the fact that war economics is a totally different thing from the economics of peace. Its purpose is not prosperity but security, a possession without price in the market place, but priceless in the other sense of the word. From this point of view, therefore, a mere balance-sheet of loss and gain is meaningless, for the competition in destruction may be the necessary, and therefore, the valid insurance of survival. The categories of normal living no longer apply.

There was no one in the academic world better qualified to deal with these questions than Professor John Bates Clark. A philosopher capable of exploring rare distances of economic history, he was free from the dogmatism which, from the days of Ricardo and Mill, had so largely colored economic thinking and made liberalism an apology for things as they are, instead of an instrument for liberation. On the other hand, he was not carried away by the new trend toward statistics, which, while furnishing a valid basis for analysis, became in second-class minds a mere science of accounting.

Conscious that the problem of human conduct is more than a mathematical equation, and unwilling to accept Mill's traditional discounting of the costs of war, Professor Clark decided that the fundamental analysis of the problem of war lay more in the field of history than of economics; that it called for a sensing of the tides of public opinion and of the mechanics of government as well as a weighting of economic facts. Therefore, he conferred with his colleagues in the Department of History at Columbia University, and they, in turn, suggested that he make a beginning by inviting the author to prepare a memorandum for the consideration of the Carnegie Endowment.

This memorandum turned out to be a preliminary outline of what was to become the *Economic and Social History of the World War*.[3] The title shows both the scope and the limitations of the work. While it covered the impact of the war upon the livelihood of both belligerent and neutral nations, sixteen of them, it avoided as far as possible the history of the war itself, leaving that for the military authorities who later wrote of it in great detail. But neither the economic nor the military history reached the fundamental political fact that war had ceased to be calculable, as it had been in the relatively static world of the past when the place of war in political theory was well defined as the recognized symbol of sovereignty in a repetitive, calculable society.

War in the scientific era follows the law of dynamics, change producing changes in geometric progression — with the whole process speeded up by the fact that the competition of war must follow a faster pace than that of peace, since in war the delay in adjustment may be fatal. The fact that the war involved so many peoples was not as significant as the fact that it involved them so completely.

There was no keeping events within bounds, as in the simple economy of the past. The shifting map of economic interests was invaded to a far greater degree than the march of armies on the geographic map, as the blockade and the financial dislocation of the war both clearly showed. . . . In its economy are combined two techniques, both of them dynamic: the technique of peace which supplies war with its resources, and the technique of destruction. Now, since both of these are progressively modified by every new development, war is as uncertain in its direction as in its intensity or spread. It is no longer a safe instrument for statesmanship under such circumstances: it is too dangerous to employ. It is no longer an *ultima ratio,* for it has lost its *raison d'être.* Victor and victim may suffer a common disaster. Its effects reach even into the unformed future and rob the savings of generations yet unborn. Time, as well as space, levels its barriers to the march of destruction. This new dynamic world, the creation of human intelligence, containing as it does the most precious things in our heritage, has no other defense against it, once it is loosed, than that which endangers it as well. It is equally clear from this anlysis that these phenomena are not merely incidental and temporary. They are typical and more and more true as civilization develops. Such are the phenomena of war as revealed by a study of the tragic years 1914 to 1918.[4]

[3] The shaping and editing of this work took some seven years. Over two hundred contributors, among them thirty-five cabinet ministers of various governments, contributed to its 150 volumes.

[4] The first developed statement of this conclusion as to the revolution in warfare in World War I was made by the writer in Berlin, at an inaugural lecture as Professor in the Hochschule fur Politik, March 1927, in the presence of the Chancellor of Germany and other high officials. *Cf. The United States in History* (New York: Simon and Schuster, 1956), pp. 128 ff.

The Wilsonian Program[5]

The full implications of the revolution in the science of warfare were first appreciated in Germany, not by the professional soldiers but by civilians like Walter Rathenau, the head of the great German electrical trust, who mobilized industry for war purposes. His vision, as he put it, was that of "marching smokestacks" across Germany, with belching furnaces instead of guns alone. By 1916 England and France had seen the fallacy of "business as usual" and had become national arsenals in the "total war," as it began to be called. New and more powerful weapons blasted not only the trenches but the countryside and cities many miles away, while on the battlefront, stretching from the forest-clad heights of Verdun to the marshes of Flanders, some two million soldiers died in the trenches. No wonder that in October of that year, the United States re-elected Wilson on the slogan "He kept us out of war." But when, to break the British sea power then blockading Germany, the Germans declared unrestricted submarine war, except for a small lane across the Atlantic, sank ships without warning and with no provision for survivors, and gave Wilson no satisfaction when he asked their war aims, the country quickly awakened to the danger that would lie in a victory of German militarism. Indeed, this prospect, in December 1916, seemed all too likely, with Russia helpless against further German invasion. The new war spirit was evident in the hostile reaction to Wilson's address on war aims to Congress on January 22, 1917, in which he called for a peace without victory:

First of all there must be peace without victory. . . . Victory would mean peace imposed upon the loser, a victor's terms imposed upon the vanquished. It would be accepted in humilation, under duress, at an intolerable sacrifice, and would leave a sting, a resentment, a bitter memory upon which terms of peace would rest, not permanently but only as upon quicksand. . . . Mankind is looking now for freedom of life, not for equiposes of power. No peace can last, or ought to last, which does not recognize and accept the principle that governments derive all their just powers from the consent of the governed, and that no right anywhere exists to hand people about from sovereignty to sovereignty as if they were property. . . . These are the principles of mankind, and they must prevail.

In other words, the real issue in the war was freedom — democratic freedom. Cynics mocked at this reminder of the primacy of morals over brute strength at the very time when the moral forces of humanity were surrendering to bleak despair. Yet even the warring nations listened. When the war had become meaningless carnage, Wilson rallied the forces of civilivation from involvement in universal destruction to a task, not of rebuilding the outworn structure of a state system using war as its ultimate instrument of policy, but of creating a world community of which mankind had until then hardly dared to dream. Even from the distance of American aloofness from the struggle, Wilson had, to the surprise of his detractors, made himself the exponent of the submerged forces of peace and freedom, upholding with

[5] There is a rich literature on this subject. This section takes that for granted, and deals only with those aspects which bear directly upon the central theme of the volume.

persistent tenacity the power of moral ideals against that of brute force. But more important still, he proposed to organize those moral ideals in an international organization:

> It will be absolutely necessary that a force be created as a guarantor of the permanency of the settlement so much greater than the force of any one nation now engaged or any alliance hitherto formed or projected that no nation, no probable combination of nations could possible withstand it. If the peace presently made is to endure, it must be made secure by the organized major force of mankind.

Here we have the germ of the Covenant of the League. This was not his first endorsement of the idea. On May 27, 1916, in an address before the League to Enforce Peace on the need for a peace based on justice and freedom, he stated, "I speak the mind and wish of the American people when I say that the United States is willing to become partner in any feasible association of nations formed to realize these objects and make them secure against aggression." But the League to Enforce Peace, although supported by men of such eminence as Elihu Root, was too legalistic for Wilson because it proposed a World Court as the substitute for war, and Wilson rightly felt that the prevention of war lay not in the rigidity of a legal structure but in the field of politics, where peace could be kept by the interplay of common interests. The causes of wars between modern nations are to be found less in the factual matters of dispute than in the hostile attitudes of nations over the disputes. Emotions and attitudes are for statesmen to deal with; courts and the procedure of arbitration are essential, but they are not enough. This was the thought that matured in Wilson's mind in the critical months of 1916. It was also the thought of the leaders of thought in Europe — such men as Lord Phillimore, Lord Robert Cecil and Gilbert Murray in England, and Léon Bourgeois in France. It was Bourgeois who had coined the name "La Société des Nations" as early as 1908. As early as 1915 the British League of Nations Society was formed, destined to become for over a decade a political power. But next to Wilson in influencing public opinion was Marshal Smuts, whose pamphlet *The League of Nations; a Practical Suggestion* matched in eloquence and elevation of thought the pronouncements from Washington.

If the origins of the movement for an international organization for peace were not Wilsonian, it readily accepted his leadership as he shaped the program in the autumn of 1918,[6] and finally made it the concluding paragraph of his Fourteen Points: "A general association of nations must be formed under specific covenants for the purpose of affording mutual guarantees of political independence and territorial integrity to great and small states alike."

Here, according to the official interpretation of the Fourteen Points, was to be "the foundation of the whole diplomatic structure of a permanent Peace."[7] The next problem was to realize this purpose in the treaty of peace.

[6] Address on the Liberty Loan, September 27, 1918.
[7] 2 U.S. Dept. of State *Foreign Relations of the United States*, Washington: U. S. Gov't. Printing Office 1918, Supplement, vol. I, p. 405 ff.

At the Paris Peace Conference, the making of a new map of Europe and of the world — with all the problems involved in so vast a reconstruction of the framework of nations, and the recovery from the disasters of the war — was the most pressing part of the peace settlement to those whose loyalties and welfare were so deeply involved. But to President Wilson and to liberal opinion in all countries, the most important task of the Peace Conference was not the political settlement of boundaries and conflicting national claims — matters on which voluntary agreement might be well nigh impossible, but which, nevertheless, would be adjusted in the process of history. The fundamental issue in the war, for the Wilsonians, was the prevention of resort to war, or the threat of it, as a means by which those adjustments would be made. To demand that nations renounce entirely the right of war, the most ancient attribute of sovereignty, and the "final argument" *(ultima ratio)* of nations, was not — as yet — practical politics. Wilson was not a pacifist, as his own crusading speeches showed during the war. But while allowing that there might be need to resort to war when the life of a nation or the principles of justice were at stake, he, although a leader of the new nationalism, proposed to curb it by erecting an international organization dedicated to the task of finding alternatives for war and obligated to suppress aggression.

The Covenent of the League of Nations, in which this ideal took final shape, was hammered into shape by a committee at the Paris Peace Conference, under the chairmanship of President Wilson and having among its leading members Lord Cecil and Marshal Smuts from the British delegation and Léon Bourgeois from the French. The actual drafting was largely the work of Sir Cecil Hurst and David Hunter Miller, the able legal adviser of President Wilson and Colonel House, who was also its historian.[8]

Far from being a daring departure from the national state system, as its enemies in the United States Senate asserted, the Covenant was an effort to strengthen that system by providing an organ, modelled after its own parliaments, with Assembly and Council, to replace the crude arbitrament of war. There was only one article in the Covenant which bore any resemblance to a super-state, Article 10:

> The Members of the League undertake to respect and preserve as against external aggression the territorial integrity and existing political independence of all Members of the League. In case of any such aggression the Council shall advise upon the means by which this obligation shall be fulfilled.

To Wilson — and to his enemies — this was the heart of the Covenant, a "Monroe Doctrine for the world." Yet it was a dead letter until the very last months of the League when, finally, Japan invoked it to keep the Western Powers out of its "sphere of influence" on the Asiatic mainland. Seldom has

[8] In *The Drafting of the Covenant* (New York: The Macmillan Co. 2 volumes, 1928), and in his monumental Diary (printed privately) which, with documents, fills twenty volumes.

so great an event depended on so mistaken an interpretation of a document as the renunciation of the League by the United States on the basis of its objection to Article 10. The League did not even make arbitration compulsory, in spite of its erection of a World Court and the fact that there were dozens of arbitration treaties in existence.

The heart of the League was not Article 10 but Article 11, which stopped more than one menace of war by the oldest of all diplomatic devices, conciliation. The text seems weak and vague, but while arbitration or the rules of the World Court led to verdicts or judgments which sovereign states accepted in theory but rejected in practice, conciliation took into account the susceptibilities of nations and used them for finding ways for accomodation on disputed issues, if not for complete agreement. It was the subtlest and most effective instrument of peace in the history of the League. The text read as follows:

1. Any war or threat of war, whether immediately affecting any of the Members of the League or not, is hereby declared a matter of concern to the whole League, and the League shall take any action that may be deemed wise and effectual to safeguard the peace of nations. In case any such emergency should arise, the Secretary-General shall on the request of any Member of the League forthwith summon a meeting of the Council.
2. It is also declared to be the friendly right of each Member of the League to bring to the attention of the Assembly or of the Council any circumstance whatever affecting international relations which threatens to disturb international peace or the good understanding between nations upon which peace depends.

Persuasion and warning were the prime methods of the League to prevent wars among its members; and even if wars broke out, provisions for its suppression showed the same kind of cautious regard for the susceptibilities of nations. The only unqualified obligation to take action against a nation going to war in violation of the Covenant was the economic sanction of complete severance with the violator. Military sanctions could only be "recommended" by the Council, leaving each government free to apply them as it saw fit (Article 16).

Criticism of these provisions as having been too weak, in view of the ultimate failure of the League, are unrealistic. The tide of nationalism was running too strong in the post-war years of resentment and distrust for public opinion anywhere to accept a "league to enforce peace" by the "organized major force of mankind." The League of Nations failed because the nations were not ready to accept even its persuasive methods to avert war. The blame rests not on the League but on its members, and especially on the one great nation which refused even membership.

The International Labor Organization

The finest sentence in the Treaty of Versailles is not to be found in the Covenant of the League of Nations but in the preamble to the constitution of the International Labor Organization: "Permanent peace can be established only if it is based upon social justice." This was the one section of the treaty which reached beyond politics to the daily interests of the common man, and equally far beyond the interests of most diplomatists and politicians at the Peace Conference. When Clemenceau, as its president, announced at the first General Session of the Conference that there would be a commission to plan an international labor organization, there was surprise and bewilderment in that part of the audience which never hesitated to express its feelings. The journalists present came away from that first general session seeking light from any and every quarter where they might find it, in order to explain to the readers "back home" how the Conference was proposing to set about the actual business of securing the peace of the world. Their surprise at the prominence of international labor legislation was not due to any lack of interest in labor problems, but to the fact that up to the very moment of this announcement no word had reached the public that the Peace Conference, which had ostensibly met mainly to draw boundaries and set nations in their places on the map, had any intention to move industrial problems to the fore. The program laid down in this solemn session was therefore far removed from what either journalists or the general public seemed to have expected.

There was two conjectures as to why the Conference had taken this step. The first was that the real masters of policy, the great Powers, had not reached agreement as to how they were to proceed in the settlement of the larger issues before the Conference, and that, as there was need to give some other indications of activity in the meantime, the public and the smaller Powers were being put off with something of general interest to keep them occupied. The other was that the governments of Europe were nervous in the face of a rising industrial unrest, with unknown Bolshevistic possibilities, and had, therefore, to offer to Labor a definite and formal recognition at the very opening of the Conference, both to justify themselves with reference to the war in the past, and to hold forth the hope of a larger measure of international labor agreements in the future.

Whether the governments of Europe were nervous or not in the winter of 1918-19, there was plenty of reason for uneasiness. We have now become so used to the Bolshevist regime that we cannot any longer realize how deeply it first stirred the passions of all classes in Europe — the bourgeois with fear, the radicals and revolutionaries with uneasy hope. Then the wild fires of revolution in Germany seemed to presage universal anarchy, and at least one or two of the governments represented at Paris were thought to stand in daily danger of being overthrown. The long shadow of Russia could not be obliterated from Europe. On May 1, 1919, the "Labor Day" of Europe, the French government showed how fearful it was of a revolution similar to those breaking out in Central Europe — stimulated by the Bolshevists — by it mobilizing 60,000 troops in Paris. Fortunately, this police measure was enough to prevent an armed outbreak.

In such circumstances the holding of international labor Conferences at Berne by the Socialists and the Syndicalists or Trade Unionists, who proposed once more to take up the broken threads of their pre-war organizations, had more than ordinary significance. This meeting was meant and taken as being more or less of a challenge to Paris — the revolutionary and industrial international organizations as against the governmental.

The work of the Commission for International Labor Legislation of the Peace Conference has first of all to be measured against that of these international organizations of European industrial democracy. Fortunately comparison is not difficult, for both Internationals, the Socialist and the Trade Union, drew up definite propositions embodying the principles upon which they wished to see world peace. When one examines these pronouncements, however, from the standpoint of labor, with reference to its own claims as such in the settlement, one is struck with the fact that a large part of the program they laid down had nothing to do with economic matters at all, but concerned things so remote from the factory and workshop as the Balkan boundaries or colonial adjustments. This in itself is a significant, and withal an inspiring fact, which seems to have attracted little attention — that the first attempt of industrial democracy to frame a program for foreign affairs should have so little to do with labor itself.

The "War Aims" which organized labor and the Socialists had put forth at various times in the latter stages of the war had covered the whole wide range of social justice and laid down general principles for international dealings without regard to the limitations of the particular demands of the workers. The leaders of industrial democracy were engaged upon the larger task of laying the basis for the new world order, which they hoped to erect, so that democracy might be safe in the future to go ahead with its plans and its dreams of economic progress. So deeply were they impressed by the interdependence of reforms at home with the international peace that their main preoccupation in the suggested settlement was to secure peace as a condition for the reforms which could then follow.

The British Labor Delegation to the Peace Conference made a proposal that instead of centering attention solely upon any specific claims of labor which might be inserted in the Treaty, there should be erected a Governing Body of ten representatives each of labor and employers, and twenty of government; an annually recurring International Labor Conference; and an International Labor Office of experts which could keep pace with the progressive changing demands of the labor world, and so secure, not one single Labor Charter, but a never-ending series.

The idea was a large and fruitful one. So far as labor was concerned, the Peace Conference of Paris would be but the first step in a continuous process; and the Treaty, instead of being a final document, was, in so far as it was concerned with industrial problems, but the first clauses of a document which was to be continued by future congresses through future treaties. It would thus be the beginning of a continuous cooperation on the part of Labor, Society, and Governments.

The International Labor Conference is a body without precedent in history, a tripartite organization composed of one representative each of workers and employers, and two for the government. For the first time in the history

434

of international law it was proposed to permit unofficial delegates — mere citizens of difference countries representing home interests in labor or capital, to vote with similar representative citizens of other countries, independently of the action of the representatives of their governments, and so to help actually to bind those governments towards certain international policies and treaties.

It was clear that some device would have to be found for the limitation of the powers of these nonofficial representatives, and yet it was necessary that the limitation should not be carried to the point of endangering in any way the reality of their work. As the Commission was warned more than once in the course of its proceedings, labor was tired of words and empty and delusive promises and would not be interested in the erection of any institution which was devoid of power. If, however, power were to be given to men irresponsible to their governments, it was taking that power from the governments themselves. This brought one into a very dangerous dilemma, for if the power to make labor treaties were to be taken over by a body containing so large an element of unofficial representatives, what about the power to enforce the treaties? Should the governments be held responsible for carrying out propositions arrived at and agreed upon in the formulation of which they had been partly shut out? The result would be to make a government little more than a police force for the administration of regulations arrived at by these Conferences; in short, there would have arisen something like a world state under the aegis of industrial democracy, and the International Labor Conference would be the most august legislating institution in the world, over-riding government not only within itself but in the subsequent carrying out of its decisions.

This dilemma gave rise to a long discussion in the Commission. The more revolutionary section, represented especially by the brilliant Secretary of the French Confédération Générale du Travail, was strongly for proceeding at once with the bolder policy which would endow the International Labor Conference with the powers of a genuine legislature and bind the constituent countries to the carrying out of its decrees. This point of view was apparently shared in greater or less extent by those qualified to speak for labor in all the continental countries — a fact of much significance in estimating how far towards industrial confederation the continental countries might proceed. Great Britain and the United States, however, and still more Japan, were reluctant even to consider such a revolutionary point of view, and stood out strongly against the notion that the time had come for the recognition of a world state, even where the impulse to common action was so strong.

For the United States, which at best had come against its will into the arena of world politics, any suggestion that its government should abrogate its control of such domestic affairs as industrial legislation seemed almost automatically to exclude it from participation in the scheme. Japan was equally reluctant, but for another reason — its industrial problems were so unlike those of Western Europe, that it could hardly be expected to place itself at the mercy of an international body in which it would have so slight a voice. Since there was no power to compel the representatives of any state in Paris to accept a body endowed with such prerogatives it was clearly necessary to find some device by which the Conference of Labor should have sufficient authority to justify its existence in the eyes of labor as a real force for securing legislation, and yet not set itself up as a super-government in opposition to existing governments.

It was this dilemma which brought forth the second and most ingenious contribution to the British scheme, namely that the power of the International Conference be limited to secure the submission of its legislation to the legislatures or other competent authorities of the participating states. In the field of international labor legislation, the Foreign Offices and other bureaucratic intermediaries cannot interfere; no recommendations of the Conference can be smothered in the files of a reactionary diplomatic official; they must be brought within a given time to the attention of Parliament or Congress or whatever lawmaking body the country may possess.

Beyond that, international compulsion cannot go towards securing the adherence of the participating Powers; all the World Conference can do is to lay its conclusions before the highest tribunal of public opinion in each country, and leave it to that body to decide whether it shall adhere or not.

In the long history of political theory it would be hard to find an experiment more interesting and suggestive than this delicate machinery for transmitting to Powers jealous of their reputation and their standards of social morality the forceful suggestion of international cooperation in matters which had hitherto lain exclusively within their jurisdiction. On the face of it there is no derogation of sovereignty whatever; the International Conference has no power to make legislation, but simply to suggest it. In reality, however, that suggestion, if passed by a two-thirds vote, comes to the various countries with an authority which somewhat resembles the device by which the British officials once governed the titular rulers of Egypt. In a word, the essence of the plan is to throw back upon public opinion in the various countries the responsibility for carrying on social legislation. By seizing upon this sound principle in the assignment of responsibility for passing legislation, it is possible to exact from the participating states a degree of responsibility for such laws as they do accept which otherwise could not have been exacted.

The results have more than justified this unique experiment. At present, one hundred and fourteen Conventions and one hundred and twelve recommendations for social legislation have been accepted by the participating governments. In 1919, when the I.L.O. was founded, there were only two treaties dealing with standards of social welfare, one prohibiting the use of white phosphorus, and the other concerning night work by women. Now the ideals of social justice are not only safeguarded by international action but by a world-wide cooperation in technical assistance for backward peoples. For the I.L.O., which was practically independent of the League of Nations, is now a specialized agency of the United Nations — the only body of the Geneva constellation to live through World War II. There are now (1959) 1932 ratifications by governments of the conventions.

436

The other economic and social aspects of the work of the League of Nations lie for the most part outside the scope of this work. Although a competent Secretariat played an important part in the rebuilding of Europe, it lacked the resources of a Marshall Plan, owing to the abstention of America.

There were also a Health Organization, world-wide in its scope and composition; an Advisory Committee on the Traffic in Opium and Other Dangerous Drugs which worked effectively in Asia; and a refugee organization set up mainly as a consequence of the revolution and civil war in Russia, when about two million people left their country and huddled in Eastern and Central Europe without resources. As Commissioner in this field, Nansen the explorer, accomplished miracles with inadequate financial support. Finally there was the Organization for International Intellectual Cooperation, designed to bring together teachers, artists, scientists and authors from different countries. Although this body drew together scholars of eminence in various branches of learning — Bergson, Einstein, Gilbert Murray, Madame Curie and others — their program of work lay for the most part outside of the political field. And yet it was this organization which became the model for the greatly enlarged organization of the United Nations, the Educational, Scientific and Cultural Organization, known as UNESCO.

In all these lines of international clarification and cooperation, pioneering bodies were created which proved of great value in developments after World War I.

CHAPTER XVIII

CRUSADES AGAINST FREEDOM

Resurgent Nationalism in Europe

ALTHOUGH World War I, by the creation of the League of Nations, brought organized internationalism for the first time into the drama of history, it also gave emphasis to the sentimental attachment to one's own country which is one of the strongest emotions of civilized man. For the European peoples as well as their governments the war was primarily a culmination of the long tragic history of militant nationalism. This was true of all European countries. The central theme of history for a thousand years had been the development of the national state.

England, shut in by the encircling seas, had been one of the first to develop a national patriotism, even during the Middle Ages fusing native British stock with Anglo-Saxon, Danish, and Norman invaders into a self-conscious nation. This fusion had been completed in the great days of Elizabeth, when England began to play its part in world trade. In the seventeenth century the struggle with the Stuart kings made the nation more self-conscious by placing political power in the hands of Parliament. In the nineteenth and twentieth centuries the rise of the middle class and then of the working class to power accentuated the sense of British nationality, and the growth of world empire strengthened instead of lessened this attachment to the homeland.

In France patriotism was even more pronounced than in England. Through the long centuries the country had been welded together by the Capetian kings, but their figures were distant and shadowy compared with the ever present memory of Joan of Arc. It was the French Revolution which added the final chapter to French nationalism. The slogan of that revolution, "Liberty, Equality, Fraternity," became, under Jacobin leadership, the voice of a new nation, for the France of today did not exist in the Old Regime, with its local customs barriers and its privileged orders. "The Marseillaise," the marching song of the revolution, became the national anthem and the tricolor a symbol of patriotic pride. There remained, however, bitter factional and class antagonisms which, in spite of the sense of a common nationalism, the French have never been able to weld into a balanced political unity. But, if public spirit — which is the key to British political capacity — is often lacking, French nationalism is much like that of Germany, a sentiment stirred mostly by militant patriotism, the kind which Bismarck used to unify his country, and which reached its climax in the Third Reich of Adolph Hitler.

Already during the Paris Peace Conference it was clear that the two principles of Woodrow Wilson's policy which had most dominated Europe — even the enemy states, in the last year of the war — the prevention of war by a League of Nations and the self-determination of Nations, were by no means on an equal footing. In Wilson's political philosophy "self-determination of nations" was another term for freedom as the foundation of an international society solving its differences by peaceful means. But in Europe, where nations had so largely won and maintained their freedom by war, "self-determination" meant nationalism with all the force of history behind it, living and vibrant in the minds of peoples, to whom it meant freedom to pursue their own way of life.

The organization of peace was a new and untried experiment. Unfortunately, although no nation cherished patriotism more than the Americans, they did not fully appreciate the problems which the new organization presented to European statesmen, especially those who had just lived through the greatest war in history. Wilson's biographer, Ray Stannard Baker, a man of genuine integrity, writing from the privileged position of one in daily contact with Wilson, depicted Clemenceau, the embodiment of French realism, but also a liberal, as a mere reactionary cynic, because he did not believe that the old antagonisms could be exorcised from war-torn Europe by a sudden conversion to the techniques of peace. Lloyd George, the practical statesman, was described as a trickster, because he was willing to make compromises with Germany, believing that the guarantee of peace lay more in the maintenance of workable relationships with nations than in the adoption of general international principles. The underlying fact which neither Wilson nor his biographer appreciated was that the nations reshaped by the World War had been shaped and reshaped by war through all the centuries, and that even under the Covenant of the League, they would inevitably grope toward the use of power, or a balance of power, upon which peace, however precarious, had been maintained through much of the nineteenth century.

As long as this trend of European policy was closely tied in with that of the League's efforts to build up collective security, as, for instance, in the case of the Little Entente or the creation of other nonagressive pacts, it was valid. But as early as 1923 Poincarè had shown once more, by his single-handed invasion of the Ruhr in order to ensure French "rights" to reparations, that the inevitable instrument of nationalism was militarism; and the lesson was not lost on Japan and Italy, which cherished dreams of empire, or on a Germany filled with resentment and thwarted ambition.

While there were in all three of these countries men and women of good will who abhorred war and looked with anxious hope to the League of Nations to strengthen the ties of international peace, so often strained to the breaking point — Italians still cherishing the ideas of Mazzini, Germans as open-minded as Goethe or Kant, and some Japanese as devoted to peace as Nitobe — they were at a disadvantage politically because they could not hope to offer to their fellow countrymen the promise of direct action. Following the world-old method of resort to war or the threat of it, at first separately and then together, these nations withdraw from the League of Nations, after some twenty years of its by no means futile history, and entered into an open conspiracy against the peace, a conspiracy which culminated in World War II, in a crusade against both peace and freedom.

The issue which Woodrow Wilson had presented to the world was finally seen, in the tragic years which followed, to be the supreme issue of all time, one from which no nation can escape. Summoning, in imagination, the serried ranks of all the soldiers and sailors of the First World War, and recalling the promises made to them that it was to be a war against war, a struggle to end "the nightmare of dread which lay upon the nations before the war came," he foretold the consequences of failure in words which were to have a pregnant and compelling meaning: "There will surely come, sometime in the vengeful Providence of God, another struggle in which not a few hundred thousand fine young men from America will have to die, but as many millions as are necessary to accomplish the final freedom of the peoples of the world." Note the final phrase!

We now turn to the prologue of this tragedy, as it was prepared in Italy, Germany and Japan.

Mussolini and Facism

The effects of World War I upon Italy were to strain its impoverished economy to the breaking point, while disillusionment over the peace settlement added a sense of futility in the management of the state itself. Then, over against the dull routine of life in an imperfectly organized society, the bugle call of romance sounded in Italian ears from the poetry and daring of d'Annunzio and the strident reminders of the glory of ancient Rome in the harangues of Mussolini.

The situation was ideal for a demagogue who could capitalize on both trends of national disaffection, attacking with brutal ruthlessness all supporters of the existing order — not only communists and conservatives, but also the middle class liberals — and appealing at the same time to a hitherto dormant spirit of devotion to Italy, of pride in its history and confidence in its future. This dualism — on the one hand resort to force and violence, with unscrupulous disregard of all the restraints of morality or even the instincts of common humanity, and on the other hand the inspiration of a call to the Italian people to realize their destiny — had been implicit in the teachings of Machiavelli. But none of his great pupils in the past, neither Frederick the Great, Talleyrand, nor Bismarck, had ever carried them so far, with such blatant boastfulness, as the founder of Italian Fascism, Benito Mussolini.

Few figures in history offer more lessons to the student of history than this son of a blacksmith, who created his own instrument of power and by it ruled Italy for twenty-three years. He lacked the vast resources of the two other outstanding revolutionists of his time, Hitler and Stalin, both of whom, as we shall see, were also Machiavellian and therefore reactionaries, in spite of their claims to be creators of a brave new world. But in the advocacy of force as a basis of power and war as an instrument of national policy, he was the first to challenge the new ideology, which linked peace with justice in the League of Nations. Moreover, his creative energy, which set going a national revival inside of Italy, and his apparent readiness, during the first years of his regime, to conduct foreign affairs within the framework of the existing European state system, led other nations to discount his militarism, and so gave him the opportunity to build it up against the time when he could defy by acts the pacific policies of nations, which from the first he had defied in words.

Mussolini's early career was a checkered one: day laborer, schoolteacher, socialist agitator, and editor of the Italian socialist newspaper, *Avanti*. But he broke with the socialists on their opposition to Italy's intervention in the war, enlisted in the army, was wounded and discharged in 1917. After the war was over he continued, in his own newspaper, *Populo d'Italia*, a passionate campaign for militant nationalism in peace time. War, he said, was a blessing in disguise, a means of uniting the nation along lines which would "ensure the moral and material greatness of the Italian people." This program of national solidarity was an appeal to the common people and was directed against both conservatives and socialists. Just what its positive content called for was not set forth in definite terms, but its two aims, some form of national, not international, socialism, and an enhancement of the power of the state, were to be achieved by the leaders of a revolutionary organization, the *Fascio di Combattimento*, composed of armed, black-shirted groups or *fasci*. The name was taken from the *fasces*, or bundles of rods carried before the magistrates of ancient Rome as a symbol of the unity and power of the state. The Fascist movement was therefore militarism in civilian life, with unquestioning acceptance of authority and direct action — meaning violence or the threat of it — against all opponents.

Finally, in October, 1922, Mussolini judged that the time was ripe for a *coup d'état*, and the black-shirted legions marched on Rome. The king, to avoid bloodshed, yielded to the demonstrators and sent for Mussolini, who had remained in Milan, and entrusted the government to him. As prime minister he was voted autocratic powers by the bewildered parliament. It was soon evident that Mussolini had learned the Machivellian craft of dictatorship. The local fascist leaders, richly rewarded with medals and specious honors, vied with each other against opponents, while Mussolini allowed them to take the blame for excesses. He did not always succeed in this, however, for in 1924 the murder of an outspoken socialist deputy, Matteotti, shocked the conscience of the nation. As for the working class, he knew how to make an asset of his humble origins: "I do not come from an aristocratic and illustrious family," he would say. "I worked with my hands. . . . I am the enemy of those who . . . try to dupe the workmen."

From the beginning of his rule, Mussolini assumed full charge of foreign and domestic affairs, and in course of time held as many as five cabinet portfolios. As Duce, or leader, he was the supreme head of the government, a title which he assumed later. With political opposition cowed by violence, or the threat of it, and local governments in the hands of fascist dictators (*podeste*) carrying out or trying to anticipate Mussolini's orders, the country began to assume, between 1925 and 1928, the form of a "corporate state." What this really meant, as Mussolini himself explained on more than one occasion, was a declaration of the omnipotence of government and a denial not only of democracy, but also of representative government. The rule of the majority was to be replaced by that of the *Duce*, who was to be regarded as the very embodiment of the nation's will. Mussolini's motto, "Believe, obey, fight," summed up what was to be expected of the common man.

By a paradox with which we are now only too familiar, Mussolini asserted that this autocracy was the "purest form of democracy," a claim repeated on every possible occasion by Hitler and Stalin. In the Italian state the denial of participation in government was also a denial of personal freedom, because the individual had no share in safeguarding his own rights. It was therefore quite in line with the development of Fascism that freedom of speech, freedom of the press, and freedom of assembly, as well as freedom from arbitrary arrest, should practically cease to exist. This meant, in fascist hands, the silencing of political opponents by violence and barbarities of all kinds. Humiliating subservience was forced on teachers in schools, and in the universities black-shirted youths laid their revolvers on their writing desks. Newspapers were heavily censored. Unyielding foes, like Count Carlo Sforza, former foreign minister, who fled the country, had their property destroyed or taken away from them, while those who failed to escape were imprisoned. There was no guarantee of personal rights in the fascist-dominated courts.

Nevertheless, from the standpoint of purely material gain, Fascism seemed to justify itself throughout the first decade of its regime. The co-ordinated effort of the nation, spurred on by means of mass demonstrations and held to its purpose by strict (though ultimately futile) measures against corrupt practices as well as against sullen opposition, increased the output of Italian industry and bettered public utilities.

But this was only one part of the story. The improved welfare of the Italian people was achieved under a system which denied that peace could be the basic principle of conduct, either within or between nations. The crude mental attitude that the rule of life is the survival of the fittest by "tooth and claw" was adopted by Fascism, especially in its glorification of war. Mussolini made this the central issue of international affairs, thus challenging the whole ideology of the League of Nations, in such passages as these: "Equally foreign to the spirit of Fascism, even though they may be accepted for their utility in meeting special political situations, are all international or political organizations which, as history proves, crumble to the ground whenever the heart of nations is stirred by sentimental, idealistic, or practical considerations. . . . War alone brings up to their highest tension all human energies and puts the stamp of nobility upon the peoples who have the courage to meet it."

Fascism carried this anti-pacifist spirit over into the lives of individuals. It was dedication for combat. The Fascist must "live dangerously" — a precept drilled into the people from the earliest years of childhood, and driven home by militarist organizations, especially those which appeal to youth — the pageantry of parading marchers and the challenge of mock warfare.

Behind all this lay the distorting perspectives of the "glorious Imperium" of ancient Rome. "Fascism sees in the imperialistic spirit — that is, in the tendency of nations to expand — a manifestation of their vitality. In the opposite tendency, which would limit their interests to the fatherland, it seems a symbol of decadence. People who rise or revive are imperialistic; renunciation is a characteristic of dying peoples. The Fascist doctrine is that suited to the tendencies and feelings of a people which, like the Italian, after lying fallow during centuries of foreign servitude, is now reasserting itself in the world."[1] The "Imperial nation" was now to expand across the Mediterranean (*Mare Nostrum*), and the non-European lands beyond it were once more to see the military might of Italy, for Fascism was "a manifestation of the power of the people which traces its own origins to Rome, and bears the triumphal and immortal insignia of the Roman lictors on the shores of the African sea."

[1] Mussolini, Benito, *The Doctrine of Fascism*, pp. 41-42.

The dream of a revival of Roman power around the Mediterranean was first tested by Mussolini in the occupation of the Greek island of Corfu in 1923, due to the murder, on Greek territory, of an Italian official. The demands of Italy upon Greece to pay an enormous indemnity, backed by the threat of war, was so much like Austria's ultimatum to Serbia in 1914, that the League of Nations intervened — though not strongly enough in the opinion of its strongest supporters — and thus became the special object of Mussolini's enmity.

The next step in his Balkan policy was the annexation of Albania, a process extending from 1927 to 1939, as a leverage against Yugoslavia, whose possession of Fiume was sorely resented by Italian nationalists. After all, there was nothing new in the power politics of European states, in this kind of intervention, as well as that in Spain in concert with Germany in 1936, in support of the Franco rebellion. Mussolini realized that his new empire must be, not in Europe but in Africa. The only African state not claimed by a European Power was Ethiopia, which had disastrously defeated an Italian army in 1896, and which, therefore, was marked out for invasion. The war of conquest began in 1935, in spite of Ethiopia's deeply moving protest in the Assembly of the League of Nations. The time for aggression was well chosen. England and France were still suffering from the Great Depression of the early thirties; and, when they held back from any attempt to restrain Mussolini, it was not to be expected that the United States, not a League member, would interfere. Even as it was, however, Secretary of State Cordell Hull did take steps to deny oil to the Italian navy.

In the wrecking of the League of Nations, Mussolini had other, more powerful partners in infamy, Hitler and the militarists of Japan. It was not by chance that all struck at the same time, in the years when the nations devoted to the maintenance of peace and freedom were economically weak; and it was inevitable that by joining an alliance as Axis Powers, they should recognize their common purpose in the suppression of freedom.

Hitler and Nazism

The simplest explanation of Fascism and National Socialism is that they were parts of the aftermath of World War I. The truer explanation is that the world of law and order into which they erupted was not only in disorder owing to the war, but that the organization of government in both Italy and Germany was inadequate for the task of safeguarding the heritage of freedom. The parliamentary system which had been adopted generally on the Continent in the nineteenth century, did not work with the efficiency of its English model. In Italy it was too much influenced by a convenient acceptance of *laissez-faire;* in Germany it was too much dominated by bureaucracy and the Hohenzollern tradition of paternalism and militarism. There, the rhapsodic philosophy of Nietzsche had already dealt armed blows on the temple of Hegel; and nationalism, school for power, but disillusioned and resentful after military defeat, threw the blame for Germany's post-war sufferings on its ex-enemies and on the Jews.

Clearing its conscience of any responsibility by a persistent propaganda of war guilt against its former enemies, and mentally and economically unprepared to grapple with the consequences of defeat, German public opinion could offer no bulwark against the steadily mounting tide of discontent, which found expression in Adolph Hitler's conspiracy against the peace of nations. It was also a conspiracy against freedom — not a secret conspiracy, any more than Mussolini's, for both were its outspoken enemies from the beginning of their careers. Deftly, both leaders (*Duce* and *Führer* are synonymous) turned the technique of Lenin against him by exploiting the fear by the middle class of Bolshevism, while using the political advantage which that claim gave them to seize power. Discipline under leadership and a totalitarian state were the aims of all of these arch enemies of freedom.

Fortunately for history, Hitler's autobiography, *Mein Kampf*, is a complete revelation of the tricks of the demagogue. There is nothing more weighted by deceit in Machiavelli's *Prince* than the chapter on propaganda in this bible of the Nazis. The chapter begins by a confession that the way to power is to win the masses, rather than to convince thoughtful people whom he calls "theorists." "Theorists," he says, are rarely great organizers, and the organizer must be a man who does not overvalue nor underestimate mankind in the mass. "On the contrary, he must try to take account of weakness and bestiality, so that he can create a formation which as a living organization is filled with the strongest and most constant force, and thus is suitable for carrying an idea and paving the way to success." An agitator is better suited to be a leader than is a "theorist" or intellectual, for to lead means to be able to move the masses. According to Hitler, the talent for shaping ideas has nothing whatsoever to do with the qualities of a leader:[2]

"When a movement harbors the purpose of tearing down a world and building another in its place, complete clarity must reign in the ranks of its own leadership with regard to the following principles:

"*Every movement will first have to sift the human material it wins into two large groups: supporters and members.*

"*The function of propaganda is to attract supporters, the function of organization to win memberss.*

"*The supporter is made amenable to the movement by propaganda. The member is induced by the organization to participate personally in the recruiting of new supporters, from whom in turn members can be developed.*

"*Propaganda will consequently have to see that an idea wins supporters, while the organization must take the greatest care only to make the most valuable elements among the supporters into members. Propaganda does not, therefore, need to rack its brains with regard to the importance of every individual instructed by it, with regard to his ability, capacity, and understanding, or character, while the organization must carefully gather from the mass of these elements those which really make possible the victory of the movement.*

"*The first task of propaganda is to win people for subsequent organization; the first task of organization is to win men for the continuation of propaganda. The second task of propaganda is the disruption of the existing state of affairs and the*

[2] Hitler, Adolf, *Mein Kampf* (translation by Ralph Manheim; Boston: Houghton-Mifflin Company, 1943), pp. 581-582, 583.

permeation of this state of affairs with the new doctrine, while the second task of organization must be the struggle for power, thus to achieve the final success of the doctrine."

The remainder of this chapter of *Mein Kampf* deals with the beginning of the organization of the National Socialist Party. Hitler left discussions to the committees and made his own decisions independently of their conclusions. Thus, "Parliamentarianism" within the party was robbed of any effective action. The keynote of the whole organization was loyalty to the leader. Already, by 1921, Hitler had prevented committees from interfering with active leadership. "In the course of two years I have enforced my opinion more and more, and today (1924) it is already a matter of course in the movement, at least in so far as the highest leadership is concerned."

Here we have the fundamental principle of totalitarian rule from which the intellectual elite of the nation is to be either excluded or brought into line, and which has no place for majority rule or dissent.

It is not easy to quote from *Mein Kampf* because of its verbosity and the way in which one paragraph rambles along to another. Yet the main ideas in it are plain enough. It starts with Hitler's own background as a poor Austrian boy who "went to Vienna with a suitcase containing some clothes and linen, and an unshakeable determination to become 'something.'" The story of his early struggles with poverty in Vienna is given with a naiveté which disarms the reader at the start; but in the second chapter, after describing his "years of study and suffering in Vienna," he quickly passes into a denunciation of the Vienna Jews and Marxian socialists, who, in his mind, were linked with them. The emotional — not to say hysterical — outburst at the end of this chapter is a key to much that follows:

If, with the help of the Marxian creed, the Jew conquers the nations of this world, his crown will become the funeral wreath of humanity, and once again this planet, empty of mankind, will move through the ether as it did thousands of years ago. Eternal nature inexorably revenges the transgressions of her laws. Therefore, I believe today that I am acting in the sense of the Almighty Creator; by warding off the Jews, I am fighting for the Lord's work.

Migrating from Vienna to Munich, Hitler found no change in the social and economic structure, because — as he saw it — there were Jews to be found in Germany as well. On August 3, 1914, Hitler petitioned to serve in a Bavarian instead of an Austrian regiment, and "joy and gratitude knew no bounds" when the permission was granted. The experience of the war itself strengthened his nationalist feeling still further, and at the close he decided to devote his life "as an orator" to the endless struggle against Marxian socialism. His first preparation for this was to study the war-time propaganda with which the British attempted to win over German opinion and thus lessen Germany's will to fight.

After the lengthy biographical sketch, Hitler turns to his central idea: that of securing the purity of the German race and ending "the rule of the Jew." The twisted and vindictive quality of this fanatic nationalism would certainly not have appealed to the majority of the German people before the

445

First World War, even though there had been some anti-Semitism in social and professional life.

At first Hitler's rantings were discounted by sensible Germans almost as much as by people of other countries, and, in spite of the trouble over reparations and the French occupation of the Ruhr, Stresemann's policy of conciliation, combined with thrift and hard work at home, seemed to be bringing back stability and even a promise of a return of prosperity to Germany from the depths of bankruptcy into which it fell in 1923. But a defeated and humiliated nation cherishes resentments of which it is sometimes not fully conscious until reminded by a demagogue of the "wrongs" which it has suffered. Hitler's charge that there had been enemies at home as well as abroad, ceaselessly repeated, struck home when the business depression of 1930 brought unemployment and hardship to the German people. Then the Nazi (as the National Socialists had come to be known) increased the number of their seats in the Reichstag from the twelve they had won in 1928, to ninety-five.

The "servitudes" of the Treaty of Versailles, the restrictions on armament and the continued occupation of the sections of territory along the Rhine, were galling to German pride; but still more bitter was the veto which the Allies, and especially France, placed in 1931 upon a proposed customs union between Germany and Austria, on the ground that it was a first step to the unification (anschluss) forbidden in the treaty. The revulsion of German nationalism against such "vassalage" was just what Hitler needed to force his party into power, and in the elections of 1932 it won 230 seats in the Reichstag, becoming the strongest party in the Reich. Although Hitler's party began to lose voting power right after the elections, political maneuvering led President von Hindenburg to accept Hitler as Chancellor in January, 1933.[3]

Then occurred the event which sealed the fate of Germany: on the eve of new elections, set for March, the Reichstag building was set on fire. The Nazis claimed that the half-witted Dutch boy who started the fire was a communist agent, but the evidence for this charge was lacking. The incident, in any case, enabled the new government to suspend civil liberties and to suppress all opposition to it. Germany had now to learn the nature of a police state, in which there was neither freedom of speech, nor of assembly, while the youth were indoctrinated with loyalty to Hitler and hatred for all opposition to his rule.

Accustomed to authority and susceptible to emotional appeal, the German people accepted the new regime, and in new elections increased the Nazi membership in the Reichstag to 288, to which might be added 52 Nationalists who were in sympathy with them. President von Hindenburg, already ill, died in August, 1934, and Hitler assumed the functions of president of the Reich as well as chancellor. A plebiscite confirmed this act by a 90 per cent majority. But the new master of Germany chose to retain the title

[3] See especially relevant chapters in A. Bullock, *Hitler: A Study in Tyranny* (London, Odhams Press, 1952).

which he had held in the Nazi party, that of Führer (the Leader), a title unique in German history.

The new state was to be both authoritarian and totalitarian. Germany's historic freedoms of thought and of public discussion were gone. Freedom of religion was outwardly recognized, but the Lutheran Church was brought under government control, as were also the labor unions. All of these suppressions were carried out with German efficiency. Two "private" armies backed the regular police: the "Storm Troopers" (the "Brown Shirts" like the black-shirted Fascists) and the "Steel Helmets." The safeguards of personal liberty being done away with, the result was an orgy of crimes, torture and the murder of innocents, which constitutes the most incredible chapter of this whole history of freedom from the Ice Age to the present time, blood-stained and heroic as that history has been.

The terrors of the Spanish Inquisition were repeated, if not outdone, in the prison chambers of Berlin. The fanatic racial attacks of the "Nordics" upon the Jews, in which an estimated four and a half million perished, surpasses in horror any other persecution, not only by its refinements of cruelty, but by the fact that it was carried out in a nation which had been leading Europe in culture and science. Nor were all the victims Jews. No opponent of Nazi rule was safe from the night-time knock of the Gestapo on his door, dragging him to prison or death. The only emancipation from this ruthlessness lay in the war with which Hitler challenged the free world; not that the war itself was a solution, but that it opened the door to policies of peace and freedom.

Before we proceed with that story, however, we must turn to Japan, the third partner in the great crusade against Freedom.

Japanese Imperialism

While Germany had its Hitler and Italy its Mussolini, Japan had its General Tojo. Hideki Tojo, a firm believer in the necessity of war with the United States if Japan were to realize her dream of world empire, became premier of Japan in October, 1941, thus assuring the complete ascendancy of Japan's military party in the government of the country and the control of its policies. The ideas of Tojo and his group were in perfect alignment with those of Germany and Italy.

Japanese militarism was not an excrescence on the body politic as it was in Italy and Germany. In our introductory chapter on Asia, we touched upon the respect paid to *Bushido* — the way of the warrior, the *Samurai*. There was nothing like it in Europe; even Sparta did not call for suicide *(hara kiri)*.[4] For seven centuries, from the eleventh century to the Meiji Restoration in 1867, Japan was ruled economically, socially and politically by a soldiery whose chieftain bore the title of *Shogun*. While this did not mean one long, uninterrupted dictatorship — for there were long intervals when

[4] The ancient Spartan "Come home with your shield or upon it" meant "Fight to victory or death in battle."

447

there was little if any central control — it did mean that militarism was the dominant force throughout practically all the history of the country. There was no *Magna Carta,* nor were there Bills of Rights, and when the institution of the *Samurai* was abolished in the Meiji revolution, its spirit lived on, not only in the reconstructed army and navy, but in a society whose leaders were determined to be modern in every way. Unfortunately, the contacts with the West, which furnished the model for a modernized system of government, also stimulated Japan's inherent militarism. European imperialism was just showing what power politics could do on the defenceless Asiatic mainland, and this brought back memories of the days when Japan itself had been forced to yield to armed might.

Japan's era of military imperialism began with the war on China in 1894-1895, which resulted in forcing that country to give up its claims to Korea and Formosa. But this was only a curtain-raiser to the war with Russia ten years later — the real turningpoint in Japan's history, when, by unprecedented victories on land and sea, it replaced Russia as the most powerful and dangerous neighbor of China, which then seemed almost on the verge of dissolution. Then, in a revolution begun on October 10, 1911, the Manchu Dynasty was overthrown. The country, however, was not yet ready for the Republic which replaced it, and on the outbreak of World War I, the Japanese imperialists moved against China, first by occupying the German holdings in Shantung, and then, in January, 1915, presenting the famous — or infamous — Twenty-one Demands, which would have transferred to Japan control of China's railways and most of the industries of Northern China and its ocean ports, forced Japanese "advisers" on the Central Government, and made way for the penetration of Japanese police into China.

The series of aggressive moves which followed lie outside the scope of this history, except insofar as they illustrate the ruthlessness of military occupation used as an instrument to terrorize the conquered. From the seizure of Manchuria in 1931, the first bombing of Shanghai in 1932, and Japan's withdrawal from the League of Nations in 1933, the militarists proceeded with their plans to dominate the Chinese mainland under the thin disguise of a "co-prosperity sphere."

But the unexpected stubbornness of Chinese resistance led to outright — if still undeclared — war, and the bombings of Shanghai, the mass murders at Nanking and the atrocities against women and children shocked the conscience of America, already made uneasy by the thought that our policy of neutrality was making our people accomplices of the Japanese by shipping war materials to Japan. The "China Incident" as Japan insisted on calling its aggression, finally merged into the open warfare of World War II, and Japan's dream of empire which at first seemed to be on the point of realization, finally ended with the unconditional surrender of Japan on the deck of the warship *Missouri* on September 2, 1945.

The dream was real enough in the minds of the Japanese imperialists. Their ideas were set forth in a document which purports to embody the decisions of a conference lasting eleven days, from June 27 to July 7, 1927, to be presented to the emperor by the Prime Minister, Baron Giichi Tanaka.[5] While the "Tanaka Memorial" is concerned mostly with measures to be taken in Manchuria, Inner and Outer Mongolia, it regards these as but the first steps on the road to world conquest. This grandiose plan runs as follows: "Japan cannot remove the difficulties in Eastern Asia unless she adopts a policy of 'Blood and Iron.' But in carrying out this policy we have to face the United States, which has been turned against us by China's policy of fighting poison with poison. In the future, if we want to control China, we must first crush the United States, just as in the past we had to fight in the Russo-Japanese war. But in order to conquer China we must first conquer Manchuria and Mongolia. In order to conquer the world, we must first conquer China. If we succeed in conquering China, the rest of the Asiatic countries and the South Sea countries will fear us and surrender to us. Then the world will realize that Eastern Asia is ours and will not dare to violate our rights. This is the plan left to us by Emperor Meiji, the success of which is essential to our national existence."

The last sentence of this incredible document is, fortunately, only part of the militarist dream; but as for the rest of it, it is surely a blueprint of the strategy of world conquest which swung the Japanese navy away from Asiatic waters to head off the United States by a surprise attack on Pearl Harbor. We must leave it at that and return to our main theme, which is the effect of such leadership on the government and people of Japan.

The cause of freedom is always at stake when militarists take control, for, by the resort to force to gain their way, they deny the first element of freedom. War is not "the final argument of kings"; it is no argument at all. It invokes a stratagem which has no relation to the issues at stake, employing strength drawn from other sources, and, in utter disregard of freedom, represses all thought or action which opposes its course. That is what happened in Japan. The new, untried experiment of representative government, which centered in the attempt to make the lower house of the Japanese Diet assume control of the government, like the House of Commons in Great Britain, met with the fiercest kind of opposition from the military cliques. Strengthened by such secret organizations as the Black Dragon Society, largely made up of poor farmers and small businessmen who had been ruined by the rise of the great monopolies and the costs of armaments, these cliques terrorized Tokyo in the 1930's by murder and the threat of it, and assassinated two prime ministers and other high officials. Hundreds of people were imprisoned for harboring "dangerous thoughts."

The heads of the army and navy had the advantage that under the Constitution of 1889 the military authorities were independent of the civil branch of the government. This followed the traditional scheme of dual government of old Japan, in which the Shogun had kept control of the military, and there was more than a reminder of that duality in the fact that the

---

[5] This document itself bears the date July 28, 1927. Whether Tanaka wrote or endorsed it, as most historians believe in spite of official denials, it is a clear statement of the policy later followed by Japan.

heads of the army and navy were on active service and could commit the government to their policies in spite of opposition in the Cabinet — of which they were members — or in parliament. With this constitutional handicap to lessen their influence, the liberal statesmen whose interest was peace and reform had only short intervals of power.

Thus the years passed in confusion. Yet such rapid economic advances were made that even the moderate political element felt the need of expansion, while the impatient militarists began to plan for a major war. Japan had not learned the lesson of World War I, that war had ceased to be a calculable instrument even of aggression, for it was the one great Power that really profited from that war. Its easy conquests in Shantung strengthened the conviction of its military and naval circles that the path of empire which they had opened up by acquiring Korea and Formosa as a result of victory over China, and getting a foothold in Manchuria by victory over Russia, was now leading them to undertake the mastery of Asia. The fallacy of Nazism and Fascism was almost inevitable in the Japan of 1939 as the dream of still greater profits from a still greater war touched the false note in that otherwise noble spirit of Japan — *Bushido* — the glorification of the profession of arms. The great crusade in the Pacific was not so much against freedoms long cherished and understood, as against the future development of freedom as a way of life.

With the signing of the peace treaty with Japan on September 2, 1945, the greatest war in history came to a close. Not only had the crusade of the Axis Powers to divide the free world ended in defeat, but it seemed as though freedom had won a universal and lasting triumph. It was soon realized, however, that these high hopes were illusory, as Russia under Stalin turned on its former allies and reached out for a world dominion of communism with a dream of ideological conquest beyond the reach even of the imagination of a Tanaka. As the plans of Moscow became more evident, and China turned to a communist form of government, many in the countries of the free world came to doubt if its victory in World War II had any meaning. Peace and freedom seemed as far off as ever, in spite of the terrible cost paid in human lives, in the destruction of so many cities and the loss of so much of the heritage of art and culture. But this is a short-sighted view. The world was saved from a tyranny under the Axis Powers, which in 1939 far outranged the ill-prepared defenses of the nations of the free world. The war not only failed to enslave the west, it freed the militarist Powers from their own tyrannies. Their militarism was destroyed, burned out in the destruction of total war, and at the end even the old military leaders realized that war in the atomic age could no longer safely be used as an instrument of policy.

The failure of fascism and national socialism to destroy the political structure of Europe and replace it by totalitarian tyrannies did not end the menace of militarism in Europe. Their place in the battle line against freedom was immediately taken by Soviet Russia. Nowhere on the long road to freedom had the shadow of impending night held greater horrors than in the torture chambers of Nazi Germany, the home of Kant and Goethe; nowhere had liberty been more reviled than in fascist Italy, the birthplace of the law of nations over a thousand years before. But in the war of deliverance from this nightmare, the Western Powers had as an ally — and a mighty one — a Communist tyranny, as ruthless and militarist as Germany had been. The full significance of this fact was not at first apparent, for victory over the Axis Powers seemed to the rejoicing Americans and British to mark the end of an era and the beginning of a new one free from the menace of war. Only one statesman, Churchill, warned that the strategy of the West had stopped short of final victory; that the overthrow of Germany should be followed up by the rise of a new Soviet empire in Eastern Europe. General Eisenhower, backed by President Truman, chose, instead to open the door to the Communist armies west of Berlin and of Czechoslovakia.

Thus, without meaning to do it, the American high command perpetuated militarist tyranny in eastern Europe, by withdrawing or holding back before the forward march of Stalin's troops.

CHAPTER XIX

THE COLD WAR

The Background of History

IT IS NOW over forty years since the U.S.S.R. was founded. While this is not a long period in the life of a nation, it is long enough to prove that the problems which it presents to the world are not merely passing incidents, but are part of the warp and woof of the fabric of history. A short analysis of that history is, therefore, essential to the understanding, not only of the cold war, but of international relations generally.

The revolution was incredible. A small band of determined men, supported by a few thousand soldiers and sailors surprised themselves as well as their enemies, by the quick success of their uprising in Petrograd; but, before they could conquer the entire country, they had to fight a dozen wars against both foreign and Russian forces. There were over twenty organized armies to overcome. The Ukraine was invaded by Deniken and Wrangel, Petrograd attacked by Yudenich; there were British and French troops in the White Sea on the north and Odessa on the South, Germans and Italians and Greeks on the southern Cossack steppes and the Ukraine. Siberia was occupied by Kolchak and Simenov, Japanese and Americans occupied Vladivostok, and many thousand former prisoners of war, like the Czech legion, crossed from the Urals to the Pacific. Yet, from the bastion of Moscow, Lenin with Trotsky, "the organizer of victory," defeated every foe and conquered an area nearly three times the size of the United States.

The explanation is only partly to be found in the militant doctrine of communism with its single purpose and strict discipline; it lay even more in the blindness of the reactionary leaders, attempting to restore the old regime, in their divided counsels and general incapacity. Nevertheless, the result was epochal. Except for a defeat from the Poles in 1920, who took over part of White Russia and the Western Ukraine, and Bessarabia on the south west, all the vast empire of the Tsars was, by 1923, the empire of the Bolshevists.

But it was a country suffering what seemed beyond the limits of endurance. While full statistics are lacking, it is estimated that more than five million deaths were due to the (first) World War, the civil wars, typhus and other diseases, and sheer privation. Industry was almost dead, only about 14 per cent of the low figure of Tsarist Russia, with hardly more industrial capital per person than in the Congo. Agriculture was producing less than half of the pre-war output; and, owing to the lack of rolling stock on the outward railways (at one time only two locomotives left on a main line), farm produce piled up to rot at country way stations instead of reaching the city markets. The crisis revealed the capacity of Lenin, for, in 1921, he inaugurated a New Economic Policy (N.E.P.) which violated doctrinaire communism by restoring the profit motive of private enterprise to stimulate industry, permitting the peasants to receive payment for their crops. The rigid communist theorists regarded this as treason to their principles, but the day was saved for the U.S.S.R. There were still many obstacles to overcome; but by 1927 Soviet Russia had restored pre-war industrial production, and by 1928 industry was socialized and ready for Stalin's test of its capacity in a Five Year Plan, which carried Russia safely over the years of the Great Depression.

The deviation of N.E.P. from orthodox communism is of special importance in the study of Soviet policy, for it was the second time that Lenin saved the day by resort to practical expedients. The original call to the war-weary soldiers in 1917 to break ranks and go home to seize their lands on the great estates had no flavor of communism, but it made a communist victory possible. The resort to the profit motive to stir the country to economic recovery was also only an expedient. But these two great examples of freedom of action by Lenin constituted models for Stalin in both domestic policy and his own devious diplomacy. Hardheaded realism, not theory, dominated in crises. This, as we shall see, is as much a rule of conduct for the Kremlin as it ever was for any government in history.

The importance of this clue to Soviet policy must be kept in mind; for while, by its very nature, expediency cannot be charted, responding as it does to changing circumstances, the clue to it lies in the actual happenings rather than the predisposition of communist theory. Now the happenings which determined the tortuous course of Soviet foreign policy are fairly clear, but we are apt to forget them in the passing events of today. First of all, there was serious trouble in the Far East. The Japanese, by conquering Manchuria in 1931, blocked the Soviet's shortest route to Vladivostok, the Chinese Eastern Railway, a heavy blow to Russia. But Stalin was not ready for a costly test of strength in the Orient and waited until Yalta for a final chance to gain much more than had been lost. The same Fabian tactics were used in China, when, in what looked like a purely benevolent act, the Soviet, in 1942-43, withdrew from Chinese Turkestan (Sinkiang) in which they had long had a sphere of interest. Such bargaining diplomacy paid off well when China became a communist ally.

Soviet policies in Europe were equally realistic. Instead of joining in with Great Britain and France in the peace settlement of Versailles, it turned to Germany and made its own treaty at Rapallo in 1922, which offered at least an open door for trade and economic relations. There was not much to be gained by either country, since both had been so badly crippled by the war, but politically it meant that Russia was aligned for the next ten years against the dominance of Great Britain and France in the councils of Europe.

All this was changed in 1933 by the rise to power of Hitler, the loudly proclaimed enemy of communism. The result was that in 1934 the Kremlin swung over to join the League of Nations, which it had long been denouncing as the instrument of capitalist imperialism. But collective security by way of Geneva was never highly rated in Moscow or Paris, and in 1935 a Franco-Soviet pact was signed, as a surer make-weight against Hitler.

While this new alignment in the foreign relations of the U.S.S.R. showed Stalin's capacity for practical adjustment to changing realities, he soon showed that he regarded it as a none-too-safe anchor to windward, for in the years 1935 to 1937 he proceeded to build a stronger defense for his rule at home by a series of "purges," a reign of terror at the top of the communist regime. The victims were chiefly those who, as leaders in the Bolshevist revolution, questioned or might question the realistic trend of the Kremlin. Stalinism was to be as solid an orthodoxy as Leninism, with which it was dialectically confused. Thus, at the critical moment, communism was invoked to cover the political realism of a Machiavelli. Then, firmly seated as both communist pontiff and politician, Stalin turned on those generals of the Soviet army and those politicians who might be accused of secret pro-German leanings, or dealings, and by their prompt execution quelled any possible disaffection.

The effect of the terror in Russia was apparently all that the Kremlin desired; there were no signs of rebellion against Stalin after it. But the effect upon the noncommunist world was an increased revulsion in public opinion against such ruthlessness, making further relations with the U.S.S.R. almost impossible. Moreover, this terror in high places was known to have followed upon the war against the "Kulaks," the independent, well-to-do peasants, who had resisted collective farming, great numbers of whom had been liquidated or exiled to Siberian slave labor camps, a crusade ruthlessly carried out under Khrushchev. All in all, at the very time when it needed most to strengthen its defenses against the future might of Nazi Germany, Soviet Russia alienated all noncommunist countries by its persecution of all "deviationists," as the opponents of Stalinism were called.

The mutual distrust was evident in the disarmament negotiations at Geneva. When Litvinov proposed universal disarmament, the Western powers suspected that this was a manoeuver designed to apply only to the highly industrialized nations, while leaving Russia's manpower practically untouched. Then, as later in the dispute over atomic weapons, confidence was lacking on both sides, and failure widened the gulf of misunderstanding.

The situation grew steadily worse as the ominous threats of a second world war developed in Spain, Ethiopia and the Orient, although in these events Soviet Russia played only a secondary part. While she helped the communists in Spain, they were never more than a minority of the loyalist forces against Franco; the intervention of Italy and the nonintervention policy of France and Great Britain were much more important. The U.S.S.R. had the distinction of standing out against the recognition of Italy's conquest of Ethiopia. But it did not have a vital interest in these distant conflicts. Even Hitler's first moves toward war, in the Rhineland and Austria, were let pass by the Kremlin. They were treated merely as a redressing of the balance of power between France and Germany and a normal fulfillment of Germany's nationalist aims by giving it sovereignty over people of German blood.

But Czechoslovakia was different. Not only was this the border-land of the Slav, but it was the key to Eastern and Central Europe, behind the bastions of the Erz mountains, with their mixed Sudeten population of Austrians, Germans and Czechs. When Hitler, claiming that the Sudeten Germans were oppressed by the Czechs, threatened invasion to "liberate" them, Soviet Russia offered before the League of Nations, in 1938, to render Czechoslovakia "immediate and effective aid, if France, loyal to her obligation, will render similar assistance." The offer was ignored and Russia rebuffed. In the judgment of Winston Churchill — no friend or dupe of communism — this was a major blunder, on the path to that greatest of all diplomatic blunders, Munich, and that "the indifference — not to say disdain" with which this offer was treated, "left a mark on Stalin's mind." In after-dinner conversations at Yalta, Stalin said that it was the Munich agreement which led him to ally himself with Hitler, the next year. The only explanation he could think of for the betrayal of Czechoslovakia by France and Britain was that they wanted to turn Hitler eastward, bringing him into conflict with the U.S.S.R., instead of attacking the Western Powers. Churchill, supreme realist, but at that time out of power, would have risked at least a test of Russia's good faith where vital interests were at stake. Instead, Chamberlain chose to take the risk with Hitler, in one of the most fateful, and fatal, of all surrenders in history.

It was not only Great Britain and France which checked Russian action in the Munich crisis; Poland and later Rumania were unyielding in their refusal to allow Russian troops to cross their territory to help Czechoslovakia. Moscow was stirred to more than resentment by all the evidences of suspicion and hostility; and its fears of encirclement by the capitalist world were increased. Therefore, Stalin started a series of manouevers to make terms with Hitler. The agent in this Machiavellian diplomacy was Molotov who, in April, 1938, replaced Litvinov at the Foreign Office. Ribbentrop conducted the negotiations for Hitler. On both sides, ideologies were discarded in hard-headed, cynical bargaining on the prizes of victory in the war, which, as the Kremlin realized, Germany was planning to begin in Poland. By August 23, the treaty was signed by which the U.S.S.R. became the accomplice of Nazi Germany in plans to divide the spoils of conquest.

The Stalin-Hitler entente, built upon this edifice of cynical diplomacy was the prelude to World War II. Stalin's share of guilt in this manoeuver is amply established by the documents subsequently published from the archives of the German Foreign Office. But the record makes it clear that he acted not as a communist but as a nationalist. It was a pure case of power politics, in which Russians and Germans linked their fortunes together in the same kind of a raid on Poland as had been done in the partition of that unhappy land in the eighteenth century. Stalin's deal with Hitler was like that of Catherine the Great with Frederick the Great; his attack upon the Baltic countries and the war with Finland were in line with the ambitions of Peter the Great to get for Russia "a window on the Baltic." The seizure of Bessarabia rounded out the Russian empire to the mouth of the Danube. This was pure Russian imperialism. It is true that it was strengthened by the cohesive force in communist discipline, which at the same time was welding the many diverse ethnic and social elements of the U.S.S.R. into a new and more vibrant nationalism; but the motive force was the nationalism, not the doctrines of Marx-Lenin.

Such was the situation in the first two years of World War II. Through the tragedy of French defeat and the great days and months of Britain's incredible defense, Stalin watched the Nazis overrun Europe without any apparent apprehension that Russia had been marked for the next victim. Then, suddenly, on June 22, Hitler, furious at a Yugoslav uprising which checked his plans for conquest in the Balkans, and confident that the time had come for him to realize his greatest dream, Germanic mastery of southeastern Europe and Southern Russia, swung his troops against his ally. His eyes were fixed on Caucasian oil and the rich wheat fields, the sugar and iron of the Ukraine and the Donetz regions. But these great prizes, opening the way to the Orient, were less important to Nazi Germany than the elimination of Russia as a power in Europe. Russia recoiled from the blow, but held at Leningrad in the north, Moscow in the center and Stalingrad in the south. Finally, in November, 1942, after over a year of desperate fighting, the tide was turned and Stalin's armies began the advance which two years later brought them to the Elbe.

The history of the war lies outside the scope of this study, except for one very important fact: that the Kremlin, instead of yielding to the forces of nationalism which it had unloosed, became more communist-conscious as the war progressed. At least that was the impression made upon Russia's allies as it accepted their munitions, tanks and guns without recognition either at home or abroad and refused to give them free access behind its lines. The use of the iron curtain is never much objected to in war-time, when military security is of supreme concern. But this was something else.

Evidently the Politburo, the all-powerful committee within the Kremlin, was determined to prevent intercourse for ideological as well as military reasons. They may have feared that their control would be endangered by the new forces, national and political, released by the war, and that foreign criticism of their ways of doing things — so different from the West — would both weaken loyalties at home and lessen the confidence of the allies in their fighting power. As the Politburo never told the reasons for holding aloof, this is mostly guess-work. But the fact remains, and it is all-important for understanding what followed, that the very men who could plan national strategy with cold-blooded realism in league with Hitler, acted during their war with him and after it as though they were not merely the defenders of their country, but the high priests of a cult which should not be profaned by the presence of unbelievers. They probably calculated that nationalism was not enough to hold the loyalties of their people; that it needed the inspiration of the golden age which they promised but which noncommunists denied. They also surely did not wish the outside world to know how far short of the desired achievement they were. To nationalist sensitiveness were added communist mistrust of the ideological hostility of their allies.

This mistrust is the key to most of the history of Soviet international relations. On the part of the Allies, there was a constantly recurring fear that Stalin would once more make peace with Hitler, that both of them would some day see how terrible a blunder the war had been, how heavy would be the cost, and how little chance there was for a victory that could repay even the slightest fraction of the enormous losses. On the Soviet side there was the equally strong feeling that Great Britain and the United States were holding back too long their attack on the Western Front. To meet this situation and hold the alliance together, the United States redoubled its efforts to supply munitions, by the perilous and costly North Atlantic and Arctic route to Archangel and by the engineering triumph which made the Persian Gulf a temporary Russian port of entry.

But diplomacy was also needed, and President Roosevelt found in Harry Hopkins a man in whom Stalin believed and whose courage, sincerity and forthrightness did much to save the situation. Molotov coming to Washington was less successful, but he won from Roosevelt the promise of a second front in 1942. When this date proved impossible, owing to the vast preparations necessary for the largest amphibious invasion in all history, someone had to explain it to Stalin. The task was taken over by Winston Churchill, who arrived in Moscow in August, 1942, while the Germans were still forcing the Russians back toward the Volga. Few episodes in Churchill's great career can match this, when he finally got Stalin to agree to the substitute front in Africa (November, 1942). But the unfulfilled promise of the second front remained a powerful irritant in Russian-Anglo-American relations, both in the war and in the peace which followed. Even after the tide of war turned, at the close of 1942, Stalin's surly attitude toward his allies was not softened, and he continued to show his temper in his objections to the Western insistence that the Italian campaign had first to be fought before the Western Front could be risked.

However, by this time, purely military planning had ceased to be the sole preoccupation of the allies, for they had now to face the problem of planning for the peace — one they were not to solve for long years after the fighting stopped in the long futilities of the cold war. It was a problem to which the United States had not given anything like the attention, up to this point, that it deserved. Churchill's strategy, on the contrary, had never lost sight of it; his insistence on striking at "the soft under-belly of Europe" was designed to reach the Balkans before the Russians could break the Nazi line, and so check the age-old Russian design of domination there and at the Straits. The failure of this plan did not lessen Stalin's mistrust of the intention behind it. It was time for full and frank discussion on all major issues. Thus began the series of conferences at Moscow, Teheran, Yalta and Potsdam, which constitute the political parallel to the military history.

The Moscow Conference

The first political conference between the allies took place in Moscow, October 19-30, 1943. It was not at the top level, but at the next to the top-level, attended by the Secretaries of State of Great Britain, the United States, the U.S.S.R. and China, instead of their chiefs. The meaning of this, in the language of diplomacy, was plain. Pioneering exploration could establish the ground for future policy without final commitment, a cautious and well-known method of diplomacy. For this first step to attempt to iron out the underlying differences with Russia and to outline the basic principles of the peace and the machinery for maintaining it, the United States was fortunate in having as its representative the veteran statesman, Cordell Hull, Secretary of State. It was the only conference on the settlement which he attended. Foreign Secretary Eden represented Great Britain, and Molotov the U.S.S.R.

Secretary Hull had sensed the mistrust of Moscow because of the delay in the invasion of northern France, and had avoided meeting Eden on the way, for fear Stalin and Molotov might think that Britain and the United States were forming a common policy in advance of discussing it with Russia. Molotov did not disguise his suspicion that the promised Western Front would not materialize as planned, and only after being reassured on this point did he move on to other matters of united policy. In view of Italy's surrender over a month previously, an Advisory Council was set up to deal with nonmilitary matters there, and a declaration on Italy called for a complete suppression of Fascism and Fascists, ending with a significant phrase that the Italian people were to be free to choose their own form of government. The status of Austria, when liberated, was conditioned by the fact that it was on Hitler's side during the war, which raised a serious matter of disagreement later as to its treatment by Russia and her allies. The only agreement reached about Germany was on the procedure for dealing with war criminals.

Slight as these items seem, in view of the vast problems of the whole post-war settlement, the air was cleared enough for Secretary Hull to carry his major point, the erection of international machinery for the long reaches of a future, the nature of which no one could foretell. First of all, there was to be a European Advisory Commission (EAC) in London, to deal with the post-war problems of Europe; then, of far-reaching importance in the opinion of Secretary Hull the acceptance of a pledge to set up a permanent organization in place of the League of Nations.

Secretary Hull was given an enthusiastic reception by both Houses of Congress when, on November 18, he reported to them on this first diplomatic conference with the U.S.S.R. Mr. Hull's reputation for sturdy, forthright Americanism gave added weight to his expressed conviction that the great task of adjustment with the Russians had begun in a manner that gave fair — if not bright — promise for the future. It was essential, he said, that, if the fruits of victory were not to be lost, there should be agreement on "those basic principles and policies which will render impossible a repetition of our present tragedy," and that, "machinery of action necessary to carry out these principles and policies" be set up at once.

Throughout his address, Mr. Hull emphasized the practical realism of his diplomacy. He was the last man to yield to wishful thinking. This gave added weight to his statement that he had secured its assent to the creation of the United Nations. This was set forth in the document which Mr. Hull then read to the Congress, of which the following conclusions are the most important.

Declaration of Four Nations on General Security, Moscow, October 30, 1943....
   4.   That they recognize the necessity of establishing at the earliest practicable date a general international organization, based on the principle of the sovereign equality of all peace-loving states, and open to membership by all such states, large and small, for the maintenance of international peace and security.
   5.   That for the purpose of maintaining international peace and security pending the re-establishment of law and order and the inauguration of a system of general security, they will consult with one another and as occasion requires with other members of the United Nations with a view to joint action on behalf of the community of nations.
   6.   That after the termination of hostilities they will not employ their military forces within the territories of other states except for the purposes envisaged in this declaration and after joint consultation.
   7.   That they will confer and co-operate with one another and with other members of the United Nations to bring about a practicable general agreement with respect to the regulation of armaments in the post-war period.

The news of Secretary Hull's evident success at Moscow had already preceded him, and already on November 5th, the Senate had passed a resolution of Senator Connally, Chairman of the Senate Committee on Foreign Relations, approving the plan for the United Nations adumbrated in the Declaration. For most people this was the first indication that the United States was again proposing something not unlike the League of Nations, which it had rejected after World War I. Even President Roosevelt had been dubious as to the reception of such an idea by American public opinion. But, for over a year, a small committee in the State Department, drawn partly from the outside,[1] had been working with Under-Secretary Sumner Welles on the blueprint of an international organization, which later became the basis for Dumbarton Oaks and the charter of the United Nations.

At Moscow, Secretary Hull took the first step toward the fulfillment of this program. Senator Connally was aware of this preparatory work, which had been carried on in secret because of possible political capital to be made by the die-hard opponents of the League of Nations, which the new organization was bound to resemble. This caution accounts for the last paragraph of the Senator's resolution, a reminder to the Senate that, when the new international organization for peace and security actually was formed, the Senate would have full opportunity to pass on it.

In the United States, public opinion felt that the success of the conference had been largely due to Secretary Hull. It was known that he shared to the full the nationwide distrust of communism, especially the Russian brand, and the revulsion of feeling against what was regarded as the mass-murders of Stalin's purge of his old associates. Now Moscow had acceded to "cooperation and collaboration" with the United States and Great Britain in the establishment of a joint commission to advise on the conduct of the war and the adjustment to peace and had joined in planning for a world-wide organization for peace in the future. For the first time, American tribute to the marvelous achievements of Russian arms, and sympathy for its terrible sufferings, were not qualified by reluctance to have it as an ally. Russia would play the game! This mood was reflected in generous outpourings of private contributions to Russian Relief and in the action of Congress in passing resolutions in both Houses endorsing the work of Secretary Hull.

In the dark years which followed, this interlude of good will, while always restrained except in radical quarters, has been forgotten. But it was shared by conservatives and liberals alike, neither of whom subscribed to the doctrines held by the Kremlin but were anxious to have an assurance that its power would be an added safeguard against a recurrence of Nazi terror and militarism. This mood lasted through the next two years, though doubts assailed it from Russia's refusal to raise its iron curtain and its unceasing intransigence as it became sure of victory. It made possible the Conferences at Teheran and Yalta.

[1] The author was one of its members.

The Teheran Conference

The way had now been cleared, both by the Moscow Conference and the progress of the war, for a meeting of the heads of state. The decisions of history are determined by a few powerful men more often than is commonly known or appreciated. At Teheran — November 28 to December 1, 1943 — three of the world's most experienced politicians and most powerful personalities faced the realities of war and peace, in the full consciousness of their responsibilities. Roosevelt had been eager for the chance to deal with Stalin personally and had once told Churchill frankly that he thought he could "handle Stalin personally better than your Foreign Office or my State Department." He was confident of his skill in dealing with men, and properly so.

But his cordial greeting to the Russians when, in the first informal meeting he welcomed them as "new members of the family of nations," was merely a good opening for putting his case before Stalin for Soviet aid against Japan. When Stalin gave assurance that he would turn on Japan as soon as Hitler was defeated, Roosevelt was then able to refuse the demands of those of his advisors who wanted to have him divert forces from the European to the Asian front. This matter of diplomatic strategy must be cleared up, because of the bitter attacks which have been made upon Roosevelt on that account. His task at Teheran was hard. The great attack on the Western Front could not be ready before May, 1944, many months after Stalin had been led to expect it. Nevertheless agreement was reached, satisfactory to all, which is more than the pessimists thought could be achieved. The first act in fulfillment of this program was the announcement by President Roosevelt that General Dwight Eisenhower was appointed commander-in-chief of the European allied armies on the west.

Outside of military matters the conference did not get very far. It rested content with a preliminary exchange of views on the post-war territorial settlement of Europe, the terms to be offered or imposed upon Germany, the structure of the United Nations and the possibility of its having a strategic basis. But the Teheran Conference seemed to its participants, and to public opinion at the time, to open the door to a new era of understanding and of joint support for a lasting peace. We must not forget that these men were among the most experienced statesmen of our time, men whose judgments had been hardened in the iron clamp of war and who realized that under such conditions self-deception is more than a crime. How was it, then, that this high promise was not fulfilled? The answer lies in the pages of history which follow.

The Yalta Conference

Fourteen months passed after the Teheran Conference before the heads of the great alliance met again, months of the most momentous military events in history. The Soviet armies had, by an incredible feat of arms, turned the German invasion into a disastrous defeat and were following up the beaten but still powerful foe with continuing and irresistible strength. Although wounded and sorely stricken by the ruthless Nazi method of war, Russia was stirred by a new sense of nationalism as the hour had at last come to wreak vengeance on the invader. Only once before, in the defeat of Napoleon, had it beaten the mightiest military combination of the age; and Hitler had been mightier than Napoleon. No wonder, therefore, that in the hour of this stupendous victory, the masters of the Kremlin found in Russian patriotism a force with which to weld the war-time loyalties into peace-time support for strengthening the autocracy of the Communist Politburo — the successor of the Tsars.

In judging what was done at Yalta — February 4 to 11, 1945 — we should remember this dominating fact, that it was a war-time conference, held while great battles were either being fought or being planned, and that Stalin timed its meeting to fit with military strategy. He had held back from any earlier meeting, while the issue on the Eastern front was in any doubt, and now was ready for it before the Americans and British had crossed the Rhine. He could not have known at the time that Hitler was contributing to his diplomatic game by timing his last great drive against the American and British in the desperate Battle of the Bulge, hoping to cut off Antwerp and the whole northern wing of the allied forces on the West. The fate of the world might have been quite different if he had thrown his reserve against Russia, instead of leaving this eastern front weakened and unable to withstand the rapid Russian advance.

But also, the Yalta Conference decisions, and the events which followed after, could have held in check Stalin's diplomacy, which, as we shall see, was closely linked with the military situation. He came to Yalta, as we can clearly see now, with the hindsight of history, in the dual role of a Russian and a Communist, and combined these into a single aim — imperialism. It does not matter much whether we call it Russian Imperialism or Communist Imperialism; he himself called it in an address to his people "Soviet Patriotism."

There can be no doubt that Roosevelt did not, and could not, negotiate at Yalta with as much confidence as Stalin. Not only was the fighting on the Western Front at a desperate stage, but the war in the Pacific was nearing its climax and was by no means decided. Yet, he too had strong cards to play. The year 1944 had witnessed the deliverance of France, beginning with the great sea invasion, OVERLORD, to the coast of Normandy in June, followed by rapid but costly battles in the weeks and months that followed. Rome was captured in June, and the forces in the Mediterranean could join with those in the north to close the ring around beleaguered Germany.

In August, Stalin, sure of his northern front, turned on Rumania and ousted all opposition there; in September he forced Bulgaria to surrender. The Danube Valley lay open, with Tito taking over Yugoslavia. The war in Europe was rapidly becoming a thing of history; the allies had a different

461

task than the one at Teheran; they had now to concentrate on reaching an agreement among themselves on the post-war settlement.

The Yalta Conference has been the subject of bitter controversy and the literature on it is heavily charged with political prejudice for and against the participants. The British and American delegations came away from it in high spirits, confident that the alliance which had stood the strain of the greatest war in history would be able to stand all the strains of peace-time relations. But this optimistic conclusion was not arrived at without great and serious disagreements in the negotiations, for in almost every question before the Conference, the differences between the Russians and their allies, seemed at first irreconcilable. The agreements, therefore, were compromises, which is a sound method of diplomacy, but only if sincerely and honestly made in the conviction that yielding one point may win others and that profit will be made from the good will thus evoked. But as we have noted above, the Bolshevists do not have that freedom to compromise which is the basis of Western diplomacy. Therefore, Stalin and Molotov were quick to take advantage of any concession made by them, while the British and Americans found themselves, both at the conference and later, yielding more than they intended. Yet, between men of good faith, the terms were reasonable and workable.

The outstanding problem was the future of Germany. Stalin's proposals were clearly stated in the opening plenary session. They were: (1) that Germany should be partitioned; (2) that a new form of Government should be set up in Germany; (3) that the terms of surrender should be defined; (4) that the amount and nature of reparations should be agreed upon. He presented these points more as a program for the future than as the agenda for the Conference itself; but there was no escaping the implication that Russia would insist on having its own way on all of them, as far as it could. Clearly the allies were not ready for such wholesale arrangements, but Stalin evidently felt strong enough to lay all his cards (concerning Germany) on the table.

The question of Poland was more pressing; it was already "liberated" by the Russians, but the Soviet liberators had been the accomplices of Hitler in 1939, having shamelessly betrayed it when Warsaw fell before the Nazi blitz. A Polish "Government-in-exile" in London, under a liberal leader, Mikolajczyk, was regarded by the British and Americans as representing the real Poland, while the Polish communists formed a Provisional Government in the City of Lubin, recognized by the U.S.S.R. As it became clear that Stalin was inflexible in his determination to have the conference accept this satellite government for all Poland, and as his armies were in actual occupation and there was no way for the British or Americans to reach them, they yielded, with the proviso that it "should be reorganized on a broader democratic basis with the inclusion of democratic leaders from Poland itself and from Poles abroad." This new government should then be called the Polish Provisional Government of National Unity. History was soon to show how worthless was this "concession to western ideals," as the communist terror enveloped Poland under the Russian occupation.

Fully as important as the imposition of a communist government on Poland was the question of its frontiers. Russia won an easy diplomatic victory in getting agreement to push Poland's eastern frontier back along the Curzon line, which had been accepted as the best ethnic dividing line between the Poles and Russians by the American and British experts at the Paris Peace Conference, when Poland was put back on the map. But Poland itself had never recognized this line and its frontier had run farther east; so, at Yalta, Stalin tried to get Roosevelt and Churchill to agree to give Poland compensation for losing what lay east of it, by extending the Polish western frontiers over into Germany as far as the Niesse River, and including Upper Silesia.

Both the President and the Prime Minister refused this extreme demand, which Stalin finally withdrew, and the future line between Poland and Germany was left to be settled at the peace conference. But as the Russians overran this territory, they permitted the Poles to move into it, and the Germans either were driven out or found conditions intolerable. Stalin undoubtedly had calculated upon this at Yalta, and so was, cunningly, content to leave the Polish-German frontier problem for a future settlement — when it would be settled by the occupation forces of the U.S.S.R., thereby securing all of Russia's demands even if no formal agreement was made.

Territorial settlement was only part of the Yalta program. While Stalin was quietly clearing the pathway through Poland for communist imperialism in Eastern Europe, Roosevelt succeeded in securing his consent to a Declaration on Liberated Europe, which was a shining document in the murk of war and desolation, but which was to prove almost as unreal as the Holy Alliance of over a century earlier. Yet, it was, in the eyes of both Churchill and Roosevelt not merely a vague assertion of agreed purpose by the allies, to be fulfilled by each in its own way and as far as suited personal interests; it contained a definite pledge to establish throughout the territory won back from the Nazis, "free elections of governments responsive to the will of the people, and to facilitate when necessary the holding of such elections." The three governments were to work out this program in consultation with each other. If Russia had kept this pledge, there would have been no cold war.

This declaration might well have served as the preface to the agreement to establish a United Nations Organization, although in the published texts it came second. Much work had already been done in planning its structure since Secretary Hull had introduced it in the Moscow Conference of 1943. The Dumbarton Oaks Conference in Washington, in August and September, 1944, had produced a detailed draft, based on that of the State Department committee referred to above. There they had come face to face with the central issue of the voting procedure in the Security Council — the problem of the veto — and had deadlocked on it. At Yalta it was solved by a compromise, proposed by the United States. A permanent member of the Security Council would not vote on the settlement of a dispute to which it was a party, but would vote on enforcement measures.

An equally difficult question was that of membership in the United Nations. Stalin was adamant in his insistence that Byelorussia (White Russia) and the Ukraine should be members, and Churchill, anxious not to have any objection to membership by the British Dominions, got Roosevelt to yield his stubborn opposition to the arrangement. Russia, as the one communist member, was well aware how often it would be in a minority. It would now have at least two additional votes to keep it company.

The controversies which have raged over the Yalta Conference have been bitter and so filled with partisan prejudices as to obscure the historical realities. It can hardly be doubted that men so experienced in the wiles of diplomacy and such doughty fighters in the arena of politics as Roosevelt and Churchill got all that could be gotten from Stalin. They knew perfectly well that he respected only power and was a master in both its use and the threat of it. But the fulfillment of Yalta was a different page of history from the conference itself, and they were not able to bring the full measure of their power to check his unscrupulous falsification of his commitments. The pathway which he chose was that which led to the cold war.

Why then did President Roosevelt in reporting to Congress speak so glowingly of the Yalta negotiations, if they were to prove so deceptive? No one at the conference table, not even Stalin, was less naive than this master of the art and science of politics. Yet he greeted Congress with these cheering words: "I have come from the Crimean Conference with a firm belief that we have made a good start on the road to a world peace." Was his judgment based upon a realistic sense of the strategic advantages which Stalin held at the time, so that the only diplomatic gains to be got from him were in the final, long term settlement when the balance of power would be on the side of the West?

Roosevelt was well aware that the timing was by no means right for him. His hand would have been stronger after Eisenhower had crossed the Rhine, which was soon to happen, but until the strong western bastion of Germany had fallen to American and British arms, the Russians were leading in the race to victory. Yet, it would not do to wait any longer, for then the military occupation would be crystallized. Therefore the allies had to accept the time and conditions as they came. It was surely something to inject into the politics of power, when engaged in the supreme crisis of all history, the assurance of an honorable and forward-looking peace. This Stalin was obliged to accept. His later betrayal of these principles constitutes another page of history.

A Difficult Ally

Soviet Russia's alliance, first with Great Britain and then with the United States, was always honeycombed by mistrust, and at times strained almost to the breaking point by acts which indicated a latent, continuing hostility. For Stalin and his associates, while fighting to save Russia from the Nazi invaders, were equally determined to save it for Bolshevist communism against the impact of their capitalist comrades-in-arms. In the light of subsequent history, it is clear that here, in this unyielding revolutionary dogmatism, the cold war had its origin.

The Russian Lend Lease operation, from the vantage point of high military position, was without parallel in history, covering over eleven billion dollars worth of supplies and services to meet every kind of military need. Convoys of over 2,000 ships (of which 77 were lost with crews and cargoes) were sent to Russia, carrying a billion dollars worth of machinery and industrial equipment, medical supplies and clothing, along with half a billion dollars worth of trucks, combat and other vehicles. These played a decisive part in the war, enabling the Russians to move rapidly across country, while the German armies were mostly held to the railroad lines, owing to the lack of gasoline and the destruction of the military roadways by allied bombing.

Yet there was no sign of appreciation for American aid. Marks and indications of foreign origins were avoided or eliminated to enhance the relative importance of domestic supplies. Joint enterprises with foreigners were prevented wherever possible, partly from suspicion of foreign motives, partly to keep for the U.S.S.R. all credit that could come from achievement of victory. Agreements were limited to predetermined decisions made by those in supreme command; the autocrat in the Kremlin dominating them all. The result was unfailing opposition to proposals and requests unless they had previously been screened and passed upon. Then, there was the doctrinal communist aloofness from contact with "effete" capitalism, combined with a complex of inferiority when faced with the superior quality of the American equipment. In short, Lend Lease to Russia had to operate through the chinks of an iron curtain, with an ally who was never willing to cooperate except on his own terms.

Language difficulties in translation added to the obstacles in negotiation. The Russian dictionary equivalent for "to propose" is a word that, to the communists, means "to direct," to give an order that cannot be disobeyed.[2] In Russian "aggressive" means only committing or planning to commit aggression, never merely "energetic" or "vigorous." "Compromise" is not a native word, and has only an evil connotation. To give up a demand once presented, even when a very minor or formalistic point, makes a Bolshevist-trained negotiator feel that he is losing control of his own will and is becoming subject to an alien will. Therefore, any point which has finally to be abandoned must be given up only after a terrific struggle. The Soviet negotiator must first prove to himself and his supervisors that he is up against an "immovable" force.

There was probably another reason for the attitude of those in the Kremlin; in addition to their communist ideology, they felt a need to maintain their own prestige with the Russian masses. While it is true that patriotism was at white heat in the early part of the war, the disasters of the German invasion could not leave the Politburo, the Communist cabinet of Stalin, free from the possibility of a revulsion against it, sooner or later, unless it could register a claim to victory in its own right. Therefore, everything Russian

[2] Reference is here made to a masterly survey of those and many other obstacles to understanding by Philip P. Moseley's *Techniques of Negotiation*, in the volume, *Negotiating with the Russians*, World Peace Foundation, 1951.

in equipment was played up, and foreign aid was played down. The deceit and disloyalty of this policy was in line with the Russian account of how the war itself was going, which also played up the Russian victories and gave only grudging credit to the prodigious achievements on the western front. This is an aspect of the war which stands out all the more strikingly when one recalls that at this very time American and British opinion was thrilling with unstinted admiration of the miracle of Russia's defense and ultimate triumph. Never was the generous outpouring of sympathy and admiration more ungenerously returned.

Stalin's hand was strengthened by a divergence in British and American points of view. At first, and until Teheran, he was evidently on his guard against the "entente cordiale" which had apparently grown up between his two capitalist allies. Roosevelt, with his intuitive insight, had divined Stalin's state of mind and won him over at Teheran — at the risk of alienating Churchill — to what seemed like a genuine, cordial understanding of the war aims of the United States. They differed from the British aims to an extent which is only now becoming clear. The United States concentrated on the purely military aim of defeating the Axis powers so thoroughly that these conspirators against its peace and security — along with that of the whole world — would never again be a threat.

Great Britain, on the other hand, did not view the war as a purely military event, but kept in mind from first to last the political consequences of strategy. That was what had lain behind Churchill's proposal to strike at "the soft, under-belly of Europe." To the British it was important to hold the Danube and the Balkans against Russian occupation, mindful, as all European statesmen must be, of the danger of Russian imperialism reaching into the heart of Europe by the century-old pathway of invasion. Churchill wanted the victorious American army in Italy to be sent into Austria before the Russians could get there; but instead, Eisenhower had them sent up the Rhone Valley to strengthen his right wing on the Upper Rhine. Subsequent criticism holds that he overestimated the strength of the German front. But the political results of the American strategy were all in Russia's favor. The same line of British reasoning led to the proposal to break rapidly through northern Germany to Berlin and East Prussia to hold the Slavic invaders back from securing a stranglehold there.

Long before Yalta, it was evident that these political war-aims of the British had been discarded for the Roosevelt-Marshall-Eisenhower plan of campaign, to end the war by knock-out blows in Germany and Japan, and then deal with political problems on a peace-time footing. Local guarantees, along European frontiers would have little meaning for Americans, eager, above all else, to leave Europe to the Europeans, once the Nazi terror has been ended. No one in public life in the United States at that time ever gave the slightest warning that we might be going back seven years later to finish the job. For no one could then foretell the future strength of Soviet imperialism or the menace of the cold war.

Instead of territorial guarantees as barriers against aggression, the United

States insisted, with even stronger emphasis, upon a universal system of collective security, based on the Principles of the Atlantic Charter, which had been accepted in the first Declaration of the United Nations. It was perhaps inevitable that it should be the leader in this world-wide movement, because no other nation had to fight the world war with equal might in Asia and Europe. The only international arrangement for enduring the continuance of our ideals of democracy and freedom was an organization like that planned in the State Department and at the Dumbarton Oaks Conference — a United Nations. When the basic principles of this were accepted at Yalta, it seemed to the Americans there that the foundations had been laid for the structure of world peace. But to the Kremlin "world peace" did not mean renunciation of the latent cold war against the capitalist nations, which was the continuing legacy of the Bolshevist revolution. Therefore, diplomacy was strategem, valid only so long as it served the Soviet interests.

The American conceptions of the war as a military expedition to overthrow the Axis powers,[3] and of peace as a cooperative enterprise on even terms, were utterly foreign to the Soviet's conception of either war or peace. The British, and indeed all Europeans, lacked the sense of security which was supplied by the mighty barrier of the Atlantic and felt the need for the substitute for distance in military defense and in the diplomacy that built strong defenses against possible attack by neighboring nations. They, therefore, could understand the Kremlin's insistence that the peace settlement should not leave open pathways of invasion on the long western frontier of Russia.

But at Yalta, while this problem was clearly foremost in Stalin's mind, he had accepted a formula granting genuine democratic regimes to the countries along that frontier. This, if carried out, would have been undoubtedly a diplomatic victory for the West, a greater one than either Roosevelt or Churchill could publicly acknowledge. For one of the chief rules of diplomacy is that a compromise must never be spoken of as a concession, lest it be withdrawn.

In these circumstances, the Yalta agreements take on added significance. On the threshold of victory the three great allies were opening the door on a new era of European peace. Yet on the very days that Churchill and Roosevelt reported to their peoples, Stalin, without a word of warning, violated the Declaration on Liberated Europe by a blow at Rumania. While the Soviet army was occupying the country, Andrei Vyshinski, Molotov's deputy, appeared in Bucharest and gave young King Michael a two hour ultimatum to dismiss his all-party Prime Minister, and four days later forced the king to accept a communist government under a Prime Minister chosen by Moscow. The United States and Britain protested and called for consultation, but no attention was paid to them, and Groza, the Communist Premier, was sworn in a few days later.

[3] G. Kennan in *Foreign Affairs*, April, 1951, refers to "the American bad habit of assuming that there is something final and positive about a military decision, — that it is the ending of something and the happy ending, rather than a beginning."

The cold war, long held in the background, was at last coming out in the open. Soviet Russia, now confident in its own strength, was reverting to the revolutionary strategy of communist imperialism. This was something quite different from Trotsky's dream of world revolution which would end the era of nationalism. On the contrary it was Russian communist imperialism, the extension of the power of the Kremlin, in the same way as the Caesars built up their empire, by setting up around its borders associated states as "friends and allies" of the Romans. It was power politics in a new setting, motored by communism but using the century-old technique of conquest. For it was closely knit to the progress of the Russian armies.

In the period before Yalta, during the summer and autumn of 1944, the Kremlin had halted their victorious advance in Poland and turned their main effort to the Danube and the Balkans. Coldly calculating that Poland was already in their grasp, while building up for their drive over into Germany, they concentrated on the invasion of southeastern Europe. So, Bulgaria was forced, by domestic conspiracy and the menace of attack, to follow the fate of Rumania and become a satellite state. With the cooperation of Tito, then a loyal ally of Moscow, Hungary was encircled and by the end of the year the new Empire of Stalin reached to the Adriatic, over seven hundred miles from the Dnieper. Then the hour struck for the great Russian advance on Prussia. In January, 1945, the German lines on the Vistula broke, and, with Poland completely overrun, the Russian armies pushed to within a hundred miles of Berlin.

Thus, so far as Soviet Russia was concerned, the Yalta Conference was an incident on the road to an incredible victory.

A Hopeful Interlude — The Hopkins' Mission

"It is not so difficult to keep unity in time of war since there is a joint aim to defeat the common enemy, which is clear to everyone. The difficult task will come after the war when diverse interests tend to divide the Allies. It is our duty to see that our relations in peacetime are as strong as they have been in war."

These are the words of Stalin as taken down by Secretary of State Byrnes at the farewell banquet of the Yalta Conference.[4] Almost before their echo had died away, the Kremlin was violating these high sentiments by its unilateral action in Poland and the Balkans and had, on wholly mistaken grounds, challenged the good faith of the United States and Great Britain in negotiations — which never came off — for ending the war in Italy by getting the Germans out of it. The concern over the new attitude in Russian diplomacy troubled President Roosevelt in the last days of his life, but, while greatly disappointed in Stalin, he did not share Churchill's opinion that they

[4] Cf. James F. Byrnes, *Speaking Frankly* (New York: Harper & Bros., 1947), p. 44. President Roosevelt had previously said almost the same thing in his speech on the State of the Union, on January 6, 1945: "The nearer we come to vanquishing our enemies, the more inevitably we become conscious of differences among the victors."

should risk an open break until it was quite clear that the Soviet policy was really a deliberate betrayal of the Yalta agreements. Secretary Byrnes comments: "He was philosophic about it. He had reached the conclusion — which I was to reach months later — that there is no easy formula to guide one in getting along with the Soviets." An hour before he died, on April 12, 1945, he cabled to Churchill: "I would minimize the general Soviet problem as much as possible because these problems, in one form or another, seem to arise every day and most of them straighten out as in the case of the Berne meeting (on the negotiations for the German surrender). We must be firm, however, and our course this far is correct."

There can be no doubt of the soundness of this line of action, firmness within reason; no Munichs, but also no lack of patience and diplomacy. This was the political strategy in which Roosevelt was a master. There was no softness in his tough Dutch fiber, but no one ever excelled him in the capacity for dealing with opponents on their own terms. Had he lived, these qualities would have been tested to the full, for Russia was already set on the course that led to the Cold War.

While Soviet policy could be flexible — doctrinaire communism yielding to expediency in achieving immediate ends — the military situation at the end of the war was so much in Russia's favor that there was little need for Russia to make concessions. With Soviet troops in occupation of the whole Danube Valley, Czechoslovakia, Poland and Eastern Germany, Stalin held an advantage without parallel in the history of diplomacy. The critics who lay the blame on the conferences at Yalta and Potsdam for the stranglehold of Soviet Russia upon Eastern and Central Europe fail to go back to the heart of the matter, which lay in the military history of the last phase of the war, when we held back, not only from Berlin and Prague, but from Leipzig and Dresden, the occupation of which would have given the American army a strategic hold in Eastern Germany. Stalin's diplomacy was, therefore carried on from behind a totally different iron curtain than the one about which Mr. Churchill warned us — an iron front of embattled communist troops from the Baltic to the Adriatic.

The occupation of this vast territory by armies under the control of Moscow determined the nature of subsequent diplomacy. With Germany destroyed, France stricken to the heart, and British power well nigh exhausted, Soviet Russia was in a position of greater advantage than when, a century earlier, the Tsar Alexander had defeated Napoleon. It was not to be wondered at, therefore, that Generalissimo Stalin should attempt to make the most of this situation, and that the only force which could hold him back from the effort to make this empire permanent was the armed might of the United States. Here, however, he found allies in those who, at Washington, were insisting upon the rapid demobilization of the American army once Germany was defeated. The American conception of the war as a crusade for the sole purpose of defeating the armies of Hitler and Mussolini was politically a fundamental blunder. For, in the chaos which the war produced, the peace settlement was bound to be determined by the politics of power. Nowhere was this hard realism better understood than in the Kremlin.

Such was the situation when Roosevelt died on April 12, 1945. No finer tribute was paid to him than Marshal Stalin's message to President Truman, given to our Ambassador in Moscow: "The President has died, but his cause lives on. We shall support President Truman with all our force and with all our will." As if to make the tribute real, he also sent word to President Truman that the U.S.S.R. would be represented by Molotov at the San Francisco Conference and would cooperate in the creation of the United Nations. But this gesture which at the time seemed well meant failed to allay the mistrust on either side. For when Molotov reached Washington on his way to the conference, President Truman took him very much to task over what the Kremlin had been doing in Rumania and Poland. Molotov reacted violently to this criticism, and Moscow supported him in hot rejoinders of protest against American interference in what it regarded as matters of prime importance for the security of Russia. American public opinion, on the other hand, strongly supported the President's insistence that the promise of genuine democratic governments in Poland, Rumania and Bulgaria be made good. But Moscow's conception of "democracy" was communism, based on the one-party system which denied the legitimacy of any major political opposition to communist rule.

From the standpoint of the U.S.S.R., it was a happy coincidence that the "democracy" which would be imposed upon the satellite countries could serve as the ready instrument for Soviet imperialism. But from the standpoint of the United States, this was all a betrayal of the Yalta Conference. The issues in this fundamental disagreement were now bound to come to the fore in two ways: first, in the conference in San Francisco called for the creation of the new world organization, the United Nations; second, in the impending peace settlements now that the war was drawing to a close.

With reference to the first of these, the creation of the United Nations, it had been clear from the beginning of the planning that the U.S.S.R. would never accept membership without taking steps to safeguard itself against the capitalist powers which would form the great majority of the membership. This situation was not wholly met by the grant of membership to the Ukraine and Byelorussia. The question of the veto, therefore, was paramount in Russia's acceptance of the Charter. This was largely ironed out at Dumbarton Oaks and Yalta by the proposal to limit the veto to the enforcement of peace while allowing free discussion on the subject matter of disputes. Nevertheless, at San Francisco this proposal was never embodied in the Charter or in the proceedings of the Conference. No hint was given at San Francisco of the way in which the veto was subsequently to be used by Russia to block action by the United Nations.

The war in Europe was over; the structure of peace now had to be rebuilt. But it could not be rebuilt along the lines of the past; the national state system which reached its climax in the nineteenth century had been shattered in World War II even more than in World War I, when three great empires had been overthrown. This time the upheaval reached deeper into the lives of all Europeans. The Nazi-Fascist revolution had been crushed, but the conquerors had not begun to reach agreement on the new state system to be established, and as they approached this problem their divergent ideas and interests proved to be greater obstacles to a solution than the situation in the defeated nations themselves. At Yalta, the shadow of these coming events could be seen, but lightly enough that it could be easily brushed aside. Now, with the war ended, it was beginning to darken the whole outlook of the peace settlement. Molotov's visit to Washington and his stay in San Francisco made matters worse instead of better, for what he saw and heard confirmed the conviction in his rigidly doctrinaire mind — perhaps the most unyielding in the Politburo — that the United States was rapidly becoming conscious of its continuing responsibilities in world affairs and that Russian ambitions would have to measure themselves against its power and not merely against the lesser might of crippled Britain.

Keenly aware of the impending danger of this critical turn in affairs, Ambassador Harriman, on his return journey from San Francisco to Washington, took up the suggestion of the adviser, Charles Bohlen, that President Truman should send Harry Hopkins to Moscow on a personal mission, to try to clear away mistrust and misunderstanding so as to prepare the way for a conference to agree on a program for the drafting of the peace treaties. Already in Moscow, Mr. Harriman had sensed a growing hostility in the "arrogant attitude" of the Kremlin, when he expressed the concern of the United States over Soviet policy in Poland and Rumania. Now it was evident that the device upon which the United States was centering its hopes for world peace, the United Nations, was, in Russian eyes, both too remote from the local issues of Eastern Europe and too heavily weighted against Soviet Russia to be accepted by it wholeheartedly as the international safeguard of peace and justice. The situation called for immediate diplomatic action along lines entirely different from those which seemed to be leading inevitably to a complete impasse in the peace settlement. What was needed was not the intrigue of a Tallyrand — for Moscow was on its guard against that kind of diplomacy — but a forthright, transparently honest effort by someone it had learned to trust.

That at once pointed to Harry Hopkins as the best possible emissary. The Kremlin, and especially Stalin, had not forgotten that it was Hopkins who negotiated the Lend Lease program for Russia in July, 1941. He had just returned from being the first administrator of Lend Lease, from March to July, when Great Britain was the chief recipient of its aid, and while on a visit to London secured Roosevelt's consent to a mission to Moscow. There he planned more generous help for Russia than military supplies, having in mind the sufferings of the civilian population as well. Stalin personally had been more accessible to him than to most other Allied representatives in Moscow, and the two men had got on well together.

Going with Roosevelt to Yalta, Hopkins had reached the conclusion that "the Russians could be reasonable and farseeing," but he added that this judgment applied chiefly to Stalin himself: "We could count on him to be reasonable and sensible and understanding." Naturally Stalin could not fail to know of this flattering — if over-optimistic — appraisal of his statesmanship. On the other hand, Hopkins was no appeaser, and never hesitated to hit hard when the subject called for frankness. Fortunately, too, this quality appealed to Stalin; both men were able to deal quickly and directly with matter which, in a full dress conference, tended to drag on or be disposed of by meaningless platitudes.

President Truman was at first reluctant to begin his administration by sending a personal emissary to Stalin, but after a few days' hesitancy he agreed to the plan, and Hopkins, although a very sick man, readily undertook the task of peace-making. His mission to Moscow was a diplomatic success, for he, like Talleyrand, had a keenly sensitive understanding of what was in the minds of those with whom he was dealing and so was able to establish a basis of mutual confidence for negotiations — or at least to get negotiations started on an even footing. But the success in diplomacy proved to be a failure in statesmanship, for Hopkins yielded too much to Stalin in order to get a settlement, as history was to prove. Seldom, however, has any one man had so many problems to negotiate for the great Powers; and Hopkins had two grave handicaps: he was bound by ties of loyalty and affection to keep to the policies held by Roosevelt up to the hour of his death; and he himself was suffering from a fatal illness which caused his own death six months later.

Stalin at first was in a surly mood, cherishing a grievance against the United States for the way in which it had cancelled Lend-Lease to Russia, President Truman having allowed the announcement to appear in the newspapers before Moscow was officially informed of it. Adding this apparent affront to his previous suspicions that the Americans were negotiating separately for the surrender of the German army in Italy and that Eisenhower's troops were making slower progress than the Russians (owing to Hitler's having thrown his heaviest forces to the western front), Stalin had come to the conclusion that the Western Allies were trying to get the better of him. These obstacles to negotiation had to be cleared away first, so Hopkins began by recalling President Roosevelt's confidence that the United States could cooperate in peace as in war, and then referred to his own part in arranging Lend Lease for Russia before the United States had entered the war.

Until very recently the American people had been overwhelmingly pro-Russian, due to the brilliant victories of the Soviet armies. But in the last month or so all this warmth of feeling for Russia had clouded over, chiefly because of the Soviet failure to carry out the Yalta agreement on Poland. President Truman shared the public sense of bewilderment over the Soviet action in interfering in the Polish question. Stalin said that the Soviet Government wanted only to insure the establishment of a friendly Poland; and that it had to counter the British plan to revive the system of the *Cordon Sanitaire* on Russia's borders. When Hopkins denied that the United States had any such plans, Stalin replied that if all three governments genuinely wished a settlement, it should be easy, but "if one of them secretly did not wish to see it settled, then the difficulties were real." Evidently this obvious platitude was meaningless if the settlement were not on Russia's terms, for, after further negotiations, Stalin made it clear that the reconstituted government of Poland should have no "fascists" in it, and on that note, Hopkins gave in and assured Stalin that the United States would not insist on having any member of the Polish Government in Exile included in the Provisional Polish Government. Stalin had won.

Germany naturally presented even harder problems, and little was done beyond the promise by Stalin of the appointment of Marshal Zukov to the Allied Control Council for Germany — a promise which was not kept during the first three weeks after the invasion of Normandy. In Asia Stalin promised an attack on Manchuria and cooperation with Chiang Kai-shek; also a quadripartite trusteeship over Korea, placing that country under the U.S.S.R., the United States, China and Great Britain, until it was capable of self-government.

The mere listing of these problems — on which epoch-making decisions had either to be made or prepared for future agreements if possible — shows how wide is the field which statesmanship must open to diplomacy. But the temporary success, in actually inducing Stalin to negotiate, must be measured against the long-range consequences of agreements. Although there was a temporary break in the darkening clouds of mistrust and hostility, yet when the three governments actually came to grips with such fundamental matters as the future of Poland and Germany, they were ultimately faced with apparently irreconcilable conflicts of interest. When a controversy ends in this sort of impasse the only solution known to history has been a resort to power politics. In years gone by, this would have meant war or the threat of it; but in a world marked by the smoldering ruins of World War II, this was unthinkable. Instead the world moved reluctantly but inexorably further into the cold war.

The Potsdam Conference

Although a diplomatic success of the first order, the Hopkins mission had only prepared the way for the negotiations of the peace treaties. It had not even solved any of the major questions concerning the great powers, such as the regime to be established in Germany or the shifting of national boundaries; it had, however, created a favorable atmosphere for their consideration, and had at least given a temporary basis for optimism that the U.S.S.R. and the United States might without too great a delay reach a workable agreement.

The first test of the validity of this hope came in the Potsdam Conference (officially known as the Berlin Conference) which was held from July 17 to August 2, 1945, in the lakeside palace of the former Crown Prince Wilhelm in suburban Potsdam. At this conference there was no change in the Russian

473

personnel, but in Roosevelt's place came President Truman and his Secretary of State, James F. Byrnes, who, at Yalta, had been on the President's staff as Director of Mobilization. Prime Minister Churchill was present at the conference until July 25, when, owing to his defeat in the British elections, he was succeeded by Clement Attlee, with Mr. Bevin as Foreign Minister in place of Mr. Eden. It may be remarked here that Mr. Byrnes noted with interest that the change in administration brought no change in British foreign policy.

"At Yalta," said Secretary Byrnes, "peace had seemed so remote that the question of how it should be brought about was not, to my knowledge, even discussed."[5] Even at Potsdam, five months later, although the war in Europe had come to an end, it was still too soon to attempt the framing of final peace treaties, for the situation was too chaotic and the problems too vast and intricate for any quick and easy solution. Foreseeing that this would likely be the situation, Secretary Byrnes had come to Potsdam with the plan for a Five-Power "Council of Foreign Ministers" (the Big Three — Russia, Great Britain and the United States — with the addition of France and China), to be set up for the purpose of studying the terms of peace to be embodied in the treaties, which would then be submitted to the nations concerned in a final peace treaty.

This plan was readily adopted at the Potsdam Conference, which thus relieved the Conference of the need for proceeding to actual treaty-making but could confine itself to an agreement upon the principles which should be embodied in the treaties when drafted. The method seemed to be a sound one, for it was designed to clear away all underlying misunderstandings so that the treaty-makers would have only the technical task of applying the principles in detail. But the history of the following years was to show the fallacy of such a device. In most of the major disputes between Soviet Russia and the Western Powers there have been constant references by both sides to what they thought the Potsdam decisions had really meant. Mr. Byrnes justified his method by stating that he was attempting to avoid the blunders of Wilsonian diplomacy when the Paris Peace Treaty of 1919 attempted to cover the details of peace settlements after World War I. But subsequent history tended, rather, to justify Wilson. The disputes between the U.S.S.R. and the Western Powers were to prove as bitter as those between the Allied Powers and the Germany of the Weimar Republic and Hitler. When there are fundamental differences in the policies and purposes of the negotiating Powers, agreements stated in general terms are more likely to prove a delusion and a snare than a basis of a workable settlement. This was the case in the agreements reached at the Potsdam Conference.

Strangely enough the first serious break occurred, as we shall see, over the nature of that very body which was designed to get rid of conflicts on details — the Council of Foreign Ministers. The Council was set up to draft peace treaties for Italy, Rumania, Bulgaria, Hungary and Finland; then it

[5] James F. Byrnes, *Speaking Frankly*, p. 70.

was to proceed to the preparation of a peace settlement for Germany "to be accepted by the Government of Germany when a government adequate for the purpose is established." Only those members of the Council were to participate in the drafting of a treaty who represented States "which were signatory to the terms of surrender imposed upon the enemy State concerned." This meant that the Chinese would participate only in the Far Eastern settlement, that France would participate in the drafting of the Italian treaty, and, it was understood, would also participate in the final settlement with Germany. In the case of Finland, with which the United States had not been at war, Great Britain and Russia alone would draw up the treaty. The reason for this complicated procedure was that Stalin, partially supported by Churchill, held that the Council should be composed only of representatives of the Three Great Powers. The Americans objected to this procedure, and the final protocol was a compromise. But, as we shall see, Stalin's concession in this regard was nothing that the Americans could build upon to widen the scope of the Council of Foreign Ministers.

Although the Potsdam Conference postponed its more serious problems, it did come to grips with some of the more immediate issues.

The central problem, in peace and in war, was Germany. In June and July a system of military occupation had been established. Dividing the country into four zones, each, with the exception of Berlin, placed under the control of a military commander, acting under orders from his own government. An Allied Control Council was set up in Berlin to secure some semblance of unity in the country along lines to be agreed upon by the Allies. The Potsdam Conference took this system for granted; but it was not long before the system broke down, first through French and then through Russian obstruction.

If this arrangement were to be left for any length of time, the effect would be a practical dismemberment of Germany, especially in view of the fact that the U.S.S.R. insisted upon giving Poland compensation in German territory for what was to be taken from it by Russia on the east. At Yalta, it had been agreed upon that "the final delineation of the western frontier of Poland should await the peace conference," but almost immediately the Soviet Union had proclaimed that all German territory east of the Oder and Neisse Rivers, as well as most of the southern half of East Prussia should be turned over to Polish administration. With reluctance the British and American delegates at Potsdam agreed to this *fait accompli*, insisting with futile repetition that a final settlement should be made at the peace conference. Meanwhile, the communist government of Poland, which had moved from Lublin to Warsaw, expelled all German settlers from the 60,000 square miles of farming country which had thus been taken over, resettled the land with Poles, and blotted out all traces of German ownership, government and language. This process was to find its logical conclusion when, in June, 1950, Soviet pressure led to the formal recognition by the communist East German Government of the Oder and Neisse line as the Polish boundary.

The other major problem affecting Germany was that of reparations for war damages. Russia had suffered losses from the German invasion far beyond anything that Germany could pay, but it was intent upon collecting reparations from post-war and future German production. The Americans and British, while sympathetic with the reasons for this demand, were anxious to restore a productive German industry so that Germany could help pay for the costs of occupation and become self-supporting as soon as possible. An intricate compromise was worked out to deal with this problem, but it was never applied because of the continuing opposition by the Soviet Government. The British and Americans were also opposed to the Soviet demand for a share in the occupation of the Ruhr Valley. Koenigsberg, ancient seat of the Hohenzollern dynasty, had already been given up for lost, and Russia had at least got full possession of that "window on the Baltic" which had been the goal of Russian diplomacy since the days of Peter the Great. The larger aspects of Russian imperialism were now becoming apparent: It was not only set upon dominating the Balkans, but at Potsdam made an unsuccessful bid for the control of one of Italy's African colonies, preferably Tripolitania.

There was full agreement on one subject: the complete disarmament and demilitarization of Germany and the elimination of the control of German industry that could be used for military production. War criminals were to be punished, denazification measures to be undertaken, and German education was to be controlled to eliminate Nazi doctrines and develop democratic ideas, but in spite of the prospects of an indefinitely long occupation, nothing was done looking toward the actual dismemberment of Germany such as had been proposed by Secretary of the Treasury Morgenthau, but strongly opposed by both the American and British Foreign Ministers. Stalin had said, in talking with Mr. Hopkins, that he would keep an open mind on the subject, but did not propose it at Potsdam.

Secretary of State Byrnes describes the Potsdam Conference as "the success that failed." The judgment of history has been definitely adverse, for although it registered the defeat of Nazi Germany, it set up no effective barrier against Soviet imperialism.

The Council of Foreign Ministers, which was to draw up the peace treaties, failed utterly in its task. The negotiations dragged on for fifteen exasperating months, through four sessions of the Council, one special meeting of the three Powers at Moscow, and one full-dress, seventy-nine-day Peace Conference at Paris, attended by twenty-one nations. At the end there was no agreement.

Churchill Warns of the Iron Curtain

The diplomatic gains that had been made in these slow and difficult negotiations and finally registered in the Peace Conference were made in spite of a mounting antagonism between both governments and peoples. Already, on February 9, 1946, Stalin, in one of his most important speeches, rededicated the U.S.S.R. to the communism of Marx and Lenin. Intended not only for Russia but for the whole listening world, the emphasis with which he repeated the fundamentals of the communist creed led some observers in Europe and the United States to think that he was defending himself against other members of the Politburo who had been disturbed over the negotiations in the peace settlement. There was nothing new in this, but the circumstance and the force with which the communist doctrine was expounded made it seem like a calculated warning note of increased hostility in dealing with the West.

The reassertion of doctrine was, however, merely a prelude to the announcement of a new five-year plan to increase production in iron, steel, coal and petroleum for defense "against any eventuality." The communist party was reorganized to make it more efficient in carrying out this program. Propaganda was stepped up against the capitalist countries, the United States in particular being charged with war-mongering, while the Soviet Union posed as the bastion for the defense of world peace.

If the Russians took this address as an epoch-making event in strengthening their ideology and their policy, in the outside world it was taken as an ominous warning of the dangers that lay ahead in a divided world. This was the setting for the speech of Winston Churchill, in Fulton, Missouri, on March 5, 1946. Although no longer in office, he spoke with great authority as the most outstanding personality in the Western world. He had been watching the discouraging drama of Russia's obstructionism in the efforts at European recovery, and had come to the conclusion that if this were to go on without public protest, Europe and the world might repeat the mistake that had been made in not appreciating the danger of Hitler's challenge which brought on World War II. Churchill has shown himself to be the supreme realist of his day, and when an invitation was extended to him to speak in the United States upon the menace of Soviet policy, he chose, with his customary astuteness, to give his address in a small college, Westminster, in the heart of the Middle West. There he delivered an historic address, the impact of which was profound upon both American and British public opinion. It was a call to "constancy of mind, persistency of purpose, and the grand simplicity of decision which should rule and guide the conduct of the English-speaking peoples in peace as they did in war." The central portion of the speech was so eloquent that it will always remain the classic statement of the opening phase of the cold war:

A shadow has fallen upon the scenes so lately lighted by the allied victory. Nobody knows what Soviet Russia and the communist international organization intends to do in the immediate future, or what are the limits, if any, to their expansive and proselyting tendencies.

I have a strong admiration and regard for the valiant Russian people, and for my war-time comrade, Marshal Stalin. . . .

We understand the Russian need to be secure on her western frontiers by the removal of all probability of German aggression. We welcome Russia to her rightful place among the leading nations of the world. We welcome her flag upon the seas. Above all, we welcome, or should welcome, constant, frequent and growing contacts between the Russian people and our own people on both sides of the Atlantic.

It is my duty, however, and I am sure you would not want me not to state the facts as I see them to you, it is my duty to place before you certain facts about the present position in Europe.

From Stettin in the Baltic to Trieste in the Adriatic, an iron curtain[6] has descended across the Continent. Behind that lie all the capitals of the ancient states of Central and Eastern Europe; Warsaw, Budapest, Belgrade, Bucharest and Sofia — all these famous cities and the population around them lie in what I might call the Soviet sphere, and all are subject, in one form or another, not only to Soviet influence but in a very high degree and in some cases, increasing measure of control from Moscow.

Police governments are pervading from Moscow. But Athens alone, with its immortal glories, is free to decide under British, American and French observation.

The Russian-dominated Polish government has been encouraged to make enormous and wrongful inroads upon Germany, and mass expulsions of millions of Germans on a scale grievous and undreamed of are now taking place.

The communist parties, which were very small in all these eastern states of Europe, have been raised to pre-eminence and power far beyond their numbers and are seeking everywhere to obtain totalitarian control. . . .

An attempt is being made by the Russians in Berlin to build up a quasi-communist party in their zone of occupied Germany by showing special favors to groups of left-wing German leaders. At the end of the fighting last June the Americans and British withdrew westward, in accordance with an earlier agreement, to a depth at some points of 150 miles upon a front of nearly 400 miles, in order to allow our Russian allies to occupy this vast expanse of territory which the Western democracies had conquered.

If now the Soviet Government tries, by separate action, to build up a pro-communist Germany in their areas this will cause new serious difficulties in the American and British zones, and will give the defeated Germans the power of putting themselves up on auction between the Soviets and the Western democracies. Whatever conclusions may be drawn from these facts — and facts they are — this is certainly not the liberated Europe we fought to build up. Nor is it one which contains the essentials of permanent peace. . . .

Twice the United States has had to send several millions of its young men across the Atlantic to fight the wars. But now war can find any nation, wherever it may dwell, between dusk and dawn. Surely we should work with conscious purpose for a grand pacification of Europe within the structure of the United Nations and in accordance with our charter. . . .

[At the close of World War I] there were high hopes and unbounded confidence that the wars were over and that the League of Nations would become all-powerful. I do not see or feel that same confidence or even the same hopes in the haggard world at the present time.

On the other hand, I repulse the idea that a new war is inevitable; still more that it is imminent. . . . I do not believe that Soviet Russia desires war. What they desire is the fruits of war and the indefinite expansion of their power and doctrines.

If we adhere faithfully to the Charter of the United Nations and walk forward in sedate and sober strength, seeking no man's land or treasure, seeking to lay no arbitrary control upon the thoughts of men, if all British moral and material forces were bound with your own in fraternal association, the high roads of the future will be clear, not only for ourselves but for all, not only for our time but for a century to come.

[6] This classic Churchillian term was first used by Mr. Churchill in a debate in the House of Commons on August 6, 1945: "Sparse and guarded accounts of what has happened and is happening have filtered through; it is not impossible that tragedy on a prodigious scale is unfolding itself behind the iron curtain which at the moment divides Europe in twain."

Churchill's address was not an attack upon communism as such; it was a warning against communist imperialism and the revolutionary doctrine of aid to the subversive elements in noncommunist countries. But Stalin chose to treat it as an instance of pure war-mongering. In an interview in *Pravda,* on March 13, 1946, he charged that Churchill, like Hitler, was ready to set war loose by a racial theory that only nations speaking the English language should decide the destinies of the entire world.

Although Churchill's speech rang like an alarm bell over the English-speaking world, it did not carry conviction in all liberal quarters, and especially in the English Labor Party, which had always cherished a reservation against his "militarism," dating from the time that he anticipated Germany's declaration of war in August, 1914, by readying the fleet to meet the German attack. He must have had this critical attitude toward him in mind, when, on another occasion, he said, with dry humor, "I have not always been wrong." As a matter of fact, few statesmen in history have been so often right on so many great and fateful issues.

The trend in American public opinion at the time was so strongly away from war that through the spring and summer months of 1946 there was a continuing hope that either the Russians would become more reasonable, or that we would find a way to compromise. This, however, was not the opinion of the Americans actually engaged in negotiations with the Russians. Secretary Byrnes was now going a long way from the genial persuasiveness of President Roosevelt, and facing up frankly to Soviet obstruction, was calling a spade a spade. As he had no successes to show for his "shirt-sleeves" diplomacy, his critics took the line that the Russians would respond to friendly treatment as they had when Harry Hopkins had got Stalin to understand the American point of view and was able to reassure him that there was no underlying hostility in the proposals offered him. The criticism of American diplomacy found expression in quarters which, although liberal, were by no means communist in sympathy.

CHAPTER XX

THE DEFENSE OF FREEDOM

The Truman Doctrine

THE YEAR 1947 was a turning point in this history of what had now become a divided world.

The events which launched this new turn of affairs were President Truman's Message to Congress on March 12, 1947, delivered to a joint session of both Houses, in which he set forth what has become known as the "Truman Doctrine" of containment against Soviet aggression; and the organization of the creation by Moscow of the Cominform, designed to coordinate communist action wherever possible throughout the world. Although the elements of this ideological and political conflict were always present in the foreign relations of Soviet Russia, both in peace and in war, obstructing and frustrating most of the efforts at European reconstruction, yet diplomacy had not wholly failed in finding at least partial solutions to the more pressing problems. The compromises which made agreement possible were in most cases to the advantage of Moscow, mainly because of its preponderant military power in eastern Europe after the close of the war. But until the end of 1946 the thrust of Soviet power, although vigorous and unrelenting, was not carried on in a way that seemed to threaten the peace.

There were two reasons for this: one was the expectation of the speedy withdrawal of American troops and of American interest in the European scene, and the other was the fact that the economic suffering of western Europe seemed to be creating the perfect breeding ground for the growth of communism, especially in France and Italy. Under these conditions the policy-makers in the Kremlin were, in the words of Secretary of State Acheson, "led to believe that they were about to win the greatest prize of history without military effort on their part; a power system extending from the Atlantic to the Pacific, including the Mediterranean and North Africa and most of the population and resources of the world."

The first outstanding event of this history was the proclamation of the "Truman Doctrine" of the "Containment" of militant communism (March 12) to check the attempt to spread communist control over both Europe and Asia. The Truman Doctrine which challenged this Soviet imperialism went far beyond that other doctrine of American history of a century earlier, the Monroe Doctrine, which had proclaimed the interest of the United States in the maintainance of free institutions in Latin America. It was not limited to any one area of the world, and, unlike the Monroe Doctrine, it was offered as a practical guarantee of freedom in other countries by American economic and military action if necessary. The United States then, as we have seen above, was not in a position to give effective support to democratic institutions in Latin America, and throughout most of the nineteenth century, it left that task to the British navy which patrolled the seas against the imperialism of reactionary governments of Continental Europe wishing to extend their power in any part of the Americas. This time, the United States undertook to guarantee the Truman Doctrine of world liberation from the threat of communist tyranny, and reluctantly but sternly accepted the leadership of free nations in meeting the threat of communist imperialism. The President's message was strongly supported by both parties in Congress, which passed the National Security Act on July 26, 1947.

This message to Congress had at first-sight borne little resemblance to a major historical document. It was almost like an incidental passage inserted in a plea to Congress for financial help to Greece and Turkey — a strange setting for a doctrine of world-wide application.

By the end of 1946, the United States was deeply involved in the effort to block Soviet influence in both Greece and Turkey. To carry out this policy, President Truman appeared before Congress on March 12, 1947, and asked for four hundred million dollars to help preserve peace in the situation in both countries. The President went on to say:

I am fully aware of the broad implications involved if the United States extends assistance to Greece and Turkey, and I shall discuss these implications with you at this time.

One of the primary objectives of the foreign policy of the United States is the creation of conditions in which we and other nations will be able to work out a way of life free from coercion. This was a fundamental issue in the war with Germany and Japan. Our victory was won over countries which sought to impose their will, and their way of life upon other nations. . . .

The peoples of a number of countries of the world have recently had totalitarian regimes forced upon them against their will. The Government of the United States has made frequent protests against coercion and intimidation, in violation of the Yalta Agreement, in Poland, Rumania and Bulgaria. I must also state that in a number of other countries there have been similar developments.

At the present moment in world history nearly every nation must choose between alternative ways of life. The choice is too often not a free one.

One way of life is based upon the will of the majority, and is distinguished by free institutions, representative government, free elections, guarantees of individual liberty, freedom of speech and religion, and freedom from political oppression.

The second way of life is based upon the will of a minority forcibly imposed upon the majority. It relies upon terror and oppression, a controlled press and radio, fixed elections, and the suppression of personal freedoms.

I believe that it must be the policy of the United States to support free peoples who are resisting attempted subjugation by armed minorities or by outside pressures.

I believe that we must assist free peoples to work out their own destinies in their own way.

I believe that our help should be primarily through economic and financial aid which is essential to stability and orderly political processes.

In other words, the United States was to be committed to a world-wide mission as the champion of freedom. "Life, liberty, and the pursuit of happiness" should be the aim, and ultimately the heritage of all mankind. But, while success crowned its efforts in Europe, the problems of Asia were complicated. Even where the old colonial system had been destroyed, resentment over past wrongs colored the new freedom. The only solution was that opened up by the United Nations, an adaptation of the Marshall Plan, offering "technical assistance to countries needing it." This was the basis of President Truman's famous "Point Four," a program for American cooperation with other nations to undo the wrongs of the past by building a better future.

We should make available to peace-loving peoples the benefits of our store of technical knowledge in order to help them realize their aspirations for a better life. And, in cooperation with other nations, we should foster capital investment in areas needing development. . . . The old imperialism — exploitation for foreign profit — has no place in our plan. . . . Democracy alone can supply the vitalizing force to stir the peoples of the world into triumphant action, not only against their human oppressors, but also against their ancient enemies: hunger, misery and want.

Gone forever was the sheltered continent of American isolation. The obstacles on the long road to freedom raised by the Kremlin also became stepping stones to further advance in Europe in NATO and the movement for European Union. There some progress was made, although the conference of President Eisenhower and the heads of government at Geneva in the summer of 1955 was a disappointment and the "new look" in Moscow after Stalin's death failed to convince those whom the Kremlin had so often tried to deceive. But if, all in all, Europe offered a measure of hope, in Asia the situation remained dark. There was frustration in relations with China and tragedy on the hills of Korea, and in the United States the opposition which had been isolationist became belligerently anti-communist, both at home and abroad, to the extent that in the name of freedom they were ready to betray it. This constituted one of the saddest chapters in its history, and in that of the country which had been its protector.

The assumptions on which the Truman Doctrine were based were made public in an anonymous article in *Foreign Affairs* for July, 1947, later revealed to have been written by a top-level official of the State Department and one time member of the American staff at Moscow, later Ambassador George Kennan. After analyzing the Soviet historical background, he turned to the present "political personality of Soviet power." In the Kremlin, he found, stress had been laid on a trio of key concepts: (1) the innate antagonism between capitalism and socialism, which, in Soviet eyes, excludes the possibility of cooperation; (2) the infallibility of the Kremlin, on which rests the rigid discipline of the Communist Party; and, (3) the use of deception, which may actually be resorted to by Soviet leaders for tactical purposes. The Kremlin, he said, was not in a hurry. "It can afford to be patient." Therefore the United States policy must be a "long-term, patient but firm and vigilant containment of Russian expansive tendencies." The Soviet power, he said, is not monolithic for the Russian people are still capable of overthrowing it some day. The United States, on the other hand, "has a spiritual vitality capable of holding its own among the major ideological currents of the time. . . ."

This summarization was everywhere taken as a semi-official view. Unfortunately, it gave a negative cast to the American plans for European recovery because it placed the accent upon opposition to Russia rather than upon either the political aim of safeguarding freedom or the economic aim of the restoration and strengthening of the productive capacity of the countries still suffering from the economic mutilations of the war. Throughout the next few years, these two currents in the thought and efforts of the American people to ensure a free and prosperous world were thus confused. In the struggle for Germany there were many examples of this dichotomy.

The European Recovery Program; The Marshall Plan

The fundamental purpose of the United States in World War II, as in World War I, was to establish a better and safer world for the common man. This found expression in a nationwide movement to help repair the loss and damage which the war had caused and to alleviate human suffering. Private contributions matched those of the government in a prodigious outpouring of generosity. The channel for this action was the United Nations Relief and Rehabilitation Administration (UNRRA) and was shared in by the other nations to the extent of their capacity. But the contribution of the United States was so much greater than all the rest combined that the organization was substantially American.

In the months following the close of the war, United States shipments of relief supplies to the liberated and war-torn countries were estimated by the Commerce Department, on February 8, 1946, to have reached the incredible sum of four billion dollars, with two billion, one hundred million going to UNRRA. This activity continued throughout 1946, and even in 1947, seven hundred and fifty million dollars more was given to UNRRA by the government. President Truman announced that during the twelve months ending June 30, 1947, the United States had shipped a record total of 18,433,000 long tons of food to the European nations, including the Soviet Union, and to China, the Philippines, India, the Netherlands, East Indies and to Latin America.

Vast as these contributions were they were mostly absorbed in the immediate task of temporary relief, and little had been done in basic reconstruction. When Secretary of State Marshall visited Europe in the spring of 1947, the situation which he found there was so serious that at the end of April he issued a call for immediate action to hold back "the disintegrating forces" in Europe "without waiting for further fruitless negotiations." "The patient [Europe] is sinking" he said, "while the doctors deliberate." On his return to Washington, he found that Under-Secretary Acheson had been studying the problem in detail, and his suggestions were embodied in an address by Secretary Marshall on June 5, at Harvard University, in which he outlined what is known as the Marshall Plan. It was an invitation to European nations to join together in a detailed study of their common needs so that the United States could consider them as a whole and not as those of separate nations. Said Secretary Marshall:[1]

Our policy is directed not against any country or doctrines but against hunger, poverty, desperation, and chaos. Its purpose should be the revival of a working economy in the world so as to permit the emergence of political and social conditions in which free institutions can exist. Such assistance, I am convinced, must not be on a piecemeal basis as various crises develop. . . .

It is already evident that, before the United States Government can proceed much further in its efforts to alleviate the situation and help start the European world on its way to recovery, there must be some agreement among the countries of Europe as to the requirements of the situation and the part those countries themselves will take in order to give proper effect to whatever action might be undertaken by this Government. It would be neither fitting nor efficacious for this Government to undertake to draw up unilaterally a program designed to place Europe on its feet economically. This is the business of the Europeans. The initiative, I think, must come from Europe. The role of this country should consist of friendly aid in the drafting of a European program and of later support of such

[1] *Department of State Bulletin,* June 15, 1947, p. 1160.

a program as far as it may be practical for us to do so. The program should be a joint one, agreed to by a number, if not all, European nations.

An essential part of any essential action on the part of the United States is an understanding on the part of the people of America of the character of the problem and the remedies to be applied. Political passion and prejudice should have no part. With foresight, and a willingness on the part of our people to face up to the vast responsibility which history has clearly placed upon our country, the difficulties I have outlined can and will be overcome.

The day after his Harvard speech Secretary Marshall held a press conference designed to reassure the U.S.S.R. and the governments of eastern Europe that his proposal fully included an invitation to them to share in the proposed American aid for economic recovery. In short, Moscow was given the choice of working for or against the economic recovery of Europe. Likewise, a bid was made to the nations of eastern Europe to cooperate with the West and to help in the up-building of a European community of nations, designed not only to restore the prosperity of the past, but to lay the basis for a future international economy with a richer promise than could have been fulfilled under the old national state system with its narrow rivalries and antagonisms. If Russia denied the satellites this opportunity, such action would at once reveal their loss of independence. But the American plan invited them to escape this fate by full cooperation with the nations of the West.

This was really a call for a new era in Europe at a time when each nation was concentrating upon its own sufferings. It was a challenge to remember those of their neighbors and to prepare jointly a program for American aid which would be fair to all of them. No wonder that voluntary agreement as to the allocation of American funds was hard to reach, especially in the face of Russian opposition.

The official British reaction was immediate and enthusiastic. Foreign Minister Bevin flew across the Channel to talk with French Prime Minister Bidault, and on their invitation Molotov met with them in a Three Power Conference on June 27, 1947. Molotov's part in this conference remains one of the puzzles of Soviet history. He brought with him to Paris a large staff of technical experts, a fact interpreted everywhere as indicating a willingness to participate in the Marshall Plan. The optimism created by this impression was strengthened by Molotov's personal attitude at the opening session of the conference with Bevin and Bidault, and his opening words were expressions of goodwill which would seem to indicate that Moscow had once more mode a *volte face* and was prepared to develop more friendly relations with its former allies.

But during a session while Molotov was speaking, a messenger delivered a sealed envelope to him. Then, without any change of expression in his impassive face, he launched into a bitter attack upon the whole American plan. From that moment on, he used the conference as a propaganda platform from which to attack the United States as an unscrupulous plotter attempting to continue its war-time dominance of western Europe by extending its capitalistic control through credits which it would later collect. He was particularly violent against international cooperation in the preparation of a joint program to be presented as a whole to the United States, insisting that each nation should decide for itself what funds it needed and how it would spend them. How could this be done in any case until an agreement was reached on the settlement of Germany? The outstanding question of reparations was evidently to the fore in this part of Molotov's argument.

It is possible that some of the bitterness in the anti-American diatribes these took shape at once in the creation of the Cominform, planned, as we have seen, to take the lead in propaganda offensive, especially for the devastation and losses of the war, it was not willing to raise the iron curtain for an inspection of its industrial and economic statistics which would have been required of it if it had entered into the Marshall program. It certainly also feared that the Soviet satellite countries might respond to the strong economic magnet of Western financing, and thus the control of Soviet Russia would be lessened. None of these satellite countries, not even Czechoslovakia or Poland was allowed to go to Paris, to learn the nature of the American proposals, but sixteen European nations met there on July 12: Austria, Belgium, Denmark, Eire, France, Great Britain, Greece, Iceland, Italy, Luxembourg, the Netherlands, Norway, Portugal, Sweden, Switzerland and Turkey. (Spain was not invited.)

This was the first step on the long and uncertain pathway toward the union of Free Europe. In his address of June 5, in which he made the offer of aid to Europe, General Marshall stipulated that "there must be some agreement among the countries of Europe as to the requirements of the situation and the part these countries themselves will take. . . . in a joint program." The Secretary of State had correctly interpreted public opinion in the United States in insisting that American aid to Europe should not be parcelled out in Washington with the inevitable result of sharp and embarrassing rivalries which would be left to Washington to settle. The making of an estimate of the amount which the European countries might need to cover their deficits over a four-year period was worked out in an organization new to history: The Committee for European Economic Cooperation (C.E.E.C.). This committee which met in Paris, had some preliminary indications of the amount the United States might possibly contribute, and in the short period of three months (July to September, 1947) it had completed a detailed, two volume report, which was sent to Secretary Marshall and made the basis of his request to Congress for a single European Recovery Fund.

The calculations involved many unknown factors, as there were no precedents to build upon, and the miscalculations of reparations after World War I, furnished an added caution in estimating the costs of rebuilding Europe after World War II. Moreover, during the four-year period of the recovery program, many unforeseen economic and political developments might change the whole situation. However, the committee reached an estimate of five billion, six hundred and forty million dollar deficit in 1948, to be met by United States aid, and an aggregate of fifteen billion, eight hundred and ten million dollars for the four years, 1948-1951. The adverse balance of

Europe with the Western Hemisphere (Canada and Latin America included) was estimated at seven billion, four hundred and eighty million dollars for 1948 and twenty-one billion, seven hundred and eighty million for the four years.

Washington at once got busy to deal with this vast problem. The President set up a committee on foreign aid under the chairmanship of W. Averall Harriman (commonly called the Harriman Committee) which reported on November 7, as its estimate for the year 1948 a maximum of six billion, three hundred and forty million dollars.

American insistence on dealing with western Europe as a whole ran into two major obstacles. In the monetary field, the currencies of the different countries were at different stages of inflation; for instance, the wholesale price level in France was twelve-fold and in Italy fifty-five fold of what it had been in 1938, while Belgium led the Netherlands and Norway in sounder finance. In Great Britain the convertibility of sterling broke down in August, 1947. In short, none of the countries of western Europe, with the exception of Switzerland, had monetary reserves available for meeting foreign indebtedness, and were making bilateral agreements among themselves for payments in dollars or gold, which further complicated the whole situation. To help stabilize world currency, Congress put into the International Monetary Fund two and three-quarter billion dollars, but even that was insufficient. The other problem of the lowering of trade barriers was naturally rendered more difficult by this monetary situation, but it was also a problem deeply rooted in history, for the control of foreign trade had long been regarded as one of the outstanding attributes of national sovereignty. This had been especially the case since 1879, when Bismarck inaugurated the protective tariff system for the German Empire, a measure paralleled in 1931, by the British preferential tariff system, which carried that ancient citadel of free trade away from its historic moorings. While the countries of western Europe were now well aware of the advantages of tariff union, the difficulties seemed almost insuperable.

Nevertheless, the need for a sound basis for western European economy was so imperative that the governments which had worked under the Committee of European Economic Cooperation, recast the complicated international machinery by a Convention on April 16, 1948, creating the coordinating central body under the title of the Organization for European Economic Cooperation (O.E.E.C.). The guiding principle which it laid down for the recovery program envisaged for the first time a general economy for western Europe.

The debates in Congress were long and thorough, and it was not until April 3, 1948, that it passed the Foreign Assistance Act, followed later by an appropriation of five billion dollars for European aid for the fifteen month period ending on June 30, 1949. It was one of the most decisive acts, not only in the history of the United States, but in that of every country of western Europe. The aftermath of the most destructive war in history was being cleared away, and out of the ruins a new Europe began to appear —

one which, as the years were more and more to disclose, was faced with the challenge of a great decision: whether to build constructively on the basis of freedom, or to accept the revolutionary leadership of Moscow.

The issue was one which, so far as the United States was concerned, had to be faced in the concrete terms of financial and economic cooperation with western Europe. It is hard, almost impossible, to translate the sufferings of a war-torn continent into authentic dollars and cents. They do not tell the story of broken lives, although they do help to measure the effort that must be made to open new horizons and to restore the faith in mankind which wars tend to destroy. In reality, if we have the imagination to see it, every figure in the international bookkeeping of the Marshall Plan stands for a human being; it measures his hopes and fears as well as the goods he buys in the market place. It is in the light of these far-reaching facts, that we shall read the story of that combination of enlightened self-interest and human sympathy and understanding that lies in the ledgers of the Marshall Plan.

The historian of the future will certainly regard these events as nothing short of revolutionary, not only in the history of the United States, which took the initiative, but also in that of western Europe, which had the hard task of fitting rival claims of nations into a single plan of economic recovery for submission to the United States. This was no mere episode in world history; in international practical politics it marked the turning point from the National State System of absolute sovereignties, which for the last four centuries had molded the thought and action of the peoples of the Western world.

It was inevitable that Soviet Russia should mobilize against the free nations in stronger and more definite movements wherever possible. The first of these took shape at once in the creation of the Cominform, planned, as we have seen, to take the lead in a propaganda offensive, especially for the strengthening of the communist movement in Europe. As these opposing forces clashed, the cold war reached into the political and economic life of Europe and America, threatening to denature the United Nations by creating within it a deepening cleavage of mistrust and fear and an unwillingness to work together on the problems of disarmament and the elimination of war.

Out of this dark picture of discouragement and danger a promise of radiant hope was born as the nations of western Europe began for the first time to lay the foundations of a real structure of international unity. Throughout history they had, like the City States of ancient Greece, developed and defended their sovereignties by the use of war as an instrument of national policy, and their relations with each other had been marked by recurring antagonisms rather than by a common effort at mutual understanding and cooperation. Now this age-long international anarchy was yielding to a sense of common interest in the face of the danger of Soviet dominance menacing the liberties that had been won in the long process of the centuries.

By a paradox which the communists had failed to foresee, their attack upon the political structure of the West tended to strengthen it by giving it a new sense of unity. Therefore they changed the direction of their propaganda away from local issues in Europe to concentrate upon American aid to the free nations in an intensified and unrelenting propaganda war on "American Imperialism." They seized upon the fact that American cooperation was military as well as economic, and by quoting irresponsible and extreme anti-communist utterances in the United States, led many sober Europeans to question "American interference" in Europe as "war-mongering" and provocative. It would be difficult to overestimate the influence of this propaganda in war-torn Europe, where a new attitude towards war had been brought about by the catastrophies of two world wars and fear of the incalculable potentialities of mass destruction in the atomic age, especially after the U.S.S.R. challenged the supremacy of the United States in hydrogen bombs. It is this problem of peace and security which, more than anything else, blocked the pathway to an understanding between the communist and the free world. But, as history has shown more than once, obstacles can be made stepping stones if there is sufficient wisdom and foresight.

The issue in the cold war, therefore, is more than the preservation of our heritage of freedom against communist aggression; out of it might conceivably come a new guarantee for the preservation of civilization itself.

CHAPTER XXI

THE BRITISH COMMONWEALTH OF NATIONS

WE HAVE traced the history of the Cold War in greater detail than that of any other conflict in the long fight for freedom, because the issue which it raised remains the supreme threat to freedom in the world today. But, to keep our bearings we must leave the confusion of this unsettled struggle, at the point where it has become an iron truce between two worlds, and turn back to review the achievements of freedom, of which the Communists have shown so little understanding.

This means going back to the revolutions for freedom and the history of the free nations, then to the extension of that freedom on the stage of world affairs in the British Commonwealth of Nations, to the troubled but inspiring drama of the United States, to a history culminating in the United Nations and then to a new pioneering age of statesmanship in the nations of western Europe, balanced against still newer experiments in government in Asia and Africa.

The first part of this chapter — and the most important — has already been given in the history of the American Revolution.[1] But as great as that revolu-

[1] Cf. Chapter XIII.

tion was, it still left the old colonial system untouched outside of its frontiers. That system was the political embodiment of modern imperialism, which began with the commercial revolution and the opening to Europe of the resources of Asia and America. All the sea-going Powers of Europe were in it, and in an era when mercantile rivalries led to war upon each other, exploited the native peoples in all possible ways. The most effective way was the establishment of colonies, bringing political support to commercial exploitation. From the seventeenth century to the nineteenth the old "colonial system" was maintained by the Spanish, the Portuguese, the Dutch, and the French, as well as the English — a system which left its bitter memories and anti-Western antagonism in the "colonial" peoples.

It was but natural that the United States should cherish this resentment against the government and people who had attempted to impose this system upon them, but it was Great Britain which led in what became a world-wide movement of emancipation from the exploiting policies of the old colonial system. Its sudden rise to world empire in the final struggle with the French in the Seven Years' War, threw upon the shoulders of the trading nation responsibilities of colonial government for which neither it nor any other nation was then prepared. It was only in the thirteen American colonies that the issues were understood by those who applied to their own homeland the principles of responsible government which had been worked out in England itself. But it was not the American Revolution which led the British Parliament ultimately to extend to their remaining colonies the principles for which the colonies had fought. The impact of the American Revolution on British thought had been rather to build a purely negative anti-imperialism which denied the value of colonies to the mother country, a movement which became dominant in the reform element of politics. This was strengthened by the fact that, owing to the industrial revolution, Britain's commerce prospered in spite of both the wars of the French Revolution and the American colonies, a prosperity which had no connection with the old colonial system.

Prophetic leadership in anti-imperialism had been given by Adam Smith in his *Wealth of Nations*, published in 1776, which, as already noted, matched in its influence on European thought the other, political proclamation of freedom of that year. The treatise which ultimately, in the first half of the nineteenth century, became the bible of economists, has a long chapter on colonies, tracing their history from ancient times, with especially trenchant criticism of the bad effects of the monopolistic policies of the mercantile system of his day. Of all the fallacies of the old colonial system the one which he emphasized most was that cost far outran the gain, which was shared by the few at the expense of the many. The expense of the protection by armies and navies was robbing the country of capital for free investment:

Great Britain derives nothing but loss from the dominion which she assumes over her colonies. . . . But . . . to propose that Great Britain should voluntarily give up all authority over the colonies, and leave them to elect their own magistrates, to enact their own laws, and to make peace and war as they might think proper, would be to propose such a measure as never was and never will be adopted by any nation in the world. No nation ever voluntarily gave up the dominion of any province, how troublesome soever it might be to govern it, and how small soever the revenue which it afforded might be in proportion to the expense which it occasioned. . . . The most visionary enthusiast would scarcely be capable of proposing such a measure with any serious hopes at least of its being adopted. If it was adopted, however, Great Britain would not only be immediately freed from the whole annual expense of the peace establishment of the colonies, but might settle with them such a treaty of commerce as would effectively secure her a free trade, more advantageous to the great body of the people, though less so to the merchants, than the monopoly which she at present enjoys.

The political results of such an emancipation might revive "the same sort of parental affection on the one side, and filial respect on the other, which used to subsist between the colonies of ancient Greece and the mother city from which they descended."

Here, tentatively but clearly stated, is the vision ultimately realized in the British Commonwealth of Nations. For the argument is rounded out by the conclusion that "the colonies may be taxed either by their own assemblies or by the Parliament of Great Britain." This development can at best be achieved at the same slow rate as the British Parliament itself, which took centuries to establish its control of the purse. The problem is not merely that of granting freedom to the colonies, but of assuring competent management of colonial affairs. Representative government would most likely succeed in a union of Great Britain with her colonies. Indeed the constitution of the empire "seems to be imperfect" without such a change in its constitution. Adam Smith continues:

We, on this side of the water, are afraid lest the multitude of American representatives should overturn the balance of the constitution, and increase too much either the influence of the Crown on the one hand, or the force of the democracy on the other. But if the number of American representatives were to be in proportion to the produce of American taxation, the number of people to be managed would increase exactly in proportion to the means of managing them; and the means of managing to the number of people to be managed. The monarchical and democratic parts of the constitution would, after the union, stand exactly in the same degree of relative force with regard to one another as they had before.

The people on the other side of the water are afraid lest their distance from the seat of government would expose them to many oppressions. But their representatives, of which the number ought from the first to be considerable, would easily be able to protect them from oppression. . . . The distance of America from the seat of government, besides, the natives[2] of that country might flatter themselves, with some appearance of reason too, would not be of long continuance. Such has hitherto been the rapid progress of that country in wealth, population and improvement, that in the course of little more than a century, perhaps, the produce of America might exceed that of British taxation. The seat of empire then naturally removes itself to that part of the empire which contributed most to the general defense and support of the whole.[3]

Here is the best liberal thought of Britain in the year of the American

[2] The first edition had "nations" instead of "natives."
[3] Adam Smith, *An Inquiry into the Nature and Causes of the Wealth of Nations*, edited by Erwin Cannon (New York: Random House, 1937), p. 590.

Declaration of Independence. The central issue is the same: the control of taxation. The federal empire which is here envisaged is a more daring concept than that which was realized in either the United States or the British Commonwealth of Nations. Plans for representation arranged progressively on an economic basis, have been recently revived in projects for reform of the United Nations, but, however logical and reasonable in themselves, they have made no headway against the political demands of equality in the sovereignty of national states. History wove a different pattern for colonial freedom than this cooperative enterprise of an empire constructed on economic lines. The only lesson which British political and economic thought took from Adam Smith was one which he did not intend to give, that the colonies were inherently a burden to the mother country. His suggestion that a properly organized empire might be profitable to all, was, as he insisted, impossible of realization as long as the business of government was hampered by the barriers of the mercantile system, under which the consumers who compose the body of the nation pay tribute to the producer, who controls policy. The closing words of *Wealth of Nations* reveal the far reach of its critical vision:

The rulers of Great Britain have, for more than a century past, amused the people with the imagination that they possessed a great empire on the west of the Atlantic. This empire, however, has hitherto existed in imagination only. It has hitherto been, not an empire, but the project of an empire, not a gold mine, but the prospect of a gold mine. . . . It is surely now time that our rulers should either realize this golden dream in which they have been indulging themselves, or that they should awake from it themselves and endeavor to awaken the people. If the project cannot be completed, it ought to be given up.

After Waterloo, and especially after the Reform Bill of 1832 put the middle class in power in England, anti-imperialism took the warning of Adam Smith to heart, but not to the extent of lessening the existing empire. The political implications of *Wealth of Nations* remained unfulfilled, while the economic reform overthrew protection in the ultimate acceptance of free trade. Of the two political parties, the Conservatives remained imperialist, the Liberals anti-imperialist. The only "empire" was India, — the title of Victoria was Queen of the United Kingdom and Ireland until Disraeli as Prime Minister had her proclaimed Empress of India at a magnificent durbar held near Delhi on January 1, 1877. But there were "Crown Colonies" flung over the seven seas, which were imperial possessions in the strict sense of the word. The government of these colonies was for the most part in the hands of the Colonial Civil Service, whose first interest was that of the natives rather than the European trader. It is only fair to the Conservatives to say that in this regard they shared the Liberal sense of responsibility for their trusteeship.

The incident which opened a new page in colonial history was a rebellion in Upper and Lower Canada (Ontario and Quebec) in the first year of Victoria's reign — 1837. The grievances of the few hundred "embattled farmers" who rose under the Scottish-born radical, William Lyon Mackenzie (grandfather of William Lyon Mackenzie King, Prime Minister of Canada for almost thirty years), and the French nationalist leader Louis Joseph Papineau, were not unlike those of the American revolutionists, charges that in the government of each colony the elected assembly was unable to assert itself against an irresponsible oligarchy termed the "Family Compact," and that no redress could be gotten from the British Government. The influence of Jacksonian democracy, then at its height across the border, stirred the leaders of the rebellion in Upper Canada more than the distant influence of British parliamentarianism, then readjusting to the new era of reform. Yet the new liberalism in Parliament took the step which it should have taken in Massachusetts after the Stamp Act; it sent an enlightened statesman to find out what was wrong and recommend the remedy. Lord Durham, chosen for this mission had been one of the chief architects of the Reform Bill. The Report, which he submitted in 1839, now stands out as "perhaps the most famous report in the English language, and the cornerstone of the present British Commonwealth of Nations."[4]

Strangely enough, this document has not kept its place among the familiar classics of the history of politics. Yet in its lengthy text — it is a whole book in itself — there are magnificent passages descriptive of the vast resources of Canada, which raise the issue of colonialism from petty politics to the level of a discussion of world affairs. The conclusion which British liberals had drawn from Adam Smith, that investment in colonies like Canada was wasteful extravagance, was met by the confident assertion that "unbounded material of agricultural, commercial and manufacturing industry are there." Instead of renouncing colonies, the mother country should develop them. "The country which has founded and maintained these colonies at vast expense of blood and treasury justly expects its compensation in turning their unappropriated resources to the account of its own redundant population. They are the rightful patrimony of the English people, the ample appanage which God and nature have set aside in the New World for whose lot has assigned them but insufficient portions in the old world." But the old colonial system must go. Canada should be freed from irresponsible government linked with London by a bureaucratic Colonial Office, through rapidly changing, ill-informed imperial governors. A new colonial regime was needed, granting to the colonists those elements of self-government which are inherent in the British system. In all matters of domestic concern the elected assembly should be supreme. This was supported by an argument based on the history of responsible government in England itself.[5]

It is not by weakening, but by strengthening the influence of the people on its government; by confining within much narrower bonds than those hitherto allotted to it, and not by extending the interference of the imperial authorities in the details of colonial affairs, that I believe that harmony is to be restored where dissension has so long prevailed, and a regularity and vigor hitherto unknown introduced into

[4] Burt, Alfred Le Roy, *The United States, Great Britain and British North America* (New Haven: Yale University Press, 1940, and Toronto: The Ryerson Press, 1940).

[5] John George, Earl of Durham, *Report on the Affairs of British North America*. (Oxford: Clarendon Press, 1912), pp. 277-279, pp. 282-283.

the administration of these provinces. It needs no change in the principles of government, no invention of a new constitutional theory, to supply the remedy which would, in my opinion, completely remove the existing political disorders. It needs but to follow out consistently the principles of the British constitution, and introduce into the government of these great colonies those wise provisions by which alone the working of the representative system can in any country be rendered harmonious and efficient. . . .

I would not impair a single prerogative of the Crown; on the contrary, I believe that the interests of the people in these colonies require the protection of prerogatives which have not hitherto been exercized. But the Crown must, on the other hand, submit to the necessary consequences of representative institutions, and if it has to carry on the government in unison with a representative body, it must consent to carry on by means of those in whom that representative body has confidence. In England this principle has been so long considered an indisputable and essential part of our constitution that it has hardly been necessary to inquire into the means by which its observance is enforced. . . .

The colonists may not always know what laws are best for them, or which of their countrymen are the fittest for conducting their affairs; but, at least, they have a greater interest in coming to a right judgment on these points, and will take greater pains to do so, than those whose welfare is very remotely and only slightly affected by the good or bad legislation of these portions of the empire.

Although this may seem a very grudging acknowledgement of the validity of democracy, British liberalism applied it not only to Canada, but by a gradual process of transforming the empire into a commonwealth of nations, in all the major colonies. It became the Magna Carta of colonial freedom. When Queen Victoria ascended the throne in 1837, there were no self-governing colonies; sixty years later, on her diamond jubilee, there were eleven, whose Prime Ministers brought to the Queen the respectful homage of young nations, whose freedom had strengthened, not weakened, their loyalty and pride in British citizenship.

The effort of Conservative statesmen to bind the colonies more closely together and to the mother country in an Imperial Federation met with little success, however, and Sir Wilfred Laurier, the eloquent French-Canadian Prime Minister, while paying glowing tribute to the empire, spoke for all the colonial statesmen when he said: "I claim for Canada this, that she shall be at liberty to act or not to act, to interfere or not to interfer, to do just as she chooses." Canada was already making its own tariffs and commercial policies and even insisting on its own decisions in matters of peace and war. But when the supreme test came in 1914, it, along with the other dominions, joined unreservedly in support of the empire. Australians and New Zealanders at Gallipoli, South Africans clearing the enemy from the African continent, and Canadians holding Vimy Ridge in France and breaking through the Hinderburg line, earned the right to participate in the Paris Peace Conference and then in the League of Nations. The most dramatic tribute to the regenerating power of freedom was the participation in both the war and the peace-making of the two leaders of the Boer War with Britain in little over a dozen years before, Generals Louis Botha and Jan Smuts. But both had joined with their late enemies to realize — though in other terms — the dream of Lord Milner, a Union of South Africa.

In the history of South Africa, Lord Milner holds the same kind of place as that of Lord Durham in Canada, only much more important because this time he changed the structure of the empire. As High Commissioner for South Africa and Governor of Cape Colony during the Boer War, he had been a proconsul of Empire, to whom Lord Roberts paid tribute for his wisdom in counsel and "unfaltering courage." But it took an equal courage to withstand the political opposition to his terms for the peace settlement, which gave the British only equal treatment with the Boers, their beaten enemies. It was the realization of that high statesmanship which Lincoln showed in his second Inaugural. In his farewell address at Johannesburg in 1905, Milner, referring to his share in the war, said: "What I should prefer to be remembered by is a tremendous effort after the war not only to repair the damage of that calamity, but to restart the colonies on a higher plane of civilization than they have hitherto attained."

Milner's place in the British scheme of things was that of an elder statesman, whose opinion bore weight on major questions of imperial policy. At the Paris Peace Conference of 1918-1919, he was a power behind the scenes in the British Delegation and at times substituted for the Prime Minister, Lloyd Goerge. As it was from this Conference that the final impetus was given to make the change from empire to commonwealth, and as I was a privileged observer of that historic event, I quote a passage from my diary, recording my impressions of Lord Milner and his ideas on colonial government:[6]

Milner said that Britain had succeeded well where it had really tried hard, in handling primitive peoples, but that was an entirely different job in colonial administration from the cooperation in government necessary where the people governed were of about the same grade of intelligence as their governors. He indicated that in his mind this second task was so different from the first as to be hardly in the same category of colonization, and said that it was so difficult a job that he wondered if the British or any other nation could ever succeed at it.

The question which required the greatest wisdom in statecraft was to determine at what stage, and how far, a people of capacity but immaturity should have their rights of self-government admitted. He said that the dividing line seemed to be reached when the governed people began to express themselves in abstract terms, that is, in the demand for constitutions and institutional bodies, instead of in terms of personalities. Colonial administration could be highly successful so long as it was a question of personal confidence in the administrator and personal rule by him. For this type of government what is needed is not so much technical knowledge as dependable character and good common sense. This is what the British public school system has developed in the young men who go out to savage tribes with training only in mathematics and the humanities, especially the classics. The strange paradox of their success in colonial administration is not so inexplicable after all, for both by position and by racial prejudice they naturally take a position of aloofness and have an innate sense of their own superiority which primitive

[6] The extract is from my volume *At the Paris Peace Conference* (now out of print). Lord Milner applied his theory of government in his Report on Egypt (1920) in which he recommended replacing the British Protectorate by an "independent" Egypt, in which Great Britain's "special interests" would be safeguarded by financial and judicial advisors and a police force to defend imperial connections but not to constitute a military occupation of the country. This was the blueprint used by Lord Allenby in negotiating the settlement of 1922.

peoples readily recognize as a sign of leadership. But Milner said that this stage of the colonial problem was rapidly narrowing down with the growth of education and he did not look for a long continuance of the old British colonial system.

I asked him if he would be a little more definite about the second stage to which he referred — that in which the natives were thinking in general or abstract terms. He said that there was no exact way to define it, but that as nearly as one could state it, it was about when a people began to demand written or formal safeguards for their rights. He said that the turning point sometimes came before the native people were really ready for the reform for which they were asking, but that even if they were not ready or able to take on constitutional government, they were likely to cause the old personal type of government to fail as soon as they ceased to look to the personal qualifications of those governing them as the essential basis of relationship.

The anti-imperialism of this pro-consul of empire shows statesmanship at its best. But, as we have seen, it could build upon over a century of liberal thought and actual experience in British colonial administration. This was lacking in France, concentrating on building a Continental rather than a world empire, which it lost in both America and India. The whole drift of its history, from Richelieu to Napoleon was toward centralization of government, a pattern into which its newly acquired colonies of the nineteenth century, in Africa and Asia, did not easily fit. For the French conception of colonial administration was entirely different from that of Great Britain or the United States. Instead of preparing its colonies for freedom, it planned to integrate them into the French nation, making their lands part of the metropole.

The most perfect example was Algeria, which was declared to be a part of France itself. The conception of colonial integration applied in principle, however, to the whole French system. French colonial experts have written volumes in defense of this unique extension of citizenship which, at first glance, seems to resemble the way Roman citizenship was extended to the peoples of the empire. It can be argued that it was a higher social and political aim than the British method of escaping the responsibility of imperial rule by the disintegration of the empire. But history is now passing adverse judgment on the French method, both in Asia and North Africa; for however much it avoided racial prejudice, so prevalent elsewhere, it did not leave the natives free to work out their destiny in their own way, and it was left to the brilliant initiative of Charles de Gaulle to change French colonialism from benevolent despotism to freedom in one of the greatest political experiments of our time.

The Belgian colonial empire in Africa began on the model of the East India Company, a corporation called The International Association of the Congo, organized and managed by King Leopold II, apart from the government of Belgium. As it established "protectorates" over a large area, the other European states took notice of this private empire of Leopold, extending through central Africa, and at a conference held in Berlin in 1884-1885, recognized the Congo Free State, with Leopold as "sovereign." It was "free" only with reference to the trading rights of other European countries; but the natives were forced to bring rubber and war products as a "tax," the penalty for failing to do so being cruel punishment, even torture and death. These "Belgian atrocities," reported by missionaries, stirred indignation, especially in the "nonconformist conscience" of England, and forced the governments of Europe to take the final step in the suppression of slavery, in the nonslavery conference of Brussels in 1890, to which all nations subsequently agreed. In 1908 the Congo Free State was annexed to Belgium as a colony and renamed Belgian Congo.

The Brussels Conference had one fatal weakness, it did not provide for an international organization to which the signatories would have to report. The result was that when the situation in the Congo deteriorated, as it did in missionary opinion, there was no international authority to which appeal could be made. It was this situation which led the American expert on colonial questions at the Paris Peace Conference in 1919, George Louis Beer, to propose the Mandate system for the League of Nations, a proposal which had the eloquent support of Marshal Jan Smuts of South Africa. Article 22 of the Covenant, has the ring of a pioneering document, which it is: "To those colonies and territories which as a consequence of the late war have ceased to be under the sovereignty of States which formerly governed them and which are inhabited by people not yet able to govern themselves under the strenuous conditions of the modern world, there should be applied the principle that the well-being and development of such people form a sacred trust of civilization and that securities for the performance of this trust should be embodied in this Covenant." The Covenant then went on to state that "the character of the mandate must differ according to the stage of development of the people, the geographical situation of the territory, its economic conditions and other similar circumstances." This principle was applied by dividing the mandate into three categories, those that had formerly been part of the Turkish Empire; those of Central Africa; those of Southwest Africa and the South Pacific Islands. In every case the mandatory Power in charge of the administration of the territory should render to the Council of the League an annual report which would be subject to the approval of the League.

The Mandate system of the League of Nations furnished the precedent for the International Trusteeship system of the United Nations. Here both the purposes and the structure of the system are spelled out: the promotion of self-government, the encouragement of respect for human rights and "equal treatment in social, economic and commercial matters for all Members of the United Nations." The oversight of all these complications, including the welfare of the inhabitants, is vested in the Trusteeship Council, except where there are strategic areas, which cases go to the Security Council. The division of authority is logical and necessary, but the fact remains that it is only in the nonstrategic areas that the nations are given a schooling in all the duties and responsibilities of freedom.

From this strange and little known story of the origins of the Mandate and Trusteeship systems we must turn back to the revolution in the colonial government of Great Britain in the nineteenth century, a chapter in the history of anti-imperialism which is one of the proudest chapters in the history of freedom — matched only in courage and far-sightedness by the revolutionary policy of France under de Gaulle, the fate of which must be left to future historians.

The transformation of the Victorian world empire, "on which the sun never sets," from colonies under imperial rule to a Commonwealth of Nations, was not entirely due to colonial statesmanship, such as we have seen in Durham and Milner. It could never have been carried through but for the conviction of British statesmen in Parliament that anything short of self-government for the Dominions was repugnant to the principles of the unwritten constitution of Great Britain itself. From the days of the Reform Bill, its supporters, the Reformers or Liberals, had been opposed to the politics of powers, either in foreign affairs or within the empire; but it was the imperialist-minded Conservatives who prepared the framework for the Commonwealth, by their advocacy of imperial federation during the last quarter of the nineteenth century.

The Diamond Jubilee of Queen Victoria in 1897 brought the Prime Ministers of the Dominions to London — and again in 1907 — in what was called an Imperial Conference.[7] But it had no power and was only a symbol of empire. The real centers of the developing history were in the member States themselves, of which Great Britain, while the most important, was only one. The senior Dominion was Canada, created out of British North America by an Act of Parliament in 1867. Australia became a federation in 1901 and the Union of South Africa in 1910. Alongside them was New Zealand, which led all the world in solving the racial problem, and a great galaxy of Crown Colonies, which remained under administration by Parliament.

This was the situation until World War I; then, as the Dominions had participated in it, they took part in the Paris Peace Conference at its close as full members. Only in the signature of the Treaty of Versailles were they grouped together in a subordinate list under the sovereignty of the British Empire. The listing was a printer's device, as there was no British Empire in international law, only a Kingdom and an Empire of India.[8] The error was corrected at conferences of the Dominions with the mother country in London in 1926 and 1930. The anomolous political structure, the nature of which the British, with their customary indifference to codification, had never clarified, was given form and a name: The British Commonwealth of Nations. This was largely due to the brilliant work of a group calling itself the Round Table, several of whom had worked with Lord Milner in South Africa. Behind the movement lay the strength of Lord Milner's position as an elder statesman, which, as we have seen, brought him into the War Cabinet in World War I, then to the Paris Peace Conference and Egypt. It is not

[7] Since the end of World War II there have been frequent Prime Ministers' Conferences, not to mention financial and foreign trade conferences.
[8] For a discussion of this point see J. T. Shotwell, *At the Paris Peace Conference* New York, Columbia University Press (1937), pp. 414.

possible, here, to single out more than one member of this group, for none of them signed their articles for their Quarterly Review *The Round Table*. But the editor, Lionel Curtis, wrote with the conviction of a major prophet, and his eloquent book, *Civitas Dei* gave the sanction of Augustine to the idea of the Commonwealth.

The Statute of Westminster of December, 1931, the charter of this new creation, is a brief but momentous historical document. In it the British Parliament gives up all claim to legislate for the Dominions unless the Dominion concerned requests and assents to an act. Parliament may not declare void and inoperative any act duly passed by the legislature of a Dominion on the ground that said act is repugnant to past or possible future acts of the British Parliament. The Dominions are united by common allegiance to the Crown and no change can be made touching the succession without the consent of all the Dominions. The word "colony" shall not be used in future references in connection with any of the Dominions. A Governor-General in each Dominion represents the Crown, but he is a figurehead, and the link with Britain is through a High Commissioner whose status in London is that of an Ambassador, alongside the other Ambassadors of the Commonwealth members at other capitals.

It should be added that the smaller old-time colonies are also sharing in the movement of self-government. Although the British Civil Service, whose record for efficiency is hard to match anywhere in history, had already inaugurated many reforms, no history of freedom could ignore the contribution of those pioneering statesmen of the jungle and forest, like Lord Lugard in Nigeria or Hubert Murray in Papua, who raised the status of the natives from primitive conditions to that of the semi-civilized, even if their initial efforts sometimes failed, as in sections of Africa. But the greatest work of the colonial administrators is with civilized but small communities, which are on the path to self-government. In these Crown Colonies, the civil service, far from being oppressors of the colonists, make it their duty to prevent exploitation by outsiders, British or others.

The Commonwealth itself defies description.[9] It is a function rather than a structure; it is the way the member nations act together rather than as a mere substitute for empire. It violates the rigid conception of sovereignty as the absolute master of a nation's fate. Its founders meant it to be the old fashioned thing, a federation. That was what they talked of at the turn of the century. But it has got beyond that now. Its members put the accent on freedom — even from the dominion of the mother country.

This strangely new device of functionalism rather than federation, so puzzling to foreigners, is nothing new in British history. It is the product of that outstanding contribution to politics of parliamentary rule, compromise — without surrender — as the recognized way of solving national problems. The tie that binds the members of the Commonwealth is loyalty to its common purpose, of which the Crown is only the exalted symbol. And that purpose is freedom exercised under due process of law, with befitting modera-

[9] Sir Drummond Shiels, M.C., M.B., *The British Commonwealth*: A Family of Peoples (Longacre, London: Odhams Press Ltd., 1952), 384 pp.

tion and statesmanlike regard for all consequences. True to the political traditions of the mother country, the Commonwealth has no written constitution. The Statute of Westminster is more like a treaty providing for independent states to work together.

The climax of this long drama came on August 15, 1947, when the Empire of India made way for a Dominion within the Commonwealth.[10] Although the word "British" has been dropped, the membership remained in that great association of free nations which has in these last years taken over the heritage of an empire which, contrary to the laws of nature, grew young instead of old and became the embodiment and champion of freedom the world over. No such device had previously been known in the history of politics as this in which India was able at once to act as a sovereign nation on equal terms with its late overlord, the United Kingdom, while mutual respect ripened into a friendship never possible under empire.

The fact that Ceylon is also a member of the Commonwealth strengthens the tie; the case of Pakistan is different, raising problems for which no solution is in sight. Here, in this conflict between Moslem and Hindu is the one reminder of the tragedy of India's past, in the divisions of its tribal wars and the taboo abhorrence of the impure or the unbeliever. Fortunately, the impact of the modern world bears in upon this persistence of ancient antagonisms. It cannot bear too heavily, for that intensifies the reaction; but, given time, the solution should not be beyond the ingenuity of those who would profit most.

It is, of course, in these interstate relations that the Commonwealth plays its part in Indian affairs. Within its own borders, each one jealously guards its newly won independence, but political nationalism does not solve the greatest problem which confronts it in its effort to take its place in a world of nations; its adjustment to the dynamics of industrialism. This is a problem common to all which no one people can solve by itself. The mere avoidance of inter-Indian wars is not enough, although even this is menaced at times. The needs of industry reach out for raw materials, for power and for markets through states that do not cease to be neighbors because they have become independent. The Commonwealth offers them a method of working together on equal terms, as partners in a common enterprise, with no derogation of sovereignty. The situation and the way to meet it was clearly set forth by an Indian writer in the *India Quarterly:*

> Commonwealth countries have to evolve a scheme of cooperative effort by which industrialization of countries like India, Pakistan and Ceylon can be promoted and very greatly accelerated. For the implementation of such schemes it would be necessary to create and administer a central pool of resources, skill and experience, which can be drawn upon for rendering assistance . . . directing economic forces consciously in relation to the needs of the less developed countries. . . . This has to be done in order to make the Commonwealth a reality in the true sense of the word, in theory and in practice.[11]

[10] Cf. Chapter XXII, "The New Asia."

[11] Gyan Chad, "Industrialization of India and Commonwealth Cooperation," *India Quarterly* (December, 1945)

The economic program of the Commonwealth is not only reason for its retention by the new Indian nations, however. The prestige of membership on even terms with Great Britain replaces the splendor of imperial durbars with something more real and more satisfying. Independence is surpassed by something more than an alliance. It is a matter of pride as well as of security to keep the shadow of the old imperial connection.

It is no wonder that the British Commonwealth of Nations puzzles European Continental politicians. It bears the mark of the outstanding quality of British policy, realism that cherishes symbols like royalty itself, but refuses to let them interfere with practical ways of getting things done. Yet it is a tribute to the universal appeal of the Commonwealth that one of the best descriptions of it is that given by Nehru, the leader of the nation that throughout history has least resembled the British. In any case, we have to go to the Indian statesman for the most penetrating analysis ever made of the Commonwealth:

> We are members of the Commonwealth — that rather strange and odd collection of nations which seem to prosper most in adversity. . . . Somehow it has found some kind of invisible link by seeing that practically there is no link and by giving complete independence and freedom to every part of it. . . . This Commonwealth has grown and changed repeatedly, and while Member nations of this Commonwealth sometimes disagree, sometimes have interests conflicting with each other, sometimes pull in different direction, nevertheless the basic fact remains that they meet as friends, try to understand each other, try to accommodate each other and try, as far as possible, to find a common way of working. It may not always happen, but what is really important is the friendly approach in this, as in every other problem of life or every problem of international affairs. That friendly approach, that sympathetic approach, that attempt to understand, that attempt, in so far as one can, to go in step, and at the same time enjoy the complete knowledge that one can take any step — a combination of these factors has led, I suppose, to the success of this rather remarkable experiment.

There are few passages in the literature of politics more meaningful than this extract from Nehru's New Delhi speech in 1950.

Such, in outline, is the Commonwealth which replaced the Empire. It is a strange story, that of this world-wide experiment in freedom. It takes us into a wholly different world from that of the Stamp Act and the soldiers of Cornwallis — one that shares the inheritance of the common law, Magna Carta, habeas corpus and representative government. No wonder the members of the Commonwealth find in it the expression of a way of life rather than a hard and fast system of government.

CHAPTER XXII

THE NEW ASIA

THE ROAD to freedom which we have been traveling has been confined, so far, to the Western world. Although it touched on the history of Asia in its opening chapters, this study has followed the path along which Europe looks back to Greece and Rome, through the Middle Ages and the modern world, with almost no mention of the problems of freedom in the Orient. The reason for this is that there was relatively little to record, compared with what happened in the West, under the shifting impact of politics, war, religion and economics. It was only in the nineteenth century that Asia began to parallel the revolution which founded politics in ancient Greece, when it replaced the ties of primitive society by a secular practice of government. It is to be hoped that in the long ranges of the future the parallel with the movement begun in Greece will hold. But the history of the West is a sobering reminder that the road to this goal is a long and difficult one, and Asia has only begun to enter on it.

Asia is too vast and varied for detailed study here. Even the three great societies which we pass in review — Indian, the Chinese and the Japanese — present so many differences among themselves that few generalizations are applicable to them without serious qualifications, and this is even truer of the miscellany of countries stretching over southeastern Asia into islands of Indonesia. Yet, there is an Asia. Compared with the changeful West it presents the hard outlines of a static society, one which has preserved until the nineteenth century an ancient mold for both thought and action. This does not mean, however, that its annals have been empty of protest or revolt against oppression by native rulers or foreign conquerors, or that in its nobler aspects it is lacking in the achievement of justice, which, as we keep repeating, is the basis of freedom. But throughout this history, there was no such challenge to the way of life as that which has now resulted from Western influences disrupting the traditional conservatism of Oriental society. The interplay of these new forces with the old is giving a new meaning not only to the history of Asia, but also, because of its magnitude, to that of the whole world.

501

We call this new era the "Awakening of Asia," but the term is inadequate and misleading. It implies that its peoples slept throughout the changeless past; but they were restless with energy in war and peace, creating empires, building cities and leaving a real heritage of culture. What is taking place today is the transfer of this energy and intelligence — for neither was ever lacking — to deal with new problems. Old Asia is touched with youth again; one of the miracles of history. It owes this to the West, but is reluctant to admit it. It also owes to the West the urge to draw together in a Pan-Asian movement, which never existed before. The consciousness of race takes on a different meaning from that of ancient tribalism or tabooed classes within a nation when it draws the line between the white race and the colored — of any color. This reaction against the whites tends to unite not only Asians with Asians, but for the present at least, with Africans as well. It is a protest movement which has deeper roots and a further reach than communism, and gives to the revolt against colonialism the strength of a moving tide. It was primarily on this racial basis that the new Asia began its political career at the conference of Bandung in 1955, a landmark in the history of the New Asia, marking the end of colonialism but, in spite of many brave words, offering no agreed program for the regime of freedom.

Behind the problems of imperialism and colonialism, and much more difficult to solve, lies this problem of race. A full discussion of it would take us outside the scope of a history of freedom into the broader field of human relationships. For here we plumb the depths that reach beyond politics and economics, beyond reason itself, to the primitive core of instinctive reactions, some of which were lodged in the taboo. Anthropologists have proved that the term "race" as commonly used is mostly misleading, for some of the tests — color, head measurements, or other physical characteristics, and more especially language — do not remain static under new environments. Language can be acquired. Whites eventually turn brown under the tropical sun, and Professor Boas, the great anthropologist, has proved by a study of Italians in New York that the impress of environment may even affect head formation.

Moreover, the political evolution of Europe from tribe to nation was, as we have seen in both ancient and modern history, a violation of the blood tie. Whatever we mean by race, the mingling of the peoples in European migration, and not consanguinity, was the basis of nationality in that part of the world where nationality first dominated politics. This was as true of Western Europe as it is of America today, the melting pot of all races. The occupants of a London bus have as many different kinds of head formation — long, round or square — as those in a New York subway. What makes them all British or American, as the case may be, is the impress of environment. But where the environment itself remains the same for centuries, both physical features and languages also remain static, although even in such cases there are minor variations. There were two such peoples in Europe which had little intermingling in the migrations of ancient or medieval history: the Jews who were excluded from Christian nations; and the Nordic peoples whose homelands were not overrun by southern or eastern invaders. Even these strains have divergent elements, however: the Jews of northern and eastern Europe differ in appearance from those of the south; and not all Nordics are blond. The fact that these two were branches of larger primitive divisions of mankind the Semites and the "Aryans,"[1] need not concern us here, for such racial formations (whatever that term implies) were already breaking up when the records of history began, as the history of Judah bears witness. This is also true of the swarthy, long-headed Mediterranean "race" which also inhabited the Atlantic seaboard, and which became politically, more than racially, self-conscious under the Roman Empire.

Until Hitler's day, the problem of western history was not race, but nationality. Then, based upon a false biological theory of race, exalting the Nordic peoples above all others, the Nazi persecution of the Jews blackened the record of the German people with deeds that surpassed in horror anything in the history of a civilized nation. The theory was set forth in the work of a Germanophile Englishman who became a German citizen, Houston Stewart Chamberlain. His book, *The Foundations of the Nineteenth Century*, first published in German in 1899, attributed everything good in the modern world to a German or Aryan (the terms were interchangeable) "race." According to Chamberlain, the moral superiority of this "race" is the hope of the world, and only by the victory of the Aryans over the lesser peoples can humanity be saved from moral decline. Therefore, when Chamberlain witnessed the defeat of Germany in World War I, it meant to him not merely a political disaster, but moral degradation for civilization.

All this, however, has little, if anything, to do with the race problem after World War II as it emerged in the new era of world politics in the United Nations. This time it is the expression of a world-wide division of mankind with regard to only one simple test: color. The white race (or races) of European stock are confronted by the colored peoples of Asia and Africa, who are determined not only to get rid of colonialism, but to establish racial relations on equal terms.

The new Asia came into being as a response to two compelling stimuli, industry and commerce, and internal economic disturbance of age-old habits of work and social organization based upon them; and an external political reaction against Western imperialism. The economic change raises the same issues as it did in the West, either that of reforms under the capitalist system or revolution under communism; the political issue is that of ending colonial imperialism. History, however, has confused these two, because the colonial powers of the era now closing were also the capitalist exploiters. The result is that communism, as a revolt against capitalism — although the greatest embodiment of imperialism in the world today — seems to talk the same language as anti-imperialism.

[1] It is almost impossible to avoid the use of this term, although it properly applies to language instead of race. The racial stock is Caucasian, and includes more than those who spread out from Iran in the invasion of India on the south and Europe on the northwest, carrying with them the basic words of their original tongue. But the anthropological problem of the mixture of races in those migrations lies outside the scope of this book, except for the racist theories of Germany.

It is this false, but almost inevitable conclusion that makes the problem of Asia so baffling. For the old colonialism left a double sting — the exploitation itself and the humiliation of the Asians in having to deal with foreigners who, holding themselves aloof socially behind a racial barrier, often wounded the native pride of those who felt themselves the possessors of a superior culture with roots deeper than those of the West. The result was to bring an alignment of the nonwhite peoples against the whites in a movement which, in the eyes of its leaders, at least, has the portentous possibilities of a mobilization of the majority of mankind. The resentment against such contacts with western "materialism" was to create a gulf of mutual misunderstanding, which the communists in their attacks on capitalism have done their best to widen. In this propaganda their success has been incredible in the case of the United States; the one nation that has fought colonialism from Concord to Manila Bay, is singled out in the communist charges as the leader of Western "imperialism," not only because of its support of the reactionary Chiang Kai-shek, but also because in its efforts to build up anti-Communist forces everywhere, it tried to mobolize Asia against the Soviet advance.

It is a naïve concept of Asia, but one widely shared, that in the new era opening before it, it will follow one of the two patterns set for it by the Western world, either that of the free economy of capitalism or communism. Even China, the avowed champion of communism is reshaping its society along Oriental lines, in violation of the Marxian theory that the communist state will "wither away" as all mankind escapes from the feudal overlordship of capitalism. For Mao's China is an all inclusive dictatorship, regimented by a militarism that is also a police force. It is this militarism which, quite apart from communism, has replaced colonialism in the rest of Asia, except for the two great countries which had already adopted free economy, Japan and India. Neither communism nor freedom but military dictatorships rules in almost a dozen countries of southeast Asia, from Pakistan, through Burma and Malaya to Indo-China and Indonesia.

Reports from Washington indicated disappointment with this development; yet Washington itself was partly to blame for its support of military planning in its world-wide policy of "containment" of communism, unmindful of the way this enhanced the importance of the military class in the new republics. But, quite apart from American influence, the army was bound to come to the fore in states that had no experience in self-government and were now suddenly forced to face national responsibilities on their own. For, as *The New York Times* has pointed out:[2] "In lands with unbalanced economies, scanty education and little administrative background, the armies became a relative elite. Their officers were healthier, more honest, more patriotic and more used to coordinated effort, than other groups. Their soldiers received at least some learning and familiarity with national problems as distinct from purely provincial problems. Officers have the habit of leadership as well as the habit of accepting authority. When political chaos appears as in Pakistan or Burma, the army discovers that it is itself the most effective instrument to move in the vacuum."

[2] Article by C. L. Sulzberger in *The New York Times*, January 5, 1959.

So far, the military dictatorships have been beneficient; Generals Aijub Khan in Pakistan, Ne Win in Burma, Sarit Thaurat in Thailand and Nasution in Indonesia have all attempted to justify their seizure of power by straightening out the inadequacies and dealing with the corrupt practices of previous governments. Yet thoughtful Asians are fully aware that, in the words of the former Premier of Pakistan, Huseyn Shaleed Suhrawardy, "the purported remedy is not a cure but the prevention of a cure; that dictatorship does not combat corruption, but erects it into a principle; that it does not widen access to talent in public service, but closes sources to talent by preempting office for a chosen inner group; that its instruments are not information, but deception and concealment, seeking not the education but the confusion and continued tutelage of the people by playing on their emotions rather than permitting the operation of reason."[3]

Such ringing denunciation reminds one of the attacks upon despotic rule in Europe before the English or French Revolutions; but nowhere in the background of these Asian nations was there a Magna Carta of the rule of law. To expect them to become efficient democracies on the Western model once they have rid themselves of colonialism is mere wishful thinking. But, while we must not expect too much too soon, we should remember that in western Europe the foundations for freedom were laid in an age of despots and that the revolutions in England and France came only after the people themselves were conscious of their rights — an entirely different thing than being aware of their grievances.

Whether southeastern Asia will repeat this history or take an entirely different path, that of communism, will largely depend upon the future of China, as the dominant power in the Orient. Before turning to it, however, and the new nations of southeastern Asia taking shape under the shadow of its imperialism, we must review the history of the two Asian Powers which have, for quite different reasons, followed the Western world, Japan and India. The contrast between them and communistic China furnishes the varied background for the new nations of the southeast.

India

India is a world of its own. A sub-continent as large as all Europe west of Russia, with a population greater than that of Europe with Russia added, and a civilization thousands of years older than that of the West — the ruins of its oldest cities date with ancient Babylon — it nevertheless played no part in the history of freedom until the twentieth century. Then, by a revolution unparalleled by any other political revolution since politics began, a new India suddenly emerged, not merely as a beneficiary of freedom but as its leader in a new strategy of moral conquest, the strategy of peace. On August 15, 1957, in a solemn ceremony at Delhi, the British flag was lowered in the presence of the last Viceroy, Lord Mountbatten, and in its place was raised the flag of the Union of India, its emblem the *charka* (wheel) of the Bud-

[3] *Foreign Affairs* (April, 1957), p. 425.

dhist emperor Asoka of the third century B.C., symbolizing India's ancient culture, replacing the spinning wheel of Gandhi on the flag of the Indian Congress of pre-independence days.[4]

The triumph of Indian nationalism had, however, been sadly marred by the breaking off of Moslem Pakistan on the northwest and east, the creation of Mohammed Ali Jinnah in a nationalist movement combined with religious fanaticism with which the British felt powerless to deal. It was a symbol of the peaceful nature of the transfers of sovereignty that both new states were to be Dominions of the British Commonwealth of Nations.

The separation of Pakistan was a grievous blow to the hopes of Gandhi for a union of all India. Apart from it, however, the rest of India was united as it had never been in all its history. There were still some 562 states, ranging in size from that of a feudal manor to a powerful principate, which were ruled by their own princes more or less in the traditional oriental way. Even the most powerful conquerors — Aryan, Moslem and British — had never been able to unify the country completely. The practical-minded British had treated the larger sovereignties, like those of the Maharajahs of Travancore and Mysore and the Nizam of Hyderabad, as "friends and allies" on the model of ancient Rome, granting them sovereignty over all but defense and foreign relations. It was one of the chief criticisms of British rule in India that it was so largely linked with the native rulers of dependent states, most of them reactionary and all of them despots in the oriental way — even the enlightened ones. The verdict of history might have been harsher, however, if the British had tried to ignore those whose titles to rule often outdated anything else in India. Such a revolution could only be carried out by the Indians themselves, and that is what happened in independent India.

The end of the British Empire of India brought a political freedom undreamed of in the past, but it also threw upon the unaccustomed shoulders of the Indians themselves the responsibility for the modernizing of their way of life. The task is incredibly difficult, for nowhere else has the servitude to superstition, which we have described in the beginning of this study, created greater obstacles to progress, cementing racial diversity and social stratification, than in India. Successive foreign conquests, from the dawn of history to modern times, have stratified the population with layers of race, while the Hindus became increasingly encased in castes held apart by the iron laws of the taboo. Of these castes there were four (or five if we count the outcaste

---

[4] As early as 1921 Gandhi had been calling for the creation of a national flag. "A flag is a necessity for all nations," he wrote. "Millions have died for it. It is no doubt a kind of idolatry which it would be a sin to destroy. For a flag represents an ideal. The unfurling of the Union Jack evokes in the English breast sentiments whose strength it would be difficult to measure. The Stars and Stripes mean a world to Americans. The Star and Crescent will call forth the best bravery in Islam. It will be necessary for us Indians — Hindus, Mohammedans, Christians, Jews, Parsis, and all others to whom India is their home — to recognize a common flag to live and die for." Then he went on to propose a flag with a spinning wheel as its only device, for "India as a nation can live and die only for the spinning wheel," its defense against industrial exploitation. (*Young India*, pp. 436 ff.) His article "The Music of the Spinning Wheel" (*Ibid.*, p. 497) has a lyric quality as it extols the part played by the spinning wheel in history.

untouchables, as the British did): the Brahmans, or priestly caste; the warriors; the merchants and landowners; and the servants or menials. The ancient Indian laws simply strengthened the caste distinctions, grading the penalties for violations of taboos or crimes according to them. For example, no Brahman could be executed for any crime, while at the other end of the scale, the cruelest of punishments were inflicted for the slightest of offenses, for example, speaking slightingly of a priest. The "laws of Manu" which codified such caste distinctions, remained in force until the British put an end to them. Untouchables were obliged to keep at a distance from other castes, not travel the same roads, or let their shadows fall on a Brahman.

All of these barriers to freedom in a common citizenship had to be swept away if Indian nationalism was to be a reality. The rule of the taboo had to be replaced by the rule of law — secular law — with equal justice for all. This had been introduced by the British — their greatest gift to India. The leaders of the new India, Gandhi and Nehru, were both trained in English law. Mohammedan law also was based on the principle of equality, but only among Believers — for it too, like the laws of Manu, was a religious code. The leaders of Indian nationalism had, therefore, a long road to go and the miracle of its history is that India, both Hindu and Moslem, has achieved so much of the transformation in so short a time.

Great as is this achievement, it was accompanied by a tragedy of even greater magnitude. For two nations were created instead of one, with terrible consequences for both. Time and again in the history of the West — and also in that of China — nationalism has stained the radiance of the freedom of which it claimed to be the champion. Never was this more clearly shown than in the Indian revolution for independence. For the creation of Pakistan was not designed for peaceful cooperation between the two new nations but was the result of a militant fanaticism, that of its founder, Jinnah, as definitely as the benign teachings of Buddha colored the thought of India.

Pakistan was a new and artificial creation covering little over half of the ninety million Moslems scattered through India. Although Moslem dynasties had ruled large portions of it for most of the thousand years between the Arab invasion in 711 and the end of the Mogul Empire in 1707, there had never been a Moslem empire of all India nor had there been partition of Moslem states from non-Moslem territories before the fateful August of 1947. During Moslem rule there had been periods of splendor — of which the Taj Mahal is the supreme witness — but there were also periods of plundering and spoliation, of looted cities and temples defiled, of massacre and enslavement and rule by the sword. If ruthlessness could have founded a nation, India ought to have been united centuries ago, for the great mass of the Moslems were of native Indian stock, not immigrants brought in by invading armies. But conversion to Mohammedanism had transformed them utterly, as in the earliest days it had transformed the Arabs themselves, and this proved to be the real barrier to unity. Islamic civilization was the very opposite of that of Hindu India. It has had much in common with seventeenth century Puritanism in Europe, not only in the austerity of its worship but in the insistence on the democratic equality of all Believers. All these qualities were foreign to Hinduism with its over-laden pantheon instead of one God, its class distinctions and its castes, iron-bound by taboos. To these religions and social differences were added economic and political antagonisms, when landlords or money lenders were Moslems and the poverty-stricken peasants Hindus, as in the United Provinces, or where the reverse was true, as in the Punjab and parts of Bengal.

Where the commonest habits and customs of each community meant sacrilege to their neighbors, riots were bound to occur, and where such fanaticism was rampant, the efforts of the British rulers to keep the peace were often equally opposed by both sides. The fact that the British were a race apart, maintaining their aloofness with rigid social rules, made them another caste, foreign, masterful, innately arrogant, yet capable of dealing fairly and sympathetically with the indigenous population. This is as far as one can generalize on the British in India, for British-Indian relations varied greatly both in history and geography, so greatly that any one characterization is misleading. Yet it is a history rich in lessons of colonial imperialism in both blundering and achievement.

It was in the year 1600, in the great era of Elizabethan expansion after the defeat of the Spanish Armada, that the British East India Company was chartered. It was not designed, like the later Virginia Company or the Company of Massachusetts Bay, to be a political as well as a commercial body. "The Governor and Company of Merchants of London trading with the East Indies" was founded to reap some of the rich harvest of trade with the Spice Islands as well as that with the mainland of India, a trade of which Portugal had had the monopoly since the sea route to the Orient was opened by Vasco da Gama a hundred years earlier. With the defeat of Spain (with which Portugal was united), these sea ways were open to an unlimited competition, and in the seventeenth century East India companies were established not only in England but also in Holland, France, Denmark, Scotland, Spain, Austria and Sweden. The colonial and maritime wars which followed lie only along the margin of this history. They belong rather with that of European nationalism in the troubled dawn of modern times described above. So far as Asia was concerned, there was at first little to choose among the westerners, for all were there for one purpose — to seize a share in the fabulous wealth of the Orient. It must be remembered, when judging this "colonialism" which has left such a bitter memory in Asia, that the orientals themselves were adepts in the art of getting the best of a bargain. Yet when the profits of the trading companies reached as much as 100 percent, as they sometimes did, more was involved than trading. Tribute was imposed on native rulers, and exploitation was backed by the superior arms and military forces of the Europeans.

The transition from commerce to conquest in India was too complicated to be reviewed here. The East India Company became a sovereign in camouflage, while British controls spread in native principates, supported by a small British army and British-trained native troops. Although corruption and exploitation were repressed by reforming governors, the steady extension of British power, repeated annexations of territory, the spread of education, the introduction of steam engines and western goods in competition with native industry stirred resentment which needed only an incident to explode. This happened when the native troops mutinied in 1857 because their cartridges, which they had to bite open, were greased with the fat of cows and pigs in utter disregard of the prescriptions of the Hindu and Moslem religions. The blind stupidity of the military mind was at a premium in the British military officers in India.

The Mutiny and its repression, terrible as they were, meant the end of the East India Company after more than two and a half centuries. Its entire administration was taken over by the Crown; and twenty years later, in January 1877, Queen Victoria was proclaimed Empress of India at a durbar held with all the magnificence of the Orient at the ancient Mogul capital, Delhi.

The Empire of India provided a unity for the sub-continent for the first time in its twenty-five hundred years of known history. It was also for the first time a purely secular rule. There remained within it hundreds of local unities, holding apart from each other but all owing allegiance to the Crown. While great affairs of state were settled in London, the government of this vast confusion of peoples came increasingly into the hands of the Indian Civil Service. Introduced in 1853, when the old system of patronage under the Company made way for selection on the basis of competitive examinations, the system was gradually opened to Indians, first to the lower offices only, but later to higher offices as well, and so prepared the way for self-government in that quiet but thorough way in which the British carry on so much of their affairs. It is important to bring this fact to the surface, for both the Indian and the Pakistani administrative systems rest on this British-built foundation, though now there is hardly a British official left in either nation.

At its best, the Indian Civil Service did for India what the British Civil Service did for Great Britain and the Empire. It administered honestly according to the standards of an enlightened bureaucracy. But even when the civil servants ran the business of government with conscientious efficiency, they unconsciously identified the interests of India with their own — a fault which only the exceptional bureaucrat can escape. A hostile English critic went so far as to term them members of "the world's most tenacious trade union," a judgment shared to the full by Nehru, who quotes it and then continues bitterly:

They ran India, they were India, and anything that was harmful to their interests must of necessity be injurious to India. From the Indian Civil Service and the kind of history and record of current events that was placed before them, this conception spread in varying degrees to the different strata of the British people. The ruling class naturally shared it in full measure, but even the worker and the farmer were influenced by it to some slight extent and felt, in spite of their own subordinate position in their own country, the pride of possession and empire. The same worker or farmer if he came to India inevitably belonged to the ruling class here. He was totally ignorant of India's history and culture and he accepted the prevailing ideology of the British in India, for he had no other standards to judge by or apply. At most a vague benevolence filled him, but that was strictly conditioned within that framework.[5]

It is sobering to find that Nehru follows this criticism of the British in India with a characterization of the British at home which is as blinded by national prejudice as that against which he bitterly protests, charging that "in our own day that curious group which has no fixed standards or principles or much knowledge of the outside world, the leaders of the British Labour Party, have been usually the staunchest supporters of the existing order in India."[6] It is hard to believe that a disciple of the generous-hearted Gandhi could have failed to appreciate the clear-sightedness and courage of the Labour Party, which was already planning the independence of India, and granting it in the Indian Independence Act of July 1947. The complete break with the past was symbolized by the retirement from the Governor-Generalship of the soldier, Lord Wavell, and the appointment of Earl Mountbatten in his place to preside over the surrender of the Indian Empire. The Labour Party, largely inspired by "the nonconformist conscience of England," put through an achievement unique in the annals of freedom when under its guidance Great Britain voluntarily renounced its sovereignty over four hundred million former subjects of the Crown.

It would be utterly unfair, however, to take the passages from Nehru's book quoted here as typical of the work as a whole, which is the product of the uninhibited outpouring of a sensitive, highly-trained mind, keenly aware of the complexities of Indian history and politics. But the resentment against the British was so deep as to fail to draw a distinction between the *burra sahib*, the vulgar type of businessman, or others on the make, and the *pukka sahib*, the perfect gentleman of the ruling class, the product of the great schools such as Eton or Winchester and the universities of Oxford and Cambridge, who, as members of the civil service did so much for India, but whose manners, though impeccable, were offensive to the Indians — their gracious aloofness bearing all the marks of a consciousness of racial superiority. Yet it should not be forgotten that it was one of this class, Allan Octavian Hume, who with the encouragement of the Viceroy, Lord Dufferin, was the founder of the Indian National Congress long before the days of Gandhi or Nehru. It was in response to his appeal to the intellectual elite of India that the Congress was created in Bombay in 1883 — long antedating any other movement for national freedom in Asia.

In moving terms, Hume wrote:

Whether in the individual or the nation, all vital progress must spring from within and it is to you, the most cultured and enlightened minds, her most favored sons, that your country must look for the initiative. In vain may aliens, like myself, love India and her children; . . . in vain may they, for her and their good, give time and trouble, money and thought; in vain may they struggle and sacrifice; they may assist with advice and suggestions; they may place their experience,

[5] Jawaharlal Nehru, *The Discovery of India* (New York: John Day Co., 1946), p. 291.
[6] *Ibid*, p. 292.

abilities and knowledge at the disposal of the workers; but they lack the essential of nationality, and the real work must be done by the people themselves. . . . Every nation secures precisely as good a government as it merits. If you, the picked men, the most highly educated of the nation, cannot, scorning personal ease and selfish objects, make a resolute struggle to secure greater freedom for yourselves and your country, a more impartial administration, a larger share in the management of your own affairs, then we, your friends, are wrong, and our adversaries right; then, at present at any rate, all hopes of progress are at an end, and India neither lacks nor deserves any better government than she now enjoys.[7]

The Indian National Congress, which was the answer to this appeal, was something new in India. In the first place, it was a secular body, keeping politics apart from religion. Secondly, it was at first not revolutionary in temper but resembled in its outlook the liberal, reformist trend of the best British thought of the nineteenth century, such as the political philosophy of John Stuart Mill.

The Indian Civil Service, which Nehru attacked, was not composed of doctrinaires, however. They were practical reformers, establishing an impartial administration of justice, eliminating corruption, insisting on strict accountability in the collection of taxes, and, above all, trying to rid India of tribal and feudal wars under a regime of peace such as the country had never before experienced. Reforms like these, they felt, were the real steps to freedom, but would be imperiled or lost if the great business of government were too suddenly turned over to vast, uneducated masses divided by history, language and religion.

It was to them, therefore, that the Secretary for India, Edwin Montagu, and the Viceroy, Lord Chelmsford, turned for support when, in 1917, they prepared a draft of a new constitution for India, which was embodied in the Government of India Act of 1919. It was intended to do for India what the Reform Bill of 1832 had done for Great Britain. Except in Burma and the North-West Provinces, both of them frontiers, moderately representative governments were to be set up with an electorate of some five million, but with the control of justice and the police remaining in the hands of the civil service, responsible to the governor alone. On paper, the powers of the legislature were large, covering all laws having to do with British India, but with a proviso that the Governor-General-in-Council could take any measures they deemed necessary "for the safety, tranquillity, or interest of British India or any part thereof."

The proposals were well meant. They were never designed to camouflage dictatorship, as their Indian critics believed.[8] But it is the fault of liberalism that in its concern for law and order it lacks the boldness of great adventure — such as was needed in India when it was touched into new life by two tremendous forces, the industrial revolution unchecked by such social legislation as had developed in Great Britain, and the disillusionment of return-

[7] Quoted in full in *Modern India* by Sir Percival Griffiths (New York: Praeger, 1957), pp. 63, 64.

[8] Comment based on conversations of the author with Edward Montagu during the Paris Peace Conference of 1919.

ing Indian soldiers, whose great services to the Empire in World War I deserved a better reward than the denial of full citizenship. These forces of discontent under foreign rule tended naturally to become forces of sedition, but when riots and murders increased, the only remedy proposed was forcible suppression by abolishing trial by jury in cases of sedition and even the right of appeal against a death sentence. These measures, proposed in the Rowlatt Acts of 1919, were never applied, but the fact that they could even be seriously considered roused men like Gandhi, who previously had hoped for reform within the empire, to realize that the only solution was independence.

There was, however, an instrument of repression more terrible than the courts — the army, Kipling's soldiers, trained only for fighting on the word of command. There had been rioting in the Punjab city of Amritsar in which some five Englishmen were murdered, and when, in violation of the law, a large crowd of Indians gathered in a city square, General Dyer, in charge of security, ordered a squad of fifty soldiers to fire on them without warning or possibility of escape, killing 379 and wounding twelve hundred, and then marched his troops away, paying no attention to the dead or dying.[9]

The effect of this atrocity was electric. The Montagu reforms had no chance of a hearing, for nationalism was no longer in a mood to compromise with the government. All India was stirred, as it had been stirred only once before, in the Mutiny and the aftermath of reprisals. But grave as it was, the crisis might have been but temporary, as had happened in the past, if India had not found a leader in Mohandas K. Gandhi, trained in both English and Hindu thought, and in the Indian National Congress, an instrument for unrelenting political battle. Indignation was canalized into political action; the Indian Revolution had begun.

It was different from any other revolution in history, so different that all the world knows about it and there is no need for a detailed description of it here. Yet its strategy is often misunderstood. The nonviolent method of resistance was not mere passive resistance of the negative type of self-abasement; it was the opposite of that — a confidence in victory by the hand of God, if one but follows God's rule of life; a discipline of righteousness, surrendering only to love, even for one's enemies. Gandhi coined a word for this method — *satyagrapha* — from two Sanskrit roots, *satya* (truth) and *agraha* (steadfast grasping).[10] It was the simplest of creeds, yet it touched

[9] British public opinion was divided on Amritsar. General Dyer was recalled from India, but the Conservative *Morning Post* opened a subscription fcr him and actually raised £26,000. There is no doubt that the mob was in a dangerous mood, and might quickly have got out of hand, as had happened elsewhere. The point has been made that Dyer had too few soldiers for his own safety, and anyone who has seen police losing their heads from fear (as the author has, in Paris, on one occasion) knows how brutal the forces of law and order can become.

[10] In *Young India* (p. 11), Gandhi makes this point clear. "Satyagraha differs from passive resistance as the North Pole from the South. The latter has been conceived as a weapon of the weak and does not exclude the use of physical force or violence for the purpose of gaining one's end, whereas the former has been conceived as a weapon of the strongest and excludes the use of violence in any shape or form."

such deep wellsprings of Hindu feeling that police measures were unavailing when, in movements of protest, thousands would block city streets submitting to beatings without attempting to retaliate, and other crowds applauded the burning of British cloth. In the eyes of authority, such acts were sedition, and when accompanied by complete noncooperation with the government in the payment of taxes or public services, the situation simply got out of control. Gandhi chose dramatic ways to illustrate this, walking with his disciples over a hundred miles to get salt from the sea in protest against the salt tax, as one example. When the government struck at his leadership in "noncooperation," he went joyfully to prison, in which he spent in all about six years and by which he gained even more moral authority over the millions now accepting his strategy of revolution. His fasting "even unto death" against government repression always had the British beaten. The ultimate result, if India stood firm, had to be the grant of its independence.

The Declaration of Independence of India, if one may term it so, was a manifesto which Gandhi issued in October, 1920, "A Letter to Every Englishman In India."[11] It begins with a recital of his own services to the Empire, in the Boer War, the Zulu War, the first World War, and in recruiting drives to build up the Indian army "all in the belief that such acts as mine must gain for my country an equal status in the Empire." But British condonation of the Punjab atrocities (the suppression of the riots after Amritsar) completely shattered his faith in the good intentions of the British. Then, as though the American Declaration of Independence were on his mind, he lists India's grievances, but instead of making his appeal to the "opinions of mankind" he addresses it to those Englishmen in India who were having to choose between freedom and force, inviting them "respectfully, to choose the better way and make common cause with the people of India whose salt you are eating. To seek to thwart their aspirations is disloyalty to the country."

These are gentle words; but the indictment of British rule has the sterner ring of revolution as it lists the grievances against it. They are:

Exploitation of India's resources for the benefit of Great Britain.
An ever-increasing military expenditure, and a civil service the most expensive in the world.
Extravagant working of every department in disregard of India's poverty.
Disarmament and consequent emasculation of a whole nation lest an armed nation might imperil the lives of a handful of you in our midst.
Traffic in intoxicating liquors and drugs for the purpose of sustaining a top-heavy administration.
Progressively repressive legislation in order to suppress an ever-growing agitation seeking to give expression to a nation's agony.
Degrading treatment of Indians residing in your dominions. . . .
And you have shown total disregard of our feelings in glorifying the Punjab administration and flouting the Muslim sentiment. . . .

And he continues:

11 *Ibid.*

Bravery on the battlefield is impossible for us. Bravery of the soul still remains open to us. . . . I am engaged in evoking that bravery. Noncooperation means nothing less than training in self-sacrifice. Why should we cooperate with you when we know that by your administration of this great country we are being daily enslaved to an increasing degree. The response of the people to my appeal is not due to my personality. . . . People flock in their thousands to listen to us, because we today represent the voice of a nation groaning under iron heels. . . . My religion forbids me to bear any ill-will towards you. I would not raise my hand against you even if I had the power. I expect to conquer you only by my suffering. . . .

You are in search of a remedy to suppress this rising ebullition of national feeling. I venture to suggest to you that the only way to suppress it is to remove the causes. . . . You can compel the Government to summon a conference of the recognized leaders of the people, duly elected by them and representing all shades of opinion, so as to devise means for granting Swaraj in accordance with the wishes of the people.[12]

Swaraj meant more than mere political independence. There must be freedom for the common man, "freedom for everyone, the smallest among us, to do what he likes without any physical interference."[13] Yet Gandhi was no advocate of anarchy, and added the all important qualification, "Where there is complete freedom of opinion, we can prove worthy of our religion by remaining true to it in the face of coercion." This was an argument addressed particularly to Moslems, to whose support he went to great lengths; but it applied as a matter of course to the attitude of the Hindus toward the millions of untouchables.

Mere political independence was not enough; there must be freedom from the hampering taboos also. Born and raised under the Brahmanical taboos, Gandhi remained convinced of the validity of the caste system as a framework for society, yet did more than anyone else to unify the Hindus, mingling freely with untouchables, performing "defiling" duties to show that they did not defile, even adopting a young "untouchable" girl as his daughter — not merely as a symbolic act but as one of sincere paternal affection. But he held to the caste system, proposing merely to merge the untouchables in it. It was on this point that B. R. Ambedkar, the leader of the untouchables, broke with him, forming a separate party from the forty-five million untouchables.[14] Gandhi's doctrine of love as the one true principle of life (shimsa) was to work through the existing social order. It was a transformation of the spirit, not an overturn of society. Sincerely held, this doctrine was nevertheless the only one which made for a unity which could even include

[12] *Ibid*, p. 570.   [13] *Ibid*, p. 281.

[14] Dr. B. R. Ambedkar (Ph.D. from Columbia University, where he was a student of the author), the head of the Scheduled Castes Federation, the strongest organization of the untouchables, entered the Indian Cabinet as Law Minister and was the chairman of the committee of distinguished Indians who drafted the Indian Constitution which went into effect in January, 1950. As a student he used to insist strongly that the untouchables could get better treatment from the Brahman-controlled native government. His experience in the government confirmed him in this conviction, and he resigned from the Cabinet in October, 1951, having found "the same old tyranny, the same old oppression, the same old discrimination which existed before, but perhaps in a worse form." In World War II he fought an election on the platform of direct alliance with the Western powers, and lost. He never returned to power, and died in 1956.

the Moslems. It was Gandhi's great grief that ultimately it did not do so.

Too humble in spirit to accept willingly the title *Mahatma* (Great Soul) which his disciples — and then all India and the world outside — bestowed on him, Gandhi yet had the true sense of leadership, which led him to hold in public his hour of prayer and meditation in the hushed presence of his followers. More endearing was the other name by which he was known in the hundreds of thousands of villages in India — *Bapu* or "Father." So great became the reverence paid him that the place where he was cremated has become a national shrine. In death he has become almost a deity.

If a new Carlyle were today to write a new *Heroes and Hero Worship,* his outstanding hero would not — or should not — be a Frederick the Great, who left his country a heritage of militarism culminating in the criminality of Nazism, but the humble, saintly figure of the man who won the freedom of a nation not by war but by the moral sovereignty of peace, who proved that the most challenging of the sayings of Jesus is true — that the meek can inherit the earth. The moral triumph of Gandhi is all the greater when we recall his physical handicaps: a figure that entirely lacked the dignity of a great personality, a dark-skinned little man with wizened face flanked by large ears, with kindly eyes and humble bearing — until confronted with the moral issues of his time and people, and then capable of the flash of command and the sense of spiritual power. To his India, the loincloth woven at his loom or those of his village neighbors became almost a regal garment, the symbol of the triumph of a great ideal, that of freedom won by the simple life and by the arts of peace. Fortunately, we may know him well and intimately, for his autobiography ranks alongside that of St. Augustine in the revelation of his inmost thoughts and acts and passes an equally severe judgment on them. Then we have his writings and speeches, almost a library in extent. One collection, his contributions to the periodical *Young India* during the fateful years 1919-1922 (when he was imprisoned), reaches almost twelve hundred pages. The editor, one of his intimate disciples who was destined to become the first president of the Republic of India, Rajendra Prasad, compared its papers with those of the American *Federalist* for its influence in the formation of a nation's outlook. The title itself was a challenge; it was not "Mother India," cherishing an ancient heritage (although that sentiment was not lacking), but *Young India,* of the new world of freedom.

In this intensely human story which we have been tracing, merging the centuries from the Rig Veda to Swaraj, the other Indian nation, Pakistan, had no part. In its final form it was an improvisation of a few months in the summer of 1947. There was, of course, nothing new in the gulf between Moslem and Hindu, and the movement for Indian freedom had met with chilling response from Moslems, fearful that as a minority of some ninety millions in a total population of three to four hundred millions they would have none of that equal status which they enjoyed under the British. The Moslem League, the organ of Moslem nationalism, under the militant leadership of Mohammed Ali Jinnah, had come out for a Pakistan as early as 1940, but it had never limited its activities to northeastern and northwestern India, the Pakistan of today. When partition came with independence in August, 1947, no provision had been made for the details of the separation. This seems incredible in view of the fact that there was continuous rioting through 1946 in Bengal, and that the Sikhs, the most militant sect of the Hindus, and the Moslems were murdering each other in the Punjab.

On August 16, the first day of India's freedom, the rioting in Calcutta reached the dimensions of a reign of terror, which speedily spread to other cities, while in once peaceful villages neighbors murdered each other in an orgy of fanaticism. There was nothing else to do than to attempt escape in a mass migration, the greatest and most terrible ordeal of migratism in modern times. About twelve million migrants in all moved from the land of one religion to another. Of these it is estimated that over two million died of disease, starvation or exhaustion or were slaughtered along the wayside by fanatic or criminal bands. The dawn of freedom, so promising of kindliness and charity to Gandhi, so bright and confident in the faith of Jinnah, was menacing the end of all their hopes. Nor was the red dawn followed by the clear sky of an untroubled day. The freedom won so easily from the British was a challenge to life in a new era — one which nations of long experience in self-government find hard to meet — and which is doubly difficult for new nations like India and Pakistan.

Only twelve years have passed since these things were done; it will take much longer before history can pass judgment on the Indian revolution for freedom. Ambedkar's disillusionment over the treatment of the untouchables, and the cold — or open — war with Pakistan show how long a road the new India has to travel before the high ideals of Gandhi can be finally achieved and safeguarded by "due process of law" under enlightened governments. The debt to the British in this regard so largely balanced the grievances listed in Gandhi's indictment, quoted above, that both new nations remained — to the puzzled surprise of the rest of the world — dominions within the Commonwealth, even after the declaration of a republic. Nor was this a meaningless gesture, as Nehru has made clear.

Fortunately for India, Gandhi's idealism was followed by Nehru's statesmanship, still holding to the fundamentals of Swaraj, finding in moderate socialism a way to maintain both parliamentary government and social reform, and much needed industrial development — with British and American aid — while holding a neutral policy in the world struggle between the two great empires of capitalism and communism. Nehru has set down his political philosophy in clear and concise form in an essay, first circulated as a confidential letter among his friends, then published in the journal of the Indian Congress and finally reprinted as an article in *The New York Times Magazine* of September 7, 1958.

The striking thing about this statement is that it does not sound like a voice from Asia:

The old civilizations, with the many virtues they possess, have obviously proved inadequate. . . . Religion gave a certain moral and spiritual discipline; it also tried to perpetuate superstition and social usages (meaning, for India, the taboos). Indeed those superstitions and social usages emeshed and overwhelmed the real spirit of religion. Disillusionment followed. Communism comes in the wake of this disillusionment and offers some kind of faith and some kind of discipline. To some extent it fills a vacuum. It succeeds, in some measure, by giving a content to man's life. But in spite of its apparent success, it fails, partly because of its rigidity, but even more because it ignores certain essential needs of human nature. . . . Communism has definitely allied itself to the approach of violence, even if it does not indulge normally in physical violence. Its language is of violence, its thought is violent, and it does not seek to change by peaceful or democratic measures, but by coercion and indeed by destruction and extermination. Fascism has all these evils of violence and extermination in their grossest forms and, at the same time, has no acceptable ideal.

This is completely opposed to the peaceful approach which Gandhi taught us. . . . I prefer the old pagan approach of tolerance, apart from its religious aspects. But whatever we may think about it, we have arrived at a stage in the modern world where an attempt at forcible imposition of ideas on any large section of people is bound ultimately to fail.

The nobility of thought which with Gandhi was instinctive is here intellectualized, ranging beyond the immediate issues of the day. Yet Nehru is also a practical politician, and his policy of neutralism in the world struggle between communism and the noncommunist nations is as firm an expression of Indian nationalism in world affairs as his unyielding attitude toward Pakistan, especially in the undeclared war over Kashmir.

Pakistan, it must be remembered, was an artificial creation, linking two areas separated by a thousand miles of Indian territory, with differing economic needs and no common political heritage. The only tie is religion, one that solves none of Pakistan's pressing economic, social and even political problems and offers no guidance in the wholly foreign device of representative government. Therefore, when in October, 1958, the semblance of freedom under a parliamentary constitution, establishing personal rule, was overthrown by army leaders, there was not even a murmur of protest in public opinion — for no public opinion existed sufficiently informed on public affairs to make protest meaningful. As a matter of fact, Pakistan is not a nation in the modern sense of the word. It is a "jumble of nationalities, Pathans, Bengalis, Sindhi, Baluchis and refugees from India" (to quote an article in *The New York Times* of October 19, 1958). "There was no truly national party, no national parliament elected by and responsible to the people. No bridge existed between the communities any more than between West and East Pakistan." In the opinion of Western observers its very survival as a single independent state is doubtful. Whether it will find in the Commonwealth a way to reconcile its differences with India is a problem too uncertain even for speculation.

China

Vast and challenging as are the potentialities of Indian civilization, emerging from its troubled centuries, and powerful as is the dynamism of an already awakened Japan, the central problem of Asia is China. It is not only that in magnitude it surpasses other countries, with a population equal to that of all other Asian countries combined — one-fifth of the human race — but that what had been the greatest reservoir of conservatism in the world has in a series of revolutions passed in hardly more than one generation from oriental monarchy to communism. How and why did this happen? Is the process only an interlude in the century-long history of the Chinese people; or is it, as some have claimed, a variant form of their social formation and therefore the culmination rather than the denial of it.

The answer to this question is fateful not only for the Chinese but for all the world. No one knows — or can know — what it will be; but already one thing seems clear. Chinese communism differs from that of the West — in spite of protestations to the contrary — because of its different setting in history and in the social system which that history produced. The clues to present and future lie, therefore, as much in the history as in the problems which China confronts today. Age-old ways of thinking and living cannot be thrown off by a people who had never known any other, as easily as by nations attuned to change throughout all modern history.

Looking back into the Chinese past for the elements that lived on, we find there, as in other early societies the potency of the taboo in all human relationships, from those of family and clan to the priestly emperor, who could communicate directly with Heaven — a term so charged with supernatural powers that it was sometimes used, somewhat vaguely for the one person who had access to it — by proper ceremonies at proper times. The status of the nobles was measured by their rights to perform the sacred rites, especially in the sacrifices to their ancestors. The hierarchy set by these priestly functions dominated the whole structure of society, which necessarily remained rigid because so largely sacred. That point is all important, for, until the impact of the West in recent years, it prevented revolutions from attempting to overthrow the institutions of government, for that would be treason not to the person of the ruler but to the Mandate of Heaven, which was the very foundation of the Celestial Kingdom. Through the changing dynasties, the traditional forms were maintained.

Under these conditions government never freed itself from taboos as it had done in Greece and Rome and all the West. The Chinese, instead, with the practical common sense typical of them, paid little attention to politics, but turned to the sages for guidance in the way of life. This is how Confucius acquired his authority, with a social system so strict, so rooted in its own past, that it furnished a substitute for politics — at least in general terms. Its chief connection with government was by way of the great civil service functionaries trained primarily to apply the moral precepts of the sage to every act of life. The training of these functionaries was unique. It was a test in scholarship, especially in the Confucian classics. The applicants had to learn the texts by heart so well that from a single reference they could bring to mind whole passages. The system was magnificent in its complete disregard of anything but the ancestral heritage. Examination halls were built or set aside in the provincial cities, and the contestants were judged by the beauty of their brushstrokes as well as by their answers. In theory all this was open to any promising lad, and the relatives of poor boys could club together to give them leisure to become scholars; but it was mostly from the leisured class itself — the mandarins — that the civil service was recruited.

For thousands of years no foreign influences — except the Buddhist religion — reached to the core of this vast, self-centered society. Mountains and deserts shut it off from the west of Asia, and on the north it was protected from the raiding horsemen by the Great Wall. Vast and immovable, it looked back on its history as the empire of Heaven itself, the "Middle Kingdom," in the center of the world. Held closely together by its hierarchy of officials and its clan and family system, it easily absorbed its conquerors, Mongol and Manchu, and paid little or no attention to the outside world. Proudly isolated from the rest of the world, the Chinese surpassed even the ancient Greeks in their disdain for foreigners. The center of the world was the Temple of Heaven in Peking, as the emperor was the son of Heaven. The claim was undisputed by those who brought the tribute of subject princes in mile-long processions along the highway to the gates of the Forbidden City.

The enduring strength of China is not to be found, however, in the pomp and circumstance of empire, but in the character of the people, 85 per cent of whom are peasants. Throughout the centuries of unchanging history, they have shown outstanding qualities of sturdy character and self-respect which makes them a very real power in the land. Moral stature was a basis for authority in the village organization, in which the elders applied local custom to keep things going with due regard for the rights of neighbors.

The people are poor, desperately poor by Western standards, for it seems to them elementary justice to divide the paternal property equally among the sons. Therefore, in the final division, the share of each son is often less than an acre. For more than four thousand years they have planted their crops in the same way in their market-garden farms, living in little villages, joined together by rambling country lanes just wide enough for a single mule cart. Their chief concern, next to making the barest living from the impoverished soil, was to escape from exploitation by the tax collector by avoiding any sign of prosperity or added comfort, thus killing any incentive to improvements. When calamities came, as they often did, the money lender took his usurious profits. Even selling girl children into slavery was sometimes resorted to as a last way out. The village elders apportioned the taxes which each family was to pay, held as trustees the title deeds to land and other village property, and saw to it that the life of the village ran on smoothly. They also had to deal with the district magistrate and arranged for inter-village activities; but they never thought of their functions as political. Politics was that framework of officialdom that reached down from the central government to the district (hsien) which corresponds roughly to the Western country. It stopped there, and left the local and intimate structure to the family, the village organization and its parallel, the guild.

The guild was, like the village, an organization of those making their living the same way, as artisans or merchants. It was much the same formation as had existed in medieval Europe. Its purpose was to ensure a livelihood for its members. Therefore there was a strict control in the enforcement of its rules. No one could work or practice a trade or profession except in his guild. There were guilds not only for merchants and bankers, but for beggars and even thieves.

This was no home for individual freedom. The only way to live was in a closely knit family formation, including so many relatives that it was more like a clan. The earnings of individuals might be recorded in their own names, but they were held in trust for the whole family. There was in this communal sharing a kind of social insurance within the family, but this did not apply as between families, for each one had to manage its narrow margin of resources to be able to meet the next crisis or disaster. The result was that the victim of an accident might be left to suffer or die on the roadside without help from passers-by, because he or his family might be held responsible for the maintenance of the victim for the rest of the latter's life, and no one had the right to saddle his family with such a responsibility. Thus the system had its bad as well as its good side. What interests us here, however, is how it tied the individual to the family organization so completely that the question of individual freedom from its settled way of life was almost never successfully challenged.

The solidarity thus achieved must not be thought of, however, as keeping the individual out of the scene. For when we turn to the law — which is the rule of conduct — we find that it is distinguished from the jurisprudence of the West in being personal, while in the West it became impersonal. It never underwent the revolution in jurisprudence which transformed Western law from its beginnings in Greece and Rome to the last judgments or practices of the British, Continental or American courts. This is so fundamental a point that we must pause over it. In his masterly survey of Chinese society, *The Great Wall Crumbles*, [15] Grover Clark summarized the two contrasting systems as follows:

The older China had nothing corresponding to Western law. It had criminal codes, administrative regulations for the officials, and edicts issued by the emperor or other high officials. But the field covered by civil law in the West lay almost entirely outside the purview of the government as such. Neither the criminal codes, the administrative regulations, nor the imperial edicts were drafted or thought of as crystallizations of abstract principles. Furthermore, such documents were not cited as precedents in any way corresponding to the citation of precedents in Western legal practices.

This did not mean, however, that China had no well established methods of settling disputes. Still less did it mean that there was no justice. It meant simply that both rules and methods functioned in terms of personal relations within the particular groups concerned or between groups, and that the purpose was not to apply abstract principles but to deal with particular situations in such a way as to secure a result which would be essentially fair to all the parties concerned. Using the Western phraseology, with due reservations: the Chinese were concerned with the equities of the situation and not with the technicalities of the law.

The rules of conduct — the "law" — on the basis of which disputes were to be settled were the local customs. These got their validity from the fact that things

15 As this book is unfortunately out of print, the whole passage is quoted here.

were done that way in that locality or within that group. The rights of land tenants, for example, were fixed in each local area not by statute or executive order but by local practice. The rights of guilds over their members and in relations to outsiders were determined by the practice of the guild and the region. Marriage and divorce were family matters and not the concern of the government. Transfer of land holdings was arranged by the parties and, though the local magistrates were supposed to register the transfer, the definitive record was in private and not official hands. When a dispute or a question of rights arose, the settlement was based on local custom and circumstances rather than on general principles of law or "legal procedures." When a magistrate had to deal with a criminal case, he gave great weight to the personal factors involved, including the character of the accused and his victim, in deciding how much mitigation should be allowed of the penalties provided in the code. The penalties laid down in the criminal code, in fact, were intended to set the extremes to which punishments might go, not to lay down the punishment in usual cases. The actual sentences regularly were much milder than the code penalties.

This being the fundamental feeling about how disputes and crimes should be handled, no special judiciary was essential.

Justice was not something to be administered by some judge sitting on a bench and from this remoteness acting as the upholder of an abstract Truth which could not concern itself with mere persons. It was something to be wrought out in the market place by the disputants and their neighbors in the light of the very personal and immediate circumstances.

From the Chinese point of view, obviously the best people to settle the dispute fairly and to deal with crime reasonably were the people who knew most about the immediate circumstances, and who had to go on living with the disputants. These neighbors might know little or nothing about any "body of law," but they did know the local situation, and it was that local situation which mattered, not abstract principles of law or ancient court decisions or imperial edicts or provisions of more or less remote statutes or codes.

The official, as distinct from the leaders of the various groups, came into the picture as a judge, if at all, when the disputants and their neighbors were unable by themselves to settle their difficulties. The official's function, however, was to restore and maintain order rather than to interpret and apply the "law." To do this, he needed to have executive and legislative as well as judicial authority — to draw the Western distinction which has almost no meaning in terms of the Chinese conception of government and social regulation.

The student of Western politics has to think in other dimensions in dealing with this way of life of the Chinese. Although there was a chance for talented peasant lads to rise to the governing class as scholar-functionaries, this did not prevent the functionaries from sharing the indifference of the monied class to the lives of the peasant farmers or the coolies of the towns and cities. There were exceptions. For instance, in World War I, an enlightened scholar, James Y. C. Yen, the founder of the Mass Education movement, learned to his surprise that the coolie laborers imported to Europe to dig or fill the trenches in northern France, were keen to learn the thousand character writing, a simplified form of writing which enabled them to read, and that these poorest of Asiatics quickly and eagerly responded to education. But the common lot of the peasant farmers, frequently the victims of money lenders or corrupt officials, was poverty and ignorance, not excluding the possibility of slavery. No wonder the European merchants living in China —

not the missionaries, who, however, had no hand in politics — shared the disdain of the upper-class Chinese for the poor yet patient peasant.

But the peasant had not always been patient. He had a strong sense of his rights in the Confucian order of society. Time and again, as late as the middle of the nineteenth century, he had fought with desperate courage to throw off the yoke of a corrupt or tyrannous government and the grinding oppression of the money lenders, and in times of national calamity rumor spread from village to village in that surprising way in which it does in all illiterate societies. Mere palace revolutions within the Forbidden City were of little concern to the peasant, but misgovernment, incompetence and weakness at the top showed itself in the whole hierarchy of officialdom, reaching down to the administration of district (*Hsien*) and village.

Such was the situation in the last years of the Manchu dynasty. There was a growing sense of humiliation as foreign governments forced upon China territorial and commercial concessions which seemed to threaten its dismemberment. This, indeed was the more or less openly declared ultimate purpose of Japan in its war with China in 1894-1895, when it not only seized Korea and Formosa but by its arrogant conduct deeply wounded Chinese pride. "Face" in the Orient is self-respect; it is essential for men and nations. The repercussion of this, and the other aggressions of foreigners, "opening up the Forbidden Kingdom," to their own advantage, was especially strong among Chinese living abroad, not only intellectuals and prosperous merchants but even laborers. Scholars trained in Western ways of thinking in America and Europe, the chief of whom was Sun-Yat-sen, came home to stir the fires of a nationalist movement against both foreign aggression and Manchu incompetence.

Before this movement could organize nationally, however, the peasants began direct action in the traditional Chinese way, by secret societies, one of which, the Boxer society, gave its name to the major uprisings of 1900. The crafty Manchu court turned the insurgents away from attack on its corrupt officials to murderous indiscriminate onslaughts on the "foreign devils," including many missionaries scattered throughout the country and the beseiged Legation Quarter in Peking. Retribution was swift. An international expeditionary force took Peking, and a heavy indemnity was imposed, with foreigners in control of China's revenues to make sure of payment.[16] The Manchus made some gestures of reform such as the abolition in 1905 of the old examination system for civil office; but high-sounding reforms, including the promulgation of a set of principles for what might look — to foreigners at least — like a limited monarchy, were never put into practice.

It only needed an incident to end the decrepit monarchy; and it happened in 1911. While republican conspirators had increased in numbers and strength among the Chinese overseas and in South China under the inspirational leadership of Sun-Yat-sen, travelling from country to country, often at the risk of his life, still it was the chance discovery of a bomb in the hands

[16] The remission of some of this to be used for educational and cultural purposes was one of the wisest acts of the Western powers in China.

of revolutionists at Wuchang, opposite Nanking, on the Yangtze, which forced them into open rebellion. It is an axiom of history that revolutions and civil wars tend to be ruthless. The Chinese Revolution was no exception. The republican rebels in South China massacred Manchus in wholesale slaughter; all opposition elsewhere was speedily overcome, and within four months the Manchu ruling family had abdicated. Insurrectionary bands meanwhile at once took over provincial governments, held meetings in Shanghai and Hankow and drafted the first constitution for the first republic of China. It had all the outer trappings of Western politics, a constitution with provision for a national assembly elected by the people, ministries under it and the president.

But the sovereign people had never had any experience in electing its government, and the revolutionary groups in the provinces simply appointed their own representatives to the body which was to set up the national government. This revolutionary body, however, went ahead and proclaimed the establishment of the Republic on the first of January, 1912, with Sun-Yat-sen, who had recently returned from America, as the provisional President. But the young republic had neither a national army to restore peace nor a trained administrative system to replace that of the old empire.[17]

Remnants of these instruments of government were still held in Peking, however, by Yuan Shih-kai, to whom the foreign powers naturally looked for the restoration of conditions more favorable to them. Sun-Yat-sen, troubled by the prevailing anarchy, with incredible short-sightedness resigned his presidency in favor of Yuan, whose real aim — frustrated by his death in 1916 — was to repeat the history of ancient China and end the anarchy by founding a new dynasty. Instead, he was the first of a series of war-lords who ruled sections of China for the next ten years, much like the feudal lords centuries earlier.

It was this crisis, threatening the partition of China by both war lords and foreigners — especially the Japanese — which revealed in Sun-Yat-sen the two essential qualities of statesmanship, a political philosophy unshaken by disaster and an equally courageous strategy in carrying it out. The philosophy had to be hammered out of Western political thought into forms which the Chinese people could recognize as their own. This finally was achieved in the series of lectures delivered in 1924, which, published under the title *The Three Principles of the People* (San Min Chu I), became the bible of the revolution. The three principles are Nationalism, Democracy and Livelihood. The book opens with a trumpet call to all Chinese, peasants as well as intellectuals, to a new patriotism, that of loyalty to China itself, the

[17] The situation was graphically summed up by Professor Paul Linebarger in *The China of Chiang Kai-shek*, (1941), p. 4. "In theory, the Chinese Republic was established January 1, 1912. In practice, the name *Republic* masked a *melee* of governments and power organizations, ranging from bandit gangs with pretentious political color to authentic regional governments administering large areas. . . . None of these governments ever held an election based on wide suffrage; none has systematically subordinated policy to law; none has possessed a treasury, fleet or air force worthy of a second class power, until the present [World]war." (Boston: World Peace Foundation. 1941. 449 pp.)

new China of the revolution, which is described in the subsequent chapters. There is no better way to rouse the spirit of a people than to remind it of its grievances, and it is from this sense of wrongs endured and wounded pride that the revolutionary doctrine starts.

What is the standing of our nation in the world? In comparison with other nations we have the greatest population and the oldest culture, of four thousands years duration. We ought to be advancing in line with the nations of Europe and America. But the Chinese people have only family and clan groups; there is no national spirit. Consequently, in spite of four hundred million people gathered together in one China, we are in fact but a sheet of loose sand. We are the poorest and weakest state in the world, occupying the lowest position in international affairs. The rest of mankind is the carving knife and the serving dish, while we are the fish and the meat. Our position now is extremely perilous; if we do not earnestly promote nationalism and weld together our four hundred millions into a strong nation, we face a tragedy — the loss of our country and the destruction of our race. To ward off this danger we must espouse Nationalism and employ the national spirit to save the country.

The nation, with its precious heritage of culture and its profound sense of social integrity, Confucian to the core, must be made safe for democracy (the phrase might have been used). The safeguards of the people's rights — that is to say their freedom — lies in the separation of the powers of government, as in the United States, into three coordinate divisions: legislative, executive and judicial. But the *San Min Chu I* goes further. "If we want to combine the best from China and the best from other countries, we must take the three Western governmental powers . . . and add to them the old Chinese powers of examination and censorship and make . . . a quintuple-power government. Such a government will be the most complete and the finest in the world, and a state with such a government will indeed be of the people, by the people, and for the people."[18]

The future of China is stated in the words of Lincoln. Nowhere in the *San Min Chu I* are the Chinese reminded of the teachings of their own sages, although there are constant reminders of the rule of good and bad emperors and their officials. There might have been such quotations from Confucius as "When the Great Doctrine prevails all under Heaven work for the common good" or the saying of Mencius, "Most precious are the people; next come the spirits of land and grain and last the princes. Heaven sees as the people see. Heaven hears as the people hear." But Sun-Yat-sen was turning from the self-satisfaction of self-centered China to the challenge of its open doors into which modern ideas were coming with modern science.

The culmination of the appeal for a new China comes in the third principle, Livelihood. It begins with an examination of Marx and Russian Communism, neither of which he accepted. Although he gave credit to the Russian revolution for "lifting up justice and overthrowing inequality for the sake of mankind," he rejected the economic theory of history which attributed the forms of society to the means of production. Instead he followed the reasoning of Dr. Maurice William, whose *Social Interpretation of History*

[18] *San Min Chu I*, Lecture 6.

challenged the Marxian theory, claiming instead that what determined the nature of a society was the sum total of its interests, including those of the consumers.[19] "The problem of livelihood is the problem of subsistence," a point which seemed as obvious to the Chinese as to the Americans. The divergence from the orthodoxy of Moscow was not destined to play an important part, however, in the development of the Chinese revolution; for, although Sun-Yat-sen rejected communism, he accepted communists in his national movement against the "imperialists" of the West and Japanese aggression, exploiting the anarchy forced upon the young republic by such scheming war-lords as Yuan Shih-kai.

Much more important than this alliance with communism, however, was the reorganization of the nationalist movement along the lines of the Russian Communist Party, in an identical structure of militancy, the Kuomintang. This step taken by Sun-Yat-sen in 1921 meant a practical — though not a theoretical — denial of the ideal of Western democracy which had been the inspiration of his early revolutionary thought. True, it was to be limited, as in Russia, to the periods of revolution and tutelage, but power tends to perpetuate itself and the new discipline of the Kuomintang gave it ultimately as undemocratic a structure as Lenin could have wished.

The way in which the vision of a free, democratic China was lost in the reactionary Kuomintang of Sun-Yat-sen's successor, Chiang Kai-shek, is one of the classics of Machiavellianism. In 1927, the revolutionary forces which had set out from southern China for the conquest of the north had tended to get out of hand in terrorist campaigns, urged on by the communists, until by the time it reached the Yangtze it had taken on almost the character of a second Boxer movement. There was, however, no Lenin to galvanize the threat of terror into a communist dictatorship; and before it could organize, as it did, the capitalists of Shanghai found a leader ready to act.[20] Chiang Kai-shek, in command of well-trained Kuomintang troops, struck suddenly and with utter ruthlessness at the communist-led working class of Shanghai and in a short time drove west and north over central China. The way was opened, by support from capitalist Chinese, for the advance on the north; and within a year the Nationalist army had expelled the last war lord (Chang Tso-lin of Manchuria) from Peking and moved the capital to central China at Nanking.

The new republican China had little resemblance to the democracy of the San Min Chu I, still less to that of Lincoln, who had been an inspiration to Sun-Yat-sen. The form of government was modeled on that of Soviet Russia, with the Nationalist Party, Kuomintang, in the same central position of power as the Russian Communist Party. Plans for developing representative

[19] As I have pointed out elsewhere (in the Political Science Quarterly for March 1932), this constitutes one of the rare romances in the history of politics. Dr. William's book received little attention in America, but Dr. Sun found a copy in Shanghai.

[20] Chou En-lai, communist organizer in Shanghai, barely escaped with his life; Mao Tse-tung was a refugee from a short-lived putsch at Hankow. Chu Teh, the military genius of the Communist Revolution, first met with Mao in 1928. The combination of these leaders later formed a kind of triumvirate.

government were talked about, and constitution-making proceeded apace, but they never were realized in a country that had had no experience in such strange, self-contradictory institutions as parliaments. No dictatorship was ever more perfectly planned than that which Lenin had initiated and which became the model for the Nationalist government. We have already seen how much Hitler and Mussolini owed to the plan of that ruthless organizing genius; but it had freer play in a society which had for centuries conditioned itself — by Confucian discipline — to life under Oriental despotism. The result was that sovereignty was vested in the National Party — no other was permitted to exist — and the real government was the Standing Committee of the Executive Committee, a general staff under the Generalissimo who was the Party head.[21] It was the capitalist copy of the regime of Lenin.

There was much to be said for this centralization of power to bring order out of chaos, especially as the Kuomintang was forced to fight two wars, one with Japan and the other with the communists. The invasion by Japan forced Chiang Kai-shek back to the mountain fastnesses of the west, where he made his captial at Chungking. But while he was losing, because he spent too much of his strength in the civil war with the communists, they kept gaining in the guerrilla warfare with Japan until they, instead of Chiang, stood out as the national defenders of China.

The story of the rise of the Chinese communists is one of the romances of history. Driven from their stronghold in Canton and south China where the Kuomintang first attempted to wipe them out in a ruthless and merciless crusade, a determined section of them showed their fanatical devotion to the cause by one of the most incredible feats in military history, the Great March across over six thousand miles of mountainous country to the border of Mongolia in the far northwest, avoiding cities but becoming masters of guerrilla warfare. For some ten years these ardent communists lost touch with that industrial society which Marxists insisted was the essential foundation for communism. It is no wonder, therefore, that to the few Americans who got in touch with them in their distant retreat, they seemed more like agricultural reformers helping the peasants to throw off an iniquitous land-lordism than like the communists whose creed they professed; but it is significant that Stalin in his conversation with Harry Hopkins should pass them by and offer instead to promote unification of China under the leadership of Chiang Kai-shek. He further stated that this leadership should continue after the war because no one else was strong enough. He specifically stated that no communist leader was strong enough to unify China.[22]

The history of the next few years in which the nucleus of communism grew into the government of all China lies at the very heart of our theme. The communists had two advantages, their combination of nationalism, shown in their successful defense against the Japanese, and their leadership

[21] Cf. *The China of Chiang Kai-shek* by Professor Paul H. A. Linebarger (World Peace Foundation, 1941).

[22] Robert E. Sherwood, *Roosevelt and Hopkins,* (New York: Harper & Bros., 1948), p. 902.

against exploitation by both reactionary Chinese and foreigners. This combination of economic and social reform with patriotism proved irresistible. So far as the autocratic structure of communist rule was concerned, there was ample precedent for it, not only in the Kuomintang but also in Chinese history. Confucians had also held that there was only one truth, one doctrine, one class.[23]

But the insistence of the Russian communists that this doctrine was to be realized only through the creation of an industrial proletariat in an industrial revolution was unrealistic in China which had far less industrial development than had been the case in even backward Russia. Therefore, while the Chinese communist leaders, Mao Tse-tung and Chou En-lai and their colleagues, accepted the theory of Marx, in practice they were too realistic and too Chinese to base their revolution on an industrial proletariat which as yet hardly existed and certainly had lacked national influence. Instead, they began with that combination of peasants and scholars which was the basic structure of Chinese nationalism. While doctrinaire communists insisted on industrial collectivism as the basis of the true orthodoxy, Mao's government, so long in close contact with the peasants, developed what was called the New Democracy, freeing the peasants from exploitation by landlords with land reform and cooperation as its aim. In practice this meant that a village of peasant private proprietors organized their economy much as would have been done in a large collective farm; and that, for the time being, was success enough for the practical-minded Chinese communists. Later, when they felt that the time had come for more orthodox communism, they carried out great collectivist drives, and finally created the rigidly disciplined society of communes described below.

As for the intellectuals, they were to enjoy a fair degree of academic freedom so long as they did not interfere with the government. There was no less freedom in the universities than there had been under the Nationalists, who had used students as spies on noncomplying professors. The communists were less crude in their methods; for, while they had no intention of allowing party discipline to disintegrate, they could offer the intellectuals new careers, as the Communist Party created a new hierarchy to replace the mandarins of the old empire. Office was open to all, even members of the Manchu Imperial family, relatives of Kuomintang politicians and war lord generals, as well as peasants and workers.

It would be hard to imagine any greater social revolution than this which cut off ties of family and clan and created a closed society dedicated to a common purpose. Sun Yat-sen, and then Chiang Kai-shek, had tried to realize it without renouncing the structure of capitalism, and the Kuomintang had been engulfed in the corruption of an outworn Chinese society. This time the mandarin officials, no longer held to their Confucian traditions, joined in

[23] This theme is ably developed by Professor C. P. Fitzgerald in *Revolution in China*, (1951). Critics have claimed that he made too much of the Confucian background, but his study clearly established the difference between the ideas of Mao and those of Lenin or Stalin. (New York: Praeger, 1951).

with the "proletariat" to base their nationalism on collectivist economy.[24]

It was undoubtedly this combination of nationalism with communism which led Mao Tse-tung, Chou En-lai and the other leaders in Peking to connive with the Kremlin in the attack upon Korea, and to extend its communist power throughout Southeast Asia.

Thoughtful students of the increasing strength of Communist China reached the conclusion that military threats, such as those in support of Chiang Kai-shek's announced purpose of invading China, merely played into the hands of the masters of united China, who then, with ready forgetfulness of their own aggressions, could pose as the defenders of the peace against Western imperialism. It was disturbing to find how ready an acceptance this claim won in such countries as India, anxious above all things to avoid war. But one thing was made increasingly clear — the only major change that might be wrought in China will be made from within, not by force or the threat of it from without.

In spite of efforts to keep closely-knit ties with Moscow and repeated emphasis on Marxism, Chinese communism reflected at that time both the subtle and national character of Chinese thought. This was evident in the famous address of Mao Tse-tung delivered before the Supreme Council of State on May 2, 1956. Taking as a Party slogan an old Chinese saying — older than Confucius — "Let a hundred flowers blossom and a hundred schools of thought contend," Mao admitted controversies within the Party, and apparently between it and other parties. But it was not long before this extension of freedom of discussion was corrected in an address (also before a closed session of the Supreme State Council) on February 27, 1957. The text of this, as revised by Mao himself, was published on June 18.[25] The guiding principle implied in this address was that communism should be built under a leadership, which, while it must be competent, must not sink back into a bureaucracy with the faults so familiar in the past. In other words, the "New Democracy" of China must not develop that kind of privileged class which Djilas so graphically described as developing in the communist countries of the West. While ideological differences among communists should be held within bounds, they should be decided by free discussion, not by "crude, coercive methods."

In Mao's original speech there was a frank admission (omitted in the official published text) that the revolution had cost the lives of 800,000 Chinese. But now there should be no more terror. "No organ of parties in government, no person regardless of rank, merits, history or past victories, has the right to silence critics. . . . The education of the masses must be carried on seriously but with the gentleness of a breeze or of a light rain. . . .

[24] This importance of point is emphasized by Professor Fitzgerald. "The new members from these mandarin families are, of course, ardent Communists, sincere believers in the New Democracy, servants of the people. They are also precisely the same group of people who have governed China for the last two thousand years. It is in their blood. They are born to rule, and whether by virtue or Confucius and the Emperor or Marx and Mao Tse-tung makes very little difference. Deep-rooted, not in any way destroyed by the Revolution, is the old Chinese conviction that government is an affair for the elite."

[25] English translation published in *The New York Times* of June 19, 1957.

Except in major offenses against law or discipline, all should be free from punitive measures. Self-criticism and criticism of others should take place in heart-to-heart talks between comrades. There must be no mass assemblies and no battles."

But the winds of opinion which blew through the door thus opened for freedom of thought among communists — Mao was talking only to them — threatened, however, to become a gale, as the "rightists" seized the occasion to reveal their hidden doubts and grievances. The "Rectification Program," with its slogan "Unite, Criticize, Unite Again" brought out genuine grievances of the kind of bureaucratic misrule that had ruled Chiang Kai-shek. But the liberal line of Peking went too far too soon. China still needed a strong government of the kind that oriental peoples — and Confucius — recognized as necessary for the maintenance of order in society. In the text of the address published in June, the responsibility for disturbances is placed upon the higher authorities. "In a big country like ours it is nothing to get alarmed about if small numbers of people should create disturbances; rather we should turn such things to our advantage to help us get rid of bureaucracy."

Foreign observers discounted this language of sweet reasonableness as an effort to make them forget the ruthlessness of the early years of the communist revolution. Upon the whole, however, this promise of a milder regime seemed at first to have been realized. Although there were numerous arrests and some executions of extreme "rightists" or "counter-revolutionists," there were numerous arrests and some executions of extreme "rightists" or "counter-revolutionists," there was no reign of terror such as in the Russian purges. Strong measures, however, were taken to prevent riots in the collectives and strikes in the factories from getting out of hand, especially at a time when hundreds of thousands of peasants were trying to escape from their misery by crowding into the cities, enticed by the promise of a Five Year Plan on the Russian model to increase industrialization which proved so tempting as to invite disaster.

The mistakes of government — some of them inherent in communism — proved less disastrous, however, than the calamities of nature, typhoons, and floods in the midst of the worst and longest drought in recent Chinese history. The effort to raise the standard of peasant economy was as inept at first, however, as the earlier drive to industrialization had been; for the government mobilized a vast army of students — with oriental disregard for arithmetic, estimated at either three or ten million, certainly much less — to give up for the time being whatever ambitions as scholars they might have cherished, and live and work as peasants. It seems incredible that a government dominated by Mao Tse-tung of peasant origin, and Chou En-lai, of a family of scholars,[26] should so far forget the realities of those two basic

[26] Mao Tse-tung's father was a well-to-do peasant, able to give his son a good start in life. Mao attended Peking University, having among his professors Hu Shi, the exponent of John Dewey's philosophy, but seems to have sunk himself in the military aspects of Chinese history. In any case, it was as a military leader that he rose in the Communist Party, steadily supplanting others. Chou En-lai graduated from Nankai University when it was under the presidency of Chiang Po-ling, an outstanding advocate of Western education and liberal thought in China.

elements of Chinese life as to force them into a condition bound to produce bickering and domestic strife. For the scholars could not readily bring themselves to the status of peasant, and the peasants hated having arrogant outsiders in their villages. Besides, the crops failed, and the student farmers had no remedy for a drought.

The government of Mao Tse-tung, however, with true Chinese persistence, was not to be turned aside by initial mistakes or calamities. At first it tried making concessions to the noncommunists, but they were more apparent than real, for "the People," who were to be granted freedom of speech included only those accepting the basic principles of socialism, not "the enemies of the People," those hostile to the socialist revolution. The bourgeoisie should be reasoned with, however, so as to prevent them from becoming really "antagonistic." There is no parallel in the Soviet Union or its satellites to this effort which the Chinese Communists made at this stage of their history to cooperate with the Bourgeois parties.

But the situation was chaotic. There were even eight noncommunist parties in the Chinese People's Democratic Front, embracing "workers, peasants, petty-bourgeois elements, the so-called national bourgeoisie and anti-imperialist and patriotic forces." To steer the Communist ship of state through such confusions and uncertainties required both tact and persuasion and an unshaken purpose. Both of these Mao and his colleagues showed to the full. The peasant masses were prepared for collectivism by experience in cooperatives. It was not long, however, before this slow way of converting the Chinese to communism by persuasion and example was given up for a policy of action and enforcement going far beyond anything tried in Russia since the first phase of the Bolshevist revolution. Lenin, though rigid in theory, was a realist in practice and saw that a sudden change into a purely communist society was more than the people could take and restored, in part at least, the stimulus of profit through competition. Mao now proved more Leninist than Lenin and in what was called a "great leap."

The growth of a vast bureaucracy, stretching down from the ministries to the villages had been already under way in this transformation of China from Confucianism to Marxism, when Mao decided to carry into effect this extreme form of communism in which all traces of private ownership, or even privacy, were to be blotted out. A detailed account of this incredible chapter of Chinese history was given in an article by Tillman Durdin in *The New York Times* cabled from Hong Kong on September 25, 1958 — a first preview of the world of the future if it were to be molded by absolute, unqualified communist ideology, as the following paragraphs show:

Under the regulations for a full-fledged commune, a few thousand to 10,000 peasant households merge their farm collectives into an organization that takes over all collective property as well as the small plots, tools, livestock and fowls the peasants have been permitted to keep individually up to now. Instead of splitting up the income of the collective as heretofore, the peasants go on a fixed wage system.

Family and individual household living virtually disappears. The commune members eat in central mess halls and live in communal housing. Nurseries take care of the children and the women do full-time work in the fields along with the men.

All means of production and all labor belong to the commune. It not only farms the large area under its control but builds and manages industries, handles trade and banking, and runs schools, irrigation systems, hospitals, posts and the telegraph.

The managements of the *hsing* (township) and of the communes become one and the same. The organization is along military lines and the communes arm and incorporate able-bodied persons into the militia.

Wages can be cut or bonuses given in accordance with the work enthusiasm of the members. Labor groups can be shifted from farm to factory or to distant construction projects whenever the commune directors will.

The communes will be under tight Communist Party rule and operate within the framework of over-all policies and plans laid down in Peiping. The commune members have the right to elect commune congresses and lower-level bodies, but the elections will be strictly controlled. The system is regarded as likely to spread eventually to the cities.

Peiping is believed to have decided to establish the communes to improve its control and increase the state's share of production, particularly of agricultural output. Under the farm collectives, the members benefited to some extent from bigger crops through sharing what was left after state collections. Under the communes, the wage system will limit the workers to fixed incomes.

The communes also will help the Government with its program of increasing local industries, and facilitate the mobility and control of labor. They will add tens of millions of women for full work away from home by freeing them from household tasks.

Such a world seems too fantastic for belief, and especially for acceptance by a people committed throughout the past to a society based on family and kinship ties. But the most enlightening comment on the communes was that of Khrushchev in his long interview with Senator Humphrey of Minnesota.

They are old-fashioned, they are reactionary. We tried that right after the revolution. It just doesn't work. That system is not nearly as good as the state farms. They are based on the principle, "From each according to his abilities, to each according to his needs." You know that can't work. You can't get production without incentive.[27]

As Senator Humphrey remarks, this criticism of Mao's communes is also a rejection of the very core of Marxian theory, like a life-long Christian saying that the Golden Rule would not work. But much more important than the question of communist heresy is the clear indication that the Kremlin was critical of Mao and by no means ready to accept this Oriental type of communism as fitted for the West. This conclusion is confirmed by the comments of Mikoyan in interviews during his visit to the United States. The divergence between China and Russia opens a world of speculations. But meanwhile a new China has already come into existence, and we have fortunately a description of it which bears no color of propaganda, that of a scientist Professor J. Tuz Wilson of the University of Toronto, who as President of the International Union of Geodesy and Geophysics travelled in the interior of China while the communist experiment was being made. His

[27] *Life*, January 12, 1959, p. 86.

description of the way China is revolutionizing its six hundred millions is a document of the first importance. The transformation of Lanchow, a small provincial city, to a metropolis of 800,000 inhabitants is even less significant than the new laboratories and libraries of a university founded in 1946. "After several millenia of the same way of life," says Professor Wilson, "the Chinese race is now stirred to its depths. Its passive religions have been suppressed in favor of vigorous activism. Its ancient ideographs are being replaced by an alphabet. Family life, government, social organizations, business — all have been profoundly altered. The whole country is being transformed at a fantastic rate. . . . What is certain is that China will never again be the same."[28]

Evidently what is taking place is not merely the transfer from Mandarin to communist bureaucracy. A great experiment in social living, far greater than that planned for the West by Karl Marx, will be tested against a different background in China — one, it must be remembered, that has had no parallel anywhere in Asia. There may be, after all, in the long reaches of the future, those "hundred flowers of thought" which were cherished before the days of Confucius, but of a kind that neither Confucius nor Marx would recognize.

Mao himself, however, has warned us against wishful thinking. After the Polish uprising in Poznan and the Hungarian revolution he made clear that he was no "revisionist." Khrushchev's attack on Stalin in February, 1956, which demolished the dogma of infallibility in the communist leadership, seemed not to have been shared by Mao — in spite of the fact that Stalin had once opposed him. There are two explanations of this reactionary move. One is that he is sincerely fearful of confusion in communism and sees in an unyielding Marx-Lenin orthodoxy the necessary discipline to prevent its disintegration in a nation which loves freedom in debate but lacks experience in its practical application. The eagerness with which the proposal to allow "a Hundred schools of thought" in communist theorizing was greeted was a revelation of the continuing vitality of Chinese thought; but it was also a warning that the movement for freedom might readily challenge the further extension of communism which Mao was planning. To meet this challenge, the government in Peking created a more efficient bureaucracy than that which had ruled Imperial China for many centuries. If history were the clue to the future — which, in the dynamic world of today, it is not — this new bureaucracy, the one organ of government familiar to the masses of China, would be a guarantee of its strength and endurance. But communist China has broken with precedent, and the tests in the orient as in Europe are those described by Djilas in his penetrating analysis of *The New Class*. Any régime which relies upon a bureaucracy becomes increasingly dependent upon it, and nowhere is that fate more likely than in China. For the immediate future, however, Mao has an instrument of government which ensures a more than imperial power, and he stands forth as the outstanding champion for communism not only in China but in all Asia.

[28] Published in *The Saturday Review of Literature*, November 8, 1958.

At the height of his power — or, perhaps, of its most critical moment — when the communes were set up all China, Mao resigned the Presidency of the Republic, keeping, however, the control of the one instrument of power, the Party. There is nothing in the history of the Chinese people like this intensive, all-embracing militarism — for it is nothing short of that, with its local militias watching over the communes. This is Prussianism far beyond the dreams of any Hohenzollern. What will become of it, no one knows. But the Chinese people have shown through many centuries of their history, an inner strength of resistance against tyranny which is not likely to be lacking in the years to come. Their path of freedom will be a different one from ours, but the ultimate goal will surely be the same — that freedom which is the final expression of both the individual and society.

Japan

From the standpoint of the West, the history of Japan is incredible. The most rigidly conservative of nations throughout the centuries, cherishing patriotism as a religion and a way of life, it rose, in a single generation out of the background of an Oriental society to be the leader in the revolutionary modernization of Asia. A people only just emerging from feudalism under the newly recovered authority of a divine emperor established parliamentary government and a code of laws on the Western model. Down to these last years it cherished the ancient myth that Japan had been created by a special act of the deities and that the emperor was the direct descendant of the Sun Goddess. Now the emperor himself leads his people to renounce his divinity; but the religious basis of society remains, linking the new industrialized nation to a philosophy of life which connects it with a mythological past. On the one side are the contacts with the Western World; on the other the all-pervading presence of that spirit world of Shinto, to whose shrines the pilgrims still come on trolley cars, in buses or on foot. For the old Japan lives on behind the modern facade.

The Japanese annalists dated the history of Japan from 660 B.C., the accepted date of the accession to the throne of Jimmu Tenno, grandson of the Sun Goddess; but reliable records begin only in the fifth century A.D. The centuries that followed were mostly filled with clan and feudal wars, with four great families leading, the Fujiwara, the Taira, the Minamoto and the Tokugawa. From the ninth to the nineteenth centuries the great feudal lords maintained the emperor as a powerless but sacred symbol of divinity, sequestered at the old capital of Kyoto, guarded against anyone but his ministers seeing his sacred face. Power passed to the chieftains of the dominant feudal family who, in the twelfth century, took over the military organization at Kamakura, or later Yeddo (now Tokyo), leaving only civil affairs for the court at Kyoto to administer. The headship of this military organization was termed *Shogun,* meaning "general" or dictator, and until 1868 it was the Shogun and not the emperor who ruled Japan.

This system reached its climax in the sixteenth and seventeenth centuries when the long series of feudal and tribal wars was brought to a close by two great statesmen, Hideyoshi and Iyeyasu, both of them outstanding figures in world history. The Shogunate which Iyeyasu founded was a system which made the chief of his family, the Tokugawa, the heritage ruler of the Empire, and relegated the emperor definitely to the position of a sacrosanct mediator between his heavenly ancestors and his subjects, which had the advantage of keeping politics free of that kind of clericalism which was so serious a problem in the West.

The principles of the system were set forth in a document known as the Testament of Iyeyasu. Although a munificent benefactor of Buddhism, the great Shogun based his political philosophy on that of Confucius. The foundation of government should be the recognition of the five relationships: between ruler and subject; between parent and child; between husband and wife; brother and sister; and friend and friend. The family was the social unit of society. No distinct line was drawn between law and morals, between the duty of citizenship and virtue in family relationships. As in China, substantive law was entirely lacking. Custom, when widely practiced and long established, was to be complied with in the civil affairs of life. Detailed exposition, however, covered criminal law, clan relations, etiquette, rank, precedence, administration and the practice of government.

The social structure of Japan under feudalism was divided into three groups: the court nobles; the military class or *samurai;* and the common people. The court nobles, who traced their descent from the imperial house, were relatively few in number, and were often impoverished, but of exalted station. The *samurai* were the hereditary soldiers, sworn to defend their feudal chieftains and their country. In spite of constantly waging feuds in which no quarter was given or expected, their code of honor, *Bushido,* was respected by the nation as a whole.[29] The common people were divided into three classes of farmers (the most respectable), artisans, including artists and ceramists, and, lowest of all, tradespeople. Below these were the "defiled," living in separate hamlets, tabooed and ostracised from generation to generation. By reason of its military element, there was a sharper distinction in social classes than in China, with a hierarchy of power and precedence that held the classes of the nation sternly to their allotted places, until the revolution of the Meiji emperor ushered in modern times.

The transformation of Japan is a complicated story. On the one hand we have the pressure from without when Commodore Perry forced it to open a few ports to foreigners in 1854, and when Consul General Townsend Harris, four years later, negotiated another treaty of commerce and diplomatic representation at the Japanese court — a treaty paralled by others with twelve Western Powers. But at the same time Japan itself was getting ready for the change. Throughout the nineteenth century, scholars sought to strengthen the cult of the emperor by reviving the study of Japan's ancient history, and undermined the Shogunate by pointing out how the country had failed, under it, to achieve its divine purpose of saving mankind. Naive as the ideal may seem, it prevented the country from falling into feudal

[29] See Chapter II.

anarchy again, when the Tokugawa Shogunate came to an end in 1867, for the whole nation supported the restoration of the emperor to supreme power. The final urge to the restoration, the greatest act in the history of Japan, was the blockade of the port of Shimomoseki by the combined fleets of the United States, Great Britain, France and the Netherlands, in retaliation for Japanese attacks on trading ships in the straits west of that seaport.

Fortunately the Meiji, the young emperor of the restoration, proved to be one of the world's great statesmen. Breaking the seclusion of the past, he moved his court from Kyoto to Tokyo, lived openly among his people, urged them along the pathway of reform and had cordial meetings with foreign representatives of the Treaty Powers. The credit for all the work of the opening years should go to a group of able young men, practically all from the *samurai* class of lower nobility, most of whom had gone abroad to study. The empire owed much to these men and to the select group of enlightened advisers, who as the years went by, came to be known as the *Genro,* or elder statesmen. The principles of the new regime as set forth in the emperor's name in a document called a "Charter Path" run somewhat as follows:[30]

The practice of argument and debate shall be adopted by all, and all measures shall be decided by impartial discussion.

High and low shall be of one mind, and social order shall thereby be perfectly maintained. It is necessary that the civil and military powers be concentrated in a single whole, that the rights of all classes be assured and the national mind be completely satisfied.

The uncivilized customs of former times shall be broken through, and the impartiality of justice displayed in the working of nature shall be adopted as a basis of action.

Intellect and learning shall be sought for throughout the world, in order to establish the foundations of the Empire.

This document contains more meaning than appears at first reading. The opening paragraph calls for parliamentary procedure. The second one lays the basis for law in Confucian ethics. The third deals with the need for a central government; the fourth proposes to substitute the "law of nature" for divers local cusotms — that same principle of Western Law to which the American Declaration of Independence refers. The authors of this document obviously had studied in Europe and America. The same holds true of the code of laws of the following years, in which the use of torture was abolished and a reformed judicial system was set up. The introduction of a parliamentary system was less important than the establishment of universal compulsory school education, which made Japan one of the most literate nations of the world. But more important still was the industrial revolution which, with almost breath-taking speed, transformed the country from complete Asiatic isolation to an economic competitor of the Western Powers and raised it to the first rank alongside them.

To understand Japan today, we must never forget what it meant to a nation to cut so many ties with the past, especially when that past was

[30] Quoted in *The History of Japan* by Kenneth Latourette, (New York: The Macmillan Co., 1947), p. 94.

hallowed with religion and the annals of war. The Japanese were called upon to make the apparently impossible adjustment between a philosophy of life which connects nation and family with a mythological past and an industrially modernized present. Ancestor worship is not a vague abstraction, but an intimate affair of the family. There is in the Japanese home, often within the house itself, a shrine where the departed still are supposed to come and visit with the living. It is seldom that the foreign visitor will find the little screen in the wall moved back to reveal the household altar, with its constantly replenished gifts of food or flowers, for the spirits to whom these gifts are made are too dearly held in loving regard to risk having the foreigner make an irreverant remark or wound the family feelings by an apparent lack of sympathy. Shrines like these are to be found in the homes of business men who have lived for years in Europe or America, but who remain linked with the social structure of an ancient past by the constant reminder of their ancestors.

It is a strange fact that those who modernized Japan, the Elder Statesmen of that generation which has now almost entirely passed away, did not think that the economic and political changes which they inaugurated would ever touch the religious and ethical bases of Japanese society. The great Meiji Emperor, who became the symbol of the modernizing forces of Japan, has had erected to him in Tokyo one of the greatest shrines in all Japan, a place for reverence and prayer set on the outskirts of the great industrial capital in an area of great silent woods surrounding the cloisters of a temple. No high official assumed office without going to the most ancient shrine of Ise, where in a little chamber of a primitive temple are kept the sacred sword and mirror said to have been given to the chief founder of the Imperial line by the Sun Goddess herself.

Acts like these were not mere formalities to those who modernized Japan. They saw no inconsistency in retaining their belief in the spiritual world of Shinto and the sacred quality of the empire, while adopting the factory system or setting up parliamentary government under a divine emperor. But if the Elder Statesmen were not troubled by the incongruity in this mixture of East and West, the Emperor Hirohito, grandson of the Meiji, apparently was. As a young man he violated the rigid court tradition and travelled abroad, taking a sympathetic interest in liberal, even democratic, politics and finally, after World War II, formally renounced the imperial claim to divinity.

Unfortunately, the contacts with the West, which supplied Japan with a modernized structure of government, also stimulated an expansion of its inherent militarism. European imperialism was just then showing what power politics could do on the defenseless Asiatic mainland. This brought back memories of how Japan itself had been forced to yield to armed might. But the military tradition of the *Samurai* was now reenforced with the economic needs of a growing population and the newly proven capacity of the industrial leaders. The result was an era of Japanese imperialism which began with the war with China in 1894. Victory in this war gave the army and navy such political influence and power that, combined with reactionary industrialists, and building on vibrant Japanese nationalism, they launched the country on one war after another. The defeat of Russia in 1904-5 and the series of aggressions against China were the prelude to World War II, when the great dramatic dream of empire over all Asia was ended in unconditional surrender on the deck of the warship *Missouri*.

The history of these wars lies outside the scope of this study. What is of interest is the effect upon the government and the people of Japan. The cause of freedom is always at stake in the struggle between militarists and liberals, for militarists deny the first element of freedom. War, as we have said before, is not "the final argument of kings"; it is no argument at all. It invokes a stratagem which often has no relation to the issues at stake, employing strength drawn from other sources, and it represses all thought or action that opposes its course. This is what happened in Japan. The new, untried experiment of democracy, which centered in the attempt to make the lower House of the Diet assume control of the government, like the House of Commons in Great Britain, met with the fiercest kind of opposition by the military cliques. In the 1930's they terrorized Tokyo by murder and the threat of it, and assassinated two Prime Ministers and other high officials. Hundreds were imprisoned for harboring "dangerous thoughts." The heads of the Army and the Navy had the advantage that under the Constitution of 1889 the military authorities were independent of the civil. This followed the traditional scheme of dual government of old Japan, in which the Shoguns had kept control of the military, and there was more than a reminder of that duality in the fact that the heads of army and navy were on active service and could commit the government to their policies in spite of opposition in the Cabinet — of which they were members — or in parliament. With this constitutional handicap to lessen their influence the liberal statesmen whose interest was peace and reform, had only short intervals of power.

Thus the years passed in confusion, and such rapid economic advances were made that even the moderate political element felt the need of expansion, while the impatient militarists began to plan for a major war. Japan had not learned the lesson of World War I, that war had ceased to be a calculable instrument even of aggression, for it was the one great Power that really profited from that war. Its easy conquests in Shantung strengthened the conviction of its military and naval circles, that the path of empire which they had opened up by acquiring Korea and Formosa as a result of victory over China and getting a foothold in Manchuria by victory over Russia, was now taking them to the mastery of Asia. The fallacy of Nazism and Fascism was almost inevitable in the Japan of 1939 as the dream of still greater profits from a still greater war touched the false note in that otherwise noble spirit of Japan — Bushido — the glorification of the virtues of those following the profession of arms.

Fortunately for the development of a Japan free from its traditional militarism, aggression in World War II did not pay. That the militarists have learned anything from defeat can hardly be expected, but three overwhelming influences turned the nation from thoughts of revenge to constructive policies of peace: the decisive nature of the defeat; the American occupation; and the enlightened leadership of the emperor. The Occupation limited its reprisals to the execution of relatively few "war criminals," then de-purged most others judged responsible in various degrees for pro-war activities. It also set about healing the wounds of the war with policies of reform and with a constitution drafted on democratic lines in place of the Prussian-modeled Constitution of 1889. The emperor accepted, in an epoch-making message of January 1, 1946, the constitutional provision which denied him the immense powers of the Meiji Constitution and described him as "the symbol of the State and the unity of the people, deriving his position from the will of the people with whom resides sovereign power." Deftly, however, the drafters of the constitution used the same term for emperor that had been used in the Meiji Constitution: *Tenno,* or "Heavenly Lord."

Laudable in purpose, but open to criticism in both its terms and its practicality, was the provision by which "The Japanese people forever renounce war as a sovereign right of the nation and the threat or use of force as a means of settling international disputes." Here we have the vague, comprehensive formula of the discarded Kellogg Pact. Like Secretary of State Kellogg, General MacArthur, in a message to the Japanese people, reserved the right to arm for national defense; but as no one had defined defense, and defense is the pretext for most wars, the text of the constitution was meaningless. The fallacy of it was driven home by the subsequent insistence of the United States that Japan should help in the defense against Soviet aggression. The real force making the revival of Japanese militarism unlikely, is the inescapable fact that in the era of atomic war, thickly populated Japan is virtually defenseless, a fact which makes it reluctant to follow the lead of America into any dangerous risks in dealing with Russia.

If militarism is lessening as an obstacle to freedom in Japan, social and economic reforms offer new spheres of action. Chief among these are the new labor laws. The factory system of Japan, dominated by the great industrial combinations (the *Zaibatsu*) — now dissolved — had repeated the worst conditions of the England of a century earlier, when little children were brought in from poverty-stricken country homes to work at starvation wages in the mills. These conditions were changed as Japan, a member of the International Labor Organization from its early days at the League of Nations in Geneva, succeeded in having its social standard raised in a series of labor laws which made labor conditions in Japan better than those of the rest of Asia. A Land Reform Act also cut down absentee landlordism and helped the peasantry. All in all, the democratization moved swifter in Japan than anywhere else in Asia — or, for that matter, anywhere in the world. Viewed in the light of its own history, it seems almost too good to be true.

Indonesia

Before the English established themselves in India, their commercial rivals, the Dutch, had taken over the "spice islands," which stretched over a thousand miles of ocean, sturdily holding these rich possessions even when they lost their American colony to the English. From the seventeenth century to the twentieth they held these islands, the richest in natural resources of all Asia, closely in their grasp, ruling them by Dutch agents and exploiting their trade to their own advantage. Unlike the British in India, they offered the natives no share in the administration except at the lowest level of purely local affairs. As late as 1938, 92.2 per cent of the higher personnel was Dutch, and only 6.9 Indonesian. Even when a revolutionary movement had begun against this regime, the Dutch Governor General, Van Mook, admitted that during an entire century, when great changes were being made in India and China, Dutch policy "was unable to visualize the inevitable emancipation of the Asiatic colonies and the growth of nationhood in these areas."[31] Like the French and unlike the English they regarded their East Indian colonies as an integral part of the mother country, to which measures of self-government could be offered, but never independence. There was no parallel to the Indian Civil Service, trained to take over the administration of the islands.

This old colonial regime was rudely broken up when, in World War II, Japan conquered the islands, welcomed at first by the mass of the people and by the lesser functionaries hoping to reach higher office under the Japanese, and nationalist leaders like Sukarno and Hatta were at first led to cooperate with them by their promises of a new era — "Asia for the Asiatics." But by August 1945 it was clear that Japan was defeated and Sukarno and Hatta issued a Declaration of the Independence of Indonesia.

Then came the strangest episode in this confused history. The British Labor Government was told by the Dutch Embassy in London that Sukarno's movement for an Indonesian republic did not represent a spontaneous nationalist movement but, on the contrary, was a Japanese puppet government of a totalitarian character, dependent on the Japanese military organization; that Sukarno had received a high decoration from the enemy and was allowed to proclaim the Indonesian Republic while the Japanese military forces were still in control of the island. This statement, broadcast by the B.B.C., that the Indonesian Republic was really a satellite of Japan still left doubts in the minds of many members of the British Labor Party, and sixty members of Parliament issued a statement urging that the problems arising from the termination of the war in the Far East should be recognized as a concern of the United Nations.

This suggestion was not acted upon until months of confused and uncertain history had passed, including an attempt of the Dutch to reestablish its old colonial system by a new attack upon the Republic, in July, 1947. This revival of colonial war was what the British had hoped to avoid by diplomacy, but while London hesitated to oppose the Dutch, India and Australia acted. Nehru sounded the new note in no uncertain terms. "No European country, whatever it may be, has any right to set its army in Asia against the people of Asia. The spirit of the new Asia will not tolerate such things." The Labor government of Australia also gave support to Sukarno. While Washington joined London in holding back, India and Australia laid the

[31] Quoted in *The Republic of Indonesia*, by Dorothy Woodman, p. 272. (London: Cresset Press, 1955. 435 pp.)

problem before the Security Council of the United Nations, which, after debate, appointed a Committee of Good Offices, as it came to be named, consisting of an Australian, to be chosen by the Indonesian Republic, a Belgian, to be chosen by the Dutch, and an American, to be chosen by the other two, to work with the consuls of the United States, Great Britain, France and Belgium already in Djarkarta. The Security Council's resolution also called for a cessation of hostilities, but this and the effort at a settlement failed and the Dutch sent in new armed forces to occupy all the large towns in Java.

Then, again the United Nations acted. On December 24, 1948, the Asian countries in the Security Council, India, Burma, Ceylon and Pakistan, using a new form of sanction, banned the Dutch airline KLM. Australian dock workers boycotted Dutch ships (as they had in 1947), and, at the suggestion of Burma, a conference of sixteen Asian nations met in Delhi and passed a series of resolutions, culminating in one recognizing the sovereignty of the United States of Indonesia by January 1, 1950. The Security Council later backed this up, but the Dutch army still stayed on until June 30, 1949. When it finally left, the Netherlands realized that their ocean empire in Asia was ended.

The terms of the settlement, arrived at by a Round Table Conference at the Hague, linked the United States of Indonesia with the Netherlands in a Union which recognized Queen Juliana as the titular head — a settlement on the British Commonwealth model. The queen, in a final ceremony, shook hands with Dr. Hatta, the Indonesian leader and, speaking with evident emotion, said "We no longer stand partly opposed to one another. We have now taken our places side by side, however much we may be bruised and torn, carrying the scars of rancour and regret." The carillon then rang out the national anthems of both nations.

Independence had been won. The newest country of Asia had now to face its own problems, and they seemed almost unsolvable. The lack of a trained civil service rendered doubly difficult the effort to create that most complicated of all systems of government, a democratic federalism, rendered still more difficult by the fact that each island had its own culture and traditions. Even more than in India, a nation had to be created. There were sixteen states in partnership and autonomous territories, to be made into a nation. In the very first parliament, President Sukarno announced a constitutional reform, and in August, 1950, proclaimed the establishment of the Republic of Indonesia as a unitary state, with a constitution to be shaped by a Constituent Assembly.

This Commonwealth did not last, however. In February, 1956, Indonesia declared Round Table Conference agreements with the Dutch abolished, and in August of that year repudiated Indonesia's debt to the Netherlands.

Such were the origins of Indonesia. It was inevitable, however, that its new freedom should, in spite of the prestige of President Sukarno, and his self-appointed parliament, reflect in its political parties and its trade unions the varied outlook of nationalism, socialism, communism and the varied interests of the far-flung archipelago. The situation became critical when an army revolt in Sumatra led Sukarno, in his capacity as Commander-in-Chief of the Armed Forces, to issue an Order of the Day in which he declared that the very foundations of the State had been shaken. In his New Year's Message to the nation he stated that the time had come to consider whether Indonesia should not frankly give up trying to copy the Western models of democracy, which had worked so badly for the last eleven years, and try another way. Maturing his "concept" of a guided democracy in cooperation with General Nasution, the Supreme Army Authority, whose chief task had been to suppress the rebellion, President Sukarno proposed an Extra-Parliamentary cabinet of experts in business to advise him in a "guided democracy which would be in accordance with Indonesia's tradition and history." In an Emergency Law of May 6, 1957, he authorized the formation of a National Advisory Council, nominated by him to help expedite matters on which the Parliament proved incapable of speedy action.

The formation of this Council was termed by President Sukarno "the first phase of the new-style democracy. . . . What I saw in Western and communist countries only served to lay the finishing touches on an idea I have long been pondering upon. In the West, freedom of speech and freedom of expression take the foremost place, while in the communist world freedom from want and freedom from sorrow are more important. For Indonesia I will take the middle path or a synthesis of these two extremes. . . . I do not have a party of my own, as India's Nehru has in the Congress Party, as Burma's U Nu has in the Anti-Fascist League or as communist and fascist countries where the leaders can easily effect thorough-going changes." The alternative, therefore, to personal rule was the Advisory Council. Parliamentarism would never get anywhere. "I am convinced that free-flight liberalism cannot produce a just and prosperous society." Guidance by functional groups in an advisory council is "real and national."

It was not long before it was evident that Sukarno's "guided democracy" would not be guided effectively by an advisory council without power supplied by an irresponsible executive or a responsible parliament. The political experience of the West could not be ignored. Again, as in six other nations of southeastern Asia, a vigorous young army general Nasution, moved his officers into key positions in the newly created Ministry of Economic Stabilization, in the nationalized Dutch Handelsband and in mining and oil exploitation, so vital to both Dutch and American firms. Nasution owed his rise to his success in fighting rebels in the jungles; he protected the republic equally against right wing revolts of generals and communist demonstrations and strikes. But the new experiment in government brought only political confusion and economic disaster. The cabinet was changed eighteen times in the ten years after the Dutch relinquished their sovereignty in 1949. Then in July, 1959, President Sukarno issued a decree abolishing the 1950 constitution, dissolving the Constituent Assembly and ending "guided democracy" by his own assumption of sovereign power. In reply to questions from reporters, he stated that he would be head of both state and government. "But one thing is sure" he added, "I am not a dictator and I will have many consultations about everything." The same news despatch which contained this gem of political philosophy announced that Indonesia had purchased abroad the largest military equipment in its history.

CHAPTER XXIII

AFRICA

THE ROAD to freedom in Africa is a short one, but today it is being crowded by millions of unaccustomed feet. Except for the Nile valley, the littoral of the Mediterranean, and the Cape, Africa remained until the latter part of the nineteenth century the habitat of primitive peoples, victims of the grossest superstitions, enslaved or decimated by tribal wars. Although some tribes excelled others in the crude beginnings of farming life, on the whole the conditions were those of brutal savagery. They were not all of one racial stock, but differed in color and looks — only a part of them negroid, but all distinctively "African" and all living, at least until recently, in primitive tribes, of which there were some eight hundred in all. Among them, war or the threat of it was constant, mostly raids for booty and slaves. The slave trade in Africans, which sullied the dawn of modern Europe, was largely based on that of the natives themselves.

The "Dark Continent" was not only darkened by these barbarities, but by its impenetrability. The Sahara Desert was blanketed on the south by hundreds, or thousands, of miles of trackless forests fed by tropical rains so fast that the native, with his primitive tools, was practically helpless against it, and, except in South Africa, the grasslands lacked the rich soils of the American prairies. Add to this the fact that the coastline has only a few, far-separated harbors, and the natural isolation of the continent shut it out of history until modern times. Then Europe opened the continent by two forceful entries and one of pure idealism — the slave trade and colonial exploitation on the one hand, and the missionary effort on the other. Over against the Portuguese, Spanish and English slavers of the seventeenth century or the Dutch, Belgian, French or German colonial exploiters of the nineteenth century, one must keep in mind the selfless, courageous work of men like Livingstone, Lavigerie and Schweitzer, to mention only three outstanding figures in a movement of emancipation from witchcraft, taboo and the other impediments to civilization in primitive life to which not enough credit is given today.

It is the tragedy of Africa that the one institution that was best known about it from ancient to modern times was slavery. In ancient Rome the African Numidians shared the servitude of the fair-haired prisoners from the north or of any other conquered country, but after the Numidian kingdom was conquered no empire rose in Africa to match the kingdoms of the emancipated German tribes. The Moorish conquerors were slavers and remained so until our own time. The color bar was the badge of slavery in Europe and its colonies. But, it was not an institution imported from without but the persisting practice of savages who never got beyond the level of tribal life. There, as elsewhere in the world, slavery was fed by intertribal wars, which were often raiding expeditions for booty. The same connection between war and slavery had once prevailed in Europe, but there it had finally yielded to the varied interplay of economics and politics, forces never strong enough to establish civilized life in Africa. This reservoir of slaves offered new temptations to native slavers when the markets of the New World were opened in the age of the explorers, although the European slavers were raiders as well. It was this involvement of Europeans in the overseas extension of slavery which aroused their conscience and led to the suppression of the slave trade and the abolition of slavery in their own lands.

We have already traced the early stages of the anti-slavery movement in Europe and the final abolition of it there and in America. But the movement to suppress the African slave trade called for international action. The Peace Treaties of 1814 and 1815 and the Declaration of the Congress of Vienna and the Declaration of Verona of 1822 denounced the slave trade as repugnant to the principles of justice and humanity. The Treaties of 1831 and 1833 between France and Great Britain and the Treaty of Washington between Great Britain and the United States in 1862 called for joint action at sea to suppress the slave trade, and provided for mutual rights to visit, search and capture ships suspected of slaving operations. The Berlin Conference of 1885 reaffirmed the suppression of the slave trade and referred to it as an established principle of international law. History does not give sufficient credit to the British navy patrol of the suspected sea routes to the African coasts. The General Act of the Brussels Conference of 1889, mentioned above, which was attended by representatives of seventeen nations, has been termed the Magna Carta of the African slave. It is a lengthy document of one hundred articles divided into seven chapters, providing in detail for the complete suppression of the slave trade and all the inhuman practices of slave dealers, and providing too, for the welfare and repatriation of fugitive slaves. Bureaus to oversee the proper execution of the Act were set up at Zanzibar and Brussels, and plans outlined for offices and institutions for the liberation and protection of liberated slaves.

After World War I, in the Treaty of St. Germain-en-Laye, in September 1919, the United States, Belgium, the British Empire, Italy, Japan and Portugal abrogated the Berlin and Brussels General Acts and substituted for them a sweeping commitment in the following terms:

The signatory Powers exercising sovereign rights of authority in African territories will continue to watch over the preservation of native populations and to supervise the improvement of conditions of their moral and material well being. They will, in particular, endeavor to secure the complete suppression of slavery in all its forms and of the slave trade by land and sea.

This promise was made too in the Mandate System of the League of Nations and in the Anti-Slavery Convention of 1926, signed in Geneva by the representative of thirty-six states. The problem of African slavery had merged into that of a world-wide movement, to which we will turn in our study of the United Nations.

It is fitting that the first section of a chapter in the history of freedom in Africa should deal with slavery. But emancipation from that once dominant evil, while not complete in the darkest part of the continent, is no longer the main issue in African affairs. It is the movement by the Africans to undo the history of the partition of Africa in the nineteenth century.

Geographically, Africa was a perfect stage for European imperialism, Asia could force it to compromise with long established native States; in Africa there were no kingdoms or empires to block the path. Under Saracen and Turkish rule the peoples along the Mediterranean, had, with the exception of Egypt, become little more than backward tribes, whose one interest in central Africa was the slave trade. The only early European settlements south of the Equator were those of the Dutch, taken over by the British in 1814 in the war with Napoleon, and the Portuguese colonies on the east and west coasts.

Then, in the eighteen seventies, Leopold II of Belgium opened the new era of partition by seizing the vast tropical regions of the Congo and securing the consent of the European Powers, after long years of negotiation, to the creation of the Congo Free State under Belgian sovereignty. The partitioning then became a race. France added Tunis alongside Algeria which it had taken in the eighteen thirties, and then parts of Morocco, while Germany in East Africa blocked both British plans for a strip "from Cape to Cairo" and French plans for reaching the Nile from the Congo. The history of this contest in power politics does not concern us here, except to note that it was imperialism almost undefiled, and that it was the extension to Africa of the rivalries of that national state system which had kept Europe in suspended anarchy.

We are now witnessing the end of this colonialism in a movement by native peoples which has spread over the whole continent, challenging all colonial rule by the assertion of new rights in a larger freedom. To measure the place of this movement in history generally, we must deal with it in its own historical setting, which is utterly different from either that of Europe or Asia. The native tribes differ widely among themselves, physically, mentally and culturally, so widely indeed that the idea now being bruited abroad of an African native federation holds little promise of realization. The slogan "Africa for the Africans" is a fighting slogan against Europeans settled or ruling by right of conquest; it is not a declaration of the recovery of fundamental freedoms, for there were none to recover. It is a challenge to an uncertain future.

The first settlers, the Portuguese on the east coast and the Dutch on the south, did little or nothing to change native conditions, holding, as was the case with slave-owners and many others everywhere, that the reason these people remained so far behind the civilized world was that they were mentally incapable. But this judgment concerning the African is disproved by recent history. It is perhaps not a fair test to point to the rapid rise of Negroes in the United States although that advance is one of the most notable of any race in history. Yet a parallel movement is now under way in Africa, touching its dormant soul with the promise of new life. The causes of it are complicated and even contradictory: occupation and colonization, exploitation and social betterment, and, above all, science and religion. The only thing these elements have in common is that they are agencies of change. They force upon natives and Europeans alike new conditions of life which bring them, if belatedly and unevenly, into the great currents of contemporary thought.

For the natives it means an awakening to rights never known before — rights to share in a civilization which they are helping to create. And above all, it means the revelation of capacities in them never suspected in the past. The son of an illiterate Masai native becomes a surgeon in a London hospital; a generation that in childhood never saw a wheel produces engineers by the hundred; millions that never had an alphabet are at schools all over the continent.

The background of history of the Masai has been summed up in a masterly survey by Sir Philip Mitchell, formerly Governor of Uganda and Kenya and for many years a colonial administrator. While admitting many evils, cruelties and injustices under European rule, he says:

But they were mild things compared with the very recent past when few men and women could roll themselves in their sleeping hides or mats in their smoky huts at night with any certainty that tribal enemies, slave-raiders, marauding elephants or lurking lions or leopards would not strike them down in the night, that sorcerers or evil spirits would not slip through between the eaves and the walls in the dangerous darkness and destroy them by magic, that smallpox or sleeping sickness would not break out among them, or drought, locusts, or flood wipe out the crops so that famine, which could not be relieved, would destroy half a tribe.

So the stage was set for the great awakening, which continues to this day — an awakening which has brought with it the vast range of problems which confronts us today in contemporary Africa. . . .

Two world wars and the continually increasing speed and range of communications, mineral discoveries, and rising prices for nearly all that Africa produces have combined to stimulate and accelerate the speed of the immense developments which have followed the missionary and exploring journeys of Livingstone, Speke, Krap, Rebmann, and many others. The sudden impact of the West brought with it a few — surprisingly few — wars of conquest, some local sorcery, and necromancy, which are, I believe, in essence, atavistic movements back into the horrors and darknesses of the past. Mau Mau, which afflicts Kenya today, is one of many such outbreaks, a septic growth in the body of society which has attracted to itself the underworld of places like Nairobi and the scum of the colony.[1] Ritual murders in Basutoland, the West African countries and elsewhere, leopard men, python cults and other disorders of the hearts and minds of people in violent transition, whose world is whirling along at a dizzy speed, whose way of living has been turned upside down in a generation — these things break out from time to time and cause great suffering and disturbances. I have no time here to do more than note them in passing, with the observation that they are, unhappily, often seized on by tendentious writers and speakers in the West and misrepresented as political revolts, liberation movements, and resistance to tyranny.

In the judgment of Sir Philip Mitchell, the chief characteristic of the African awakening is not its material demands, but its spiritual outlook, which was the work of the missionaries.

I believe that, fundamentally, it was the Bible, the Bible and the brave, determined, merciful men and women who carried it and its message of hope — hope of the end of the slave trade, of prevention of epidemics and relief of famine, of protection from the savage whims of tyrants or the obscene orgies of sorcerers — to a people who were living in a brutish lethargy induced by continuous danger, horrors and sufferings. Maybe a generation has grown up which has forgotten these things, both in Africa and Europe, but I served in Africa forty-two years ago when they were still very recent, still actively operative in many places, still decisive of the attitudes of the mass of the people toward me and my fellows who had come to deliver them from the great man-hunt which was life in Central Africa. My eyes have seen it and my ears have heard, and I take leave to say that it is not necessary to seek further for the prime mover.

This tribute to the emancipating power of Christianity is not completely shared by the African leaders of the nationalisms of today for they recall that the political and social ideas of the missionaries were too often — even in men like Dr. Schweitzer — an acceptance of the "status quo." The practice of the Christian virtues needs to be applied and enforced by an enlightened administration. This has by no means been lacking in the history of Africa. No greater help up the path of peace and freedom has been found than in the life work of Lord Lugard in the early colonial days of British East Africa and Nigeria. But just as the history of religion has its dark chapters of intolerance and racial discrimination, the history of colonial governments has its tyrannies and exploitations, in a record now happily narrowing down to one major issue, that of *apartheid* in South Africa and also in Southern Rhodesia and Nyasaland. This policy of segregating the blacks in separate areas and denying them status in the areas reserved for the whites is one of the most heartless chapters in the history of racial prejudice.

The Belgians in their vast Congo domains concentrated upon the exploitation of the rich resources of that country, and after an initial stage of cruel oppression under the management set up by King Leopold II, devel-

[1] It would be hard to compress more history into a single sentence than has been done in this reference to Mau Mau, an outbreak of savagery in one of the more capable of the native tribes, the Kikuyu. The impression that this was merely a reaction to the dislocation caused by pioneering under British rule was belied by the fact that while Mau Mau terrorists killed some 30 whites, the number of natives killed was estimated to be 30,000 or even double that number. But it must be remembered that this includes the natives who were killed by the government troops — or police.

oped enlightened policies for the cultural and educational advance of the natives. These measures for social betterment were not accompanied, however, by the growth of self-government. The natives remained wards, well taken care of, but not sharing in the rights of political citizenship. This paternalism succeeded so long as the Congo economy prospered in the world mineral market, but when it slumped, thousands of native workers, were thrown out of work, just at the time when the African nationalist movement was sweeping over the adjoining French territories. Although from December 1957 the Belgian Government allowed municipal councils to be elected in the capital, Leopoldville. The political tension there was intensified by the prevalence of unemployment, and rioting broke out when a native meeting was prevented by the police. The number of casualties were not large but the incident was such that an emergency session of the Belgian Chamber of Representatives decided unanimously to send a commission of investigation.

The report of this commission, while lauding the loyalty of the native troops, called for a gradual evolution towards independence of the Congo. This action of the Chamber was hailed by King Baudouin as a definite recognition of the future independence of the Congo. "It is our firm resolution," said King Baudouin, "to lead the peoples of the Congo to independence in prosperity and peace, without petty recriminations but also without ill-considered haste. In a civilized world, independence must combine and guarantee freedom, order, and progress. We must give the Congo firm and well-balanced institutions, an experienced administration, a solid social economic and financial organization, and the intellectual and moral education of the people without which democracy is both a mockery and a tyranny. We are pledged to the realization of these basic aims. We intend to consecrate ourselves to them in enthusiastic, cordial, concerted efforts with our African peoples. Far from imposing purely European solutions on them, we intend to favour original adaptions in conformity with their character and the traditions which they cherish. For this purpose, a large measure of decentralization, combined with a rapid extension of the electoral system and the abandonment of all discrimination between black and white, will allow the development of the various regions to take place in various ways, in accordance with their geographical, cultural, and racial characteristics as well as their economic development. . . ."

The history of French African colonization has been touched upon above. But it is now completely overshadowed by the revolutionary remaking of the Republic and its "empire" by General de Gaulle. The vast French empire in tropical Africa was broken up and given the choice of independence or remaining as autonomous "republics" within the French "Community" (or commonwealth). It is a tribute to French rule that only one small African colony, Guinea, chose independence. Then, to the bewilderment of Paris and London, its Marxist-trained Premier proposed joining with the Republic of Ghana, which had stayed within the British Commonwealth, joining with Nkrumah, the "liberator" of Ghana, in an effort to create a great federation of native African states. The neighboring state of Liberia, however, the one free native state in West Africa, which had matured under American tutelage, refused to join in what its President called "an unrealistic and utopian" federation.

With the exception of Guinea, the whole vast equatorial empire of French Africa chose to remain inside the French community — Madagascar, tropical Gabun, the mineral-rich French Congo and the vast stretches of French Equatorial Africa, Senegal and the French Sudan along with the Islamic Republic of Mauritania with its walled and modern cities of Marrakesh, seat of the medieval Almoravides who once conquered Spain. The mere listing of these former colonies, now communities (or Departments) of France shows the extent of the French colonial revolution in Africa, but the greatest problem of all remained unsolved — Algeria. For it had been a part of France for a century with about one-seventh of its population French, who never fused with the Moslem and cherished a nationalism which rejected with fanatic zeal any lessening of French sovereignty. But with even greater fanaticism the Moslem fighters carried on their war of liberation. The statesmanship of de Gaulle prevented the French extremists from civil war in France itself, but in Algeria even his great prestige failed at first to force "freedom" on either faction — the French Algerians regarding it as a surrender to Moslem rule, the Moslems regarding it as a device for depriving them of full sovereignty. However, in the Senatorial elections in Algeria in June 1959, the "moderates," who supported de Gaulle's compromise measures, won out against both the European "ultras" demanding integration with France or Moslem extremists favoring immediate independence. It has long been evident that most Algerians are utterly weary of the cruel war which has continued for four and a half years. Nevertheless, the Algerian rebels did not vote, but went on fighting.

The goal which President de Gaulle has sought for Algeria has been an ideal one for both that troubled land and France itself. When he assumed office he stated that goal in terms which embody the finest ideals in the history of France, "what the government wants is for Algeria, through her trials and in spite of all delays, little by little to reveal, thanks to the action of all France, her essential self." It has been his consistent conviction that this "self" is a state of mind which will bring economic well-being and juridical equality to Algerians and Frenchmen alike.

This is statesmanship of high quality, for it embodies a constructive conception of freedom lifting that much misused word from the slogan of politics to a historical reality.

One thing is clear, the era of European imperialism in Africa is over. But if the process of partitioning the continent has come to an end, this is by no means true of racial problems which it has left — wherever the white man remains. While these problems remain to some extent wherever there are European settlements, they are most crucial in South Africa, both by the extent of the conflicts which have emerged, and their intensity. It must be remembered that the Dutch settlers held to the practice of slavery long after the British had abolished it, and that one of their reasons for the great trek into the Transvaal was their determination to keep slaves. Their racial prejudice did not prevent racial intermixture, but the Boers of today are forcing those of mixed blood into the category of the stateless Negroes.

Apartheid has been the official policy of the South African Government since 1948. It either forces them to migrate into their own reservations, where there is little chance for a livelihood, or crowds them into shanty-town city slums, unsanitary and disease-ridden, victims of a civilization in which they have almost no share. One of the most shocking incidents was the trial for high treason in Johannesburg of those who were protesting or refusing to accept this racial discrimination. Yet the situation as described by a competent, open-minded authority, Cornelius W. De Kiewiet, the South African-born president of Rochester University, is not wholly discouraging. Labor leaders have been able to organize successful strikes and boycotts in a number of cities. A shrewd leadership has learned that civil disobedience is more powerful than riots. When the natives were thrust into the alien environment of the white man's economy and legal system, the inevitable consequence was crime and political discontent, but the gulf between the native and European is now as wide as might be expected, for the native is deeply drawn into the framework of white society.

In an increasing degree the native population is being detribalized and Westernized, urbanized and industrialized, inextricably intertwined with the white community. . . . It is too simple to say that African natives are restless merely because they are oppressed. Africa has been going to school with the West, with its industrialism and its political thought. There is the story of a young Nigerian who enrolled at the famous London School of Economics in the days when Harold Laski and others of his persuasion were assailing the capitalist system and all of its works. After a term or two an acquaintance asked him how he was getting on. "Oh, famously," he replied, "I have learned what my grievances are." There is restlessness because there is enlightenment. Men see opportunities to which they were blind in their primitive state, and they reach after them because of the discernment the West has taught them. . . .

The noise of speeches on apartheid leads to the impression that the relations between the races can only be described in the language of breakdown and conflict. But these are manifestations of a deeper process of adjustment and assimilation. His dirty shack on the slums of Johannesburg, his pyorrhea instead of the fine teeth of his tribal days, his acquisition of the goods of white society by work or theft, his religious cults, the invasion of his language by new and strange expressions — all these and much more are the signs that the native has moved in large numbers well within the frontiers beyond which the laws of apartheid now wish to thrust him. That it is easy to demonstrate the powerful hold that the old beliefs and habits of the tribe still have upon him cannot disprove that he is a member of the total South African community, unripe as yet for its highest privileges and opportunities, weighed down by his illiteracy, a clumsy fit, demoralized and often frightened yet irreversibly a part of the total life of South Africa. The true problem of South Africa is to what degree and by what means the process of adjustment and integration is to be continued. It would be easier to drive the white man out of South Africa than the black man out of the society that the white man has created.[2]

[2] See Chapter by Cornelius W. De Kiewiet, entitled "Fears and Pressures in the Union of South Africa," in *Africa Today*, C. Grove Haines (ed.) (Baltimore: The Johns Hopkins Press, 1954), p. 213.

The contrast to the ruthless methods of the Boers was, until recently, to be found in the British colonies. These still cover most of Central Africa. The most important of them on the west coast is Nigeria, with a population of over thirty millions; those on the east coast are Uganda, Kenya, Tanganyika, and North and South Rhodesia — a territory as large as all Europe west of the Oder. In West Africa the enlightened colonial administration of Lord Lugard literally created Nigeria out of its many war-like tribes, and made it a land without a color bar. West of it, the Gold Coast and part of Togoland worked their way up to freedom in the newly created state of Ghana, which, in March, 1957, became a republic within the British Commonwealth. The problems of East Africa have proved more difficult, as racial discrimination was accentuated by the immigration of East Indians, mostly laborers. The optimism of Sir Philip Mitchell, which shines through his sympathetic statement quoted above, was not wholly shared by the Royal Commission of 1955, whose long and elaborate report was hailed as "marking rather than making a revolution in colonial history."[3] Taking this judgment at face value, one thinks back to that other great document which did transform British colonial history, the Durham Report on Canada. The two Reports are fundamentally different, however. The prime question in Africa was not the political issue of self government — although that is in the offing; it was the ownership of land. Tribal ownership, which Lugard left untouched and untouchable in Nigeria, had once been a constant cause of war between neighboring tribes, and an impediment to progress. The natives, however, were attached to it, as the basis of their traditional way of life, and the British recognized this paramount interest in such laws as the Native Land Trust Ordinance of 1930 which "set aside reserves for the native population forever." But agrarian reforms were not the widened conception of the Commonwealth of Nations. As this is the goal of British West Africa, where Ghana has been granted independence within the Commonwealth, we have here in the backward parts of the Dark Continent a beacon to light the path of freedom in the earliest stages of its long pioneering journey.

This short sketch of the recent history of Africa bears out its opening sentence, that the road to freedom has been a short one. But in that fact lies a clue to the future, which should serve as a warning to those Americans and others who tend to regard all colonial governments as remnants of oppressive regimes and fail to examine the experience in or the capacity for freedom of the native races. Commenting on this, Dr. De Kiewiet, from whose authoritative survey of African affairs we have quoted above, reminded us in an article in *Foreign Affairs* in April, 1955, that "American public opinion is very prone to analysis by slogan and platitude, and some of the slogans and platitudes commonly applied to colonial issues are simply shortcuts to misunderstanding." The slightness of the history of Africa south of the Sahara is the key to any understanding of the continent's present problems. The

[3] Cf. *A New Deal in East Africa*, by Philip Mason, Royal Institute of International Affairs, 1955.

land has always been poor and powerless, and politically and culturally empty. It is therefore "incapable of generating its own renaissance, as it is incapable of generating the capital needed to finance for all its peoples even the lowest standard of living that could still be called modern."

Dr. De Kiewiet finds that "in the cultural and historical emptiness of Africa there is, however, some potential advantage. There are no ancient and deep philosophic and religious contradictions such as divide India from China, or the Mediterranean shores of North Africa and the Levant from the neighboring European shore. Africa has its hates, of course, but they are local and tribal. New political and cultural combinations in Africa are entirely possible. That is why federation movements make sense.

"Africa has finally entered the stream of change that is coursing so strongly in most of the non-Western world, and therefore there is need to consider closely what will be the African territorial and political units in the future. Federation and consolidation can be important allies of effective modernization, for they produce a diversified framework on which viable states may be built. Parliamentary statutes and constitutional instruments such as created the Central African Federation are not an answer in themselves. They acquire meaning only to the extent that they have available the means and instruments of modern progress and can apply them to meet the needs of their populations."

From even this hurried survey it is clear that there has never been one Africa. To the diversity of native tribes the European exploiters and colonizers added their own diverse patterns of customs, languages and governments. The grant of independence, therefore, opens up old problems in a new setting, especially where industrialization has taken root, as in parts of South Africa, and economic grievances are joined with racial ones. The situation is one which lends itself to communist propaganda, for the base of tribal life is communal. Yet the pathway to industrial communism is somewhat uncertain in the African forests. Even Nkrumah, the creator of the independent state of Ghana, although a professed Marxist, has a fetish libation poured before he makes a political speech. If this is the accepted protocol for a former divinity student, graduate of Harvard and professed follower of Jefferson, who aspires to leadership throughout West Africa, political independence still leaves a wide gap to be filled before the achievement of that truer freedom which denies the tyranny of the taboo.

Yet this is the road which Africa is now entering, and no force can ever again hold it back.

CHAPTER XXIV

THE UNITED STATES OF AMERICA

W E MUST now turn from our wanderings to the history and problems of today in the United States of America.

The heroic age of American history was quick to surround with myth the lives of those who founded the Republic. Supreme above them all stood the figure of George Washington, and a kindly fancy surrounded his life, even in childhood, with appropriate legend. In course of time the other Founding Fathers — especially Jefferson and Hamilton — became Olympian figures as well. But in their own lifetime they did not escape calumny — not even Washington — for partisan strife ran high in the politics of the new nation, so high that it threatened at times to disrupt it, and continued until it finally culminated in the greatest civil war in history.

It was but natural and inevitable that the time should come when the critics would question this or that fact in the accumulated popular belief. But most of this criticism lies rather in the field of biography than of history, having to do with personal incidents which have little bearing upon national happenings. The historian has only a casual interest in controversies of this kind. His problem is a different one. It is to recover not merely the personalities of the past, which is the task of the biographer, but to recover as well the conditions of the time in which they lived, the society with which they were surrounded and their effect upon it, as well as its effect on them.

Historical characters have a three-fold existence: they live on as individuals in the relatively simple narratives of their lives; they live as well in the structure of the institutions which they have helped to create; and also, their influence survives through the statement of their own philosophy and ideals or the advice which they have given to others. The nation which honors them with continuing remembrance does not really distinguish between these three aspects or elements of personality. The thoughts of great men live after them in an independent life apart from the circumstance which first stimulated them into being, and then become attached to other times and circumstances, bearing still the name of their originator but with a changed meaning as the tone and accent changes from age to age. The historian, therefore, has a double task to trace the doctrines back to their source and make sure what they meant in terms of their own time, and then to note as well the historical influences that have come from even a misunderstanding of the original texts.

It is the first of these two tasks which is by far the most difficult — the tracing of doctrines back to their source and relearning them in terms of their own time. It calls for the historical imagination at its best, recreating those conditions and recalling to life the actors in the scene. Fortunately for the United States, the men who formulated the ideas at the founding of the Republic were individuals of such decisive character as to leave the impress of their personality on their own and succeeding generations. The historical imagination, therefore, is stimulated by contact with forceful individuals and moves in an atmosphere of reality when grappling with the political thought of the formative period. Real men are thinking real things, talking outright to each other in no uncertain terms. The political scene in which this drama is cast is equally clear-cut and definite: a group of colonies is taking shape in terms of nationhood, and the ideals which this movement expresses are current in the Old World as well.[1]

Time and again the far-flung fabric of federal union had to stand the strain of diverse interests: frontiersman against the "money power" of the eastern cities, the agrarian south against the industrialized north, and above all the irreconcilable conflict over slavery. In Washington's Farewell Address, so often quoted for its warning against foreign entanglements, the first in the list of the dangers confronting the republic was internal division and the possibility of disruption. "It is of infinite moment that you shall properly estimate the immense value of your national union to your collective and individual happiness . . . accustoming yourselves to think and speak of it as the palladium of your political safety and prosperity . . . indignantly frowning upon the first dawning of every attempt to alienate any portion of our country from the rest or to enfeeble the sacred ties which now link together the various parts."

The "first dawning" of disruptive plans was not long delayed. Aaron Burr's conspiracy to set up a state of his own in the Louisiana Territory was followed shortly by threats from New England that it might forcibly resist President Madison's Nonintercourse Act, by which he hoped to avoid war with England. But these were minor incidents in the current of American history. Much more serious was the cleavage between north and south as revealed in the fight over the tariff — which was bitterly opposed by the south. It rallied to the support of South Carolina's threat to nullify the federal law, while the north equally rallied behind Daniel Webster's famous call to the loyalty for which Washington had pleaded: "Liberty and Union, now and forever, one and inseparable."

Meanwhile, behind these debates in Congress, the power of the central

[1] The text of this chapter owes much to my book *The United States in History* (New York: Simon and Schuster, 1956).

government was quietly but firmly defined and established by the greatest of American jurists, John Marshall, who held the office of Chief Justice of the Supreme Court from 1801 to 1835 and made it "the living voice of the Constitution" both in strengthening the federal government and in safeguarding the rights and liberties of the citizens against abuse of its power. Never was politics more soundly based upon the rule of law; and never has history more clearly shown that the rule of law is not enough unless it guarantees the rights of all. And slaves were, in the great essentials of civilized life, outside the law. Here, then, lay the gravest issue of all.

By what now seems like an incredible contradiction, the nation which was dedicated from its birth to freedom was the last great repository of slavery in the civilized world. The explanation of this anomaly lies as far back in history as the discovery of America. For, although serfdom had disappeared in the advanced countries of Europe, Portugal and Spain, and then Elizabethan England, developed the African slave trade with the American colonies. The seamen of Elizabeth had no scruples against this inhuman commerce. Sir John Hawkins, knighted for his services against the Spanish Armada, began his career by robbing a Portuguese slaver and smuggling the slaves into Spanish colonies. The crest on his coat of arms was a chained Negro. Both by licensed companies and private adventurers the English slave trade reached such proportions that between 1680 and 1700 it exported to America over 300,000 slaves. Under Elizabeth all this trade was with the Spanish colonies, and it was not until 1620 that a Dutch ship brought the first cargo of slaves to Jamestown and sold them to the Virginia tobacco planters. As the slave market grew with the growth of the plantations in the southern English colonies, the merchants from Bristol were joined by those of Boston and New York, laying the basis for fortunes, some of which remain today. By 1783 over two million Negroes had been sold to American buyers. Although mere cupidity was some check upon the cruelty of this traffic — due to the value of the cargo — yet every ship was a death-house for the weakest of the slaves.

That this iniquitous trade was not only tolerated but shared in by the English colonists in America was not due to any special moral blindness on their part. It was commonly shared in Europe in the early eighteenth century, as is evidenced by the clause in the Treaty of Utrecht in 1714, one of the most important in European history, which stipulated that Spain should grant to Great Britain a contract (assiento) for supplying 4,500 Negroes annually to the Spanish colonies. In the course of the "century of enlightenment," however, the liberalizing movement of the philosophes in France led in protest against slavery, and in 1788, just before the Revolution, a Société des Amis des Noirs was founded for the abolition of both slavery and the slave trade. Lafayette was a member of this body and Mirabeau was an active sympathizer. In England the first to speak against slavery anywhere under the British flag were the Quakers, who in 1783 set up a society "for the relief and liberation of Negro slaves in the West Indies and for the discouragement of the slave trade on the coast of Africa." In 1789, the year of the opening of the French Revolution, William Wilberforce, "the Liberator," supported by his friend the Prime Minister, William Pitt, raised the issue in Parliament, which finally abolished the slave trade in 1807, thus enabling Great Britain at the Congress of Vienna to secure the assent of the other Powers to its abolition. Slavery itself still persisted in the colonies, especially the West Indies and South Africa, until the final Emancipation Act was passed in 1833, the year after the Reform Bill. It was a typically British act: recognizing that slaves were property, it compensated the owners, and to make the transition to a free society possible without too violent an economic revolution, kept the Negroes on an apprenticeship basis for seven years. Slavery officially ended in the whole of the empire on January 1, 1834.

The contrast between the history of emancipation in Europe and the tragic story of the United States is due not only to the relative slightness of the problem of slavery there compared with its magnitude here, but even more to the fact that the Constitution had by implication left the matter in the hands of the states. Although anti-slavery sentiment was shared by most of the framers of the Constitution, the opposition of South Carolina and Georgia prevented any reference to it in that document, except in the provision for the return of fugitive slaves from one state to another (Article IV, Section 2), a clause which later led to the Dred Scott decision, on the pathway to the Civil War. The Quaker, John Woolman, had led the first anti-slavery movement in the United States before the Revolution, and Benjamin Franklin joined in it after independence. Washington in his will provided for the emancipation of his own slaves, and he said to Jefferson that it was "among his first wishes" to see some plan adopted by which slavery in his country could be abolished by law. Hamilton and Madison denounced the principle of slavery; but no one had a remedy. Jefferson was more forthright in his comment on it, "I tremble for my country when I reflect that God is just." But the division of powers in a federal system of government left the states to deal with slavery within their boundaries as they saw fit. There were only two unquestioned fields where federal authority could deal with it — in the territories not yet formed into states, and in the control of foreign trade. In 1787 the North West Ordinance forbade slavery in the North West Territory, and in 1794 the slave traffic was forbidden with foreign countries.

The long struggle over the extension of slavery to the Louisiana Purchase and beyond was the fundamental political issue of United States history for the next half-century. The south, with its great estates, could only keep its balance of power with the growing industries of the north if it were allowed to expand as the lands opened up across the Mississippi. To head off the threatening conflict of interests between the free-soilers and slaveowners, in the Compromise of 1820 Missouri was admitted as a slave-owning state to balance the entry of Maine, while slavery was prohibited in the Louisiana Purchase north of Missouri's southern boundary. John Quincy Adams wrote in his diary, "I take it for granted that the present question is a mere preamble, a title page to a great tragic volume." The day of decision was postponed, but the issue grew as the nation expanded, and the territory taken from Mexico had to be brought into balance by the Compromise of 1850. It was passed by Congress after the greatest debates in its history, by the greatest debaters, John Calhoun, Henry Clay, and Daniel Webster, whose voices were to be heard no more, while the Fugitive Slave Law stirred the embers of conflict into flames in the north. The effort of Stephen Douglas to compromise once more by squatter sovereignty was no solution, and the final word was spoken by Abraham Lincoln in 1858: "A house divided against itself cannot stand. I believe this government cannot permanently endure half slave and half free."

Nevertheless, the secession movement, led at first by South Carolina, swept over the states of the Deep South, where "cotton was king" and slavery a basic fact in economic life. In February 1861 delegates of these states met in Montgomery, Alabama, and formed a provisional government for the "Confederate States of America." The final constitution, adopted in March, was largely copied from the constitution of the United States, only expressly maintaining state sovereignty. The border states, of which the most important was Virginia, hesitated to join, but did so when the Federal Government called on them for troops to suppress the rebellion.

Lincoln's Inaugural Address gave the country the measure of the man to whom its destinies were entrusted in the hour of crisis. He denied any thought of disturbing the institutions of the south, but declared that he must uphold the laws of the nation. "In your hands, my dissatisfied fellow-countrymen, not in mine, is the momentous issue of civil war. . . . You have no oath registered in heaven to destroy the government, while I have the most solemn one to 'preserve, protect and defend it.'" The common memories of the north and south were "mystic chords stretching from every battlefield and patriot grave to every living heart and hearthstone all over this broad land." But before dawn on April 12, 1861, the Confederates at Charleston fired on Fort Sumter in its harbor and forced its surrender the next day. From that hour until the final scene of Lee's surrender at Appomattox, the country suffered four years of the terrible scourges of civil war.

This was not the first war in which free men fought over the meaning of freedom, but in the vastness and desperate character of the conflict it outranged all others previous to it. Our interest here, however, is not in the military history but in the fact that the victory of the north not only brought emancipation of the slaves but placed new and far-reaching responsibilities on the government of the federal republic. The Confederacy had carried the States' Rights doctrine to the point of national disruption. Now the nation had decided, by the terrible arbitrament of war, that its sovereignty extended over the whole range of freedom. This was expressed, once and for all, in the immortal words of Lincoln's Gettysburg address: "that this nation, under God, shall have a new birth of freedom — and that government of the people, by the people, for the people, shall not perish from the earth." The "new birth of freedom" thus interpreted meant more than freedom for the slaves. The "unfinished task" for which those honored dead had given "the last full measure of devotion" was much more than that; it was the perfecting of a federal republic so that all its varied elements would have a common goal, linking freedom and responsibility, "with charity for all and malice toward none." These words from Lincoln's second Inaugural Address give Lincoln's own interpretation of democratic freedom. It was for democracy as well as freedom that the war was fought.

Although the war put an end to slavery, Lincoln's Emancipation Proclamation was limited to slaves in those states which were "in rebellion against the United States" and was applied as military success permitted. It was not until the war was over that Congress passed the Thirteenth Amendment to the Constitution, providing that "Neither slavery nor involuntary servitude, except as a punishment for crime whereof the party shall have been duly convicted, shall exist in the United States or any place subject to its jurisdiction." This reads more like a great principle of law than a provision for practical application. To bring it down from generalities that thundered without an accompanying stroke of lightning, the Fourteenth Amendment was passed three years later, and its ratification by the secessionist states was made a condition of their readmission to the Union. Its opening paragraph, combined with the Fifteenth Amendment of two years later (1870) constitute the strongest guarantee against racial and political injustice in any document in the history of freedom. Amendment Fourteen provides that:

All persons born or naturalized in the United States, and subject to the jurisdiction thereof, are citizens of the United States and of the States wherein they reside. No State shall make or enforce any law which shall abridge the privileges or immunities of citizens of the United States; nor shall any State deprive any person of life, liberty, or property, without due process of law; nor deny to any person within its jurisdiction the equal protection of the laws.

And the Fifteenth Amendment provides that:

The rights of the citizens of the United States to vote shall not be denied or abridged by the United States, or by any State, on account of race, color or previous condition of servitude.

These three amendments to the Constitution constituted a charter of liberty for the slaves and their children. But it was a liberty for which they were in no way prepared — the privilege and responsibility of citizenship in a republic, which until then had been as alien to them as though it had been a foreign land. Nor were the emancipated Negroes given any example of what that freedom meant, as they watched the abuse of it in the high-handed reconstruction of the south, which lasted for a decade and more and deepened the cleavage between North and South. The South showed little opposition to the first phase of Northern rule, that by generals of the occupying army, for the war had made it familiar with military necessities. But this was followed by the imposition of rule by "carpetbag" politicians, often corrupt and seldom representative of the best traditions of American politics. Although the North as a whole was not vindictive in its treatment of the South, the extremists won out in Congress and it was they who forced along the Fourteenth and Fifteenth Amendments, more in reprisal against the south than with regard to the preparedness of the Negroes for citizenship. Angered by their helplessness, the southern whites took the law into their own hands in the Ku Klux Klan and other vigilante movements.

It took more than two generations for the south to escape from the anarchy and sporadic incidents of terror, such as the lynching of Negroes, which continued in this aftermath of the war. Yet this era was already passing when the twentieth century raised new ones, owing to the surprising advances made by the Negroes in the face of many handicaps. The new issues have lost even any lingering echoes of slavery, but arise from the problem of racial integration, which we have already treated in the chapter on "New Aspects of Freedom."

We return now to the normal life and development in the nineteenth century United States.

From Laissez Faire *to the New Freedom*

Nowhere, not even in the England of the Industrial Revolution, was the principle of *laissez faire* — or, in the American idiom, "rugged individualism" — more generally accepted than in the United States. This was especially the case while there were still farms to open on the prairies, towns to be created and railroads to be built to link the country in a national economy. So strong was this principle in the minds of the people that the Bill of Rights was almost never invoked as the palladium of liberty — not until after a new era dawned at the close of the nineteenth century, when the United States began to lead the world in inventions and to apply those of Europe to change the conditions of life not only in the new industrial cities, but on the farms as well. Nowhere else did the static mold of agricultural society break-down so rapidly under the dynamic impact of the machine age as in the country of farmers whom Jefferson called "the Chosen People of God," for whom he foretold that there would be room enough for "the hundredth and thousandth generation."

But within two generations after Jefferson's death manufacturers were already producing three times the value of the products of the farms, and it was an industrialized north that won the Civil War. But the war that saved the Union left a legacy of economic ruthlessness and corruption less evident in the exhausted south than in the victorious north, where "rugged individualism" had free play along the railroads of the west and in the immigrant-filled cities of the east. The era of southern "reconstruction" was also that of the new capitalism, still mainly centered in the eastern states, with money yielding usury rates, and tariffs continuing after the war for protection against foreign competition. The decline in the moral stature of the fast-growing states was evidenced by the lowered standards, which made success rather than integrity a widely accepted standard in business, especially in big business. Unscrupulous masters of capital carried on warfare — not always purely economic — against competitors, almost like the feudal barons before the national state put an end to this anarchy.

The new baronies were the "trusts," corporations for controlling not only industries but the markets for their products as well, creating monopolies, which justified their ruthlessness by their success. Standard Oil claimed that its elimination of backward competitors was in the public interest; it was certainly in the interests of the owners of corporate stock. The American steel furnaces, which by 1900 were producing as much steel as Great Britain and Germany combined, brought fabulous wealth to investing capitalists. But the "Triumphant Democracy" which Andrew Carnegie hailed in this new combination of science and management over the less competent or less fortunate ironmasters, brought a new industrial proletariat into existence, a group for whom the "land of unlimited opportunity" became more and more limited, as contract labor from Europe poured into the slums of cities and along the hill-slopes by the mines.

The curtain was going down on the first act of the great American drama. The day's work, the most important thing in the lives of most people, was being taken over from them in ways outside their control. Then the curtain began to rise on Act II, in which the actors — the American people themselves — undertook to recover their birthright of freedom. But it was not the kind of freedom they were accustomed to, handed down in the precepts of the past, personal insistence on each man's rights in the narrow setting of individual lives, but a new freedom based on closer integration in the social life not only of the community, but of the nation as a whole.

The new era was not to recover the title deeds of an outworn past, but to write new ones for an ever changing future.

The New Freedom

The dawn of the new industrial age was a troubled one as intrenched capitalism imposed an economic tyranny on labor,[2] which, feeling that it had no redress in legislation or the courts, turned to the only weapon left: the strike. This universal weapon of unarmed labor had been used before, but only after the Civil War did it become a threat to national peace and security, both on the part of the strikers and that of the resort to force and even bloodshed on the part of the employers backed by the State.

The first national conflict was the railroad strike of 1877, when wages were cut below a decent living standard. The incipient rebellion, which flared up in most cities dependent on railways for supplies, was finally suppressed by militia or federal troops. And the owners, blind to their own responsibility, persuaded public opinion that the strike had been fomented by foreign agitators, an ominous forecast of similar stifling of social and national conscience in the future.

Turbulent years of industrial strife followed — the Homestead Steel plant

[2] The hours of labor were excessive, twelve a day in a seven-day week in the steel industry (until 1923), sixty to eighty-four a week in textiles, eighty-four to one hundred or more in New York bakeries and over seventy for trainmen. Wages of unskilled workers were less than ten dollars a week and of skilled workers rarely more than twenty; while women earned as low as $3.91 in Richmond and as high as $6.91 in San Francisco.

near Pittsburg and the Pullman works near Chicago were battlefields where men died for economic justice and freedom because they knew no other way to win it. By 1898, however, when the President of the Pennsylvania Railroad defied the United Mine Workers' strike by claiming that "God in his infinite wisdom had given (to the owners) the property interests of the country," public opinion could not stomach such "un-American" feudalism, and President Theodore Roosevelt had public opinion behind him when he threatened to take over the mines, and so enabled the miners to gain their demand for arbitration.

The years which produced the trusts thus became years of challenge to the American conscience. Its awakening was due less to the appeals of labor leaders than to the writings of a galaxy of social reformers whose place in the history of justice and freedom is only a little lower than that of the *philosophes* who roused France to the faults of its social system in the eighteenth century. The chief organ of these "muckrakers," as Theodore Roosevelt called them, was *McClure's* magazine, but it was a new day in journalism when the criticism of American life was based on such sound scholarship as Ida Tarbell's great series of articles on Abraham Lincoln, the same kind of research as she put into her classic *History of the Standard Oil Company,* telling how the competitors were driven to the wall by the corrupt use of public utilities by the new trust. Lincoln Steffens struck behind economic wrongs to corruption in local government in his *Shame of the Cities,* while Ray Stannard Baker and others covered the whole front. The country was roused to a keen sense of responsibility for conditions which everyone — or nearly everyone — felt were "un-American." In *The Jungle* Upton Sinclair described the defenseless condition of immigrant labor, a book which especially stirred President Roosevelt.

Opposition to the trusts remained a keynote of reform. It came in the first instance, not only from labor, but from the business world as well, based as it was on competition, and from public opinion generally. From the first years of the Republic, and even before it, there had always been a stalwart opposition, especially in farm and country, against "money power." It showed itself in the opposition to the "bank" for stabilization of national finance. The protests of the farmers of the middle west against "Wall Street" were intensified by the fact that the holders of mortgages on their farms were "soulless corporations."

The Populist Movement, mostly drawn from the Democratic party, or at least from those bred in the Jeffersonian tradition, finally found an eloquent voice in William Jennings Bryan, whose address at the Democratic Convention of 1896, while narrowly directed to free silver, was really a proclamation of the independence of farming and middle class Americans from the dominance of big business. "I come to speak to you in defense of a cause as holy as the cause of liberty — the cause of humanity. . . . We say to you that you have made the definition of a business man too limited in its application. The man who is employed for wages is as much a business man as his employer. . . . We have petitioned and our petitions have been scorned;

we have entreated and our entreaties have been disregarded; we have begged and they have mocked when our calamity came. We beg no longer; we entreat no more; we petition no more. We defy them." The ringing peroration against the gold standard: "You shall not press down upon the brow of labor this crown of thorns; you shall not crucify mankind upon a cross of gold" — while it held the convention spellbound, voiced only a passing phase of social discontent, compared with the demand for a redress of economic grievances.

That these grievances were real was proved by the long history of the efforts to get rid of them. Bryan's campaigns in the Democratic party through the next twelve years were matched by Theodore Roosevelt's "trust-busting" reforms and the religious fervor of his Progressive Movement. In Congress, the strongest voice of protest was that of Senator Robert La Follette, whose attacks upon the controlling interests in lumbering and railroading in Wisconsin drew national attention to that state in the way Bryce said that state politics could be laboratories for the nation, and gave him a leading place among the reformers in Washington. It was a long reach from securing justice for the farmers of the middle west to the La Follette Seaman's Act, but nowhere was freedom more violated than in the two-shift regime of ship-hands at sea. Not only for Americans but for competitors in other lands, the three-shift day made life more endurable on all the seven seas, abolished the crime of desertion in the Merchant Marine and "elevated the seamen for the first time to the full status of free men."[3]

It was this question of the length of the working day which, along with the demand for better wages, was the heart of the program of the American Federation of Labor from the time of its foundation by Samuel Gompers in 1886. An eight hour day and a six-day week was all that the A.F.L. could hope for, and even that was gained only after years of struggle. The twelve-hour day, or longer, which was the rule of the nineteenth century, left little freedom to enjoy — or even see — the world. From whistle-blow at six in the morning, during all the winter months, the worker never saw the daylight of the outside world. For the economists, his labor was a property which he sold to make a living. But Gompers got the United States to deny this in what he called "Labor's Magna Carta," the insertion in the Clayton Anti-Trust Act of 1914 of the phrase "the labor of human beings is not a commodity or an article of commerce." President Wilson's comment on signing the Clayton Act was that: "Justice has been done to the laborer. His labor is no longer to be regarded as if it was merely an inanimate article of commerce disconnected with the fortunes and happiness of a human being to be dealt with as an object of sale and barter. But that, great as it is, is hardly more than the natural and inevitable corollary of a law whose object is industrial freedom and initiative as against any kind of private domain."

But this item of national legislation hardly touched the real problem of economic justice in labor problems, which lay within the jurisdiction of the

[3] S. E. Morison and H. S. Commager, *The Growth of the American Republic* (1937), Vol. II, p. 168. New York: Oxford University Press, 1951.

states, with the one exception, in a Constitutional amendment in 1924, which gave Congress "the power to regulate and prohibit the labor of persons under eighteen years of age." The constitutional problem involved was one that can never be wholly solved in a federal system of government, but must be worked out by constant adjustment as the nation grows increasingly welded closer together by economic forces.

The prime purpose of a federal system is the preservation of local liberties within the national framework, leaving the states or local authorities to deal with those questions which lie close to the individual lives and interests of the citizens and which vary with local circumstances and ways of life. This meant that during the long period of predominantly agricultural economy, when each section of the country had to rely upon itself for essentials, most law-making in economic and social matters, including education, started within the state and was jealously preserved against any tendency toward federal "intervention." The boundary between national and local spheres of government was hard to draw. The issue of slavery was but the greatest one of many which kept arising as the nation grew more unified. On the whole, free economy was left to local regulation. This meant, in the self-reliant communities making their own way in the world, only that minimum of regulation which was necessary to keep things going on the line and under the spur of individual initiative.

When, therefore, the new social conscience of the country found expression in politics — in sections of both political parties — it marked a vital turning point in the history of the United States. It inaugurated an era — long and troubled — of emancipation from the tyranny of uncontrolled capitalism, which ultimately culminated in a whole series of acts by which the Federal Government built up a system of social legislation reaching to every citizen everywhere. If, as we have maintained time and time again throughout this study, freedom is but another name for social justice, this chapter of United States history is one of the most important in this whole survey.

The "Square Deal" of Theodore Roosevelt and the Progressive Wing of the Republican Party which followed him — meaning a four-square attitude of government to both capital and labor — seemed to conservatives to be a denial of the fundamental principles of competition in a free society. Under President Taft they held back the tide of social legislation, which had lagged almost half a century behind that of Germany under Bismarck. Then came Woodrow Wilson. If the World War had not come in 1914, he would have been known in history, not as an international leader against militarism on the fields of France and in the creation of the League of Nations, but as a leader in political and economic reform at home. In his first inaugural address to Congress in 1913, there was not a word on foreign affairs, but a program of constructive reform to secure a new freedom for the common man.

This inaugural address is one of the great state papers of American history, standing in the same high rank as Jefferson's First and Lincoln's Second Inaugural. Nowhere else in all the rich literature which this new life — this *vita nuova* — of the United States produced, is there a clearer vision of its meaning or a more moving statement of its mission:

We have been refreshed by a new insight into our own life.

We see that in many things that life is very great. It is incomparably great in its material aspects, in its body of wealth, in the diversity and sweep of its energy, in the industries which have been conceived and built up by the genius of individual men and the limitless enterprise of groups of men. It is great, also, very great, in its moral force. . . .

We have built up a great system of government which has stood through a long age as in many respects a model for those who seek to set liberty upon foundations that will endure against fortuitous change, against storm and accident. Our life contains every great thing and contains it in rich abundance.

But the evil has come with the good and much fine gold has been corroded. . . . We have been proud of our industrial achievements, but we have not hitherto stopped thoughtfully enough to count the human cost, the cost of lives snuffed out, of energies overtaxed and broken, the fearful physical and spiritual cost to the men and women and children upon whom the dead weight and burden of it all has fallen pitilessly the years through. The groans and agony of it all had not yet reached our ears, the solemn, moving undertone of our life, coming up from output of the mines and factories and out of every home where the struggle had its intimate and familiar seat. . . .

At last a vision has been vouchsafed us of our life as a whole. We see the bad with the good, the debased and decadent with the sound and vital. With this vision we approach new affairs. Our duty is to cleanse, to reconsider, to restore, to correct the evil without impairing the good, to purify and humanize every process of our common life without weakening or sentimentalizing it. There has been something crude and heartless and unfeeling in our haste to succeed and be great. Our thought has been "Let every man look out for himself, let every nation look out for itself," while we reared giant machinery which made it impossible that any but those who stood at the levers of control should have a chance to look out for themselves. . . .

We have come now to the sober second thought. The scales of heedlessness have fallen from our eyes. We have made up our minds to square every process of our national life again with the standards we so proudly set up at the beginning and have always carried at our hearts. Our work is a work of restoration. . . .

This is the high enterprise of today: to lift everything that concerns our life as a nation to the light that shines from the hearth fire of every man's conscience and vision of the right. . . .

The nation has been deeply stirred, stirred by a solemn passion, stirred by the knowledge of wrong, of ideals lost, of government too often debauched and made an instrument of evil. The feelings with which we face this new age of right and opportunity sweep across our heartstrings like some air out of God's own Presence, where justice and mercy are reconciled and the judge and the brother are one. We know our task to be no mere task of politics but a task which will search us through and through, whether we be able to understand our time and the need of our people, whether we be indeed their spokesmen and interpreters, whether we have the pure heart to comprehend and the rectified will to choose our high course of action.

The "high course of action" was not to be a revolution but a series of reforms adopted by a government responsive to an enlightened public opinion. Too often "the great Government we loved has been made use of for private and selfish purposes and those who used it had forgotten the people," but the recovery of the title deeds to citizenship in a free republic must come by deliberate reforms. The things which ought to be altered were listed: a tariff which makes the Government a facile instrument in the hands of private interests (reformed in the Underwood Tariff); a banking and currency system perfectly adapted to concentrating cash and restricting credits (reformed by the Federal Reserve System); control of the trusts without denying the right of labor to combine (The Clayton Anti-Trust Act of 1914); control of interstate commerce to prevent unfair competition (The Federal Trade Commission Act); aid to the farmer (by a federal farm loan act), and other similar legislation, greater in scope and more important than the legislation of any president since Lincoln.

It was when this new freedom was being realized that its leader found himself drawn into the war in Europe. At its outbreak in 1914, President Wilson invoked the historic American doctrine of neutrality, but carried it a stage farther than ever before. "The United States must be neutral in fact as well as in name during these days that are to try men's souls. We must be impartial in thought as well as in action, must put a curb on our sentiments as well as upon every transaction that might be construed as a preference of one party to the struggle before another." This call to absolute, personal neutrality was not based on moral indifferences to the issues of the war, but on a belief, widely shared throughout the country, that both sides in the conflict were imperialistic.

After two years of war, however, Wilson came to the conclusion that "there is a deeper thing than even the equality of right among organized nations. No peace can last, or ought to last, which does not recognize and accept the principle that governments derive all their just powers from the consent of the governed." There must be a "peace without victory"; and it should be made secure "by the organized major force of mankind." This was in January, 1917; by April he called on Congress to declare war on Germany as the only way to preserve the "rights of nations great and small and the privileges of men everywhere to choose their way of life and obedience. The world must be made safe for democracy. Its peace must be planted upon the tested foundations of political liberty."

This most compelling of all calls to war ended on a note of tragedy, but also one of high resolve:

It is a fearful thing to lead this nation into war, into the most terrible and disastrous of all wars, civilization itself seeming to be in the balance. But the right is more precious than peace, and we shall fight for the things which we have always carried nearest in our hearts. . . . — for democracy, for the right of those who submit to authority to have a voice in their own governments, for the rights and liberties of small nations, for a universal dominion of right by such a concert of free peoples as shall bring peace and safety to all nations and make the world itself at last free. To such a task we can dedicate our lives and fortunes, everything that we are and everything that we have, with pride of those who know that the day has come when America is privileged to spend her blood and her might for the principles that gave her birth and the peace which she has treasured. God helping her, she can do no other.

As stirring as this call for a crusade for democracy and freedom was, the country was not ready for such high emprise. Although loyalty to the flag filled up the draft of civilian soldiers in sections of the country dominated by isolationist sentiment, yet the issues of war were not understood by any but a minority and, in spite of government propaganda, the great ideals of

1917 were tarnished in two years of deadly conflict by popular reversion to the one mood which wars impose on a people, the single aim of victory. It was a stern mood of denunciation of the barbarities of "the Hun," and suppression of suspected disloyalty by an Espionage Act and a Sedition Act made the champion of freedom abroad its oppressor at home. Not only were "conscientious objectors" sent to prison — over four hundred of them — but "witch-hunters" informed on independent-minded citizens who were not carried away by war hysteria. While a national Board of Historians warned their colleagues throughout the country not to write anything of which they would be ashamed ten years after the war was over, such objectivity was little observed. No one saw this trend more clearly than Wilson, realizing that war meant "force to the utmost, force without stint or limit,"[4] and that the result would be that "the spirit of ruthless brutality will enter into the very fibre of our national life, infecting Congress, the courts, the policeman on the beat, the man on the street."[5]

Under these pressures the new freedom ceased to advance along the pathway of reform. Its leaders saw from the very entry into the war that this would be the result, and, although accepting Wilson's call — sometimes literally in tears — tended to become isolationists in the post-war years, giving full vent to sentimental pacifism, which refused responsibilities abroad. Thus the 1920's became a dark era of American liberalism. While America slept, dreaming the golden dream of unexampled prosperity, selling its surpluses in the world market gutted by the war, militarism took new and more sinister form under Hitler and Mussolini, and communism emerged for the first time as a sovereign force among the nations.

At last, through the darkness of a second world war and the murk of a cold war, the age-long issue of Marathon, Runnymede and Yorktown, that of freedom, stood out clearly in its world-wide setting as the living embodiment of peace against militarism, of justice against exploitation, of individual and social security against despotism. It was, or should be, equally clear that this far goal could not be reached by war, nor forced upon nations still unaware that its inherent elements are peace and justice. It also had to be embodied in an international organization not thwarted in its purpose nor falsified in its design by the anarchy of unlimited national sovereignties.

The New Deal

For ten years after World War I it seemed as though it had been immensely profitable for the United States. The gutted markets of devastated lands were filled with American goods, and, though the war debts of its allies, like the reparations due them from their late enemies, remained largely unpaid, American capital went abroad to aid in world recovery. As in the period after the Civil War, rugged individualism reigned in the busi-

[4] Address at Baltimore, April 6, 1918.
[5] Interview with Frank Cobb, editor of The World, in William Allen White's Woodrow Wilson. (Boston and New York: Houghton-Mifflin Co., 1925.)

ness of government as in private business. The "normalcy" of Harding and Coolidge seemed under Hoover to have reached the climax of a golden age when spectacular fortunes were made overnight in the confidence that the new industrialism would know no limits. The bankruptcy of Germany and Austria and the devaluation of the French franc were ominous signs that the cost of the greatest war in history would have to be liquidated. But still the "economic vacuum" which the war had created in Continental Europe stimulated mass production of factory and farm in the United States until ten years after the war, when, suddenly, in October, 1929, the gleaming structure of credit on which prosperity rested, crashed, carrying with it most of the economy of the nation. Hundreds of thousands of families, the well-to-do along with the wage-earners, lost their homes and all their savings, and as the crisis continued, by 1932 over twelve million were hopelessly out of work. By the time the depression ended, some ten years later, it had cut the national income by half.

It is not the extent of the national catastrophe which concerns us here, but its effects on the national character and outlook of the American people. The permanent result was political, the opening of a new chapter in the history of freedom in America. The "New Deal" which Franklin Roosevelt promised the country as he swept into power in the election of 1932, with a majority of seven million votes, was a revolution in the eyes of those who, like President Hoover, still cherished the *laissez-faire* philosophy as the one valid principle of "the American way of life," and history will almost certainly agree. Holding firmly to the conviction that for politics to get into business would endanger the liberty of the citizen by interfering in his private affairs, Hoover had failed to see that the depression was not a normal part of the business cycle in which hard times alternated with prosperity, but a delayed consequence of World War I, accentuated by nationalist legislation hampering freedom of trade. He was right, however, in his apprehension that an extension of governmental powers for an emergency would have long range consequences in both the economics and politics of the United States.

The Republican Party, which had been the traditional spokesman for federal sovereignty, now held that the problems of economic and social welfare were the responsibility of local authorities or private charity. The Democrats, the old party of States' Rights, became the advocate of the new nationalism, which the New Deal carried far beyond anything dreamed of by Theodore Roosevelt or Woodrow Wilson, to whose nineteenth-century liberalism the idea of a "welfare state" was anathema. Both the Square Deal and the New Freedom had been inherently conservative, in spite of their apparent radicalism. They were designed to make the old freedom work, strengthening it by redress of evils and the elimination of corruption. They had no thought of creating a welfare state; one had to look to Europe to see that development, and few Americans cared to see it.

Great Britain, suffering heavily in two world wars, met equally desperate unemployment by public works, strict control of banking, heavy income taxes on those able to pay and a whole program of economic planning. The British people were restive under the strain of these measures, but as a politically mature people, their national solidarity held, and Conservative opposition, while watchful and keen, interpreted their ancient freedoms in terms of social justice and welfare. This, the opponents of the New Deal were hardly prepared to do, because the whole ghastly episode of the great depression still seemed too much of an exception to American conditions of life to be made a starting point for a really new regime. Roosevelt, however, from the very first, held that relief measures offered no solution to the problem of unemployment, and insisted that they should be followed by a permanent system of social security.

The full force of the economic revolution was concentrated in the National Recovery Act of June, 1933, which has been described as "in some respects the most remarkable law passed by an American Congress.[6] It had been preceded by various measures, reaching from emergency farm relief to the creation of the Tennessee Valley Authority and the abandonment of the gold standard. But the National Recovery Act covered the entire industrial structure of the country, giving federal control by codes drawn up and administered by New Deal officials or those collaborating with them. It was not surprising that the Supreme Court, by unanimous vote, invalidated the code system on the ground that federal regulation of wages and hours of labor would call for control of "the processes of production and distribution that enter into cost," and "override the authority of the States to deal with problems arising from labor conditions in their internal commerce." As a result of this action by the Supreme Court, the President terminated the National Recovery Act, but its program of finding jobs, increasing wages, shortening the day's work, ending child labor, and guaranteeing collective bargaining, was the basis of the Wagner-Connery Act of 1935, creating a permanent Labor Relations Board. The Fair Standards Act "put a ceiling over hours and a floor under wages," fixing forty hours a week as standard, and a minimum wage of forty cents an hour.

The greatest achievement, however, was the Social Security Act of 1935, providing old age pensions and unemployment insurance, payments to the blind, dependent mothers and children, and a wide range of benefits, thus bringing the United States for the first time in line with European social legislation. The country which recovered from the Great Depression was no longer the same, and its government, with a vast bureaucracy to control its economy was utterly unlike anything in its past. Opposition developed, voicing the fear that the vital principles of American freedom, self-reliance and distrust of power in high places were being undermined. Yet when the scaffolding of emergency measures was removed, the social guarantees of freedom from want remained and in the following years it was the Republican Party which extended social insurance, in 1955, twenty years after its enactment.

[6] Henry Steele Commager, *Documents in American History*, New York: Appleton-Century-Crofts, 1958.

Franklin Roosevelt's statesmanship was that of a man of action rather than a political philosopher, but he was gifted with political intuition, and the keynote which he gave to the New Deal had a deep and poignant meaning at a time when well-to-do citizens were reduced to beggary. It was "freedom from want." The phrase does not occur in his first inaugural, which concentrated on the first obstacle to recovery: fear. But the want was sketched in short, grim paragraphs. "The withered leave of industrial enterprise lie on every side; farmers have no markets for their produce; the savings of many years in thousands of families are gone. More important, a host of unemployed face the grim problems of existence, and an equally great number toil with little return." Yet, "compared with the perils which our forefathers conquered because they were not afraid, we still have much to be thankful for. . . . Plenty is at our doorstep, but a generous use of it languishes in the very sight of supply. Primarily this is because our rulers of the exchange of mankind's goods have failed. . . . True they have tried, but their efforts have been cast in the pattern of an outworn tradition. . . . The measure of the restoration lies in the extent to which we can apply social values more than monetary profit. . . . These dark days will be worth all they have cost us if they teach us that our true destiny is not to be ministered unto but to minister to ourselves and our fellow-men."

Sobered and matured by adversity, the county realized that its freedom must be protected against the anarchy of unrestricted individualism and that the government must take measures to guarantee a national security which would make "freedom from want" a reality.

World War II

In 1931, when the United States was in the depth of the great depression and Great Britain was going off the gold standard, the first step toward a second world war was taken by Japan in its seizure of Manchuria, followed by the invasion of northern China and Japan's withdrawal from the League of Nations when faced with censure by it. The United States, not being a League member, could only offer it moral support, stating that it would "endeavor to reinforce what the League does."

But even if it had been a member, it could hardly have taken effective measures to stop war. Japan had timed its stroke well. The Great Depression in the United States and Great Britain gave it its opportunity for undeterred conquest. Then Italy invaded Ethiopia, Germany tore up the Treaty of Locarno, fortified the demilitarized Rhineland, occupied Austria, dismembered Czechoslovakia, and finally in league with Stalin, overran Poland. Great Britain and France then saw the legions of Hitler turning west, and all Europe was in flames. Alliance with Japan threw the Axis Powers into a world-wide conspiracy against peace and freedom.

Never were the liberties of the modern world so threatened with extinction as in World War II. The ruthless tyranny of Nazi Germany, with its millions of victims at home and in the conquered territories, was matched only in less degree by its allies. Their victories threatened to envelop the free nations of western Europe in a web of oppression and to rebuild Asia into a vast military empire. While the American people were horrified at the atrocities and disturbed by the military might of the Axis Powers, they did not realize that the menace to the freedom of the world menaced their own freedom as well. Yet the isolationist sentiment, which bound the country to neutrality in case of war between other nations, did not take the extreme form which Woodrow Wilson had given it at the outbreak of World War I — neutrality in thought as well as in action. Already, in 1938, the German aggression drew from Roosevelt the warning that "even a neutral cannot be asked to close his mind or his conscience."

But the pacifist reaction after World War I had indiscriminately grouped all European nations as militarist and blamed the late allies for having misled the United States into a war which settled nothing. And though both the President and his Secretary of State, Cordell Hull, early became convinced that the aggression of the Axis Powers might lead to attack on the United States, the most that Congress would do was to amend the neutrality laws to permit belligerents to buy munitions at their own risk. It was not until June, 1940, that the country became genuinely alarmed. France had been stricken to the heart, the Germans were in Paris, the British army had been cut off from its retreat and was saved only by the miracle of Dunkirk; Mussolini had declared war to share in the Nazi spoils of victory. In an address at the University of Virginia, Roosevelt laid bare the dread realities of the hour and at last there was almost universal approval of his warning that it was a delusion to imagine that the United States can become "a lone island in a world dominated by the philosophy of force."

Such an island may be the dream of those who still talk and vote as isolationists. Such an island represents to me and to the overwhelming majority of Americans today a helpless nightmare, the helpless nightmare of a people without freedom. Yes, the nightmare of a people lodged in prison, handcuffed, hungry and fed through bars from day to day by the contemptuous, unpitying masters of other continents. . . .

Overwhelmingly we, as a nation, and this applies to other American nations, are convinced that military and naval victory for the gods of force and hate would endanger the institutions of democracy in the western world. . . .

Once more the future of the nations is at stake. We need not, and we will not, in any way, abandon our continuing efforts to make democracy work within our own borders. We insist on the need for vast improvements in our social and economic life. . . . The program unfolds swiftly and into that program will fit the responsibility of every man and woman in the land to preserve our heritage in days of peace.

I call for effort, courage, sacrifice, devotion. Granting the love of freedom, all of these are possible.

And the love of freedom is still fierce, still steady in the nation today.

With the fall of France, Great Britain remained the only bastion of freedom in western Europe, hard pressed in the air and at sea. The air battles were won in spite of terrible devastation. Churchill voiced the judgment of the world and history in his tribute to the British airmen: "Never have so many owed so much to so few." But the very life of Britain depended on its overseas trade, and to protect it, in September, 1940, fifty American destroyers were exchanged for leases on British Atlantic naval bases, which, the government announced later, were made available to all American Republics for the common defense of the hemisphere. By October, the first peace-time conscription in United States history was put into operation and over thirty-one million men were classified, and over seventeen million were drafted for military service. By November, Congress voted almost eighteen billion dollars for rearmament.

Almost immediately, Germany, Italy and Japan published their alliance. Japan recognized and respected the leadership of Germany and Italy in the establishment of a new order in Europe; Germany and Italy recognized and respected the leadership of Japan in the establishment of a new order in Greater East Asia, and all three countries would assist one another with all political, economic and military means when one of them was attacked by a Power not then involved in Europe or the Chinese-Japanese conflict. This reference to the United States was clearly intended as a threat. Secretary Hull warned that the oceans were no longer barriers to "the avalanche of conquest" which was planned to submerge the free world, and that the savage excesses of the war were only a prelude to those of the peace which the Axis Powers would impose, if victorious.

This time the warnings were heeded, as the country showed by the re-election of Roosevelt in November, 1940, for a third term, unprecedented in United States history. At once the rearmament, begun before, was stepped up, so that the United States could really be the great "arsenal of democracy," and the neutrality legislation was by-passed by the Lend-Lease Act of January, 1941, which authorized the government to lend or lease any defense articles or facilities to any nation whose defense was vital to the United States.

The Four Freedoms

It was time to proclaim the principles of democratic freedom. Roosevelt did so in his address to Congress on January 6, 1941. It was not a well-rounded statement of political philosophy, but one which everyone could understand and remember, that of the Four Freedoms. The text of this historic statement runs as follows:

In the future days which we seek to make secure, we look forward to a world founded upon four essential freedoms:
The first is freedom of speech and expression — everywhere in the world.
The second is freedom of every person to worship God in his own way — everywhere in the world.
The third is freedom from want, which, translated into world terms, means economic understanding which will secure to every nation a healthy peacetime life for its inhabitants — everywhere in the world.
The fourth is freedom from fear, which, translated into world terms, means world-wide reduction of armaments to such a point and in such a thorough fashion

that no nation will be in a position to commit an act of aggression against any neighbor — anywhere in the world.

That is no vision of a distant millenium. It is a definite basis for a kind of world attainable in our own time and generation. That kind of world is the very antithesis of the so-called "new order" of the tyranny which the dictators seek to create with the crash of a bomb.

Of the four freedoms, the last two are not to be found in the history of human rights in either the English or the French Revolution or in the United States Bill of Rights. Freedom from fear and want were forced on the conscience of Americans by the Great Depression and voiced by Roosevelt in the New Deal. In the opening of his first inaugural address he singled out fear as the first evil to overcome: "First of all, let me assert my firm belief that the only thing we have to fear is fear itself — nameless, unreasoning, unjustified terror which paralyzes needed efforts to convert retreat into advance." But this is not the kind of fear referred to in the Four Freedoms. It was not the fear of economic helplessness on the part of individuals, but the political danger of aggression and war, to be countered by disarmament among the nations. Also, freedom from want is, to use another of Roosevelt's terms, the international policy of the "good neighbor" in operation; a political rather than an economic concept. The document would have been stronger if the explanations had been omitted; and as a matter of fact public opinion took the bolder view, which Roosevelt, as a practical politician did not open up to Congress.

The next, and only other, statement of the principles of freedom for World War II, was the Atlantic Charter, formulated in a dramatic interview of Roosevelt and Prime Minister Churchill on board a cruiser off Newfoundland in August, 1941. It referred especially to only the last two of the four freedoms, although Roosevelt in his message to Congress reporting it, suggested that the first two freedoms were also implied in it. "It is also unnecessary for me to point out that the declaration of principles includes of necessity the world need for freedom of religion and freedom of information. No society of the world organized under the announced principles could survive without those freedoms which are a part of the whole freedom for which we strive."

The Atlantic Charter began with a renunciation of imperialism, with "no territorial changes that do not accord with the freely expressed wishes of the people concerned; respect for the right of all peoples to choose the form of government under which they will live. . . . After the final destruction of the Nazi tyranny, they hope to see established a peace which will afford to all nations the means of dwelling in safety within their own boundaries, and which will afford assurance that all the men in all the lands may live out their lives in freedom from fear and want." This time it is not merely the freedom of nation as against nation, but for "all men in all the lands." The phrase sounds Churchillian.

The issue was now clearly joined. By October, 1941, a Nazi submarine torpedoed an American destroyer, and Roosevelt commented that "history has recorded who fired the first shot." But the Axis Powers left it for their one great sea power, Japan, to open the war on the United States by its attack on Pearl Harbor; not that its decision to strike was not its own, but that the Axis grand strategy included Asia — and all the world. It was in line with Hitler's attack on Russia, as Roosevelt said when, in an address to the American people, he stated that, as Germany and Japan were acting in accordance with a joint plan, the war across the Pacific meant war across the Atlantic as well. American isolationists in their bitterness over the outbreak of the war, blamed Roosevelt for it rather than the Japanese, and the echo of their accusation can still be heard. But the Report of the Congressional Joint Commission on the investigation of the Pearl Harbor attack, which, together with its documentary exhibits, covers over forty volumes, leaves no support for the view that the Roosevelt Administration either plotted war with Japan or wished for one.

At once the United States moved to bring the nations then arrayed against the Axis Powers into a great coalition, pledged to the defense of freedom in peace as well as in war. This pledge, signed by the representatives of twenty nations in Washington on January 1, 1942, bore a name new to history. It was a "Declaration by the United Nations." In it the signatory governments subscribed to the common program of purposes and principles set forth in the Atlantic Charter, "convinced that complete victory over their enemies is essential to defend life, liberty, independence and religious freedom, and to preserve human rights and justice in their own lands as well as in other lands, and that they are now engaged in a common struggle against savage and brutal forces seeking to subjugate the world."

Thus the United Nations made its first, war-time appearance as a mobilization for freedom. But, as Briand said of the Paris Peace Pact, which was to bear his name along with that of Secretary of State Kellogg, "it was one thing to proclaim peace; another thing to organize it." The organization of peace and freedom in the United Nations was yet to be achieved. But the war had still to be won, and in the winning of it the road was open to another war — this time a cold war — by a mistaken strategy and a mistaken conception on the part of the United States of the nature of war itself — mistakes from which Soviet Russia profited. Viewing the war as a purely military event and a temporary interruption of its peaceful pursuits, the American leadership refused to accept the European concept of it as an instrument of policy, and planned for victory in the simplest, most direct way — by a head-on attack on the western front. Churchill urged that when Italy was conquered the Americans and British should strike at the enemy's flank by a march on Vienna and the Danube, and thus head off a Soviet advance. The British also wanted to outrace the Russians to Berlin. But Eisenhower, Marshall and Roosevelt concentrated only on the defeat of the main German forces in the center, accepting the advance of their Russian allies as good military strategy, with the result that all eastern Europe was occupied by them, and when peace came they remained in occupation, while the United States prepared, as at Appomattox, to leave for home, and for their own "spring ploughing."

But wars are political as well as military. They are not mere interruptions in the life of nations. They create new situations and call for continued adjustments to them. This the United States realized later. But the mistake which set the pattern for the future was made before the conferences at Yalta and Potsdam met, and it was Russia's pattern. The second great crusade had failed within sight of its goal — like that of Richard Coeur de Lion who, almost eight centuries ago, had to turn back from the holy city of his dreams when just in sight of its walls. The full extent of the frustration was not felt at once, in the happiness of peace; but, both in Europe and Asia, the war which beat down the most terrible attack on human freedom left the final problem still unsolved, with a cold war instead of peace.

Tests

The cold war was not only a defense of freedom; it was also a test of its defenders, a test which for a while the United States, or at least its most vocal politicians, failed to meet. The same arguments which had supported the Inquisition of the Middle Ages were again advanced by men and women convinced that communism was treason, and tolerance of it, and anything even distantly resembling it, must be crushed out — this time out of loyalty to the State instead of to the Church.

The parallel may seem overdrawn, for no physical penalties were imposed except for overt acts or complicity in them. But the procedure of investigation by congressional committees was very like that of the Inquisition: denial of confrontation of witnesses and the withholding of specific charges. The penalty for the heresy of communism, even in some cases for having been a communist years ago, or having the members of one's family known to have associated with those suspected of heretical views, might be dismissal from any position of public trust, notably in the government, but also in the teaching profession. It will be strange reading in future histories of this period that for an accused to invoke the clauses of the Bill of Rights was taken as added proof of guilt. Freedom of thought cannot flourish where freedom of speech is violated, and both suffered at the hands of those to whom any form of collectivism was anathema. The crisis showed that the upholders of the sacredness of things as they were and are could be as rigidly doctrinaire as the communists themselves, or as the medieval theologians.

This incredible lapse from the ideas of the Founding Fathers and from what the United States had always regarded as a sacred trust — the guardianship of freedom — this betrayal of human rights, needs explanation, although it can never be explained away. It was partly due to the fact that the United States had been forced into a position of chief opponent of the communist advance both by reason of its power and its unswerving conviction that communism was its one irreconcilable enemy — a conviction reinforced by the communists themselves. In the case of China there was added a bitter resentment against a nation for which the American people had long cherished friendly regard, and on behalf of which much missionary effort and educational cooperation had been expended. For the United States, which had never joined in the imperialist raid of the capitalist West on Asia, to be singled out by the Chinese as the chief enemy was too much to bear. Even before the attack on Korea, the opponents of the New Deal were blaming our failure in China on the government in Washington, when the real reason was that the Chinese Government which the American opposition supported, that headed by Chiang Kai-shek, was rejected by the Chinese people themselves. To charge General Marshall, the liberator of Europe, with treason to American interests because he failed in his mission to China marked the depth of infamy to which partisan politicians can descend. The country waited for Eisenhower to say so.

The war in Korea not only reinforced the resentment against communist China; it, along with the communist attack on the French possession in Indo-China and such sabre-rattling in Europe as the blockade of access to Berlin, gave the cold war the sinister aspect of the prelude to World War III. Such a dread event was only averted, in the judgment of Winston Churchill, by the American predominance in nuclear weapons. If that were the only guarantee of peace, the situation became more perilous still when Russia narrowed and then erased the margin of American atomic supremacy. But, whatever the strategic situation, the threat of war was always there, always behind the bland words of diplomacy, always making the cold war a dangerous game with loaded weapons. This is the one, only possible reason for the betrayal of the Bill of Rights and the cherished freedom of American history. For there is one virtue more necessary to the State than freedom — it is loyalty. From the days of the ancient Greeks and even before them in the structure of primitive society, the bond that held tribesmen to chieftains and citizens to the State was held a sacred one. Violation of it was treason and the penalty for treason everywhere has been death. When, therefore, the issue becomes one between freedom and loyalty to the State against forces threatening to denature or destroy it, freedom must yield.

But did this issue arise within the United States? Were the forces of subversion dangerous? What is subversion? Is it an insistence on the right to criticize government or society? Or, should the charge of subversion be limited to those who advocate the use of force to overthrow government or society? The answer to these questions was, to say the least, not made easier by the communists in the Kremlin. It had been laid down by Lenin, whose prophecies no Soviet partisan would dare to contradict, that the Marxian revolution would not stop until it had conquered the world; that it would use force when necessary, but above all, it would use guile. Diplomacy would be used as a technique of revolution, and the infiltration of communist agents into noncommunist countries would prepare the way. Now the world was seeing this revolution spread to an incredible degree. The resort to force had been tried and succeeded in Russia, eastern Europe and China. Was Soviet Russia using the interval of an uncertain peace to plan for further wars by disarming suspicion in the nation at a time when they should be alert? These were some of the doubts in American minds which led them to give popular support to demagogues like Senator McCarthy in their "crusade for freedom," in which the fundamentals of freedom were consistently violated in its name.

Far more serious than the mouthings of the rabble-rousers, however, was the extent to which the country responded to their call. This was due largely to the confusion in the public mind created by the communist propaganda protesting innocence and pacific intent while Soviet policy was persistently waging the cold war with provocative strategy. It was natural that a people whose treasured isolation had been twice violated by European militarists should be suspicious of the camouflaged militarism of Soviet Russia. But it was also due to a quality in the American mind which has to be noted here. In many ways, we are a tolerant, kindly people, with the kindliness of neighborhoods linked together when they have grown into nationhood. But we are also intolerant of deviation from the accepted standards of living, insisting on orthodoxy in conduct and belief, and tending to resent the intrusion of new — especially foreign — ideas. These are but a few of the many elements in the confusion of a strangely new chapter of United States history.

But while the analysis explains in part the sultry atmosphere of intolerance in the treatment of those who insist on their right to know more of communism, or even of those who find in it a challenging if extreme philosophy of social welfare, it does not justify persecution by processes outlawed long ago, and against which the United States has raised the bulwark of a constitution — a noble structure of law and of courts, which fortunately are still there as a last and strong resort.

Besides this, in spite of our boldness in invention and efforts to capture the future before it arrives, we are essentially conservative. The courts are largely governed by precedent, the precepts of the past are national treasures; above all, the Bible rules in the United States more than any other authority, dictating the stern righteousness of the Old Testament as much as the teachings of the Sermon on the Mount. Indeed it had been a Christian priest — later disowned by his church — who prepared the way for intransigence in dealing with communism by a gospel of extreme nationalism, directed against those fellow citizens who were of different political or religious beliefs. The spread of such doctrines in the name of national security would have been like a devastating army of occupation in the spirit of America, if it had found lodging there.

The pathway to such obscurantist ideas leads toward the worst of all despotisms: that in which the victims themselves destroy their own liberties in the mistaken belief that the demagogues are rescuing them from the social and political evils which are present in the world today. It is the democratic parallel to communist tyranny. If these preachers of nationalism could mobilize the discontent into forces of constructive statesmanship and build firmer foundations for the institutions designed to protect the inherent rights of life, liberty and the pursuit of happiness; if their aspirations were as enlightened as their attack was vindictive, there would be no need for apprehension. But the fundamental principle of freedom is magnanimity. It cannot build the structure of its desire if the eye of the architect is distorted by envy and hatred. Only the generous are free in spirit; and this is true of nations as well as of individuals. Generosity, of course, can be carried to extremes and become a weakness if one's concern about others reaches a point where one neglects to think of one's own legitimate interests. Altruism is a noble sentiment, but no lasting social order was ever built upon it alone. To find the equilibrium between our own rights and those of our neighbors is the fundamental problem of statesmanship. It follows from this that the maintenance of our liberties lies in so maintaining the balance between ourselves and others as to weaken and destroy the appeal of the demagogue. This cannot be done by attempting to outrival him in vituperative attack. It cannot be done by stirring up against him similar, but opposing, passions; for ignorance and prejudice provide a stronger arsenal in such a conflict than reason and intelligence. The path which reason must take to make liberty secure is that which leads toward fair dealing and social justice.

The real answer to the doctrinaire, whether he be communist, fascist, or one who masquerades under the guise of democracy, is to redress the conditions which give his teachings their appeal. In other words, the maintenance of our own liberties depends on a quickened conscience as to our own duties. Unfortunately this formula does not say all that it should to us. Duty is an abstraction rather than a catalog of things to do. That "stern daughter of the voice of God" is mostly listened to as the prompter for doing immemorial tasks. It speaks for habit more than for reason. This was all right as long as habit was reasonable; and throughout the long past, in which the conditions of life repeated themselves generation after generation and century after century, the wisdom of the Fathers was a ready guide for the present. But with the coming of modern science these conditions are in eternal flux. Invention and discovery bring increasing change with the increase in control of time and space, and the ever-shifting nature of the day's work. The performance of one's duty to society, upon which rest the opportunities for freedom, is therefore no longer the unquestioned acceptance of routine, either in economic relations or in government itself. The only safety for the Republic, the only guarantee for our individual liberties from now to the end of time lies in the constant, if conservative, criticism of the institutions, as well as the habits, which we have inherited from the past. If we cannot resolve this problem so as to satisfy the inmost needs of our fellow citizens, our liberties either will be lost in the riot of anarchy or suppressed by the tyranny of the demagogue.

Never in all the history of civilization was there such a challenge to the most precious possessions of the spirit of man. Again we come back to say that the chief problem of our time has not been Nazi or Fascist developments in Europe nor the communist empires in Russia and Asia, for these are temporary manifestations; it is the adjustment of men to the machine. For untold millennia before the Ice Age down to yesterday, man made his way in the world with strength of body rather than by the subtle processes of thought. The claw which he inherited from his prehensile ancestors be-

576

came a marvelously accurate instrument for mastering the crude forces of nature; but now, just in our time, we are turning into a new era which has only just begun but will never end: the era in which we must think our way through rather than grapple with nature by animal strength.

The prime duty, therefore, of the citizen of today is to direct his own life and that of society in terms of their innermost needs, as those needs shift with the advances made in the arts and sciences in the different corners of the world. Inventions are, by their nature, of world-wide application, and the nation that attempts to cut itself off from the progress of science will be ruined by it. Therefore, merely to stand on the sacred institutions of the past is to create a maladjustment with the present, the kind of maladjustment which breeds blind discontent. The institutions of government, as well as those of economic and social life, must henceforth be conceived in increasingly dynamic terms. It is not enough for freedom to broaden out from "precedent to precedent" if such advance is forced on it from without. It must take its stand on the basis of social justice and see to it that there is an adequate instrumentality for making that justice effective.

The curtailment of liberty in the United States due to the cold war with communism is not so serious as that which remains as the aftermath of slavery. Economic and social forces shift with the dynamics of applied science, creating new situations and a world of new ideas — in spite of the statics of either doctrinaire communism or conservatism. But much more stubborn is the problem of an under-privileged race, the Negro, which the Civil War did not solve but only opened. The fourteenth and fifteenth amendments, following the lines laid down by Chief Justice Marshall, made the Federal Government the protector of the rights of citizens against invasion by State Government. For the first time the Constitution defined citizenship in terms of freedom. To the south, even after the war and "reconstruction" had passed into history, these amendments were never accepted as valid, lacking endorsement by duly elected state legislatures. Such was the view of even so moderate a southerner as Cordell Hull, Secretary of State. Negroes were denied not only the right to vote but opportunity for social and educational advancement. They were no longer held down by terror of the threat of lynching, but still faced the obstacles of poverty and social ostracism. And yet in the twentieth century they have won their way up to take a distinct place in American culture and thought. But it remained distinct, never fully integrated with that of the whites, which meant a continuing disadvantage to the Negro. This remained true of communities in the northern states, but it was only custom, not law.

In the south, however, especially where the Negroes predominated as in Mississippi and parts of Alabama, the law held the two races apart, not only in schools but in public conveyances. The National Association for the Advancement of Colored People (N.A.A.C.P.), which includes many prominent whites among its members, fought this condition in the courts, invoking the Fourteenth Amendment, and finally, in 1954, the Supreme Court in one of the most important decisions in its history outlawed segregation wherever the public authority extended. This unanimous judgment of the Supreme Court was a clear, legal assertion of equal rights of all citizens, Negro as well as white, to the same public schools. It stirred white opposition in the south to the point of violence, especially in Arkansas, where federal troops were called out to protect the Negro students in what had been a school for white children. The result there as in other southern states, especially Virginia, was an effort to avoid "integration" by creating a private school system sanctioned by the state government. This revival of the doctrine of nullification of over a century ago, led to long and bitter controversies in Congress on almost the same lines of states rights against federal laws as in the days of Calhoun and Webster.

Outwardly it seemed as though the progress which the American Negro had been making in recent years had suddenly met a check, and that the racial taboos that were the heritage of slavery were gaining rather than losing strength. But the real situation was less a retrogade movement — for anti-integration had been an unbroken tradition — than a forward movement of the Negro, reaching out to new appreciation of economic, social and intellectual possibilities. In the deep south, the Negro demand for "integration" is a revolutionary break with long-established folkways, but even there the forces of progress are at work.

It was at Montgomery, Alabama, the cradle of the Confederacy, that Negro public opinion found a leader in a young Baptist minister, Reverend Martin Luther King, who in a few months rose from obscurity to a position among his people which resembled, in a small but genuine way, that of Gandhi in India, whose teachings he followed literally, along with those of Jesus. Non-violence was the answer to violence. Speaking from his own front porch which had been shattered by a bomb, he pleaded for peace, law and order. "We are not advocating violence. We want to love our enemies. Be good to them. Love them and let them know you love them. . . . I want it to be known the length and breadth of this land that if I am stopped this movement will not stop. . . . For what we are doing is right — and God is with us."

It was a strange coincidence that this call for a peaceful revolution came from Montgomery, the cradle of a slave-owning Confederacy. The call was heard wherever there were Negroes living in the United States, and the combination of Christian charity and firm resolve won it the adherence of militant Negro leaders in the south. This movement of desegregation left threats and violence behind and became a challenge to all Americans. In the words of a northern journalist, it became a "spiritual force that aspired even to ending prejudice in man's mind."

The racial question in the United States will not be wholly solved for a long time. Nowhere else, outside Africa, does it exist in anything like the same proportions. And yet, by contrast with what South Africa is doing, the United States stands well. The social prejudices are lessening in the younger generation. There is no color line in sports, except in the deep south. The achievements of Negroes are recognized in the nation generally. The old idea of inherent Negro incapacity has been broken down by such educational leaders as Booker T. Washington, such scientists as George Washington Carver, such statesmen as Ralph Bunche, such artists as Marian Anderson, of whom the whole nation is proud.

It was not by southern recognition of achievements by Negroes, however, that relief came in this racial cold war, but by action of the courts, following up the historic decision of the Supreme Court. The governor of Arkansas was the first to defy this decision and the situation was made more serious by the uses of federal troops to force integration in the schools. But the leadership in the south was soon taken over by the state that had the tradition of southern leadership — in war and peace — Virginia. The governor and assembly organized "massive resistance" to what they regarded as federal invasion of states' rights, but finally, in January 1959, Virginia's own Supreme Court ruled that the laws closing public schools to exclude Negroes were contrary to the state constitution requiring the state to "maintain an efficient system of public free schools throughout the state." Other decisions of federal courts followed and the governor and Legislature surrendered to the rule of law. The importance of this conclusion can hardly be overestimated. It was far more than a victory for the rights of Negroes as citizens; it was a vindication of the great principles which the Founding Fathers took over from the champions of English freedom, Chief Justice Coke's reliance on the Common Law and John Locke's treatise on government.

CHAPTER XXV

THE UNITED NATIONS

Origins

IN 1939, WHEN once more as in 1914 "the lights were going out all over Europe," the American League of Nations Association, deeply concerned over the failure of the free nations to support the League when defied by Japan and denounced by Mussolini and Hitler, formed a Commission to Study the Organization of Peace, to plan in the hour of disaster a "more perfect union." It was not a propaganda body except as objective studies, published from time to time, appealed to thoughtful people, and yet it exercised a considerable influence on public opinion and ultimately at Washington.[1]

[1] Sections of this Chapter were originally written for the author's volume *The Great Decision* (New York: The Macmillan Co., 1944), now out of print.

Other bodies with similar aims were also at work in other countries as well, not only in the field of international law and in the Churches, but also in commerce, industry and labor. The deeply rooted isolationist sentiment in the United States for neutrality "in other peoples' wars" was still so strong, however, that the adverse reaction to a single sentence in a speech of President Roosevelt, referring to the need for a "quarantine" against the contagion of war caused that sensitive politician to hold back from following in the footsteps of his one-time chief, Woodrow Wilson. Even when the country gave signs of a change of mind on this fundamental problem, Roosevelt limited his suggestions to the creation of economic and welfare bodies, like a world bank, possibly in London; an organization for world health, possibly at Paris, and one for food and agriculture with a center in Iowa or Nebraska.

Planning for an international political organ for collective security was left for a committee working secretly at the State Department, under the chairmanship of Under Secretary Welles.[2] There was an additional reason for secrecy in that the United States was by that time at war. But in all the early planning Roosevelt never encouraged the creation of a world-wide *political* organization with the obligation to enforce peace by collective action.

Throughout the tragic months and years of the second World War the members of the alliance of the United Nations found themselves confronted with many unforeseen problems, concerning both the conduct of the war and its subsequent liquidation. Under the stress of the need for immediate action, little if anything could be done about them, or at least so it seemed to the governments concerned. Even relatively innocent questions, like those of food and agriculture, were handled delicately by foreign offices careful not to raise any political issues that might in any way impede action by the joint military staffs, while anything resembling outspoken criticism of foreign policy was disavowed by public opinion, and properly so, for its possible bad effect on the military effort.

Such was the situation after almost three years of war, a situation that left much to be desired in the clarification of ultimate war aims and the relation of the powers with reference to them. Then, on November 1, 1943, dawn broke over the world from the walls of the Kremlin, when the Tripartite Conference of the Foreign Secretaries of the United States, Great Britain,

[2] It was in this committee of the State Department that the blueprints of the Charter of the United Nations were prepared, first for the preliminary international conference at Dumbarton Oaks, and then at the San Francisco Conference. The attempt of this committee to build on lines other than those of the Covenant of the League of Nations was illustrated by Chairman Welles' request that no member of it re-read the Covenant or League literature while at work on the new plan. Yet when the draft was completed, it resembled the constitution of the League in all important points. There was no other form of universal political organization possible, so long as the basis was the sovereignty of national states. The present author, as a member of this State Department planning committee, had already seen the same conclusions reached by the Commission to Study the Organization of Peace, of which he was Chairman. Later, as Chairman of the Consultants at San Francisco, it fell to him to help in strengthening the economic and social elements in the Charter, along the Rooseveltian lines.

and Russia issued a communiqué which, as we have already seen, contained the promise of a world organization "for the maintenance of peace and security."

The wide reach of this agreement took the world by surprise. Public opinion had not been prepared for it because the press in both England and the United States had made much of the fact that the Soviet Government would not meet at some more convenient spot in a relatively neutral territory like northern Africa or Egypt, but insisted upon having the delegates take the long journey to Moscow, as though Soviet Russia were the leader of the alliance. Once more, however, experience showed that the way to test the reality of Soviet policy was to meet it frankly face to face and by personal contact dissipate the fog of distrustful surmise in people's minds.

Whatever Roosevelt thought of Stalin, Churchill's suspicions of Soviet diplomacy were never wholly allayed by verbal agreement on the aims of war and peace. He had wanted the one sure guarantee against Russian imperialism, occupation of at least a bastion in Eastern Europe by the Western armies. Roosevelt, however, supported by his military advisors, refused to accept this strategy in order to avoid doing anything which might result in continuing American involvement in the affairs of the Continent. This was one of the vital decisions of history, a tragic blunder in American statesmanship, for events were to justify Churchill's judgment. There were those in each nation who kept questioning whether the forces of freedom were really bound together by more than a common danger. Although the leaders of these nations had emblazoned the high ideals of international freedom and justice on their oriflamme of battle, there was as yet no clear assurance of their fundamental harmony with the ultimate aims of the war.

In spite of the military need for unity of purpose, there were still many points of possible misunderstanding among the three Great Powers. There was a persistent trend of public opinion in the United States which distrusted the fundamental motives of the British and held back the fullest measure of cooperation with them because of a fear of British imperialism in the Orient. In Great Britain there was fully as strong a current of doubt as to whether the United States could be counted upon to make good in the post-war period its wartime protestations that it supported a structure of world cooperation.

Nevertheless, American public opinion, forced by the war to reconsider its isolationist policies, and historically adverse to alliances with single states, began definitely to swing toward a permanent world organization. Measurements like those of the Gallup poll taken every few months throughout 1941 and 1943 showed a steady increase in the number of those favoring a post-war international organization "with power to maintain peace." These polls finally registered between 75 and 80 per cent of acceptance of the very kind of international obligation which had kept the United States out of the League of Nations. The result was that after the Moscow Conference a resolution was passed by over 90 per cent of the total membership of Congress, fully endorsing the principle of collective security. This trend got important support by the Latin-American states Conference at Chapultepec, Mexico, in March 1945, which requested the Inter-American Juridical Committee to draw up a Declaration of the International Rights and Duties of man as a basis of the solidarity of American states.[3]

The Charter of the United Nations

While these events were under way, plans went ahead for the meeting of the San Francisco Conference, in April, 1945, to shape the Charter of the United Nations. As the Drafting Committee of the State Department had found out,[4] the structure of the United Nations Organization (as it is still called in Europe) turned out to be necessarily almost a replica of that of the League of Nations, with the General Assembly as the sovereign body and the Security Council, like the Council of the League, to deal with war or the threat of it. In its statement of Purposes and Principles (Chapter I), the Charter made it clear that the Organization was not the constitution of a world government, but was designed, like the League, to strengthen the sovereign independence of its members. There is even an echo of Wilson's phrase in the pledge "to develop friendly relations between nations, based on respect for the principle of equal rights and self-determination of peoples."[5] To make the point clearer still, Article 2 begins with the unqualified statement that "the Organization is based on the principle of the sovereign equality of all its members."

With such a basis for membership, it was natural that the General Assembly, composed of ambassadorial representatives of sovereign states, should be limited to the making of resolutions and the promotion of international cooperation instead of acting like a world parliament with power to enforce its will. History was soon to show the inadequacy of such a structure for international peace, and ways were devised for strengthening action by the Assembly, including such far-reaching suggestions as one by Sir Winston Churchill for weighted voting, but no responsible statesman is ready to accept the full alternative of a world state composed of peoples narrowly nationalistic at heart or largely inexperienced in world affairs.

The one most practical measure to enable the Assembly to perform more effectively the functions entrusted to it in the Charter was that proposed by the United States in the fifth Assembly session in three resolutions grouped under the heading United Action for Peace. The first of these provided for emergency sessions of the General Assembly on twenty-four hours notice by any seven members of the Security Council or by a majority of the members of the United Nations, in case of a threat to the peace, breach of the peace or act of aggression. It also called for the establishment of a Peace

[3] The work of these jurists was embodied in the American Declaration of the Rights and Duties of Man, adopted at the Bogota Conference of American States, March to May, 1948.

[4] *Cf.* above, p. 000, n.   [5] Chapter I, Articles 1, 2.

Observation Commission to report on international tensions, the creation and maintenance by member states of elements of their armed forces for prompt use as United Nations units, and the establishment of a Collective Measures Committee to study and report on ways to strengthen international peace and security. The other two resolutions bore more directly upon the functions of the Security Council, and need not concern us here. It was the resolution strengthening the Assembly which took the first step toward world mobilization of peace efforts under the United Nations.

In presenting this proposal to the General Assembly of the United Nations, Secretary of State Dean Acheson spoke less about "the strength to prevent aggression" than "the war against want." "Just as Korea has become the symbol of resistance against aggression, so it can become also the vibrant symbol of the renewal of life." There was an echo here of the creative work of the Marshall Plan; but Secretary Acheson went farther. Economic recovery was the basis of "a larger freedom":

In building a more secure and prosperous world we must never lose sight of the basic motivation of our effort: the inherent worth of the individual human person. Our aim is to create a world in which each human being shall have the opportunity to fulfill his creative possibilities in harmony with all.

It is our hope that the relaxation in international tension, which we seek, will be accompanied by a great restoration of human liberty, where it is now lacking, and progress everywhere toward the "larger freedom."

But the safeguarding of human freedom is not a distant goal, nor a project for the future. It is a constant, immediate, and urgent concern of the United Nations.

The United Nations should keep forever in mind the objectives set forth in the universal declaration of human rights, and we should press forward with the work of our distinguished Human Rights Commission.

While we are engaged in creating conditions of real peace in the world, we must always go forward under the banner of liberty. Our faith and our strength are rooted in free institutions and the rights of man. . . .

The peace the world wants must be free from fear — the fear of invasion, the fear of subversion, the fear of the knock on the door at midnight.

The peace the world wants must be free from want, a peace in which neighbors help each other, and together build a better life.

The peace the world wants must be a moral peace, so that the spirit of man may be free, and the barriers between the hearts and minds of men may drop away and leave men free to unite in brotherhood.

This is the task before us.[6]

We shall see later on how this task has been carried out by the United Nations. The Security Council, which Secretary Acheson sought to sidestep in his resolution in the Assembly, became more and more the symbol of futility, owing to the vetoes of the communist members. But, it must be remembered that in the absence of a world state, the veto is the legitimate instrument of a sovereign state. The veto cannot be eliminated until war as an instrument of national policy is definitely outlawed, not only in government pronouncements but by the public opinion of mankind.

[6] *The Department of State Bulletin*, Vol. XXIII, No. 587, p. 529.

If the prevention of war by force or the threat of it presents problems as yet unsolved, there is promise of a solution by following the long road which this study has traced, that of the new freedom which lies in the betterment of human relations the world over — not an unreal altruism, but a recognition of common interests between nations as well as within them. Here the United Nations has pioneered beyond anything attempted by the League of Nations.

This extension of its sphere of activity was chiefly due to the influence of an awakened public opinion in the United States. For by this time American public opinion was becoming alert to the idea of a world community and, in addition to government delegates at the San Francisco Conference, the State Department, with some bureaucratic reluctance, invited representatives of some forty-two national bodies in business, labor, education, religion and public affairs to serve as Consultants with it. The Consultants left their mark on the Charter in various clauses, but especially in Article 71, which provided for similar nongovernmental bodies under the Economic and Social Council.

But more direct results were embodied in the Charter of provisions for human rights, culminating in the proposal (submitted the Commission to Study the Organization of Peace) for a permanent commission on human rights as an integral part of the United Nations Organization. This is one of the first instances in history of an unofficial body determining the text of a treaty in an international conference of governments.[7]

Not too much, however, should be claimed for the Consultants of the United States delegation. Liberal thought had its advocates in many countries, especially in the British Commonwealth of Nations, of which Marshal Smuts was once more an eloquent exponent. It was a Belgian, Senator Henri Rolin, who insisted on the insertion in the opening of the charter of the familiar words of the United States Constitution, "We the people of the United Nations," instead of the stereotyped phraseology of treaties. Most significant of all is the fact that, in spite of the fact that the Charter was primarily, like the Covenant of the League, a guarantee of collective security against the threat of war, the pledge in the Charter that its members "promote universal respect for, and observance of, human rights and fundamental freedoms for all without distinction as to race, sex, language or religion," is not linked up with the threats to peace under the Security Council, but under the program of the Economic and Social Council. This wise move made it an organ for the development of peaceful societies instead of merely a concern of war prevention. The United Nations was not to lose sight of the fundamental basis of domestic peace, the consent of the governed.

The Charter of the United Nations states these larger purposes and principles in language which matches in nobility of thought any other charter

[7] There are, however, numerous instances of the influence upon such official bodies of unofficial leaders of public opinion, such as that of Robert Owen on the Congress of Vienna or English nonconformists on the Brussels Conference.

in the history of freedom. However familiar it has become it should be quoted here:

We, the peoples of the United Nations determine

to save succeeding generations from the scourge of war, which twice in our lifetime has brought untold sorrow to mankind, and

to reaffirm faith in fundamental human rights, in the dignity and worth of the human person, in the equal rights of men and women and of nations large and small, and

to establish conditions under which justice and respect for the obligations arising from treaties and other sources of international law can be maintained, and

to promote social progress and better standards of life in larger freedom, and for these ends

to practice tolerance and live together in peace with one another as good neighbors, and

to unite our strength to maintain international peace and security, and

to ensure, by the acceptance of principles and the institution of methods, that armed force shall not be used, save in the common interest, and

to employ international machinery for the promotion of the economic and social advancement of all peoples.

This program of human betterment was implemented by an international structure designed to cover all of the vast field which it outlines.

These were the ideals of the League of Nations, spelled out in more moving eloquence than the sober preamble to the Covenant which had limited itself to the formula of a treaty:

THE HIGH CONTRACTING PARTIES,

In order to promote international cooperation and to achieve international peace and security

by the acceptance of obligations not to resort to war,

by the prescription of open, just and honorable relations between nations,

by the firm establishment of the understandings of international law as the actual rule of conduct among Governments, and

by the maintenance of justice and a scrupulous respect for all treaty obligations in the dealings of organized peoples with one another,

Agree to this Covenant of the League of Nations.

This coldly legal wording of the preamble to the Covenant is in striking contrast to the wide reach of the ideals set forth in the Charter of the limited Nations. But when we turn from these far horizons to the means for reaching them we find that the simpler organization of the League had an advantage over the elaborate structure of the limited Nations.

The most serious fault in the Charter was one which at first thought seems merely verbal. The Council of the League became the Security Council in the Charter. While the Council of the League was chiefly concerned with war or the threat of it, it was also an organ for a wide range of problems, such as the treatment of minorities and the economic recovery of distressed areas. This meant that its members were chiefly concerned in applying the technique of conciliation — as in the settlement of a dispute between France and Germany over the administration of the Saar territory, when the Italian (Vittorio) Scialoja wrote a formula on the back of an envelope and passed it to Stresemann and Briand who nodded in agreement. The case was serious, for Germany was threatening to leave the league. As it was, the whole incident hardly got a paragraph in a newspaper. Such common sense methods are almost impossible when the issue is the security of nations. This implied criticism of the narrowing field of what should have been a general executive council is still valid although, as we shall see, the other functions were taken over by other United Nations bodies, the Economic Council and the Specialized Agencies. This leads to compartmentalization, however, and the approach to the Assembly is inadequate.

The Security Council remains, as was intended, the supreme body for the maintenance of peace and security.

Naturally during the debate on atomic energy and on the political settlement after the war, public attention has been centered upon the work of this vital organ of the United Nations. But in the longer perspective of the stabilization of peace, the Economic and Social Council, and more especially the Commissions and Specialized Agencies working for the most part under it, have been blazing the trail of pioneers in regions never fully explored. Under them, practically all of the major activities of mankind have been surveyed in the interest of human betterment.

Toward a Democracy of Nations

In the closing days of 1955 a new era began in the history of the United Nations when, in a single session of the General Assembly, sixteen nations were admitted as members. In the Assembly hall itself, and still more in the corridors and Delegates' Lounge, this decisive act was termed revolutionary, because it ended a long stalemate by invoking the principle of universal instead of selective membership. The fact that this apparently basic change was not complete did not lessen but rather accentuated its significance by the continued concentration upon it, especially in respect of the three great Powers, Japan, Communist China, and Germany.

Actually, the change was less a revolution than a clarification of principles which had never been thoroughly worked out either at the foundation of the United Nations or during its ten years of troubled history.

It must be remembered that the name United Nations was first borne by the military alliance which the United States drew together at a meeting in Washington in January 1942, shortly after our declaration of war. The twenty-six nations represented at that conference subscribed to the "common program of purposes and principles" of the Atlantic Charter, thus not only excluding the enemy states, but setting up standards of international behavior in peacetime. The first attempt to embody these principles in an international organization was made by the small committee of the State Department previously referred to, working under the Under Secretary, Sumner Welles. But this remained a wartime secret until Secretary Hull secured agreement at the Moscow Conference of October 1943 that Great Britain and the USSR would join with the United States to establish "a general international organization, based on the principles of the sovereign equality of all peace-loving States, and open membership by all such States, large and small, for the maintenance of international peace and security."

The Moscow Conference was at first hailed as the dawn of a new day in international relations, but only a few months later darkness settled down on Eastern Europe as Stalin prepared to demand extended multiple representation for the USSR in the United Nations and then proceeded to violate the "Declaration on Liberated Europe" of the Yalta Conference by establishing Communist control in each satellite state. From this time on, throughout almost the whole ten years of United Nations history until 1955 the USSR, by the use of its veto power in the Security Council, sought to prevent the admission of other noncommunist States. The line of division thus drawn was equally accepted by Russia's opponents, and the stalemate continued with little change. Finally, on motion of Canada, the solution was found in the compromise which admitted twelve "free" nations and four communist.[8] Unlike most political compromises, however, this one reached beyond the practical dispute to the underlying principle, that of universality, as the basis for action in completing the full roster of the member-states of the United Nations.

It is interesting to note that no one raised the question as to whether or not the new arrangement was in violation of the Charter which limits membership "to all peace-loving states which accept the obligations of the Charter" and "in the judgment of the organization are able and willing to carry out these obligations." The answer, which apparently seemed self-evident, is that the only sure test of membership is the fulfillment of all its obligations, and this can be applied only within the organization itself.

Thus, a new meaning may be given to the clause which stipulates that a member may be expelled if it "has persistently violated the Principles contained in the Charter." A member in good standing is not only "peace-loving" but a loyal supporter of the "purposes and principles" set forth in Article I, including those of "justice and international law, respect for the principle of equal rights of peoples, international cooperation in solving international problems of an economic, social, cultural, or humanitarian character, and in promoting and encouraging respect for human rights and for fundamental freedom for all without distinction as to race, sex, language, or religion."

While there is always a risk in extending the rights and privileges of citizenship to those inexperienced in its exercise, the blunders of democracy are more readily redressed by an awakening of public opinion than in a government by an elite intent on preserving for itself the best of all possible worlds; and what is true of the relationship of citizen to citizen within the state is also true of the relationship of one State to another.

On the other hand, this is no time for wishful thinking. The new era of

8 At the end of Dec. 12, 1958, the total number of members was 82.

the United Nations not only increases its membership; it also greatly increases its problems. The argument implicit in the foregoing analysis is that in this widened field of activities in the arts of peace, rather than merely in the head-on operation of policing against war, lies the hope of the future. But it would be a mistake to expect a speedy fulfillment of so vast and varied a program as that outlined in the Aims and Purposes of the Charter. For one thing, it will take time for the nations which have no common heritage of culture or political institutions to understand and agree upon the meaning of the great ideals there set forth. A more dangerous obstacle to fulfillment is the possible misuse of the newly acquired freedom, since it might be used as a license for revenge on exploiters of the past. Yet, at the first Assembly of the enlarged United Nations, the Asian Powers, while at first they seemed to be satisfying an anti-European prejudice, finally acted as freely and independently as the European ones in the condemnation of the U.S.S.R. for the massacres in Hungary.

The Commission on Human Rights

The "new dimensions of peace" still lack any adequate survey. How far do its boundaries run along those of national states, and how far do they reach beyond them into the lives of men? It is significant that, even with the experience to draw upon of those nations already having bills of rights of their own for the protection of their citizens, the makers of the Charter were not ready to insert one in the text. For, as we have seen time and again, the more conscious a nation is of the rights which its citizens have acquired, the more sensitive it is of any external intervention. This proved to be the case with the United States, because of the provision in the Constitution that treaties are "the supreme law of the land" and the fact that most social and personal relations lie within the jurisdiction of the states.[9]

It was under these conditions that the United Nations began the implementation of its great design, not merely to save the world from war, but to make it a world worth saving. The Economic and Social Council, at its meeting in February, 1946, established a "nuclear" commission on human rights, and a "nuclear" commission on the status of women. The term "nuclear" which has come into common use since the dawn of the atomic age, is used to describe preliminary bodies drawing up the constitutions of permanent ones. The recommendations of this nuclear commission were accepted by the Economic and Social Council and passed on to the General Assembly for its endorsement.

Closely connected with their work was that of the Conference on Freedom and Information in press, radio and motion pictures. There was also the parallel Subcommission on the Prevention of Discrimination and the Protection of Minorities. A Trusteeship Council was set up to deal with the international oversight of non-self-governing peoples, and the Interna-

[9] The issues thus raised are of vital importance to the future relations of the United States to the United Nations, as was evidenced by the proposal by Senator Bricker for an amendment to the Constitution designed to limit treaties to matters of diplomatic expediency.

tional Labor Organization was once more set to work on the problems of economic and social justice. The list is by no means complete, for the program is a concrete expression of the awakening conscience of mankind.

The Commission on Human Rights, when finally established, was composed of eighteen members of the United Nations, selected by the Economic and Social Council for three-year terms. It is thus a highly official body of government appointees, and on this account was criticized by some as being too political in character. A proposal to have it composed of distinguished individuals representing various cultures, much as in the case of the World Court, was, however, voted down. The argument which prevailed was that the Commission should not be an academic body exploring theories of government, but a responsible organ of the United Nations. Fortunately, the representatives measured well up to the desired standard. The Commission originally consisted of distinguished jurists, like M. René Cassin, head of the Conseil d'Etat, the highest tribunal in France, and other experts in this field, as well as representatives of governments. Its most influential member, Mrs. Franklin D. Roosevelt, was elected Chairman by unanimous vote, a position she held until the election of President Eisenhower.

It would be a mistake to regard the task of the Commission on Human Rights as that of an emergency body concentrating upon the elimination of such gross violations of the dignity and worth of the human person as characterized the Nazi and Fascist dictatorships. It is true that these cruel and despotic acts were responsible for bringing the subject into the arena of international affairs. But the remedy does not lie in applying coercion against coercion under conditions which by their very nature will not last. It lies in the upbuilding of new conceptions of political morality and the recognition of the common interest of all mankind in their emergence and development everywhere.

Seen in this light, the work of the Commission on Human Rights reaches beyond all the externals of international organization to supply the vital principle of international justice by extending its guarantee over the lives of all men everywhere. In its historical perspective, the international movement for human rights, if its program is to be fully achieved, is a revolutionary challenge of the United Nations to that greatest political creation of modern times, the state system of today. It is true that it is hedged about by qualifications respecting national sovereignty, but if it is to prove effective, these qualifications will be less and less heard of in the coming years. Compared with it, even the effort to control atomic energy, novel and revolutionary as the proposal seems, has less of history behind it and is more limited in its scope.

We must not, therefore, expect so much immediately of the United Nations as to suffer the blight of disillusionment in cases of unforeseen impediments or delays. On the other hand, we must maintain our faith in the ultimate triumph of this movement, for in it resides the spiritual power which alone can achieve and maintain permanent peace among nations. Fortunately, already the conscience of mankind has been touched and awakened as never before. Upon this fact we may base our hopes, if along with the spiritual awakening there is a parallel development of intellectual under-standing. Join these two forces of the mind and the spirit of man and they become invincible. The legalistic mind which has been developed in Amer-ican education, owing to the federal character of our government, tends to blind us to such far-reaching realities. The law that embodies human rights is not an artificial creation of political mechanics; it is the expression in defi-nite terms of the will to enforce the moral purpose of a people.

It is as a first tentative start in this clarification that we should regard the efforts of today to prepare an international bill of human rights. No such formulation in these pioneering days of the United Nations can be thought of as embodying the final statement either of doctrine or practice in this vast new field. Yet, worthwhile efforts have been made to draw together the fundamental principles of such a declaration of human rights and the extent to which they can be embodied in legal obligations; and these efforts should be studied, not in that dogmatic temper which insists on having its own way, but in the generous spirit of human understanding.

The United Nations Commission on Human Rights prepared three docu-ments: A Universal Declaration of Human Rights, consisting of some thirty articles; a Draft Covenant on Civil and Political Rights, of fifty-four articles; and a Draft Covenant on Economic and Social Rights, of eighty-nine arti-cles.[10] The reason for this division and arrangement goes to the heart of the whole problem. The Covenants list the items which might be made binding, enforceable, legal obligations; the Declaration is a statement of both present and ultimate aims. The United States, as indicated above, was reluctant to prepare a treaty which the Senate might refuse to ratify and concentrated on the Declaration, contending that if it could win unanimous or nearly unanimous approval by the Assembly, it would further the cause of freedom more than a covenant accepted by only a limited number of States. Great Britain, on the other hand, took the line it has always followed in interna-tional dealing, skeptical of the value of declarations unless nations were really willing to act on them. It therefore came to the Commission with a draft of a convention, in precise legal terms. The Commission solved the problem by working on separate drafts for the Declaration and two Draft Covenants, one on Civil and Political Rights, and the other on Economic, Social and Cultural Rights.

The labor involved in the preparation of these pioneering drafts was prodigious. The basic collection of documents prepared by the United Na-tions Secretariat was a volume of 408 pages, but that was only a reminder of the fact that the problems confronting them covered human experience in all parts of the world throughout history. The Declaration, for example, had to consider what weight should be given, for example, to a precept of Confucius which had molded the ideas of China, or the five virtues with their corresponding freedoms, in the teaching of Buddha, or the canons of

[10] The texts are given in the Appendix of "The United Nations and Human Rights," by James Frederick Green, The Brookings Institution, Washington 6, D.C., pp. viii.

conduct in the Koran.[11] In contrast with the wide scope of these ethical concepts, the fundamental rights cited by the Western nations were essentially political and social, such as had been set forth in declarations or bills of rights or were incorporated in laws or constitutions.

Such divergent approaches made the problem of drafting difficult enough, but the greatest obstacle to agreement came from the communists, who insisted on the economic basis of all political and social institutions, and, therefore, on the priority of the economic freedom, which was summed up in "the right to work." Everyone knew that the importance given this right by the Soviet delegates was because it could not be implemented without regimentation of the state; therefore it was strongly opposed — in its unqualified form — by the Western nations. In the end, the West won out, for while they listed the right to work as universal, they added in the Declaration that there should be free choice of employment. The result was that the communist bloc refused to sign.[12]

The "right to work" raises a fundamental issue in the minds of communists. In the dialectic of their philosophy, they regard this aim as the one great advance over capitalist thinking. For, while we in this country think of human rights in their political and legal setting, as the assertion of the rights of the individual within the State, the communists feel that such assertion of intellectual and spiritual freedom as the laws provide is unreal unless it is geared into the economic life of the common man. They insist, with the strongest of moral convictions, that the high goals we have set for ourselves can be achieved only by breaking down the obstacles to social and economic justice, and that this can be achieved only in a collectivist society.

It would be blindness not to realize that here we come again upon the great divide between the communist and noncommunist worlds. The economic interpretation of history denies the immutable character of the rights of man which have voiced the aspirations of the great movements of the past. The communists insist that these have merely reflected the demands of a class dominant at the time, and therefore lacked the universality of communism, based on the one deciding element in life and society: productive work. The dictatorship of the proletariat thus becomes for the convinced communist a synonym for the ultimate freedom which noncommunist countries never reach. Moreover, the great ideals of former movements for freedom seem to him to have been not merely partial, as an expression of one

[11] These were summarized in *Human Rights, Comments and Interpretations*, edited by UNESCO (New York: Columbia University Press, 1949).

[12] Article 23 of the Universal Declaration of Human Rights reads as follows:
1. Everyone has the right to work, to free choice of employment, to just and favourable conditions of work and to protection against unemployment.
2. Everyone, without any discrimination, has the right to equal pay for equal work.
3. Everyone who works has the right to just and favourable remuneration ensuring for himself and his family an existence worthy of human dignity, and supplemented, if necessary, by other means of social protection.
4. Everyone has the right to form and to join trade unions for the protection of his interests.

section of the nation, but, by supporting the claim of that section — mainly capitalistic exploiters — to have blocked the path to the one lasting and universal right, that of economic justice.

The great revolutionary movements for freedom, viewed in the light of this dialectic materialism *(diamant* for short) which is the foundation of the U.S.S.R., merely turned the national state over to the owners of the means of production at a time when the Industrial Revolution was reducing the mass of workers to wage slavery. The escape from this new tyranny of capitalism by socializing the means of production is, therefore, according to *diamant,* the only way mankind generally can acquire those "fundamental rights and freedoms" which the propertied class in the advanced nations have won for themselves.

If the Communist interpretation of history were a mere ideological conception, it could be of interest only to theorists and historians, but it is the working basis of government, the bulwark of a system which definitely rejects democracy by its refusal to allow political parties within the State. Never was casuistry put to more powerful use than in the claim that opposition to policies of state is treason because in theory the collectivist economy includes everyone, whereas in noncommunist countries there must be provision for opposing political parties. Party freedom is meaningless in theory and treasonable in practice if it disrupts the harmony of a classless society. This is the law and the gospel as taken from Marx and Lenin and applied by Stalin in the 1936 constitution of the U.S.S.R. "In the U.S.S.R., political liberty is regarded chiefly as the right to break free from a capitalist state, because in socialist society the individual has no desire for liberation from the State. Individual liberty — individualism in all its forms — looks quite different when it is considered from the standpoint of the enslavement of the individual in a capitalist State. . . . The concept of liberty as determined by the socialist form of society completely upsets the definition of the rights of man."[13]

"In a socialist society the individual has no desire for liberation from the State." In this sentence the apologist for communism summarizes his whole case. But the Soviet Government itself has acted in contradiction to it, not only in its ruthless reign of terror against its enemies in the early days of the Soviet revolution, but in the continuance of the legal agency of that terror, the Cheka — the All-Russian Extraordinary Commission for Combatting Counter-revolution, Profiteering and Sabotage. This revolutionary tribunal, with its secret police, spies and informers, carried over into the Soviet regime the worst methods of the Tsarist repression, formally ordering some thirteen thousand executions in addition to uncounted thousands of unrecorded victims in the years 1918 to 1922. The terrorist police system of the period when Lenin was in control continued under various names: GPU, NKV and MVD[14] and was the arm of the Stalinist persecution of Bolshevik

[13] Boris Techkchko, *The Conception of the Rights of Man in the U.S.S.R. Based on Official Documents, in Human Rights,* edited by UNESCO (New York: Columbia University Press, 1959.)

[14] The initials of the Russian words have become so well known that it is unnecessary to give the names of these organizations in full.

comrades accused of heresy, but really liquidated because of their opposition, real or falsely charged, to the new autocracy in the Kremlin. To these victims must be added the continuing exile or murder of the Kulaks, the peasants who clung to individual ownership of the land.

The Communist world, which has accepted the regime of cruel suppression on the grounds of revolutionary necessity, was shocked when, after Stalin's death, his former colleagues, especially Khrushchev and Bulganin, denounced, or confessed, before the Soviet Congress this continued terror as the madness of unrestricted tyranny. The claim that human rights had been respected in Soviet Russia was thus denied by Stalin's successors. But no sooner had they made this gesture of repentance than they showed how false it was by their murderous and ruthless suppression of the revolt of freedom-loving Hungarians against communist rule. The falseness of the Russians' claim that they were the liberators of oppressed peoples was at last apparent even to leading communists in Western Europe, who recoiled against the horrors of Budapest. The Western world looked on in detestation at a crime it was powerless to avert.

From this analysis of Soviet tyranny, we turn back to the United Nations Declaration of Human Rights. It was approved by the General Assembly on December 10, 1948, after eighteen months of study and debate, revised and redrafted by the Commission, debated word for word in the Economic and Social Council and rewritten by a committee of the Assembly. In the final test, no nation voted against it, but the communist countries abstained, as did also Saudi Arabia on the ground that it was too largely an expression of Western ideas, and South Africa because it went too far for that racially divided country.

The Declaration was now before the world for judgment. It had been translated into 46 languages and distributed throughout the world by both the United Nations and many other agencies. But while its statement of principles is generally accepted by the nations, the Covenants which seek to apply them into law have had hard going. The heaviest blow dealt them was their repudiation by the United States Government in 1953. This does not mean that the States rejecting them or reluctant to accept them refuse to enforce them in domestic law. But it does mean that apart from the Soviet objections, one of the greatest limitations to freedom lies in freedom itself, jealous of its political rights and its way of life. The only adequate remedy for this situation lies in the schooling of intelligence to appreciate the various achievements of peoples who have to work out their destiny under diverse conditions of history and physical environment, and to keep before them the inspiration of a common purpose. The future of civilization depends upon that exercise of intelligence. It is in this field, equally with that of war prevention, that the United Nations faces its supreme test, as the guardian of freedom.

The Welfare of Nations

While the Commission on Human Rights deals with the traditional aspects of freedom and therefore has precedence in this description of the

nonpolitical activities of the United Nations, more important than any formulation of the rights of man are the provisions for the realization of "life,
liberty and the pursuit of happiness" in the daily life of men and nations.
The communists were right in insisting that a charter of freedom should include the most important thing to most people in the world — work — although they were wrong in insisting on only one way for dealing with it.
But freeing the pathways of life for the pursuit of happiness means more
than the right to work; it means a world-wide cooperative effort to make life
more worthwhile — the ultimate goal of freedom.

The program for this new world was set forth in Chapter IX of the
Charter, under the heading "International Economic and Social Cooperation." The purpose is stated in article 55:

With a view to the creation of conditions of stability and well-being which are
necessary for peaceful and friendly relations among nations based on respect for
the principle of equal rights and self-determination of peoples, the United Nations
shall promote:
a. higher standards of living, full employment, and conditions of economic and
    social progress and development;
b. solutions of international economic, social, health, and related problems; and
    international cultural and educational cooperation; and
c. universal respect for, and observance of, human rights and fundamental
    freedoms for all without distinction as to race, sex, language, or religion.

A central organ, the Economic and Social Council, was provided for in
the Charter to coordinate the "international machinery for the promotion of
the economic and social advancement of all peoples." History was soon to
show, however, that this machinery tended to coordinate itself, and that the
commissions and agencies set up to deal with conditions of life, health, labor
and cultures became vital organs in themselves, so important that the General Assembly took an interest in them. Alongside some twelve commissions
of the Economic and Social Council, of which the Commission on Human
Rights is one, there are the Specialized Agencies, which have become of outstanding importance in the nonpolitical activities of the United Nations; for
they extend its sphere of action, are semi-autonomous, and are fitted into the
structure of the United Nations in a relationship which is more like that of a
federal system than the term agency would seem to imply. The only model
from previous history was that of the autonomous relationship between the
International Labor Organization and the League of Nations; and, as it is a
specialized agency of the United Nations — the only Geneva organization to
live on through World War II (although without the membership of the
Axis powers) — we may begin with it.

During the war years, the I.L.O., as it is popularly termed, concentrated
on plans for the future, and at its twenty-sixth Conference at Philadelphia in
April 1944 issued a Declaration which President Roosevelt said "future generations will look back upon as a landmark in world thinking." The declaration affirmed that "all human beings, irrespective of race, creed or sex, have
the right to pursue their material well-being and their spiritual development

594

in conditions of freedom and dignity, of economic security and equal opportunity." There being at that time no League or United Nations, the I.L.O. stated that, "It is a responsibility of the International Labor Organization to examine and consider all international economic and financial policies and measures in the light of this fundamental objective." This was going too far; and the politically minded, inside and outside of government, agreed that the I.L.O. should keep within its sphere of social welfare by way of conventions or recommendations for legislation of national governments. But within these established limits, it has fulfilled all the hopes of its founders. Member goverments have adopted 114 international labor conventions and 189 recommendations. These instruments, embodying improved labor conditions, constitute what has become known as the International Labor Code. This record of success is all the more astonishing in the light of history; for there were only two treaties dealing with labor conditions when the I.L.O. was founded.

Of the other Specialized Agencies the only one which lies directly within the horizon of this work is the United Nations Educational, Scientific and Cultural Organization (UNESCO). The furtherance of international understanding had been recognized, though, in a somewhat left-handed manner, by the League of Nations in its Organization for International Intellectual Cooperation.[15] The United States had had no official connection with this body owing to nonmembership in the League, but in the Pan-American Union it had seen the importance of cultural relations between nations, and in recent years there had been a great increase in unofficial international organizations dealing with academic and social problems. Even within the State Department a committee was organized on educational and cultural relations. It was, therefore, natural that under the United Nations there should be established a much more important body than had existed under the League of Nations, and in November, 1945, a Conference held in London drew up the constitution of a body which bears the awkward title of United Nations Educational, Scientific and Cultural Organization. The constitution of this body states its purposes in an eloquent preamble, which needs little further explanation:

. . . Since wars begin in the minds of men it is in the minds of men that the defenses of peace must be constructed; the ignorance of each other's ways and lives has been a common cause throughout the history of mankind of that suspicion and mistrust between the peoples of the world through which their differences have all too often broken into war; that the great and terrible war which has now ended was a war made possible by the denial of the democratic principles of the dignity, equality and mutual respect of men and by the propagation in their place through ignorance and prejudice of the doctrine of the inequality of men and races; that the wide diffusion of culture and the education of humanity for justice and liberty and peace are indispensable to the dignity of men and constitute a sacred duty which all the nations must fulfill in a spirit of mutual assistance and concern; that a peace based exclusively upon the political and economic arrangements of governments would not be a peace which could secure the unanimous, lasting and sincere

15 See Chapter XVII.

support of the peoples of the world and that peace must, therefore, be founded, if it is not to fail, upon the intellectual and moral solidarity of mankind. *For these reasons* the States parties to this Constitution, believing in full and equal opportunities for education for all in the unrestricted pursuit of objective truth and in the free exchange of ideas and knowledge, are agreed and determined to develop and to increase the means of communication between their peoples and to employ these means for the purpose of mutual understanding and a truer and more perfect knowledge of each other's lives. *In consequence whereof,* they do hereby create the United Nations Educational, Scientific and Cultural Organization for the purpose of advancing through the educational and scientific and cultural relations of the peoples of the world the objectives of international peace and of the common welfare of mankind for which the United Nations Organization was established and which its Charter proclaims.

The program of UNESCO at first included many activities in the field of post-war reconstruction, supplying reading material to war-devastated areas, and helping intellectual leaders displaced by the war. Its chief activities have been in the field of education, in which it has maintained advisory commissions in underdeveloped countries, sponsored seminars on international understanding in Europe, and a critical examination of the teaching of the social and political sciences, among other activities. In the field of the natural sciences it has installed equipment to make possible laboratory work, and given grants-in-aid to scientists. It has maintained cultural exchanges between member nations and given full access to the art and literature of other countries. It also has undertaken, by a survey of press, film and radio facilities throughout the world, to develop means of communication among those countries which permit the free exchange of information, and distributes films and broadcasts "designed to promote peace and human welfare."

Two other Specialized Agencies call for mention here, for, although outside the direct interests of this study, they have done and are doing work of great importance in the upbuilding of a world community; these are the World Health Organization and the Food and Agriculture Organization.

The World Health Organization also profited from the pioneering work of the League of Nations. Its function, as far as possible, is to fight preventable diseases, stopping the course of plagues at their source, and thus make for that strength of body and mind by which man is able to enjoy the rights and freedoms to which civilization makes him heir. Disease is another dread dictator, sometimes torturing the body and sometimes, like the "thought police," preying on the mind. Political and social human rights can have very little meaning unless the body and mind are equipped to enjoy them.

The Food and Agriculture Organization deals with the distribution of the world's food supply so that both the producer and consumer may profit. It is trying to see not only that there is enough food at the right places and at the right time, but that the kind and quality of food are adequate for a healthful diet. There is no dictator so terrible as hunger. In its relentless power a man sinks to the level of an animal. If we are to live up to the Charter of the United Nations, we must deal with this problem, not with the casual interest of those who have no experience with suffering, but with the sympathetic insight of those who can realize the prime need of the under-privileged in all countries. At the same time, we have to admit that the terms of the problem itself are so new that we do not know how best to deal with them. We can learn that lesson by recognizing the supreme importance to the world at large of the Food and Agriculture Organization, and participate loyally in it.

Through agencies like these, the functional, if not the political, unity of civilization is under way; for economic cooperation there are the International Bank for Reconstruction and Development, the International Monetary Fund, the International Trade Organization, and the International Civil Aviation Organization, while a branch of the Secretariat itself is in charge of the vastly important field of Technical Assistance, to plan and supervise the application of western science to the problems of peoples who, in the words which years ago Marshal Smuts put into the Covenant of the League, "are not yet able to stand by themselves under the strenuous conditions of the modern world."

Finally, there is one agency which has not yet fully taken shape, but may be of more importance than all the rest, the International Atomic Energy Agency. It is not yet possible to comment upon it in detail, but if the negotiations now under way succeed, it will have the supreme task of establishing a control of atomic energy which will eliminate the menace of destruction and assure its development for purposes of peace. If this body is established and fulfills its purpose it will be the most important of all organs of government, because upon its decisions will rest the possibilities of the future.

All of these organs of the United Nations, and others as well, should be kept in mind in any discussion of human rights and fundamental freedoms, for the assertion of these rights is a statement of a way of life, a goal towards which we are striving. In order to achieve this goal, we must do more than draft pious resolutions or even attempt to set up the principles of a new international law. We must make sure that there is a decent way of life for all before we can set about safeguarding it, and until there is freedom from fear and freedom from want, the achievement of human rights will be incomplete. Neither freedom from fear nor want can be legalized out of existence. They exist because of certain defects in our civilization. To remedy these defects should be one of the great tasks of the United Nations, established, as the Charter states, "to reaffirm faith in the dignity and worth of the human person."

CHAPTER XXVI

ON THE RIM OF THE FUTURE

THE LAST TWO chapters open alluring horizons on a new world; but in the fateful autumn months of 1956 those horizons were lost in darkness, as the liberties of Hungary were stamped out in blood and the cloud of war rose in Egypt. In disheartening confusion the free world saw the very structure of international relations threatened by the forces of Soviet tyranny in the heart of Europe, while at the gateway between East and West, Israel, France and Great Britain, in disregard of the pledges in the Charter of the United Nations, resorted to the arbitrament of arms in a desperate but blundering attempt to speak to the reactionary nationalism of the Arab world in the only language which they believed it would listen to: that of military power. The catastrophic consequences to Western Europe of the small-scale attack on Egypt which followed almost reached the dimensions of a major war, as the greatest source of its power, oil, was cut off by the blocking of the Suez Canal. But the blow to Western economy, disastrous as that was, was less vital to the free world than the loss of moral authority which amounted to a betrayal of its professed ideals.

History records no sadder moment in the history of France and Great Britain than the scene in the United Nations, when practically all America, Asia and Africa, along with most of the other nations of Europe, demanded a humiliating cessation of aggression and a withdrawal of the invading forces from Egypt "forthwith." This was not the language of conciliation or even of diplomacy, as Paul-Henri Spaak pointed out in an eloquent but vain appeal to the General Assembly. It had the harsh tones of an ultimatum, doubly searing in its effect, because for the first time the United States voted with the U.S.S.R. in favor of it; and this at the very time that the Soviet army was crushing the uprising in Hungary against Communist tyranny — of which we shall have more to say later on.

Undoubtedly, Secretary of State Dulles was sincere when he said that, as spokesman for the United States, he intervened in the debate "with a very heavy heart." That certainly was the case with all true friends of freedom, for the unqualified denunciation of the invasion of Egypt held long-reaching consequences both for the Western alliance of NATO against Soviet aggression in Europe and for the United Nations, in which the U.S.S.R. could pose as the protector of Asia and Africa against "colonialism." It should have been a sobering thought that these nations readily accepted the Soviet charge that what the British and French regarded as a holding operation at the Suez Canal was really a glaring revival of "colonial imperialism." Actually, the demand for international — not British or French — control of the Canal had nothing to do with colonialism, but the slogan stirred smouldering resentments which, as the Russians never forget, could burst into flaming nationalism in Asia, Africa and South America.

Deeper still than the memory of economic exploitation, racial antagonism — mostly that of color — added to the anti-Western demonstrations. The white race, once master, was being put in its place. The fact that anti-imperialism had been the guiding principle of Great Britain in recent years, as we have seen in previous chapters, was lost sight of by the representatives of the country that had profited most from it, India. For it was Krishna Menon of India who led the attack on the "colonial" powers. The United States, traditionally anti-colonial, but not too discriminating in the support of native governments, good or bad, and also not unmindful, perhaps, of its investments in Arabian oil, joined with the U.S.S.R. in support of the harsh ultimatum that the invaders of Egypt leave "forthwith" without any guarantee of an ultimate settlement of the issue at stake. How far they were from that judicious temper which is the indispensable basis of statesmanship, was evident in the remark of an Indian delegate after the Assembly meeting, when, in a sudden outburst of candor while speaking to me, he summed up the situation by a comment which was also a threat: "The target is Europe."

A major test of the United Nations had now come in the first session of the enlarged Assembly. Was it to link the upsurging nationalism of the newest — and oldest — nations with the communist war on capitalism and serve as a recruiting ground for those who would make Europe the target? If the nations which brought freedom into the world were to be supplanted by those which had acquired it only recently, and they in turn were to follow the lead of the U.S.S.R., at least in its militant anti-Western policy, the days of the United Nations were numbered.

But that was not what happened. Although Moscow quickly took every advantage offered it by the disunion of the Western Powers over the war on Egypt, the hollowness of its pretenses as the champion of the small nations was revealed to the whole world by its ruthless suppression of the liberties of the Hungarian people. The two crises — in Egypt and Hungary — coincided, and the result was not an increase in Soviet strength, but an awakening to the danger of an imperialism as despotic as any in history. The bitterness of Arab hostility against Israel, Britain and France was understood throughout the Orient, and this sentiment blurred sympathy for the Hungarians fighting against Soviet occupation of their country — one that cherished a glorious history of its defense of its freedom. Yet as the heroic uprising of the Magyars was only slowly suppressed, its full significance became evident to the Western nations, if not to Asia and Africa. It widened the crack in the monolithic empire of Moscow, which had been opened first by Yugoslavia, and then, in more recent months, by Poland.

This did not really mean that the empire of the Kremlin showed signs of dissolving like that of Kipling's Britain. Those who shared this optimistic forecast, including highly-placed officials in Washington, pointed to the fact that the movements in Poland and Hungary were largely shared in by youths who had never lived under a regime of freedom. There were even signs of unrest in the student body inside the U.S.S.R. itself. If these movements were actually directed against the Communist system, they would evidently disprove the Jesuit saying that the education of a child to the age of seven would determine its outlook through life. Could it be true that indoctrination in communist orthodoxy, with its falsification of history and its promises for the future, was yielding to the heresy of nationalism, not only in the satellite countries, but even in Russia itself?

The answer is that we cannot be sure that anything happened in all this testing of mind and character behind the iron curtain to justify the conclusion that the Jesuits were wrong. According to their own account in their student paper — the reliability of which is perhaps open to question — the youths of Russia indignantly answered an American radio claim that they were forsaking communism. They insisted that they were critical only of the failure of the Kremlin to reap the full benefit of the crisis forced on the world by the action of the British and French in Egypt. That was evidently not the way the Kremlin understood the situation, however, for it began a full dress inquiry into the whole educational system to find out what was wrong with it. The chief grievance of the students seemed to be an overdose of communism, forcing the student youths to combine work on farms or in factories with their studies, a program too severe for some of them. The refusal to accept this party discipline unhesitatingly was denounced in the communist press as a tendency toward "individualism." But the students had no political program of their own, for nothing in the past or present of Russia gave them any idea of how a State could be organized under freedom.

The situation in Poland was somewhat similar in that its leader, Gomulka, kept Polish nationalism within the communist regime. A convinced communist himself, he mobilized the forces of discontent along the age-old lines of history, against Russian interference in Polish affairs, without risking a return to the old regime, which, it must be recalled, had never given freedom to the common man. Freedom from Russian domination in Poland's internal affairs was all that was sought by Gomulka, and if that was partly gained, it was because of the general uncertainty which the Kremlin faced in the satellite nations. But Polish nationalism is a vital force, and today the future is by no means certain, although Gomulka proved to be more a communist than a nationalist.

Hungary was different. There, the youths had studied from their youngest years the epic of their defiance of the greatest empire of the later Middle Ages, that of the Turks, their proud kingdom ranking with the Empire of Austria, and their heroic fight against Russian invaders in the great days of Kossuth. Here was something to outrival the propaganda of the communists. In short, the unrest in Eastern Europe seems to have meant anticommunism only in Hungary, and even there the nation was split in a civil war.

It was the heroism of the Hungarians which forced the Assembly of the United Nations to face up to Soviet imperialism, which it did by four almost unanimous resolutions in the General Assembly (only the communists voted against them), calling upon the government of the U.S.S.R. to desist from its intervention in the internal affairs of Hungary, to withdraw its forces from Hungary, and to cease its repression of the Hungarian people.[1] The puppet government of Hungary avoided possible expulsion by withdrawal from the Assembly, and put itself further outside the pale by refusing the United Nations officials, even the Secretary-General, admittance to the country to report on conditions there. With thousands killed and more thousands exiled to unknown prison camps, the heroic workers faced a winter's cold with a general strike to show their unconquered spirit. This was and will always remain, one of the noblest and most tragic episodes in the history of freedom.

The significance of what is happening to the communist empire of the U.S.S.R. must be left to experts familiar, not only with international problems, but with the history of Eastern Europe. The first notable analysis of Soviet polity was an article in the magazine *Foreign Affairs* for July, 1947, "The Sources of Soviet Conduct." It soon became known that the anonymous author was none other than the chief Russian expert in the State Department, George Kennan. While the analysis covered many points, the one most important conclusion was stated in a single sentence: "The possibility remains (and in the opinion of this writer it is a strong one), that Soviet power, like the capitalist world of its conception, bears within it the seeds of its own decay, and that the sprouting of these seeds is well advanced." Studies of the communist crises in Poland and Hungary tended to verify, at least in part, this forecast of the troubles developing in the Soviet system.

It has been charged by those unfriendly to the United Nations that that body showed its futility in both Egypt and Hungary. But it can be argued with equal force that in using only a moral sanction, instead of taking military measures, as in Korea, it won a great and bloodless victory. The campaign of Communist propaganda failed to prevent most of the Asian block in the United Nations from turning against the U.S.S.R. on its action in Hungary.[2] But the Egyptian crisis showed that the United Nations needed to implement its strategy of peace, even if it did not resort to force. The statesman who seized the occasion for this reform was Lester Pearson, the Minister for External Affairs of Canada. Doubly disturbed not only because the

[1] Resolutions of the General Assembly, November 4, 9, 21, and December 4, 1956.
[2] It is a sad commentary on India's vaunted devotion to democracy and democratic ideals that it refrained from voting a censure of the U.S.S.R. in the Hungarian crisis.

Charter had been violated, but also because the very existence of the British Commonwealth had been endangered by the disaffection of its Asian members, he proposed the creation of a U.N. Emergency Force to keep peace in Egypt between the belligerents. Unfortunately, the resolution was not clearly framed,[3] and while the United Nations force remained along the disputed frontier, the creation of a permanent international police continued to be studied; for it raised the fundamental question whether the United Nations is a sovereign superstate in its maintenance of peace, or only the embodiment of a moral force — which often suffers eclipse when nations clash.

It probably would have been too much to expect of an Assembly so strongly imbued with nationalism that it would set up local bodies to oversee the application of its resolutions, except under strictly defined conditions. There was more than nationalism to overcome, however, if the United Nations were to make its agencies not only advisory but compulsory as well, in a police force to preserve the peace. The technical difficulties in the creation of such a force have long been subjects of study in the Military Staff Committee of the Security Council. It would not do to have anything resembling a standing army, with quotas filled at all times and equipment always ready to deal with any kind of emergency, for such a development would be readily accepted only by nations with military traditions and might prove to be a tool in the hands of reactionaries, making the United Nations resemble the Concert of Europe under Metternich. On the other hand, the infrequent use of a United Nations police force, used only when all peaceful measures failed, raises questions of morale in the ranks and of costs of maintenance. The provisions in the Charter for contingents from the Member States when necessary were wisely limited to temporary arrangements; what was lacking was the political agreement in the United Nations to ensure their use when the crises came.

There is, however, as we have said before, another and stronger defense of peace by the United Nations than police action or the threat of reprisals against an agressor. It is the upbuilding of common interests in welfare. The new members of the United Nations are not merely jealous of their sovereignty, they are also intent on fitting themselves for a world dominated by the newest world power: science. While they cherish their grievances against the colonial powers which had so long kept the monopoly of this new power, they will have the chance to see that the path to peace, as far as they are concerned — and they are the great majority of mankind — is by cooperation under freedom. The United Nations has already been pioneering along this line, but without a clear appreciation of the fact that only in this way can its new members avoid making an alliance between anti-colonialism and communism, in which the United Nations police force would become an instrument of discord instead of world unity. Such, in broad terms, is the

[3] The newspapers at the time stated that Egypt and its supporters took it to mean only a police force to oversee the withdrawal from Egypt of the invading troops, and that the Secretary-General of the United Nations accepted this interpretation. Fortunately, this report was not true.

one promising program within the United Nations for the nations of Asia, Africa and South America.

Europe and North America have their full share in this problem, but they have also the major responsibilities for keeping the peace while the world grows up to political as well as economic and cultural maturity — not as overlords of the less advanced countries, but as members of the community of Europe and the Atlantic. Fortunately these Western nations can bring to the support of the peace purposes of the United Nations its most important ally — NATO. The development of this great military alliance into a political and economic union, for which provision has been made in Article 2 of the North Atlantic Treaty — the proposal of Lester Pearson of Canada — was strongly advocated by forward-looking sections of public opinion in Great Britain as well as on the Continent. Inter-parliamentary groups met unofficially at the NATO headquarters in Paris in 1955 to urge action along these lines.

But when Great Britain and France invaded Egypt without informing their allies of their plans, the first reaction was that the very existence of NATO had been imperiled, not to speak of the greater Atlantic unity built on it. But at a fateful meeting of the NATO Council in December, 1956, it not only showed its power to survive, but took a first, if tentative step away from the purely military alliance to the wider program of North-Atlantic-European integration. The shadows of disagreements still lie ahead, but the light was at least breaking through on a larger horizon than before. While military planning remained strictly defensive, NATO was strengthened by proposals for the coordination of the economic and political forces of the free nations. To bring this vision of a new Europe down from the clouds and make it a practical program, the NATO Council turned to the Belgian statesman, Paul-Henri Spaak, the man who took over from Winston Churchill the leadership of the European Movement, to embody it in the Council of Europe.

Great movements need great men. Carlyle was not wholly wrong in his theory of history as the creation of leaders, although he overstated his case, and it is now the fashion to denounce him as a proto-fascist. The solution for most of the crises in history has been found by men of superior insight, capacity or power. In turning the secretaryship of NATO over from a professional soldier like Lord Ismay to one of the most experienced statesmen in Europe, more was done to further the unity of Western Europe than in the passage of any number of pious resolutions. Even before being installed in office, M. Spaak showed at once the clarity of his vision, when he flatly turned down the suggestion of the British Foreign Secretary, Mr. Lloyd, that NATO have a parliament of its own, which, said M. Spaak, would "only clutter up" the already existing machinery for European unity. The thing to do is to make the already existing institutions work, as recent history has shown they could.

Thus the menacing shadow of disagreement among the free nations was largely dissipated. But progress is slow by the very fact that freedom is jealous of power. Governments which depend upon public opinion cannot go beyond the desires of the people they represent. The situation in NATO was well summed up by C. L. Sulzberger, correspondent of *The New York Times:* "This [dependence on public opinion] is the essential political weakness of NATO, and the reason it cannot tidily agree on every matter. But it is also NATO's essential strength, for the populations of the West believe in the North Atlantic Community. They are, if necessary, ready to fight for it. This, as demonstrated in Hungary and Poland, is not the spirit of the Warsaw [communist] Pact, so patently an instrument of imperial oppression."

In other words, the free nations not only make discouraging blunders, but the national independence which they cherish is an obstacle to the larger freedom. The ultimate aim is too remote for a nationalist Europe to achieve by the accustomed way of states still clinging to sovereignty as the very symbol of their being. That way to the unity of the free world will be darkened by misunderstanding and mistrust before the goal is reached. Yet, absolute state sovereignty which for so long tended to create international anarchy is no longer possible. The way to the unity of Western Europe is still darkened by misunderstanding and mistrust, and yet a new sense of common interests has developed to the point where it challenges the prejudices of history. Just as in the world of engineering the imperfections of a machine call for rectification and improvement, so in that great engineering process which history has become, the imperative need in the spirit of man for a fuller and richer life will some day reach its ultimate goal, in a commonwealth, not merely of Europe and North America, but of free nations everywhere.

This is not whistling in the dark; it is a recognition of the fact that the two major conflicts of 1956 over Hungary and Egypt, which seemed at one time to block the road to peace and freedom — however tragic in themselves and however important the outcome — were but passing incidents in history, compared with the transformation of practically all the conditions of life on this planet which has been ushered in by the control of the atom. On October 6, 1956, at the very time when the Israelites were moving in on the Sinai peninsula, seventy nations signed, at the United Nations, the Statute of an International Atomic Agency for the peaceful uses of the atom. The United States offered to contribute 5,000 kilograms of uranium-235 to its "pool" or bank of nuclear fuel and as much more as would be needed to match all contributions to July, 1960. The comment on this by a writer in the *Bulletin of the Atomic Scientists,*[4] on the launching of President Eisenhower's Atoms-for-Peace Agency goes to the heart of things:

If, at the outset of the industrial revolution, the world community had set up an agency to guide and influence the mining and sale of coal, the operation of steam generators, and the uses of steel, our world today would have been a very different place in which to live. Among other things, the whole nineteenth-century pattern

[4] "The Atomic High Road," by William R. Frye, *Bulletin of the Atomic Scientists* (December, 1956).

of empires might have been different, if, indeed, there had been any colonialism at all as we have known it. The atoms-for-peace agency, established this fall, is empowered to do for us in the atomic revolution of our time what mankind failed to do in the industrial revolution of the eighteenth and nineteenth centuries. . . .

The statute provided that there should be a staff of inspectors with authority to penalize any nation violating it by refusing further assistance. The danger that the U.S.S.R. might attempt by propaganda to persuade the "have-not" nations that it was offering more than the United States was met by the provision that the United States would match the contributions of any other nation. This provision alone was worth all the propaganda that the communists could devise. It opened the perspective of an atomic age with the real promise of a better life. But the promise remains unfulfilled so long as neither side in the cold war trusts the other. The issue at stake is not communism versus capitalism but power politics, darkened with the menace of war, yet held back from the catastrophe by the changed nature of war itself.

The only hope for the future lies in turning from the negative of mutual fears to the positive of mutual understanding. Then, with minds freed from fanatic ideologies — on both sides — a civilization can be built different from any recorded here.

CONCLUSION

More potent than all the armies of all the nations, thought is grappling with human destiny. As Marshal Jan Smuts has so eloquently put it, mankind has struck its tents and is on the march in a vast unending trek of pioneers into a new civilization, of which only the distant outlines lie before us, indistinct but shining far away. But we cannot leave history behind us as we make it. It still stays with us, to warn and to inspire. "The past is prelude. . . ." That greatest line of the greatest English poet is inscribed on the National Archives Building in Washington; but it does more than remind us of a nation's achievement; it is a summary of the long story we have been telling here: for the story of freedom is the story of all mankind.

We have traced it in three great eras: that of the haunting tyranny of the taboo; that of militarism and the politics nurtured by it; and that of economic exploitation. We have seen that escape is not enough; that there are positive steps to be taken at each stage of emancipation, as superstition gives way to intelligence in religion and morals; as war changes its nature under science and ceases to be a directable instrument of politics; and finally as economic and social justice become the accepted basis of the common life.

The process of emancipation is two-fold: it does not stop with the elimination of evils of the past. It must offer substitutes for them, for what is now an evil was once a felt need. It is this second phase of the transformation of society from primitive elements to civilization which is the problem of today and tomorrow.

We have seen how in the prehistoric ages the human pack and horde merged into the tribe and the tribe into the city-state or the military structure of empire, and then, in the centuries of our own history, how the national state became the sovereign political unit. Each of these social groupings cherished its own way of living and maintained it in the unending repetition and rhythm of the seasons through untold generations. The enemy to this sacredness of custom was the foreigner who had other habits and other gods. In the realm of taboo, his very presence might be sacrilege. Therefore, the magician and the priest, with the support of the warrior class, guarded against the dangers from without. But war brought slaves as well as booty, and as the artisans hammered out their tools or trinkets, shy but persistent merchants spread their wares outside the sacred city walls or in the bazaars of the Orient. Then culture traveled with the exchange of goods and the intermingling of the peoples.

With the growth of property came the growth of law, a process older than Hammurabi, which in the ancient world finally broke through the old taboos into the noble expression of human rights in Roman law. The only fitting law for a world empire was the Law of Nations (*jus gentium*) instead of the municipal law of Rome, for, in the creation of the universal code, the Roman jurists could call upon the experience of all mankind. Thus the Roman law in its final form was not purely Roman in origin; it was also the embodiment of Stoic philosophy and Christian morals. Because it drew from so many diverse sources and was applied to the citizenship of a universal empire, it proved to be the one contribution of ancient Rome which lives on in the world today.

Now the time has come for a new law of nations. The mingling of the peoples and the interplay not only of their cultures but of their rights in society are fully as great as was the case in those far-off days when the Roman jurists began their work. For they began it while Rome was still a Republic and the process of world conquest was in its early stages. Today the forces of science, stronger than all of Caesar's legions, are welding the world into a new formation which has no parallel in all the past.

There have been two main patterns offered us to follow, and our choice was made in the tragic but irrevocable decisions of the second World War. On the one hand, there was the German peace (*pax Germanica*), a crude or rather a superficial imitation of the *pax Romana* based upon power but not implemented by justice; on the other hand, there was the cooperation of the freedom-loving nations. The German peace, military in conception, had no tolerance for variant forms of society and regarded opposition to its political will as treason. This is the inevitable outcome of military control, as Rome itself was to learn when the iron clamp of the dictator crushed out not only the liberties of Roman citizens but their very means of livelihood. The Roman Empire fell to the barbarians not as a powerful state pulsating with vitality but as a hollow shell decked in the outworn trappings of Byzantium. The same fate would ultimately befall any modern imitation of Roman militarism. The *pax Germanica* might have conquered the world in our time but it could not have furnished a fitting political embodiment for the dynamic forces of the world of science, the first condition of which is freedom.

The accent upon freedom, therefore, in our war aims was not mere rhetoric. In fighting for freedom, we were fighting for the only possible basis for the future — that which guarantees to each individual the open pathways of the mind and the free choice of a career. There is no hope for a society which revives the penalties of the taboo against the independent thinker; nor can justice develop under military regimentation. There must be freedom for the individual to experiment and to explore, to think and to express his thought, and that freedom must be safeguarded by both law and custom so long as it is not anti-social. This is what we mean by democracy, not the rule of the many but rather the safeguarding of their freedom, a freedom that justifies itself by providing disciplined intelligence in its leadership and a critical, open-minded citizenship. It is worse than useless to create a vast system of international diplomacy and government if its control is to rest in the hands of those who are unfit for such high responsibilities, and that will be the case if the citizens are not alertly aware of their own interests and free to insist upon them.

Civilization is not a mechanism but a vital principle, or rather an embodiment of many varied principles of life, which have their roots in diverse soils and their expression in divers cultures. It cannot flourish, it cannot even survive, if those in the seats of power deny it the fundamental freedoms of life itself. Therefore, tyranny, which denies these freedoms, is not so much a method of government as a crime against society.

From this survey we draw one conclusion: that as tyranny is the worst school for freedom, freedom itself is the best. The test of its maturity is the way in which the safeguarding of fundamental freedoms has been carried out. For the significance and unique contribution of a true democracy is the use it makes of minority opposition. The bi-partisan system organizes this opposition to take part in the play and counterplay of politics much better than the more logical multi-party system which tends to block action by wrangling stalemates. But, however the opposition takes shape, it must be accepted and recognized as a legitimate organ of democratic government. It was the violation of this principle in the one party system of the Kuomintang' in China, Fascism in Italy, National Socialism in Germany, and Sovietism in Russia which confused loyalty to party with loyalty to State and, thereby, while apparently exalting the power of the State, in reality made it subservient to a single, uncompromising element in it. Thus, by a paradox, the totalitarian regimes are their own ultimate enemies by the denaturing of loyalty.

From what has just been said, it is clear that democracy, which seems to us the normal way of life, is neither applied nor understood in large sections of the world today. Even in the nations which share the political heritage of Greece and Rome, the relation between the citizen and his government varies greatly. Democratic countries which were largely shaped in the Roman tradition — not only the so-called Latin countries of Europe and America, but the Germanic countries as well — expect government to govern and to invoke bureaucracy as the necessary implement. The emphasis is on law and order, which tends to make major changes take the form of revolution. The contrast with British democracy has appeared from time to time in the course of this survey; but the main reason for it is that Continental governments were never wholly free from the threat of war, and government had to be strong enough to deal with national emergencies. Nowhere was there a successful experiment in Jeffersonian democracy. Masaryk tried it in Czechoslovakia, but in spite of his great prestige, he could not get his people, long subject to Austrian or Hungarian bureaucracy and divided in former loyalties, to work together with their neighbors in a regime of freedom. Democracy will succeed only where opposition to the government is permitted, and only as long as it does not become sedition against the State itself.

If the uses of democracy vary so much in Europe and America, they are still less understood in Asia and the other parts of the world where the great experiment of self-government by the people themselves has never been tried. The greatest fallacy in American thinking today is the failure to appreciate the fact that even the most friendly, best disposed peoples of non-European cultures cannot be made over by any political legerdemain for the model set by Magna Carta and the Bill of Rights. Time and experience are needed. If time can be guaranteed, the experience will follow.

We must be careful, however, not to lose our way at the end of this long journey and confuse freedom with democracy. If, as we have pointed out at every stage of this long road, freedom is the fullness of life for the individual — the *summum bonum* to use the classical term — then it is the nature rather than the form of government which counts. The test of this has now been formulated in the Universal Declaration of Human Rights of the United Nations, but the failure to incorporate it in a Convention, establishing these rights under the rule of law for all nations shows how far we still are from agreement, not only on the form but also the content of a universal guarantee of freedom. The rise of military dictatorships in Asia and the possibility of similar developments in Africa are happily countered by a lessening of such dictatorships in Latin America, a trend of which the United States has not been sufficiently aware.

For the present, the horizon is obscured by both the immaturity of the new nations and the surging strength of communism. The future, however, assured for freedom is an assertion of life itself. Its well-springs may be poisoned by disregard of the rights of others, they may erupt into crime or overflow into anarchy; but they can be and will be controlled. That was the lesson of the revolutions for freedom which ushered in our world of today. It is also that of the hidden force in that perverse faith in communism which accepts tyranny in the name of human rights and freedom. But the goal of full achievement will never be reached by the mere assertion of ideals. Freedom must be clothed with authority and embodied in institutions dedicated to its sovereignty. But sovereignty in the world of science is not what it once was in the long eras of agricultural living. It is an interplay of interests, for that is the way people will be living from now until the end of time. The only prosperity, the only happiness for mankind will be found in the interplay of human interests — in short in the application of the golden rule.

So, in the long future, the city of man will be the embodiment of the City of God. Augustine's conception would never have challenged the best thought of the Western world, if the City of God had been modeled on the city state of ancient Greece, narrowly cherishing its own rights against those of its neighbors and waging war to maintain them. By his time the city state had become the world, the *orbis terrarum*. Now, once more, the national sovereignties, which have had the right of war and peace, are being forced by a greater sovereignty, that of science, to merge their interests and respect the rights of others. The City of Man raises its shining ramparts over the national state system which history prepared as the embodiment, imperfect but inspiring, of the aspirations of man for independence and freedom.

Civilization is only just beginning to show the glory and nobility of man in a world in which freedom is another name for justice. It will be his task to the end of time to establish and maintain that world, so that freedom also becomes another name for history.

INDEX

INDEX

A

Aachen, 175
Abba, 152
Abelard, 209
Aborigines, 50
Abraham, 72
Achilles, 302
Acquitaine, 162
Acropolis, 83
Act of Supremacy, 311
Act of Toleration of 1685, 324
Acton, Lord, 95, 207, 272, 305, 409
Acts of the Apostles, 139
  Acts 23: 24-29, 182
Adams, John, 345-348
Adams, John Quincy, 555
Ad extirpanda, 214
Address to the Christian Nobility of the German Nation, 308-311
Addresses to the German People, 383
Adoptionism, 212
Adrianople, 161
Adriatic, 113
Advice to Ruined France, 318
Aegean Sea, 75-76, 90
Aetolian and Achaean Leagues, 99
Africa, 542-551
  South, 23, 112, 114, 126
Agamemnon, 77, 230
Agincourt, 79, 268, 334
Agôge, 88
Ahriman, 61

Ahuramazda, 61, 107
Aijub Khan, 505
Aiken, Dr., 399
Aisne, 425
Akhenaton, 59
Alaric, 161, 195
Albania, 443
Albi, 212
Albigenses, 211
Aldus, 265
Alexander the Great, 43, 46, 73, 75-107, 115, 123
Alexander 1, 386
Alexander VI, 282, 284
Alexandria, 38, 123, 213
Alfred the Great, 164, 167
Algeria, 495, 544, 548
Alhambra, 240
Allah, 71-74
Allemanis, 172
Allied Control Council, 473
Alps, 58
Amalekites, 64
Ambedkar, B. R., 514
Amendments to the Constitution, 377
Amenhotep, *see* Amenophis IV
Amenophis IV, 59
America, 18-22, 42
American Commonwealth, 364
American Federation of Labor, 40, 561
American Revolution, 292, 320, 488
Amon Re, 59

B

Baal, 64

Babylon, 38, 45, 60, 66, 75, 84, 91, 107

Babylonia, 38, 45, 59-60

Babylonian Captivity of the Church, 308

Babylonians, 35, 105

Bacon, Francis, 300

Bacon, Roger, 210

Baghdad, 73, 159

Baker, Ray Stannard, 438, 560

Ball, John, 187

Balliol College, 306

Baltic Sea, 44, 158-159

Baptists, 320-324

Barclay, Sir Thomas, 424

Basel, 298

Basil, 152

Basques, 239

Bastille, 331, 357

Battle of the Lechfeld, 173

Baudouin, King, 547

Bayeux, 198

Beard, Charles and Mary, 376

Beaton, Cardinal, 313

Beccaria, 185, 354

Bedouins, 70

Becker, Carl, 347-349

Beer, George Louis, 496

Beethoven, 386

Before History, 22-42

Beginnings of the American People, 349

Belgian Congo, 495-496

Bellarmin, Cardinal, 299

Benedict, 153

Benedictine Rule, 153, 196-197

Bengals, 508

Bentham, Jeremy, 370

Bergson, Henri, 396, 437

Bernard, St., 154

Berne, 423

Bethmann-Hollweg, 424

Berthold, Elector of Mainz, 278

Bessarabia, 455

Bevin, 474, 484

Bidault, Georges, 484

Bill of Rights, 375

Bismarck, 19, 243, 269, 280, 389, 403, 407, 421-422, 427, 438, 440, 486, 562

Black Dragon Society, 449

Black Death, 186, 255, 259

Black Monks of Benedict, 153

Black Sea, 76, 97, 115, 161

Blackstone, 348

Blanc, Louis, 390

Blois, 169

Bloody Tenent of Persecution for the Cause of Conscience, 322

Boas, Professor, 502

Boccaccio, 297

Bodin, Jean, 290-291

Boer War, 493-494, 513

Boers, 550

Bogomils, 212

Bohlen, Charles, 471

Bolivar, 388

Bologna, 227

Bolshevism, 413-421

Bolshevists, 411-421

Boniface VIII, 203, 228, 237, 310

Borgias, 269, 282

Born, Bertrand de, 386

Boroughs, 224

Bossuet, 291

Boston "Tea Party," 345

Botha, Louis, 493

Boulanger, General, 403

Boule, 93

Bourbons, 326

Bourgeois, Léon, 430-431

Bourges, 224

Bowen, Catherine Drinker, 330-331

Bowle, John, 292

Boxer Rebellion, 522

Bracton, 229

Brahmanism, 50, 62

Bradford, William, 343

Brehaut, Ernest, 210

615

617

Machiavelli, 18, 185, 245, 261, 304, 408, 414, 440, 444
  Italy and, 281-289
Mackenzie, William Lyon, 491
MacMahon, President, 392, 403
Madagascar, 548
Madison, James, 376, 381, 553, 555
Magna Carta, 171, 184, 231, 233, 249, 271
Magnum Concilium, 231
Magna Graecia, 83
Magyars, 159
Mahan, Captain, 265, 404
Maitland, F. W., 231, 330
Malatesta, 297
Malenkov, 415
Man:
  brotherhood of, 17
  primitive, 22-32
Mana, 29
Manchu Dynasty, 448, 522
Mani, 61
Manichaeanism, 61, 149, 151, 212
Manu-captum, 121
Mao Tse-tung, 414, 525, 527-532
Manicipium, 121
Maoris, 29
Macaulay, 401
MacArthur, General, 338
Marathon, 86, 90, 106
Marcel, Etienne, 225
Marcus Aurelius, 123
Marduk, 60
Mare Nostrum, 442
Margraves, 172
Maria-Theresa, 189
Marie Antoinette, 357, 360
Marius, 114, 156
Mark 13: 7-8, 192
Marlborough, Duke of, 425
Marne, 425
Marseillaise, 361, 438
Marseilles, 80
Marshall, Chief Justice, 377, 554, 577
Marshall, George C., 485-486, 572, 574

Marshall Plan, 437, 481, 482-488
Marsilius of Padua, 245-246, 261, 296, 310
Marston Moor, Battle of, 333
Martin of Tours, St., 149
Marvin, F. S., 300
Mary, "Bloody," 312, 313
Mary of Burgundy, 278
Mary, Queen of Scots, 291, 326-327
Mary (William and), 338
Maryland, 323
Marx, Karl, 246, 248, 355, 402, 406-411, 412-421, 528, 532
  and the Communist Manifesto, 406-411
Masaryk, Thomas G., 307, 608
Mason, George, 249, 350-352, 364, 375-377
Mason, Philip, 550
Mass Education Movement, 521
Massachusetts, 322, 327
Massachusetts Bay, 343, 508
Mather, Frank Jewett, Jr., 304
Matteotti, 441
Matthew 5:38-48, 191
  22:15-22, 192
Mau Mau, 545-546
Maur, St., 298
Maurice of Orange, Prince, 316
Mauritania, 548
Maximilian, 277, 298
Maximilian, Duke of Bavaria, 28
Maximus, 151
Mayfield, 230
Mayflower Compact, 342
Mazarin, 382
Mazini, 439
McCarthy, Senator, 575
McKenzie, 330
Mecca, 70-75
Medes, 38, 105
Medici, Lorenzo di, 284
Medicis, 260, 282
Medina, 72
Mediterranean Sea, 43, 58, 76-77, 80, 82, 105, 107-133
Meiji Restoration, 36, 447, 538

N

O

Philip II, 225, 265, 275, 313
Philip IV, 199, 221, 237, 310
Philip the Fair, 228-229, 252
Philistines, 64, 87
Phillimore, Lord, 430
Philosophes, 18, 124, 188-189, 340, 352, 354-355, 382, 554, 560
Phoenicia, 119
Picts, 161
Pilate, 148
Pilgrim's Progress, 337
Pitt, William, 555
Place, Francis, 369
Plato, 82-107, 122-123, 130, 139, 176, 179, 289, 297, 408
Platonic Academy of Florence, 297
Plebs, 36
Plotinus, 297
Plutarch, 86
Plymouth, 227, 322, 342
Po, 157
Podestàs, 242
Poincaré, 439
Point Four Program, 481
Poitiers, 238
Poland, 416, 455, 600
Polis, 76, 99
Politburo, 411
Political Testament, 291
Politics, 15-22
  beginnings of, 75-85
  of power, 85-90
  in theory, 99-104
  medieval, 18
Politics, 89, 101, 103
Polybius, 124
Pompey, 114, 126
Pontifex Maximus, 116, 149, 174, 200
Poor Laws, 258
Populist Movement, 560
Populo d'Italia, 440
Populus Romanus, 109
Portugal, 508
Potsdam Conference, 473-476
Poznan, 416, 532

Praeger, Frederick A., 417
Praetor peregrinus, 118
Praetor urbanus, 118
Praetorian Guard, 117
Presbyterians, 309, 320-324, 327
Prester John, 264
Primitive Man, 22-32
Prince, 245, 281-289, 444
Priscillian, 151
Progressive Movement, 561
Protestant Revolt, 188
Protestant Theory of Persecution, 305
Provisions of Oxford of 1258, 233
Pukka sahib, 510
Punic Wars, 113
Punjab, 508
Pupin, 220
Puritans, 309, 320-324, 326-327
Pym, John, 333
Pyrenees, 162
Pythagorean Theory, 299

Q

Quakers, 208, 212, 320-321, 337, 554
Québec, 491
Quesnay, Francis, 372
Questor, 82

R

Rabelais, 298
Rainbow Series, 423
Rajendra Prasad, 515
Raleigh Tavern, 345
Rapello, 453
Raphael, 304
Rashdall, 195
Rathenan, Walter, 429
Reasonableness of Christianity, 319
Rebmann, 545
Red Sea, 70

Virginia Company, 341, 508
Visconti, 281-282
Visigoths, 157
Vladivostok, 452
Vogelweide, Walter von der, 386
Voltaire, 352-365, 382
Vosges, 424
Vyshinski, Andrei, 467

W

Wagner-Connery Act, 567
Waldenses, 211, 308
Waldo, Peter, 211, 308
War, 32-35
    and economics, 32-35
    New Age in Peace and War, 393-405
    Science and War, 402-405
    Cold War, 21, 451-477
    World War I, 421-437
    World War II, 568-570
    system, 15-22
    Napoleonic Wars, 19
    Peloponnesian, 19
War of 1812, 404
War of Italian Liberation, 422
War of the Latin Allies, 111
Warburg Castle, 308
Warfare, Revolution in, 421-422
Wars of the Roses, 270, 305, 312, 325
Washington, Booker T., 579
Washington, George, 346, 348, 379-381, 395, 552-553
Waterloo, Battle of, 363, 386, 491
Wavell, Lord, 510
Wealth of Nations, 372, 489-491
Webster, Daniel, 380, 553, 556, 578
Welfare, 15-22, 27
    of nations, 593-597
Welles, Sumner, 459
Wellington, Duke of, 370, 373, 401, 425
Western Political Thought, 292
Westphalia, Treaty of, 281, 306

Whigs, 341, 366, 379
White Sea, 451
White, William Allen, 565
Wilberforce, 370, 555
Wilhelm II, 423
William I, 232
William and Mary College, 351-352
William, Maurice, 524
William of Orange, 316, 338
William the Conqueror, 164, 172, 198, 202, 228, 270
William the Silent, 276
Williams, Roger, 318-323
Williamsburg, 345, 350
Wilson, James, 348, 352, 531-532
Wilson's First Inaugural Address, 562-563
Wilson, Woodrow, 421-438, 561, 564-565
Wilsonian Program, 429-430
Winchester, 510
Winthrop, John, 341, 343
Witanagemot, 231
Wittenberg, 279, 307
Wolfe, Bertram D., 415
Wolsey, Cardinal, 312, 317, 368
Woodman, Dorothy, 539
Woolman, John, 555
Wordsworth, 360, 386
Work Houses, 398
Works and Days, 103
World Health Organization, 437, 596
World War I, 19, 130, 421-437
    and the League of Nations, 421-437
World War II, 20, 568-570
Wrangel, 451
Wyclife, John, 187, 214, 246, 306-307
Wythe, George, 352

X

Xenophanes, 82-83, 89
Xerxes, 79, 104, 105

Y

Yahweh, 64, 68
Yalta Conference, 453, 460-464
Yangtze, 75, 523
Yeddo, 533
Yen, James Y. C., 521
Young India, 512, 515
Yuan Shih-kai, 523, 525
Yudenich, 451
Yugoslavia, 416-417, 443, 461

Z

Zen Sect, 57, 63
Zeno, 123
Zeus, 97, 302
Zoroaster, 60
Zoroastrianism, 60-62
Zukov, Marshal, 473
Zulu War, 512